SCOTLAND

OWNERS OF LANDS AND HERITAGES
(17 & 18 VICT., CAP. 91)

1872–1873
RETURN

I.

OF THE NAME AND ADDRESS OF EVERY OWNER OF ONE ACRE AND UPWARDS IN EXTENT (OUTSIDE THE MUNICIPAL BOUNDARIES OF BOROUGHS CONTAINING MORE THAN 20,000 INHABITANTS), WITH THE ESTIMATED ACREAGE, AND THE ANNUAL VALUE OF THE LANDS AND HERITAGES OF INDIVIDUAL OWNERS;

AND OF THE NUMBER OF OWNERS OF LESS THAN ONE ACRE, WITH THE ESTIMATED AGGREGATE ACREAGE AND ANNUAL VALUE OF THE LANDS AND HERITAGES OF SUCH OWNERS IN EACH COUNTY.

II.

A SIMILAR RETURN FOR MUNICIPAL BOROUGHS CONTAINING MORE THAN 20,000 INHABITANTS

Presented to Both Houses of Parliament by
Command of Her Majesty
Queen Victoria

HERITAGE BOOKS
2011

HERITAGE BOOKS
AN IMPRINT OF HERITAGE BOOKS, INC.

Books, CDs, and more—Worldwide

For our listing of thousands of titles see our website
at
www.HeritageBooks.com

A Facsimile Reprint
Published 2011 by
HERITAGE BOOKS, INC.
Publishing Division
100 Railroad Ave. #104
Westminster, Maryland 21157

Originally published
Edinburgh:
Printed by Murray and Gibb,
Printers to Her Majesty's Stationery Office
1874

— Publisher's Notice —
In reprints such as this, it is often not possible to remove blemishes from the original. We feel the contents of this book warrant its reissue despite these blemishes and hope you will agree and read it with pleasure.

International Standard Book Numbers
Paperbound: 978-0-7884-2738-1
Clothbound: 978-0-7884-8893-1

LIST OF COUNTIES, ALPHABETICALLY ARRANGED,

WITH BOROUGHS CONTAINING MORE THAN 20,000 INHABITANTS.

		PAGE
1. ABERDEEN		1
Do.	BOROUGH OF ABERDEEN	9
2. ARGYLL		11
3. AYR		17
Do.	BOROUGH OF KILMARNOCK	29
4. BANFF		30
5. BERWICK		32
6. BUTE		37
7. CAITHNESS		39
8. CLACKMANNAN		42
9. CROMARTY		44
10. DUMBARTON		45
11. DUMFRIES		52
12. EDINBURGH		60
Do.	BOROUGH OF EDINBURGH	66
Do.	Do. LEITH	69
13. ELGIN		71
14. FIFE		74
15. FORFAR		90
Do.	BOROUGH OF DUNDEE	98
16. HADDINGTON		101
17. INVERNESS		105
18. KINCARDINE		109
19. KINROSS		112
20. KIRKCUDBRIGHT		115
21. LANARK		122
Do.	BOROUGH OF GLASGOW	140
22. LINLITHGOW		144
23. NAIRN		148
24. ORKNEY		150
25. PEEBLES		157
26. PERTH		160
Do.	BOROUGH OF PERTH	172
27. RENFREW		173
Do.	BOROUGH OF PAISLEY	180
Do.	Do. GREENOCK	182
28. ROSS		184
29. ROXBURGH		188
30. SELKIRK		194
31. STIRLING		196
32. SUTHERLAND		204
33. WIGTOWN		206
34. ZETLAND		208
ABSTRACT		211

PREFATORY REMARKS.

This Return sets out the estimated acreage of owners of lands and heritages in Scotland; and the annual value of the same. The names and addresses of owners of one acre and upwards are given, together with the extent and annual value of their lands and heritages, and the number of owners of less than one acre of land, with the aggregate extent and annual value of their property.

The Return is made up in Counties; with separate Returns for Boroughs containing 20,000 inhabitants.

The estimated acreage has been obtained by the Surveyors of Stamps and Taxes from inquiry on the spot, and from the best resources at their command.

The duty imposed on these officers in ascertaining the estimated extent or acreage of properties was one of considerable difficulty, and, occasionally, of some delicacy.

The following was the course adopted:—

Early in January 1873 a circular was addressed by me to the known agents of landed proprietors, setting forth the nature and particulars of the Return sought, and requesting such information as could be conveniently furnished as to the areas of estates under their charge. In many cases, prompt and satisfactory replies were received; but not unfrequently my correspondents referred me to local factors, occupying tenants, and other persons, with an occasional intimation that there was no survey of the estate or estates of their constituents, who could not be reasonably expected to incur the trouble and cost of obtaining the information sought by the Officers of the Government.

On the 10th of February the Surveyors were instructed, when no satisfactory information could be obtained from owners, factors, farmers, or others, to select persons of local knowledge and skill to aid them in ascertaining the acreage of properties. 'A scientific survey,' it was intimated, 'is
' of course out of the question; but persons may no doubt be found, who, for a moderate fee, will
' visit the lands and make tolerably accurate estimates of the acreage of the several properties
' that will fall to be dealt with in that way. As such process, however, of survey and estimate will
' be an expensive one, it must not be resorted to until all other efforts to obtain information shall
' have failed, or until the estimated cost shall have been submitted to me, through the Inspector
' of the Division, and shall have been formally sanctioned.'

Shortly thereafter schedules were furnished to each Surveyor, to be addressed by him to owners, occupiers, and other persons, in his district, soliciting the requisite information.

Schedules were, at the same time, furnished to all parties so addressed, on which answers to certain queries were to be returned, so as to give the least possible trouble to the public in filling up and thereafter posting the schedules to the Officers by whom they had been issued.

Besides the difficulty, in the absence of authentic *data*, of estimating the extent of lands and heritages, the labour (largely shared by the in-door Officers) of ascertaining correctly the names

PREFATORY REMARKS.

and addresses of owners of an acre and upwards in extent was very great; but it is believed that the general accuracy of the result will be found to justify the attention and care bestowed on that branch of the Return.

With reference to the matter of annual value, the Valuation Rolls of Counties and Boroughs, made up towards the close of 1872, being authentic documents, have been followed. Such Rolls were prepared by Assessors appointed by the Commissioners of Supply for Counties, and by Magistrates for Boroughs, under the provisions of the Acts 17 & 18 Vict. cap. 91, and 20 & 21 Vict. cap. 58.

The Valuation Roll made up in 1872 by the Assessor of Railways and Canals, appointed under the 20th section of the former Act, has been adopted as representing the true annual value of the property of which that Officer is the Assessor.

When, from whatever cause, lands and heritages have been omitted from the Valuation Roll of a County or Borough, the omission has been supplied by the insertion in this Return of the estimated acreage, and of the annual value of the property, as fixed by experienced and competent persons.

The reason why the annual value of property has been taken from the Valuation Rolls of 1872, is that the compilation of this Return, having been commenced during the early part of 1873, the Valuation Rolls then in force were those made up in autumn 1872, 'for the year commencing ' at the term of Whitsunday immediately preceding, and ending at the term of Whitsunday im- ' mediately following,'—17 & 18 Vict. cap. 91, sec. 12.

In the category of 'Owners' are included Feuars, Leaseholders of 99 years or upwards, and Liferenters, whether in virtue of office or otherwise.

The extent of lands has been estimated in imperial acres. It has not been considered necessary to give fractional parts of an acre; and in stating the annual value, it has been deemed sufficient to give the result in pounds and shillings.

The duties assigned to Inspectors and Surveyors of Taxes in connection with this Return have been discharged with zeal, intelligence, and discretion; and equally satisfactory has been the performance of the duties which devolved on the in-door Officers of Stamps and Taxes, by whom each Return as received was carefully examined and checked. It is satisfactory to be enabled to add, that the services of the several Officers engaged in the work have been given heartily, faithfully, and with a meritorious desire, to the utmost of their power, to promote an object which is felt to be one of national importance and interest.

ANGUS FLETCHER,
Comptroller-General of Inland Revenue
for SCOTLAND.

Inland Revenue, Edinburgh,
25th February 1874.

LIST OF OWNERS OF LAND.

SCOTLAND.

1873.

ABERDEEN.

Population in 1871,	244,603.
Inhabited Houses,	34,589.
Number of Parishes,	85.

Name of Owner.	Address of Owner.	Estimated Acreage of Property.	Gross Annual Value.	Name of Owner.	Address of Owner.	Estimated Acreage of Property.	Gross Annual Value.
		Acres.	£ s.			Acres.	£ s.
Abercromby, Sir Robert John, of Birkenbog and Forglen, Bart.	Forglen House, Turriff	1,942	1,669 4	Allan, Mrs. Margaret	Potterton, Belhelvie	835	769 15
				Alsop, James	Inverurie	1	20 15
Aberdeen, Earl of	Haddo House, Aberdeen	63,422	40765 11	Anderson, Rev. Alexander	The Manse, Rhynie	14	40 10
Aberdeen Asylum for the Blind	Aberdeen	90	162 —	Anderson, Rev. Alexander	Old Aberdeen	3	90 —
Aberdeen, Dean of Guild of	Aberdeen	634	605 3	Anderson, Trustees on Estate of Sir Alex., Kt.	Aberdeen	267	1,155 4
Aberdeen, Magistrates and Town Council of	Aberdeen (Water Reservoirs)	4	544 —	Anderson, Alexander	Aucharnie, Forgue	343	208 14
	(Aqueduct, Water and Gas Pipes, underground)	—	3,505 —	Anderson, George	Nether Aucharnie, Forgue	207	207 10
	(Other Property)	132	203 —	Anderson, James	Angusfield, Aberdeen	67	229 6
Aberdeen, Synod of	Aberdeen	195	184 15	Anderson, John, of Westhill	Westhill, Skene	552	644 6
Aberdeen Town and County Banking Co.	Aberdeen	1	175 —	Anderson, John	Balmoral Ter., Aberdeen	1	150 5
Aberdeen, University of	Aberdeen	3,708	4,400 18	Anderson, Trs. of late John	Auchleuchries, Cruden	927	684 1
Aberdeenshire, Commissioners of Supply of	Aberdeen	3	138 —	Anderson, Michie Forbes	Deebank, Aberdeen	110	212 11
Aberdein, Alexander	Inveramsay, Pitcaple	76	130 —	Anderson, Mrs. Margaret	Ellishill, Peterhead	165	271 15
Aberdein, George and Jean	Dykeside, Newhills	85	103 —	Anderson, Catherine, and others	Peterhead	28	25 —
Abernethy, James	Ferryhill, Aberdeen	4	78 15	Annand, Rev. John	Manse, Cairnie	15	40 —
Abernethy, James, & Co.	Ferryhill, Aberdeen	1	200 —	Annand, John	Kintore	1	142 8
Abernethy, Representatives of Mrs. Ann	Ferryhill, Aberdeen	2	77 19	Arbuthnot, James	Invernettie, Peterhead	145	627 4
Aboyne and Braemar Railway Company	Aberdeen (Railway)	54	1,093 —	Arbuthnot, James	Nether Kinmundy, Longside	2,122	1,843 8
Adam, Andrew	Donbank Cot., Aberdeen	1	25 —	Arbuthnot, Trustees of late William	Dens, Peterhead	792	881 —
Adam, George	Beltie, Torphins	200	164 —	Arbuthnot, Trustees of late Jane	Willowbank, Peterhead	14	47 —
Adam, George	Inverurie	1	33 8	Bain, Alexander	Ferryhill Lodge, Aberdeen	2	100 —
Adam, Rev. Jas., per P. Cooper, Curator Bonis	Newhills	1,407	681 3	Bain, James	King St. Road, Aberdeen	2	69 —
Adam, Janet M.	Inverurie	1	33 10	Baird, Trustees of late George, of Strichen	Strichen House	11,248	9,048 18
Advocates, Society of	Aberdeen	2,405	2,052 5	Baird, Trustees of George Alexander, of Strichen	Strichen House	16	45 —
Ainslie, A. Douglas, of Delgaty	Delgaty Castle, Turriff	2,822	1,768 5	Baird, James, of Auchmedden	Cambusdoon, Ayr	5,979	2,704 8
Airth, John	Fernielee, Aberdeen	20	60 —	Baird, Thomas	Enfield, Aberdeen	50	166 —
Aitken, John	Harthill, Newhills	5	26 —	Bannerman, Sir Alexander, of Elsick and Crimonmogate, Bart.	Elsick House and Crimonmogate	7,660	7,744 16
Aiton, William, of Boddam	Sandford Lodge, Peterhead	467	1,114 13	Barclay, William	Haugh, Kincardine O'Neil	50	33 —
Alcock, Benjamin	Schoolhouse, Cruden	2	10 —	Barkway, Rev. Alex. B.	F. C. Manse, Culsalmond	1	52 10
Alexander, John	Inverurie	1	37 10	Barnett, Alexander	Backward, Kemnay	132	348 —
Alexander, William, of Springhill	Whitehill, Peterhead	435	553 —	Barron, Alexander	Summerfield, Aberdeen	25	82 —
Allan, James	Templand, Auchterless	240	187 —	Beattie, Mrs. Jane	Middlefield, Inverurie	6	33 5
Allan, Trs. of late James	Midbeltie, Kincardine O'Neil	1,066	791 6	Begg, Charles	Milton of Towie, Strathdon	97	70 —
Allan, Rev. John	The Manse, Peterculter	4	35 —	Beveridge, Robert	Beith Villa, Aberdeen	1	65 —
Allan, John, as Judicial Factor on the Estates of Balmaud, &c.	Banff	496	517 1	Birnie, John B. L., of Johnstone	Edinburgh	23	190 —
Allan, Mrs. Jane G.	Outseats of Pitmuxton, Aberdeen	37	136 18	Bisset, John	Fraserburgh	2	200 —

A

ABERDEEN—continued.

Name of Owner.	Address of Owner.	Estimated Acreage of Property.	Gross Annual Value.	Name of Owner.	Address of Owner.	Estimated Acreage of Property.	Gross Annual Value.
		Acres.	£ s.			Acres.	£ s.
Bisset, Mordaunt F., of Lessendrum	Lessendrum	2,682	2,582 17	Carnegy, Ann G., and Thomas M'P. Grant	Edinburgh } Craig }	1,918	1,440 5
Bisset, Mrs. Elizabeth	Pontefract, Yorkshire	4	36 15	Cassie, Rev. James F.	Beechgrove, Aberdeen	4	170 —
Black, Rev. John	Old Aberdeen	2	50 —	Catto, John	Cattofield, Aberdeen	20	147 —
Black, William, & Co.	Devanha, Aberdeen	2	120 —	Chalmers, Charles, of Monkshill	Rothiebrisbane, Fyvie	538	473 10
Blaikie, Dame Agnes, Executrix of late Sir Thomas, Kt.	Aberdeen	335	252 8	Chalmers, Trustees of late George, James, & Alexander	Aberdeen	1,997	1,362 13
Blake, James & Alexander	Miltown of Pitfodels, Aberdeen	10	65 —	Chalmers' Hospital, Trs. of	Banff	110	55 15
Boddie, Mrs. William	Inverurie	5	124 4	Chalmers, James	Westburn, Aberdeen	22	165 —
Booth, John	Old Aberdeen	1	16 10	Cheves, Robert, of Gateside	Longside, Mintlaw	118	166 1
Boyd, Andrew	Peterhead	30	125 —	Cheyne, James	Inchgreen, Turriff	610	716 15
Boys' and Girls' Hospital, Trustees of	Aberdeen	2,089	1,803 16	Christie, Alexander	Huntly	2	174 14
Brand, Mrs. Elspet	Auchinten, Cruden	262	441 —	Christie, Alexander	King St. Road, Aberdeen	4	75 —
Brebner, James	Greens of Savock, Ellon	3	16 10	Christie, Rev. Andrew	The Manse, Kildrummy	9	36 —
Brebner, Rev. James	The Manse, Forgue	18	45 —	Chrystall, William	Gateside, Aberdeen	102	261 10
Bremner, Alexander, of Glasslaw	Port-Elphinstone, Inverurie	1,024	724 16	Clark, James	Louisville, Aberdeen	12	100 —
Bremner, Rev. John	The Manse, Glenbucket	11	26 —	Clark, Sir John F., of Tillypronie, Bart.	Tillypronie, Tarland	649	350 9
Bremner, Thomas John	Peterhead	356	349 16	Clark, John Moir	Garthdee, Aberdeen	17	170 —
Bridges, Rev. Alex. H., of Fedderat	Beddington House, Surrey	4,456	2,816 19	Clark, William	Woodhill, Kinellar	8	25 14
Brown, Alexander	Aberdeen	1	19 —	Cobban, Representatives of Agnes	Inverurie	9	34 10
Brown, Rev. George	Tanfield, Woodside	13	111 6	Cochran, Alexander, of Balfour	Aberdeen	1,259	336 18
Brown, George	Mount Street, Aberdeen	7	89 11	Cochran, Trustees of late Francis J., of Balfour	Aberdeen	39	197 —
Brown, John	Howe o' Buchan, Peterhead	68	212 —	Cochran, Mrs. Elizabeth	Balfour House, Aboyne	5	42 —
Brown, Rev. William	F. C. Manse, Rayne	1	18 —	Cock, Rev. John F. M.	The Manse, Rathen	7	32 —
Brown, Mrs. Rebecca	Old Aberdeen	1	43 10	Collie, Alexander	Harlaw, Pitcaple	1	25 —
Bruce, Alexander, William, and George	Fraserburgh	3	199 10	Collie, Alexander	Oakbank, Aberdeen	28	164 —
Bruce, George	Heatherwick, Keith-hall	4	60 —	Collie, George	West Cults, Aberdeen	37	210 15
Bruce, James	Old Meldrum	1	76 15	Collie, George	Morkeu, Aberdeen	21	96 —
Bruce, James, of Inverquhomery and Longside	Inverquhomery, Mintlaw	1,300	1,649 8	Collie, James	Cults, Aberdeen	118	525 —
Bruce, William	Inverurie	1	21 —	Collie, Robert, senior	Braeside of Pitfodels, Aberdeen	8	101 15
Bruce, Rev. Wm. R.	The Manse, Newmachar	21	50 —	Collie, Ann	Merchiston, Edinburgh	1	14 —
Bruce-Hay Girls' School, Trustees of	Slains	1	9 —	Coltman, Wm. Bachelor, of Deskrie and Blelack	London	7,484	2,376 16
Buchan Combination Poor House, Managers of	New Maud	5	80 —	Compton, Mrs. Jessie T.	Gloucester	180	140 —
Buchan, James, of Auchmacoy	Auchmacoy House, Ellon	3,408	2,972 12	Cook, Charles	Ballater	1	235 10
Buchan, Elizabeth	Kintore	2	16 5	Cook, Rev. George	Manse, Kincardine O'Neil	7	42 5
Burgess, Alexander	Gordon Place, Dyce	1	75 10	Cook, John	Ashley, Aberdeen	24	200 —
Burgess, James	Countesswells, Aberdeen	7	22 —	Cooper, George	Wracs, Kennethmont	90	83 15
Burness, Reps. of Alexander, of Mastrick	Mastrick, Aberdeen	126	214 —	Cooper, Charlotte and Sophia	Homewood, Aberdeen	2	70 —
Burnet, Peter, of Elrick	Elrick House, Summerhill	1,487	1,864 17	Corbet, Rev. Adam	The Manse, Drumoak	281	622 18
Burnett, Alexander	Old Meldrum	3	27 7	Corbet, James	Cairnlee, Peterculter	2	37 —
Burnett, Alex. George, of Kemnay	Kemnay House, Aberdeen	4,486	2,719 7	Cordiner, Wm. Fraser, of Cortes	Mormond House, Lonmay	1,585	1,320 12
Burnett, Charles John	Old Aberdeen	2	61 —	Couper, John Cardno, of Craigiebuckler	Craigiebuckler, Aberdeen	420	1,057 4
Burnett, Sir James Horn, of Leys, Bart.	Crathes Castle	84	108 16	Coutts, George	Stonefield, Inverurie	3	15 —
Burnett, Trustees of late John, of Dens	Aberdeen	732	769 4	Coutts, William	Alford	1	117 —
Burnett, Newell	Aberdeen	1	35 —	Coutts, Mrs. Elizabeth	Dyce	9	21 12
Burnett, Rev. Thomas	The Manse, Daviot	10	36 —	Craigie, John Burnet, of Linton	Linton House, Cluny	1,515	1,701 16
Burnett, Rev. Thomas	The Manse, Kennethmont	12	32 —	Crawford and Balcarres, Earl of	Dunecht House	8,855	6,160 2
Busfeild, Rev. Harcourt	The Parsonage, Lonmay	8	22 10	Cromar, Mrs. Grace	Old Aberdeen	1	50 16
Byres, James G. Moir, of Tonley	Tonley, Whitehouse	4,623	3,527 1	Crombie, Alexander, of Thornton and Leddach	Thornton Castle, Laurencekirk	659	671 13
				Crombie, Alexander	Grubb Lodge, Cults	4	51 —
				Crombie, James	Goval Bank, Aberdeen	5	48 —
				Crombie, James and John	Grandholm Mills, Aberdeen	43	751 5
Cadenhead, Lt.-Col. James	Summerhill, Aberdeen	41	178 10	Crombie, John	Balgownie Lodge, Aberdeen	13	112 —
Calder, Rev. John	Manse, Leochel Cushnie	26	35 —	Cruickshank, Rev. John	The Manse, Turriff	10	45 —
Caledonian Railway Co.	Glasgow { (Railway) (Other Property) }	1 1	621 — 30 —	Cruickshank, William	Fraserburgh	127	90 12
Cameron, William H.	Morefield, Aberdeen	2	45 10	Cruickshank, Mrs. Sarah, of Piltochie	59 Queen Anne Street, London	171	185 —
Campbell, Alexander	Ruthrieston, Aberdeen	1	76 —	Culter Paper Mills Company (Limited)	Peterculter, Aberdeen	28	600 —
Campbell, Rev. Archibald A.	The Manse, Lonmay	17	42 —	Cumine, James, of Rattray	Rattray House, Peterhead	1,696	1,292 14
Campbell, Rev. Peter Colin	Old Aberdeen	1	65 —	Cushny, Rev. Alexander	The Manse, Rayne	10	32 —
Campbell, Captain Robert	Cloghill, Newhills	250	281 8	Cushny, Rev. John	The Manse, Huntly	9	39 —
Campbell, William	Cortiebrae, Rathen	112	113 13				
Campbell, Reps. of William	Kenfield, Aberdeen	10	108 —				
Campbell, Mrs. Mary	Argyle Cottage, Cults	1	40 —				

ABERDEEN—continued.

Name of Owner.	Address of Owner.	Estimated Acreage of Property.	Gross Annual Value.
		Acres.	£ s.
Dalrymple, Charles E.	Kinnellar Lodge, Blackburn	135	241 6
Davidson, Alexander, of Desswood	Desswood House, Kincardine O'Neil	40	112 —
Davidson, Charles	Forresterhill, Aberdeen	44	215 5
Davidson, Charles, & Sons	Mugiemoss, Aberdeen	21	769 —
Davidson, Duncan, of Tillychetly	Tillychetly, Alford	200	170 —
Davidson, Trustees of the late Duncan, of Overboddam	Overboddam, Insch	1,934	1,569 —
Davidson, George	Wellwood, Aberdeen	28	264 10
Davidson, Rev. George	Manse, Logie Coldstone	14	38 —
Davidson, James	Inverurie	4	72 —
Davidson, Rev. John	The Manse, Inverurie	7	44 —
Davidson, John, junior	Old Meldrum	3	49 15
Davidson, Patrick, of Inchmarlo	Inchmarlo, Banchory	1,422	872 5
Davidson, William	Pt. Elphinstone, Inverurie	2	140 15
Davidson, William	Kintore	2	15 —
Davidson, Rev. Wm. L.	The Manse, Bourtie	12	38 —
Davidson, Mrs. Anne, and Captain Alex. Sharp Thain	Auchaber, Huntly	1,070	828 10
Daviot, Kirk-Session of Parish of	Daviot	2	20 14
Dawson, Mrs. Mary	Kintore	3	43 19
Deeside Railway Company	Aberdeen (Railway)	120	6,222 —
Dingwall, Trustee of Alex., of Rannieston	Edinburgh	470	530 —
Donald, Rev. James	The Manse, Keith-hall	24	45 —
Donald, James	Cullerlie, Echt	76	246 5
Donald, William	Cults, Aberdeen	1	25 —
Donald, Mrs. Frances	Inverurie	2	48 10
Donald, Ann, Isabella, and Barbara	Kintore	22	105 18
Douglas, Thomas	Airyhall, Aberdeen	35	157 —
Downie, Alexander	Burnieboozle, Aberdeen	8	30 —
Downie, Trustees of late Charles	Broomhill, Aberdeen	46	216 5
Downie, Mrs. Mary	Aberdeen	14	70 —
Drain, William	Old Meldrum	2	43 —
Duff, Archibald	Annfield, Aberdeen	8	72 —
Duff, Garden Alex., of Hatton	Hatton Castle, Turriff	11,576	9,661 18
Duff, Major Lachlan Duff Gordon, of Drummuir	Drummuir Castle, Keith	4,328	2,356 14
Duff, M. E. Grant, of Eden, M.P.	Eden House, Banff	1,013	1,294 4
Duff, Robt. Wm., of Fetteresso, M.P.	Fetteresso Castle, Stonehaven	1,588	1,747 6
Duff, Trustees of late Mrs. J. C. C. Grant, of Greenness	Aberdeen	913	302 19
Duff, Mrs. P. H. Sterrit, of Corsindae	Corsindae House, Aberdeen	4,481	2,171 4
Duff, Mrs. T. F.	Chantilly, France	41	28 5
Duguid, Rev. James E.	F. C. Manse, Newmachar	1	21 —
Duguid, John	Inverurie	7	31 12
Duguid, Peter, of Bourtie	Auchlunies, Aberdeen	1,325	1,521 —
Duguid, Rev. William	The Manse, Glass	18	33 —
Duguid, William	Ballater	1	118 5
Duguid, Elizabeth & Margt.	Newlands, Aberdeen	17	106 —
Dunbar, Peter	Dysart Bank, Aberdeen	25	45 —
Duncan, Joseph	Countesswells, Aberdeen	1	10 —
Dunn, Rev. Charles	The Manse, Birse	5	35 —
Duthie, Alexander, of Ruthrieston	Edinburgh	217	995 18
Duthie, William, of Cairnbulg	Ashley Lodge, Aberdeen	1,018	1,427 —
Duthie, Mrs. Matilda, of Cairnbulg	Albyn Place, Aberdeen	277	523 17
Easton, Rev. James C.	The Manse, Meldrum	10	49 —
Edmond, Francis, of Kingswells	Kingswells, Aberdeen	813	1,133 5
Edwards, Trustees of Alex.	Old Aberdeen	1	21 5
Ellis, Mrs.	Miltown, Leochel Cushnie	6	5 —
Elmsly, George	Woodside, Aberdeen	76	250 3
Elphinstone, Sir James D. Horn, of Horn and Logie Elphinstone, Bart., M.P.	Logie Elphinstone	5,524	5,107 1
Emslie, Joseph	Camphill, Lumphanan	3	8 —
Emslie, Mrs. Margaret, of Tullochvenus	Tullochvenus, Lumphanan	385	233 —
Episcopal Church, Trustees of	Meiklefolla, Rothie	2	15 —
Erroll, Earl of	Slains Castle	4,249	4,268 3
Erskine, Mrs. Mary A. Knight, of Pittodrie	Pittodrie House, Pitcaple	3,270	4,250 2
Erskine, Mrs. Mary A. Knight, and Mrs. Margaret J. Dundas	Pittodrie House, Pitcaple	8	14 12
Esplin, William	Cults, Aberdeen	1	30 —
Ewan, Rev. William	F. C. Manse, Fyvie	1	21 —
Ewen, George	Whitemyres, Newhills	5	19 —
Farquharson, Trustees of late Andrew, of Breda	Breda, Alford	1,761	929 7
Farquharson, Andrew, of Whitehouse	Whitehouse, Tough	690	508 7
Farquharson, Francis, of Finzean	Finzean, Aboyne	16,809	6,166 12
Farquharson, Lieut.-Col. Geo. M'Bain Barnes, of Breda	Breda, Alford	120	120 15
Farquharson, Col. J. Ross, of Invercauld	Invercauld, Braemar	87,745	9,567 3
Farquharson, Reps. of Lieut.-Colonel John, of Corrachree	Corrachree House, Tarland	695	462 17
Farquharson, Peter	Ashley Road, Aberdeen	1	109 10
Farquharson, Robert O., of Haughton	Haughton House, Alford	4,500	3,773 14
Farquharson, Trustees of late Robert, of Allargue	Allargue, Strathdon	5,700	599 5
Ferguson, Lieut.-Colonel George A., of Pitfour	Pitfour House, Mintlaw	12,305	10,492 3
Ferguson, Rev. John	The Manse, New Pitsligo	10	33 —
Ferguson, Rev. Wm.	F. C. Manse, Ellon	1	25 —
Ferguson, William, of Kinmundy	Kinmundy House, Mintlaw	4,068	3,555 6
Fiddes, Rev. Robert	The Manse, Kinellar	12	40 —
Fife, Trustees of Earl of	Duff House, Banffshire	139,829	17,740 5
Finnie, Mrs. Agnes	Peterhead	47	140 —
Fisher, Marriage Contract Trustees of Capt. Chas. B. and Mrs.	Aberdeen	165	313 5
Fisher, John	Aberdeen	1	51 4
Fisher, Mrs. Basil	Cuparstone Rd., Aberdeen	1	100 —
Fleshers, Incorporation of	Aberdeen	4	120 —
Flockhart, Alexander	Belmont, Aberdeen	11	153 10
Forbes, Sir Charles, of Newe, Bart.	Castle Newe	29,238	5,992 7
Forbes, Hon. Charles Murray Hay	Brux, Strathdon	3,852	1,278 —
Forbes, Duncan, of Balgownie	Balgownie, Aberdeen	900	2,367 6
Forbes, George Stuart, of Asloon	Asloon, Alford	1,674	1,025 17
Forbes, Lt.-Col. Henry E., of Easter Kinmundy	Easter Kinmundy, Skene	723	980 16
Forbes, James Ochoncar, of Corse	Corse, Lumphanan	1,946	1,500 16
Forbes, Rev. James B.	The Manse, Leslie	12	28 —
Forbes, John, of Haddo	Haddo, Huntly	161	178 15
Forbes, John, of South Auchinclech	South Auchinclech, Skene	172	134 —
Forbes, General John, of Invernernan	Invernernan, Strathdon	15,336	865 13
Forbes, Lord	Castle Forbes	13,621	5,675 15
Forbes, Heirs of Rev. Robert	Aberdeen	5	67 6
Forbes, Sir William, of Craigievar and Fintray, Bart.	Fintray House, Aberdeen	9,347	8,539 8
Forbes, William N., of Auchernach	Auchernach, Strathdon	1,300	163 18
Forbes, William	Seaton Dykes, Aberdeen	2	11 —
Forbes, Wm., & Co.	Invernettie, Peterhead	8	51 —

ABERDEEN—continued.

Name of Owner.	Address of Owner.	Estimated Acreage of Property.	Gross Annual Value.		Name of Owner.	Address of Owner.	Estimated Acreage of Property.	Gross Annual Value.
		Acres.	£ s.				Acres.	£ s.
Forbes, Mrs. Annabella	Boyndlie House, Fraserburgh	35	63 3		Gordon, Heirs of Arthur Forbes, of Rayne	Mavisbank, Banchory	830	999 1
Forbes, Mrs. Jane O., of Boyndlie	Boyndlie, Fraserburgh	3,325	2,040 —		Gordon, Carlos Pedro, of Wardhouse and Kildrummy	Wardhouse, Insch, and The Lodge, Kildrummy	13,427	6,876 2
Forbes-Mitchell, Mrs. M., of Easter Beltie	Easter Beltie, Torphins	1,361	642 8		Gordon, Charles	Aberdeen	2	46 —
Fordyce, James Dingwall, of Culsh	Edinburgh	1,757	1,260 15		Gordon, Trustees of late Rev. Charles	Mannofield	20	72 1
Fordyce, W. Dingwall, of Brucklay, M.P.	Brucklay Castle	20,899	12743 19		Gordon, Trustees of late Francis, of Kincardine	Aberdeen	1,716	1,047 9
Foulerton, General Thos.	Rubislaw Park, Aberdeen	1	60 —		Gordon, George J. R., of Ellon	Ellon Castle	5,556	6,194 19
Fowler, Andrew	Brodiach, Skene	95	115 —		Gordon, George Milne	Rosehearty	1	57 —
Fowler, John	Harthill, Newhills	4	21 10		Gordon, Gordon E.	Mosstown, Udny	235	254 6
Fowler, Robert	Upper Corskie, Cluny	4	69 14		Gordon, Sir Henry Percy, of Niton, Bart.	Knockespock, Aberdeen, and North Court, Newport, Isle of Wight	6,709	3,438 7
Fowler, William, of Asleid	Ardmiddle Mains, Turriff	316	256 —					
Fowler, William	Middlemuir, Inverurie	3	9 —					
Fraser, Rev. Andrew	The Manse, Oyne	9	38 —		Gordon, Henry Wolrige, of Hallhead and Esslemont	Esslemont House, Ellon	4,962	4,502 17
Fraser, Angus	Woodbank, Aberdeen	14	86 —					
Fraser, David	Derncleugh, Aberdeen	7	49 —		Gordon, James, of Manar	Manar, Inverurie	2,260	2,114 15
Fraser, Edward, of Williamston	Williamston House, Insch	1,297	1,725 19		Gordon, James F. G. S., of Craig	Craig Castle	3,333	1,139 5
Fraser, Francis G., of Findrack	Findrack, Torphins	1,600	895 —		Gordon, James W., of Cairness	Cairness House, Lonmay	4,100	3,476 5
Fraser, Col. Fred. M., of Castle Fraser	Castle Fraser	4,247	3,697 8		Gordon, John, of Cluny	Cluny Castle	20,395	13713 10
Fraser, Capt. Geo. C., of Sheddocksley	Sheddocksley, Aberdeen	533	901 13		Gordon, John, of Craigmyle	Craigmyle, Torphins	3,200	1,884 3
Fraser, William James, of Park	Park, Lonmay	454	267 5		Gordon's, John, Charitable Fund, Trustees of	Aberdeen	3,345	2,323 5
Fraser, William N., of Tornaveen	Edinburgh	250	207 15		Gordon, Patrick Pirie, of Buthlaw	London	1,124	1,287 17
Fraserburgh, Magistrates and Town Council of	Fraserburgh	52	287 11		Gordon, Peter	Bonnymuir, Aberdeen	4	31 —
Fraserburgh, Trustees of Harbour of	Fraserburgh (Quays & Harbour Basins)	3 / 23	341 1 / 1,743 18		*Gordon's, Robert, Hospital, President and Governors of*	Aberdeen	5,283	5,473 5
Free Church of Scotland, Trustees of	Edinburgh	8	289 8		Gordon, Theodore, of Dunnydeer	Dunnydeer, Insch	727	616 11
Friends, Society of	Aberdeen	3	26 10		Gordon, Thomas	Upper Kaimhill, Aberdeen	82	267 —
Fyfe, John	Village, Kemnay	2	156 —		Gordon, Col. Wm. Cosmo, of Fyvie	Fyvie Castle	11,700	8,741 9
					Gordon, Mrs. Ann, of Glasgoforest	Glasgoforest, Aberdeen	1,970	2,144 15
Galloway, Robert	Lumbs, Lonmay	98	78 —		Gordon, Mrs. Margaret, of Sandfordhill	Albyn Place, Aberdeen	399	370 5
Galloway, Mrs. George	Inverurie	3	60 —		Gordon, Salvadora Maxwell, & others, & Lieut.-Col. James A. West	London	305	209 10
Gammell, Major Andrew, of Countesswells	Countesswells, Aberdeen	3,946	3,396 2					
Gammell, James, of Ardiffery	Bath	2,193	2,168 16		Grant, Sir Archd., of Monymusk, Bart.	Monymusk House	14,881	7,698 13
Gammie, John	Braeside, Pitcaple	5	8 5					
Garden, Trustees of late George, of Lairshill	Lairshill, Aberdeen	240	384 13		Grant, D. R. Lyall, of Kingsford	Kingsford, Alford	320	323 10
Garden, James	Deebank, Aberdeen	20	4 5		Grant, Robert, of Druminnor	Druminnor, Rhynie	4,197	2,901 15
Garden, Trustees of John, of Millfield	Millfield, Turriff	685	420 —		Grant, Trustees of late Robert Charles	Balgowan, Keig	600	390 10
Garden, Mrs. Christian, of Springbank	St. John's Wood, London	26	90 18		Grant, Mrs. Ann	Whitemyres, Newhills	97	181 —
Gardner, Rev. Archibald	F. C. Manse, New Deer	1	20 —		Gray, Alexander, sen.	Inverurie	5	52 10
Garioch, Trustees of late Rev. George, of Gariochsford	Gariochsford, Huntly	389	307 10		Gray, Rev. Alexander	The Manse, Auchterless	7	41 —
					Gray, John	Keithney, Inverurie	3	30 14
Gerrard, George	Hayfield, Peterhead	63	130 —		Gray, Mrs. Helen	Maryfield, Inverurie	5	16 —
Gibb, George G. S., of Cults	Cults House, Aberdeen	981	1,668 17		Gray, Mrs. Jane	Westpark, Cults	2	44 —
Gibb, James Shirra, of Nether Contlaw	Nether Contlaw, Peterculter	259	315 14		Gray, Mrs. Mary	Ellangowan, Aberdeen	22	84 —
					Gray, Elspet & Helen	Whitemyres, Newhills	14	30 —
Gibb, William	Rubislaw Quarries, Aberdeen	20	322 8		*Great North of Scotland Railway Company*	Aberdeen (Railway) (Other Property)	1,054 / 5	31853 — / 90 —
Gill, David, of Blairythan	Aberdeen	853	810 1		Gregor, Rev. Walter	The Manse, Pitsligo	13	32 —
Gillan, Rev. James	The Manse, Alford	6	35 —		Grubb, Anthony, jun.	Inverurie	2	77 10
Glenny & Cruickshank	Lethenty Mills, Inverurie	1	97 10					
Glover, Capt. Thos. B.	Braehead, Bridge of Don	1	40 —					
Gordon, Adam Hay, of Avochie	Mayen House, Rothiemay, Huntly	850	675 10		Hadden, Alex., & Sons	Green, Aberdeen	21	653 6
					Hall, Alexander Harvey	Campfield, Banchory	2	41 10
Gordon, Alexander	Inverurie	1	22 —		Hall, George	Whitemyres, Newhills	12	25 —
Gordon, Trustees of late Alexander, of Ellon	Ellon Castle	6,092	3,652 14		*Hammermen, Incorporation of*	Aberdeen	48	212 7
Gordon, Alexander M., of Newton	Newton, Culsalmond	3,369	2,989 4		Harper, John	Seafield, Aberdeen	20	166 —
Gordon, Rev. Andrew	The Manse, Logie Buchan	7	35 —		*Harrow's Mortification, The Trustees of*	Old Aberdeen	16	60 —

ABERDEEN—continued.

Name of Owner.	Address of Owner.	Estimated Acreage of Property.	Gross Annual Value.	Name of Owner.	Address of Owner.	Estimated Acreage of Property.	Gross Annual Value.
		Acres.	£ s.			Acres.	£ s.
Harvey, Trustees of late Peter, of Ardo	Ardo, Belhelvie	960	1,102 1	Johnston, James	Moreseat, Cruden	251	130 —
Harvey, William, James, and Susan	Middlemuir, Belhelvie	185	165 —	Johnston, John	Inverurie	1	14 15
Hay, Alexander	Old Aberdeen	1	46 6	Johnston, William	Heathcot, Lumphanan	50	43 5
Hay, Col. Alex. S. L., of Rannes	Leith-hall, Kennethmont	12,546	7,916 8	Johnston, Reps. of Wm.	Brandsbutts, Inverurie	10	52 4
Hay, Trustees of late James	Bellfield, Aberdeen	107	240 —	Johnston, Sir William, of Hilton, Bart.	Hilton House, Aberdeen	308	765 14
Hay, James Gordon, of Seaton	Seaton, Aberdeen	3,342	5,960 13	Johnston & Fullerton	Woodside	3	195 —
Hector, Trustees of James	Aberdeen	13	62 —	Johnston, Elisabeth	King St. Rd., Aberdeen	9	38 —
Hector, Mrs. Susan	Udny	1	44 —	Jopp, Trs. of late Alex.	Woodhill, Aberdeen	45	230 —
Henderson, Alexander	Mile End, Aberdeen	1	19 —				
Henderson, Trustees of late Alexander, of Caskieben	Caskieben, Aberdeen	1,850	1,263 14	Keay, Rev. W. Murray	The Manse, Foveran	7	32 —
Henderson, Heirs of John	Cairncry, Aberdeen	22	72 —	Keith, William	Old Aberdeen	1	61 —
Henderson, Robert R.	Blackhill, Peterhead	25	73 15	Keith, William, jun.	Aberdeen	10	237 15
Henderson, William	Devanha House, Aberdeen	8	110 —	Keith, Mrs. Isabella	Stockethill, Aberdeen	45	221 —
Henderson, Trustees of late William	Abbothall, Aberdeen	42	92 —	*Keith-hall, Kirk-Session of Parish of*	Keith-hall	1	14 12
Henry, William Leslie	Findracy, Echt	1	34 10	Kemp, Rev. John Syme	The Manse, Dyce	6	30 —
Hepburn, Alexander	Parkhill, Turriff	50	63 —	Kilgour, Patrick	Upper Middlefield, Aberdeen	20	68 —
Hepburn, George, of Bogside	Dublin	308	93 19	Kilgour, William, of Tulloch and Balgaveny	Tulloch Cottage, Old Meldrum	2,740	2,018 —
Hepburn, George	Liverpool	6	76 —	King, Lieut.-Col. William Ross, of Tertowie	Tertowie House, Blackburn	381	481 15
Hepburn, James	Little Swanford, Turriff	40	48 —	*King Edward, Heritors of Parish of*	King Edward	1	43 —
Hill, William James D.	Kintore	17	72 16	Kinloch, Alex. John, of Park	Park House, Drumoak	1,681	1,118 10
Hogarth, Mrs. Thomas	Elmfield, Aberdeen	3	65 —	Kintore, Earl of	Keith-hall, Inverurie	17,021	15801 17
Horn, James, of Pitmedden	Pitmedden, Oyne	805	956 9	*Kirk Work Fund*	Old Machar	2	190 —
Howie, Alex., & Sons	Buxburn, Aberdeen	7	270 —	Knight, Reps. of William	Hillhead, Old Meldrum	1	24 19
Humphrey, John	Guildhall, Dyce	47	90 —	Knox, Mrs. Ann	Old Meldrum	2	22 6
Humphrey, John, of Comalegy	Balmoral Pl., Aberdeen	304	375 12	Kyle, Capt. John, of Binghill	Binghill, Aberdeen	212	320 —
Hunter, Alexander	Inverurie	2	45 2				
Hunter, Capt. Alexander Chambers, of Tillery	Tillery House, Newburgh, Aberdeen	3,687	3,146 16				
Hunter, Mrs. Isabella	Janefield, Cults	5	30 —	Lamond, William, of Stranduff	Stranduff, Kincardine O'Neil	809	457 19
Huntly, Marquis of	Aboyne Castle	80,000	11215 3	Lamond, Mrs. Margaret, of Pitmurchie	Pitmurchie, Torphins	380	319 12
Hutchison, Alexander	Cocklaw, Peterhead	511	528 2	Lawson, John	Blackhills, Skene	2	18 —
Hutchison, Thomas	Richmond Hill, Peterhead	20	60 —	Leith, Alexander, of Freefield and Glenkindy	Freefield, Insch	8,566	4,217 —
Hutchison, William, of Cairngall	Cairngall, Longside	810	1,336 15	Leith, James Forbes, of Whitehaugh	Whitehaugh, Alford	3,864	2,852 10
Hutchison, Christian's Representatives, and Mrs. Jane Bruce	Peterhead / Burntisland	2	299 9	Leith, Trustees and Executors of John, of Balcairn	Balcairn, Aberdeen	1,046	1,391 10
Imray, James and John Imray	Elmhill / Aboyne	6	25 10	Leith, Lady, of Westhall	Westhall, Oyne	474	683 10
Infirmary, President and Managers of Royal	Aberdeen	1,566	1,566 17	Lendrum, George, of Stirling Brae	Pothead, Cruden	158	366 —
Innes, Lieut.-Col. Thomas, of Learney	Learney, Torphins	6,923	3,264 5	Leslie, Rev. Alexander	Parsonage, Meiklefolla, Rothie	8	18 —
Innes, Thomas G. Rose, of Netherdale	Netherdale House, Turriff	3,744	2,448 3	Leslie, Trustees for Alex. Milne	Udny	211	322 11
Innes, Thomas	Middlemuir, Inverurie	11	29 —	Leslie, Trustees of late Colonel Charles, of Balquhain, K.H.	Fetternear House, Inverurie	8,940	7,388 —
Innes, Mrs. Agnes	Kintore	2	15 —	Leslie, Captain Hans Geo., of Dunlugas	Dunlugas House, Turriff	64	32 —
Insch, Parochial Board of	Insch	6	17 —	Leslie, Heirs of Hugh Fraser, of Powis	Powis, Old Aberdeen	132	1,154 12
Inverurie Gas Light Company	Inverurie	1	71 —	Leslie, Heirs of James	Old Meldrum	3	37 2
Inverurie, Heritors of Parish of	Inverurie	1	40 —	Leslie, John	Holm Cottage, Inverurie	6	48 10
Inverurie, Magistrates of Burgh of	Inverurie	45	201 19	Leslie, Rev. John	The Manse, Udny	13	59 —
Irvine, Rev. Alexander	The Manse, Crimond	7	32 —	Leslie, Trustees for John	Udny	257	331 18
Irvine, Alex. Forbes, of Drum and Schivas	Drum Castle	7,689	5,209 13	Leslie, Lt.-Col. Jonathan Forbes, of Rothie and Badenscoth	Rothie-Norman	7,164	4,628 11
Jack, John	Whitecairns, Belhelvie	1	9 10	Leslie, Lieut.-Col. Lewis Xavier	Tillydrone, Old Aberdeen	4	107 —
Jackson, George	Inverurie	1	72 10	Leslie, William, of Warthill	Warthill, Pitcaple	3,960	4,486 18
Jackson, Henry	Loch-head, Aberdeen	3	112 —	Leslie, William, of Nethermuir	Albyn Place, Aberdeen	2,298	2,659 2
Jamieson, Alexander	Peterhead	208	404 12	Leslie, Heirs of Mrs. Barbara, of Meadaple	Kinbroon House, Rothie	295	380 —
Jamieson, George	Drumgarth, Aberdeen	10	77 —	Leslie, Trustees for Annabella	Udny	124	165 17
Jamieson, George, of Rosebank	Albyn Place, Aberdeen	199	184 12				
Jamieson, James	Prospect Hill, Aberdeen	50	227 10				
Johnston, Alexander	Johnston Place, Crimond	244	333 —				
Johnston, Rev. James	F.C. Manse, Belhelvie	2	15 —				

ABERDEEN—continued.

Name of Owner.	Address of Owner.	Estimated Acreage of Property.	Gross Annual Value.	Name of Owner.	Address of Owner.	Estimated Acreage of Property.	Gross Annual Value.
		Acres.	£ s.			Acres.	£ s.
Leslie, Trustees for Barbara Janet	Udny	167	167 17	Maitland, William	Rothney Inn, Premnay	1	79 —
Leslie, Isabel	Aberdeen	1	7 —	Mann, William	North Braco, Cruden	245	206 10
Leslie, Trustees for Susan Hector	Udny	142	223 2	Mann, Mrs. Jessie	South Braco, Cruden	125	74 14
Lessel, Reps. of Mrs. Mary	Inverurie	1	52 10	Manson, Alexander, of Kilblean	Kilblean Cottage, Old Meldrum	360	432 10
Ligertwood, John	Buxburn, Aberdeen	181	569 3	Manson, James	Cromblethill, Old Meldrum	4	114 10
Littlejohn, William	Camphill House, Aberdeen	18	95 —	Manson, John, of Fingask	King Street, Aberdeen	585	860 15
Lizars, Mrs. Mary	Arnlee, Cults	14	50 —	Manson, John, & Co.	Glengarioch Distillery, Old Meldrum	3	71 10
Low, Rev. Alexander	The Manse, Keig	16	38 —				
Low, Rev. Alexander	The Parsonage, Longside	1	15 —	Manson, Reprs. of Rev. John	Banff	200	149 —
Low, Mrs. Jane	Inverurie	5	14 —	Marr, George, of Hatton	Cairnbrogie, Old Meldrum	633	520 12
Lumsden, Rev. Edward	The Manse, Midmar	15	44 —	Marr, John	Cliff House, Cults	11	65 —
Lumsden, Edward James, of Bethelnie	Auchry House, Turriff	620	1,077 —	Marr, Mrs. Jean and Mrs. S. Davidson	Cromblet, Old Meldrum } North Coullie, Udny }	3	23 15
Lumsden, Frederick C., of North Bethelnie	Auchry House, Turriff	745	706 12	Martin, James	Aberdeen	62	150 10
Lumsden, Henry, of Pitcaple	Pitcaple Castle	1,410	1,680 12	Masson, Rev. Wm.	The Manse, Culsalmond	13	35 —
				Matthews, Alexander	Kirkton of Tough	2	17 —
Lumsden, Hugh Gordon, of Clova and Auchindoir	Clova, Lumsden	15,499	6,886 11	Matthews, William, jun.	Polmuir, Aberdeen	20	126 4
Lumsden, John Farquhar, of Auchry	Auchry House, Turriff	615	804 —	Mearns, Rev. William, of Disblair	The Manse, Kinneff	1,012	1,342 3
Lumsden, Richard W., of Cuminestown	Auchry House, Turriff	892	736 15	Meldrum, Heritors of Parish of	Meldrum	1	30 —
				Melvin, William	Patie's Mill, Keith-hall	2	20 —
Lumsden, Colonel Thos., of Belhelvie, C.B.	Belhelvie Lodge, Aberdeen	717	814 8	Menzies, Mrs. Thomas	Summerfield, Aberdeen	5	24 10
Lumsden, William James, of Balmedie	Balmedie House, Aberdeen	7,397	6,728 10	Merchant Maiden Hospital, Governors of	Edinburgh	2,674	4,126 11
Lumsden, Mrs. Jane	Glenbogie Cott., Rhynie	5	35 —	Merchant's Society	Old Aberdeen	11	68 —
Lumsden, Mrs. Susannah, of Cushnie	Cushnie House, Alford	5,000	2,588 8	Mess, Jonathan	Gordon's Mills, Aberdeen	12	455 16
				Michie, Mrs. James	Lumsden Village	2	51 —
Lunatic Asylum, Managers of Royal	Aberdeen	42	1,050 —	Middleton, Alexander	Tillymorgan, Culsalmond	7	40 —
Lyon, Alexander	Lillybank, Aberdeen	2	85 —	Middleton, Francis	Tillymorgan, Culsalmond	131	138 —
				Middleton, George	Balnagowan, Aboyne	100	45 —
				Middleton, Rev. John	The Manse, Glenmuick	8	35 —
				Milligan, Rev. William	Old Aberdeen	1	48 —
Macandrew, Daniel	Firhill, Aberdeen	6	120 5	Milne, Rev. Alexander	The Manse, Tyrie	7	30 —
M'Allan, Mrs. Helen	Fountainhall, Aberdeen	4	52 —	Milne, Rev. Alexander	The Manse, Tough	6	32 —
M'Bain, George	Seafield, Aberdeen	7	63 15	Milne, Rev. And. Jamieson	The Manse, Fyvie	8	39 —
M'Combie, Rev. Charles	The Manse, Lumphanan	1,707	1,051 12	Milne, David	Greenfield, Turriff	174	112 10
M'Combie, Jas., & Co.	Peterhead	2	50 —	Milne, John Duguid, of Melgum	Ardmiddle House, Turriff	2,568	1,423 19
M'Combie, William, of Easter Skene	Easter Skene, Lynturk	2,179	1,992 19	Milne, John Henderson, of Craigellie	Craigellie House, Lonmay	714	922 13
M'Crie, Rev. George	F.C. Manse, Clola, Mintlaw	5	19 —	Milne, John and Wm. Ramsay	Mains of Laithers, Turriff } Cupar-Fife }	3	70 —
Macdonald, Alexander	Kepplestone, Aberdeen	16	81 —	Milne's Mortification	Aberdeen	8	47 —
M'Donald, Ewan	Johnstone, Skene	85	128 19	Milne, Rev. Robert	The Manse, Towie	6	28 —
M'Donald, F. K., and Rev. George Davidson	Pitmuxton, Aberdeen	25	119 —	Milne, William	Burnrigs, Inverurie	1	15 —
M'Donald, Rev. John	F. C. Manse, Kinellar	1	20 —	Milne, William	Burnland Cott., Inverurie	8	33 5
M'Hardy, David	Cranford, Aberdeen	4	52 —	Milne, Mrs. Barbara, of Ardmiddle	Ardmiddle House, Turriff	1,100	1,070 4
Mackintosh, John	Peterhead	13	14 —				
M'Intosh, Rev. James M.	F. C. Manse, Skene	1	25 —	Milne, Mrs. Isabella	Turtory House, Marnoch	927	649 —
Mackenzie, James T., of Kintail and Glenmuick	Glenmuick House, Ballater	25,000	1,116 —	Milne, Mrs. Margaret	Kinaldie, Blackburn	295	455 10
				Milne, Mrs. Susan	Comers, Midmar	3	26 —
Mackenzie, John, of Glack	Glack House, Daviot	4,036	3,825 3	Mitchell, Alexander, of Kincraig	Ythan Lodge, Newburgh	489	508 12
Mackenzie, John Russell	Thorngrove, Aberdeen	2	50 —	Mitchell, Andrew	Logierieve, Udny	295	364 9
Mackenzie, William, of Fortrie	Mount St. Ternan, Banchory	836	651 19	Mitchell, Rev. Henry	The Manse, Monquhitter	11	49 —
Mackenzie, Mrs. Elizabeth	Friendville, Aberdeen	28	137 10	Mitchell, John Forbes, of Thainstone	Thainstone House, Kintore	1,107	1,123 7
Mackenzie, Trs. of late Christina, of Foveran	Foveran House, Aberdeen	1,486	1,732 —	Mitchell, Thomas Walker	Maryhill, Turriff	212	242 —
M'Kenzie, Rev. James	The Manse, Aboyne	30	30 —	Mitchell, William	Glendaveny, Peterhead	7	19 —
M'Kerran, Rev. Robert	The Manse, Clatt	5	33 —	Mitchell, William	Elmbank, Aberdeen	2	60 —
Mackie, Alexander	South Mile-end, Aberdeen	4	38 —	Mitchell and Rae	Newburgh, Foveran	6	204 —
				Mitchell, Mrs. Helen	Berryhill, Peterhead	202	460 13
Mackie, Elisabeth	Inverurie	5	22 —	Moir, Alexander	Granitehill, Aberdeen	22	72 —
M'Laren, Rev. Peter	The Manse, Fraserburgh	6	59 —	Moir, Trs. and Executors of late Colonel George, C.B.	Scotstown, Aberdeen	626	1,533 —
M'Lennan, Mrs. Jane	Camphill, Lumphanan	555	317 19				
M'Leod, Rev. Nicholas K.	The Parsonage, Ellon	2	21 —				
M'Nab, Alexander, of Techmuiry	Middleton Kerse, Clackmannan	1,933	1,650 3	Moir, Trustees of John, & Sons	Aberdeen	219	554 18
M'Naughton, Archibald	Balgairn, Ballater	1	30 —	Moir, Trustees of late Robert	Howe of Tarty, Ellon	450	405 10
Macpherson, Rev. W. Mearns	The Manse, Monymusk	9	36 10	Moir, William	Calfward, Inverurie	8	26 —
M'Pherson, James	Mile-end, Aberdeen	2	45 —	Moir, Margaret	Muirfield, Aberdeen	2	10 —
M'Pherson, Trustees of late John	Springhill, Aberdeen	131	322 15	Morgan, Alexander	Kintore	3	33 —
				Morgan, Duncan C.	Causewayend, Lonmay	17	20 10
M'Willam, Rev. Alex	Ythan Wells, Forgue	4	28 —	Morrice, David R.	Old Aberdeen	1	70 14

ABERDEEN—continued.

Name of Owner.	Address of Owner.	Estimated Acreage of Property.	Gross Annual Value.	Name of Owner.	Address of Owner.	Estimated Acreage of Property.	Gross Annual Value.
		Acres.	£ s.			Acres.	£ s.
Morrison, Alexander, of Bognie	Mountblairy House, Turriff	10,251	7,128 9	Queen, Her Majesty The	Balmoral Castle	25,350	2,392 16
Morrison, George	E. Whitemyres, Newhills	10	20 —				
Morrison, George	Forbes-field, Aberdeen	14	80 —	Rae, Alexander	Pimlico, London	1	64 2
Morrison, Harry L. L., of Blair	Newton of Struthers, Forres	1,187	1,214 13	Rae, Alexander	Kintore	4	15 14
				Rainy, Rev. Alexander	The Manse, Drumblade	11	35 15
Morrison, Mrs. Agnes	Old Meldrum	3	39 —	Rainy, Trustees of late Dr.	Middlefield, Aberdeen	58	319 16
Morrison, Mrs. Mary	Clerkhill, Peterhead	6	8 —	Ramsay, Lieut.-Col. John, of Barra and Straloch	Straloch and Barra Castle	3,056	2,716 3
Mortimer, Arthur	Old Aberdeen	1	70 —	Rankine, Rev. Edward	U. P. Manse, Shiels	1	13 —
Morton, Mrs. Elizabeth	43 Dee Street, Aberdeen	1	25 —	Redhyth's Mortification, Trustees of	Aberdeen	457	423 17
Muirs School, Trustees of	Fyvie	6	5 —	Reid, Trustees of late James	Muirtown, Aberdeen	622	815 10
Murdoch, Rev. James	F. C. Manse, Rosehearty	1	20 —	Reid, Rev. John	The Manse, Savock	4	26 —
Murray, Andrew, of Allathan	Belmont St., Aberdeen	1,250	1,729 10	Reid, John	Rubislaw, Aberdeen	8	78 10
Murray and Hutton's Mortification, Trustees of	Concraig, Skene	466	491 19	Reid, Robert	Woodside, Kintore	3	54 10
Mutch, John	Philipston, Old Meldrum	75	75 —	Reid, Rev. William	The Manse, Auchindoir	15	34 —
				Reid, Trustees of late Mrs. Elspet	Westburn, Inverurie	2	15 15
Napier, Charles	Links, Aberdeen	2	25 —	Rennie, John T.	Deemount, Aberdeen	8	180 5
National Bank of Scotland	Edinburgh	36	160 3	Richards and Company	Broadford, Aberdeen	32	482 —
New Pitsligo, Trs. of Q. S. Established Church of	New Pitsligo	1	20 —	Richmond, Duke of	Gordon Castle	69,660	24747 15
Nicol, Robert and Alex.	Auchentarf, Rayne	197	253 18	Ritchie, Rev. Andrew	The Manse, Coull	6	29 —
Nicol, William Edward, of Ballogie	Ballogie, Aboyne	7,219	2,558 6	Robb, George, of Pittrichie	Pittrichie House, Udny	1,019	1,040 —
Nicol, Christina	Inverurie	3	11 —	Robb, Rev. John	The Manse, Longside	370	430 16
Niven, Alexander	Woodside, Aberdeen	196	215 14	Robbie & Murray	Dyce	1	20 —
North of Scotland Banking Company, Trustees of	Aberdeen	1,736	1,554 9	Robertson, Andrew, of Hopewell	Indego, Tarland	520	352 10
Northern Agricultural Company	Aberdeen	1	52 —	Robertson, George	Inverurie	1	15 —
				Robertson, George	Schoolhouse, Lonmay	1	10 —
Northern Lights, Commissioners of	Edinburgh	10	84 —	Robertson, James	Huntly	4	239 5
				Robertson, Peter	Wellbank, Peterhead	41	68 —
				Robertson, William	Invernorth, Rathen	23	26 —
Obrist, Trustees of Mdme. Alice Jane	Auchleuchries, Cruden	910	946 16	Robertson, Mrs. Isabella, of Persleyden	Huntly	146	351 5
Ogilvie, Rev. William	The Manse, Fintray	10	48 17	Robertson, Jane	Bridgefield, Aberdeen	4	45 —
Ogston, James	Norwood Hall, Cults	16	115 —	Robinson, Hardy, of Denmore	Denmore, Aberdeen	286	564 11
Old Meldrum, Superior and Feuars of	Old Meldrum	81	10 —	Rodger, Trustees of Jas.	Whitemyres, Newhills	10	28 10
Old Mill Reformatory, Directors of	Aberdeen	56	185 —	Roger, Marriage Trustees of James and Mrs.	Aberdeen	45	145 —
Orrok, Trustees of late John G. B., of Orrok	Orrok, Belhelvie	1,026	1,103 8	Roman Catholic Congregation, Trustees for	Strichen	9	35 —
				Rose, Executors of Donaldson, of Hazlehead	Hazlehead, Aberdeen	832	1,130 8
				Rose, Hugh	Mains of Shiels, Whitecairns	47	97 10
Panton, Patrick	Eden Bank, Roxburgh	1	25 —	Ross, James	Donneside, Tarland	118	127 —
Park, John and Thomas	Fraserburgh	2	128 10	Ross, John L., of Arnage	Arnage House, Ellon	2,050	2,003 8
Paterson, Rev. John	U.P. Manse, Whitehill	1	22 —	Ross, Major John, of Tillycorthie	Albyn Place, Aberdeen	220	296 10
Paterson, William	Auldtown of Carnousie, Turriff	60	125 —	Ross, Rev. Robert	The Manse, Cruden	10	32 —
Paterson, William	Rose Cottage, Kinellar	28	45 —	Ross, Rev. William	The Manse, Kintore	10	49 13
Paton, Lieut.-Col. John, of Grandhome	Grandhome, Aberdeen	1,745	2,849 10	Ross, Mrs. Elizabeth, and Isabella Lawson	Elgin	434	263 7
Paull, Rev. William	The Manse, Tullynessle	14	35 —	Rough, Alexander	Newpark, Newhills	113	175 4
Pegler, George	Kepplestone, Aberdeen	15	144 10	Rough, Mrs. Jane	Mill of Lumphart, Daviot	3	28 —
Perry, Eliza	Maida Vale, Stonehaven	1	18 —	Roy, Trustees of late James	Rotunda Place, Aberdeen	18	125 —
Peter, Rev. George	The Manse, Kemnay	12	33 —	Russell, James, of Aden	Aden, Mintlaw	8,402	6,989 6
Peter, Rev. James	The Manse, Old Deer	36	76 15	Russell, William	Kinninmonth House, Mintlaw	675	462 12
Peterhead, Trustees for Community of Feuars of	Peterhead	52	344 12	Rust, Rev. James	The Manse, Slains	7	32 —
Peterhead, Trustees of Harbours of	Peterhead (Quays & Harbour Basins)	2 / 22	249 13 / 2,934 —	Rust, Williamson, of Auchinclech	Gilcomston Park, Aberdeen	150	252 10
Philip, Alexander	Yonderton, Cruden	700	514 10	Rutherford, George David	Deebank, Aberdeen	28	15 —
Philip, Johnston	Inverurie	13	89 10	Ruxton, Thomas	Craigton, Aberdeen	25	110 —
Philip, Rev. Wm.	The Manse, Skene	15	41 —				
Philip, Mrs. Ann	Loan Cottage, Inverurie	2	70 2				
Philip, Mary and Cath.	Inverurie	6	42 5	Saltoun, Lord	Philorth House, Fraserburgh	10,082	10967 3
Phillip, Reprs. of Colin A.	Pitmuxton, Aberdeen	26	68 —	Saltoun, Trustees of late Lord	Memsie, Fraserburgh	700	962 18
Phillip, John	East Middlefield, Aberdeen	18	46 —	Sangster, Alexander	Stonehousehill, Cruden	144	84 —
Pirie, Alex., and Sons	Stoneywood, Aberdeen	263	3,292 5	Sangster, Trustees of late Alexander	Westburn, Inverurie	8	40 —
Pirie, Francis	Marchfield, Inverurie	4	15 —	Sangster, James	Newfield of Invernettie, Peterhead	101	75 —
Polson, Robert L.	Old Aberdeen	2	91 18				
Polson, Jessie and Grace	Old Aberdeen	1	39 7				
Pringle, Rev. John	The Manse, Tarves	8	37 —				
Prott, William	Huntly	1	79 —				

ABERDEEN—continued.

Name of Owner.	Address of Owner.	Estimated Acreage of Property.	Gross Annual Value.	Name of Owner.	Address of Owner.	Estimated Acreage of Property.	Gross Annual Value.
		Acres.	£ s.			Acres.	£ s.
Scott, Trustees of late Alexander	Huntly	585	898 17	Stewart, Rev. James	The Manse, Peterhead	14	88 15
Scott, Mrs. Elizabeth I. J., of Gala	Gala House, Galashiels	190	150 —	Stewart, Executors of late Marjory	Caernaveron, Alford	418	384 —
Scott, Wilhelmina Ann, of Campfield	Campfield, Banchory	1,057	723 1	Still, Charles Stewart	Richmond Hill, Aberdeen	5	110 —
Seton, David, of Mounie	Portobello	1,336	1,967 4	Still, James	Burnbank, Aberdeen	8	18 —
Seton, Sir William Coote, of Pitmedden, Bart.	Pitmedden House	662	996 10	Still, Robert, of Millden	London	800	789 8
Shand, Alex. Sharp, of Templand	Templand, Forgue	620	685 —	Stirling, Reps. of George	Westerton, Cults	7	82 —
Shand, Sir C. Farquhar, Kt.	Mauritius	2	45 7	Storie, Rev. Archibald	The Manse, Insch	10	37 —
Shaw, Farquharson, of Auchinhove	Auchinhove, Lumphanan	350	289 —	Strachan, William	Mill of Balmaud, Turriff	248	185 —
Shaw, Robert	Kepplestone, Aberdeen	5	16 10	Strachan, William	Moreseat, Aberdeen	8	76 15
Shaw, Elizabeth O.	Aberdeen	1	44 —	Stronach, Alexander	Sunnypark, Old Aberdeen	6	60 —
Shepherd, James, of Aldie	Aldie, Cruden	1,750	1,154 3	Struthers, John	Old Aberdeen	1	70 —
Shepherd, Trustees of late James, of Aldie	Longhaven, Cruden	3,173	2,422 4	Stuart, Alexander, of Inchbreck and Laithers	Laithers House, Turriff	1,191	987 10
Shepherd, Capt. Thomas, of Kirkville	Kirkville House, Skene	442	728 5	Stuart, Lieut. Eustace R. Burnett, of Dens and Crichie	Cork	1,262	1,516 10
Sheriffs, Lieut.-Col. Alex.	Torryburn House, Kintore	3	25 —	Stuart, Margaret C. D.	17 Newbie Ter., Liverpool	1	67 —
Shier, David	Kepplestone Cottage, Aberdeen	2	30 —	Stuartfield, Feuars of Village of	Old Deer	28	6 7
Shipmasters, Society of	Aberdeen	1	434 14	Sutherland, James	Seafield, Aberdeen	14	180 —
Shirreffs, Trustees of late Miss Shirreffs Lumsden	Blairmormond, Lonmay	898	1,083 15	Summers, George	Whitehouse, Keig	1	40 —
Shives, James	New Pitsligo	42	66 —	Swan, Alexander	Eastfield, Aberdeen	1	27 12
Sim, James	Cornhill, Aberdeen	159	784 18	Symmers, Alex. A.	Glenburnie, Aberdeen	389	240 17
Sim, John	Holborn, Aberdeen	3	18 —	Symmers, George S. A.	Glenburnie, Aberdeen	445	314 2
Simpson, Reps. of late Alex.	Hole, Fochabers	19	27 —				
Simpson, Alex., junior	Deebank, Aberdeen	13	63 —	Tailors, Incorporation of	Aberdeen	10	42 14
Simpson, Alex., junior, and others	Glenythan, Forgue	850	572 13	Tailors, Incorporation of	Old Aberdeen	1	42 4
Simpson, Trustees of late Alex., of Colyhill	Colyhill, Aberdeen	1,882	1,739 9	Tait, Wm., and others	Crichie, Kintore	66	731 2
Simpson, Rev. James	F. C. Manse, Monquhitter	1	22 —	Tayler, George Skene, of Inchgarth	Inchgarth, Aberdeen	118	353 —
Simpson, Rob., of Cobairdy	Cobairdy, Huntly	1,703	1,660 9	Taylor, George	Mill of Allathan, New Deer	44	111 10
Simpson, Thomas	Old Meldrum	4	33 7	Taylor, George	Inverurie	4	92 10
Sinclair, Alexander	Inverurie	2	19 10	Taylor, Rev. Malcolm C.	The Manse, Crathie	8	52 —
Sinclair, William	Morningside, Aberdeen	2	26 10	Taylor, Mrs. Elspet	Ellon	1	80 15
Singer, Mrs. Mary	Hatton, Fintray	1	5 —	Thain, Alex. Sharp	Drumblair, Forgue	30	46 —
Skelton, Jas., of Sandford	Gogar House, Edinburgh	118	235 —	Thom, William	Outseats, Pitmuxton, Aberdeen	4	77 —
Skene, Trustees of late George, of Skene	Skene House	3,849	2,950 4	Thompson, George, of Pitmedden	Pitmedden, Dyce	1,308	1,671 1
Skene, J. Gordon Cumming, of Pitlurg and Dyce	Pitlurg House, Ellon	8,992	6,362 4	Thomson, Alexander	North Street, Inverurie	1	85 10
Skene, Wm. Abraham, of Lethenty	Bath	900	1,201 6	Thomson, Alexander	Redhouse, Bourtie	3	95 10
Skinner, James, senior	Westfield, Inverurie	10	45 —	Thomson, David	Old Aberdeen	2	60 —
Skinner, James	Woodside, Aberdeen	2	54 10	Thomson, Trustees of late George	Boynsmill, Forgue	18	333 —
Skinner, Rev. William	The Manse, Tarland	9	50 —	Thomson, John	Schoolhouse, Turriff	3	16 10
Smart, Rev. Gordon	The Manse, Cabrach	27	22 10	Thomson, Rev. William	The Manse, Belhelvie	10	33 —
Smith, Francis	Balnagarth, Aberdeen	8	42 10	Thurburn, Representatives of late Mrs., of Murtle	Murtle House, Aberdeen	500	807 13
Smith, James	Wester Ord, Skene	150	140 —	Trades Widows' Fund	Aberdeen	12	50 8
Smith, Rev. Jas. M'Gavin	The Manse, Millbrex	3	16 10	Trefusis, Hon. C. J. R. H. S. F., of Pitsligo, and Lord Clinton as his administrator in law	Heanton Satchville, Devon	6,730	4,760 4
Smith, John	Old Aberdeen	1	24 15	Turner, Major John, of Turnerhall	Turnerhall, Ellon	2,970	3,087 19
Smith, Trustees of late John	Easter Ord, Skene	151	200 —	Turner, Helen C. and Robina R., of Menie	Menie, Belhelvie	1,694	1,709 5
Smith, Robert, of Glenmillan	Glenmillan House, Lumphanan	665	490 11				
Smith, Rev. Robert	Chanonry, Old Aberdeen	10	81 14	Udny, John Henry, of Udny and Dudwick	Udny Castle	9,225	9,041 7
Smith, William	Muir of Kinellar	28	28 —	Union Bank of Scotland, Trustees of	Glasgow	1	168 —
Smith, Trs. of late William	Jericho, Insch	355	472 —	Urquhart, B. C., of Meldrum and Byth	Meldrum House	5,837	6,707 4
Smith, Mrs. Mary	Edinburgh	3	40 —	Urquhart, Mrs. Mary I. P., of Craigston	Craigston Castle, Turriff	3,998	2,856 2
Spottiswood, Henry A. F., of Muiresk	Aberdeen	1,491	1,396 19				
Sprott, Rev. George W.	The Manse, Chapel of Garioch	20	55 —	Wales, H.R.H. The Prince of	Birkhall, Ballater	6,810	816 12
Stables, Mrs. Ann	Old Aberdeen	3	36 15	Walker, Alexander, of Grange	Richmond Cott., Peterhead	202	509 —
Stein, John and Mrs.	Berryden, Aberdeen	10	98 —	Walker, George	North Balmoor, Peterhead	186	398 —
Stephen, George	Damhead, Cults	13	76 3				
Stephen, William	West Cults	130	275 —				
Stephen, Trustees of late William, of North Kinmundy	North Kinmundy, Summerhill	517	501 9				
Stevenson, A. Ogilvie	Ashgrove, Aberdeen	17	125 10				
Stevenson, William	Viewfield, Aberdeen	23	110 7				
Stewart, Rev. Charles	The Manse, Strichen	10	31 —				
Stewart, Rev. Donald	The Manse, King Edward	21	40 —				

ABERDEEN—continued.—(Municipal Borough of ABERDEEN.)

Name of Owner.	Address of Owner.	Estimated Acreage of Property.	Gross Annual Value.	Name of Owner.	Address of Owner.	Estimated Acreage of Property.	Gross Annual Value.
		Acres.	£ s.			Acres.	£ s.
Walker, George	North Mains of Barra, Old Meldrum	2	40 –	Whyte, Rev. James	The Manse, Methlic	10	40 –
Walker, James D., of Blairton	5 Oxford Square, Hyde Park, London	386	482 –	Whyte, James	Little Clinterty, Blackburn	250	277 10
Walker, John	Whitemyres, Newhills	2	8 –	Will, John H., & Co.	Peterhead	1	50 –
Walker, John and Peter	North Culmellie, Leochel Cushnie	53	38 –	Williamson, Alexander	Westhill, Skene	3	8 –
				Williamson, Arthur S.	Arthurseat, Aberdeen	24	90 9
Walker, Robert, of Richmond	Richmond, Peterhead	74	140 –	Williamson, John	Old Meldrum	3	45 –
Walker, Robert	Portlethen, Aberdeen	3	22 10	Williamson, Trustees of late Peter	Craigbank, Aberdeen	45	150 10
Walker, Thomas	Fraserburgh	2	241 10	Williamson, Jane, Margaret, and Eliza	Beech-hill, Aberdeen	20	127 –
Walker, William	Old Culmellie, Leochel Cushnie	61	48 –	Wilson, Alexander	Kirkhill, Old Meldrum	6	54 –
				Wilson, James	Crombletbank, Old Meldrum	1	32 –
Walker, William	Old Meldrum	1	25 –				
Walker, William, junior	Kepplestone, Aberdeen	1	24 –	Wilson, Rev. James	The Manse, Aberdour	12	45 –
Walker, Jane	Aspenbank, Ballater	1	25 –	Wilson, Rev. John	The Manse, Premnay	8	27 –
Wallace, Rev. David	Whitehall, Aberdeen	4	70 –	Wilson, Peter	Old Meldrum	4	65 10
Wallace, Rev. John	The Manse, New Deer	9	45 –	Wilson, Mrs. Elizabeth	North Kinmundy, Summerhill	27	65 10
War, Secretary of State for	London	1	160 –				
Watson, John Paton, of Blackford	Blackford House, Rothie	1,300	1,101 15	Wilson, Mrs. Margaret	Waterside, Forbes, Alford	1	25 –
				Wright, Rev. Maxwell	The Manse, Echt	5	39 –
Watt, George	Inverurie	2	21 3	Wrights and Coopers, Incorporation of	Aberdeen	15	101 –
Watt, Rev. John	The Manse, Strathdon	3	25 –				
Watt, John	Mains of Seaton, Aberdeen	1	78 9				
Weavers, Incorporation of	Aberdeen	148	275 –	Yeats, William, of Auquharney	Auquharney, Ellon	1,500	1,034 4
Weavers, Incorporation of	Old Aberdeen	1	47 10	Young, Alex., of Mount Pleasant	Mt. Pleasant, Peterhead	227	400 –
Webster, George	Durno, Pitcaple	71	117 11				
Webster, George	Bloomfield, Aberdeen	1	78 –	Young, Rev. Thomas	The Manse, Ellon	9	51 –
Webster, Rev. John	The Manse, Cluny	16	38 15	Youngson, T. A. W. A.	Southfield, Aberdeen	6	44 –
Webster, John	Longcroft, Oyne	60	80 –				
Webster, John	Aberdeen	16	109 –	Total Owners of Land of one Acre and upwards		869	1,252,100 768,791 4
Webster, Robert	Woodhead, Turriff	250	236 –				
Webster, William	Inverurie	1	20 –	Total Owners of Lands of less than one Acre in extent		3,620	1,258 82,724 19
Whyte, Alexander B.	Dalhibity Cottage, Peterculter	8	40 –				
Whyte, George	Meethill House, Peterhead	25	110 –				
Whyte, Trustees of late George, of Meethill	Meethill House, Peterhead	152	548 16	Grand Total		4,489	1,253,358 851,516 3

MUNICIPAL BOROUGH OF ABERDEEN.
Population over 20,000.

Name of Owner.	Address of Owner.	Estimated Acreage of Property.	Gross Annual Value.	Name of Owner.	Address of Owner.	Estimated Acreage of Property.	Gross Annual Value.
		Acres.	£ s.			Acres.	£ s.
Aberdeen Association for Improving the Dwellings of the Labouring Classes	Aberdeen	1	300 6	Black, William, & Co.	South Bridge	2	120 –
				Blaikie Brothers	St. Clement Street	6	657 10
Aberdeen Commercial Coy.	Aberdeen	2	441 10	Blind Asylum, Managers of	Huntly Street	1	300 –
Aberdeen Co-operative Building Coy.	Aberdeen	2	90 5	Bon-Accord Terrace, Proprietors of	Bon-Accord Terrace	2	14 –
Aberdeen County and Municipal Buildings, Commissioners of the	Aberdeen	1	1,792 10	Boys' and Girls' Hospital, Directors of	King Street	4	200 –
				British Linen Company Bank	Edinburgh	1	236 10
Aberdeen Harbour Commissioners	Aberdeen (Quays, Harbour, and Docks)	72	10783 12	Brown, George	Rosemount	4	461 16
	(Other Property)	60	3,331 –	Bryce, James	Westbank	1	176 11
Aberdeen Lime Company	Aberdeen	1	429 4	Byres, Trustees of James Gregory Moir, and Mrs.	Tonley, Whitehouse	1	40 7
Aberdeen, Magistrates and Town Council of	Aberdeen (Water and Gas Pipes, underground)	80	4,829 9	Caledonian Railway Coy.	Glasgow (Railway)	12	2,992 –
		–	7,246 –		(Other Property)	1	489 –
				Catto, Robert	Wallfield	5	102 10
Aberdeen Town and County Bank, Directors of	Aberdeen	8	1,165 13	Chalmers' Trustees	Sandilands	2	548 15
Adam, Trs. of late Robert	Jack's Brae	2	211 1	City of Glasgow Bank	Glasgow	1	859 12
Advocates, Society of	Aberdeen	10	298 –	Collie, Robt., junior	Cults	2	220 –
Anderson, Trustees of Sir Alexander, Kt.	Aberdeen	103	431 12	Commercial Bank of Scotland	Edinburgh	1	175 –
				Cumine, James, of Rattray	Rattray House, Peterhead	1	120 –
Bakers, Incorporation of	Aberdeen	10	722 18	Crown Property	Inland Revenue, Post-Office, and Custom-House	1	626 –
Bank of Scotland	Edinburgh	1	623 –				
Bannerman, Georgina	18 Albyn Place	1	120 –	Davidson, R. W. Duff	Hardgate	3	73 –

B

ABERDEEN—continued.—(Municipal Borough of ABERDEEN.)

Name of Owner.	Address of Owner.	Estimated Acreage of Property.	Gross Annual Value.	Name of Owner.	Address of Owner.	Estimated Acreage of Property.	Gross Annual Value.
		Acres.	£ s.			Acres.	£ s.
Deeside Railway Company	Aberdeen (Railway)	3	165 —	Northern Agricultural Co.	Waterloo Quay	1	595 10
Donaldson, George	Summerfield	2	44 —	Northern Assurance Co.	Aberdeen	1	200 —
Downie, Trustees of late Charles	Duff's Park	9	705 3	North of Scotland Banking Company	Aberdeen	1	441 —
Dunn, William	Fonthill Place	1	600 8				
Edwards, Trustees of late Alexander	George Street	2	557 18	Ogg, Henry, & Co.	Cuparston	2	581 13
				Ogston, Alex., & Sons	Loch Street	3	273 3
Falconer, Catherine	Belvidere	3	87 —	Old Machar, Parochial Board of Parish of	St. Machar Place	4	260 11
Ferguson, Rev. Alex.	Leadside	1	36 7				
Fisher, Trustees of late William	Ferryhill House	14	125 —	Pirie, Alex., & Sons	Stoneywood	2	460 —
Fordyce, W. D., M.P.	Brucklay Castle	4	224 19				
Fraser, David	Broadford Cottage	1	50 —				
Fraser, John, & Son	Hutcheon Street	4	125 —	Reith, Mrs. Margaret	Cuparston	1	32 15
				Richards & Co.	Broadford Works	13	2,101 10
				Robinson, Crum, & Co.	Bannermill	14	1,056 12
Gordon's, Robert, Hospital, Governors of	Schoolhill	3	533 5	Reid, George and Joseph S. Sams	Justice Mill Lane	1	85 —
Gash, John	St. Clair Street	1	34 —	Runcy, Charles	Barkmill	3	135 13
Gill, David	Skene Terrace	1	274 —	Runcy, Theophilus	Millbank	13	121 —
Gray, Margaret	King Street	2	369 10	Royal Bank of Scotland	Edinburgh	1	140 —
Great North of Scotland Railway Company	Aberdeen (Railway) (Other Property, under an acre)	37 —	2,455 — 324 15				
				Sangster, Alexander	Nellfield Place	2	208 15
				Scottish Provincial Assurance Company	Aberdeen	1	280 —
Hadden, Alex., & Sons	Green	3	1,000 —	Shipmasters, Society of	Aberdeen	7	333 5
Hadden, James Farquhar	Union Grove	12	150 —	Shoemakers, Incorporation of	Aberdeen	11	316 15
Hall, Russell, & Co.	York Place	1	445 —				
Henderson, James and William	Westfield	6	210 10	Sim, Heirs of Major-Gen. Duncan	Holburn Street	2	131 3
Henderson, John Sharp	Willowbank	1	255 —	Sim, John	Millbank	2	289 18
Henderson, Mrs. Jane	Loanhead	5	118 10	Smith, George	Mounthooly	1	305 5
				Spark, Henry Smith	Craigie Park	7	137 15
				Stevens, Robert	Rosemount	2	349 13
Incurables' Hospital, Directors of	Aberdeen	3	77 15	Stevenson, William	Viewfield	2	1,044 —
Industrial School, Directors of	Skene Square	2	319 —	St. Nicholas, Parochial Board of Parish of	Nelson Street	6	716 —
Infirmary, Managers of Royal	Woolmanhill	2	628 14	Sutherland, James	Seafield	1	428 10
Ironside, William	Causewayend	1	112 6	Summers, Elsie	Summerfield	6	70 —
				Tailors, Incorporation of	Aberdeen	6	25 5
Jamieson, George	Langstane Place	2	1,031 —	Trades' Hospital of Aberdeen	Aberdeen	45	805 10
Keith, William, junior	Roslin Terrace	4	249 14				
				University of Aberdeen	Aberdeen	10	1,534 13
				Union Bank of Scotland	Glasgow	1	355 —
Laing, John	Granton Lodge	2	100 —				
Leslie, William	Albyn Place	1	301 1				
Lumsden, William	Eastbank	2	288 —	War, Secretary of State for	London	2	500 —
				White, James	Millbank	1	45 —
				Williams, William	Catto Square	3	1,145 8
Macdonald, Field, & Co.	Constitution Street	3	270 —	Wood, Trustees of Henry and Mrs.	Leadside	1	25 10
M'Gregor, Mrs. Ann	Summer Street	4	736 6	Wrights and Coopers, Incorporation of	Aberdeen	4	182 14
M'Kenzie, George	Rosemount Place	2	108 —				
Melville, Thomas	Westfield	2	80 —				
Militia Barracks, Commissioners of Supply of the County of Aberdeen for	King Street	3	350 —	Yeats, William, of Auquharney	Aberdeen	11	578 14
Miller, John, & Co.	Sandilands	7	460 6				
Milne, George	Queen's Cross	2	150 —	Total Owners of Land of one Acre and upwards		111 764	72,907 17
Mitchell, Adam	Charlotte Street	2	314 10	Total Owners of Lands of less than one Acre in extent		2,872 1,016	194,425 3
Morton, John Thomas	Mount Street	3	306 18				
National Bank of Scotland	Edinburgh	1	409 17				
Nicol, Alexander	29 Albyn Place	1	202 14	GRAND TOTAL		2,983 1,780	267,333 —

ARGYLL.

Population in 1871, - - - - - - - **75,679.**
Inhabited Houses, - - - - - - - **13,497.**
Number of Parishes, - - - - - - - **40.**

Name of Owner.	Address of Owner.	Estimated Acreage of Property.	Gross Annual Value.		Name of Owner.	Address of Owner.	Estimated Acreage of Property.	Gross Annual Value.
		Acres.	£ s.				Acres.	£ s.
Airston, Mrs. Mary Hunter	Blairmore	1	48 –		Buchanan, Trs. of late Robt.	Ardfillan, Dunoon	8	70 –
Alexander, Thomas	Kirn	2	40 –		Buchanan, William	Sandbank	1	26 –
Allan, Thomas W. Murray, of Glenfeochan	Glenfeochan, Oban	10,000	1,525 –		Buchanan, Jess	Munroy, Campbeltown	3	19 –
Alston, Mrs. Mary	Kilmun	1	45 –		Bulloch, Lade, & Co.	Campbeltown	1	154 –
Ancell, John	Castleton, Innellan	1	229 –		Burnley, William F.	Ericht Bank, Kirn	11	150 –
Anderson, Alexander	Hillside Cottage, Kirn	1	40 –		Caddow, John	Oban	1	20 –
Anderson, Alexander Dunlop, of Ardsheal	Ardsheal House, Fort-William	1,345	444 5		Cairns, John	Briarbrae, Innellan	1	55 –
Anderson, Reps. of John	Ashgrove, Innellan	1	347 –		Caldwell, Frederick Wm., of Mishnish	Mishnish, Tobermory	3,444	746 15
Anderson, John	Hunter's Quay	5	100 –		Caledonian Canal Commissioners	Kilmallie	252	210 –
Anderson, Heirs of William	Avondale Lodge, Dunoon	1	55 –		Callander, George F. W., of Ardkinglass	Ardkinglass, Cairndow	51,670	5,626 –
Andrew, Matthew	Anderston, Campbeltown	14	39 –		Cameron, Donald, of Lochiel, M.P.	Auchnacarry Castle, Fort-William	16,000	2,462 9
Annan, William	Fairfield, Kirn	1	85 –		Cameron, John	Lochaline, Fort-William	2	29 –
Arbuckle, Heirs of James	Joppa Lodge, Innellan	2	70 –		Cameron, Rev. John	Campbeltown	8	48 –
Ardrishaig Free Church, Trustees of	Ardrishaig	1	20 –		Cameron, Mrs. Mary, of Barcaldine	Barcaldine House, Taynuilt	20,000	2,078 19
Argyll and Bute, Lunacy Board of	Lochgilphead	50	500 –		Campbell, Alexander, of Auchindarroch	Auchindarroch, Lochgilphead	7,017	1,599 14
Argyll, Duke of	Inveraray Castle	168,315	45672 –		Campbell, Heirs of late Alexander C., of Monzie	Inverawe House, Bonaw	13,000	1,042 12
Austin, Henrietta, Elizabeth, and Margaret Isabella	Bellwood, Innellan	2	60 –		Campbell, Lt.-Col. Arch., of Glendaruel	Glendaruel House, Colintraive	14,032	2,361 –
Bain, Rev. James	Manse, Kilfinan	5	46 –		Campbell, Rev. Archibald	Assapoll, Bunessan	125	30 –
Bald, Peter	Fairy Knowe, Blairmore	2	100 –		Campbell, Rev. Colin	Kilninver, Oban	18	16 –
Ballantyne, Heirs of Thomas	Lochgoilhead	1	45 –		Campbell, Trustees of Colin, of Highwood	Highwood, Oban	4,067	983 8
Bamford, Thomas	Lochgilphead	1	50 10		Campbell, Colin G., of Stonefield	Stonefield, Tarbert	35,186	5,813 7
Barnett, Rev. John	Manse, Kilbrandon, Oban	23	35 –		Campbell, Campbell Macpherson, of Ballimore	Ballimore House, Tighnabruaich	9,521	1,933 –
Barr, John	Innellan	2	30 –		Campbell, Admiral Colin Yorke, of Barbreck	Barbreck House, Lochgilphead	10,369	2,461 9
Barrie, Robert	Sandbank	1	13 6		Campbell, Donald	Barcaldine	3	13 –
Beaton, Kenneth A.	Muckairn, Taynuilt	1	13 –		Campbell, Sir Donald, of Dunstaffnage, Bart.	Dunstaffnage Castle, Oban	3,000	915 10
Beaton, Murdoch	Ledaig, Taynuilt	5	11 –		Campbell, Rev. Donald	Kilmichael, Glassary	17	45 –
Beattie, Mary S., of Glenmorven	Glenmorven, Fort-William	9,354	915 –		Campbell, Donald A.	Dungallan, Oban	5	88 –
Begg, Heirs of Thomas	Springbank, Dunoon	2	105 –		Campbell, Trustees of Donald A. Barriemore	Airds, Taynuilt	8	45 –
Bell, Mrs. Margaret	Hunter's Quay	1	60 –		Campbell, Captain Donald P., of Baleveolan	Baleveolan, Appin	3,500	784 6
Bellardie, Trustees of John	Lochgoilhead	1	40 –		Campbell, Dugald, of Ardlarach	Glasgow	500	135 –
Benzie, James	Tighnabruaich	1	33 –		Campbell, Dugald, of Strachur	Strachur Park	24,593	3,286 16
Beresford, Lady de la Poer, and others (in trust), of Ballachulish	Ballachulish House, Fort-William	5,198	2,804 –		Campbell, Rev. Dugald	Southend, Campbeltown	12	40 –
Berry, Walter, of Glenstriven	Glenstriven House, Toward	4,500	530 –		Campbell, Duncan, of Lochnell	Lochnell House, Bonaw	39,000	6,801 2
Birkmyre, Mrs. Margaret	Leonard Bank, Innellan	6	138 –		Campbell, Lieut.-Col. Duncan, of Southhall	Southhall, Colintraive	19,736	2,245 –
Black, Trustees of George	Tobermory	1	113 –		Campbell, Duncan MacIvor, of Asknish	Manor House, Inveraray	8,838	1,682 19
Black, Heirs of John R.	Lochgoilhead	2	40 –		Campbell, Capt. Farquhar, of Aros	Aros House, Tobermory	46,000	3,691 11
Blackie, John S.	Altnacraig, Oban	2	55 –		Campbell, Sir George, of Cumlodden, Bart.	Garscube House, Glasgow	6,787	1,209 4
Boyd, Adam	Hunter's Quay	2	145 –		Campbell, Hugh	Tarbert	2	144 –
Boyd, James	Oban	1	68 –		Campbell, James A., of New Inverawe	New Inverawe House, Kilchrennan, Inveraray	900	270 –
Breadalbane, Earl of	Taymouth Castle	179,225	21165 –		Campbell, James A., of Inverneil	Inverneil, Ardrishaig	11,810	2,977 4
Breadalbane, Trustees of First Marquis of	Bolfracks, Aberfeldy	24,967	1,150 –					
Broadfoot, John	Lillybank, Blairmore	2	81 –					
Brodie, John	Cairndow	2	10 –					
Brown, Alexander	Oban	2	15 –					
Brown, Isabella	Colliebeg, Kilmun	2	50 –					
Bruce, Henry, of Ederline	Ederline House, Lochgilphead	12,000	912 –					
Buchanan, Daniel	Tighnabruaich	1	86 –					
Buchanan, Duncan, of Achadochyearnbeg	Auchinbreck, Colintraive	946	105 –					
Buchanan, Col. David C. R. C., of Carradale	Glen Carradale House, Campbeltown	18,000	2,575 –					

ARGYLL—continued.

Name of Owner.	Address of Owner.	Estimated Acreage of Property.	Gross Annual Value.	Name of Owner.	Address of Owner.	Estimated Acreage of Property.	Gross Annual Value.
		Acres.	£ s.			Acres.	£ s.
Campbell, Rev. James R.	Manse, Clachan, Tarbert	4	25 —	Coulter, Thomas	Lochgilphead	5	99 10
Campbell, John, of Kilberry	Kilberry, Tarbert	20,000	2,173 —	Crawford, Archibald	Strathlachlan	1	12 —
Campbell, John, Heirs of	Strachur	1	25 —	Crawford, Donald	Tighnabruaich	1	102 —
Campbell, Rev. John	F. C. Manse, Tarbert	1	25 —	Crawford, Robert, of Lochsanish	Lochsanish, Campbeltown	458	550 —
Campbell, John B., of Drimnamuchloch	Carse House, Tarbert	2,880	660 —	Crichton, Heirs of David	Auchincraig, Kirn	1	60 —
Campbell, John B., of Lerags	Lerags, Oban	1,500	458 —	Crinan Canal Commissioners	Ardrishaig (Canal)	172	1,638 —
Campbell, Rev. John G.	Tyree	38	30 —	Crown, The		118	944 10
Campbell, John Graham, of Shirvain	Castleton, Lochgilphead	10,841	1,756 —	Curdie, Rev. James	Manse, Gigha, Kintyre	8	30 —
Campbell, Captain James C., of Ardpatrick, R.N.	Ardpatrick, Tarbert; and Filkings Hall, Lechlade, Oxon	1,250	384 —	Currie, Daniel	Ardrishaig	1	45 —
				Curtis & Harvey	Glenlean, Sandbank	40	450 —
				Cuthbert, Hugh	Kilmun	2	35 —
Campbell, Kenneth and David Watson, of Ardow	Ardow, Tobermory	1,300	155 —	Dalgleish, Trustees of late Jas., of Ardnamurchan	22 Coates Crescent, Edinburgh	55,000	5,962 —
Campbell, Sir Louis H. D., Bt., and Dowager-Lady Campbell of Auchinbreck	Kildaloig, Campbeltown	1,340	380 —	Davison, Thomas G.	Oakbank, Kirn	3	100 —
				Davys, Richard C., of Askomil	Askomil, Campbeltown	2,287	975 —
Campbell, M'Ivor F. M., of Ballochyle	Ballochyle, Dunoon	3,613	550 —	Dawson, William	Rosemount, Kirn	3	50 —
				Dennison, Mrs. Janet	Tighnabruaich, Greenock	2	55 —
Campbell, Lieut.-Colonel Philip A. P. Bouverie, and Mrs. Caroline M. H. Campbell, of Dunoon	Hyde Lodge, Winchester	11,404	1,841 —	Dewar, Rev. Duncan	Appin	4	20 —
				Dick, John	Hunter's Quay	1	30 —
				Dickson, Andrew	Dunoon	1	179 —
				Dickson, William	Underwood, Dunoon	8	70 —
Campbell, Richard D., of Jura	Ardfin House, Jura	55,000	2,914 14	Dobie, Jessie	Tighnabruaich	1	55 —
Campbell, Robert, of Sonachan	49 Minto St., Edinburgh	666	210 10	Douglas, George	Strone, Greenock	1	17 7
				Douglas, Major-Gen. Sir John, of Glenfinart, K.C.B.	Glenfinart House, Ardentinny	15,579	2,589 16
Campbell, William, of Ballinaby	Ballinaby, Bridgend, Islay	1,800	377 10	Douglas, John B.	Ardrishaig	5	72 —
Campbell, William	Blaich, Fort-William	3	10 —	Douglas, Robert	Kilmun	1	52 —
Campbell, William	Quarry Road, Dunoon	1	20 —	Douglas, Mrs. Ann	Kirn	8	115 —
Campbell, William A., of Ormsary	Ormsary House, Ardrishaig	11,000	1,480 15	Douglas, Mrs. Margaret	Bayvyaich, Dunoon	1	64 —
				Downie, Georgina, of Appin	Appin House, Appin	37,000	2,264 18
Campbell, Mrs. Ann M., of Melfort	Melfort, Oban	1,000	135 —	Duncan, Jas., of Benmore	Benmore House, Kilmun	12,260	2,483 17
				Dunlop, George	Strone	1	117 —
Campbell, Mrs. Christina C., of Fassifern	Fassifern, Fort-William	9,500	831 —	Dunlop, Thomas	Bencoram, Dunoon	9	72 12
				Dunlop, Thomas	Kilmun	1	30 —
Campbell, Mrs. Margaret, of Ormidale	Ormidale, Colintraive	8,828	976 —	Dunoon Free Church, Deacons' Court of	Dunoon	2	130 —
Campbell, Christian	Lochgilphead	2	25 —	Dunoon Parochial Board	Dunoon	2	15 —
Campbell, Margaret, of Dunmore	Dunmore, Tarbert	2,200	526 —	Eddington, Lt.-Col. Smollett M., of Glencreggan	Glencreggan, Campbeltown	584	378 —
Campbell, Susan, of Bragleen	15 Palmerston Place, Edinburgh	1,350	215 —	Erskine, John	Kirn	1	11 —
				Ewing, William	Sandbank	7	88 —
Campbeltown Free Church, Trustees of	Campbeltown	1	40 —	Eyre, Most Rev. Charles	248 West George Street, Glasgow	2	69 —
Campbeltown, Parochial Board of	Campbeltown	2	24 —	Fell, Rev. James Alex., of Lismore	Lismore, Appin	1,800	1,274 —
Carswell, Trs. of Allan	Kirn	3	75 —	Ferguson, Alexander	Lochgoilhead	2	35 —
Chalmers, John	Corriesyke, Lochgoilhead	3	75 —	Ferguson, Rev. Alexander	Tayvallich, Lochgilphead	1	15 —
Cheape, Colonel Charles, of Killundine	Killundine, Fort-William	4,553	615 —	Finlay, Alexander S., of Castle Toward	Castle Toward, Innellan	6,758	2,867 —
Cheyne, Trustees of late Mrs. Francis C., of Lismore	10 Drummond Place, Edinburgh	2,400	1,527 5	Finlay, Kirkman, of Dunlossit	Dunlossit, Islay	17,676	2,882 —
Clark, Arch., of Garrachra	Garvie, Colintraive	3,153	300 —	Fleming, Alexander, of Kilmaho	Glasgow	390	297 —
Clark, Donald	Portnahaven	4	16 —	Fleming, Jas. N., of Keil	Keil House, Campbeltown	945	368 —
Clark, Francis W., of Ulva	Ulva House, Aros	8,000	1,525 9	Fleming, Jas. W., of Creegan	Creegan, Appin	500	131 —
Clark, John	Ardnadam	1	15 —	Fletcher, Angus, of Dunans	Dunans House, Colintraive	4,000	655 —
Clark, Reps. of Rev. John	Dunoon	13	129 —	Fletcher, Donald	Altamore, Tighnabruaich	6	60 —
Clark, Robert	Dunoon	1	77 —	Fletcher, Duncan, of Glenaros	Glenaros, Aros	2,800	299 —
Clark, William	Dunoon	3	71 5	Fletcher, Mrs. Agnes	Blairmore	1	10 —
Clayton, John	Sandbank	1	24 —	Forbes, Charles H., of Kingairloch	Kingairloch House, Fort-William	30,000	1,837 10
Clerk, Rev. Archibald	Kilmallie, Fort-William	180	80 —				
Clerk, Rev. Duncan	Torosay, Mull	30	40 —	Forbes, Rose	St. Catherine's	2	39 —
Colquhoun, Thomas	Hunter's Quay	1	40 —	Forlong, Wm., of Erins	Erins, Tarbert	2,500	288 —
Colville, David, & Co.	Campbeltown	1	216 —	Forman, John N., of Staffa	Edinburgh	60	40 —
Colville, John, of Muasdale and Machrihanish	Muasdale, Campbeltown	1,518	1,030 17	Forsyth, Representatives of James, of Glengorm	Glengorm Castle, Tobermory	13,600	2,129 9
Colville, Robert	Campbeltown	1	96 —	Fraser, Donald	Lochgilphead	3	25 —
Colville, Robert, of Drumore	Drumore, Campbeltown	611	180 4	Fraser, Rev. William	F. C. Manse, Lochgilphead	1	25 —
Compton, Lord William M'Lean, of Torloisk	Torloisk, Tobermory	8,000	1,221 10	Fraser, Rev. William	Ulva, Aros	1	18 —
Cook, James	Innellan	1	65 —				
Cooper, James	Dunoon	1	114 —	Gardiner, James	South Park, Campbeltown	3	50 —
Corkindale, Donald, of Ballygreggan	Trinity, Edinburgh	309	275 —	Gardyne, Lieut.-Colonel Charles G., of Glenforsa	Glenforsa House, Aros	20,000	1,907 16

ARGYLL—continued.

Name of Owner.	Address of Owner.	Estimated Acreage of Property.	Gross Annual Value.	Name of Owner.	Address of Owner.	Estimated Acreage of Property.	Gross Annual Value.
		Acres.	£ s.			Acres.	£ s.
Gascoigne, Frederick C. T., of Craignish	Craignish Castle, Lochgilphead	5,591	1,013 10	*Kames Powder Company*	Millhouse, Tighnabruaich	74	1,000 —
Gemmill, James	Ardenslate, Dunoon	2	16 —	Kay, John C., of Achlian	Fairfield Hall, Addingham, Skipton	8,000	851 10
Gemmell, Mrs. Agnes	West Bank, Innellan	2	50 —	Kelly, Adam L.	Lochgoilhead	1	15 —
Gibb, Trustees of Elias	Rhuebeg, Strone	3	75 —	Kent, Thomas	Dunoon	2	119 10
Gibb, John	Innellan	2	92 —	Kerr, John	Kirn	2	16 3
Gibson, Heirs of James	Innellan	6	80 —	*Killarrow and Kilmeny Free Church, Trustees of*	Killarrow and Kilmeny	1	20 —
Gilchrist, Archibald	The Castle, Dunoon	7	114 18	*Kilmore and Kilbride Pennyfair Cemetery Trustees*	Oban	3	30 —
Gilchrist, David	Ardrishaig	2	40 —	Kinghorn, David	Ardnadam	1	40 —
Glasgow, Magistrates of	Glasgow	1,429	278 —	Kirkwood, William	Lochgoilhead	1	50 —
Glassary and South Knapdale, Parochial Board of	Lochgilphead	7	22 17	*Kirn Pier Company*	Kirn	2	555 —
Glenorchy and Inishail Free Church, Trustees of	Glenorchy and Inishail	5	15 —				
Good Templars	Campbeltown	1	3 3				
Gordon, Charles, of Drimnin	Drimnin House, Fort-William	7,422	852 12	Laidlay, John W., of Drumore	Seacliff House, North Berwick	750	1,198 14
Gordon, Thomas	Ardnadam	1	50 —	Laird, Mrs. Jane	Kilbride, Dunoon	1	40 —
Gordon, Mrs. Lillias	Huntly Cottage, Kirn	2	60 —	Lamb, George	Melbourne Cottage, Innellan	2	58 —
Gow, Alfred W. J. Steuart, of Little Colonsay	Fowlers Park, Hawkhurst, Staplehurst	110	47 —	Lamont, James, of Knockdow	Knockdow, Toward	6,277	1,775 15
Graham, Heirs of Alex.	Dunclutha, Kirn	19	200 —	Lamont, John Henry, of Lamont	Ardlamont House, Kilfinan	12,000	2,959 —
Graham, Trs. of Robert C., of Skipness	Skipness Castle, Whitehouse, Kintyre	15,000	1,876 2	Lauder, Rev. William	F. C. Manse, Strachur	2	22 —
Gray, David	Dunoon	1	50 —	Lawrie, William L.	Drumneil, Airds	5	40 —
Greaves, Edward, of Glenetive, M.P.	Glenetive, Taynuilt; and Avonside, Barford, Warwick	10,000	791 —	Lecky, Francis B.	Hunter's Quay	2	40 —
Greenlees, Daniel and Samuel, of Moy	Campbeltown	335	572 9	Leny, Mrs. Mary Agatha M'A., of Duror	31 Great Cumberland Place, London	8,000	958 12
Greenlees, John	Stewarton, Campbeltown	1	25 —	Levack, Rev. John G.	Barmolloch, Kintyre	32	30 —
Gregorson, Angus	Oban	1	210 —	Livingstone, Alexander	Buchuil, Taynuilt	10	30 —
Greig, David, of Cheskan	Cheskan House, Campbeltown	277	591 10	Livingstone, Malcolm	Kirkapoll, Tyree	7	11 —
Grieve, David	The Ferns, Innellan	2	60 —	Livingstone, Trustees of late Ronald, of Drimsynie	Drimsynie, Lochgoilhead	5,360	922 —
Guthrie, Arbuthnot C., of Duart	Duart, Achnacraig	23,012	3,217 —	*Lochgilphead Burgh Commissioners*	Lochgilphead	1	13 —
				Lochgilphead Free Church, Trustees of	Lochgilphead	1	25 —
Hall, James M., of Tangy and Killean	Campbeltown	7,450	2,500 —	*Lochgilphead Poorhouse Committee*	Lochgilphead	6	150 —
Hally, George	St. Catherine's, Strachur	2	30 —	Lochhead, Heirs of Wm.	Ardrishaig	2	115 —
Hamilton, James	Darmead, Blairmore	2	65 —	Lockett, Heirs of Joseph	Sghor Bheann, Dunoon	2	75 —
Hamilton, James	Lochgoilhead	1	33 —	*Lorn Combination Poorhouse Committee*	Oban	3	250 —
Hamilton, Captain John, R.N.	Oban	2	48 —	Lothian, Helen	Kirn	1	50 —
Harkness, Thomas, of Clachaig	Clachaig, Sandbank	700	140 —	Love, Alexander	Campbeltown	1	50 —
Harvey, Alexander	Ashgrove, Kirn	4	105 —	Lumsden, David	Wellpark, Tighnabruaich	2	80 —
Hay, Heirs of William	Glengilp, Ardrishaig	10	240 —				
Hendry, Neil	Kirn	1	18 —				
Highgate, John	Blairmore	1	42 —	M'Adam, Mrs. Margaret	Innellan	2	61 10
Hill, Mrs. Janet	Blairmore	3	95 —	MacAlister, Major Charles B., of Crubisdale	Crubisdale House, Tarbert	990	540 —
Houldsworth, James, of Glencruitten	Coltness House, Wishaw	1,849	515 —	MacAlister, Keith, of Glenbar	Glenbar Abbey, Greenock	17,235	2,617 10
Hunter, James, of Hafton	Hafton House, Dunoon	5,740	3,569 —	M'Arthur, Rev. James	Manse, Kilmodan	13	32 —
Do. Do.	Do. (Dunoon Pier)		1,000 —	M'Arthur, John, of Ardmeanach	Inveraray	4,976	735 —
Hunter, James	Dunoon	1	97 —	M'Bean, David	Bowmore	4	12 —
Hunter, James & Wm. F.	Ardnadam	1	160 —	M'Beth, John G.	Ardowe, Tobermory	3	10 —
Hunter, John	Innellan	2	60 —	M'Brayne, John B., of Glenbranter	Glenbranter, Strachur	2,400	425 —
Hunter, John	Kindrochit, Lochgilphead	2	23 —	M'Caig, Rev. Donald	Muckairn Manse, Oban	7	16 —
Hunter, Robert	Sandbank	6	150 —	M'Callum, Heirs of Alex.	Oban	5	957 —
Hutchison, George	Greenock	1	41 10	M'Callum, John	Lochilphead	1	46 3
Hutchison, Mrs. Isabella	Lochgoilhead	1	45 —	M'Callum, John	Tighnabruaich	5	55 —
				M'Callum, John	Oban	1	35 —
Inveraray, Burgh of	Inveraray	600	56 —	M'Calman, Heirs of Rev. Donald, of Drishaig	Drishaig, Ardchattan	2,574	255 —
Islay Combination Poorhouse, Committee of	Islay	3	150 —	M'Calman, Donald	Kintalien, Lochgilphead	8	10 —
				M'Coll, Heirs of Dugald	Rosehill, Tighnabruaich	1	24 —
				M'Coll, Duncan	Luing, Easdale	18	12 —
Jack, Matthew	Tennyson Villa, Kirn	1	52 —	M'Corkindale, Rev. John	Lochgilphead	31	45 —
Jackson, Rev. Donald	Kilmartin	17	40 —	M'Cowan, John	Ardnamurchan	2	16 —
Jenkins, Walter	Tarbert	3	17 —	M'Cuaig, Rev. Angus	Manse Oa, Port Ellen	8	18 —
Johnstone, Archibald	Blairmore	1	64 —	M'Cubbin, Heirs of David	Chirnside, Innellan	1	40 —
Johnstone, Charles	Kirn	2	19 —	M'Cunn, Mrs. Ann G.	Ardhallow, Dunoon	10	112 —
Johnstone, James	Oban	1	36 —	M'Donald, Angus	Campbeltown	2	366 19

ARGYLL—continued.

Name of Owner.	Address of Owner.	Estimated Acreage of Property.	Gross Annual Value.	Name of Owner.	Address of Owner.	Estimated Acreage of Property.	Gross Annual Value.
		Acres.	£ s.			Acres.	£ s.
M'Donald, Archibald Burns, of Glencoe	Perth	6,305	715 —	M'Kenzie, Rev. Neil	Manse, Kilchrenan	10	27 —
M'Donald, Charles M., of Largie	Largie Castle, Tayinloan	12,775	4,025 —	M'Kenzie, Rev. Thomas	F. C. Manse, Muckairn	10	20 —
M'Donald, Donald	Fracadale	1	10 —	M'Kercher, Rev. Peter	Manse, Kilmore	59	55 —
M'Donald, Douglas J. K., of Sanda	Sanda, Southend	667	200 —	M'Kichan, Rev. Peter N.	Manse, Lochgilphead	1	25 —
M'Donald, Hector	Tighnabruaich	1	48 —	M'Kinnon, John	Cothouse, Sandbank	1	52 —
M'Donald, Rev. Hugh F.	Strachur	16	30 —	M'Kinnon, Peter	Rosemount, Campbeltown	1	55 —
M'Donald, James	Tighnabruaich	6	60 —	M'Kinnon, William, of Loup	Ballinakill, Tarbert	4,183	1,235 3
M'Donald, Heirs of James, of Dalness	Dalness, Taynuilt	5,000	575 —	M'Kinnon, Isabella	Campbeltown	2	45 —
M'Donald, John, of Garrochorran	Dunoon	700	135 —	M'Lachlan, Rev. Donald	Kilmichael, Lochgilphead	30	50 —
M'Donald, Neil M'L., of Dunach	Dunach House, Oban	463	409 —	M'Lachlan, Dugald	Lochgilphead	5	117 —
MacDougall, Alex. W., of Soroba	Battle Fields, Bath	600	304 10	M'Lachlan, Rev. Hugh	Tarbert	1	25 —
M'Dougall, Alexander	Torosay, Mull	1	13 —	M'Lachlan, John B., of Craigenterve	Craigenterve, Lochgilphead	2,900	581 —
M'Dougall, Allan, of Ardincaple	Ardincaple House, Oban	861	659 —	M'Lachlan, Robert, of M'Lachlan	Castle Lachlan, Strachur	12,000	2,005 10
M'Dougall, Rev. Arch.	Tighnabruaich	1	28 —	Maclaine, Angus	Fascadale, Ardrishaig	4	65 —
MacDougall, Col. Charles A., of MacDougall	Dunolly Castle, Oban	3,339	1,302 6	Maclaine, Trustees of Donald of Lochbuy	Lochbuy House, Oban	26,843	2,067 —
M'Dougall, Rev. James	Duror, Fort-William	2	19 10	Maclaine, Lillias and Jane, and Mary Anne Maclaine	Java Lodge, Auchnacraig London	2	45 —
M'Dougall, John, of Kilmun	Kilmun, Kilchrenan	1,000	195 —	M'Laren, Trustees of Alex., of Sunderland	Bridgend, Islay	5,509	2,151 —
M'Dougall, Heirs of John, of Lunga	Lunga, Lochgilphead	2,700	1,131 7	M'Laren, Mrs. Elizabeth	Chalet, Tighnabruaich	2	57 —
M'Dougall, Major John, of Gallanach	Gallanach House, Oban	2,636	775 10	M'Laverty, John F.	Longrow, Campbeltown	2	294 —
M'Eachran, Charles	Campbeltown	1	50 —	M'Lean, Alex., of Ardgour	Ardgour House, Fort-William	40,000	2,514 14
M'Ewan, Hugh	Ayr	2	35 —	M'Lean, Archibald	Coalhill, Campbeltown	1	9 —
M'Fadyen, Rev. James	Manse, Kildalton	80	65 —	Maclean, Archibald J., of Carsaig	Carsaig, Auchnacraig	2,700	269 —
M'Farlane, Rev. Donald	Killean, Tayinloan	13	40 —	Maclean, Rev. Donald	Manse, Colonsay	5	20 —
M'Farlane, John	Carradale, Campbeltown	1	11 —	M'Lean, Hector	Ballygrant	4	10 —
M'Farlane, Rev. Robt. M.	Manse, Glenorchy	21	40 —	M'Lean, James	Ardrishaig	1	10 —
M'Fie, Rev. Daniel	Portnahaven, Bridgend	6	16 —	M'Lean, Rev. John	Kilchoman, Islay	30	40 —
Macfie, Dugald	Gairhallow, Dunoon	3	60 —	M'Lean, Rev. Lachlan	Strontian	37	20 —
Macfie, Robert, of Airds	Airds House, Appin	6,700	2,027 —	M'Lean, Peter and John, of Gomatra	Gomatra, Aros	900	250 —
Macfie, Mrs. Agnes Farrie	Dalnashean Villa, Appin	3	35 —	M'Lean, Trs. of William	Tighnabruaich	1	42 10
M'Gibbon, Margaret	St. Catherine's	20	87 —	M'Leish, James	Strone	1	75 —
M'Gilchrist, Rev. John	Bowmore, Islay	10	28 —	M'Lellan, Allan H.	Oakleigh, Blairmore	1	55 —
M'Gillivray, Rev. Donald	Kilmelford, Lochgilphead	1	20 —	M'Lellan, John	Fanmore, Tobermory	6	7 —
M'Gregor, Alexander	Kilbride, Coll	4	10 —	M'Leod, Rev. Alexander	F. C. Manse, Strontian	12	12 —
M'Gregor, Rev. Alex.	Manse, Iona	2	15 —	M'Leod, Rev. John	Morven, Fort-William	69	40 —
M'Gregor, Duncan	Kilchrenan	1	10 —	M'Leod, Kenneth M.	Gairhill, Dunoon	2	25 —
M'Gregor, Duncan	Oban	1	132 —	M'Lugash, Duncan	Portaskaig, Islay	1	4 —
M'Gregor, Rev. Gregor	Lismore, Appin	13	25 —	M'Lurkin, Mrs. Jane	Blairmore	1	45 —
M'Gregor, John	Annfield, Kirn	3	120 —	M'Michael, Rev. Neil	Craignish, Lochgilphead	17	35 —
M'Intosh, Alexander B.	Ardenlee, Dunoon	3	110 —	M'Nab, Archibald, of Penmore	Penmore, Ardrishaig	718	282 10
M'Intyre, Rev. Alex. C., of Barmaddy	Coll, Tobermory	600	70 —	M'Naughton, John C., of Killellan	Killellan House, Campbeltown	681	697 —
M'Intyre, Rev. Angus	Auchnacraig	2	18 —	Macneal, Captain Hector, of Ugadale	Losset Park, Campbeltown	11,000	3,778 10
M'Intyre, Duncan	Rhunahorine, Kintyre	2	11 —	M'Neill, Donald, of Canna	Canna, Tobermory	2,843	574 —
M'Intyre, John, of Bragleenbeg	Bragleenbeg, Oban	500	100 —	M'Neill, Dugald, of Kintarbert	Saddell House, Campbeltown	12,805	2,935 —
M'Intyre, John	Oban	1	82 —	M'Neill, Rev. Hector, of Ardnacross	Campbeltown	594	400 —
M'Intyre, Malcolm	Achalevan, Taynuilt	4	10 —	M'Neill, Right Hon. Sir John, of Colonsay and Oronsay, G.C.B.	Kiloran House, Colonsay; and Burnhead, Liberton, Edinburgh	11,262	2,172 —
M'Intyre, Nicol, of Burgh	Burgh, Aros	1,200	116 —	M'Neill, Trustees of John, of Glenmore	Glenmore House, Kilmelford	6,466	1,022 —
M'Kay, Captain Alexander Forbes, of Carskey	Carskey House, Campbeltown	2,076	687 —	M'Neill, Col. John C., of Ardlussa, V.C.	Ardlussa, Jura	17,939	903 —
M'Kay, Charles	Campbeltown	1	25 —	M'Neillage, John and Archibald	Sandbank	1	28 —
M'Kay, Colin	Lochgilphead	1	6 —	M'Niven, Catherine	Blairmore	1	51 —
M'Kay, David	Kirn	1	77 —	M'Onie, Mrs. Mary, and Mrs. Agnes M'Ewan	Lochgoilhead	1	99 —
M'Kay, Captain George, of Morinish	Morinish, Oban	1,931	415 —	M'Phee, Daniel	Newton Bank, Innellan	1	48 —
M'Kay, George G., of Ardconnell	Inverness	500	501 10	M'Pherson, Alexander	Sandbank	3	60 —
M'Kay, Hugh	Oban	1	159 —	M'Pherson, Allan	Auchoisnish, Strontian	1	10 —
M'Kay, John	Kilbride	1	30 —	M'Quilkan, Dugald	Cuilandrynich, E. Tarbert	322	38 —
M'Kay, Trustees of John	Oban	3	487 —	M'Taggart, Trustees of Daniel, of Kilkivan	Campbeltown	313	490 —
M'Kechnie, Charles	Lochgilphead	2	73 —	M'Tavish, Flora	Kilchrist, Campbeltown	11	35 —
M'Kellar, Heirs of Mrs. Christina	Hazelbank, Innellan	1	24 —	M'Vean, Rev. Donald	F. C. Manse, Catchean	2	17 —
M'Kenzie, Rev. Alex.	Auchoish, Ardrishaig	19	35 —	M'Vean, Rev. Duncan	Manse, Sunart	8	15 —
M'Kenzie, Donald	Strontian	9	13 —				
M'Kenzie, John, of Knipoch	Knipoch, Oban	300	112 —				
M'Kenzie, John Munro, of Morinish	Wishaw	6,000	737 —				
M'Kenzie, Rev. Lachlan	Manse, Jura	12	28 —				

ARGYLL—continued.

Name of Owner.	Address of Owner.	Estimated Acreage of Property.	Gross Annual Value.	Name of Owner.	Address of Owner.	Estimated Acreage of Property.	Gross Annual Value.
		Acres.	£ s.			Acres.	£ s.
M'William, John and James, of Uigle	Campbeltown	400	125 –	Pirrie, John and James N. Fleming, of Pennygown	Glasgow Campbeltown	279	183 –
Malcolm, John, of Poltalloch	Poltalloch, Lochgilphead; and 7 Great Stanhope Street, London	82,579	18200 –	Pitkethley, James	Strone	1	50 –
Malcolm, John Wingfield, (vr. of Poltalloch,) of Achnabreck, M.P.	Poltalloch, Lochgilphead; and Carlton Club, Pall Mall, London	700	140 –	Pollock, Allan, of Ronachan	Ronachan, Campbeltown	5,046	800 –
				Popham, Mrs. Jane E. Mary, of Ardchattan	Ardchattan Priory, Bonaw	8,000	1,341 10
Malcolm, Trustees of William	Glenmoraig, Dunoon	19	380 –	Port Charlotte Free Church, Trustees of	Port Charlotte	2	20 –
Marquis, Mrs. Isabella	Oban	1	165 –	Port Ellen Free Church, Trustees of	Port Ellen	1	20 –
Marshall, David	Innellan	2	42 –	Powell, Francis	Torr-a-luin, Dunoon	4	100 –
Mathieson, William	Invereck, Kilmun	3	32 –	Powell, William F.	Cluinetter, Dunoon	6	80 –
Maxwell, Thomas	Woodlee, Innellan	1	30 –	Purves, Robert	Ardenslate, Dunoon	6	38 9
Melfort Gunpowder Coy.	Melfort	5,613	1,095 –				
Melville, George	Campbeltown	1	35 –				
Menzies, William	Kilbride, Dunoon	5	80 –	Ramsay, John, of Kildalton	Kildalton, Port Ellen, Greenock	54,250	8,226 –
Millar, Trustees of James	Rockvale, Innellan	1	56 –	Rankine, Dugald	Sandbank	1	24 –
Millar, James, jun.	Innellan	2	152 –	Rankine, James, of Ardnackaig	Dykehead, Stonehaven	334	135 –
Mitchell, Heirs of James	Hunter's Quay	1	67 –	Rankine, Patrick, of Otter	Otter House, Tighnabruaich	4,200	1,552 10
Mitchell, Peter James, of Kinloch	Kinloch, Auchnacraig	2,500	375 13	Rankine, Ann	Edinburgh	2	45 –
Moir, Trs. of the late John M'Arthur, of Milton	Dunoon	4,000	554 19	Readman, George	Kilbride, Dunoon	5	118 –
Morrison, Charles, of Islay	Basildon Park, Reading, and 93 Harley Street, London	67,000	16439 19	Reid, Hugh	Glenconner, Blairmore	1	65 –
				Reid, Heirs of James, of Auchinellan	Auchinellan, Ford Lochaw, Lochgilphead	1,200	300 –
Morrison, Henry, of Belnahua	Glasgow	6	50 –	Reid, Robert	Slatefield, Kirn	2	50 –
Morton, Earl of	Conaglen House, Ardgour, Fort-William	46,883	1,685 –	Reid & Colvilles	Campbeltown	1	124 –
				Richmond, John	Sandbank	1	15 –
Morton, Earl of, and Lord Aberdour	Do. do.	2,931	180 –	Riddell, Sir Thomas M., of Sunart, Bart.	Strontian	54,418	3,672 18
Mowbray, Mrs. Mary	Strone	2	80 –	Ritchie, Heirs of David	Blairbeg, Blairmore	3	70 –
Muir, William, of Innistrynich	Innistrynich House, Inveraray	4,250	1,259 10	Roberts, Mrs. Christina	Glenacre, Innellan	5	115 –
				Robertson, Alexander	Colinton House, Edinburgh	1	79 10
				Do.	Kilmun & Strone (*Piers*)	–	300 –
Mull Poorhouse, Committee of	Tobermory	5	100 –	Robertson, Donald, of Pennyghael	13 Inverleith Row, Edinburgh	6,080	490 –
Munro, Duncan C., of Kinlochlaich	Gourock	4,000	764 15	Robertson, Rev. Frederick L.	Kilmun	5	115 r
Munro, Rev. Hugh, of Barnalien	Kilmory, Arran	2,000	176 –	Robertson, Heirs of Patrick	Dailing Lodge, Dunoon	1	75 –
Murray, Captain John H., R.N.	Ardrishaig	1	55 –	Robertson, Robert Wm., of Glenshellish	Haughhead, Gourock	2,200	328 –
				Robin, Robert, & Son	Goatfield, Lochgilphead	16	185 –
				Rodger, Mrs. Jane	Auchnastruan, Innellan	1	40 –
*Neill, Robert	Thornbank, Blairmore	1	38 –	*Roman Catholic Church*, Trustees of	Oban	1	100 –
Newton, Rev. Wm., Rev. Horace, & J. H. G., of Glencreepesdale	Strontian	34,335	1,821 –	Ross, Rev. Duncan C.	F. C. Manse, Airds	1	20 –
				Ross, Hugh	Tobermory	1	25 –
				Ross, John M'Donald	Dailing, Kirn	2	75 –
Nicol, John, of Ardmarnock	Ardmarnock House, Tighnabruaich	4,013	1,008 6	Ross, Heirs of William	Innellan	1	45 –
Nisbet, Trustees of Henry	Tobermory	4	45 –	Ross, Mrs. Jane	Hunter's Quay	1	70 –
Niven, Mrs. Isabella	Kilbride, Dunoon	4	54 –	Rowand, Mrs. Marion	Avonholm, Strone	1	83 –
Norman, William	Norwood, Kirn	2	40 –	Russell, Rev. James C.	Campbeltown	18	34 –
Oban, Magistrates of	Oban	4	39 –	Scarlett, Jas. W., of Gigha	Gigha House, Tayinloan	3,679	2,288 14
Orde, Sir John P., of Kilmory, Bart.	Kilmory, Lochgilphead	3,094	1,218 –	Scoular, Arthur, of Tighnabruaich	Tighnabruaich	1,400	540 –
				Shaw, Thomas	Larkholm, Dunoon	1	74 –
Orde, Captain John W. P., of Blairbuie	Auchnaba, Lochgilphead	1,552	190 –	Shearer, Allan	Innellan	4	140 –
Outram, Heirs of George	Rosemore, Ardnadam	4	60 –	Simpson, Rev. Murray	Acharacle, Strontian	6	15 –
				Sinclair, Duncan	Barr	4	15 –
				Smith, Heirs of John	Tighnabruaich	1	85 –
Park, Rev. George	Manse, Inverchaolain	4	28 –	Smith, Thomas V., of Acharanich	Acharanich, Fort-William	22,050	1,800 –
Parr, Thomas P., of Killiechronan	Killiechronan House, Aros	9,000	992 10	Smith, William	Ladybank, Innellan	1	34 –
Paterson, Robert	32 Charlotte St., Leith	2	40 –	Smith, William W.	Darnley Cottage, Kirn	1	35 –
Patten, John	Bullwood, Dunoon	2	80 –	Somerville, Archibald	Hunter's Quay	2	231 10
Patten, Mary	Garail, Dunoon	5	120 –	Somerville, William	Lochgoilhead	1	28 –
Patterson, Mrs. Magdaline of Lochaline	Lochaline House, Fort-William	5,976	1,490 11	Sproat, William	Tobermory	1	30 –
				Stark, Rev. Joseph	Tighnabruaich	1	30 –
Pearson, Heirs of Adam	Ardenslate, Kirn	1	60 –	Stephen, Alexander	Fearn Coille, Dunoon	9	125 –
Pearson, Rev. James	Skerrolls, Islay	4	26 –	Stephenson, George R., of Glen Caladh	Glen Caladh, Tighnabruaich	1,000	285 –
Pender, John, of Minard, M.P.	Minard Castle, Inveraray, and 18 Arlington St., London	5,285	1,474 10	Stevenson, James	Lochgoilhead	2	33 –
				Stevenson, William	Wyndham Bank, Innellan	1	40 –
Phillips, Charles	Ardenslate, Dunoon	2	16 –	Stewart, Alexander	Hunter's Quay	1	50 –
Pirie, Rev. Henry G.	Parsonage, Dunoon	2	35 –	Stewart, Rev. Alexander	Ardgour, Fort-William	1	10 ..

ARGYLL—continued.

Name of Owner.	Address of Owner.	Estimated Acreage of Property.	Gross Annual Value.	Name of Owner.	Address of Owner.	Estimated Acreage of Property.	Gross Annual Value.
		Acres.	£ s.			Acres.	£ s.
Stewart, Charles A., of Achnacone .	Achnacone House, Appin	2,200	252 15	Thorpe, James, of Ardbrecknish	Ardbrecknish House, and Beaconfield, Newark-on-Trent .	1,300	190 —
Stewart, Colonel Charles A.	Bellgrove, Campbeltown	1	55 —	Tolmie, Alexander .	Newton, Innellan .	3	93 10
Stewart, Daniel .	Miller Street, Glasgow .	6	120 —	Torrie, Rev. Donald K. .	Glencoe, Fort-William .	1	10 —
Stewart, Rev. David	Darrochmore, Dunoon .	2	55 —	Tulloch, William .	Dunoon .	1	137 —
Stewart, James .	Prospect Villas, Strone .	1	80 —	Turnbull, Mrs. Jane	Millhouse, Tighnabruaich	1	4 —
Stewart, John .	Acharacle, Strontian .	1	13 —	Turner, Rev. Duncan	Kilmore, Tobermory .	12	36 —
Stewart, John .	Appin .	1	12 —	Turner, James .	Feorline, Toward .	1	25 —
Stewart, John .	Tighnabruaich .	1	51 —				
Stewart, Rev. John	Ardrishaig .	1	20 —				
Stewart, John C., of Fasnacloich .	Fasnacloich House, Appin	5,000	736 —	Walker, James .	Lochgoilhead .	1	50 —
Stewart, John Lorne, of Coll and Knockrioch	Stronvar House, Campbeltown .	14,247	4,118 17	Walker, John .	Holyrood, Innellan .	1	40 —
				Wallace, Matthew .	Dunallen, Innellan .	1	50 —
Stewart, James and Peter	Auchenlochan, Kilfinan .	1	46 —	Wallace, William .	Greenbank Cottage, Kirn	1	25 —
Sutherland, Rev. John .	F. C. Manse, Barcaldine .	1	15 —	Watson, John H. .	Hopehill, Kilmun .	2	120 —
Swan, David .	Lochgoilhead .	1	30 —	Webster, Mrs. Margaret, of Invercreran	Invercreran, Appin .	850	110 —
Swinburne, Captain Thomas, of Muck, R.N.	Ellanshona, Strontian .	1,299	325 —	West of Scotland Convalescent Sea-Side Homes	Dunoon .	4	220 —
Sword, Archibald	Tighnabruaich .	2	30 —	White, Henry .	Lismore, Appin .	1	3 10
Syme, Mary G .	Alvernia, Innellan .	1	45 —	White, Robert .	Ardrishaig .	2	60 —
				Wilson, John .	Garvan, Fort-William .	1	3 —
Tant, Rev. Alex. J. W. .	Manse, Kilmeny, Islay .	10	14 —	Wood, Robert B. .	Dunfeurach, Innellan .	3	96 —
Tarbert Free Church, Trs. of	Tarbert, Lochfine .	1	10 —	Wright, Duncan A. .	Rosemount, Innellan .	1	60 —
Tarratt, D. Fox, of Ellarie	Ellarie, Lochgilphead .	1,050	189 —	Wyllie, Mitchell, & Co. .	Campbeltown .	1	51 —
Taylor, Matthew S. .	Lillybank, Innellan .	2	60 —				
Teacher, William .	Craigbet, Blairmore .	1	70 —				
Templeton, Archibald	Beneli, Ardnadam .	1	65 —				
Templeton, James .	Dunfillan, Dunoon .	4	80 —	Total Owners of Land of one Acre and upwards .		581	2,030,148 359,181 4
Tennant, Robert, of Ardsheal .	Scarcroft Lodge, Leeds .	5,800	681 1	Total Owners of Lands of less than one Acre in extent .		2,283	800 70,970 6
Thomson, Heirs of George	Dalingmhor, Kirn .	10	200 —				
Thomson, Heirs of John	Ardrishaig .	1	149 —	GRAND TOTAL .		2,864	2,030,948 430,151 10
Thomson, Robert .	Shuna, Oban .	2	130 —				

AYR.

Population, - - - - - - - 200,908.
Inhabited Houses, - - - - - 26,798.
Number of Parishes, - - - - - 46.

Name of Owner.	Address of Owner.	Estimated Acreage of Property.	Gross Annual Value.	Name of Owner.	Address of Owner.	Estimated Acreage of Property.	Gross Annual Value.
		Acres.	£ s.			Acres	£ s.
Adam, William Parker, of Tour	Tour, Kilmarnock	280	739 10	Anstruther, Sir Windham C. J. Carmichael, of that Ilk, Bart.	Westraw House, Lanark	589	98 —
Adam, Mrs. Jane	Ardrossan	28	216 —	Do. do.	Do. (Minerals)	—	197 —
Ailsa, Marquess of	Culzean Castle, Maybole	76,015	35825 —	Arbuthnot, George C.	Beachhouse, Skelmorlie	3	200 —
Do. do.	Do. (Minerals)	—	14 —	Archibald, Daniel	Baidland, Dalry	20	33 —
Aird, Trustees of Hugh Howie, of Corseflat	Muirkirk	631	280 —	Archibald, Hugh	Baidland Mains, Dalry	180	307 —
Aitchison, John	Parkhead, Glasgow	2	75 —	Archibald, John	High Baidland, Dalry	21	40 —
Aitken, Andrew	Little Carleith, Galston	52	37 —	Ardeer Foundry Company	Stevenston	1	50 —
Aitken, Andrew Blair, of Yonderton	Yonderton, Dalry	135	439 —	Ardrossan, Burgh of	Ardrossan	2	95 —
Aitken, Mrs. Margaret, and others	Blythswood Square, Glasgow	70	128 —	Ardrossan, Heritors of Parish of	Ardrossan	1	20 —
Aiton, Thomas	Grange, Kilmarnock	2	4 —	Ardrossan Parochial Board	Ardrossan	2	24 15
Alexander, Archibald, of Boydston	West Kilbride	271	503 —	Ardrossan Water Company	Ardrossan	17	240 —
Alexander, Colonel Claud, of Ballochmyle	Ballochmyle, Mauchline	4,332	4,195 —	Arnott, Hugh	Stoneyhall, Newmilns	74	135 —
Do. do.	Do. (Minerals)	—	6,182 —	Auld, James and Euphemia	Doonbrae, by Ayr	2	125 —
Alexander, John, James, and Stephen	Waterside, Fenwick	3	114 —	Auld, Mrs. Janet	Bankhead, Dreghorn	5	27 —
Alexander, Amelia, of Blackshaw	West Kilbride	353	256 —	Auld, Margaret, and Mrs. Janet Rose	Irvine	4	37 —
Allan, Trustees of James	Kilwinning	236	301 —	Ayr Academy Directors	Ayr	2	100 —
Do. do.	Do. (Minerals)	—	100 —	Ayr Burgh	Ayr	100	1,466 10
Allan, James	Byres of Bankhead, Loudoun	150	105 —	Ayr Cemetery Proprietors	Ayr	3	15 —
Allan, James	Clauchlands, Lamlash	2	14 —	Ayr District Board of Lunacy	Ayr	40	650 —
Allan, John, and John Boyd and others	Largs	5	79 10	Ayr Fever Hospital Directors	Ayr	1	100 —
Allan, Trustees of John	Largs	3	50 —	Ayr Gas Company	Ayr	2	1,030 —
Allan, John	Bridgend, Kilbirnie	23	195 —	Ayr Harbour Trustees	Ayr	4	951 10
Allan, John	Old Cumnock	2	236 —	Ayr, Heritors of	Ayr	2	20 —
Allan, John	Minuntion, Barr	386	265 —	Ayr Incorporation of Shoemakers	Ayr	6	103 —
Allan, Malcolm	Kilbirnie	1	49 10	Ayr Kirk-Session, for Sessionfield	Ayr	144	87 10
Allan, William	Fairliebog, Kilwinning	42	81 —	Ayr Water Company	Ayr	6	847 5
Allison, James, of Tardoes	Tardoes, Muirkirk	600	413 —				
Allison, Robert Dunlop	Balgray, Irvine	103	212 —	Baird, James, of Cambusdoon	Cambusdoon, Ayr	19,599	8,043 —
Do. do.	Do. (Minerals)	—	96 10	Do. do.	Do. (Minerals)	—	1,000 —
Allison, William, of Bonnyton	Chivalry Green, Cambridge	1,500	860 —	Baird, John	Old Cumnock	3	134 —
Alston, Rev. Andrew	Newmilns	1	24 —	Baird, Robert	Cassillis Mill, Dalrymple	2	6 10
Alston, Trustees of Gavin	Yondercroft, Newmilns	110	100 —	Baird, Thomas	Comberbach, Northwich, Cheshire	14	42 —
Alston, George	Loudounhill, Newmilns	80	80 —				
Alston, James	Yondercroft, Newmilns	120	100 —	Baird, Trustees of William, of Rosemount	Rosemount, Symington	61	180 10
Alston, William	Carcluie, Dalrymple	1	15 —	Balderston, Robert Glass	Bishopbriggs, Glasgow	176	130 —
Alston, Mrs. Margaret	Newlands, Newmilns	122	200 —	Balfour, Robert	Lochfaulds, Beith	2	55 —
Anderson, Andrew	Kirkland, Dunlop	23	83 —	Ballantine, Andrew Rollo Bowman, of Castlehill	Castlehill, Ayr	1,174	2,099 —
Anderson, Cuthbert	Netherhill, Dunlop	39	70 —	Ballantine, James, of Boig	Greenock	260	601 —
Anderson, James	Blockmill, Stewarton	10	57 —	Do. do.	Do. (Minerals)	—	100 —
Anderson, Trustees of James A.	Carlung, West Kilbride	346	938 —	Bank of Scotland	Edinburgh	1	155 —
Anderson, Thomas, of Waterhead	Kilmarnock	2,282	832 10	Barclay, Andrew	Kilmarnock	2	109 10
Anderson, William, and others	Beith	99	102 —	Barclay, Hugh, and Heirs of Peter Barclay	Ardrossan	2	421 10
Andrew, Trustees of Allan	Leahead, Dunlop	59	174 —	Barclay, John	Gierston, Kilbirnie	112	55 —
Andrew, Trustees of David	Crosshill, Kirkmichael	1	31 —	Barr, Alexander	Nettlehirst, Beith	52	55 —
Andrew, John	Irvine	8	51 —	Barr, Allan	Beanscroft, Fenwick	101	131 —
Andrew, Robert	Townhead, Troon	65	258 —	Barr, Trustees of Hugh	Dykehead, Dalry	164	295 —
Andrew, Walter	Girvan	3	20 —	Barr, John	Knockentibber, Kilmaurs	13	94 15
Andrew, Mrs. Agnes	Main Street, Newton, Ayr	2	30 —	Barr, John	Ardrossan	4	2,002 —
Andrews, Thomas Bishop	Kilmarnock	9	30 —	Barr and Shearer	Ardrossan	3	500 —
				Barr, William	Dunlop Villa, Beith	6	67 —
				Beaton, Rev. Lewis	Manse, Muirkirk	16	50 —

C

AYR—continued.

Name of Owner.	Address of Owner.	Estimated Acreage of Property.	Gross Annual Value.	Name of Owner.	Address of Owner.	Estimated Acreage of Property.	Gross Annual Value.
		Acres.	£ s.			Acres.	£ s.
Beckett, Hugh	3 Windsor Terrace, Glasgow	1	70 –	Boyle, Mrs. Agnes, of Langlands, wife of Captain Alexander Boyle, R.N.	38 Prince's Gate, Kensington, London	271	586 –
Beith, Heirs of James	Middleton, Largs	76	75 –				
Beith, Trustees of John	Middleton, Largs	1	51 10				
Beith, Heirs of Robert	Bute Cottage, Largs	5	26 –	Boyle, Augusta	Skelmorlie, Largs	40	110 –
Beith, William	Middleton, Largs	3	18 –	Brackenridge, John	Ballig, Ballantrae	2	18 15
Beith, Parochial Board of	Beith	62	92 10	Brackenridge, William	Newyards, Maybole	2	15 –
Bell, John	Craigview, Prestwick	18	64 –	Brash, Walter	Largs	2	100 –
Bell, John, of Enterkine	Enterkine, Tarbolton	2,256	2,950 –	Brisbane, Charles T., of Brisbane	Brisbane, Largs	6,933	2,050 –
Do. do.	Do. (*Minerals*)	–	1,699 10				
Bell, Robert, of Knockbrake	Dale Street, Liverpool	2,991	730 –	Brisbane, Charlotte A. A.	Prestbury, Cheltenham	49	107 10
Bennie, William	Dalblair, Ayr	4	110 –	*British Dynamite Company*	Stevenston	100	200 –
Bickett, John	Kirkford, Stewarton	5	10 –	Brodie, Robert	Lower Canada	58	73 –
Bickett, John	Megswell, Kilwinning	51	56 –	Brodie, William	Paisley	10	15 –
Biggart, Robert	Burnhouse, Beith	88	208 –	Broom, William	182 Hope St., Glasgow	60	141 –
Biggart, Thomas	Oldmill, Beith	70	100 –	Broom, Margaret, and others, as Heirs of William Broom	Moniaive, Dumfriesshire	1,008	130 –
Biggart, Thomas, of Highgate	Bridgend, Dalry	1,119	1,193 15				
Blackburn, Sir Colin, of Doonholm, Kt.	Doonholm, Ayr; and 10 Prince's Gardens, London, W.	154	344 –	Brown, Allan	Raws, Kilmarnock	9	21 –
				Brown, Rev. Andrew	Beith	45	140 –
Blair, Trustees of Charles	Galston	13	281 –	Brown, Trustees of Andrew, of Auchentorlie	Auchentorlie, Stewarton	380	265 –
Do. do.	Do. (*Minerals*)	–	317 –	Do. do.	Do. (*Minerals*)	–	27 –
Blair, David Hunter, of Dunskey, Brownhill	Dunskey, Portpatrick	807	811 15	Brown's Charity, Trustees of	Newmilns	36	52 –
				Do. do.	Do. (*Minerals*)	–	352 –
Blair, Sir Edward Hunter, of Blairquhan, Bart.	Blairquhan Castle, Straiton	12,610	7,133 15	Brown, David	Maybole	4	68 –
				Brown, George	Burnside, Irvine	3	96 –
Blair, James	Kilmaurs	4	10 10	Brown, George	Glasgow	6	16 –
Blair, Rev. John	Manse, Straiton	8	38 –	Brown, Hugh, of Broadstone	Broadstone, Beith	329	715 10
Blair, Robert	Blackdales, Largs	10	177 –				
Blair, Thomas	Kirklands, Maybole	1	5 –	Do. do.	Do. (*Minerals*)	–	60 –
Blair, Captain William Fordyce, of Blair, R.N.	Blair, Dalry	6,680	5,828 10	Brown, James	Glasgow	7	24 –
				Brown, James	Kilmaurs	14	53 10
Do. do.	Do. (*Minerals*)	–	2,202 10	Brown, James	Rodingloft, Mauchline	1	22 –
Blair, Mrs. Mary	Harrington, Cumberland	16	93 –	Brown, James Matthew, of Greenockmains	Auchenskeith, Dalry	395	308 –
Blakeney, John	Saltcoats	1	146 10				
Blyth, Charles	Muirkirk	1	9 10	Brown, John	Hill, Dunlop	314	510 –
Bone, Trustees of William	Newton-on-Ayr	16	75 –	Brown, John	Blacklaw, Stewarton	243	163 –
				Brown, John	Shedog, Arran	12	112 –
Bone, Mrs. Janet, and Mary Bowie	Newton-on-Ayr	7	22 –	Brown, Representatives of John	Miller Road, Ayr	63	89 10
Borland, Robert	North Kilbride, Stewarton	4	15 –	Brown, Robert	New Cumnock	2	3 –
Borron, William G.	Seafield, Ardrossan	8	135 –	Brown, Robert Glasgow	Nettlehirst, Beith	59	102 –
Boswell, Patrick Charles Douglas, of Garrallan	Garrallan, Old Cumnock	594	723 –	Brown, William, of Corphin	Maybole	1,527	652 15
				Brown, William	Lodgebush, Craigie	1	5 –
Do. do.	Do. (*Minerals*)	–	1,015 –	Brown, William	Turkey	4	27 –
Boswell, Mrs. Christina	Sandgate Street, Ayr	4	99 –	Brown, William	Loanhead, Galston	72	40 –
Boswell, Lady Jessie Jane, of Auchinleck	Auchinleck House, Mauchline	11,977	8,256 –	Brown, William	Glasgow	24	46 –
				Brown, William	8 Bridge Street, Glasgow	1	20 –
Do. do.	Do. (*Minerals*)	–	3,633 –	Brown, Trustees of William, junior, of Parkend	Parkend, Saltcoats	40	375 –
Bourtreehill Coal Company	Dreghorn	1	76 10				
Bowie, Campbell Tait	26 Bothwell Street, Glasgow	2	56 10	Brown, Mrs. Grace, and others	Lugtonridge, Beith	69	138 –
Boyd, Charles, of Ladybank	Ladybank, Girvan	311	406 –	Brown, Martha, of Waterhaughs	Lanfine, Galston	9,713	6,173 –
Boyd, David	Prestwick	17	37 –	Brown, Mary, and Trustees of Mrs. Barclay Murdoch, of Capelrigg	Capelrigg, Mearns	111	220 –
Boyd, Hugh	Prestwick	10	11 –				
Boyd, Hugh	Rosemeadow, Dreghorn	3	29 15	Bruce, Margaret G., and others	31 Royal Ter., Edinburgh	1	95 –
Boyd, James	Orchard, West Kilbride	72	295 –				
Boyd, Lieut.-Col. James George Hay, of Townend	Townend, Symington	2,300	1,634 –	Bryson, William	Priestland, Darvel	8	25 –
				Buchanan, Trustees of Neil Griffiths, of Knockshiffnock	New Cumnock	2,900	1,409 –
Boyd, Rev. John	West Kilbride	1	55 –				
Boyd, John	Waterside, Largs	23	205 10	Do. do.	Do. (*Minerals*)	–	250 –
Boyd, John, and James Greig	Largs	198	46 –	Buchanan, Trustees of Walter	Downieston, Dalmellington	233	307 –
Boyd, Mrs. Jean	East Auchengree, Beith	33	50 –				
Boyd, Mrs. Mary Ann, and others	Largs	2	152 –	Do. do.	Do. (*Minerals*)	–	843 –
Boyd, Alice, of Penkiln	Penkiln, Dailly	513	373 10	Buchanan, Elizabeth, of Bellfield	Bellfield, Riccarton	298	770 –
Boyd, Jane	Springfield, Largs	3	155 –				
Boyle, Commander David, younger of Shewalton, R.N.	Shewalton, Irvine	14	24 –	Burnett, Major-General Francis C., of Gadgirth	Gadgirth, Coylton	1,500	1,236 –
				Do. do.	Do. (*Minerals*)	–	870 –
Boyle, John	Brompton	7	12 –	*Burns Monument Trustees*	Ayr	2	17 10
Boyle, John	Raith, Tarbolton	8	62 –	Burns, Patrick	Kilwinning	205	316 10
Boyle, Patrick, of Shewalton	Shewalton, Irvine	2,344	2,684 –	Do.	Do. (*Minerals*)	–	30 –
				Burns, William, senior	Nettlehirst, Beith	22	36 –
Boyle, Patrick David, younger of Langlands	38 Prince's Gate, Kensington London	5	11 10	Burns, Mrs. Elizabeth	Lasswade Cot., Lasswade	32	85 –
				Burns, Jane	Lasswade Cot., Lasswade	33	71 –

AYR—continued.

Name of Owner.	Address of Owner.	Estimated Acreage of Property.	Gross Annual Value.	Name of Owner.	Address of Owner.	Estimated Acreage of Property.	Gross Annual Value.
		Acres.	£ s.			Acres.	£ s.
Bute, Marquess of	Dumfries House, Cumnock	43,734	22756 10	Clark, George	Townhead of Drumley, Tarbolton	143	338 —
Do. do.	Do. (*Minerals*)	—	2,506 —	Clark, James, of Blanefield	Ayr	359	302 —
				Clark, John	4 Inverleith Row, Edinburgh	413	839 —
Cairnie, Trustees of Stephen Millar	Largs	2	100 —	Clark, John Fleming	Auchinhean, Lochwinnoch	30	55 5
Calderwood, Hugh	Irvine	2	47 —				
Calderwood, William	Easter Highgate, Beith	22	45 —	Clark, Mrs. Mary	Gogo Villa, Largs	2	66 —
Calderwood, Margaret, Agnes, Janet, and Jean	Fenwick	331	200 5	*Clydesdale Banking Co.*	Glasgow	2	477 —
				Coats, Sir Peter, Kt.	Auchendrane, Ayr	67	157 10
Caldwell, John	Middleton, Beith	105	208 —	Cochrane, Alexander	Grange, Dunlop	200	250 —
Caldwell, John	Australia	80	95 —	Cochrane, James	Barcosh, Dalry	147	240 —
Caldwell, John, and John Carswell	Largs	1	8 —	Cochrane, John	Mains, Dunlop	98	180 —
				Cochrane, Peter	Oldhall, Dunlop	84	165 —
Caldwell, Robert	Knockshoggle, Tarbolton	28	56 15	Colmonell, Heritors of Parish of	Colmonell	1	14 —
Caldwell, Thomas	Coldstream, Beith	18	55 —				
Caldwell, Mrs. Elizabeth C.	East Middleton, Beith	40	60 —	Colmonell, Heritors and Kirk-Session of	Colmonell	130	100 —
Caledonian Railway Company	Glasgow (*Railway*)	40	*	Colquhoun, John	Kilmaurs	8	26 10
Cameron, John	Loudounhill, Newmilns	98	111 —	*Commercial Bank of Scotland*	George St., Edinburgh	2	230 —
Campbell, Arthur, senior, of Catrineholm	Edinburgh	472	639 —	Congregational Church, Trustees of	Stewarton	59	140 —
Campbell, Arthur, junior	Edinburgh	9	36 —	Conn, Heirs of Hugh	Kilwinning	10	96 —
Campbell, Major Charles Vereker Hamilton, of Netherplace	Netherplace, Mauchline	1,627	2,654 —	Cooper, William, of Failford	Failford, Tarbolton	1,666	1,881 —
Campbell, David	Ayr	3	30 —	Cooper, William Samuel, younger of Failford	Failford, Tarbolton	5	5 15
Campbell, George James, of Treesbank	Treesbank, Kilmarnock	1,049	1,732 —	Corson, Rev. William	Manse, Girvan	3	36 —
Do. do.	Do. (*Minerals*)	—	150 —	Cousin, David	Edinburgh	107	235 15
Campbell, James	Saltcoats	1	150 10	Cowan, Andrew	Ayr	1	82 —
Campbell, James and David	Crofthead, Kilmaurs	7	34 —	Cowan, Cuthbert	Hartley, Ayr	1	95 —
				Cowan, George	Lanfine, Galston	1	69 —
Campbell, Trustees of James, of Craigie	Craigie, Ayr	323	488 —	Cowan, Mrs. Marion	Wheatriggs, Kilmaurs	20	83 —
				Craig, Hugh, and others	Raithburn, Fenwick	3	12 5
Campbell, James S. Deans, of Curreath	Curreath, Troon	229	490 —	Craig, James	Borlandhills, Dunlop	25	42 —
				Craig, James	Polquheys, New Cumnock	2,831	325 —
Campbell, Captain Leveson-Granville-Alexander, of Fairfield	Kiddleston House, Great Malvern	2,463	723 —	Craig, John	Drumshang, Ayr	158	140 —
				Craig, John	Westfield, Tarbolton	11	24 —
Do. do.	Do. (*Minerals*)	—	150 —	Craig, Robert	West Kirkland, Dalry	41	85 —
Campbell, Richard Frederick Fotheringham, of Craigie	Craigie, Ayr	2,099	3,770 —	Craufuird, Thomas M'Miken, of Grange	Grange, Maybole	1,697	2,174 —
				Craufurd, Edward Henry John, of Auchenames, M.P.	Belgrave Road, London	3,440	3,710 —
Campbell, Captain Robert M., of Auchmunnoch	Auchmunnoch, Old Cumnock	3,928	2,156 —				
Do. do.	Do. (*Minerals*)	—	12 10	Craufurd, James, of Ardmillan (Lord Ardmillan)	Ardmillan, Girvan	2,248	1,423 10
Campbell, Trustees of Thomas	Annfield, Irvine	120	278 —	Craufurd, John Reginald Howison, of Craufurdland	Craufurdland Castle, Kilmarnock	1,876	1,988 5
Campbell, William	Longcroft, Straiton	1	42 —				
Campbell, William, of Skerrington	Skerrington, Riccarton	1,594	1,815 —	Craufurd, Mrs. Jane M'Knight	Edinburgh	56	126 —
Do. do.	Do. (*Minerals*)	—	1,320 —	Crawford, Daniel	Blairside, Kilwinning	30	137 —
Campbell, William	Nurseryhall, St. Quivox	384	150 —	Crawford, David	Woodside, West Kilbride	53	150 —
Campbell, Trustees of William G., of Fairfield	Fairfield, Monkton	685	1,227 —	Crawford Brothers	Barmill, Beith	6	412 —
Campbell, Heirs of Agnes	Bank Cottage, West Kilbride	9	29 10	Crawford, Hugh, of North Barr	North Barr, Beith	257	435 —
				Crawford, Rev. James	Crosshill	5	23 10
Carmichael, Mrs. Mary M'Queen Thomson, of Castlemains	Carmichael, Lanark	1,812	1,628 —	Crawford, James	Beith	20	124 10
				Crawford, James	Harplaw, Largs	130	60 —
Do. do.	Do. (*Minerals*)	—	339 —	Crawford, John	Milstonford, West Kilbride	82	150 —
Carrick, Rev. John	Maybole	2	31 —				
Carsewell, Rev. William	Eaglesham	92	205 —	Crawford, John, and others	North Whittleburn, Largs	54	181 —
Caskie, John	Stewarton	3	168 —	Crawford, Robert	Beith	2	250 —
Cathcart, Hon. Augustus Murray	Berbeth, Dalmellington	1,000	360 —	Crawford, William	Royal Bank, Maybole	3	227 10
				Crawford, William	Raillies, Largs	83	65 —
Cathcart, Elias, of Auchendrane	Auchendrane, Ayr	327	522 —	Crawford, William	Dalry	3	24 10
				Crawford, Mrs. Elizabeth	Loans, Troon	5	15 —
Cathcart, Sir John A., of Carlton and Killochan, Bart.	Killochan, Dailly	13,118	6,386 —	Crichton, Hew	Park Place, Edinburgh	1	196 —
				Crichton, John, of Linn	Linn, Dalry	335	1,139 —
Cathcart, Honourable Mrs. Jean Macadam	Berbeth, Dalmellington	35,960	9,427 —	Crichton, Robert Orr, of Dalgarven	Linn, Dalry	93	255 —
				Cross, Mrs. Marion	South Lodge, Ayr	4	114 —
Do. do.	Do. (*Minerals*)	—	8,734 —	*Crown, The*		5	334 —
Catrine, Heritors of	Catrine	1	5 —	Cruickshanks, Rev. James	Stevenston	6	56 15
Chalmers, John	Camreggan, Girvan	25	60 —	Cruickshanks, Matthew	99 Hill Street, Glasgow	1	25 —
Chapman, James	Bridgend, Airdrie	10	33 —	Crum, Jessie	Thornliebank, Glasgow	1	137 —
Chrystal, Rev. James	Manse, Auchinleck	9	32 —	Cumnock United Presbyterian Congregation, Trustees of	Cumnock	2	30 —
City of Glasgow Bank	24 Virginia St., Glasgow	2	177 —				

* No Valuation of this portion of Railway yet made, the line being in course of formation.

AYR—continued.

Name of Owner.	Address of Owner.	Estimated Acreage of Property.	Gross Annual Value.		Name of Owner.	Address of Owner.	Estimated Acreage of Property.	Gross Annual Value.	
		Acres.	£	s.			Acres.	£	s.
Cuningham Combination Poorhouse	Irvine	11	250	–	Dobie, Bonella and Mary	Coupar-Angus	187	350	–
Cunningham, John	Trees, Maybole	1	39	–	Donald, James, and others	Kilwinning	62	62	10
Cunningham, John, of Carmel Bank	Carmel Bank, Kilmaurs	90	224	–	Donald, William	Broomhill, Kilwinning	40	64	–
Do. do.	Do. (*Minerals*)	–	191	10	Donaldson, John Ure, of Auchearne	Auchearne, Ballantrae	1,741	939	–
Cunningham, John, Jean, and Mary	Stewarton	4	17	–	Donaldson, T. Leverton	London University, London	284	511	15
Cunningham, Trustees of Major William	Prestwick	4	21	10	Donaldson, Mrs. Margaret	18 Southampton Street, Bloomsbury Sq., London	357	631	10
Cunningham, Hon. Mrs. Margaret, of Hapland	Moray Place, Edinburgh	242	345	15	Do. do.	Do. (*Minerals*)	–	3	15
Do. do.	Do. (*Minerals*)	–	5	–	Douglas, Trustees of John	Heaton, Mersey	80	150	–
Cunninghame, Arthur Wellesley Robertson, of Auchenharvie	Auchenharvie, Stevenston	650	1,519	10	Douglas, William	Crosshouse, Kilmaurs	3	48	10
Do. do.	Do. (*Minerals*)	–	2,609	–	Douglas, Margaret, and others, of Brownhill	Brownhill, Dalry	122	171	10
Cunninghame, John Wm. Herbert, of Lainshaw	Lainshaw, Stewarton	4,642	7,285	10	Do. do.	Do. (*Minerals*)	–	40	–
Do. do.	Do. (*Minerals*)	–	740	–	Douglas, Margaret	Brownhill, Dalry	2	25	–
Cunninghame, William A., of Logan	Logan, Cumnock	3,783	1,976	–	Drennan, John	Viccarton Row, Girvan	2	18	15
Do. do.	Do. (*Minerals*)	–	860	–	Drysdale, William, and others	Ronaldshaw Park, Ayr	4	120	–
Cunninghame, Wm. Cathcart Smith, of Caprington	Caprington Castle, Kilmarnock	4,888	5,098	5	Dun, Alex. Campbell	Hampstead, London	4	94	–
					Duncan, Allan	Hillhead, Coylton	2	6	–
Do. do.	Do. (*Minerals*)	–	2,918	10	Duncan, John Cochrane	America	111	145	–
Cuninghame, Sir William J. Montgomery, of Corsehill, Bart.	Maybole	1,338	1,321	15	Duncan, William	Brockwellmuir, Dunlop	43	55	–
					Dundonald, Earl of	12 Queen's Gate, South Kensington, London	12	25	–
Do. do.	Do. (*Minerals*)	–	572	–	Dundonald, Parochial Board of	Troon	1	5	–
Cuninghame, Dowager Lady Charlotte Montgomery Niven	Maybole	1,871	1,856	–	Dunlop, Alexander, of Doonside	Doonside, Maybole	875	1,197	15
					Dunlop, Alexander, of Cairnduff	Priory Lodge, Largs	2	90	–
Currie, James	Gree, Fenwick	50	50	–	Dunlop, Andrew	High Guardrum, Fenwick	22	35	–
Currie, Ronald	Skelmorlie, Greenock	2	210	–	Dunlop, Gabriel	Stewarton	103	194	–
Currie, Robert Irvine	Glasgow	4	9	10	Dunlop, James	Alton, Kilmaurs	3	12	–
Currie, Wm. Campbell	Ayr	2	30	–	Dunlop, John	Stewarton	125	373	–
Cuthbert, Alexander	Newton, Ayr	6	29	–	Dunlop, John, of Fardenreoch	Fardenreoch, Colmonell	333	295	–
Cuthbert, Mrs. Janet	Ochiltree	25	81	–	Dunlop, Robert, senior	Kilwinning	56	98	–
Cuthbertson, Trustees of James	Yardside, Kilmaurs	43	150	–	Dunlop, Robert, junior	Woodside, Kilwinning	24	55	–
Cuthbertson, John	Barrassie, Troon	2	25	–	Dunlop, William Henry, of Annanhill	Annanhill, Kilmarnock	186	453	10
					Do. do.	(*Minerals*)	–	604	–
					Dunn, David	Largs	3	100	–
Dale, Matthew	Beith	6	49	5	Dunn, Jessie Herron Violet, of Dalmore	Dalmore, Stair	93	90	–
Dalglish, William, of Roughdyke	Douglas, Lanark	130	115	–	Do. do.	Do. (*Minerals*)	–	400	–
Dalmellington Iron Co.	Waterside, Ayr	259	6,255	–	Dykes, Rev. Thomas	Manse, Ayr	4	60	–
Dalry Gas Light Company	Dalry	1	100	–					
Dalry, Heritors of Parish of	Dalry	2	30	–	Earl, Mary and Jane	Lagganwhilly, Girvan	1	39	10
Dalry, Parochial Board of	Dalry	4	12	–	Easton, Walter	Glasgow	46	134	–
Davidson, Rev. John	Manse, Symington	6	35	–	Eaton, James, of Darnaconner	8 Alva Street, Edinburgh	1,200	72	5
Davidson, Thomas	Kirkoswald	19	10	–	Eck, Frederick A., of Hollybush	Hollybush, Dalrymple	680	761	–
Davidson, William R., of Drumley	Shanghai	306	561	–	Eckford, Capt. Alexander H., and another	Largs	2	100	–
Davidson, William	Kirkoswald	13	31	–	Edmonston, Mrs. Henrietta Jane H. Smith	Hayocks, Stevenston	21	12	–
Dempster, James, of Ladyton	Ladyton, Loudoun	70	150	–	*Eglinton Chemical Company*	Halfway, Irvine	16	168	–
Do. do.	Do. (*Minerals*)	–	2,130	–	*Eglinton Iron Company*	Kilwinning	2,168	13035	10
Dennison, John	Skelmorlie, Greenock	1	70	–	Do. do.	Do. (*Minerals*)	–	1,668	10
Dick, James	Blair, Dailly	10	51	–	Eglinton and Winton, Earl of	Eglinton Castle, Irvine	23,585	32504	15
Dick, Mrs. Catherine, and Margaret Wilson	Maybole	3	18	–	Do. do.	Do. (*Harbours*)	46	4,525	10
Dickie, Rev. David	Fenwick	11	42	–	Do. do.	Do. (*Minerals*)	–	9,520	10
Dickie, James	Bogside, Dreghorn	22	51	–	Einsiedel, Countess of	Adamton, Monkton	685	1,304	–
Do.	Do. (*Minerals*)	–	25	15	Elder, George, of Knock	Knock Castle, Largs	153	418	–
Dickie, James	Kilbirnie	2	32	–	Erskine, Mrs. Janet Blane	Cassillis Street, Ayr	12	209	–
Dickson, James, of Duchray	Glasgow	139	150	–	Ewen, Robert	Ewenfield, Ayr	27	305	10
Do. do.	Do. (*Minerals*)	–	231	–	Ewen, Stephen	Woodbank Villa, Largs	1	90	–
Dickson, Colonel John, of Glenbuck	Glenbuck, Muirkirk	600	165	–	Eyre, Most Rev. Charles, and others, Trs. of Roman Catholic Congregation	West George St., Glasgow	1	42	–
Dinning, James and John	Girtrigmill, Dundonald	1	60	–					
Dixon, William Smith	Glasgow	2	60	–					
Dixon, Janet	Skelmorlie	2	80	–					
Dobie, John Sheddan	Morrishill, Beith	3	38	–	Fairlie, Rev. Henry	Manse, Kirkmichael	20	65	–
Dobie, William H.	Gartferry, Ayr	1	90	–	Fairlie, Rev. James	Manse, Mauchline	10	45	–
Dobie, Mrs. Margaret	Morrishill, Beith	272	487	–	Fairlie, William, of Holmes	Holmes, Galston	545	1,094	–
Do. do.	Do. (*Minerals*)	–	90	10	Do. do.	Do. (*Minerals*)	–	3,491	–

AYR—*continued.*

Name of Owner.	Address of Owner.	Estimated Acreage of Property.	Gross Annual Value.	Name of Owner.	Address of Owner.	Estimated Acreage of Property.	Gross Annual Value.
		Acres.	£ s.			Acres.	£ s.
Farquhar, Mary Gray and Jane	Gilmilnscroft, Sorn	2,386	741 –	Galston, Heritors and Minister of	Galston (Minerals)	–	307 –
Do. do.	Do. (Minerals)	–	330 –	Garland, Margaret, and others	High Street, Irvine	86	62 10
Farquharson, Col. James R., of Invercauld, and Honourable John Manners Yorke	Invercauld . . Folkestone . .	1,760	1,899 10	Garroway, Robert	Thorndale, Skelmorlie	2	100 –
				Gauchalland Coal Company	Kilmarnock	10	324 10
				Gaw, William	Prestwick	4	17 –
Faulds, Andrew Wilson	Knockbuckle, Beith	18	56 15	Gebbie, Rev. William	Manse, Dunlop	10	47 –
Faulds, James	Beith	17	104 10	Gemmell, Andrew	Capelaw, Neilston	70	90 –
Ferguson, Alexander	Borland, Kilmarnock	52	122 15	Gemmell, Andrew	Dalloy, Newmilns	2	5 15
Ferguson, Alexander	Auchentiber, Stewarton	77	150 –	Gemmell, John	Fenwick	2	43 –
Ferguson, Trs. of Alexander	Oldhallside, Dunlop	44	82 –	Gemmell, Patrick	Templehouse, Dunlop	52	92 10
Ferguson, James	Roanhill, Dundonald	20	28 –	Gemmell, Robert	West Kilbride	2	48 –
Ferguson, John, of Fulwood	Fulwood, Stewarton	135	167 10	Gemmell, Robert	Oxenward, Kilwinning	11	118 –
Ferguson Bequest Fund, Trustees of	Irvine and Glasgow	155	206 10	Gemmell, Thomas	Dalloy, Newmilns	2	9 –
				Gemmell, Thos. Macmillan	Frankville, Ayr	653	507 –
Ferguson, Mrs. Ann	Tillington, Stafford	29	76 –	Gemmell, William	Auchentiber, Kilwinning	70	148 –
Fergusson, Daniel	Halfway, Irvine	10	68 –	Gemmell, William	Deepstone, Beith	70	90 –
Fergusson, James	Ayr	9	199 –	Gemmell, William	Clunes Vennal, Newton	6	9 –
Fergusson, James Murray	Ayr	52	165 –	Gemmell, Mrs. Jane	Templehouse, Dunlop	26	47 10
Fergusson, Sir James, of Kilkerran, Bart.	Kilkerran Ho., Maybole	22,630	13334 15	Gemmell, Mrs. Jean	Kilmarnock	7	25 –
				Gemmell, Mrs. Marion	Newmilns	1	1 10
Do. do.	Do. (Minerals)	–	204 –	Gibb, Heirs of William	Milton Mill, Kilmarnock	9	24 –
Fergusson, Peter	Ayr	3	10 –	Gibson, Alexander	Springfield, Tarbolton	8	24 –
Fergusson, William	Ballochneal, Girvan	1	20 –	Gibson, Rev. Henry	Glenapp, Ballantrae	39	34 10
Ferrier, William Cochrane	Meikle Corsehill, Dunlop	141	200 –	Gibson, Heirs of John	Brackenhill, Kilmaurs	5	17 –
Fettes, Trs. of Sir William, of Comely Bank, Bart.	Edinburgh	13,905	2,652 –	Gillies, Robert, senior	Dochra, Beith	73	115 –
				Gillilan, Hugh	South Border, Beith	17	26 10
Findlay, James	Westfield, Greenock	94	270 –	Gilmour, Alexander	Annfield, Irvine	3	75 –
Findlay, Rev. John	Kirkoswald	8	35 –	Gilmour, Alexander	Bottoms, Beith	33	55 –
Findlay, Matthew	Lyonstone, Maybole	82	74 –	Gilmour, Allan	Netherhouse, Dunlop	88	226 15
Findlay, Robert	Thorn, Dunlop	91	153 –	Gilmour, Allan	Woodend, Kilmarnock	1	81 –
Findlay, Robert	Slacks, Darvel	6	17 –	Gilmour, Allan, and Robert Rankine's Heirs	Hairshaw, Stewarton	90	38 –
Findlay, William	Crofthead, Darvel	80	90 –				
Findlay, Heirs of William	Thornhill, Hillhead, Glasgow	36	112 10	Gilmour, Andrew, of Broadlie	Broadlie, Neilston	138	260 –
Finlay, James, & Company	Catrine, Mauchline	103	2,476 –	Gilmour, Boyd, & Co.	Hurlford, Kilmarnock	4	215 –
Finnie, Archibald, of Springhill	Springhill, Kilmarnock	45	361 10	Gilmour, James	Glasgow	64	100 –
				Gilmour, John	Townhead, Fenwick	32	81 –
Do. do.	Do. (Minerals)	–	59 10	Gilmour, John	Gree, Beith	21	35 –
Finnie, Archibald, & Son	Kilmarnock	1	195 –	Gilmour, John	Irvine	1	168 –
Finnie, William, of Newfield, M.P.	Newfield, Kilmarnock; and 95 Eaton Place, London	677	1,351 –	Gilmour, Matthew	Nethergree, Beith	70	105 –
				Gilmour, Robert	Hessilhead, Beith	49	63 –
				Gilmour, Thomas	Brae, Fenwick	51	53 –
Fleming, Hugh	Bentfaulds, Kilwinning	55	45 –	Gilmour, William	Habbieauld, Kilmaurs	29	58 15
Fleming, James Nicol, of Knockdon	Knockdon, Maybole	1,033	2,549 –	Gilmour, William	Leahead, Dunlop	80	127 –
				Gilmour, Mrs. Elizabeth	Netherhouse, Dunlop	37	80 –
Fleming, Robert	Fergushill, Kilwinning	6	19 15	Gilmour, Mrs. Mary	Bogside, Stewarton	16	42 –
Fleming, Mrs. Jane	Bridgend, Kilwinning	33	37 –	*Girvan Harbour Trustees*	Girvan	3	35 –
Forbes, William, of Callendar	Callendar House, Falkirk	603	1,235 15	*Girvan, Heritors of Parish of*	Girvan	1	18 –
				Girvan, Parochial Board of	Girvan	2	16 –
Forgan, Charles, of Towerhill	Towerhill, Kilmaurs	90	401 –	*Girvan & Portpatrick Junction Railway Company*	Stranraer (Railway)	160	*
Foulds, Alexander R.	Clerkland, Stewarton	60	100 –	Glasgow, Earl of	Kelburn House, Largs	24,968	13855 15
Foulds, John	Lochridgehills, Dunlop	120	140 –	Do. do.	Do. (Minerals)	–	4,503 –
Fraser, William and Archibald	Largs	4	67 –	Glasgow, Rev. James	Manse, Coylton	9	44 –
				Glasgow, Robert Bruce R. of Montgreenan	Montgreenan, Kilwinning	2,645	2,408 –
Freebairn, William	Drumilling, West Kilbride	98	225 –	Do. do.	Do. (Minerals)	–	167 10
Free Church Congregation	Barr	1	40 –	Glasgow, Countess Dowager of	Fairliecraig House, Largs	4	50 –
Free Church Trustees	Maybole	1	18 –				
Frew, William	Kayshill, Stair	2	28 –	*Glasgow & South-Western Railway Company*	Glasgow (Railway)	1,593	130232 –
Fullarton, Alexander	Ferguslie Place, Paisley	5	9 15				
Fullarton, Alexander	Graham's Castle, Ardrossan	2	95 –	*Glasgow, Barrhead, and Kilmarnock Joint Railway Company*	Glasgow (Railway)	195	4,502 –
Fullarton, Gavin, of Kerelaw	Kerelaw, Stevenston	896	1,944 10	Glen, David G.	Largs	3	51 10
Fullarton, Trustees of Capt. John	Overton, West Kilbride	25	81 –	Goodwin, James, Francis, David, and John	Ardrossan	1	235 10
Fulton, Trs. of Robert	Broadley, Beith	243	501 10	Goudie, Andrew	Maybole	1	66 15
Do. do.	Do. (Minerals)	–	220 –	Goudie, Robert	Ayr	1	200 –
Fulton, William and Janet	Tower of Auchenbathie, Howwood	55	65 –	Gourlay, Rev. William Edmond Crawford Austin	Stoke Abbot Rectory, Dorset	52	86 15
				Gow, Mrs. Margaret	Wester Highgate, Beith	118	202 –
Gaa's Charity Trustees	Dalmellington	2	30 –	Graham, John	City Bank, Glasgow	1	49 –
Gairdner, Trustees of Major-General	Monkton	126	90 –	Graham, John Graham Barns, of Craigallion	Fereneze, Barrhead	609	1,047 –
Galbraith, Mrs. Jane	Nether Berbeth, Dalmellington	164	175 –	Graham, Thomas D. C., of Dunlop	Dunlop House, Stewarton	1,473	3,170 10
Galloway, Andrew	Glasgow	4	12 10	Graham, Mrs. Susan	Brooksby, Largs	2	150 –

* No Valuation of this Railway yet made, the line being in course of formation.

AYR—continued.

Name of Owner.	Address of Owner.	Estimated Acreage of Property.	Gross Annual Value.	Name of Owner.	Address of Owner.	Estimated Acreage of Property.	Gross Annual Value.
		Acres.	£ s.			Acres.	£ s.
Gray, Archibald	Cranberry Moss, Kilwinning	37	149 —	Hendry, James	Kilwinning	4	82 —
Gray, David	Irvine	38	155 —	Heron, Matthew	Kilwinning	6	16 —
Gray, James	Ayr	7	18 —	Highet, David	Ayr	1	629 —
Gray, James	Mosside, Tarbolton	10	15 —	Hillcoat, Robert	Jackson Street, Glasgow	1	25 —
Gray, John Barton Farquhar, of Glentig	Kirkhill Castle, Colmonell	1,525	1,329 15	Home, Trs. of Sir George, of Blackadder, Bart., and others	Inveraray	2	83 —
Gray, John	Prestwick	9	23 —	Home, Countess of, wife of Earl of Home	Douglas Castle, Bothwell	2,271	567 —
Gray, John	Maybole	2	69 10				
Gray, John	Glasgow	36	181 —	Do. do.	Do. (Minerals)	—	.800 —
Gray, Robert	Little Scoutts, Tarbolton	26	58 —	Honeyman, John	Largs	4	100 —
Gray, Robert	New Road, Newton	9	90 —	Houldsworth, Henry	Carrick House, Ayr	3	150 —
Gray, Heirs of Mrs. Jean	Ayr	4	88 —	Houldsworth, William Henry, of Coodham	Coodham, Kilmarnock	585	1,151 —
Greenshields, John Blackwood, of Kerse	Kerse, Lesmahagow	408	224 —	Houston, Gavin	Gowanlea, Dalry	80	153 —
Gregg, James	Meiklemyre, Dalry	3	14 —	Houston, John	Gowanlea, Dalry	47	55 —
Gregg, James, and others	Meiklemyre, Dalry	70	100 —	Houston, Robert and Alexander	Lugtonridge, Beith	70	102 —
Do. do.	Do. (Minerals)	—	473 15				
Gregg, James, and John Boyd	Waterside, Largs	61	75 —	Houston, Robert, and others	Beith	55	50 —
Gregg, William	Eastmains, Kilbirnie	8	60 —	Howatson, Charles, of Dornal	Daldorch, Mauchline	1,888	738 —
Greig, James	Langside, Dalry	117	190 —	Howie, James	India Street, Kilmarnock	14	50 —
Greig, William	Langside, Dalry	76	137 10	Howie, John	Hurlford	15	503 —
Do.	Do. (Minerals)	—	20 —	Howie, Heirs of William	Hurlford	2	309 —
Gregory, Captain John Jarvis, R.N.	Blackburn, Ayr	26	120 —	Howie, Mrs. Agnes	Seamill, West Kilbride	1	30 —
Guthrie, Alexander	Monkton	1	11 —	Hume, Archibald	Auchindolly, Castle-Douglas	61	381 —
Guthrie, Andrew	Monkton	4	20 —	Hunter, Charles	Prestwick	26	28 —
Guthrie, John	Braehead, Prestwick	33	27 —	Hunter, David	Newton	8	36 10
Guthrie, Heirs of Mrs. Frances	Ayr	2	14 —	Hunter, James	North Kirkland, Dalry	27	82 —
				Do.	Do. (Minerals)	—	21 15
Guthrie, Mrs. Christina, of The Mount	The Mount, Kilmarnock	50	211 —	Hunter, James	Church Street, Prestwick	23	42 —
				Hunter, James, of Glenapp	Newmains, Motherwell	8,580	2,705 —
				Do. do.	Do. (Minerals)	—	400 —
Haddow, Robert, senior	Newmilns	280	104 —	Hunter, James	Burnscourt, Ireland	2	32 —
Haddow, William	Riggfoot, New Cumnock	160	102 —	Hunter, John	Farewell Cot., Prestwick	2	43 —
Halbert, David	Dundonald	25	38 —	Hunter, John	Poundland, Colmonell	250	117 —
Haldane, Capt. Alex., and Adriana Kerr	Largs	2	100 —	Hunter, Trustees of John	Smiddybank, Dalry	16	65 —
Halket, Colonel James	Surrey	78	50 —	Hunter, Robert, of Hunter	Hunterston House, West Kilbride	881	1,874 —
Hall, Heirs of Charles	Newton, Ayr	4	64 —	Hunter, William	Clunes Vennal, Newton	5	20 —
Hamilton, Alexander R., of Hillerhirst	Retreat, Devon	100	242 —	Hunter, William, and Mrs. Janet Bone	Newton Burnside, Newton	6	24 —
Hamilton, Captain Alex., of Rozelle, R.N.	Ayr	1,805	2,691 —	Hunter, William	Everton Cot., Prestwick	19	70 —
Hamilton, Representatives of Dougald	Mauchline	616	172 —	Hunter, Mrs. Rachel	Corsehill, Kilwinning	2	6 —
				Hunter, Mrs. Mary	Prestwick	2	11 —
Hamilton, Trustees of Hill, of Kildonan	Kildonan, Colmonell	3,683	1,519 —	Hunter, Agnes, Janet, and Thomasina	Cassillis Street, Ayr	10	9 10
Hamilton, Captain Hugh, of Pinmore	Pinmore, Girvan	8,441	3,833 —	Hutchison, Trustees of Agnes	Riccarton	20	58 —
				Hutchison, Lilias	The Knowe, Ayr	8	140 —
Hamilton, John Wallace Ferrier, of Cairnhill	Cairnhill, Craigie	1,719	2,687 —	Hyndman, Henry Cooper, of Springside	Springside, West Kilbride	413	680 —
Hamilton, John, of Sundrum	Sundrum, Coylton	2,944	3,280 —	Hyslop, Alexander	Townend, Maybole	6	52 —
				Hyslop, John, of Bank	Bank, New Cumnock	250	388 —
Do. do.	Do. (Minerals)	—	1,000 —	Do. do.	Do. (Minerals)	—	651 —
Hamilton, John	Hamilfield, Irvine	24	119 —	Hyland & Co., Thomas	Wallacetown, Ayr	4	377 10
Hamilton, Thomas	Skelmorlie	2	60 —				
Hamilton, William Finlay	Carlisle	1	12 —				
Handyside, Peter David	11 Hope St., Edinburgh	1,390	224 —	Imrie, Mrs. Eliza	Bourtreepark, Ayr	3	55 —
Hanna, Thomas Chalmers	5 Nelson St., Edinburgh	106	132 —	Inglis, Rev. Alexander	Manse, Kilmaurs	6	40 —
Hannah, David	Montgomerie St., Girvan	3	47 —	Inglis, Trustees of Thomas Hutton	Hutton Park Villa, Largs	4	105 10
Hannah, Trs. of Robert	Girvan	300	97 10				
Hart, George	Corsehill, Ayr	20	143 —	Innes, John	Highroad, Skelmorlie	1	149 —
Harvey, William	Hellier, Sorn	126	40 —	Irvine, Burgh of	Irvine	696	1,419 —
Harvie, Andrew	Parkmill, Tarbolton	2	113 —	Do.	Do. (Minerals)	—	391 —
Harvie, Mrs. Jean	Auchingree, Dalry	35	79 —	Irvine Gas Light Company	Do.	2	183 —
Hay, Mrs. Georgina	The Gondola, Fairlie	57	158 —	Irvine Harbour Trustees	Do.	8	100 —
Hay, Mrs. Jane Baird, and James George Baird Hay, spouses	Belton, Dunbar	833	1,535 —	Irvine, Parochial Board of	Do.	7	28 10
				Ivory, Mrs. Janet Hunter Rankine, and others, of Stonecalsey	Edinburgh	162	272 10
Hazel, David	Threethorus, Straiton	3,300	355 —				
Heggie, James and John	Goldcraig, Kilwinning	130	200 —				
Do. do.	Do. (Minerals)	—	80 —				
Henderson, William	Williamfield, Irvine	10	55 —				
Henderson, William, & Co.	Halfway, Irvine	27	216 —	Jack, Alexander	Maybole	3	124 —
Henderson, Mrs. Margaret	Arrochar, Helensburgh	2	10 —	Jack, Trustees of John	Warrenhill, Largs	22	45 —
Hendrie, John	Oldhall, Dunlop	25	45 —	Jackson, James	Gabreochhill, Stewarton	51	55 —

AYR—continued.

Name of Owner.	Address of Owner.	Estimated Acreage of Property.	Gross Annual Value.		Name of Owner.	Address of Owner.	Estimated Acreage of Property.	Gross Annual Value.
		Acres.	£ s.				Acres.	£ s.
James, Hugh Septimus, of Martnaham	Martnaham, Ayr	330	184 –		Kilmaurs, Magistrates of, in trust for the Poor	Kilmaurs	1	13 –
Jamieson, Andrew	Paris	4	33 –		Kilmaurs, Ministers and Bailies of, in trust	Kilmaurs	13	39 –
Jamieson, Trustees of James	Ladeside, Kilbirnie	14	244 –		Kilpatrick, Mrs. Margaret	Miller Road, Ayr	12	133 –
Jamieson, William	Chapelton, Kilbirnie	74	91 –		Kilwinning, Heritors of Parish of	Kilwinning	2	13 10
Jamieson, William	Skelmorlie, Largs	1	35 –		Kilwinning Parochial Board	Kilwinning	117	183 15
Jamieson, Annie and Isabella	Gogoside, Largs	5	49 10		King, Rev. Alexander	The Manse, W. Kilbride	6	58 –
Jardine, James	N. Whittlieburn, Largs	211	122 –		King, Daniel	Old Cumnock	2	182 –
Jeffrey, Rev. William	Manse, Riccarton	2	3 –		King, Hugh	Kilwinning	325	327 10
Johnston, William	Dalry	2	47 10		King, Patrick	Prestwick	4	2 –
Johnston, William	New Cumnock	7	44 –		King, Robert	Burnhouse, Beith	53	135 –
Johnston, Mrs. Elizabeth	16 Park Terrace, Glasgow	1	100 –		King, William	Whang Street, Beith	1	30 –
Johnston, Mrs. Agnes	Rosebank Ter., Glasgow	5	19 …		King, William, and John Wilson	West Kilbride	21	70 –
Johnston, Mrs. Margaret	Wellington Square, Ayr	375	219 –		Kinross, Trustees of John	Alloway Place, Ayr	2	117 –
Johnstone, Agnes and Jane H.	Murray Park, St. Andrews	5	25 –		Kinross, Rev. John	The Manse, Largs	11	77 –
					Kirkmichael, Heritors of Parish of	Kirkmichael	1	15 –
Kay, John	Pettoch, Coylton	110	176 –		Kirkwood, James Dunlop	Park Grove, Govan	2	16 –
Kelso, Walter Edward Utterson, of Dankeith	Dankeith, Symington	370	557 –		Knox, James	Muirhouse, Symington	1	12 –
Kennedy, Rev. Alexander	The Manse, Stewarton	7	53 –		Knox, James	Riverside, Kilbirnie	64	131 –
Kennedy, David Archibald Dalton, of Craig	Craig, Colmonell	1,390	630 –		Knox, Robert William	Moorpark, Kilbirnie	39	205 –
Kennedy, David H. C.	Exchange Buildings, Glasgow	44	112 10		Knox, William and James	Kilbirnie	4	690 –
					Kyle, David	Davidshill, Dalry	69	261 10
Kennedy, Trustees of Hew Fergusson, of Finnart	Finnart, Ballantrae	3,713	1,619 10		Do. Do. (Minerals)		–	51 –
Kennedy, John, of Underwood	71 Great King St., Edin.	557	923 –		Kyle Union Poorhouse	Ayr	5	200 –
Kennedy, Trustees of Robert T., of Daljarrock	Daljarrock, by Girvan	1,940	1,512 –		Kyle, William	Mosside, Dalry	150	257 15
Kennedy, Thomas	Kilmarnock	1	2 –		Lade, James	154 St. Vincent Street, Glasgow	259	282 –
Kennedy, Right Hon. Thomas F., of Dunure	Dalquharran, Dailly	4,141	5,990 10		Lade, Mrs. Mary, and John Crawford	Raillies, Largs	2	47 10
Do. do.	Do. (Harbour)	1	5 –		Lamb, James, of Dalquhairn	Maybole	781	180 –
Do. do.	Do. (Minerals)	–	900 –		Lamb, James	Dalquhairn, Barr	7	20 –
Kennedy, Lady Mary Primrose Shaw, of Kirkmichael	Kirkmichael	1,689	2,601 –		Lanemark Coal Company	Bankglen, New Cumnock	3	276 –
					Lang, Arthur	Ayr	30	698 –
					Lang, Hugh Morris	Broadmeadow, Selkirk	501	325 –
Kenneth, Archibald	Kilwinning	16	421 –		Lang, James, of Ferrolside	Largs	380	277 –
Do.	Do. (Minerals)	–	180 –		Lang, John	Warrenpark, Largs	3	105 –
Kent, William	Mid Cutstraw, Stewarton	8	17 10		Lang, William, of Groatholm	Mansfield House, Largs	989	1,112 –
Ker, Rev. William	Manse, Stair	38	74 10		Lang, Heirs of William	Hardcroft, Dalry	100	250 –
Ker, Rev. William Lee	Manse, Kilwinning	8	50 –		Do. do.	Do. (Minerals)	–	45 –
Kerr, Heirs of Daniel	Meadowhead, Dalry	20	54 –		Largs Harbour Company	Largs (Harbour)	2	679 –
Kerr, James	Sidehouse, Dalry	65	98 –		Largs, Heritors of Parish of	Largs	2	10 10
Kerr, John	Fulwoodhead, Beith	87	107 –		Latham, David M.	Greenock	3	110 –
Kerr, John	Gateside, Stewarton	63	100 –		Latta, John	Prestwick Toll, Newton	2	20 –
Kerr, Trustees of John	Trochrague, Girvan	721	1,423 –		Latta, William	Whitletts	19	16 10
Kerr, John B.	Halket, Dunlop	3	17 –		Langhland, John and Thomas	91 Hope Street, Glasgow	9	30 –
Kerr, John James of Robertland	Woodside Ter., Glasgow	1,421	1,916 15		Laurence, James	Stepends, Cumnock	1	198 –
Kerr, Matthew	Killumpha, Kirkmaiden	1	22 10		Laurie, Trustees of Alexander	Sornhill, Riccarton	1	43 –
Kerr, Richard, of Cunninghamhead	Cunninghamhead, Dreghorn	560	1,440 –		Laurie, Trustees of John, of Whitehill	Ayr	230	230 –
Kerr, Robert, of Auchengree	Auchengree, Dalry	152	243 –		Laurie, Nathaniel Donaldson, of Lauriston	Ravenscroft, Irvine	206	175 –
Do. do.	Do. (Minerals)	–	144 –		Lawrie, Rev. George James	Manse, Monkton	10	65 –
Kerr, Robert, of Chapeldounan	Chapeldonnan, Girvan	1,407	2,028 10		Lawson, Robert	Australia	10	68 –
Kerr, Heirs of Robert	Villas, Largs	4	125 –		Lawson, Rev. Roderick	Maybole	1	20 –
Kerr, Thomas	Newington, Edinburgh	15	32 –		Leck, Henry	170 Hope St., Glasgow	75	101 –
Kerr, William	Milton, Kilmarnock	40	44 10		Lees, John	Millburn, Tarbolton	50	50 –
Kerr, William	Townhead, Beith	18	28 5		Leggat, John	Galston	52	65 –
Do.	Do. (Minerals)	–	18 –		Do.	Do. (Minerals)	–	135 –
Kerr, Mrs. Janet	Gallowberryhill, Stewarton	6	21 –		Leiper, James	Little Glen, Newmilns	117	110 –
Kerr, Mrs. Margaret	Redwells, Kilwinning	66	75 –		Leiper, John	Onthank, Strathaven	151	141 15
Kerr, Janet	New Cumnock	3	48 –		Lennox, John	Newmilns	4	13 –
Kerr, Margaret and Isabella	Rosebank, Largs	8	126 –		Lindsay, James	Outstraw, Stewarton	18	36 –
Kidd, John	Mount Ellis, Roseneath	9	20 –		Lindsay, Robert	Guardrum, Fenwick	80	120 –
Kidney, James	Manchester	90	140 –		Lindsay, Thomas Spencer	Ireland	20	11 –
Kilbirnie, Heritors of Parish of	Kilbirnie	4	20 –		Lindsay, William	Hallhouse, Fenwick	10	53 15
Kilmarnock Water Company	Kilmarnock	3	100 –		Linn, Galbraith, & Co.	Irvine	9	72 –
Kilmaurs, Burgh of	Kilmaurs	1	4 10		Little, Rev. Simon	Manse, Ballantrae	9	46 15
					Lockhart, Adam	Sandgate Street, Ayr	6	9 10
					Lockhart, William	Mayfield, Stevenston	18	407 –
					Do.	Do. (Minerals)	–	27 10
					Logan, Mrs. Ann	Wattfield Cottage, Ayr	2	122 15

AYR—continued.

Name of Owner.	Address of Owner.	Estimated Acreage of Property.	Gross Annual Value.
		Acres.	£ s.
Logan, Mrs. Janet	Hawhill, West Kilbride	10	56 —
Longmuir, John	Irvine	67	217 —
Loudoun, Countess of	Loudoun Castle, Galston	18,638	15286 —
Do. do.	Do. (Minerals)	—	2,259 —
Loudoun, James	Loudoun Mill, Newmilns	2	14 —
Loudoun, Heirs of James	Braehead, Kilmaurs	7	13 —
Love, Alexander	Beith	4	25 15
Love, Andrew	Beith	10	18 —
Love, Hugh	Beith	2	65 —
Love, James	Beith	56	113 —
Love, Trustees of John	Beith	320	242 15
Love, Thomas	Bunswynd, Beith	2	33 —
Love, William Fulton	Beith	15	105 —
Love, Trustees of William	Nethermill, Beith	27	93 10
Love, Mrs. Mary	Hamilfield, Beith	3	46 —
Lusk, Robert	Stanleybank, Dalry	1	30 10
M'Adam, Trustees of William, of Ballochmorrie	Ballochmorrie, Girvan	976	476 10
M'Alester, Colonel Charles S., of Kennox	Kennox, Stewarton	1,012	1,441 15
M'Alester, Major Charles S., yr. of Kennox	Ayr	23	113 —
M'Alester, James, of Chapelton	Chapelton, Stewarton	175	425 —
M'Alister, John	Stockbridge, Symington	72	191 5
M'Alister, Trustees of William	Dalrympleyard, Irvine	22	107 —
M'Call, Alexander	Glasgow	6	16 —
M'Clelland, James	Ayr	14	79 10
M'Clelland, James and Walter	Glasgow	28	48 —
M'Clelland, Thomas	Kossuth Place, Greenock	1	4 —
M'Clung, James, of Pinnwherry	Daljarrock, Girvan	416	313 —
M'Colm, William	Prestwick Road, Newton	2	26 —
M'Comb, Thomas	Glasgow	1	20 —
M'Connell, William, of Knockdolian	Knockdolian, Colmonell	3,230	2,030 15
M'Cosh, James	Dalry	614	797 10
Do. do.	Do. (Minerals)	—	185 —
M'Cosh, Mrs. Agnes	54 South Quay, Ayr	23	46 —
M'Creadie, James	Ayr	3	95 —
M'Creadie, John	Drummuckloch, Stranraer	240	261 —
M'Credie, Mrs. Rachel Ann Mure, of Perceton	Perceton, Irvine	451	1,599 15
M'Crie, Rev. James	Lugar Vale, Colmonell	100	114 —
M'Crie, James	Broughton Mains, Whithorn	694	273 —
M'Cubbin, Trustees of Alexander	Ayr	21	12 —
M'Culloch, Trustees of John	Glasgow	106	150 —
M'Culloch, Heirs of Thomas	Grangemuir, Prestwick	4	90 —
M'Derment, James Inglis	Ayr	2	161 —
M'Derment, Margaret H.	8 Alva Street, Edinburgh	133	189 —
M'Donald, Archibald G.	Glasgow	1	100 —
M'Donald, Rev. James Stewart	F.C. Manse, Ochiltree	2	27 10
M'Ewan, James, of Bardrochwood	Edinburgh	205	213 10
M'Ewan, John	Prestwick	8	38 —
M'Fadyean, James	Cairnwhin, Barr	280	145 —
M'Gavin, Trustees of John	Shalimar House, Ayr	2	110 —
M'Geoch, John	Barbae, Colmonell	70	70 —
M'Ghee, John	13 Abbey Street, Paisley	19	59 15
M'Gibbon, David, of Laggan	89 George Street, Edinburgh	1,077	1,446 —
M'Gill, Thomas	Kirkmichael	2	73 —
M'Grigor, Thomas	Tarbolton	3	18 10
M'Haffie, Alexander and M'Haffie, William	Brighton, Sussex / Tranmere Park, Birkenhead	431	410 —
M'Harg, James	Dalrymple St., Girvan	1	14 —
M'Ilwraith, James, of Auchinflower	Auchinflower, Ballantrae	274	206 —
M'Ilwraith, John and John Lusk	New Luce / Girvan	2,270	302 —
M'Ilwraith, John	Ayr	2	426 —
M'Ilwrick, Gilbert	West Altercannock, Colmonell	550	173 —
M'Innes, John	Paisley	3	105 —
Mack, Anthony	South Crescnt., Ardrossan	1	70 —
Mack, Thomas	Kilmarnock	7	21 10
M'Kechnie, Thomas	Dalrymple Street, Girvan	2	205 5
M'Kenzie, James Whiteford, and others	Edinburgh	51	268 —
Do. do.	Do. (Minerals)	—	411 —
M'Kerral, William, of Hillhouse	Hillhouse, Troon	876	1,148 —
Mackie, Daniel and William, of Knockgerran	Knockgerran, Dailly	1,422	740 —
Mackie, James	Ivy Cottage, Irvine	4	66 —
Mackie, Robert	Loudoun Cott., Galston	98	216 —
Mackie, William	Glasgow	185	275 —
Do. do.	Do. (Minerals)	—	5 —
M'Kinlay, William	Caldwell Villa, Irvine	2	55 —
M'Kinnon, John	Glasgow	1	100 —
M'Kirdy, Charles C.	Glasgow	215	493 15
M'Kissock, Robert	Glasgow	3	9 —
M'Knight, James	Edinburgh	128	140 —
M'Knight, John, of Plan	Plan, Kilmaurs	107	332 —
Do. do.	Do. (Minerals)	—	1,152 —
M'Knight, Mrs. Jane M.	Ayr	114	110 10
M'Lachlan, Alexander	Blair, Kirkoswald	304	196 —
M'Lachlan, James	Irvine	1	32 —
M'Latchie, Thomas	Prestwick	29	51 —
M'Limont, John	Girvan	391	438 —
M'Lounan, James	Lugtonridge, Beith	70	65 15
M'Lymont, Trustees of Samuel	Girvan	1	94 —
M'Millan, James	Craigmalloch, Barr	400	140 —
M'Millan, James	Joppa, Coylton	3	33 —
M'Millan, John	Wallacetown, Ayr	3	86 10
M'Millan, Heirs of Thomas, of Changue	Changue, Barr	2,300	550 —
M'Moreland, Trustees of Andrew	Prestwick	19	12 —
M'Moreland, Trustees of John	Prestwick	21	10 —
M'Murtrie, Alexander	Ladyton, Prestwick	2	57 —
M'Murtrie, Rev. John	Edinburgh	5	12 —
M'Nab, Rev. David E.	Manse, Ardrossan	5	61 —
M'Naughton, James	Standalane, Stewarton	160	267 —
M'Neill, Roderick	Girvan	1	25 —
M'Neillie, John	Ayr	2	160 —
M'Quatter, James	Enterkine Saw Mills, Tarbolton	2	15 —
M'Quhae, Heirs of Rev. Stair	Monkton	48	51 —
M'Quere, Burnett	Prestwick	3	19 —
M'Taggart, Reprs. of John Orr	Seafield, Ayr	53	210 —
M'Tyre, William	Redbrae, Maybole	6	49 —
M'Whinnie, William Townsend	Prestwick	48	178 —
M'Whirter, Rev. John	London	6	12 —
Maider, Robert	Auchinleck	1	18 —
Maider, George	Aitkencleugh, Muirkirk	250	69 —
Mair, Trustees of Alexander	Darvel	91	278 10
Mair, James	Wallacetown, Ayr	7	16 —
Mair, Matthew	Newmilns	65	139 —
Mair, Robert, Heirs of, and Matthew Mair	Newmilns	6	43 —
Manson, David	Prestwick	20	20 —
Manson, John	Prestwick	19	11 —
Manson, Robert, junior	Prestwick	32	21 —
Manson, Thomas	Prestwick	1	40 —
Marr, John	Auchmillan, Mauchline	15	24 —
Marshall, John	Newyards, Maybole	2	5 —
Maybole, Heritors of Parish of	Maybole	3	16 —

AYR – continued.

Name of Owner.	Address of Owner.	Estimated Acreage of Property.	Gross Annual Value.	Name of Owner.	Address of Owner.	Estimated Acreage of Property.	Gross Annual Value.
		Acres.	£ s.			Acres.	£ s.
Maybole, Kirkmichael, and Kirkoswald Combination Poorhouse Committee	Maybole	1	40 –	Morton, William	Oldham St., Manchester	3	48 –
				Morton, Mrs. Frances Ann	Main Street, Newmilns	2	49 –
Maybole, Parochial Board of	Maybole	1	10 –	Morton, Mrs. Ann	Highside, Newmilns	185	183 –
				Motion, Heirs of Hugh	Hapland, West Kilbride	90	150 –
Maybole Water Company	Maybole	3	33 –	Motion, William	Gateside, West Kilbride	47	145 –
Maxwell, Rev. James	Kilmaurs	2	27 10	Muir, Alexander	Broomfield, Largs	3	120 –
Maxwell, Thomas	The Cottage, Irvine	4	51 15	Muir, David	Weirholm, Irvine	6	16 –
Meikle, David	Ayr	1	120 –	Muir, James	Meiklelaw, Saltcoats	6	13 –
Meikle, John	Easington, Durham	2	42 –	Muir, John	Bonnyhill, Kilmarnock	11	40 –
Meikle, Thomas	Strath, Galston	62	81 –	Muir, Robert	Nether Raith, Fenwick	40	54 –
Merry and Cunningham	Glasgow	173	7,360 15	Muir, William	Mains, Beith	96	241 10
Miller, Alexander	Kilmaurs	9	35 –	Muir, William, junior	Thirdpart, Beith	55	105 –
Miller, James	Bankhead, Symington	2	4 10	Muir, William H.	Edinburgh	62	200 –
Miller, John	Fort, Ayr	5	111 –	Muir, William and Samuel	Hayocks, Stevenston	25	62 –
Miller, John	Robbsland, Ayr	1	114 –	Murdoch, James Fergusson	Fairfield, Ayr	8	165 –
Miller, Trustees of John	Blacklaw, Stewarton	224	212 –	Murdoch, John	Ayr	6	145 –
Miller, John S.	54 Gordon St., Glasgow	3	60 –	Mure, David (Lord Mure)	Edinburgh	10	12 –
Miller, Sir Thomas M'Donald, of Barskimming, Bart.	Barskimming, Mauchline	4,453	3,823 –	Mure, John Macredie	Warriston Villa, Largs	1	80 –
				Mure, Thomas Mure, of Perceton	Edinburgh	110	365 –
				Do. do.	Do. (*Minerals*)	–	554 15
Miller, William S.	Leigh, Staffordshire	268	190 –	Mure, Colonel William, of Caldwell	Caldwell, Beith	1,400	1,861 –
Miller, William White	Edinburgh	6,000	750 –	Do. do.	Do. (*Minerals*)	–	645 5
Miller, Mrs. Catherine	Alloway Place, Ayr	8	334 –	Murray, Rev. James	Manse, Old Cumnock	15	57 –
Miller, Mrs. Cecilia B., and Peter Drew	Ardencaple House, Row, Helensburgh	156	239 10	Murray, Rev. Robert Elliot	Manse, New Cumnock	12	66 –
Do. do.	Do. (*Minerals*)	–	200 –	Mutter, William, of Meiklelaught	Ardrossan	302	506 –
Milroy, Rev. James	Dreghorn	5	42 –	Do. do.	Do. (*Minerals*)	–	8 –
Milroy, Rev. James W.	Colmonell	9	35 –				
Milroy, John, and William Muir Milroy	8 Salisbury Road, Edinburgh	350	377 10	Nairn, John	Blockhillhead, Stewarton	8	30 –
				Nairn, Robert	Chapelhouse, Dunlop	14	45 –
Mitchell, Alexander, of Sauchrie	Sauchrie, Maybole	794	440 –	*National Bank of Scotland*	Edinburgh	1	215 –
Mitchell, Andrew	Broomfield House, Ayr	417	678 –	Neill, James	Greenock	2	6 –
Mitchell, John and James	Hareshaw, Stewarton	91	78 –	Neill, Captain William James Smith, of Swindridgemuir	Swindridgemuir, Dalry	1,275	2,765 –
Mitchell, William	Cumberland Villa, Largs	2	45 –				
Mitchell, William	Egidia Villa, Irvine	1	30 –	Do. do.	Do. (*Minerals*)	–	978 5
Moffat, John	Ardrossan	2	90 –	Neilson, George Mackintosh	Ardrossan	1	50 –
Montgomerie, Capt. Alexander, of Annick	Annick Lodge, Irvine	337	715 5				
Montgomerie, James	Penzance, Cornwall	105	111 15	*New Cumnock, Heritors of*	New Cumnock	1	15 –
Do. do.	Do. (*Minerals*)	–	364 15	*Newmilns, Burgh of*	Newmilns	9	40 10
Montgomerie, Robert	Whiteridding, Kilbirnie	25	44 –	*Newmilns New Gaslight Co.*	Newmilns	1	70 –
Montgomerie, Trustees of Robert	Craighouse, Irvine	90	201 –	*Newton-on-Ayr, Burgh of*	Newton-on-Ayr	12	8 –
				Newton-on-Ayr, Freemen of	Newton-on-Ayr	2	3 10
Montgomery, Hugh	Kilmaurs	3	91 10	*Newton-on-Ayr, Magistrates of*	Newton-on-Ayr	1	17 –
Montgomery, John	Todhills, Kilwinning	33	65 –	Nicholson, John Ross	Barns House, Ayr	6	71 –
Monteith, Lady James	Mansfield House, New Cumnock	2,846	1,867 –	Nimmo, Michael	Glasgow	9	13 –
Do. do.	Do. (*Minerals*)	–	31 –	Nixon, Rev. John	Barrhill	2	21 –
Moore, John Carrick, of Corsewall	Corsewall, Stranraer	2,069	1,726 10				
Moore, Sarah	Newroad, Newton	5	28 –				
Moravian Congregation	Ayr	1	62 –	*Ochiltree, Heritors of Parish of*	Ochiltree	2	15 –
Moreton, Hon. Captain Reynolds	York Terrace, Worthing	140	280 –	Oliver, George	Manchester	12	19 –
Morris, Allan Pollok, of Craig	Craig, Kilmaurs	982	2,061 10	Onslow, Arthur Hughes, of Balkissock	Balkissock	14,426	3,235 –
Do. do.	Do. (*Minerals*)	–	1,070 15	Oranmore and Browne, Lady, wife of Lord Oranmore and Browne	Castle Macgarette, Mayo, Ireland	2,720	3,203 –
Morris, Rev. George	Dalry	2	10 –				
Morris, Hugh Baxter	Clyde View, Partick	675	529 –	Do. do.	Do. (*Minerals*)	–	1,534 –
Morris, James	Wellington Square, Ayr	2	344 –	*Original Secession Congregation*	Wallacetown, Ayr	1	5 –
Morris, William H.	Glasgow	3	80 –				
Morris, Heirs of Mrs. Jane	Millburn, Largs	2	134 10	Orr and Browns	Halfway, Irvine	18	144 –
Morris, Mrs. Janet Pollok, of Craig	Craig, Kilmaurs	165	385 10	Orr, Trustees of Alexander	Lambroughton, Dreghorn	110	290 –
Do. do.	Do. (*Minerals*)	–	100 5	Orr, Hugh	Gateside, Kilbirnie	71	93 –
Morrison, James	Greenfield, Irvine	4	42 –	Orr, James	Blackburn, Kilbirnie	22	32 –
Morrison, Robert	Tribbochmains, Stair	97	155 –	Orr, James	New Intax, Galston	2	18 –
Morrison, Thomas C.	Newton, Ayr	2	35 –	Orr, James	Craigie	21	49 10
Morrison, Margaret and Jane	Elgin Villa, Ayr	77	136 –	Orr, James	Gree, Beith	60	68 10
Morton, George	Fergushill, Kilmarnock	19	10 –	Do.	Do. (*Minerals*)	–	118 10
Morton, James	Eaglesham	20	33 –	Orr, John	Highfield, Dalry	70	76 10
Morton, John	Gorsebraehead, Galston	64	30 –	Do.	Do. (*Minerals*)	–	143 10
Morton, John Morton Mathie, of Belmont	Ayr	567	1,277 –	Orr, Rev. John	Manse, Kilbirnie	10	53 –
				Orr, Trustees of Robert	Beith	6	8 –
Morton Thomas	Ladybrow, by Darvel	50	60 –	Orr, Mrs. Margaret, and John Blakeney	Raise Street, Saltcoats	10	22 10
Morton, Thomas	55 John St., Sunderland	77	56 –				

D

AYR—continued.

Name of Owner.	Address of Owner.	Estimated Acreage of Property.	Gross Annual Value.	Name of Owner.	Address of Owner.	Estimated Acreage of Property.	Gross Annual Value.
		Acres.	£ s.			Acres.	£ s.
Orr, Mrs. Mary and Mrs. Agnes Munro	Bogend, Stevenston	5	14 10	Rae, Archibald	Ayr	2	368 —
Orr, Jane, Margaret, and Martha	Gree, Beith	38	46 —	Raeburn, James and Robert	Gorbals, Glasgow	8	36 —
Osborne, William	Westport, Tarbolton	24	61 —	Raeburn, William	Hurlford	4	18 —
Oswald, Richard Alexander, of Auchincruive	Auchincruive, Ayr	11,004	14296 10	Ralston, James Innes	Old Faskally, near Pitlochrie	2	13 5
Do. do.	Do. (Minerals)	—	3,530 —	Ralston, Mrs. Margaret Fullarton M'Dougall	Warrickhill, Dreghorn	300	653 —
				Do. do.	Do. (Minerals)	—	225 —
				Ramsay, Thomas Kennedy	Maybole	2	5 10
Pagan, George	New Cumnock	1	22 —	Ramsay, Mrs. Helen	Maybole	10	56 10
Paisley Water Commissioners	Paisley	22	80 —	Ranken, Andrew Archibald	19 Lansdowne Road, Wimbledon	5	110 —
Park, Charles	164 Campbell's Row, Bow, London	6	7 10	Rankine, Trustees of Adam	Maybole	5	24 —
Parker, Charles Stuart, M.P.	Fairley House, Largs	2	100 —	Rankine, Trs. of James	New Cumnock	1,192	1,139 —
Parker, Hugh, senior	West Broadston, Beith	8	16 10	Do. do.	Do. (Minerals)	—	2,481 —
Parker, John	Roughwood, Beith	66	160 —	Rankine, John, of Beoch	Beoch, Maybole	330	282 10
Parker, Harriet, of Assloss	Assloss, Kilmarnock	170	349 —	Rankine, Rev. John	Manse, Sorn	14	57 —
Paterson, Andrew	Victoria Park, Ayr	141	520 —	Rankine, Trustees of John A. and John M'Kenzie	Irvine Edinburgh	32	108 —
Paterson, John	Kilmarnock	6	24 —				
Paterson, John	Avondale, Strathaven	27	30 —				
Paterson, Joshua, and Alex. Macintosh	Glasgow	5	40 —	Rankine, Robert Kerr	Crawlaw, Loudoun	55	55 —
Paterson, Thomas	Longmuir, Kilmaurs	138	280 —	Reid, Adam	Allison Street, Newton	4	8 —
Paterson, William, of Coilsfield	Coilsfield, Tarbolton	2,552	3,127 —	Reid, James	Sanquhar, St. Quivox	64	82 —
				Reid, John	Ayr	2	153 10
Paterson, William, of Paterson	Paterson, Maybole	1,492	1,893 —	Reid, John Dunlop	Bordland, Dunlop	42	94 —
				Reid, Robert	Balgray, Irvine	120	180 —
Paton, Cook, & Co.	Glengarnock, Dalry	5	533 —	Reid, Robert	Bollingshaw, Stewarton	90	126 —
Paton, James	Alloway Place, Ayr	203	345 —	Reid, Robert	'Davies at the Mill,' Beith	10	16 —
Paton, James, & Sons	Ayr	2	230 —	Reid, Thomas	Glasgow	8	14 10
Paton, Theophilus, of Swinlees	Swinlees, Dalry	245	328 5	Reid, William, of Merryhill	Paisley	104	210 —
Paton, William	Hillend, Dalry	47	121 —	Reid, Mary, of Chapelton	Chapelton, Irvine	216	349 —
Do.	Do. (Minerals)	—	342 —	Rendlesham, Lord and Lady	Rendleshamhall, Woolbridge	190	249 5
Patrick, David	Dalry	110	156 —				
Patrick, Henry Gairdner, of Trearne	Trearne House, Beith	910	1,201 10	Rennie & Brown	Maybole	1	25 —
				Rennie, Thomas	Maybole	1	119 15
Patrick, James	Glasgow	146	187 15	Richmond, Francis Findlay	Newmilns	8	145 —
				Richmond, John	84 John Street, Glasgow	2	18 —
Patrick, John Fullarton, of Grangehills	Grangehills, Beith	342	481 10	Riddett, Robert	Cubeside, Dalry	42	99 —
Patrick, Matthew	Kilwinning	11	42 10	Rintoul, Robert	8 Cookridge Street, Leeds	68	100 —
Patrick, Robert William Cochrane, of Woodside	Woodside, Beith	1,249	1,554 10	Ritchie, Rev. David	Manse, Tarbolton	7	42 —
Do. do.	Do. (Minerals)	—	36 5	Ritchie, Francis Caldwell, of Kirktonhall	Kirktonhall, West Kilbride	162	405 —
Patrick, William Ralston, of Roughwood	Roughwood, Beith	2,506	3,262 5	Ritchie, John	Glasgow	41	65 —
Do. do.	Do. (Minerals)	—	1,986 5	Ritchie, John	Seamill, West Kilbride	9	81 —
Patrick, Mrs. Agnes Cochrane	Woodside House, Beith	1,574	386 —	Robb, Mrs. Janet	Smith's Place, Newton	1	19 —
				Robertson, Alexander H., of Duncanziemore	65 St. Vincent Street, Glasgow	734	560 —
Patrick, Mrs. Elizabeth Burns	Greenbank, Dalry	122	317 —	Robertson, James	Maress, Irvine	1	40 —
Peden, John	6 Bank Street, Paisley	47	40 15	Robertson, John	West Halket, Dunlop	120	170 —
Peebles, John	Burnside, Kilbirnie	56	55 —	Robertson, Rev. John	Manse, Loudoun	17	96 —
Pettigrew, Robert, of Tarshaw	Troon	103	182 —	Robertson, John, and John Thom	Kelburne, Largs	116	110 —
Picken, James Hunter	Hillhousehill, Fenwick	147	255 —	Robertson, Mrs. Jessie, and Mary Robertson	Ayr	24	46 —
Picken, John	North Glassock, Fenwick	13	22 10				
Pollock, Alexander	Gillsyard, Lochwinnoch	50	65 —	Robertson, Mrs. Isabella, and others	Kilmaurs	4	30 —
Pollock, Allan, of Broom	Lesmany, Balinasloe, Ireland	702	268 —	Robertson, Heirs of Mary, Elizabeth, and John	Northfield, Largs	3	105 —
Pollock, Andrew	Mauchline	2	45 —				
Pollock, Robert	Dalry	105	127 —	Rodger, David	Penkiln, Garliestown	1,300	700 —
Do. do.	Do. (Minerals)	—	244 —	Rodger, Robert	Dalry	8	55 —
Pollock, William	Ayr	2	78 —	Ronald, Hugh	Duchray Mains, Balmaghie	107	220 —
Pollok, Robert Morris, of Middleton	Middleton, Ayr	165	485 10	Rose, Heirs of William	Savoy Cottage, Ayr	7	82 —
Do. do.	Do. (Minerals)	—	200 —	Ross, James	Titwood, Dunlop	11	18 —
Porter, Rev. George	Maybole	14	70 —	Ross, John, junior	Glasgow	20	11 —
Portland, Duke of	Fullarton House, Troon	24,787	33625 15	Ross, William	Boghall, Beith	41	85 —
Do. do.	Do. (Harbour)	64	10708 —	Rouet, Robert	Bankend, Dunlop	27	53 —
Do. do.	Do. (Minerals)	—	16199 5	Rowand, Thomas	Greenock	1	35 —
Potter & Murray	Kyle Street, Ayr	2	33 —	*Royal Bank of Scotland*	Edinburgh	3	595 —
Potts, George C.	Craigievar, Skelmorlie	2	125 —	Russell, Archibald, jun., and Lewis Fullarton	Ardrossan	2	170 —
Prison Board Commissioners	Ayr	1	260 —				
Provan, David, of Lochridge	Lochridge, Stewarton	313	680 —	Russell, Francis	Kirkland, West Kilbride	146	256 10
Provan, Mrs. Emma	Lochridge, Stewarton	4	40 —	Russell, Mrs. Catherine	7 Royal Crescent, Ramsgate	178	307 10
Prestwick, Burgh of	Prestwick	2	4 —				

AYR—continued.

Name of Owner.	Address of Owner.	Estimated Acreage of Property.	Gross Annual Value.
		Acres.	£ s.
St. Quivox, Parochial Board of	St. Quivox	1	16 10
Salmond, Robert	Rankineston, Patna	1,600	600 —
Samson, Alexander Murdoch	Irvine	2	30 —
Samson, Charles	Irvine	1	42 —
Scott, Charles Cunningham, of Hawkhill	Hawkhill, Largs	2,320	1,435 —
Scoullar, James	Milton Mill, Gatehead	2	82 —
Sellars, William	Smithstonridge, Craigie	45	57 —
Service, Trustees of David Dunlop	Kilwinning	1	150 —
Service, William, senior	Saltcoats	1	52 10
Shand, Garden, and another	London	138	200 —
Shankland, Robert	Ayr	25	100 —
Shanks, James	Pathfoot, Kilwinning	143	114 —
Shaw, Mrs. Janet, and John Shaw	Muirkirk	2	10 10
Shearer, Andrew	Main St., Newton, Ayr	2	191 —
Shearer, Trs. of James	Ardrossan	1	491 —
Shedden, Alexander	Crummock, Beith	13	26 —
Shedden, Roscoe	Cowes, Isle of Wight	73	114 —
Sheddon, Arthur William	Middlerigg, Kirkoswald	148	109 10
Sheddon, William George, of Springhill	Springhill, Craigie	349	570 —
Do. do. (*Minerals*)	Do.	—	54 —
Shields, Maria, and others	Prestwick	2	20 —
Sime, Rev. John	Manse, Dundonald	6	42 —
Simpson, James Yates	Largs	3	179 5
Sinclair, George Lewis, of Dalreoch	Edinburgh	1,020	593 —
Sinclair, Trustees of James	Orangefield, Monkton	106	440 —
Sinclair, Robert	Stafford	11	24 —
Skeoch, Charles	Stewarton	36	261 —
Skeoch, David	Stewarton	1	21 —
Skeoch, William	Gameshill, Stewarton	23	164 —
Sloan, Fergus	Craigbank Cottage, Maybole	19	36 —
Smith, Alexander	Croft Inn, Dreghorn	1	51 —
Smith, Trustees of Andrew	Mauchline	2	181 —
Smith, James	Wheatfield, Ayr	5	174 —
Smith, James	Bushgrove, Prestwick	21	19 —
Smith, John	Windyedge, Kilmaurs	91	155 —
Do.	Do. (*Minerals*)	—	22 —
Smith, John	Fenwickland, Ayr	10	137 —
Smith, Trustees of John	Irvine	13	74 —
Smith, John, and Mrs. Agnes	Dalry	95	181 —
Do. do.	Do. (*Minerals*)	—	100 —
Smith, Peter	Prestwick	1	18 —
Smith, Thomas	Cross Street, Galston	2	28 —
Smith, William	Dalry	5	62 —
Smith, William	Townhead, Newmilns	200	296 —
Smith, William, junior	208 Adelaide Place, Glasgow	8	130 —
Smith, Heirs of Mrs. Isabella	Smith Villa, Ayr	2	50 —
Smith, Mrs. Elizabeth	Newmilns	2	49 —
Smith, Mrs. Janet	New Road, Newton	12	3 10
Smith, Mrs. Janet	Rosebank, Stair	6	15 —
Smith, Mrs. Margaret	Newlands, Kilmaurs	13	48 10
Smith, Ann, Elizabeth, and Abigail	Sandgate Street, Ayr	7	56 10
Snodgrass, James A.	Stewarton	2	50 —
Somervell, Graham, of Sorn	Sorn Castle, Mauchline	6,245	3,775 —
Do. do.	Do. (*Minerals*)	—	12 10
Somerville, Rev. James	Manse, Irvine	10	80 —
Somerville, William	Haplandmill, Dunlop	3	100 —
Somerville, William, junior	East Halket, Dunlop	100	174 —
Spier, John	Burn, Dalry	66	115 —
Do.	Do. (*Minerals*)	—	25 —
Spier, Robert	Newside, Dalry	60	90 —
Do.	Do. (*Minerals*)	—	25 —
Spiers, Trustees of Alex.	Newton-on-Ayr	3	66 —
Spiers, Robert	Blairpark, Dalry	238	316 10
Spiers, Trustees of Margaret, of Marshalland	Marshalland, Beith	445	769 15
Spiers, William, Robert, Hugh, and John	North Camphill, Dalry	210	200 —
Do. do. (*Minerals*)	Do.	—	6 —
Spiers, Ann G. and Helen	Largs	1	120 —
Sprott, John	South Park, Ayr	2	100 —
Sprott, Rev. William	Glasgow	500	203 10
Stair, Countess of, wife of Earl of Stair	Bargany, Girvan	19,266	12763 15
Do. do. (*Minerals*)	Do.	—	852 —
Stair, Earl of	Bargany, Girvan	492	940 —
Steele, James	Loanfoot, Galston	102	56 —
Steele, William	Drygatehead, Newmilns	3	13 —
Steele, Mrs. Mary	Whang Street, Beith	50	60 —
Steven, Hugh	Kilmarnock	6	20 10
Stevenson, Allan	Springfield, Dunlop	119	233 —
Stevenson, James, junior	Glasgow	5	184 —
Stevenson, John	Whitelee, Stewarton	100	100 —
Stevenson, Heirs of John	Harelaw, Paisley	53	62 15
Stevenson, Mrs. Maria Eliza, and Mrs. Margaret	2 Strathearn Road, Edinburgh	240	290 15
Stevenson, Rev. Robert	Manse, Dalry	12	55 —
Stevenson, William Cuthbertson	Balgray, Beith	99	130 —
Stewart, Trustees of Charles, of Friarland	Friarland, Ayr	278	506 —
Stewart, David Yuille	St. Rollox, Glasgow	2	60 —
Stewart, John and Rev. Richard M. Stewart	Kincardine Galashiels	175	190 —
Do. do.	Do. (*Minerals*)	—	2 —
Stewart, John	Thorn, Dunlop	17	35 —
Stewart, Sir Michael Shaw, of Ardgowan, Bart.	Ardgowan, Inverkip	92	140 —
Stewart, Paul Amedee Francis Coutts	Coylton	1,484	1,250 —
Stewart, William	Gearholm, Ayr	24	166 —
Stewart, William	Corsehill, Kilwinning	10	52 —
Stewart, William, of St. Fillans	St. Fillans, Largs	1,344	1,493 —
Stewart, Helen and Margaret	Ashcraig, Largs	40	201 —
Stewarton, Heritors of Parish of	Stewarton	5	25 —
Stirling, Rev. David	Manse, Craigie	6	32 —
Stirling, John	Bridekirk, Cockermouth	529	612 —
Stirling, John	Parkhouse, Whitehaven	206	329 10
Stirling, Rev. Robert	Manse, Galston	15	40 —
Stirrat, John	Birkhead, Saltcoats	184	309 —
Straiton, Parochial Board of	Straiton	1	8 —
Strang, Robert	Glasgow	3	90 —
Strathearn, George	Ochiltree	1	6 —
Strong, Rev. David	Manse, Barr	13	52 —
Struthers, James	Avonholm, Hamilton	100	37 —
Stupart, Trustees of Major Francis	Kilmaurs	370	963 —
Sturrock, Peter	Hurlford	2	200 —
Sym, Mrs. Margaret	Bath Place, Ayr	1	224 —
Tait, Captain Alexander Duncan, of Millrig	Millrig, Galston	183	266 —
Taylor, John	Islay	4	25 —
Taylor, John	Girvan	4	36 —
Taylor, Robert, of Darwhilling	Darwhilling, Kilmarnock	416	515 10
Taylor, William, of Blackwood	Bustonend, Kilmaurs	227	392 —
Taylor, William	Kilmarnock	7	20 —
Templeton, James	Ayr	65	1,097 —
Templeton, James	Tower, Dalry	21	32 —
Tennant, George, of Creoch	Creoch, Ochiltree	288	350 —
Tennant, William	Eaton Villa, Ayr	2	65 —
Tennent, Trustees of Charles S. P.	20 Buchanan Street, Glasgow	2	100 —
Thom, James	Corsehill, Coylton	76	66 —
Do.	Do. (*Minerals*)	—	50 —
Thom, John	Bowmanston, Coylton	1	50 —
Thomson, Allan	University, Glasgow	6	120 —
Thomson, Rev. Edward L.	Manse, Newton-on-Ayr	4	35 —

AYR—continued.

Name of Owner.	Address of Owner.	Estimated Acreage of Property.	Gross Annual Value.	Name of Owner.	Address of Owner.	Estimated Acreage of Property.	Gross Annual Value.
		Acres.	£ s.			Acres.	£ s.
Thomson, David	Shallochmill, near Girvan	5	24 10	Whyte, Thomas, of Sawerston	Catrine	126	208 —
Thomson, Joseph, Mortification of	Symington	210	326 —	Wilkie, James	Acre Villa, Largs	3	105 —
Thomson, Heirs of John A.	Wardhouse, Kilmarnock	20	37 —	Wilkinson, John	Kingston, Glasgow	6	9 —
Thomson, Nisbet	Johnston	4	11 —	Willison, James P., of Threave	Threave, Maybole	916	912 10
Do. do.	Do. (Minerals)	—	10 —	Wilson, Adam	Broom, Stevenston	2	126 —
Thomson, William	Brocklees, Loudoun	162	60 —	Wilson, Alexander	Netherhill, Dunlop	41	93 —
Thomson, William and Matthew	Crookedholm, Kilmarnock	2	205 10	Wilson, Andrew	Goatfoot, Muirkirk	7	30 —
Thomson, Jessie	9 Kew Terrace, Glasgow	58	159 —	Wilson, George	View Lane, Dunse	6	61 —
Traill, Adam	Crossbush, Riccarton	3	25 —	Wilson, Rev. James	Manse, St. Quivox	6	42 —
Turnbull, Rev. George	Dailly	12	48 —	Wilson, John	75 Union St., Glasgow	7	14 —
				Wilson, John	New York	25	40 —
				Wilson, John Pettigrew, of Polquhairn	Rosebank, Ayr	1,800	1,243 —
Union Bank of Scotland	Glasgow	4	547 —	Wilson, Robert	Burnhouse, Dunlop	1	32 —
United Presbyterian Church, Trustees of	Beith	13	105 —	Wilson, John, senior	Kilwinning	3	18 —
				Wilson, Robert	Kirkmichael	2	6 5
				Wilson, Rev. Robert M'Nair	Maryhill, Glasgow	8	26 10
Vass, Hugh	Failmains, Tarbolton	8	8 —	Wilson, Heirs of William	Baidland Mill, Dalry	12	55 10
				Wilson, Trustees of William Kerr	Thirdpart, Beith	80	148 —
				Do. do.	Do. (Minerals)	—	20 —
				Wilson, Mrs. Annabella	Golf House, Prestwick	4	70 —
Walker, Alexander	Kilmarnock	44	60 —	Wilson, Mrs. Isabella	Kirkmichael, Maybole	16	42 5
Walker, Hugh	Bridgend, Kilbirnie	56	94 10	Wilson, Mrs. Jane, of Haylee	Haylee, Largs	187	275 —
Walker, Hugh	Greenock	1	110 —	Wilson, Mrs. Isabella	Rosebank, Ayr	8	60 —
Walker, Peter, of Balrazie	Warrington	986	230 —	Wilson, Mrs. Jean	West Kilbride	3	61 —
Walker, Rev. Thomas	Manse, Dalmellington	9	54 —	Wilson, Mrs. Jean	Corsehill, Kilwinning	5	43 10
Walker, Thomas	Hazelbank, Dunlop	77	104 —	Wilson, Jane	Smithybrae, Maybole	6	30 —
Walker, Rev. William M.	Manse, Ochiltree	9	51 —	Wood, John	Passford, Loudoun	73	131 10
Walker, Mrs. Janet	Fernbank, Kilbirnie	2	49 —	Wood, William	Woodville, Newton	13	79 —
Wallace, James	Glasgow	11	33 —	Woodrow, William	Kilmaurs	8	56 10
Wallace, Rev. John	Manse, Dalrymple	6	30 —	Wrey, George Edward Bourchier, of Caddell and Thornton	Addington Ho., Reading	826	1,334 10
Wallace, Robert	Damhead, Mauchline	61	69 —				
Wallace, Heirs of Thomas	Blackburn, Stewarton	130	105 5				
Wallace, William, of Cloncaird	Cloncaird, Kirkmichael	2,584	1,601 —	Do. do.	Do. (Minerals)	—	1,144 15
Wallace, William, of Busby	Wester Dalry House, Edinburgh	616	1,232 15	Wright, John, & Son	Halfway, Irvine	2	53 —
Do. do.	Do. (Minerals)	—	317 5	Wright, Matthew	Halfway, Irvine	1	45 —
Walnut, Mrs. Maria E. L., and Mrs. Alexandrina G. Macalister, wife of Keith Macalister, of Glenbarr	Edinburgh			Wright, Margaret and Anne	Largs Castle, Largs	9	113 —
				Wylie, Mrs. Margaret	Oakly Terrace, Glasgow	23	58 —
				Do. do.	Do. (Minerals)	—	45 15
	Glenbarr Abbey, Kintyre, Argyll	797	1,126 —	Wylie, William	Paris	6	90 —
				Wyllie, James	Stewarton	83	120 —
Do. do.	Do. (Minerals)	—	260 —	Wyllie, John	Mosside, Stewarton	39	92 10
Walsh, Edmund James	Neufchatel, Travers	4	27 —	Wyllie, Janet	Cutstraw, Stewarton	4	10 —
Wardrope, John, and others	Burnbank, Loudoun	52	155 —				
Do. do.	Do. (Minerals)	—	294 —	Young, Adam	Kilwinning	11	154 —
Wark, John, James, and Margaret	Montreal, Canada	23	34 5	Young, George K., of Glendoune	Glendoune, Girvan	505	581 —
Warner, Patrick, of Ardeer	Ardeer, Stevenston	2,075	2,009 —	Young, James	Largs	3	221 —
Do. do.	Do. (Minerals)	—	1,697 —	Young, James, of Kelly	Wemyss Bay, Greenock	190	138 —
Wason, Rigby, of Corwar	Corwar, by Girvan	4,290	1,894 —	Young, James, and Mrs. Marion Blair	Mosside, Kilmarnock	7	30 —
Watson, Rev. Charles	Largs	3	105 —				
Watson, Trs. of James	Ayr	2	129 —	Young, John	Townhead, Irvine	5	9 —
Watson, John	Ayr	2	170 —	Young, John and Thomas	Newton	2	224 —
Watson, Neil	Auchenhuive, Kilbirnie	37	33 —	Young, John Hogarth	Milgartholm, Irvine	34	100 —
Watson, William	127 Argyle Street, Glasgow	1	180 —	Young, Heirs of Matthew	Langlands, Symington	21	51 —
Weir, Alexander	Falkland House, Ayr	40	832 —	Young, William	Barns Street, Ayr	2	47 10
Weir, Hugh Ferry	Kirkhall, Ardrossan	25	68 —				
Western Meeting Club	Ayr	1	60 —				
West Kilbride, Parochial Board of	West Kilbride	1	4 —	Total Owners of Land of one Acre and upwards		1,272	718,788	900,523 5
White, Matthew	Glasgow	6	24 —				
White, Mrs. Janet	Main Street, Prestwick	1	11 —	Total Owners of Lands of less than one Acre in extent		7,098	2,122	161,380 10
Whyte, James	Muirkirk	2	67 10				
Whyte, John, of Grougar	70 Wilson St., Glasgow	3,349	4,425 —				
Do. do.	Do. (Minerals)	—	2,182 —	GRAND TOTAL		8,370	720,910	1061903 15

MUNICIPAL BOROUGH OF KILMARNOCK.
Population over 20,000.

Name of Owner.	Address of Owner.	Estimated Acreage of Property.	Gross Annual Value.	Name of Owner.	Address of Owner.	Estimated Acreage of Property.	Gross Annual Value.
		Acres.	£ s.			Acres.	£ s.
Adamson, Alexander	Kilmarnock	4	254 10	Hamilton, Rev. James B.	The Manse, Kilmarnock	16	81 —
Andrew, John	Glencairn Mill, Kilmarnock	5	207 —				
Andrew, Trustees of John	Kilmarnock	18	219 —	Jeffrey, Rev. William	The Manse, Riccarton, Kilmarnock	8	50 —
Andrews, Allan, & Co.	Kilmarnock	2	100 —				
Barclay, Andrew	Caledonian Foundry, Kilmarnock	2	262 —	*Kennedy's Patent Water Meter Company*	Low Glencairn Street, Kilmarnock	1	86 —
Bickett, John	Portland Terrace, Kilmarnock	1	773 15	*Kilmarnock, Burgh of*	Kilmarnock	16	1,417 —
Blackwood, James	Gillsburn House, Kilmarnock	4	90 —				
Brown, Heirs of James	Bellsbrae, Kilmarnock	2	348 —	Lee, Thomas	Morton Pl., Kilmarnock	1	350 10
Buchanan, Elizabeth, of Bellfield	Bellfield, Kilmarnock	6	36 —				
				Mills, James	Kilmarnock	2	180 —
Campbell, George James, of Treesbanks	Riccarton, Kilmarnock	12	50 5	Muir, John	10 Merchiston Avenue, Edinburgh	9	45 —
Campbell, John	Kilmarnock	1	281 10	M'Culloch, Thomas, & Sons	Vulcan Foundry, Kilmarnock	1	230 —
Campbell, Mrs. Margaret, and others	Bridge of Allan	4	73 5	M'Kenzie, John W., and others	Edinburgh	25	36 —
Carstairs, William W.	Hawket Park, Kilmarnock	2	34 —				
Clark, Andrew L.	Portland Road, Kilmarnock	2	86 —				
Crooks, John	Flowerbank, Kilmarnock	4	340 15	Paxton, George	Richardland Brewery, Kilmarnock	1	192 —
Cunninghame, John W.H., of Lainshaw	Lainshaw, Stewarton	35	125 10	Paxton, Mrs. Janet M.	Richardland, Kilmarnock	1	42 —
Cunninghame, William C. S., of Caprington	Caprington Castle, Kilmarnock	16	59 —	Portland, Duke of	Fullarton House, Troon	518	1,499 —
Cuthbertson, Thomas	Kilmarnock	1	119 5	*Portland Forge Company*	Kilmarnock	2	60 —
Cuthbertson & Taylor	Kilmarnock	3	367 5				
				Ramsay, William	Kilmarnock	1	160 15
Deans, James Young, of Kirkstyle	Kirkstyle, Kilmarnock	43	178 10	Smith, John F.	Cringlebers, Milling, Manchester	2	416 15
Donald, James	Kilmarnock	2	277 —	Smith, Mrs. Janet	Smithshill, Kilmarnock	4	20 —
Dunlop, William Henry, of Annanhill	Annanhill, Kilmarnock	17	384 15	Stewart, Heirs of William	London Road, Kilmarnock	1	181 15
				Stewart, Janet and Agnes	Gardenhill, Kilmarnock	3	184 —
Ferguson, Thomas and James	Kilmarnock	2	400 —				
Ferguson, Mrs. Ann	Tillington, Stafford	6	29 —	Thomson, Heirs of James	Kilmarnock	2	297 15
Finnie, Archibald, of Springhill	Springhill, Kilmarnock	10	442 —	Thomson, Robert	Kilmarnock	25	88 —
				Turnbull, Andrew	Kilmarnock	2	64 —
Gilmour, John	Kilmarnock	7	128 10	Wallace, John	Kilmarnock	2	373 10
Glasgow and South-Western Railway	Glasgow (Railway)	31	5,312 —	Waugh, Thomas	Kilmarnock	2	303 10
Glasgow, Barrhead, and Kilmarnock Joint Railway Company	Glasgow (Railway)	14	43 —	Webster, Rev. Alexander	Kilmarnock	3	52 10
Glenfield Iron Company (Limited)	Kilmarnock	3	191 —	Total Owners of Land of one Acre and upwards		54	908 17,997 15
Gregory, Thomsons, & Company	Kilmarnock	1	374 —	Total Owners of Lands of less than one Acre in extent		952	129 41,350 10
				Grand Total		1,006	1,037 59,348 5

BANFF.

Population in 1871, 62,023.
Inhabited Houses, 11,603.
Number of Parishes, 30.

Name of Owner.	Address of Owner.	Estimated Acreage of Property.	Gross Annual Value.	Name of Owner.	Address of Owner.	Estimated Acreage of Property.	Gross Annual Value.
		Acres.	£ s.			Acres	£ s.
Abercromby, Sir Robert John, of Forglen and Birkenbog, Bart.	Forglen House, Turriff	8,053	6,290 2	Fraser, Rev. Hugh Fraser, Mrs. Elizabeth, of Thorax	Manse, Alvah F.C. Manse, Kirkwall	10 171	40 — 164 10
Allan, Rev. James	Manse of Keith	7	49 10				
Anderson, Rev. Alexander	Manse of Marnoch	11	35 —	Gamrie Parish, Heritors of	Gamrie	2	2 —
Andrew, Trustees of Alexander, of Easterfield	Easterfield, Inverkethney	108	105 —	Gariock, Trustees of Rev. George, of Gariochsford	Gariochsford, Old Meldrum	275	148 —
Asher, Rev. William	Manse of Inveravon	8	32 —	Geddes, James	Portsoy, Fordyce	1	23 10
				Glennie, Rev. James	Chapelton, Inveravon	7	10 —
Banff Brewery Company	Banff	14	126 —	Glenrinnes, Trustees of Church of	Glenrinnes, Mortlach	3	15 —
Banff, Burgh of	Banff	46	255 8				
Banff Cemetery Company	Banff	6	15 —	Gordon, Adam Hay, of Avochie	Mayen House, Huntly	2,171	1,528 15
Banff Harbour Trustees	Banff (Harbour)	4	104 —				
Banff, Kirk Session of	Banff	6	17 —	Gordon, Heirs of Rev. Alexander	Manse, Forglen	10	35 —
Banffshire Lunacy Board	Boyndie	20	260 —				
Barclay, James, of Buchromb	Buchromb, Mortlach; and 1 Cushion Court, Old Broad St., London	253	213 15	Gordon, John, of Cluny	Cluny Castle, Cluny, Aberdeen	2,734	2,724 9
				Gordon, John, of Cairnfield	Cairnfield House, Fochabers	3,175	1,362 12
Bartlett, Trustees of late William	Banff	2	82 10	Gordon, John	Macduff, Gamrie	2	215 —
Bisset, James	Macduff, Gamrie	2	6 13	Gordon, Sir Robert G., of Letterfourie, Bart.	Letterfourie, Buckie	1,715	1,957 3
Boyd, Andrew	Castlebrae, St. Fergus	2	21 8				
Boyndie Parish, Heritors of	Boyndie	1	1 —	Do. do.	Do. (Harbour)	5	25 —
Bruce Rev. William S.	Banff	9	44 —	Grant, Sir Geo. Macpherson, of Ballindalloch, Bart.	Ballindalloch Castle, Inveravon	14,223	3,616 16
				Grant, Rev. James	Manse, Kirkmichael	14	30 —
Campbell, F. W. Garden, of Troup	Troup, Gamrie	9,546	5,712 9	Grant, Rev. James	Manse, Fordyce	10	46 —
Do. do.	Do. (Harbour)	1	82 —	Grant, Hon. Lewis A., of Grant	Hopeman Lodge, Elgin	31	25 —
Cassie, Trustees of James	Banff	2	33 5	Grant, William, of Wester Elchies	Carron Cottage, Craigellachie	4,212	1,285 —
Chalmers, Trustees of late Alexander, of Cluny	Cluny, Marnoch	3,009	2,505 13	Grant, Trustees of William, of Beldorney	Beldorney House, Huntly	3,449	1,098 18
Clapperton, Rev. William	Buckie	2	53 —				
Clark, Alexander	Macduff, Gamrie	1	10 —	Grant, Margaret G. M'Pherson, of Aberlour	Aberlour House, Craigellachie	855	722 15
Colville, Alexander	4 Low Street, Banff	2	70 5				
Cowie, George	Dufftown, Mortlach	2	80 —	Great North of Scotland Railway Company	Aberdeen (Railway)	321	10696 —
Cruden, Rev. James	Manse, Gamrie	17	35 —				
Cruickshank, Rev. J. A.	Manse, Mortlach	5	35 —	Green, William	Lynburn, Aberlour	1	26 —
Cullen, Parochial Board of	Cullen	2	10 —				
Cumine, James, of Rattray	Rattray House, Peterhead	700	675 2	Harvey, John, of Carnousie	Carnousie, Turriff	3,424	3,296 13
				Hay, George P., of Edintore	Lagmore, Ballindalloch	350	150 —
				Henderson, Rev. George	Manse, Cullen	7	49 —
Duff, Major L. D. Gordon, of Drummuir and Park	Drummuir Castle, Keith	13,053	7,418 —	Highland Railway Co.	Inverness (Railway)	22	605 —
Duff, M. E. Grant, of Eden, M.P.	Eden House, Banff	7	20 6	Hunter, Rev. William	Manse, Macduff, Gamrie	4	34 —
Duff, Robert W., of Fetteresso, M.P.	Fetteresso Castle, Stonehaven	2,671	2,346 19	Innes, Sir James M., of Edingight, Bart.	Edingight, Keith	3,100	1,882 16
				Innes, Lieut. Robert	Charlestown, Aberlour	1	12 —
				Innes, Thomas G. R., of Netherdale	Netherdale House, Turriff	3,771	2,690 6
Ferguson, Lieut.-Col. George A., of Pitfour	Pitfour, Mintlaw	10,845	9,446 12	Inveravon Parish, Heritors of	Inveravon	2	10 —
Fife, Trustees of Earl of	Duff House, Banff	72,027	35879 13	Invermarkie, The Suckeners of	Invermarkie, Mortlach	2	2 —
Do. do.	Do. (Harbour)	5	500 —				
Fife, Trustees of Earl of; and James Barclay, of Buchromb	Duff House (Commonty) Buchromb, Mortlach	400	Included in values of Estates	Johnston, John	Brockholes House, Salop	2	24 —
Forbes, James	Portsoy, Fordyce	1	45 15	Keith Parish, Heritors and Parochial Board of	Keith	2	2 —
Forbes, John, of Haddo	Haddo, Huntly	4,773	3,991 7				
Forglen, Trustees of Free Church of	Forglen	1	10 —	Kinloch, Mrs. Marjory A. Grant, of Arndilly	Arndilly House, Craigellachie	5,895	2,864 10
Forsyth, John	Old Keith	1	54 —				

BANFF—continued.

Name of Owner.	Address of Owner.	Estimated Acreage of Property.	Gross Annual Value.	Name of Owner.	Address of Owner.	Estimated Acreage of Property.	Gross Annual Value.
		Acres.	£ s.			Acres.	£ s.
Kynoch, Trustees of Alex., of Greentown	Greentown, Keith	221	103 —	Richmond, Duke of	Gordon Castle	159,950	23831 18
Kynoch, Geo. & Geo.	Keith	15	256 —	Do. do.	Do. (Harbour)	2	10 —
Kynoch, Geo., Junior	Keith	3	16 —	Ross, Heirs of William	Cullen	1	50 —
				Russell, Rev. John	Manse, Grange	9	34 —
				St. Fergus Free Church, Trustees of	St. Fergus	1	15 —
Laing, John	Charlestown, Aberlour	2	64 10	Seafield, Earl of	Cullen House	48,939	33878 6
Lawtie's Mortification, Trustees of	Cullen	9	51 1	Do. do.	Do. (Harbours)	7	390 —
Ledingham, Rev. James	Manse, Boyndie	11	32 —	Sellar, Rev. James	Manse, Aberlour	6	35 —
Leslie, Geo. A. Young, of Kininvie	Lesmurdie Cottage, Elgin	1,941	996 12	Shand, Robert S. Kynoch	Keith	5	11 —
				Shand, Ann	Wellfield, Banff	5	20 —
Leslie, Capt. Hans G., of Dunlugas	Dunlugas House, Turriff	1,568	1,477 6	Shanks, Rev. Robert	F.C. Manse, Buckie	1	135 10
				Simpson, James	Banff	11	171 5
Longmore, Andrew, of Linksfield	Rettie, Banff	51	83 —	Simpson, Robert, of Cobairdy	Cobairdy House, Huntly	631	495 —
Longmore, William	Keith	4	112 10	Smith, William	Schoolhouse, Gartly	1	16 —
Lorimer's Mortification, Trustees of	Cullen	3	10 —	Smollett, George	Hilton of Blacklaw, Banff	4	11 —
				Souter, Heirs of James	Banff	1	163 5
				Souter, Rev. John	Manse, Inverkethney	14	35 —
				Stephen, Rev. George	Schoolhouse, Fordyce	17	25 —
M'Culloch, Donald	Asylum, Banff	5	40 14	Steuart, Andrew, of Auchlunkart	Auchlunkart House, Keith	6,329	4,440 13
M'Donald, Peter	Charlestown, Aberlour	1	63 19				
Macduff Commercial Co.	Macduff, Gamrie	2	193 7	Stewart, Alexander, of Laithers	Laithers, Turriff	3	10 —
Macduff, Magistrates and Town Council of	Macduff, Gamrie	2	4 —	Stewart, Capt. James, of Lesmurdie	Friars Park, Elgin	2,075	460 9
M'Intosh, Rev. James	Manse, Deskford	7	25 —				
M'Lachlan, Rev. James	Manse, Rathven	13	40 —	Tayler, William Jas., of Glenbarry	Rothiemay House, Huntly	313	264 —
M'Lennan, Rev. John	Manse, Tomintoul	2	13 —				
M'Vicar, Rev. William	Manse, Ordiquhill	8	30 —	Taylor, James, of Greenskairs	Portobello, Edinburgh	406	388 —
Marshall, William	Buckie	3	35 5				
Masson, Rev. Alexander	Manse, Boharm	5	6 12	Taylor, John F. S.	London	3	78 10
Masson, Rev. William	Manse, Botriphnie	8	23 —	Thomson, Rev. James	Manse, Gartly	15	47 —
Mitchell, Rev. John	Manse, St. Fergus	11	34 —				
Moir, Rev. Robert	Manse, Rothiemay	9	35 —	Urquhart, Mrs. Mary Isabella Pollard, of Craigston	Craigston Castle, Turriff	16	22 10
Morayshire Railway Co.	Elgin (Railway)	2	351 —				
Morrison, Alexander, of Bognie	Mountblairy House, Turriff	4,154	3,002 4	Walker, Alexander	Banff	3	167 5
Morrison, James, of Culvie	Culvie, Marnoch	582	321 15	Walker, Peter	Dufftown, Mortlach	1	43 5
Morrison, Joseph J. L. L., and Maria C. J.	Bombay, East Indies	398	310 12	Watt, Alexander	Macduff	8	69 10
Morrison, of Tollo	Paris			Watt, Trustees of Charles	Crombie	627	624 12
Mortlach Parish, Heritors of	Mortlach	1	2 —	Watt, James, of Whitehill	Auchinhalrig, Fochabers	474	290 14
Murdoch, Alexander	Banff	9	52 5	Wilson, Alexander	Inchgower, Rathven	7	158 —
Muterer, James	Old Manse, Boharm	16	18 —	Wilson, Alexander F.	Banff	20	137 4
				Wilson, Trustees of James	Banff	4	42 4
Nicol, James	Turriff	4	11 10				
Ord, Trustees of Church of	Ord, Banff	2	2 —	Total Owners of Land of one Acre and upwards		142 406,939	190,681 —
				Total Owners of Lands of less than one Acre in extent		3,883 562	36,344 —
Ramsay, John, of Straloch	Straloch, New Machar	2,088	1,888 13				
Rannie, Henry Alex., of Greenlaw	187 Hill Street, Glasgow	260	265 —				
Rathven Parish, Heritors of	Rathven	1	1 —	GRAND TOTAL		4,025 407,501	227,025 —
Reid, Daniel	Hazlewood, Blackhillock	5	46 —				

BERWICK.

Population in 1871, - - - - - - - **36,486.**
Inhabited Houses, - - - - - - - **6,491.**
Number of Parishes, - - - - - - - **33.**

Name of Owner.	Address of Owner.	Estimated Acreage of Property.	Gross Annual Value.	Name of Owner.	Address of Owner.	Estimated Acreage of Property.	Gross Annual Value.
		Acres.	£ s.			Acres.	£ s.
Aberdour, Lord	Cranshaw Castle, Dunse	2,551	1,050 3	Bruce, Henry	Kinleith, Currie	11	15 —
Aitchison, William	Kaimes, Coldstream	3	10 —	Buchan, Trustees of late Col. George William			
Aitken, Mrs. Catherine	Holytown	6	52 —				
Allan, Adam	Hutton, Berwick	6	64 —	Fordyce, of Kelloe	Kelloe, Dunse	824	2,121 10
Allan, James	Westruther	14	30 —	Buchan, Lady Laura, of			
Allan, John, of Peelwalls	Billie Mains, Reston	701	1,720 10	Reedyloch	London	155	410 —
Allan, Trustees of late Joseph	Quixwood, Dunse	1,663	1,015 —	Cairns, Heirs of Thomas	Buskinbrae, Coldingham	69	65 —
Allan, Capt. Henry John, of Trabroun	East India Club, London	100	211 13	Campbell, Sir Hugh Hume, of Marchmont, Bart.	Marchmont, Dunse	20,180	17976 12
Allan, William	Bowshiel, Grant's House	3	46 —	Cameron, Rev. Daniel	Manse, Ayton	15	72 —
Allan, William Henry, of Allanbank	Lauder	561	567 13	Carnegie, Jas., of Edrom Newton	Edinburgh	327	499 15
Allison, John	Coldstream	1	18 —	Carter, Walter	Ayton	2	90 10
Anderson, Thomas, of Shawbraes	Coveyheugh, Reston	196	958 11	Cathcart, Col. the Hon. Adolphus F., of Caldra	Caldra, Dunse	152	237 10
Annandale, Alexander	Bielside, Dunbar	23	35 —	Chartres, Howe	Ayton	2	35 —
Annandale, Jas. Hunter	Polton, Lasswade	23	35 —	Chirnside, George, of Edrington	Edrington, Berwick	260	595 16
Ayton Gas Company	Ayton	1	30 10	Chisholm, Walter	Lauder	3	8 —
				Christison, Rev. Alex.	Manse, Foulden, Berwick	8	58 —
Baird, Trustees of late George, of Stitchell	Stitchell House, Kelso	1,500	2,532 6	*Church of Scotland*		43	54 10
Balfour, Arthur James, of Whittinghame	Whittinghame, Prestonkirk	2,014	2,549 13	*Coldingham Village Feuars*	Coldingham	300	10 —
				Commissioners of Supply of Berwickshire	Dunse	1	191 —
Balfour, Heirs of Charles, of Newton Don	Newton Don, Kelso	919	1,763 —	Cook, Rev. George	Manse, Longformacus	20	45 —
Ballantyne, James	Lauder	3	115 10	Cormack, Mrs. Isabella	Coldingham Hill	14	12 10
Bell, Rev. Stephen	Manse, Eyemouth	10	75 —	Cotesworth, Robert	Cowdenknowes, Earlston	4	10 10
Bertram, John	Reston	10	14 —	Cotesworth, Trustees of late Robert, of Cowdenknowes	Earlston	911	1,297 11
Berwickshire Railway Coy.	Edinburgh (Railway)	105	3,083 —				
Berwickshire Road Trustees		1	46 —	Coulson, Mrs. Sarah, of Houndwood	Houndwood, Reston	1,183	1,241 16
Bisset, Mrs. Jane	Alderney	4	14 —				
Blake, Rev. James L.	Manse, Gavinton	11	68 10	Cowe, John	Luffness, Haddington	3	15 —
Blantyre, Lord	Erskine House, Glasgow	2,878	1,175 19	Cowe, Mrs. Mary	Luffness, Haddington	3	19 10
Borthwick, John, of Crookston	Crookston House, Stow	4,484	1,484 11	Cowe, Margaret	Chirnside	12	17 —
				Craig, Andrew	Scoutscroft, Coldingham	60	152 10
Boswell, Sir George A. F. Houstoun, of Blackadder, Bart.	Blackadder, Chirnside	5,309	8,746 2	Craig, George	Norham	5	25 —
				Craig, Robert	Springhill, Coldingham	11	15 —
Bowhill, James	Ayton	1	5 —	Craig, Robert	Berryhaugh, Reston	100	269 11
Bowhill, Trustees of late Thomas	Ayton	1	35 —	Cranstoun, George C. Trotter, of Dewar	Gorebridge	3	530 —
Broadwood, Thomas, of Fulfordlees	Crawhill, Dunbar	316	500 —	Crawford, Alexander	Dunse	1	52 10
				Crichton, James	Edinburgh	3	24 —
Broomfield, William John, of Old Greenlaw	Greenlaw	330	480 —	Crichton, Robert	Birgham, Eccles	3	6 —
				Crichton, William	Birgham, Eccles	2	19 10
Broomfield, Thomas	Lauder	3	51 —	*Crown, The*	(Crown Property)	2	18 —
Broomfield, Mrs. Caroline C., of Hassington Mains	Eccles	351	812 —	Cunningham, William	Coldstream	2	118 19
				Curle, Alexander, of East Morriston	Melrose	319	449 —
Broughton, Robt. Henry, of Rowchester	Rowchester House, Greenlaw	926	1,889 15	Curle, James, of Evelaw	Melrose	400	294 15
Brown, Robert Brown Forsyth	Whitsome, East Newton, Chirnside	271	864 2	Cuthbertson, William	Lauder	3	32 —
Brown, Rev. Archibald	Manse, Legerwood	13	45 —				
Brown, David Hepburn, of Park	Preston Lodge, Corstorphine	586	527 —	Dale, Mrs. Barbara	Auldhame, No. Berwick	4	27 10
				Dalrymple, James, of Greenknowe	Langlee, Galashiels	2,217	2,274 18
Brown, Forbes Scott	Longformacus, Dunse	3	85 —				
Brown, George	Bogbank, Coldingham	44	38 —	Darling, Trs. of late John	Gavinton, Dunse	9	40 15
Brown, Mrs. Margaret, of Longformacus	Longformacus	2,600	1,619 15	Darling, Trustees of late John	Gordon	2	21 —
Brown, Madeline	Trinity Lodge, Dunse	11	85 5	Darling, William	Reston	3	37 —
Brown, Margaret	Trinity Lodge, Dunse	11	85 5	Darling, Mrs. Eliza	Dublin	2	164 13
Browne, John	Longformacus	1	10 —	Darling, Mrs. Mary	Reston	3	23 —
Brownlow, Earl	Belton House, Grantham	536	1,340 10	Davidson, James	Edingtonhill, Chirnside	1	10 —

BERWICK—continued.

Name of Owner.	Address of Owner.	Estimated Acreage of Property.	Gross Annual Value.	Name of Owner.	Address of Owner.	Estimated Acreage of Property.	Gross Annual Value.
		Acres.	£ s.			Acres.	£ s.
Davidson, Major James	Nottingham	2	24 —	Gray, William	East Gordon	8	24 —
Davidson, Agnes	Coldingham	2	7 —	Gray, Mrs. Agnes	Gordon	8	35 —
Denholm, Heirs of David	Howburn, Reston	85	85 —	Greenfield, James	Reston	80	168 —
Denholm, George	Woodside, Coupar-Angus	4	20 —	Greig, James L., of Eccles	Eccles	363	871 10
Denholm, Heirs of George, of Broomhill	Broomhill, Dunse	349	811 —	Grieve, John M'Lean M'K., of Huttonhall	Huttonhall, Berwick	630	1,587 18
Dickson, Adam	Lauder	5	63 10	Griffiths, George Waldie, of Burnhall	Hendersyde Park, Kelso	298	506 5
Dickson, Alexander	Lauder	2	6 —	Gunn, Rev. George G.	Manse, Edrom	12	55 —
Dickson, Archibald	Bughtrigg, Coldstream	5	20 —				
Dickson, James, of Castle Law	Bughtrigg House, Coldstream	1,367	2,237 —	Haddington, Earl of	Mellerstain, Kelso	14,279	15099 6
Dickson, Trustees of late Richard	Lauder	2	6 —	Haig, Joseph	Kaysmuir, Dunse	5	15 —
Dickson, William, of Whitecross	Alnwick	337	551 1	Haig, Heirs of Barbara, of Bemersyde	Bemersyde House, St. Boswells	1,357	2,009 12
Dickson, William, junior	Alnwick	7	10 —	Hall, Sir James, of Dunglass, Bart.	Dunglass, Cockburnspath	7,948	8,029 11
Dobie, Rev. William	Manse, Ladykirk	11	53 —	Hardie, Captain Henry Robert, of Stoneshiel	Stoneshiel, Reston	191	475 —
Dobson, Mrs., Mrs. Macpherson; and Heirs of Catherine Purves	Pittlesheugh, Eccles	316	695 —	Haswell, Archibald	London	1	19 15
Dodds, William	Lauder	2	18 10	Hay, John	Gordon	30	87 15
Donaldson, Peter	Houndslow, Gordon	24	34 15	Hay, William	Birgham	6	19 —
Drummond, George Stirling Home, of Northfield	Blairdrummond, Stirling	1,494	1,586 13	Hay, William	Edenside, Gordon	8	16 —
Dryburgh, Thos., of Press	Edinburgh	664	860 —	Hay, Colonel William, of Dunse Castle	Dunse Castle	5,812	10093 19
Dunglas, Lord	Newton-Don, Kelso	20	35 —	Henderson, George	Lauder	1	13 6
Dunlop, Rev. John	Manse, Bunkle, Dunse	46	84 —	Henderson, John	Lauder	2	6 —
Dunlop, Geo., of Mayfield	Mayfield, Dunse	249	270 —	Henderson, Richard	Lauder	1	5 —
Dunse Feuars	Dunse	9	46 10	Henderson, William	Horndean	1	34 —
				Henry, Hon. Mrs. Louisa H., of Redpath, wife of Col. C. S. Henry, R.A.	West Green House, Winchfield, Hants	4,056	1,256 6
Earlston, Inhabitants of	Earlston	2	9 10	Herriot, James, of Coldingham Law	Coldingham Law	253	485 —
Edington, James	Lumsdaine, Coldingham	6	15 10	Herriot, Heirs of James	Herriotbank, Whitsome	102	235 —
Elliot, John	East Cruicksfield, Dunse	52	140 —	Hogg, James	Reston	3	65 —
Elliot, Robert	Edinburgh	2	25 —	Hogg, Thomas	Coldstream	6	169 5
Erskine, Charles	Melrose	7	10 —	Hoggarth, Mrs. Isabella	Kelso	5	20 —
Erskine, George Oswald H. E. B., of Dryburgh	London	359	977 9	Home, Hon. Cospatrick Douglas	The Hirsel, Coldstream	3	25 —
Erskine, Jas., of Shielfield	Melrose	808	1,002 10	Home, David Milne, of Milne Graden	Paxton House, Berwick	843	1,715 10
Eyemouth Harbour Trustees	Eyemouth (Harbour)	1	60 —	Home, David Milne, yr. of Milne Graden	Paxton House, Berwick	4	16 10
Fair, John	Buenos Ayres	4	139 16	Home, Mrs. Jean, of Wedderburn, wife of David Milne Home of Milne Graden	Paxton House, Berwick	9,145	15379 10
Fairholme, Trustees of late William, of Chapel	Chapel, Earlston	858	870 18	Home, Earl of	The Hirsel, Coldstream	2,597	5,244 17
Fettes, Trustees of late Sir William, of Comely Bank, Bart.	Edinburgh	593	1,086 3	Home, Countess of	The Hirsel, Coldstream	7,804	7,602 11
Fiddes, William	Edinburgh	10	23 —	Home, Rev. Frederick	Australia	44	105 —
Fife, Robert	St. Boswells	22	73 —	Home, Geo., of Newmains	Newmains, Reston	178	348 —
Fish, Alexander	Coldstream	1	193 15	Home, John	Fairlaw, Reston	94	105 10
Ford, James	Westruther	6	12 —	Home, Major John H. F., of Bassendean	Bassendean House, Gordon	775	890 7
Ford, Thomas	Fountainside, Coldingham	20	15 —	Home, Patrick Anderson, of Gunsgreen	Gunsgreen, Ayton	520	851 18
Fortune, James	Longformacus	5	18 15	Home, Rev. Robert	Manse, Swinton	22	103 —
Fortune, John	Reston	1	19 —	Home, Rev. Walter	Manse, Polwarth, Dunse	16	54 —
Foster, Ralph, of Whitsomehill	Sanson's Seal, Berwick	631	1,208 —	Home, William James, of Broomhouse	Broomhouse, Dunse	308	856 5
Free Church of Scotland		2	20 10	Home, Wm., of Fairlaw	Fairlaw, Reston	306	831 7
Fyfe, Isabella	Wark, Coldstream	84	51 —	Hood, John, of Stoneridge	Kames, Coldstream	690	1,614 10
Gardner, Burnet Gilroy	Coldingham Hill	16	55 —	Hood, Heirs of William, of Sunnyside	Sunnyside, Reston	317	693 —
Geddes, William Spence	Lauder	2	8 —	Hood, Mrs. Janet, of Mains, wife of Robert Hood	Edinburgh	680	1,307 —
Gibb, Mrs. Isabella	Dunse	7	73 —				
Gibson, George	Gordon	5	23 —				
Gibson, James	Gunsgreenhill, Ayton	2	91 —				
Gillie, Home Purves	Berwick	12	133 15				
Gillies, Thomas	Lauder	2	19 —	Hood, Mrs. Elizabeth, of Kames	Kames, Coldstream	500	1,132 15
Gillies, Heirs of William	Coldingham Loan	16	15 —	Hope, George, of Sunwick	Bordlands, Noble House	674	950 —
Glendinning, William	Earlston	6	31 —	Hudson, John	Dunse	50	113 10
Gordon, John, of Belchester	Cluny Castle, Aberdeen	484	1,145 19	Humble, George & John	Kelso	19	55 6
Gordon, Village Feuars	Gordon	44	6 —	Hume, James Alexander Ross, of Ninewells	Ninewells, Chirnside	1,024	2,161 15
Gordon, Lady Frances, of Blackburn	5 Wilton Cres., London	539	667 —	Hunter, George	Lauder	2	25 10
Graham, Rev. Henry G.	Manse, Nenthorn	8	41 —	Hunter, Hugh	Lauder	2	5 —
Graham, James	Lauder	3	33 10	Hunter, James	Godscroft, Dunse	153	30 —
Graham, Mrs. Margaret, wife of Thomas Graham	Thornielaw, St. Boswells	4	22 16	Hunter, James William, of Thurston	Thurston, Dunbar	1,220	1,280 8
Grant, William	Grant's House	1	68 5				

E

BERWICK—continued.

Name of Owner.	Address of Owner.	Estimated Acreage of Property.	Gross Annual Value.	Name of Owner.	Address of Owner.	Estimated Acreage of Property.	Gross Annual Value.
		Acres.	£ s.			Acres.	£ s.
Hunter, John	Muirhouse, Coldingham	3	3 —	M'Alister, Rev. Dugald	Manse, Stitchell	3	11 —
Hunter, Rev. Joseph	Manse, Cockburnspath	8	46 —	M'Braire, James, of Broadmeadows	Broadmeadows, Berwick	1,843	4,340 9
Hunter, Martin, of Antonshill	Antonshill, Coldstream	474	940 5	M'Donald, Alexander	Easter Flemington, Ayton	94	180 —
Hunter, Trustees of late William King	Dunse	114	258 —	M'Dougal, Thomas	Eskmills, Penicuik	12	15 —
Hutchinson, Representatives of late John	Ruthven, Coldstream	188	280 —	M'Dougall, David	Langlee Mains, Galashiels	55	185 —
Hutton, Rev. William M.	Manse, Cranshaws, Dunse	14	42 17	M'Dougall, George	Blyth, Lauder	135	263 15
				M'Dougall, James	Edinburgh	7	29 —
				M'Dougall, James	Lylestane, Lauder	12	44 8
Innes, Alexander Mitchell, of Ayton	Ayton Castle	5,780	10949 15	M'Dougall, John	Gordon West Mains	2	99 —
				M'Dougall, Robert	Fouldenhill, Berwick	28	65 —
				M'Gall, John	Hallydown, Coldingham	2	20 10
Jamieson, Alexander	Lauder	1	4 10	Mackenzie, Rev. Ewen, of Abbey Park	Kirkhill, Inverness	175	205 5
Johnston, William	South Shields	2	15 —	M'Lachlan, Mrs. Janet	Lauder	2	17 10
				M'Laren, Rev. Alexander	Manse, Mertoun	18	63 —
Kelly, John	Lauder	2	11 5	M'Leod, Rev. John	Manse, Dunse	15	85 —
Kerr, Joseph	Earlston	7	47 —	Marjoribanks, Trustees of late Lord, of Ladykirk	Ladykirk	979	1,763 7
Kerr, Thomas, of Craighouse	Earlston	150	189 —	Marjoribanks, Lady, of Ladykirk	Ladykirk	5,853	9,991 17
Kerr, Trustees of late Thomas	Dunse	11	175 18	Mack, William, of Berrybank	Berrybank, Reston	303	506 —
Kirke, Rev. Robert	Manse, Hutton, Berwick	14	57 —	Mair, Rev. William	Manse, Earlston	25	54 15
Kirkwood, Margaret	Gordon	2	18 10	Maither, William	Houndslow	1	10 10
Knight, Henry, of Flemington	Blandford	24	39 13	Marjoribanks, Sir John, of Lees, Bart.	Lees, Coldstream	3,332	6,063 10
				Martin, Heirs of William	Auchencraw	4	25 5
				Mason, Robert	Lothian Burn, Edinburgh	65	120 10
				Mason, Mrs. Isabella	Gorebridge	16	55 10
Laidlaw, Alexander	Lauder	2	5 —	Meiklam, John, of Gladswood	Gladswood, Melrose	258	426 —
L'Amy, Major John Ramsay, of Netherbyres	Netherbyres, Ayton	65	228 16	Meikle, Gilbert	Inveraray	24	39 13
Landale, Trustees of late Thomas	Templehall, Coldingham	175	452 6	Meikle, Henry	Banks, Linlithgow	24	39 13
				Meikle, John	Peelwalls, Ayton	45	40 —
Landells, Adam, of Bankend	Abroad	87	87 —	Meikle, Robert	Langton, Dorset	24	39 13
Lauder, Trustees of late George Dick, of Huntlywood	Huntlywood, Gordon	559	628 —	Meikle, Thomas	Edinburgh	24	39 13
				Meikle, Thomas M'Crie	Australia	24	39 13
				Meikle, William	London	24	39 13
Lauder, Magistrates and Council of Burgh of	Lauder	2,202	945 —	Melrose, Jonathan, of Monynut	Coldstream	527	220 10
Lauder, Trustees of late William	Lauder	3	74 1	Mercer, Trustees of late William	Earlston	2	32 —
Lauderdale, Earl of	Thirlstane Castle, Lauder	24,681	16096 8	Middleton, Rev. James	Manse, Lauder	8	59 10
Lawton, Mrs. Mary	Melrose	11	152 —	Millar, Andrew	Lauder	2	11 —
Leitch, Mrs. Margaret, wife of George Leitch	Spittal, Berwick	1	87 17	Miller, Rev. David	Manse, Mordington, Berwick	16	84 10
Leith, Lady Eliza C., of Kirklands, wife of Sir George H. Leith, of Burgh St. Peter's, Bart.	Drygrange, Melrose	128	275 6	Miller, William, of Manderston, M.P.	Manderston, Dunse	961	2,969 13
				Milne, Nicol, of Howpark	Faldonside, Melrose	644	527 3
				Mitchell, Heirs of Alexander, of Stow	Carolside, Earlston	2,455	2,635 9
Liddell, Mark	Lauder	2	38 10	Moffat, Heirs of James	Ayton	1	90 12
Lillie, Allan	Yarlside, Earlston	510	308 18	Monro, Trustees of late James, of Cockburn	Cockburn, Dunse	2,616	1,358 —
Little, Heirs of Mrs. Margaret	Chesterfield, Berwick	15	48 —	Morrison, Wightman	Myrtlehall, Coldingham	63	26 —
Lockie, Rev. Alexander	Gordon	10	41 —	Munro, Andrew	Lauder	2	19 —
Lockie, Robert	Gordon	8	12 —	Munro, Rev. David	Manse, Coldingham	12	47 —
Lockie, Thomas	Gordon	8	11 —	Murray, Robert	Lauder	2	17 —
Lockie, William	Lauder	2	8 —	Murray, Thomas	Lauder	3	26 16
Logan, Abraham, of Burnhouses	Caverton Mill, Kelso	514	752 —	Murray, William	Lauder	3	6 —
				Murray, William	Lauder	2	14 —
Logan, George J. Ninian, of Edrom	Edrom, Chirnside	467	1,142 10	Mushet, Mrs. Janet, of Chesterfield, wife of Robert Mushet	Dalkeith	15	48 —
Logan, Catherine	Cairnbank, Dunse	12	70 10				
Logan, Georgina	Cairnbank, Dunse	12	70 10				
Logan, Eliza Helen	Dunse	3	80 —				
Low, James, of Laws	Berrywell, Dunse	679	1,380 16				
Lugton, William	Hillburn, Ayton	1	33 —	Ness, William	Lauder	2	6 —
Luke, Trustees of late Robert	Ladywell, Dunse	161	355 —	Niddrie, Mrs. Grace, of Over Howden, etc.	Dromore West, Ireland	590	699 7
Lumsdaine, Heirs of Rev. Francis G. S., of Blanerne	Blanerne House, Dunse	2,603	2,364 6	Nisbet, Rev. Archibald	Manse, Coldstream	10	95 —
				Nisbet, Trustees of late Robert, of Lambden	Greenlaw	555	1,000 —
Lundie, William C., of Spital	Spital, Berwick	572	1,655 —	Nisbet, Trs. of late Major Thomas, of Mersington	Mersington, Eccles	551	1,722 —
Lunham, James, and Mrs. Mary	Birgham, Eccles	3	12 —	North British Railway Co.	Edinburgh	6	15 12
				Do. do.	Do. (Railway)	376	11311 —

BERWICK—continued.

Name of Owner.	Address of Owner.	Estimated Acreage of Property.	Gross Annual Value.
		Acres.	£ s.
Oswald, Heirs of James Jeffreys, of Edrington Castle	Edrington Castle, Berwick	163	450 -
Ovens, John	Gunsgreen, Ayton	4	11 -
Parker, Mrs. Hannah, of Justice Hall	Edinburgh	62	156 -
Paterson, Trustees of late Alexander	Lauder	4	48 -
Patterson, Margaret	Coldingham	3	28 9
Peacock, George	Wooden Mills, Kelso	2	11 10
Peat, Trustees of late George	Walnage, Dunse	4	61 17
Polwarth, Lord	Mertoun House, St. Boswells	4,714	6,843 16
Pringle, Lady Elizabeth, of Langton	Langton House, Dunse	8,121	8,500 16
Proudfoot, Rev. Robert F.	Manse, Fogo, Dunse	12	52 -
Purves, Heirs of Andrew	Lauder	4	23 5
Purves, Charles H. H., of Springwells	Hampton Court Palace	750	1,236 10
Purves, Robert	Eyemouth	4	24 16
Purves, Robert	Moorpark, Coldingham	9	16 -
Purves, Mrs. Agnes, of Harelaw	Dunse	88	269 10
Purves, Alison	Coldingham Muir	2	3 -
Rae, James	Lauder	2	6 -
Ramsay, Mrs. Georgina H., of Old Linthill	Cheltenham	25	47 15
Rankine, John, of Bassendean	Edinburgh	901	905 1
Rattrey, Alexander Wellwood, of Fellowhills	Ladykirk	242	307 -
Renton, David, of Chesterbank	Chesterbank, Ayton	80	150 -
Renton, Major Charles F. Campbell, of Lamberton	Mordington, Berwick	2,487	2,699 5
Renton, Thomas	Coldingham	1	36 -
Richardson, Mrs. Mary, of Nansfield	Edinburgh	65	120 -
Riddell, Captain George Wm. Hutton, of Muselee	Newport Lodge, Melton-Mowbray	119	417 10
Robertson, Rev. Andrew B.	U.P. Manse, Coldingham	1	18 -
Robertson, James	Woodside, Coldingham	32	22 -
Robertson, Rev. John A.	Manse, Whitsome	30	106 -
Robertson, Thomas Fair	Hermitage, Kelso	68	156 -
Robson, Rev. George	U.P. Manse, Lauder	2	30 -
Robson, James C.	Southfield, Dunse	1	60 -
Rocheid, Curators of Charles H. A. F. C. E. J., of Hawkslaw	Trinity College, Oxford	401	485 -
Romanes, Trustees of late Rev. George	Lauder	2	8 -
Romanes, John	Edinburgh	11	22 10
Romanes, Robert, of Harryburn	Lauder	36	208 5
Romanes, Jane, of Buskinburn	Kelso	64	35 -
Roxburghe, Duke of	Floors Castle, Kelso	6,096	816 -
Roy, Captain Frederick L., of Nenthorn	Nenthorn House, Kelso	1,778	2,955 -
Runciman, John	Earlston	8	56 5
Runciman, Richard	Lauder	2	6 -
Rutherford, Heirs of Robert	Chirnside	1	47 14
Sanderson, Mrs. Mary	Lauder	2	24 17
Sandison, Heirs of Magnus, of Highlaws	Highlaws, Ayton	180	656 5
Scott, John	Dunse	1	39 4
Scott, Peter	Chirnside	50	140 -
Scott, Lady Alicia Ann, of Spottiswoode	Spottiswoode House, Stow	11,412	5,425 14
Scoular, John	Paxton, Berwick	2	21 10
Selby, Ephraim	Hassendeanbank, Hawick	7	84 10
Seymer, Mrs. Gertrude C. Ker, of Swintonhill, etc., wife of Henry E. C. Ker Seymer	Handford	4,681	5,570 13
Shiel, Alexander	Lauder	2	8 -
Shiels, George	Galashiels	2	17 -
Shirriff, Mrs. Jane M., of Bastleridge and Fleurs, wife of Thomas W. M. Shirriff	Uxbridge	558	819 15
Simson, Reps. of late Rev. Charles	Blainslie, Melrose	2	31 17
Simson, Trustees of late Charles, of Threepwood	Lauder	2	4 10
Simpson, Robert	Earlston	1	12 -
Sinclair, Lord	Nisbet House, Dunse	1,550	3,355 2
Sleigh, Peter	Lauder	3	18 5
Smail, William	Lauder	2	7 10
Smail, William Archibald, of Overmains	Eccles	360	910 -
Smart, Rev. Alexander F.	Manse, Chirnside	8	66 -
Smeal, Adam	Lauder	2	26 15
Smellie, Trustees of late Rev. James	Reston Mains, Reston	140	400 -
Smith, Major William H., of West Cruiksfield	West Cruiksfield, Dunse	42	164 5
Smith, Mrs. Agnes	Lauder	2	19 -
Smyth, James, of Whitchester	Whitchester, Dunse	983	835 10
Somerville, George	Lauder	2	18 10
Spence, William Robertson	Lauder	3	15 -
Spottiswoode, Helen	London	14	27 -
Stalker, James	Galashiels	10	48 7
Stark, John, of Flemington	Flemington, Ayton	24	39 13
Stevenson, Robert, of Plumburn	Barnstaple	16	24 -
Stewart, Walter	Coldingham	1	12 -
Stewart, Mrs. Dorothy, of Belmont, wife of Basil Stewart	Orchard Dell, Lanark	85	190 -
Stirling, Mary E., of Renton	Renton House, Grant's House	2,674	2,987 8
Stobbs, Rev. William	Manse, Gordon	12	41 -
Stodart, Robert	Lauder	2	21 3
Stuart, Alexander Chas., of Rawburn	Eaglescairnie, Haddington	4,828	1,219 15
Suttie, Sir George Grant, of Preston Grange and Balgone, Bart.	Balgone, Drem	2,275	1,779 5
Swan, John, & Sons	Edinburgh	1	20 -
Swan, Robert	Kelso	1	12 -
Swinton, Archibald Campbell, of Kimmerghame	Kimmerghame, Dunse	1,845	3,887 13
Swinton, Mrs. Ann Elizabeth, of Swinton	Swinton House, Coldstream	1,161	2,808 3
Swinton, Catherine C.	Dunse	1	27 10
Swinton, Mary C.	Dunse	1	27 10
Symington, Robert, jun.	Lauder	3	17 -
Symington, Robert, sen.	Lauder	5	30 -
Tait, James, of Langrig	Kelso	133	283 10
Talbot-de-Malahide, Lord	Malahide Castle, Ireland	806	2,063 10
Taylor, Rev. Henry	Manse, Westruther	20	35 -
Taylor, James, of Threeburnford	Catcune, Gorebridge	400	180 -
Thomson, Alexander C., of Grueldykes	London	175	478 18
Thomson, Andrew	Lauder	2	30 8
Thomson, James	Pathhead	4	15 6
Thomson, James	Dunse	2	79 10
Thomson, Thomas	Ayton	1	17 -
Thorburn, Alexander	Coldingham	20	12 -
Thorburn, James	Coldingham	4	6 10
Thorburn, Peter	Coldingham	6	14 -
Thorburn, Robert	Eyemouth	6	45 -
Thorburn, William	Coldlands, Reston	11	9 -
Tinlin, Mrs. Mary	Earlston	2	20 -
Torrance, Mrs. Frances, wife of George Torrance	Sisterpath, Dunse	6	97 12

BERWICK—continued.

Name of Owner.	Address of Owner.	Estimated Acreage of Property.	Gross Annual Value.	Name of Owner.	Address of Owner.	Estimated Acreage of Property.	Gross Annual Value.
		Acres.	£ s.			Acres.	£ s.
Trotter, Charles Young	Chirnside	3	530 –	Weatherhead, Heirs of George Hume, and Alexander Fish	Coldstream	15	148 9
Trotter, Lieut.-Col. Henry, yr., of Mortonhall	Mortonhall (Grenadier Guards)	16	34 –	Webster, George, of Hallydown	Edinburgh	302	618 –
Trotter, Lieutenant John Oswald	Mortonhall (5th Dragoon Guards)	16	34 –	Webster, James	Fairlaw, Reston	2	15 –
Trotter, Richard, of Charterhall	Mortonhall, Edinburgh	6,780	12703 3	Wemyss and March, Earl of	Gosford, Drem	1,261	747 –
Tullis, William, of Springhill	Auchmuty, Markinch	11	15 –	White, Robert	Ryselaw, Dunse	5	22 10
Turnbull, James, of Hillend	Edinburgh	501	470 10	White, William	Lauder	2	18 10
Turnbull, John, of Abbey St. Bathans	Edinburgh	4,842	2,525 12	Wightman, Thomas	Comely Bank, Coldingham	3	6 –
Turnbull, Trustees of late Richard	Eyemouth	4	83 –	Wilkie, John, of Foulden	Foulden House, Berwick	2,550	5,244 12
Turnbull, Jane	Dunse	1	50 10	Williamson, George, of Swansfield	Edinburgh	96	140 –
Turner, James	Cockburnspath	1	42 –	Wilson, Charles	Earlston	9	199 –
Tweeddale, Marquis of	Yester House, Haddington	18,116	9,572 3	Wilson, Charles, & Sons	Earlston	2	340 –
				Wilson, George, of Georgefield	Coldstream	151	293 10
United Presbyterian Church, Trustees of	Various, Berwickshire	2	31 10	Wilson, James	Lauder	2	4 –
Usher, Mrs. Margaret	Chirnside	1	10 –	Wilson, James and Charles	Earlston	17	60 –
				Wilson, John, of Cumledge	Cumledge, Dunse	277	605 –
				Wilson, Philip	Dunse	1	48 –
Vallance, William	Lauder	2	7 –	Wilson, Robert F. R.	Tweedmouth	15	72 5
				Wilson, Jane	Coldingham	1	13 10
				Winton, George Hay	Westruther	1	11 5
Waldie, George	Gordon	4	16 –	Wood, Robert	Whitecross, Coldingham	5	29 –
Walker, Rev. James	Manse, Channelkirk	9	38 –	Wood, Mrs. Isabella	Canada	4	57 10
Walker, Rev. John	Manse, Greenlaw	11	50 –	Wright, Hugh, of Blackburn	Alticry, Glenluce	2,104	1,463 –
Wallace, John	Grant's House	2	12 –				
Weir, Trs. of late Robert Cosens, of Bogangreen	Bogangreen, Coldingham	710	849 12				
Waters, Thomas	Lauder	2	27 5	Total Owners of Land of one Acre and upwards		453	291,836 355,118 10
Watson, Adam	Oxton	1	18 –	Total Owners of Lands of less than one Acre in extent		1,290 303	22,092 13
Watson, Andrew	Dumfries	1	27 10				
Watson, George	Abbey St. Bathans, Dunse	12	10 –				
Watson, James	Lauder	2	13 –	Grand Total		1,743 292,139	377,211 3
Watson, Rev. James R.	Manse, Eccles	18	69 8				

BUTE.

Population in 1871,	16,977.
Inhabited Houses,	2,433.
Number of Parishes,	6.

Name of Owner.	Address of Owner.	Estimated Acreage of Property.	Gross Annual Value.	Name of Owner.	Address of Owner.	Estimated Acreage of Property.	Gross Annual Value.
		Acres.	£ s.			Acres.	£ s.
Anderson, Hugh	Rothesay	1	42 —	Kerr, James and Mary Jane	West Stuart St., Greenock	5	13 —
				Kilbride, Heritors of Parish of	Arran	2	85 —
Bartholomew, Robert	Ascog	5	75 —				
Beith, Heirs of John	Rothesay	4	691 5	Kilmory, Heritors of Parish of	Arran	2	33 —
Bell, Benjamin B.	Glasgow	2	70 —				
Birrell, Thomas	Serpentine Rd., Rothesay	3	153 —				
Bruce, Mrs. Mary Anne	High Craigmore, Rothesay	1	50 —				
Bute, Marquess of	Mountstuart, Rothesay	29,279	19574 10	Macbeth, Daniel	Rothesay	34	417 10
Bute, Trustees of late Marchioness of	Rothesay	6	32 10	Macbride, Rev. Alex.	F.C. Manse, Rothesay	3	151 —
				Macfie, Hector	Ardbeg, Rothesay	1	239 —
				MacGillivray, Martin	Rothesay	2	21 —
				MacIlwraith, James	Kamesburgh	1	96 —
				MacIntosh, John	Rothesay	7	111 5
				MacIver, Charles	Liverpool	1	66 —
Campbell, Arthur P. B.	Ardbeg, Rothesay	99	151 —				
Campbell, Rev. Colin F.	Lamlash, Arran	21	60 —	MacKay, Mrs. Elizabeth	South Garrochty, Rothesay	65	66 —
Campbell, Hugh	Rothesay	1	40 —				
Campbell, Heirs of Neil	Rothesay	5	786 —	MacKechnie, John A.	Rothesay	3	509 —
Corbett, John Stuart	Mountpleasant, Rothesay	6	18 —	Mackim, John	Anderston, Glasgow	3	25 —
Craig, Mrs. Flora	Mountpleasant, Rothesay	2	69 10	MacKirdy, Archibald	Rothesay	24	145 10
Croill, Thomas	Rothesay	13	140 —	MacKirdy, John	Rothesay	37	187 5
Crown, The	Whitehall, London	28	100 10	MacKirdy, Mrs. Ann	Bishop Terrace, Rothesay	2	468 5
Cumbrae Lighthouse Commissioners	Robertson St., Glasgow	2	100 —	Macnab, Rev. James	Cumbrae	9	70 —
Cumming, John	Rothesay	2	60 —	Millar, Mrs. Mary S.	Craigmore Road, Rothesay	2	77 —
				Miller, Trustees of late James	Cumbrae	1	40 —
				Mitchell, David	Montague Street, Rothesay	3	35 5
Dalrymple, Charles, of Hailes, M.P.	Ardencraig, Rothesay	33	130 10				
Duncan, Charles	Rothesay	15	387 10	Mutrie, Mary and Agnes	Bogany Road, Rothesay	1	54 —
Duncan, John, senior	Bridge St., Rothesay	2	177 15				
				Ogilvy, Walter B.	Ardentigh, Kamesburgh	1	38 —
Eglinton and Winton, Earl of	Eglinton Castle, Irvine	671	184 15	Orkney, John	Rothesay	3	1,229 15
				Orr, Robert	Rothesay	2	75 —
Fullarton, Mrs. Jane A. Bowden, of Kilmichael, wife of Menzies J. Bowden Fullarton	150 Bath Street, Glasgow	3,632	622 —	Paterson, Adam	Silverbank, Lamlash	4	34 —
				Paterson, William	Rothesay	1	170 —
				Peddie, Ellen	Mountpleasant, Rothesay	1	152 10
				Pollok, Rev. Alex.	Rothesay	1	48 —
Gibb, Mrs. Robina	Kamesburgh	4	100 —				
Glasgow, Earl of	Kelburn House, Fairlie	1,833	1,979 5	Reid, Mrs. Jessie	Cumbrae	1	129 —
Glen, Mrs. Christina	Craigmore Rd., Rothesay	2	50 —	Reid, Jessie and Georgina	Craigmore Road, Rothesay	1	70 —
Goold, Trustees of William	Ardbeg, Rothesay	2	50 —				
Graham, William, M.P.	Swanstonhill, Rothesay	16	100 —	Revie, Andrew	Rothesay	1	15 —
				Revie, John	Airdrie	2	2 10
				Rothesay, Burgh of	Rothesay	274	907 5
Hamilton, Duke of	Brodick Castle, Arran	102,210	18702 —	Do. Do.	Do. (Harbour)	6	703 —
Hamilton, Heirs of late Robert	Kames Cottage, Rothesay	2	70 —	Rothesay, Trustees of Cemetery of	Rothesay	2	15 —
Hamilton, Mrs. Jane	Ascogbank, Rothesay	5	90 —				
Harley, Andrew	Bath Street, Glasgow	1	60 —				
Heaton, Robert	Rothesay	3	554 10	Salmond, Duncan, and Co.	Rothesay	10	230 —
Herbert, William	Rothesay	1	45 —	Scoullar, Rev. John G.	Kingarth, Rothesay	14	42 —
				Sharp, Robert	Rothesay	2	654 15
				Smith, David A.	Park Terrace, Glasgow	7	65 —
Kelly, Ronald	Mountpleasant, Rothesay	1	313 —	Spencer, William	South Park, Ascog	3	90 —

BUTE—continued.

Name of Owner.	Address of Owner.	Estimated Acreage of Property.	Gross Annual Value.		Name of Owner.	Address of Owner.	Estimated Acreage of Property.	Gross Annual Value.	
		Acres.	£	s.			Acres.	£	s.
Stevenson, Henry	Craigmore Rd., Rothesay	3	116	–	Wilson, John	Rothesay	2	55	–
Stewart, Alexander B.	Langside, Glasgow	9	247	–	Wilson, John T.	Rothesay	1	30	–
Stewart, Ninian B.	Buchanan St., Glasgow	1	60	–	Wilson, Neil	Rothesay	2	32	–
Stewart, Rev. Charles	Kilmory, Arran	12	45	–					
Tait, William	Ravenscraig, Cumbrae	1	105	–	Young, Adam	Ardbeg Road, Rothesay	1	55	–
Thom, Trustees of late Robert	Ascog, Rothesay	300	672	–					
Thomson, John	Cliff Cottage, Cumbrae	1	57	10					
Thomson, Rev. Peter	North Bute, Rothesay	1	25	–	Total Owners of Land of one Acre and upwards		89	138,805	55,038	5
Thomson, Rev. Robert	Rothesay	13	98	10	Total Owners of Lands of less than one Acre in extent		648	167	31,140	1
Watson, Robert	High Craigmore, Rothesay	1	30	–	Grand Total		737	138,972	86,178	6

CAITHNESS.

Population in 1871, - - - - - - - **39,992.**
Inhabited Houses, - - - - - - - **7,474.**
Number of Parishes, - - - - - - - **10.**

Name of Owner.	Address of Owner.	Estimated Acreage of Property.	Gross Annual Value.	Name of Owner.	Address of Owner.	Estimated Acreage of Property.	Gross Annual Value.
		Acres.	£ s.			Acres.	£ s.
Adam, Thomas, of Lynegar	Lynegar, Wick	1,129	676 —	Gemmell, Rev. James	Manse of Watten, Wick	23	27 —
Anstruther, Sir Robert, of Balcaskie, Bart., M.P.	Balcaskie, Pittenweem, Fife	36,597	5,673 1	Gerry, James	Thurso	2	19 —
Do. do.	Do. (Quarries)	—	19 10	Gerry, Heirs of William	Thurso	50	82 9
				Gibson, John	Hillhead, Wick	1	23 —
				Gilbertson, Isabella	Halkirk	3	18 10
				Gordon, George M., of Swiney	Swiney, Lybster	9,072	1,355 11
Bain, James	Staxigoe, Wick	1	8 15	Grant, William	Broadhaven, Wick	1	8 —
Bain, James	Breckigoe, Wick	3	24 10	Gray, David, senior	Halkirk	3	4 5
Bain, William	Halkirk	3	5 —	Gray, David, junior	Hill of Sordale, Halkirk	2	12 10
Bain, Mrs. Janet	Thurso	2	38 —	Gray, Donald	Halkirk	2	6 15
Bain, Mary Ann	Thurso	30	100 10	Gray, Mrs. Elizabeth	Hill of Sordale, Halkirk	2	16 —
Begg, Trustees and Executors of the late David	Thurso	6	28 17	Gunn, Rev. Alexander	F.C.Manse, Watten, Wick	1	16 —
				Gunn, Trs. of late Alex.	Thurso	32	107 5
Bower, Canisbay, Dunnet, Halkirk, Olrig, Reay, Thurso, and Watten, Parochial Boards of Parishes of	Combination Poorhouse, Halkirk	5	52 10	Gunn, Donald	Staxigoe, Wick	2	20 10
				Gunn, John (shoemaker)	Halkirk	2	4 15
				Gunn, John (mason)	Halkirk	2	13 —
				Gunn, John	Reay, Thurso	1	6 15
Bremner, James	Kirkhill, Wick	2	32 10	Gunn, Mrs. Christina, and son, David	Dovecot Hall, Cockburnspath	1	17 5
Bremner, John	Newton, Wick	1	9 5	Gunn, Mrs. Margaret, of Latheron	Swiney, Lybster	1,502	709 17
Brims, James	Thurso	2	53 —				
Brims, William	Wick	1	341 10	Guthrie, Colonel Charles S., of Scotscalder	Achavarn, Thurso	13,934	2,631 11
British Fisheries Society	Wick	387	1,228 12	Do. do.	Do. (Quarries)	—	130 —
Brock, George	Greenland, Thurso	2	85 18				
Brown, Robert, of Campster	Watten, Wick	225	117 —				
Bruce, David	Wick	} 2	12 15	Hamilton, Angus	East Banks, Wick	1	22 15
and Mrs. John Mowat	Halkirk			Hamilton, Donald	Thurso	27	30 —
Buik, John H.	Wick	4	35 —	Hamilton, William	Hill of Forss, Thurso	2	73 15
				Henderson, Alexander, of Stemster	Stemster House, Halkirk Road	4,039	1,918 9
Caithness, Earl of	Barrogill Castle, Mey, Wick	14,460	4,478 14	Henderson, Alexander	Halkirk	1	3 10
Cameron, Ewan	Olrig, Thurso	2	12 —	Henderson, Trustees of late Alexander	Thurso	11	35 —
Campbell, Robert	Sandside, Reay, Thurso	1	6 —	Henderson, James, of Bilbster	Rosebank House, Wick	2,175	1,846 6
Campbell, William	Halkirk	1	4 10				
Campbell, Elizabeth	Halkirk	1	6 15	Henderson, James, of Westerdale	Westerdale, Halkirk	1,420	228 10
Campbell, Mrs. Margaret	Halkirk	2	16 —				
Clyne, Barbara	Halkirk	1	5 —	Henderson, John	Halkirk	5	15 13
Coghill, Harry	Newcastle-under-Lyne	1	18 —	Henderson, Wm. (feuar)	Halkirk	5	26 19
Cormack, Alexander	East Banks, Wick	4	165 9	Henderson, Wm. (mason)	Halkirk	3	27 12
Cormack, Francis	Pulteneytown, Wick	4	148 14	Henry, Donald	Hillieclay, Wick	1	5 11
Cormack, Heirs of John	Forse, Lybster	2	10 —	Horne, Major James, of Stirkoke	Stirkoke House, Wick	7,117	2,476 14
Coul, Mrs. Elizabeth	Louisburgh, Wick	4	18 —				
Craig, George, and Son	Thurso	21	49 10	Hossack, Charles	8 Kirk Street, Leith	1	5 10
Crawford, James	Pulteneytown, Wick	1	271 14				
Crown, The	London	9,167	2,098 9	Innes, Alexander	Halkirk	1	7 5
				Innes, James	Halkirk	2	14 10
				Innes, William	Halkirk	1	7 —
Davidson, Alexander	Newton, Wick	1	8 —	Innes, Mrs. Frederick S. Bentley, of Thrumster	Thrumster House, Wick	7,400	1,931 17
Davidson, Thomas	Ramsgoe, Wick	1	27 —				
Davidson, Mrs. Elizabeth	Staxigoe, Wick	1	10 —				
Dunbar, Sir George, of Hempriggs, Bart.	Ackergill Tower, Wick	26,880	11045 12	Jack, Alexander	Halkirk	1	3 —
Dunnet, Andrew	Halkirk	2	15 2	Jolly, Rev. Peter	Manse of Dunnet, Thurso	11	32 —
Dunnet, James	Assery, Thurso	4	23 5				
Durran, George	Thurso	1	41 10				
				Larnach, William	Halkirk	1	17 5
				Leitch, Neil	Louisburgh, Wick	3	28 10
Fergus, Rev. John	Manse of Bower, Wick	39	27 —	Leith, Mrs. Margaret	Langley Park, Wick	5	172 —
Ferryman, Augustus H.	Thurso	1	47 10	Leslie, Robert	Louisburgh, Wick	2	21 10
Flett, David	Newton, Wick	1	8 —	Levack, David	Inkerman, Wick	4	68 —
Free Church, Trustees of	Edinburgh	14	250 —	Lillie, Rev. William	Manse, Wick	38	69 10

CAITHNESS—continued.

Name of Owner.	Address of Owner.	Estimated Acreage of Property.	Gross Annual Value.	Name of Owner.	Address of Owner.	Estimated Acreage of Property.	Gross Annual Value.
		Acres.	£ s.			Acres.	£ s.
Loag, Mrs. Hugh	Wick	2	185 –	Ronaldson, John	Newton, Wick	1	6 15
Louttit, Daniel	Norland Cottage, Lybster	2	48 –	Ronaldson, William	Lybster	1	6 10
Louttit, James	Wick	4	461 –	Ross, John	Halkirk	1	12 –
Lyall, David	Papigoe, Wick	1	12 –	Ryrie, Heirs of late Stewart	Halkirk	3	19 15
MacAdie, George	Bridge Street, Wick	7	342 –	Sanderson, Agnes L.	Berwick-on-Tweed	1	27 –
M'Calman, Rev. Hugh	Manse of Latheron	18	43 10	Sanderson, Stephen	Berwick-on-Tweed	1	29 15
M'Culloch, Rev. James D.	F.C. Manse, Latheron	1	14 –	Sharp, Adam, of Clyth	Rothes, Morayshire	12,850	3,531 16
M'Donald, Heirs of Donald	Thurso	1	6 10	Do. (Quarries)	Do.	–	50 –
M'Donald, William, senior	Thurso	4	90 5	Simpson, George	Wick	1	213 –
M'Donald, Mrs. Janet	Thurso	4	49 4	Sinclair, Trustees of late Sir John, of Dunbeath, Bart.	Barrock House, Bower	6,900	2,354 17
M'Ewan, Alexander	Wick	2	153 –				
M'Ewan, Mrs. Rachel	George Street, Wick	5	18 –				
M'Gregor, George H. C. and Forbes C.	Ferintosh, Ross-shire	3	47 15	Sinclair, Sir John G. Tollemache, of Ulbster, Bart., M.P.	Thurso Castle	78,053	12833 14
M'Gregor, Rev. Roderick	F.C. Manse, Canisbay, Wick	1	14 –	Do. (Quarries)	Do.	–	1,378 –
M'Kay, Andrew	Papigoe, Wick	1	10 5	Sinclair, Sir Robert Chas., of Stevenston and Murkle, Bart.	Reay Lodge, Thurso	18,874	5,285 4
M'Kay, Donald	Thurso	3	135 –				
M'Kay, James	Thurso	96	149 18				
M'Kay, Mrs. Elizabeth	Forse, Lybster	33	23 –	Sinclair, David	Thurso	2	171 2
M'Kay, Sarah	Aimster, Thurso	1	27 –	Sinclair, James, of Forss	Forss House, Thurso	12,700	5,117 14
M'Kay, Mrs. Williamina	Halkirk	1	8 –	Do. do. (Quarries)	Do.	–	492 –
M'Kenzie, Jane	Milton, Wick	1	8 7	Sinclair, James	Halkirk	1	8 –
M'Lean, Rev. Alex.	Manse of Halkirk	7	29 –	Sinclair, Heirs of James	Wick	1	6 –
M'Leod, Donald	Halkirk	1	5 –	Sinclair, Mrs. Barbara Thomson, of Freswick	Dunbeath Castle	57,757	6,207 3
M'Leod, Mrs. Ann	Halkirk	2	9 –				
M'Pherson, Executors of late Innes	Moray St., Pulteneytown	4	33 5	Do. do. (Quarries)	Do.	–	27 15
M'Pherson, Rev. James	Manse of Canisbay	28	30 –	Sinclair, Mrs. Janet	High Street, Wick	1	44 –
M'Pherson, William	Halkirk	2	6 10	Sinclair, Trustees of late Janet, of Freswick; and A. Hamilton Ferryman	Thurso	2,373	911 3
Malcolm, Trustees of late Donald	Pulteneytown, Wick	5	10 11				
Manson, Alexander	Wick	1	50 10	Sinclair, Jessie C.	Pulteneytown	3	15 –
Manson, David	Calder, Halkirk	1	4 15	Smith, Hector W. P.	Australia	3	124 11
Manson, Representatives of late Mrs. Fanny	Halkirk	2	8 10	Smith, James, of Olrig	Olrig House, Thurso	2,734	2,274 19
				Do. do. (Quarries)	Do.	–	50 –
Manson, Mrs. Janet	Newton, Wick	1	8 –	Smith, John	Thurso	2	155 9
Matheson, Evander	Shebster, Thurso	3	2 10	Smith, Thomas	Bardnaclavan, Thurso	1	5 5
Meiklejohn, Donald	Halkirk	1	10 –	Steven, George	Louisburgh, Wick	1	14 –
Meiklejohn, James	Newlands of Geise, Thurso	2	10 –	Steven, James (carter)	Halkirk	1	11 12
Miller, Rev. John S.	The Manse, Thurso	16	63 –	Steven, James (grocer)	Halkirk	1	6 5
Miller, William	Bellevue, Wick	2	28 –	Steven, Mrs. Fanny	Halkirk	1	4 15
Miller, Trustees of late George	Tister, Watten	300	70 –	Stewart, Mrs. Catherine	Louisburgh, Wick	2	54 –
				Stewart, Williamina	Halkirk	2	9 15
Miller, Mrs. Elizabeth	Louisburgh, Wick	1	23 15	Stobie, Rev. Robert	Manse of Keiss, Wick	1	13 –
Mitchell, John	Halkirk	3	5 –	Stocks, Major Michael, of Latheronwheel	Latheronwheel House	13,600	1,744 1
Mowat, William	Halkirk	1	6 5				
Munro, Rev. Donald	F.C. Manse, Shebster, Thurso	2	10 –	Strong, Leonard, of Camster	Camster Cottage, Lybster	4,337	300 –
				Sutherland, Alexander	Halkirk	1	13 –
Murray, Heirs of Benjamin	Melvich, Thurso	7	28 2	Sutherland, Geo., of Forse	Forse House, Lybster	8,000	2,482 4
				Sutherland, James	Reay, Thurso	1	10 –
Murray, Rev. James	Manse, Reay, Thurso	89	46 –	Sutherland, John	Halkirk	2	4 –
Murray, James	Thurso	1	51 10	Sutherland, John	Greenigoe, Wick	2	30 10
Murray, Christina	Halkirk	1	10 17	Sutherland, John M.	Wick	1	10 –
				Sutherland, William	Thurso	1	301 15
				Sutherland, William	Milton, Wick	1	11 –
Northern Lighthouses, Commissioners of	Edinburgh	101	116 –	Sutherland, Janet, jun.	Halkirk	1	8 –
				Sutherland and Caithness Railway Company	Inverness (Railway)	281	Under construction.
				Swanson, John	Thurso	37	93 8
Oag, Alexander	Oag's Lane, Wick	1	52 10	Do.	Do. (Quarries)	–	30 –
Oag, Margaret	Oag's Lane, Wick	2	220 –	Swanson, John	Louisburgh, Wick	1	35 12
Oman, James, junior	Papigoe, Wick	1	4 10	Swanson, William	Weydale, Thurso	2	25 1
Paul, David	Buckies, Thurso	1	7 10	Tait, Donald	Halkirk	3	16 10
Phimister, Mrs. John	Louisburgh, Wick	1	18 –	Tait, John	East Banks, Wick	1	46 10
Phin, Rev. William	Olrig Manse, Thurso	15	37 15	Tait, William Reid	Mina Villa, Thurso	7	41 14
Portland, Duke of	Langwell, Berriedale	81,605	7,902 8	Taylor, John	America	1	2 –
				Taylor, Joshua	Thurso	1	52 15
				Taylor, Rev. Walter R.	Castlegreen, Thurso	1	28 –
Quoys, John	Wick	1	82 10	Taylor, William	Halkirk	3	10 10
				Threipland, Sir Patrick Murray, of Fingask and Toftingall, Bart.	Fingask Castle, Errol, Perthshire	10,942	2,077 17
Rae, Mrs. Margaret	Wick	1	10 10				
Rae, Thomas	Borlum, Reay, Thurso	1	20 15	Do. do. (Quarries)	Do.	–	118 –
Rae, William	Wick	1	278 6	Thurso, Magistrates of	Thurso	3	13 –
Reiach, John	Staxigoe, Wick	1	4 10	Thurso, Parochial Board of	Thurso	5	34 –

CAITHNESS—continued.

Name of Owner	Address of Owner.	Estimated Acreage of Property.	Gross Annual Value.	Name of Owner.	Address of Owner.	Estimated Acreage of Property.	Gross Annual Value.
		Acres.	£ s.			Acres.	£ s.
Traill, Trustees of late George, of Ratter	Thurso	15,263	7,981 18	Wick and Latheron, Parochial Boards of	Combination Poorhouse, Latheron	5	28 —
Do. do.	Do. (Quarries)	—	1,713 —	Wick Harbour Trustees	Wick (Harbour)	13	3,850 —
Traill, Margaret, of Ratter	Castlehill, Thurso	50	62 10	Williamson, Trustees of James, of Banniskirk	Thurso	1,375	697 8
				Do. do.	Do. (Quarries)	—	150 —
				Williamson, Curator for William	Rugie, Halkirk	1	5 —
Waters, Donald	Staxigoe, Wick	3	27 15	Wright, Mrs. Susan	Thurso	1	34 10
Waters, Mrs. Elizabeth	Halkirk	1	5 10				
Waters, Mrs. Mary	Dundalk, Ireland	1	14 10				
Weir, Mrs. Christina	Halkirk	1	6 10	Total Owners of Land of One Acre and upwards		221	471,584	118,193 19
Wemyss, David Sinclair, of Southdun	Ackergill Tower, Wick	7,000	1,636 8	Total Owners of Lands of less than One Acre in extent		809	179	18,691 14
Wick, Burgh of	Wick	6	67 5				
Wick and Pulteneytown Rope Company	Wick	3	45 10	GRAND TOTAL		1,030	471,763	136,885 13
Wick, Parochial Board of	Wick	13	24 —				

CLACKMANNAN.

Population in 1871, — 23,747.
Inhabited Houses, — 3,316.
Number of Parishes, — 6.

Name of Owner.	Address of Owner.	Estimated Acreage of Property.	Gross Annual Value.
		Acres.	£ s.
Abercromby, Lord	Airthrey Castle, Stirling	3,707	5,199 19
Alloa Harbour Trustees	Alloa (Harbour)	3	571 —
Alloa Gas Company	Alloa	2	288 —
Archibald, James	Beechwood, Tillicoultry	2	80 —
Archibald, John	Banchory, Tullibody	11	22 —
Archibald, Robert, & Sons	Tillicoultry	2	263 —
Arrol, Archibald	Alloa	5	492 —
Bald, John, & Co.	Alloa	17	1,165 5
Blair, James, of Glenfoot	Glenfoot, Tillicoultry	81	227 —
Bruce, John	London	4	23 —
Bryson, Rev. Alex.	The Manse, Alloa	14	130 2
Buchanan, John, of Powis	Powis, Stirling	296	750 10
Burleigh, Lord	Kennet Ho., Clackmannan	943	2,003 11
Do.	Do. (Coal)	—	904 5
Burn, Trs. of Ebenezer W.	Stirling	34	160 —
Calder, James	Alloa	2	478 —
Campbell, Jas. & Geo.	Holehead, Stirling	26	104 12
Campbell, Trustees of John	Cambus	4	19 —
Cameron, Margaret	Clackmannan	6	45 —
Carmichael, William, Robert, & John	Alloa	36	110 10
Christie, James, of Hillend	Hillend, Clackmannan	276	202 10
Clark, James	Clackmannan	11	108 —
Clark, William Bennet	Marshill, Alloa	1	80 —
Cowane's Hospital, Patrons of	Stirling	260	885 12
Devon Valley Railway Co.	Tillicoultry (Railway)	38	516 —
Dickie, Mrs. Isabella	Kincardine-on-Forth	3	10 —
Dickson, Mrs. Jeanette Helen	Greenfield, Alloa	9	90 —
Dollar Institution, Trustees of	Dollar	20	668 —
Drummond, Rev. Jas.	Clackmannan	2	23 10
Drysdale, Alexander	Devonside, Tillicoultry	3	277 15
Duncanson, John	The Walk, Alloa	3	224 —
Duncanson, Trs. of Mrs. Catherine	Alloa	35	107 10
Fraser, Donald	Clackmannan	1	17 —
Gibson, Sarah	Devonside, Tillicoultry	4	18 2
Gilchrist, Rev. John	The Manse, Clackmannan	6	40 10
Greig, John	Bridgend, Tullibody	66	202 —
Gunn, Rev. Angus	The Manse, Dollar	6	53 —
Haig, William James, of Dollarfield	Dollarfield, Dollar	331	792 5
Harrower, Catherine, and others	Dunfermline	12	63 9
Johnstone, James, of Alva	Alva House, Alva	1,587	721 —
Johnstone, James	Alloa	5	444 10
Kellie, Earl of	Alloa Park	6,163	8,256 15
Do.	Do. (Coal)	—	1,260 —
Knox, Robert, & Sons	Cambus	5	230 10

Name of Owner.	Address of Owner.	Estimated Acreage of Property.	Gross Annual Value.
		Acres.	£ s.
Lambert, Mrs. Mary Ann Archibald	Gaberston, Alloa	4	404 10
Leishman, James	Broomrigg, Dollar	3	478 18
Mackie, Alexander	Alloa	3	24 10
M'Laren, David	Bridge of Allan	3	75 —
M'Laren, John	Alloa	4	168 5
M'Nab, Alexander	Glenochil, Menstry, Stirling	77	803 10
Malcolm, Mrs. Jane, and James Syme	Dollar	10	50 —
Mansfield, Earl of	Schaw Park, Clackmannan	1,705	1,751 —
Do.	Do. (Coal)	—	1,866 9
Mathie, Margaret	Dollar	5	14 —
Meiklejohn, John	Coalsnaughton	1	138 17
Meiklejohn & Son	Alloa	3	160 —
Melvin, John	Alloa	5	866 10
Miller, John, of Sheardale	13 York Pl., Edinburgh	158	307 10
Mitchell, Andrew	Alloa	3	122 10
Mitchell & Mowbray	Alloa	43	589 10
Moir, Archibald	Alloa	5	72 —
Moir, James	Alloa	1	3 10
Moir, John M'Arthur, of Hillfoot	Hillfoot, Dollar	637	420 15
Mowbray, Robert	Cambus	76	640 11
Murray, Trs. of Robert, of Dollarbeg	Dollarbeg, Dollar	480	455 —
North British Railway Co.	Edinburgh (Railway)	152	6,582 —
Orr, Sir Andrew, of Harviestoun, Kt.	Harviestoun Castle, Dollar	4,726	3,912 15
Do. do.	Do. (Coal)	—	100 —
Paterson, Andrew, & Sons	Tullibody	2	158 10
Paton, John	Westbourne, Tillicoultry	2	80 —
Paton, John, Son, & Co.	Kilncraigs, Alloa	3	1,031 2
Paton, Catharine	Cowden, Alloa	3	90 —
Ramsay, Robert Balfour Wardlaw, of Tillicoultry	Whitehill, Lasswade	4,147	2,429 15
Do. do.	Do. (Coal)	—	1,000 —
Rennie, Mrs. Mary	Gowanbank, Falkirk	47	115 —
Robertson, Mrs. Helen	Stirling	7	50 —
Scottish Pulp and Fibre Company	Edinburgh	35	545 10
Shand, Geo., & others	Causewayhead, Stirling	9	63 —
Smeaton, David	Clackmannan	2	26 —
Smith, Rev. David	The Manse, Tillicoultry	13	88 —
Steuart, Trustees of Alex. Seton	Touch, Stirling	5	327 —
Stevenson, Mrs. Isabella	Edinburgh	5	60 —
Stirling, Mrs. Mary Wedderburn Morries, of Northfield and Garnel	9 South Eaton Place, London	578	1,364 10

CLACKMANNAN—continued.

Name of Owner.	Address of Owner.	Estimated Acreage of Property.	Gross Annual Value.		Name of Owner.	Address of Owner.	Estimated Acreage of Property.	Gross Annual Value.	
		Acres.	£	s.			Acres.	£	s.
Thomson, Andrew	Alloa	4	206	10	Younger, George, & Sons	Alloa	2	782	10
Thomson Brothers	Alloa	3	728	9					
Thomson, John F.	Alloa	3	65	—	Zetland, Earl of	Kerse House	2,726	3,272	10
Thomson, Watson	Alloa	2	65	—	Do.	Do. (*Coal*)	—	2,635	—
Tillicoultry, Heritors of Parish of	Tillicoultry	4	62	—	Total Owners of Land of One Acre and upwards		90		
Walker, Robert	Devonside, Tillicoultry	4	342	10				29,864	64,428	4
Wallace & Knox	Cambus	1	144	6	Total Owners of Lands of less than One Acre in extent		1,137	325	33,054	2
White, George	Clackmannan	3	20	—						
White, James	Meadowend, Clackmannan	3	20	—	GRAND TOTAL		1,227	30,189	97,482	6
Wright, William, of Broom	Stirling	105	320	—						

CROMARTY.

Population in 1871, - - - - - - - **3,362.**
Inhabited Houses, - - - - - - - **685.**
Number of Parishes, - - - - - - - **2.**

Name of Owner.	Address of Owner.	Estimated Acreage of Property.	Gross Annual Value.	Name of Owner.	Address of Owner.	Estimated Acreage of Property.	Gross Annual Value.
		Acres.	£ s.			Acres.	£ s.
Archie, Alexander	Cromarty	4	35 —	Munro, George M. G., of Poyntzfield	Poyntzfield House, Invergordon	1,776	1,870 15
Fletcher, James, of Rosehaugh	Rosehaugh House, Inverness	880	105 —	Noble, Hugh, of Gordonsmill	Gordonsmill, Invergordon	43	46 —
Fraser, Tutors of Hugh Kenneth, of Braelangwell	Cromarty	820	505 —	Resolis Parish, Heritors of	Resolis, Invergordon	2	1 10
Graham, Alexander G.	Cromarty	2	70 10	Ross, Colonel George W. H., of Cromarty	Cromarty House, Cromarty	7,437	5,348 5
				Ross, Robert	Cromarty	5	82 17
				Russel, Rev. George	Manse, Cromarty	14	49 —
Macdougall, Rev. Robert	Manse, Resolis, Invergordon	49	50 —				
Mackenzie, Colin Lyon, of St. Martins	Inverness	191	151 —	Total Owners of Land of one Acre and upwards 14		18,184	10,268 1
Mackenzie, John A. Shaw, of Newhall	Newhall House, Invergordon	6,590	2,203 4	Total Owners of Lands of less than one Acre in extent 217		22	1,696 7
Mackenzie, William Ord, of Culbo	Culbo, Invergordon	371	250 —	GRAND TOTAL . . . 231		18,206	11,964 8

DUMBARTON.

Population in 1871, — 58,857.
Inhabited Houses, — 7,638.
Number of Parishes, — 12.

Name of Owner.	Address of Owner.	Estimated Acreage of Property.	Gross Annual Value.	Name of Owner.	Address of Owner.	Estimated Acreage of Property.	Gross Annual Value.
		Acres.	£ s.			Acres.	£ s.
Abercromby, Alex. A.	Craigrownie House, Cove	5	140 —	Borland, John C.	Garelochhead	1	36 —
Aitken, Barton	Kipperoch, Dumbarton	356	403 —	*Bowling Club*	Helensburgh	2	40 —
Aitken, George	New Kilpatrick	2	52 —	Boyd, Heirs of George	Renfrew	2	208 —
Aitken, James	Langlands, Cumbernauld	7	24 —	Boyd, Mrs. Agnes	Comely Park St., Glasgow	12	98 5
Aitken, John	Succoth, Dumbarton	172	510 —	Breingan, Alexander	Helensburgh	4	412 10
Alexander, Alexander J., of Airdrie House	Airdrie House, Airdrie	431	849 10	*British Sea-Weed Co.*	Whitecrook, Yoker	12	671 10
				Brock, William	Millig Toll, Helensburgh	1	4 —
Do. do.	Do. (*Minerals and Way-leave*)	—	527 10	Brown, Alexander	Helensburgh	1	255 —
				Brown, Alexander	Greenock	2	60 —
Alexander, Henry	Woodside Lodge, Cove	2	80 —	Brown, Alexander	Charleston, Alexandria	2	95 10
Alexander, James	Queen St., Helensburgh	1	100 —	Brown, A. J. D., of Balloch Castle	Balloch Castle, Balloch	893	1,274 —
Alexander, Mrs. Christina	Cowgate, Kirkintilloch	1	95 —				
Allan, William, and others	Kirkintilloch	9	108 15	Brown, John	Helensburgh	1	95 —
Anderson, David	Knockderry House, Cove	6	115 —	Brown, Trustees of John	Dumbarton	1	222 —
Anderson, John	James St., Helensburgh	2	115 —	Brown, Robert	Millig Road, Helensburgh	1	90 —
Anderson, William	New Kilpatrick	5	125 6	Brown, Robert Bennett	Bendarroch, Garelochhead	10	130 —
Anderson, Christina	Helensburgh	1	32 —				
Andrews, John F.	1 Prince's Sq., Glasgow	1	16 —	Brown, Mrs. Mary	Oxgang, Kirkintilloch	158	466 10
Angus, George	Helensburgh	1	16 —	Brownlie, Thomas	Edinburgh	9	22 —
Angus, Ritchie	56 Hope St., Glasgow	3	110 —	Bryce, John	Braehead, Bonhill	1	100 10
Arbuckle, Matthew	7 Grey Place, Greenock	2	217 —	Buchanan, Andrew, of Auchintorlie	Auchintorlie, Bowling	2,014	2,820 10
Argyll, Duke of	Roseneath Castle, Roseneath	6,799	5,170 18	Buchanan, Colonel D. C. R. C., of Drumpellier	Drumpellier House, Coatbridge	97	140
Armstrong, William J.	New Kilpatrick	2	90 —	Buchanan, Gilbert	Kirkintilloch	1	21
Arnott, Brothers, & Co.	Whitehill, Kirkintilloch	13	60 —	Buchanan, John	Dam, Kilmaronock	135	160 —
Arrochar, Heritors of Parish of	Arrochar	9	68 —	Buchanan, Robert	Cardross	4	25 —
Auchterlonie, Thomas D.	Westermains, Kirkintilloch	1	45 —	Buchanan, Heirs of Robert	Knoxland, Dumbarton	11	81 —
				Buchanan, William	Croftfoot, Kilmaronock	126	78 —
				Bunten, Robert	Kilmaronock	3	47 —
Babtie, William	Kirkton, Dumbarton	1	60 —	Burns, George	Dumbarton	3	560 —
Babtie, William and John	Dumbarton	8	30 —	Burns, John William, of Kilmahew	Kilmahew, Cardross	1,670	3,393 10
Bain, Mrs. Jane	Helensburgh	1	55 —				
Baird, William, & Co.	Gartsherrie	460	1,278 —	Burtis, Mrs. Elizabeth	America	2	7 —
Baker, Richard	17 Tobago St., Glasgow	38	80 —	Butt, Edward	Helensburgh	1	85 —
Bannerman, Walter	Glasgow	142	174 —				
Barlas, William	Alexandria	1	210 —	Caird, Edward	Finnart, Garelochhead	79	200 —
Barony Parish, Parochial Board of	Glasgow	168	216 —	Callen, Mrs. Agnes	Dumbarton	3	273 —
				Caldwell, James	Auchingare, Row	8	105 —
Do. do.	Do. (*Quarry*)	—	800 —	*Caledonian Railway Co.*	Glasgow	150	166 10
Barr, James	Clydeside, Uddingstone	9	50 —	Do. do.	Do. (*Railway*)	46	22454 —
Barr, John	Ardrossan	1	15 —	Do. do.	Do. (*Canal*)	195	*
Barr, Trustees of Thomas	West George Street, Glasgow	5	53 —	Cameron & Roberton	Canal Bank, Kirkintilloch	5	240 —
				Campbell, Alexander	Garelochhead	1	50 —
Barr, Mrs. Anne	Carnarvon St., Glasgow	154	244 5	Campbell, Archibald	7 Steven Street, Glasgow	1	44 —
Barry, William	Airdrie	469	175 —	Campbell, Arthur	22 Dublin St., Edinburgh	380	437 15
Bartholomew, Representatives of Robert	1 Dundas Street, Glasgow	78	255 —	Campbell, Charles	Warrambeen, Craigrownie	3	60 —
Beattie, John	Helensburgh	2	45 —	Campbell, Colin, of Camieseskan	Camieseskan, Cardross	2,124	2,419 —
Bell, John	Clydeview, Dumbarton	2	564 —				
Biggart, Robert, & Co.	Milton, Bowling	2	350 —	Campbell, Sir George, of Succoth, Bart.	Garscube House, Maryhill, Glasgow	2,395	2,767 15
Bird, Gregory	Grafton Lodge, Cove	2	80 —	Do. do.	Do. (*Quarry*)	—	933 1
Birkmyre, Mrs. Margaret	Dumbarton	3	89 —	Do. do.	Do. (*Minerals*)	—	2,554 14
Black, James	Glenarbuck, Bowling	615	774 15	Campbell, Hugh	Crossewan, Roseneath	2	8 —
Black, James, & Co.	Dalmonach, Bonhill	70	1,491 10	Campbell, James, junior, of Tillichewan	Tillichewan Castle, Alexandria	1,112	1,820 15
Black, John	Anderston Quay, Glasgow	2	64 —				
Blackie, Robert	36 Frederick St., Glasgow	4	90 —	Campbell, J. D., of Peaton	Clachan, Roseneath	710	350 —
Blair, Alexander and Jane	France, Kilmaronock	20	20 —	Campbell, Malcolm	Roseneath	1	25 —
Blantyre, Lord	Erskine, Paisley	2,946	3,435 10	Campbell, Neil Colquhoun, of Barnhill	81 Great King Street, Edinburgh	150	236 —
Bonhill, Heritors of Parish of	Bonhill	7	50 —	Campbell, Peter	Garelochhead	1	91 —
				Campbell, Robert Orr	London	14	148 —
Bontine, William C. Graham, of Ardoch	Gartmore, Stirling	1,940	2,561 10	Campbell, William	Annfield Terrace, Partick	1	92 5
Do. do.	Do. (*Quarry*)	—	100 —	Campbell, Elizabeth	St. George's Road, Glasgow	1	68 —
Bontine, Mrs. Margaret	Back Street, Renton	1	29 —				

* Value included in Railway Valuation.

DUMBARTON—continued.

Name of Owner.	Address of Owner.	Estimated Acreage of Property.	Gross Annual Value.	Name of Owner.	Address of Owner.	Estimated Acreage of Property.	Gross Annual Value.
		Acres.	£ s.			Acres.	£ s.
Carnachan, Gordon	Alexandria	1	199 15	Denny & Company	High Street, Dumbarton	3	680 —
Carron Company	Falkirk	759	765 3	*Dennystoun Forge Co.*	Dumbarton	4	500 —
Carson, Samuel	Cove	1	208 —	Dick, Alexander	Queen St., Helensburgh	1	110 —
Carss, John	New Kilpatrick	3	93 —	Dick, Matthew	75 Hill Street, Glasgow	264	260 —
Caven, Rev. James	Kirkintilloch	11	61 —	Dickie, James	Yoker	3	7 —
Caw, David	86 Wilson St., Glasgow	3	24 —	Dickie, Trs. of Robert	Helensburgh	1	121 —
Cemetery Company	Helensburgh	3	16 —	Dismor, James Stewart	42 Windmill Street, Gravesend	1	55 —
Chalmers, Archibald	Clynder, Roseneath	5	351 —	Dixon, Robert	Dumbarton	64	254 —
Clark, Robert	Ivyhill, Kilcreggan	3	245 —	Do.	Do. (*Quarries*)	—	240 15
Clark, Robert	Greenbank, Arrochar	2	87 —	Dixon, Mrs. Marion	Glasgow	2	90 —
Clyde Navigation, Trs. of	Glasgow	8	1,100 —	Dodds, James	Arrochar	1	56 —
Do. (*Bowling Harbour*)	Do.	12	500 —	Donald, William M'Alister, of Lylestone	Argyll St., Helensburgh	531	637 10
Cochrane, Archibald	Shandon Row	1	29 —	Donaldson, Alexander	Heathfield, Kilcreggan	3	95 —
Cochrane, James	Duntyblae, Kirkintilloch	10	100 4	Donaldson, James, of Keppoch	Keppoch, Cardross	417	429 10
Colquhoun, Henry	Helensburgh	1	34 —	Donaldson, Robert	Woodbine, Kilcreggan	2	87 —
Colquhoun, Sir James, of that Ilk, and of Luss, Bart.	Rossdhu, Luss	67,041	12845 10	Douglas, Archibald C., of Mains	Mains, New Kilpatrick	1,284	1,368 10
Do. do.	Do. (*Quarries*)	—	97 —	Do. do.	Do. (*Minerals*)	—	324 —
Colquhoun, Rev. J. E. C., of Killermont	Killermont House, Maryhill	2,019	4,555 6	Douglas, George	Hardgate, Duntocher	8	24 —
Do. do.	Do. (*Minerals*)	—	2,072 2	Douglas, George & James	Duntocher	2	69 15
Do. do.	Do. (*Quarries*)	—	19 5	Douglas, William M'A.	Glasgow	71	185 —
Colquhoun, Robert	Helensburgh	1	35 —	Do. do.	Do. (*Minerals*)	—	5 —
Colquhoun, Trustees of Thomas	Helensburgh	3	225 —	Downie, James	Northbank, Kirkintilloch	4	10 15
Colquhoun, Trustees of Mrs. Elizabeth	Edinburgh	112	130 —	Drew, Peter	Ardencaple, Row	2	85 —
Do. do.	Do. (*Minerals*)	—	313 6	Drummond, Jane Catherine	Glenmallen, Garelochhead	6	59 —
Colquhoun, Mrs. Jean, and others	Alexandria	1	103 10	Drysdale, Arch. Browning	Helensburgh	1	80 —
Combination Poorhouse Commissioners	Dumbarton	3	250 —	Drysdale, William	Helensburgh	2	170 —
Commissioners of Supply	Dumbarton	2	217 —	*Dumbarton, Burgh of*	Dumbarton	2	675 —
Comrie, Thomas	Old Kilpatrick	2	215 15	*Dumbarton Free Church Congregation*	Dumbarton	2	45 —
Connall, William	Hillfoot	20	180 —	*Dumbarton Gas Company*	Dumbarton	3	897 —
Cooper, Mrs. Margaret	Overcroy	33	58 10	*Dumbarton Harbour Commissioners*	Dumbarton (*Harbour*)	36	250 —
Do. do.	Do. (*Minerals*)	—	23 12	*Dumbarton Water Commissioners*	Dumbarton	19	295 —
Corbett, Thomas	85 Gracechurch Street, London	5	105 —	Duncan, James	Glasgow	28	90 —
Corbett, Marianne	Millbrae, Helensburgh	33	75 —	Duncan, James	Tweichar, Kirkintilloch	123	153 2
Do.	Do. (*Minerals*)	—	60 —	Do.	Do. (*Minerals*)	—	404 16
Couper, William	Woodstone, Row	8	182 —	Duncan, James	Auchinbee, Cumbernauld	156	131 10
Couper, William and Charles	Woodstone, Row	2	130 —	Duncan, John	Gushetfaulds, Glasgow	32	54 —
Cove and Kilcreggan Gas Company	Glasgow	3	40 —	Duncan, John	Newbigging, Carnock, Dunfermline	134	170 —
Cowan, John Bell	Shandon	2	135 —	Duncan, Reps. of John	Glasgow	153	294 5
Craig, William	Dumbarton	3	250 —	Do. do.	Do. (*Minerals*)	—	140 —
Craigrownie Church Trustees	Craigrownie	2	45 —	Duncan, John T.	Lucern Villa, Cove	1	70 —
Crawford, William	Garelochhead	2	50 —	Duncan, George	Auchindavie, Kirkintilloch	50	90 —
Cree, Alexander & R. T.	Rahane, Roseneath	1	50 —	Dundas, Margaret, Mary, and Elizabeth	Row	1	52 —
Crown, The	(*Crown Property*)	10	235 —	Dunlop, Alex. Murray, of Edinbarnet	Edinburgh	1,364	922 —
Cruickshanks, James	Hazlewood, Kilcreggan	1	113 —	Dunlop, John	60 George St., Glasgow	50	60 —
Cruickshanks, Mrs. Margaret	3 Apsley Place, Glasgow	2	121 —	Dunlop, Robert	Helensburgh	2	183 —
Crum, William G.	Mere Old Hall, Knutsford, Cheshire	3	80 —	Dunlop, Robert B., of Drumhead	Park House, Sutton, Surrey	178	534 —
Cunningham, James	West Arthurlie, Barrhead	129	150 —	Dunn, Trs. of Alexander	Glasgow	41	2,400 —
				Do. do.	Do. (*Quarry*)	—	1 10
Dalglish, Robert, M.P.	Kilmardinny, New Kilpatrick	112	440 —	Dunn, Rev. William	Cardross	9	60 —
Dalglish, Jane	Torwood, Row	1	60 —	Dymock, Mrs. Eliza	Kilcreggan	1	85 —
Dalrymple, James, of Woodhead	Woodhead, Kirkintilloch	316	551 17				
Davidson, Thomas	Craigend, Cardross	2	70 —	Eadie, John	Lenzie	2	8 —
Dennistoun, Alexander	Lagarie, Row	6	160 —	Edmiston, Helen and Eliza	Glasgow	1	56 —
Dennistoun, Alexander, junior	Roslea, Row	3	110 —	Edmond, William and Robert	Croftamie, Drymen	12	111 —
Dennistoun, Mrs. Constance Mary	Armadale, Row	6	160 —	*Episcopal Church Trustees*	Dalreoch	1	35 —
Dennistoun, Margaret, Mary, Elizabeth, and Camilla	Auchinlea, Row	1	105 —	Ewing, Archibald Orr, of Ballinkinrain, Stirlingshire, and Lennoxbank, Dumbartonshire, M.P.	Ballinkinrain, Stirlingshire, and Levenbank, Bonhill	201	4,320 5
Denny, Heirs of James	Dumbarton	3	90 —	Do. do.	Do. (*Quarry*)	—	20 —
Denny, John	Dumbarton	5	58 —	Ewing, Humphrey E. Crum, of Strathleven, M.P.	Ardencaple Castle, Row	231	50 —
Denny, Peter	Helenslee, Dumbarton	43	2,014 —				
Denny, Trustees of Peter	Dumbarton	79	422 —				
Denny, Heirs of William	Glasgow	36	1,923 —	Do. do.	Do. (*Quarry*)	—	60 —

DUMBARTON—continued.

Name of Owner.	Address of Owner.	Estimated Acreage of Property.	Gross Annual Value.
		Acres.	£ s.
Ewing, John	3 Strathleven Place, Dumbarton	2	25 —
Ewing, John Orr, & Co.	Alexandria	45	2,030 10
Ewing, Mrs. Jane T.	Strathleven, Dumbarton	9,180	3,623 10
Ewing, Mary	Townend, Dumbarton	1	10 —
Faill, A. & J.	Craigpark, Duke Street, Glasgow	197	210 16
Do.	Do. (*Quarry*)	—	50 —
Farquhar, John	62 Hope St., Glasgow	2	80 —
Fergus, Andrew	Glasgow	1	95 —
Fergus, Walter	Largs	1	14 —
Ferguson, Archibald	Dumbarton	1	202 —
Ferguson, R. & J.	127 Cambridge Street, Glasgow	3	4 —
Ferrier, James	Croy	1	30 —
Filshie, James	Mount Pleasant, Kilpatrick	2	203 —
Findlay, Charles B.	Boturich Castle, Kilmaronock	1,046	1,037 10
Findlay, David	Barleybank, Kirkintilloch	3	111 10
Findlay, Colonel John, of Boturich	Boturich Castle, Kilmaronock	265	103 —
Finlay, James	Millbrae House, Helensburgh	2	145 —
Finlay, John	Auchnacloich, Garelochside	3	100 —
Finlay, Martha	Holm Cottage, Kirkintilloch	22	78 —
Fisher, Peter	Glasgow	3	20 —
Fisken, Archibald	Helensburgh	1	75 —
Fleming, Hon. Cornwallis, of Cumbernauld House	Edinburgh	3,520	3,477 5
Do. do.	Do. (*Minerals*)	—	1,181 14
Fleming, James S.	Royal Bank, Edinburgh	5	13 —
Flemyng, Rev. Francis P.	Lenzie, Glasgow	6	135 —
Fletcher, Nicol B.	Ardoch, Cardross	1	25 —
Foote, Agnes	Helensburgh	4	122 10
Forbes, William, of Callander	Callander House, Falkirk	199	30 —
Forsyth, David	Kirkintilloch	8	60 —
Forth & Clyde Railway Co.	Glasgow (*Railway*)	83	1,616 —
Fraser, Alexander	Denniston, Glasgow	1	21 —
Fraser, John	43 Argyle St., Glasgow	12	180 —
Fraser, Mrs. Janet	Helensburgh	1	210 —
Freeland, Alexander B.	Glasgow	107	225 —
Freeland, Agnes	Kirkintilloch	2	133 5
Frew, John	Helensburgh	1	59 —
Fyfe, Mrs. Margaret	Condorrat, Cumbernauld	1	21 —
Galbraith, David	45 Whitevale Street, Glasgow	2	59 —
Galbraith, James, of Townfoot	Gartochraggan, Kilmaronock	150	189 —
Galloway, George	East King Street, Helensburgh	1	16 —
Galloway, John, & others	Kirkintilloch	9	180 15
Gardner, James, & Sons	Kirkintilloch	100	255 —
Do. do.	Do. (*Minerals*)	—	250 —
Gardner, John	Nether Shannachhill, Port-of-Menteith	7	17 —
Gardner, John	Aber, Kilmaronock	15	23 10
Gardner, Robert	New Kilpatrick	1	40 —
Gartshore, James	Waterside, Kirkintilloch	2	15 —
Gas Company	Glasgow	27	405 —
Geils, John Edward, of Dumbuck	Dumbuck, Bowling	655	1,199 10
Do. do.	Do. (*Quarry*)	—	10 —
Geils, Mrs. Euphemia J.	Ardarden, Cardross	176	578 —
Geils, Charlotte E. E.	Ardarden, Cardross	235	413 10
Gibb, Trustees of Robert	Glasgow	64	100 10
Gilchrist, Archibald	Kirkintilloch	13	267 —
Gilchrist, George B.	Kirkintilloch	5	13 —
Gilmour, Alexander	Garelochhead	1	25 —
Gilmour, John	Mount Vernon, Row	7	150 —
Gilmour, Mrs. Elizabeth	Havelock Street, Helensburgh	1	80 —
Glasgow Corporation	Glasgow (*Water Works*)	—	1,607 —
Glasgow, Earl of	Kelburne Castle, Ayrshire	175	359 —
Do. do.	Do. (*Minerals*)	—	4,205 6
Glen, Mrs. Beatrice	Bankend, Dumbarton	1	18 —
Goodwin, John	Back o' Loch, Kirkintilloch	25	81 10
Gordon, Mrs. Agnes M.	Scapesland, Dumbarton	1	50 —
Gordon, Trs. of Agnes	Cove	1	70 —
Gorebooth, Mrs. Isabella	Helensburgh	5	222 —
Gourlie, James	Ardconnell, Row	14	181 5
Govan, Mary	Bankend, Dumbarton	1	29 —
Gow, James	Drumbog, Drymen	3	21 —
Gow, John	Waterside, Kirkintilloch	22	50 10
Gow, Mrs. Bridget S.	Kilcreggan	1	115 —
Gow, Mrs. Isabella	Helensburgh	1	96 —
Graham, Alexander	Ardoch, Cardross	2	75 —
Graham, Trustees of Alex.	Milngavie	2	67 10
Graham, David	Duntyblae, Kirkintilloch	2	17 15
Graham, Heirs of Robert	Claremont Cottage, Alloa	1	93 —
Gray, James	Glasgow	2	8 —
Grindlay, Representatives of Charles	Denny	1	89 10
Grozier & Martin	Kirkintilloch	1	30 15
Hall, William	Dubside, Cumbernauld	1	5 —
Hamilton, John Buchanan, of Leny	Leny, Callander	150	220 —
Hamilton, Trustees of John George	Lagarie, Row	26	208 —
Hamilton, Matthew	8 Royal Parade, Cheltenham	1	140 —
Hamilton, John and David	Glasgow	68	110 —
Hamilton, Mrs. Margaret	Glasgow	1	100 —
Hamilton, Mrs. Mary	Dumbarton	3	72 —
Hamilton, Anna Maria	Helensburgh	1	80 —
Hamilton, Grace, of Cochno	Cochno House, Duntocher	2,615	1,896 5
Hannay, Alexander	76 Buccleuch St., Glasgow	4	275 —
Hardie & Gordon	West Bridgend, Dumbarton	3	143 —
Harrower, David	Kilcreggan	2	165 —
Hartley, Mrs. Fanny C.	Shandon	4	125 —
Harvie, Robert	Cove	1	152 —
Harvie, Walter	Kirkintilloch	2	119 6
Hatrick, Trs. of William	Glasgow	1	52 10
Hay, William	Kirkintilloch	2	32 16
Hay, Mrs. Mary Ann	Drumglass, Cumbernauld	32	40 —
Helensburgh Free Church Congregation	Helensburgh	3	97 —
Do. do.	Helensburgh	1	65 —
Helensburgh Harbour Trs.	Do. (*Harbour*)	2	1,140 —
Henderson, Robert	Ledcameroch, New Kilpatrick	3	93 —
Henderson, Mrs. Jean	Viewpark, Row	4	150 —
Henry, Barclay	Arrochar	1	55 —
Henry, Mrs. Jane	Annaghmore, Kilcreggan	1	50 —
Hill, Trustees of Ninian	Greenock	5	28 —
Hill, James	96 Garngad Hill, Glasgow	4	90 —
Holmes, Heirs of R. R.	Glasgow	47	112 —
Horne, Robert	Boghouse Locks, Duntocher	1	15 —
Hume, William	Arns, Cumbernauld	30	30 —
Hunter, William	Maybank, Kilcreggan	1	60 —
Hutcheson, Graham	Glasgow	2	125 —
Inglis, John	London	89	201 15
Ismeredes, Trustees of Antonio	Glasgow	8	116 17
Jack, James	Saddlebrae, Kirkintilloch	21	38 —
Jack, Margaret, and Mrs. Jean Hutcheson	Cowgate, Kirkintilloch	5	48 8
Jackson, Richard	68 Renfield St., Glasgow	2	20 —
Jamieson, William	Shandon	42	290 —
Jeffray, Mrs. Susanna	New Kilpatrick	1	60 —
Johnston, David	Croy, Shandon	11	170 —
Johnstone, Mrs. Elizabeth	Kilcreggan	4	545 —

DUMBARTON—continued.

Name of Owner.	Address of Owner.	Estimated Acreage of Property.	Gross Annual Value.	Name of Owner.	Address of Owner.	Estimated Acreage of Property.	Gross Annual Value.
		Acres.	£ s.			Acres.	£ s.
Kerr, Peter C.	Inverness	1	123 —	M'Call, Samuel	5 Balmano St., Glasgow	1	70 —
Kerr, Charlotte	Springfield, Roseneath	1	33 —	M'Call, William	Glasgow	1	65 —
Keyden, James	186 West George Street, Glasgow	8	210 —	M'Callum, Peter	Helensburgh	1	210 —
Kibble, John	Coulport, Cove	5	200 —	M'Callum, Trs. of Robert	Rahane, Roseneath	4	165 10
Kidston, Charles	Ardencaple, Row	16	223 —	M'Cash, Robert	Gallowhill, Kirkintilloch	5	13 —
Kidston, Catherine	Ferniegair, Row	15	200 —	M'Cash, Mrs. Margaret	Gallowhill, Kirkintilloch	1	17 5
Kilmaronock, Heritors of Parish of	Kilmaronock	8	45 —	M'Cash, Mrs. Elizabeth	Gallowhill, Kirkintilloch	1	16 10
King, Rev. James W.	New Kilpatrick	10	44 10	M'Corquodale, John	Airdlamont, Greenock	2	101 —
Kinloch, Heirs of Graham	Crosshill	1	91 7	M'Culloch, J. W.	Helensburgh	1	352 10
Kinnear, C. G.	Edinburgh	462	478 16	M'Culloch, Samuel and William	16 Hutcheson Street, Glasgow	1	70 —
Do.	Do. (*Minerals*)	—	144 1	M'Culloch, William	Helensburgh	1	16 —
Kippen, James Hill, of Westerton	Westerton, Bonhill	733	867 15	M'Donald, Trs. of John	Belmore, Garelochhead	11	175 —
Kirk, Agnes and Helen	Arrochar	1	45 —	M'Dougall, Alexander	Row	1	87 —
Kirkintilloch Gas Company	Kirkintilloch	1	459 —	M'Elroy, John	Gleneden, Kilcreggan	6	739 15
Kirkwood, Heirs of John	Kirkintilloch	6	17 —	M'Farlane, Alexander	Oakbank, Kilcreggan	1	51 —
				M'Farlane, Heirs of William	Glasgow	150	211 10
Laird, Alex. Allan	Helensburgh	2	100 —	M'Farlane, George, junior	18 Elmbank Crescent, Glasgow	5	105 —
Lang, George	Heathfield, Kilcreggan	1	18 —	M'Farlane, James	Woodbank, Cove	1	12 —
Lang, James	Birdston Bank, Kirkintilloch	5	14 —	M'Farlane, John	Faslane, Garelochhead	1	40 —
Lang, Heirs of James	Dumbarton	1	25 —	M'Farlane, William	Cove	1	26 —
Lang, Heirs of Robert	Dumbarton	1	48 —	M'Farlane, Trs. of William	Kilmaronock	3	68 10
Lang, Walter	Chapelton, Dumbarton	35	189 —	M'Farlane, Elizabeth	Cove	1	22 —
Latta, John	Church St., Dumbarton	13	173 —	M'Gaan, Andrew	Annfield, Dumbarton	1	65 —
Latta, Robert	Church St., Dumbarton	2	9 10	M'George, Andrew	91 West Regent Street, Glasgow	10	90 —
Learmonth, Robert	Viewfield, Kilcreggan	1	45 —	M'Gill, J. W.	6 Hamilton Drive, Glasgow	2	20 —
Leckie, Alexander	9 Carlton Place, Glasgow	3	189 10	M'Gown, Mary	Gartenwall, Kilmaronock	9	16 —
Leith, Sir George Hector, of Burgh St. Peter's, Norfolk, Bart.	Ross Priory, Kilmaronock	1,778	1,416 —	M'Gown, Jane, Janet, Mary, and Rachel	Helensburgh	2	155 —
Lennox, Hon. C. S. H. H., of Lennox Castle	Woodhead, Campsie	80	140 —	M'Gregor, Adam, & Co.	Redcraig, Bonhill	5	95 —
Lennox, Duncan	100 West Regent Street, Glasgow	79	100 —	M'Indoe, John and George P.	Glasgow	556	1,537 10
Lennox, Peter	Bell Street, Helensburgh	2	184 —	M'Indoe, Trs. of Walter	Glasgow	100	138 —
Leny, James Cunningham, of Gartocharn	Gartocharn, Kilmaronock	397	291 —	M'Indoe, Mrs. Janet	Glenmollochan, Luss	4	53 —
				M'Intyre, James	Lyleston, Cardross	2	33 —
Lenzie Episcopal Church, Trustees of	Lenzie	2	12 —	M'Intyre, John	Cawdor Lodge, Helensburgh	1	132 —
Leresche, Mrs. Isabella, M. M.	Langside, Glasgow	3	85 —	M'Isaac, Mrs. Ann	Helensburgh	2	54 —
Leven Gas Company	Alexandria	2	446 10	M'Kay, W. W. and George	99 Cowcaddens, Glasgow	30	75 —
Liddell, William	New Kilpatrick	2	32 —	M'Kean, James	Gartocharn, Kilmaronock	52	86 15
Little, Robert	Ardencaple, Row	5	75 —	M'Kean, James	Tullochan, Kilmaronock	44	75 —
Livingstone, Mrs. Agnes J.	Queen St., Helensburgh	2	32 —	M'Kellar, John	Greenbank, Kilcreggan	2	84 —
Logan, William	Garelochhead	3	222 —	M'Kenzie, Alexander	Colquhoun Street, Helensburgh	1	120 —
Lochhead, John	Helensburgh	2	110 —	M'Kenzie, James, of Glentore	24 Stockwell Street, Glasgow	771	805 —
Luke, Alexander	Culross, Perthshire	32	67 —	M'Kenzie, R. D., of Caldervan	Caldervan, Kilmaronock	1,139	893 —
Lumsden, Sir James, of Arden, Kt.	Queen Street, Glasgow	1,447	923 —	Do. do.	Do. (*Quarry*)	—	25 —
Luss Free Church Congregation	Luss	2	20 —	M'Kenzie, Mrs. Elizabeth	Auchenheglish, Bonhill	20	151 —
Luss, Heritors of Parish of	Luss	16	64 —	M'Kinlay, Andrew	Blairquhanran, Kilmaronock	70	70 —
				M'Kinlay, Duncan	Summerhill, Shandon	1	97 10
M'Adam, Mrs. Margaret	Mains, Kilmaronock	145	380 —	M'Kinlay, George	14 St. James Street, Kingston, Glasgow	148	120 —
M'Allister, James	Tamadhu, Bonhill	3	24 —	M'Kinlay, Mrs. Lillias	Draught House, Roseneath	1	20 —
M'Allister, Trustees of Margaret	Dalvait, Balloch	145	96 —	M'Lachlan, Lachlan	Helensburgh	2	268 —
M'Arthur, Donald	Peaton Villa, Pollockshields	2	69 —	M'Lachlan, Mrs. Elizabeth	Helensburgh	1	40 —
M'Arthur, Mrs. Elizabeth B.	Cove	1	10 —	M'Lachlan, Ann, and Mrs. Janet B. M'Kinlay	Alexandria	1	185 —
M'Arthur, Mrs. Mary	Rahane, Roseneath	1	12 —	M'Lachlan, John and Marion	Dumbarton	3	44 —
M'Arthur, Mrs. Mary	2 St. James' Terrace, Hillhead, Glasgow	1	65 —	M'Lay, James	Ardoch, Kilmaronock	4	21 —
M'Aulay, Aulay	34 Ann Street, Greenock	1	85 —	M'Lean, Alexander	Glendhualt, Cove	3	90 —
M'Auslan, Trs. of James	Row	1	176 10	M'Lean, Allan	Dumbarton	1	134 —
M'Auslan, John	201 High St., Dumbarton	2	618 —	M'Lellan, Duncan	Helensburgh	1	85 —
M'Ausland, Archibald	Helensburgh	7	186 —	M'Lellan, John	Craigmore, Shandon	2	90 —
M'Ausland, David	Middlemuir, Kirkintilloch	12	56 —	M'Lellan, Walter	Blairvaddick, Row	44	300 —
M'Ausland, John	West Bridgend, Dumbarton	3	75 —	M'Leod, Allan	Dumbarton	5	93 —
M'Bean, Lachlan	Queen St., Helensburgh	2	120 —	M'Leod, George H. B.	Finnery, Shandon	6	85 —
M'Brayne, John Burns	Glasgow	20	28 —	M'Leod, James	Scapesland, Dumbarton	1	50 —
M'Call, Archibald	Glasgow	1	50 —	M'Leod, William	West Bridgend, Dumbarton	3	297 —
M'Call, Frederick	Lochbrae, New Kilpatrick	3	130 10	M'Lure, Hugh Heugh	New Kilpatrick	1	80 —

DUMBARTON—continued.

Name of Owner.	Address of Owner.	Estimated Acreage of Property.	Gross Annual Value.	Name of Owner.	Address of Owner.	Estimated Acreage of Property.	Gross Annual Value.
		Acres.	£ s.			Acres.	£ s.
M'Lure, John	New Kilpatrick	4	110 —	Ogilvie, Trs. of Thomas, & Company	Glasgow	4	110 —
M'Lure, Robert	3 Woodside Crescent, Glasgow	2	72 10	Old Kilpatrick, *Heritors of Parish of*	Old Kilpatrick	10	85 —
M'Micking's Trustees	Helensburgh	3	150 —	Orr, Robert	Meikle Aiden, Kilcreggan	1	138 —
M'Millan, Archibald, & Son	Dumbarton	5	500 —	Orr, Trustees of Robert	Helensburgh	1	95 —
M'Millan, Daniel	Helensburgh	1	100 —	Osborne, Alexander	5 Oakley Terrace, Glasgow	3	155 —
M'Millan, John	Dumbarton	4	241 —	Oswald, Andrew	Helensburgh	2	130 —
M'Millan, William	Greenock	2	24 —				
M'Murrich, James, of Stuckgoun	Stuckie, Arrochar	851	814 —				
M'Nair, John F., of Auchineck	Auchineck, New Kilpatrick	631	282 —				
M'Neil, Thomas	Dumbarton	1	639 —	Paisley, Rev. John	Glenald, Garelochhead	2	50 —
Macome, Trs. of Robert	Glasgow	2	72 —	Park, Rev. Hugh	Manse, Cumbernauld	16	50 —
M'William, Richard	Clydeshore, Dumbarton	1	57 —	Park, William	Torwood, Row	9	195 —
Magistrates and Town Council of Dumbarton	Dumbarton	147	122 —	Park, Curators of William	Glasgow	584	1,772 10
Maitland, James	Balgrochan, Torrance of Campsie	168	220 —	*Partick, Hillhead, and Maryhill Gas Company*	Glasgow	6	96 —
Malloch, John	12 Garden St., Glasgow	2	20 —	Paterson, Alexander	Dumbarton	2	8 —
Marshall, James	Glentore, Airdrie	31	38 —	Paterson, George	Helensburgh	1	90 —
Marshall, John	Avonbridge, Falkirk	1	7 —	Paterson, John	Kilcreggan	1	70 —
Marshall, John D.	Broadcroft, Kirkintilloch	6	75 —	Paterson, Joseph	Garelochhead	2	24 —
Marshall, Robert	Birkfell, Helensburgh	1	75 —	Paterson, William	Church St., Dumbarton	2	57 —
Marshall, Helen and Janet	Glasgow	98	75 —	Paterson, William and Mary	Murligan, Arrochar	1	27 —
Martin, George, of Auchindennan	Auchindennan, Alexandria	571	596 —	Paton, Robert	Old Kilpatrick	1	26 10
Martin, James	Claremont Villa, Cove	2	65 —	Patrick, John	Bilsland, Kirkintilloch	17	12 —
Martin, Trustees of James	Linn Villa, Cove	3	85 —	Pattison, Alexander D., of Mountblow	Mountblow, Dalmuir	250	778 15
Martin, Robert	Cowgate, Kirkintilloch	6	54 5	Paul, Andrew	Kirktonhill, Dumbarton	1	65 —
Mathie, John	Hardgate, Duntocher	1	70 10	Paul, Matthew	West Bridgend, Dumbarton	1	240 —
Mathieson, John, junior	142 West George Street, Glasgow	14	200 —	Pollock, John, of Auchineden	Auchineden House, Strathblane	350	46 —
Maughan, Wm. Charles	Roseneath	2	50 —	Potter, Mrs. Colville S.	Suffolk Street, Helensburgh	2	125 —
Maxwell, Andrew	Bonhill	1	178 15	Primrose, Adam	Helensburgh	1	121 —
Melville, Andrew	Garbet, Cumbernauld	328	46 —	Provan, George and John	Gallowhill, Kirkintilloch	5	19 —
Millar, Gavin Bell	Hazlewood, Cove	7	155 —				
Millar, Hugh	Broomfield, Shandon	7	122 —				
Millar, William	Knockderry Castle, Cove	6	135 —				
Milngavie Railway Co.	Glasgow (*Railway*)	20	579 —				
Moffat, Rev. William	Kirkintilloch	46	315 12	Rae, Gavin	Rahane, Roseneath	1	21 —
Moncrieff, Paterson, Forbes, & Barr	45 West George Street, Glasgow	59	95 —	Rae, Mrs. Helen	Clynder, Roseneath	2	60 —
Monteith, Mrs. Jane	Helensburgh	1	164 —	Ralston, James	Gartshore, Kirkintilloch	76	92 —
Montgomery, Martha M.	Arrochar	1	48 —	Ramsay, James	West Montrose Street, Helensburgh	2	90 —
Montrose, Duke of	Buchanan House, Drymen	2,588	1,807 10	Ramsay, Margaret	Lindowan, Kilcreggan	1	97 —
Do. do.	Do. (*Quarry*)	—	30 —	Rankin, George	Newarthill	20	35 —
Moore's Trust	Dumbarton	135	379 —	Rankin, James	Hillhead, Kirkintilloch	1	23 —
Morrison, Henry	Dumbarton	1	54 —	Rankin, Patrick	Garngibbock, Airdrie	335	375 —
Morton, Charles	Glenloin, Arrochar	9	70 —	Reid, Andrew Paterson	Tighnamorn, Roseneath	3	65 —
Morton, Creditors of John	West Bridgend, Dumbarton	1	564 —	Reid, James	Berridale, Row	1	58 —
Motherwell, John	Rawyards, Airdrie	550	100 —	Reid, John	Torrance of Campsie	32	100 —
Muir, John	New Kilpatrick	3	90 —	Reid, Robert	Eastfield, Cumbernauld	1	14 —
Muir, Matthew Andrew	Ardenvohr, Row	6	240 —	Reid, Robert Douglas	Helensburgh	1	70 —
Muir, Robert	Helensburgh	1	163 —	Reid, William	Luss Road, Helensburgh	1	45 —
Munro, John	Boghead, Kirkintilloch	15	44 —	Reid, William	52 Grove St., Glasgow	2	120 —
Do.	Do. (*Quarry*)	—	30 —	Richard, B. M.	Kirkton, Dumbarton	1	179 —
Murchie, John	Deep Den, Cove	2	143 —	Richardson, David	89 Wilson St., Glasgow	13	220 —
Murdoch & Rodger	West Nile Street, Glasgow	85	73 —	Richardson, John	9 Park Street, Grosvenor Square, London	705	1,287 10
Murphy, Henry	Springhill Terrace, Crossmyloof	2	210 —	Do. do.	Do. (*Minerals*)	—	444 —
Murray, D. & P.	Helensburgh	1	243 —	Rigby, Mrs. Jane	Dunard, Row	3	120 —
Murray, James	New Kilpatrick	2	75 —	Risk, Trustees of Charles	Helensburgh	1	90 —
Muter, Andrew	Milton, Bowling	9	184 10	Risk, James B.	Gilmore Pl., Edinburgh	6	983 —
				Rodger, Reps. of John	Westermains, Kirkintilloch	26	91 —
				Robertson, Andrew C.	Helensburgh	3	15 —
				Robertson, Archibald	Dalreoch, Dumbarton	2	88 —
Nairn, Archibald	Glasgow	4	45 —	Robertson, George	Stroul, Roseneath	10	186 —
Nairn, John	Dalvait, Balloch	5	318 10	Robertson, James	Sutherland Crescent, Helensburgh	1	97 —
Napier, Robert	Shandon	44	433 5				
Newman, Edward	12 Annfield Terrace, Partick	2	80 —	Robertson, James	Luss Road, Helensburgh	1	100 —
Noble, Andrew	Lesmund, Dene, Newcastle-on-Tyne	16	104 —	Robertson, John W.	New Kilpatrick	30	57 10
				Robertson, Robert Wm.	Rockingham, Kilcreggan	2	84 —
North British Railway Company	Edinburgh	2	435 10	Robertson, William	Struan, New Kilpatrick	1	65 —
				Robertson, Mrs. Mary C.	Garelochhead	1	70 —
Do. do.	Do. (*Railway*)	481	15566 —	Robson, John	Kirkton, Dumbarton	2	65 —

G

DUMBARTON—continued.

Name of Owner.	Address of Owner.	Estimated Acreage of Property.	Gross Annual Value.	Name of Owner.	Address of Owner.	Estimated Acreage of Property.	Gross Annual Value.
		Acres.	£ s.			Acres.	£ s.
Roman Catholic Church Trustees	Alexandria	1	10 –	Stuart, John, and Steven Thomas	Helensburgh	1	336 –
Roseneath Free Church Congregation	Roseneath	2	30 –	Swan, William D.	Glasgow	280	230 –
Roseneath, Heritors of Parish of	Roseneath	7	83 –	Swan, Mrs. Georgina F. D.	Ardchapel, Shandon	6	100 –
Ross, Alexander	Arrochar	2	40 –				
Row, Heritors of Parish of	Row	3	86 –				
Russell, James C.	London	2	78 –	Tannahill, Robert D.	Glasgow	1	85 –
Russell, John	Falkirk	365	105 –	Tarbet Free Church Congregation	Tarbet, Arrochar	1	25 –
Russell, Mrs. Janet	Arns, Cumbernauld	45	35 –	Taylor, Henry J.	Glasgow	5	75 –
				Taylor, Trustees of Henry	Stuckinduff, Shandon	3	50 –
Samuel, James	26 Great George Street, Westminster	4	105 –	Taylor, Robert	Cardross	1	60 –
Sandeman, David	Woodlands, Kirkintilloch	4	120 –	Taylor, William M'N.	Helensburgh	1	285 –
School Trustees	Row	23	22 –	Thom, Robert, of Barremman	Barremman, Roseneath	597	288 –
Scott, George	18 St. Enoch Square, Glasgow	1	109 –	Thomson, Alexander	80 West King Street, Helensburgh	1	95 –
Scott, John	Woodside, Bowling	6	235 10	Thomson, George	Barroncliff, Cove	3	95 –
Do.	Do. (Quarry)	–	60 –	Thomson, James	Fairfield, Helensburgh	1	90 –
Scott, Walter	Old Kilpatrick	4	40 –	Thomson, John	78 High St., Dumbarton	2	912 10
Scott, William	Kirkintilloch	1	21 2	Thomson, J. & G.	Barns o' Clyde, Yoker	31	2,607 –
Scott, William	Bowling	9	159 10	Thomson, Robert, senior	Dalshannon	5	121 –
Scott, Mrs. Agnes	Blantyre Farm	209	334 10	Thomson, Robert and Charles	Warrambeen, Craigrownie	3	120 –
Scott, Mrs. Agnes	Little Mill, Bowling	2	131 10	Thomson, Representatives of William	Stirling	81	228 5
Scott, Jane	Castlecarry, Cumbernauld	1	45 –	Thomson, Mrs. Grace	Linburn, Shandon	7	100 –
Scoullar, Representatives of Alexander	Glasgow	1	15 –	Todd, Trustees of John	Finnich, Drymen	12	40 –
Service, John	Woodside, Cardross	1	80 –	Town Council of Helensburgh	Helensburgh	5	507 –
Shandon Free Church Congregation	Shandon	1	62 –	Turnbull, Andrew	Portobello	270	128 –
Sharpe, James	Leabank, Cardross	4	75 –	Turnbull, David	Balloch	1	25 –
Sharpe, Agnes and Jane, and Mrs. Helen Edgar	Woodburn, Kilcreggan	2	75 –	Turnbull & Company	Millburn, Renton	11	205 10
Shaw, Archibald	Gallowgate, Glasgow	2	25 –	Turner, Coll James	Garelochhead	2	70 –
Shearer, John M.	Gallowhill, Kirkintilloch	36	46 10	Turner, Duncan	Shandon	4	140 –
Sheddon, Thomas	Arrochar	3	110 –	Turner, Neil	Clynder, Roseneath	1	26 –
Skating Pond Club	Helensburgh	5	30 –	Turner, Robert	Clynder, Roseneath	2	152 –
Skene, Trustees of John	Helensburgh	1	297 –	Union Poorhouse Committee	Kirkintilloch	6	9 –
Sloan, William K.	Kirktonhill, Dumbarton	1	144 –	United Presbyterian Church	Cove	1	60 –
Sloss, William	Glasgow	3	60 –	Do. do.	Kilmaronock	19	48 –
Smith, Adam	Falkirk	400	150 –	Ure, John	119 Stockwell Street, Glasgow	24	75 –
Smith, Archibald	Govan	1	190 –				
Smith, David R.	Calfmoor, Kirkintilloch	34	58 15	Ure, John	Helensburgh	9	72 10
Smith, Edward Turner	Hillfoot, New Kilpatrick	2	80 –	Urie, Thomas	New Kilpatrick	1	75 –
Smith, Trustees of James	Glasgow	2	80 –				
Smith, Trustees of John	Helensburgh	2	112 –				
Smith, Robert	Faifley, Duntocher	30	110 15				
Smollett, Alexander, of Bonhill	Cameron House, Alexandria	1,733	3,336 –	Walker, David	Kilcreggan	2	161 –
Do. do.	Do. (Quarry)	–	24 –	Walker, Trustees of George L.	Woodburn, Shandon	6	145 –
Snell, Mrs. Mary	Helensburgh	1	75 –	Walker, James	Tchermavado, Kirkintilloch	7	383 10
Sommerville, James	Helensburgh	2	125 –				
Spence, William	Helensburgh	1	155 –	Walker, James K.	Woodburn, Kirkintilloch	24	392 –
Stead, Mrs. Susan	Hermitage, Helensburgh	18	392 –	Walker, John	Eastfield, Cumbernauld	1	12 10
Steele, W. C.	Westonlee, Dumbarton	4	97 –	Walker, John	Ardpeaton, Cove	12	300 –
Steele, Trustees of Mrs. Isabella	Glasgow	83	95 7	Walker, Peter	E. Clyde Street, Helensburgh	3	359 2
Do. do.	Do. (Minerals)	–	126 8	Walker, Robert	108 W. George Street, Glasgow	130	230 –
Steven, Thomas	Helensburgh	2	130 –				
Stevens, Archibald	Oakbank, Alexandria	2	83 –	Walker, Trustees of Robert	Helensburgh	3	85 –
Stewart, Adam	Kilcreggan	1	72 –				
Stewart, Alexander	Helensburgh	1	412 15	Walker, William	Barbegs, Cumbernauld	19	30 –
Stewart, Charles	High St., Kirkintilloch	3	67 –	Wallace, Daniel M'K.	Edinburgh	15	53 –
Stewart, James	Greyshill, Kirkintilloch	78	100 –	Wallace, James	Middlemuir, Kirkintilloch	16	40 –
Stewart, John	Helensburgh	2	194 –	Wallace, James	Kilsyth	25	48 17
Stewart, Walter	Haghill, Glasgow	416	334 –	Wallace, Matthew	52 Renfield St., Glasgow	44	85 –
Stewart, Walter	Queen Street, Helensburgh	1	55 –	Wallace, William, of Auchinvole	Auchinvole, Kilsyth	434	774 5
Stewart, William	Barbeth, Kirkintilloch	103	140 –	Do. do.	Do. (Minerals)	–	257 –
Stewart, William Arthur	Dalmuir	1	40 –	Wallace, William	Solsgirth, Kirkintilloch	74	258 –
Stirling, Patrick J.	Dunblane	33	156 19	Do. do.	Do. (Minerals)	–	290 –
Stirling, William, & Sons	Dalquhurn, Renton	51	2,378 –	Wallace, Mrs. Margaret	Hillhead, Kirkintilloch	10	70 17
Stobcross Railway Company	Glasgow (Railway)	11	35 –	Walls, John	Glenrowan, Cove	2	78 –
Stott, John	Rowmore, Garelochhead	1	45 –	Walters, Andrew	Glenample, Lochearnhead	20	50 –
Strang, Peter	Church St., Dumbarton	3	154 –	Water Company	Alexandria	2	33 7

DUMBARTON—continued.

Name of Owner.	Address of Owner.	Estimated Acreage of Property.	Gross Annual Value.	Name of Owner.	Address of Owner.	Estimated Acreage of Property.	Gross Annual Value.
		Acres.	£ s.			Acres.	£ s.
Watson, James	Aldonick, Row	4	110 —	Wink, James	Rowmore, Shandon	2	60 —
Watson, Robert	Hazlecliff, Cove	1	97 —	Wood, John Muir	Armadale, Cove	2	70 —
Watson, Robert B.	Glenowan, Roseneath	2	40 —	Wright, Robert	Whistlefield, Garelochhead	1	32 —
Watson, Thomas	50 W. Regent Street, Glasgow	8	380 —	Wright, Rev. Thomas	Helensburgh	4	175 —
Watt, Representatives of Jane	Victoria Road, Helensburgh	2	120 —	Wylie, James	Ardoch, Cardross	1	35 —
Wemyss, Robert	Luss Road, Helensburgh	1	105 —				
Wemyss, Trustees of John	Helensburgh	1	88 —	Young, Andrew	Condorrat, Cumbernauld	1	12 —
				Young, James	New Kilpatrick	1	65 —
White, James, of Overton	Overton, Dumbarton	910	1,031 10	Young, James	Helensburgh	2	120 —
White, John, of Ardarroch	Ardarroch, Row	35	180 —	Young, Trustees of John	Row	9	180 —
				Young, Thomas	Condorrat, Cumbernauld	1	50 —
White, William	Lilybank, Kilcreggan	1	57 —	Young, William	Longmuir, Kirkintilloch	24	30 —
Whitelaw, Alexander, of Gartshore	Gartshore	1,710	1,913 16	Do. do.	Do. (Minerals)	—	50 —
Do. do.	Do. (Minerals)	—	3,781 12	Yuille, A. B., of Darleith	Darleith, Cardross	1,292	845 —
Do. do.	Do. (Quarry)	—	60 2				
Whitelaw, Thomas	Kirkintilloch	1	23 10				
Wield, William	Summerhill, Shandon	4	104 —	Zetland, Earl of	Kerse House, Falkirk	162	12 —
Williamson, John	Craigendarroch, Cove	1	60 —	Zinkiesen, Theodor Victor	Luss Road, Helensburgh	2	120 —
Wilson, Alexander	Craigend, Airdrie	5	25 10				
Wilson, Trs. of Andrew	Glasgow	2	50 —				
Wilson & Brodie	Ferryfield, Alexandria	7	761 —				
Wilson, Charles H. H.	Endrick Bank, Drymen	253	292 10	Total Owners of Land of one Acre and upwards		706	152,968 251134 —
Wilson, Trustees of James	Arrochar	2	45 —				
Wilson, Trustees of Peter	Cardross	4	108 10	Total Owners of Lands of less than one Acre in extent		1,640	768 74,273 —
Wilson, Trs. of Samuel	Port-Dundas, Glasgow	2	272 —				
Wilson, William	Edinburgh	530	499 10				
Wilson, Margaret K.	Chapelacre, Helensburgh	7	120 —	**Grand Total**		2,346	153,736 325407 —

DUMFRIES.

Population in 1871,	74,808.
Inhabited Houses,	13,646.
Number of Parishes,	44.

Name of Owner.	Address of Owner.	Estimated Acreage of Property.	Gross Annual Value.		Name of Owner.	Address of Owner.	Estimated Acreage of Property.	Gross Annual Value.	
		Acres.	£	s.			Acres.	£	s.
Adair, Thomas	Dumfries	1	253	–	Beattie, Trustees of John	High Kelton, Dumfries	77	100	–
Adamson, David	Parkfoot, Lochmaben	7	11	10	Beattie, Patrick Tod	Millmeadows, Moffat	3	34	–
Adamson, John	6 West Street, Rochdale	69	70	–	Beattie, Rev. William	Sinclairburn, Ecclefechan	16	25	–
Adamson, Heirs of Wm.	Collin, by Dumfries	1	13	7	Beattie, Wm., of Newton	Newton, Dunscore	108	154	–
Airston, William Glen, of Broomrig	Broomrig, Holywood	645	1,145	10	Beattie, Mrs.	Lochmaben	2	7	5
Aitken, James	The Hill, Dumfries	1	80	–	Beattie, Mary S., of Crieve	Crieve, by Lockerbie	11,159	3,105	–
Aitken, J. G., of Holmpark	Southfield, Stirling	200	182	–	Beck, John	Lochside, Lochmaben	2	4	10
Aitken, Robert Nicol, of Laggan	Laggan, Glencairn	465	302	7	Beck, William	Barras, Lochmaben	3	5	–
Aitken, William	Glenhill, Kirkmahoe	1	7	–	Bell, Heirs of Benjamin	Rosebank, Dumfries	64	223	–
Anderson, Andrew, of Stockbridge	Woodburn, Hawick	167	136	–	Bell, Christopher	Farthingwell, Dunscore	25	40	–
Anderson, Edward	Heck, Lochmaben	21	70	4	Bell, David	Annan	3	6	–
Anderson, George, of Woodhouse	Woodhouse, Ecclefechan	564	766	7	Bell, David	Barras, Lochmaben	1	3	10
Anderson, James	Taylorland, Dumfries	1	7	10	Bell, George	Corsefield, Dunscore	89	70	–
Anderson, Sir James, Kt.	London	4	25	–	Bell, George, of Carruthers	Carruthers, Middlebie	106	100	–
Anderson, Rev. John	Manse, Dornock	21	55	–	Bell, George Graham, of Castleoer	Castleoer, Eskdalemuir	2,850	784	–
Anderson, John Still, of Whiteside	Dalhousie, Dalkeith	346	178	–	Bell, James	Conhess, Ecclefechan	1	22	5
Anderson, William, of Netherwood	Netherwood, Dumfries	84	201	–	Bell, James	Elizafield, Collin	6	13	4
Anderson, Heirs of W.	Smallholm, Lochmaben	30	68	10	Bell, John, of Whiteknowe	Whiteknowe, Lockerbie	199	145	–
Annan, Burgh of	Annan	11	330	–	Bell, John, of Broats	Broats, Annan	550	550	–
Annan Parochial Board, for Cemetery Company	Annan	3	22	–	Bell, John and George, of Carruthers	Carruthers, Middlebie	630	400	–
Armstrong, Abel, of Williamsfield	Scales, Gretna	236	233	–	Bell, Richard	Shawhill, Tundergarth	32	20	–
Armstrong, Alexander	KirkbymoonBar, Brampton	9	12	5	Bell, Robert, of Milton	Santiago, Chili	261	275	–
Armstrong, Francis	West Craigs, Middlebie	21	18	–	Bell, Thomas, of Cressfield	Ecclefechan	121	205	–
Armstrong, James	Westgill, Annan	15	21	–	Bell, Thomas	Brydekirk, Annan	4	64	10
Armstrong, John	West Craigs, Middlebie	9	11	–	Bell, Thomas, of Torbeckhill	Torbeckhill, Ecclefechan	523	400	–
Armstrong, John	North Craigs, Middlebie	45	42	–	Bell, Thomas and George, of Minsca	Minsca, Ecclefechan	695	275	–
Armstrong, Thomas	West Craigs, Middlebie	8	11	–	Bell, William, of Auchencairn	Auchencairn, Kirkmahoe	192	152	10
Armstrong, Trustees of Isabella	Riggfoot, Middlebie	31	72	–	Bell, William	Holmhead, Mouswald	69	95	–
Arnot, Francis, of Kirkconnell Hall, C.B.	Kirkconnell Hall, Ecclefechan	394	529	10	Bell, Rev. William	Manse, Gretna	18	51	–
Arundell, Wm. F. H., of Barjarg	Barjarg, Keir	1,947	1,689	5	Bell, Heirs of Wm.	Dornocktown, Annan	100	165	–
					Bell, Mrs. Janet	Bloomfield, Annan	13	37	–
					Bell, Mrs. Kenneth	Collin, Dumfries	1	7	–
					Bell, Elizabeth	Dumfries	3	17	–
					Bell, Helen	Ecclefechan	3	13	10
					Bell, Jean, and John Blacklock	Netherhall, Kirkmahoe	395	325	–
					Bell, Martha and Janet	Racks, Dumfries	1	4	3
					Benson, Lawrence G.	Windermere	35	80	–
Baird, Hamilton, and Andrew Johnstone	Lockerbie	12	37	10	Berwick, Mrs. Jessie	Allanbank, Dumfries	3	150	–
Baird, John	Blackford, Lockerbie	122	225	–	Berwick, Mrs. Margt.	Albany Bank, Dumfries	3	80	–
Baird, Representatives of George	Stitchell, Kelso	59	120	–	Biggar, James	Wallaceton, Dumfries	15	18	5
Baird, Robert Bruce, of Over Courance	Bellevue Terrace, Edinburgh	108	348	–	Biggar, William C.	Rosefield, Annan	32	70	–
Baird, Mrs. Robert	Springbank, Moffat	12	34	–	Black, Captain Archibald, of Hazelbrae	Kirkmichael, Castle-Douglas	285	372	5
Ballantyne, James	Greenlea, Collin	2	14	5	Black, Rev. A. D.	Virginhall, Penpont	2	20	–
Barber, John, of Tererran	Tererran, Moniaive	1,277	450	–	Black, Thomas	Crawston, Dunscore	30	45	–
Barber, John, David, Wm. and Margaret	Benbuie, Moniaive	887	190	–	Blacklock, Jacob	Lochmaben	1	54	10
Barber, J., J. Harkness, and J. Wilson	Heck, Lochmaben	10	34	11	Blacklock, John	Annan	33	41	10
Barclay, Rev. James	Manse, Dumfries	8	78	–	Blacklock, Heirs of Mrs., of Craighouse	Craighouse, Middlebie	125	140	–
Barrie, Andrew D.	Elmbank, Dumfries	2	125	–	Blaikie, Thomas	Patrickholm, Middlebie	40	42	–
Bate, John, of Broadchapel	Broadchapel, Lochmaben	342	464	–	Bogie, Agnew B., of Fruidspark	Fruidspark, Annan	238	600	10
Baxter, John and Mrs.	Raeburn, Ecclefechan	8	20	–	Borrowman, Trustees of Robert	Holmend, Moffat	6	24	–
Baxter, Mrs.	Greencroft, Annan	6	10	–	Borthwick, Robert	Sprucebank, Moffat	5	10	–
Beattie, James, of Davington	Davington, Eskdalemuir	755	275	–	Borthwick, William	Peebles	16	36	6
Beattie, John, & Mrs. Bell	Kelton, Dumfries	26	27	–	Borthwick, Mrs.	Longwood, Langholm	3	78	–
Beattie, Trustees of John, of Crawston	Crawston, Dunscore	151	216	–	Boustead, John	Annan	6	11	–
					Bowman, James, and Sons	Langholm	1	200	–
					Bowness, John, of Springvale	Springvale, Kirkmahoe	26	186	10

DUMFRIES—continued.

Name of Owner.	Address of Owner.	Estimated Acreage of Property.	Gross Annual Value.
		Acres.	£ s.
Boyd, Samuel, of Marchmont	Marchmont, Dumfries	48	270 —
Boyes, Andrew, of Whitehill	Whitehill, Ecclefechan	85	48 —
Bramwell, John, of West Galloberry	W. Galloberry, Kirkmahoe	71	140 —
Bridges, Thomas	Dumfries	1	42 10
Brodie, Charles, of Bush	Bush, Lochmaben	141	134 —
Broom, Heirs of James, of Dalwhat	Dalwhat, Moniaive	1,123	732 10
Broun, Sir William, Bart.	Irving Street, Dumfries	11	70 —
Brown, Adam	Bennan, Tynron	38	120 —
Brown, David, of Ellerslie	Ellerslie, Kirkmahoe	259	170 —
Brown, Heirs of David	High Kelton, Dumfries	44	85 —
Brown, Heirs of D. B.	Carthagena, Dumfries	81	98 —
Bruce, James, of Castledykes	Castledykes, Dumfries	30	188 —
Bryson, John	Lowtherton, Dornock	2	8 —
Buccleuch and Queensberry, Duke of	Drumlanrig Castle, Thornhill	253,514	94518 5
Do. do.	Do. (*Coal & Lead Mines*)	—	3,012 —
Buchanan, Mrs. Mary, of Hetland	Hetland, Dalton	1,030	1,096 —
Burnett, Rev. William	Manse, Half Morton	5	25 —
Burnie, William	Bradford, Yorkshire	8	20 —
Byers, Andrew, and Sons	Langholm	3	217 10
Byers, Heirs of W.	Ecclefechan	2	15 5
Byers, Jessie	Greenwrae, Half Morton	7	16 —
Byrne, John William, of Elshieshields	Elshieshields, Lochmaben	823	963 —
Cadien, Mrs. Jessie, of Riddingwood	Riddingwood, Kirkmahoe	91	150 —
Caesar, John	Delvin Cottage, Tinwald	20	30 —
Caledonian Railway Company	Glasgow (*Railway*)	589	47962 7
Cameron, John, of Knockhornock and Kelton	London	163	470 8
Campbell, David	Campbelltown, Dumfries	6	33 10
Campbell, James Grubb, of Killyleoch	Edinburgh	280	495 —
Campbell, Heirs of Thomas	Glencairn	320	343 16
Carlisle Building Society	Lockerbie	2	169 —
Carlyle, David Scott	Carlisle	7	21 —
Carlyle, Robert	Waterbeck, Ecclefechan	112	255 10
Carlyle, Robert	Plea Lodge, Ecclefechan	6	18 —
Carlyle, Thos., of Craigenputtock	Chelsea	773	250 —
Carlyle, Thomas J., of Templehill	Templehill, Waterbeck	280	393 —
Carlyle, Thos. and Robert	Waterbeck, Ecclefechan	2	53 5
Carlyle, William J.	Langholm	156	142 —
Carruthers, Francis, of Dixons	Dixons, Lockerbie	285	264 10
Carruthers, George, of Stenrieshill	Stenrieshill, Moffat	618	345 —
Carruthers, James	Annan	15	34 4
Carruthers, John, of Kirkhill	Kirkhill, Moffat	304	115 —
Carruthers, John	Albie Chapel, Waterbeck	65	118 10
Carruthers, John H., of Denbie	Denbie, Dalton	709	806 —
Carruthers, Joseph	Broomrig, Lochmaben	5	10 10
Carruthers, Matthew	Watchhill, Lochmaben	6	7 —
Carruthers, Matthew, sen.	Trailflat, Tinwald	5	4 10
Carruthers, Richard B.	Dumfries	2	140 —
Carruthers, William F., of Dormont	Dormont, Lockerbie	6,355	4,698 2
Carruthers, Janet	Dumfries	4	10 —
Carson, Trustees of Mary	Stoop, Dumfries	9	59 10
Cavens, Robert, of Snaid	Snaid, Glencairn	561	560 —
Cavens, Thomas, of Birkshaw	Birkshaw, Glencairn	189	190 —
Chalmers, Walter, of Prestonhall	Prestonhall, Annan	184	196 —
Chesney, John, of Lochenhead	Lochenhead, Dunscore	70	140 —
Clapperton, Duncan, and Nelson's Heirs	Annan	7	40 —
Clark, Andrew	Lowtherton, Dornock	7	29 10

Name of Owner.	Address of Owner.	Estimated Acreage of Property.	Gross Annual Value.
		Acres.	£ s.
Clark, Rev. Henry, of Gallabank	Gallabank, Annan	413	781 16
Clark, John Gilchrist, of Speddoch	Dabton, Thornhill	1,499	1,275 —
Clark, Mrs. Elizabeth	Dumfries	1	115 —
Colville, Rev. George	Manse, Canonbie	20	50 —
Colvin, Rev. Robert F.	Manse, Kirkpatrick-Juxta	6	43 —
Colvin, William, of Craigielands	Craigielands, Moffat	812	415 —
Combined Parishes	Kirkpatrick-Fleming	4	60 —
Combined Parishes	Morton	2	60 —
Connell, Arthur	Langholm	1	6 —
Connell, James, of Conheath	Irvine House, Langholm	520	701 10
Connell, James W. F., of Auchenchain	Irvine House, Langholm	3,140	1,216 —
Copland, Charles, of Colliston	Colliston, Dunscore	2,554	1,995 1
Copland, John	Mount Sydney, Dumfries	3	38 —
Copland, John	Mainshead, Dumfries	1	272 —
Corrie, John, of M'Cubbington	M'Cubbington, Dunscore	98	214 —
Corrie, John, of East Galloberry	East Galloberry, Kirkmahoe	78	150 —
Corson, James	Dumfries	8	142 —
Corson, Samuel, of Craigenputtock	Corsock, Dumfries	700	133 —
Costine, Trustees of J., of Lochvale	Lochvale, Dumfries	96	260 —
Cotts, William	Shinnelforge, Tynron	2	33 —
Coulthart, William	Carronbridge, Thornhill	91	56 10
Couper, Rev. David	Manse, Tynron	15	45 —
Cowan, John	Allansfield, Dumfries	3	8 4
Cowan, Robert	Birkhill, Dumfries	1	50 —
Cowie, Mrs. Jane	Infirmary, Dumfries	3	5 —
Cox, James	Gatehouse	16	64 —
Craig, William, of Carse of Ae	Dumfries	181	449 —
Cranstoun, James T.	Nithbank, Dumfries	8	35 5
Cranstoun, William S.	Moffat	14	264 —
Creighton, Margaret	Gasstown, Dumfries	10	19 5
Crichton Institution, Trs. of	Dumfries	112	1,060 —
Crichton, Rev. James A.	Manse, Annan	16	79 —
Crichton, James M'M.	Barkerland, Dumfries	106	160 —
Crichton, John Pritchard, of Friars Carse	Edinburgh	267	457 —
Crichton School, Trustees of	Sanquhar	1	18 —
Cron, William	Greenfield, Kirkpatrick-Fleming	2	25 —
Croom, Rev. David	Edinburgh	14	122 —
Crosbie, George	Collin, Dumfries	1	8 —
Crosbie, James	Lantonside, Caerlaverock	1	35 8
Crosbie, Joseph	Lagganlees, Dunscore	14	21 —
Crosbie, Theodore	Annan	3	8 —
Crosbie, William	Laurelmount, Dumfries	12	128 —
Crown, The	(*Crown Property*)	1	395 —
Cruickshanks, J. M., of Broomhill	Broomhill, Lochmaben	365	501 —
Cruickshanks, John, of Trailflat	The Mount, York	272	373 5
Cruickshanks, Allison, of Robbiewhat	Mouswald	119	120 —
Currie, David, of Craigshields	Annanholm, Moffat	1,291	200 —
Currie, James	Dumfries	1	15 10
Currie, Rev. John R.	Manse, Hutton & Corrie	37	45 —
Currie, Mrs. Joan	Clerkhill, Dumfries	4	209 10
Currie, Mary, H., & G., of Newfield	Newfield, Ecclefechan	178	110 —
Dalgleish, Mrs. D.	Annan	35	135 2
Dalgleish, Heirs of Mrs. Mary	Annan	27	78 —
Dalkeith, Earl of, and Lord Henry Scott	Boatford, Penpont	25	35 —
Dalrymple, Charles	Shrawhead, Annan	45	48 —
Dalziell, David B., of Glenae	Glenae, Tinwald, Dumfries	1,234	943 —
Davidson, James	Hass, Middlebie	2	13 10
Davidson, James	Summerville, Dumfries	48	140 —

DUMFRIES—continued.

Name of Owner.	Address of Owner.	Estimated Acreage of Property.	Gross Annual Value.	Name of Owner.	Address of Owner.	Estimated Acreage of Property.	Gross Annual Value.
		Acres.	£ s.			Acres.	£ s.
Davidson, John	Lowthertown, Dornock	2	11 5	Edgar, Mrs. William	Lochenlee, Dunscore	70	76 —
Davidson, Rev. Robert	Manse, Holywood	9	40 —	Elliot, William Scott, of Arkleton	Edinburgh	2,163	760 —
Davidson, Thomas	Langholm	1	106 10	Ellis, George Henry	Langlands, Ecclefechan	5	22 10
Davidson, William, of Marchhill	Marchhill, Dumfries	83	302 —	Ensor, William	Heathfield, Annan	7	40 —
				Ensor, Mary	Heathfield, Annan	5	6 —
Davidson, Mrs., of Rosebank	Rosebank, Lockerbie	290	305 —	Ewart, David	Lockerbie	8	34 —
Davidson, Mrs. Simon	Lowthertown, Dornock	1	6 3	Ewart, Robert Wm., of Allershaw	Allershaw, Moffat	110	110 —
Denholm, John	Moffat	1	11 10				
Denholm, Walter	Moffat	3	47 —	Ewart, Mrs. Alicia	Nithbank, Thornhill	24	63 5
Dewar, Peter	Collin, Dumfries	1	7 10				
Dick, Mrs. Joanna, and others	Croydon, London	60	84 —	Farish, Harvey	Racks, Dumfries	2	9 10
Dickie, William	Greystone Bank, Dumfries	1	160 —	Farish, Samuel, of Todhillmuir	Kirklands, Kirkmichael	126	195 —
Dickson, Jacob	Woodside, Mouswald	2	7 10				
Dickson, James	Locharbriggs, Dumfries	1	12 —	Farish, Samuel	Racks, Dumfries	1	7 10
Dickson, John G.	Chapelknowe, Half Morton	40	50 5	Farish, Mrs. Jane	Howgill, Annan	4	21 —
Dickson, Robert	Eaglesfield, Ecclefechan	3	5 —	Fell, John, Trustees of	Woodside, Mouswald	1	6 —
Dickson, William Clark, of Upper Locharwoods	Upper Locharwoods, Bankend	374	210 —	Fergusson, Rev. John	Edgerston, Jedburgh	10	42 10
				Fergusson, Curators of Robert Cutlar, of Craigdarroch	Craigdarroch, Moniaive	2,264	1,755 —
Dickson, W., & D. Scott, of Craigenvey	Edinburgh	1,100	345 —				
Dinwiddie, James, of Whitehall	Whitehall, Kirkmahoe	237	168 —	Fergusson, R. D. G., of Isle	Chester St., Edinburgh	1,009	1,118 10
				Fergusson, Thomas	Sanquhar	2	17 —
Dinwiddie, Mrs. Ann	Greenbrae, Dumfries	7	30 —	Fergusson, William, of Springfield	Rochester	165	130 4
Dinwiddie, Mrs. Mary	Scaleyhills, Kirkmahoe	17	30 —				
Dirom, Lieut.-Col. Thos. Alex. Pasley, of Mount Annan	Mount Annan, Annan	1,502	1,480 2	Fergusson, Mrs.	Sunnyrig, Longtown	4	11 10
				Fergusson, Mrs. Jos.	Rosedale, Collin	4	14 —
				Fergusson, Mrs. Ellen	Dowievale, Dumfries	60	80 10
Dirom, Leonora	Cleuchhead, Annan	2	25 —	Fergusson, Janet	Dumfries	1	348 —
Dixon, Mrs. Isabella	Annan	5	5 —	Fergusson, Wilhelmina	Dumfries	1	10 —
Dobbie, William	Greencroft, Annan	3	72 —	Fleming, John	Marionburgh, Ballindalloch	12	15 —
Dobie, Andrew L., of Glenholm	Glenholm, Lockerbie	125	132 —	Fletcher, Major Joseph, of Kelton Mains	Kelton House, Dumfries	167	456 15
Dobie, David	Collin, Dumfries	1	9 9				
Dobie, Francis Jardine	Lockerbie	165	200 —	Forbes, Wm., of Callendar	Callendar House, Falkirk	2,416	732 —
Dobie, Hugh	Langholm	2	30 10	Forfar, Mary	Auchencairn, Kirkmahoe	27	50 —
				Forrest, Andrew T.	Arken Terrace, Langholm	30	78 10
Dobie, Trustees of Thomas, of Scalehill	Scalehill, Tundergarth	142	180 —	Forrest, William John	Longmeadow, Annan	13	84 10
Dobie, Rev. William	Kinghorn	26	64 10	Forsyth, Heirs of Rev. James	Oakfield Ter., Glasgow	34	56 —
Dobie, William	Broombush, Lockerbie	14	45 —				
Dobson, William	Sanquhar	11	17 10	Fraser, Wm. Newby	Penrith	39	75 —
Donaldson, Rev. John	Manse, Kirkconnel	24	47 —	Fraser, Katherine Ann, Margaret J., and Mary, of Glenmaid	Glenmaid, Kirkmahoe	428	140 —
Doughty, William	Canonbie	6	31 16				
Douglas, A. H. J., of Lockerbie	Lockerbie House, Lockerbie	2,336	3,345 2				
Douglas, James D. S., of Craigs	Baads, Haddington	6,629	6,013 4	Gardiner, Rev. Alexander, of Esbie	Brechin	250	420 —
Douglas, Mrs. Janet	Milliganton, Holywood	98	70 —	Gardiner, Rev. George	Westerhill, Annan	9	76 15
Douglas, Mrs. Robert	Burnfoot, Holywood	37	176 10	Gardner, William	Burnfoot, Applegarth	2	11 10
Dow, Trustees of William	Mountainhall, Dumfries	43	124 —	Geddes, Matthew, jun.	Vine Cottage, Lochmaben	2	6 —
Dryfesdale United Presbyterian Church, Trustees of	Dryfesdale, Lockerbie	5	47 —	Gillespie, James	Annanbank, Moffat	16	40 10
				Gillespie, Rev. John	Manse, Mouswald	25	50 —
Dudgeon, Patrick, of Cargen	Cargen, Dumfries	4	12 10	Gillespie, Thomas	Beckfoot, Annan	87	125 —
Dumfries, Burgh of	Dumfries	135	727 —	Gillison, John	Islesteps, Troqueer	43	100 —
Dumfries, Commissioners of Supply for County of	Dumfries	2	285 —	Gladstone, Steuart, of Lannhall	Lannhall, Tynron	446	356 —
Dumfries and Galloway Infirmary, Directors of	Dumfries	4	120 —	Gladstone, Thomas S., of Capenoch	Capenoch, Thornhill	1,302	1,256 15
Dumfries Gas Light Co.	Dumfries	2	338 —	Glaister, John	Ecclefechan	2	18 —
Dumfries Hospital, Directors of	Dumfries	66	130 —	Glasgow and South-Western Railway	Glasgow (Railway)	639	49753 —
Dumfries Parochial Board	Dumfries	8	185 —	Glover, John	Dumfries	8	28 3
Dumfries Police Commissioners	Dumfries	2	5 —	Glover, Newall Irving	Dumfries	42	81 —
				Gordon, Henry	Moatbrae, Dumfries	1	90 —
Dunbar, William, of Langshaw	Langshaw, Ecclefechan	200	245 —	Gordon, James	Dumfries	1	115 —
				Gordon, John Henry, of West Skelston	West Skelston, Dunscore	745	651 —
Duncan, Rev. J. Rogers	Manse, Torthorwald	15	50 —				
				Gordon, Sir R. G., of Gordonston and Letterfourie, Bart.	Letterfourie, Banffshire	151	300 —
Ecclefechan and Lochmaben Congregation and Hightae School	Lochmaben	6	11 5				
				Gordon, William	Nunbank, Dumfries	7	67 —
Edgar, David	Beltenmont, Ecclefechan	2	35 10	Gourlay, Rev. John H.	Manse, Brydekirk, Annan	1	22 8
Edgar, John, of Mid-Locharwoods	Locharwoods, Dumfries	514	353 —	Gowanlock, J. and W.	Broom, Saint Mungo	115	150 —
				Graham, Andrew	Lochmaben	5	47 —
Edgar, John	Frankfield, Dumfries	2	10 —	Graham, Archibald	Langholm	9	72 —
Edgar, Wm. Schlinder, of Kirkland	London	202	300 —	Graham, Sir F. U., of Netherby, Bart.	Netherby, Longtown	33	40 —
				Graham, Isaac	Troqueer	3	28 10

DUMFRIES—continued.

Name of Owner.	Address of Owner.	Estimated Acreage of Property.	Gross Annual Value.		Name of Owner.	Address of Owner.	Estimated Acreage of Property.	Gross Annual Value.	
		Acres.	£	s.			Acres.	£	s.
Graham, James, of Callside	Dumfries	50	161	10	Hoggan, George, of Waterside	Waterside, Keir	2,032	1,585	5
Graham, Trustees of James, of Dunnabie	Dunnabie, Lockerbie	999	898	–	Hope, David Boyle	Oakfield, Dumfries	2	60	–
Graham, John, of Shaw	Shaw, Lockerbie	1,415	702	–	Hope, Rev. John	Manse, Dunscore	68	87	–
Graham, John	Lockerbie	3	66	10	Hopetoun, Earl of	Hopetoun, Queensferry	2,549	634	–
Graham, John	Balstacks, Lockerbie	52	72	–	Horner, Heirs of Mrs.	Rosedale, Collin, Dumfries	1	6	–
Graham, Robert, jun., and Ann and Jane Graham	Broomhill, Lochmaben	105	230	–	Hotson, James	Langholm	1	191	15
Graham, Col. William, of Mossknow	Mossknow, Ecclefechan	4,019	4,993	6	Howat, Mrs. J.	Douievale, Dumfries	8	47	–
Graham, William	Ecclefechan	3	42	–	Hunter, Rev. David, of Killylung	Killylung, Holywood	349	478	–
Graham, William	Lochmaben	12	75	–	Hunter, Heirs of W. G., of Burnhead	Burnhead, Lockerbie	298	355	–
Graham, William	Eaglesham, Glasgow	13	28	10	Hunter, Mrs.	Milnton, Thornhill	8	38	–
Graham, Wm. Grierson	Smallholm, Lochmaben	117	230	10	Hutchison, David, James, and Joseph	Racks, Dumfries	1	13	10
Graham, Mrs. Janet	Ecclefechan	4	28	–	Hutchison, Robert	Collin, Dumfries	3	7	10
Graham, Ann	Gateside, Dumfries	1	12	–	Hutchison, Robert	Racks, Dumfries	1	4	10
Grahame, Trs. of W. R.	Moat House, Annan	37	190	–	Hutchison, Mrs.	Racks, Dumfries	1	9	–
Grant, Rev. J. D.	West Calder, Edinburgh	10	10	–	Hutton, Mrs. Janet, of Castramond	Maxwelltown	226	82	–
Gregan, William	High Street, Dumfries	3	186	–	Hyslop, James	Schoolhouse, Kirkmichael	2	6	5
Grierson, Sir A. W., of Rockhall, Bart.	Rockhall, Dumfries	3,514	3,084	–	Hyslop, John	UpperStepford, Dunscore	61	55	–
Grierson, Thomas B.	Thornhill	1	70	–	Hyslop, Trustees of Wm., of Mid-Locharwoods	Mid-Locharwoods, Bankend	314	305	–
Grierson, James, of Dalgoner	Dalgoner, Dunscore	800	1,117	–					
Grierson, John, of Muirside	Muirside, Holywood	286	310	–	Inglis, Rev. John	Manse, Sanquhar	22	100	–
Grierson, John	Dumfries	2	185	–	Inglis, Margaret	Auchencrieff, Dumfries	1	4	10
Grierson, Thomas	Mossfoot, Lochmaben	2	5	10	Irving, Representatives of H. B., of Milkbank	Milkbank, Lockerbie	254	353	–
Grierson, Mrs. Edward	Sauchtree, Dumfries	1	206	10	Irving, John	Annan	2	13	–
Grierson, Grace D.	Mount Charles, Moffat	1	50	–	Irving, John	High Street, Annan	5	12	–
Gunning, Mrs. Ann S.	Cresswell, Dumfries	27	203	–	Irving, John, of Burnfoot	Burnfoot, Ecclefechan	4,868	3,683	5
					Irving, John	Kenziels, Annan	2	13	–
Hair, John, of Fleuchlarg	Fleuchlarg, Moniaive	155	122	–	Irving, John	Roundknowe, Annan	5	7	–
Halbert, John Potts, of Ashbygrange	Ashbygrange, Annan	356	1,078	12	Irving, Jonathan	Sandhills, Annan	33	69	9
Hall, John	Cockieshill, Lochmaben	3	6	10	Irving, Rev. Lewis H., of Hazelberry, etc.	Arnot Hill, Falkirk	471	350	–
Hall, William	Barnkin, Dumfries	1	10	10	Irving, Nathaniel	Annan	11	29	–
Halliday, David	Lowthertown, Dornock	1	5	–	Irving, Nathaniel	Kenziels, Annan	8	22	–
Halliday, James	Meikleholmside, Moffat	18	22	–	Irving, Robert	Plumdon, Annan	15	65	–
Halliday, John	Jonesfield, Lockerbie	3	10	5	Irving, R. Nasmyth, of Bonshaw	Bonshaw, Ecclefechan	1,435	1,325	10
Halliday, Joseph W.	Coopwood, Lockerbie	64	65	–	Irving, William	Westgill, Annan	22	38	15
Halliday, Peter	Boghall, Moffat	1	117	–	Irving, Wm. O. B., and John B., of Whitehill	Whitehill, Lockerbie	193	220	–
Halliday, William	Newfieldbank, Moffat	10	25	–	Irving, Mrs. Susan	Eaglesfield, Ecclefechan	1	9	5
Halliday, Mrs., of Whinnyrig	Whinnyrig, Annan	239	495	8	Irving, Mary Anne	Fish Cross, Annan	4	7	–
Halliday, Mrs. Jane	Stakeford Cot., Dumfries	2	140	–					
Halliday, Mrs. Jane	Dumfries	2	8	–	Jackson, John, of Amisfield	Amisfield, Dumfries	445	783	–
Hamilton, Heirs of B.	Townfoot, Sanquhar	2	6	6	Jackson, John	Solway Bank, Annan	84	100	–
Hamilton, John	Cockwell, Lochmaben	14	15	–	Jackson, Robert	Newton, Dumfries	5	10	–
Harkness, James	11 Wood Street, Bolton	62	70	–	Jackson, Thos. and Janet	Paulsland, Ecclefechan	45	69	–
Harkness, John	Albany House, Dumfries	1	60	–	Jamieson, William	Shuttlefield, Lockerbie	55	64	5
Harkness, Joseph	Lochmaben	25	40	–	Jardine, Alexander	Glenstuart, Annan	1	10	–
Harkness, Joseph	Mid-Crossleys, Holywood	25	52	–	Jardine, Alexander	Dumfries	3	10	10
Harkness, William	Lochmaben	2	8	10	Jardine, Andrew, of Corrie	Lanrick Castle, Stirling	9,838	5,569	5
Harrison, William	Gullielands, Annan	245	273	5	Jardine, Rev. David	Manse, Keir	14	46	–
Heck, Heritors of	Lochmaben	3	8	–	Jardine, George	Hightae, Lochmaben	24	27	–
Henderson, George	Ivy Lodge, Dumfries	47	311	–	Jardine, Heirs of Robert, of Balgray	Balgray, Lockerbie	850	705	10
Henning, Thomas, of East Skelston	East Skelston, Dunscore	302	206	–	Jardine, James	Bishopcleuch, Lockerbie	58	100	–
Heron, James, of Duncow	Duncow, Dumfries	737	1,363	–	Jardine, James, of Dryfeholm	Dryfeholm, Lockerbie	761	1,118	–
Herries, Lord	Everingham Park, York	5,814	6,257	–	Jardine, James	Parkhead, Dumfries	12	39	–
Hewatson, Jas., of Swyre	Auchenbainzie, Thornhill	466	353	5	Jardine, James	Racks, Dumfries	4	9	–
Hewatson, James	Grennan, Penpont	25	40	–	Jardine, John	Blaemeadow, Lochmaben	4	5	10
Hewatson, Thomas, of Broomfield	Broomfield, Penpont	402	215	–	Jardine, Robert	Haggrigg, Lockerbie	3	8	–
Hewison, Alexander	Thornhill	7	23	–	Jardine, Robert, of Castlemilk, M.P.	Castlemilk, Lockerbie	7,714	8,598	–
Hiddleston, James	Moniaive	3	38	10	Jardine, Sir William, of Applegarth, Bart.	Applegarth, Lockerbie	5,538	5,813	5
Hiddleston, Thomas	Boddinlea, Dumfries	6	16	–	Jardine, Trustees of William, of Granton	Granton, Moffat	2,212	883	10
Hiddleston, Trs. of John	Kilroy, Dunscore	131	231	–	Jardine, William	Dryfebridge, Lockerbie	2	114	–
Hiddleston, William	Riddingwood, Kirkmahoe	44	75	–	Jardine, William	Eaglesfield, Ecclefechan	5	17	5
Hightae and others, Heritors of	Lochmaben Mosslands	146	60	–	Jardine, Wm. Alex.	Queen St., Edinburgh	12	10	–
Hill, John	Bowerhouses, Ruthwell	6	16	10	Jardine, Mrs. Christiana, of Beattock	Beattock House, Moffat	680	400	–
Hobkirk, Robert	Southburn, Lockerbie	69	85	–					
Hoddam United Presbyterian Church	Hoddam, Ecclefechan	7	39	–					
Hogg, Rev. David	Manse, Kirkmahoe	10	36	–					
Hogg, Thos. and Wm.	Castle-Douglas	6	45	–					

DUMFRIES—continued.

Name of Owner.	Address of Owner.	Estimated Acreage of Property.	Gross Annual Value.	Name of Owner.	Address of Owner.	Estimated Acreage of Property.	Gross Annual Value.
		Acres.	£ s.			Acres.	£ s.
Jardine, Reprs. of Mrs.	High Street, Lochmaben	2	4 5	Landale, Rev. David	Manse, Applegarth	9	39 -
Jardine, Mary, and John Johnstone	Innerfield, Lochmaben	23	14 10	Lang, James Innes, of Sunnyhill	Sunnyhill, Holywood	266	306 10
Johnstone, Alexander	High Street, Moffat	1	236 -	Lattimer, George	Lowthertown, Annan	2	10 -
Johnstone, Christopher, of Croftheads	Dinwoodie Lodge, Lockerbie	100	158 10	Laurie, Mrs. Isabella, of Maxwelton	Maxwelton, Moniaive	1,810	1,531 -
Johnstone, George	Waterside, Terregles	4	18 -	Learmont, George	Barkerland, Dumfries	27	177 -
Johnstone, Heirs of Patrick Maxwell	Bankhead, Kirkmahoe	2	15 -	Learmont, William	Dumfries	7	85 -
Johnstone, Hon. Henry B., of Corehead	Corehead, Moffat	2,960	1,575 -	Leny, Wm. Macalpine, of Dalswinton	Dalswinton, Dumfries	5,724	4,282 -
Johnstone, Jas., of Gibsons	Gibsons, Lockerbie	146	220 -	Leslie, Richard	Heck, Lochmaben	2	6 10
Johnstone, John	Northburn, Lockerbie	108	71 -	Liddell, Rev. Thomas	Manse, Lochmaben	8	41 10
Johnstone, John, of Halleaths	Halleaths, Lochmaben	2,122	2,734 -	Lightbody, Thomas	Langholm	1	105 -
Johnstone, John J. H., of Annandale	Raehills, Moffat	64,079	27884 -	Linton, Sir Wm., K.C.B.	Skairfield, Lochmaben	13	45 -
Johnstone, James and Walter, of Bodesbeck	Bodesbeck, Moffat	3,050	694 -	Little, James	Corriehill, Lockerbie	58	55 -
				Little, John	Annan	23	22 10
Johnstone, Major-General Thomas Henry, of Carnsalloch	Carnsalloch, Dumfries	2,409	2,821 -	Little, Heirs of John M.	Maryfield, Dumfries	33	164 -
				Little, William	Loganbrae, Half Morton	1	10 -
				Little, Mrs. Georgina	Droveroad, Langholm	5	32 -
Johnstone, Rev. Wm.	Manse, Cummertrees	31	50 -	Little, Mrs. Jane, of Wicketthorn	Annan	240	220 10
Johnstone, Sir Fred. John William, of Westerhall, Bart.	Westerhall, Langholm	17,064	6,834 -	Little, Mrs. Janet	Annan	4	8 -
				Lochmaben, Burgh of	Lochmaben	2	3 5
				Lockerbie, William	Eastfield, Dumfries	81	452 10
				Lockerbie, Mrs. David	Rosedale, Collin	2	7 10
Johnstone, Thomas, Geo., and John	Waterside, Terregles	84	114 -	Lockerbie, Mrs. John	Trench, Dumfries	2	10 -
				Lorimer, Andrew	Lauriston House, Moniaive	182	102 10
Johnstone, Thomas	Middleshaw, Lockerbie	33	40 -	Lorraine, Rev. Jos. C.	Manse, Caerlaverock	21	50 -
Johnstone, Thomas	Malton, Yorkshire	3	12 10	Lyon, George Francis, of Kirkmichael	Kirkmichael, Dumfries	2,994	2,532 -
Johnstone, Trustees of D.	Riggheads, Lochmaben	339	470 -	Lyon, Lieut.-Col. George, of Dalruskin	Bellfield House, Cupar-Fife	410	407 -
Johnstone, William, of Cowhill	Cowhill, Holywood	230	426 -				
Johnstone, William	Shawhill, Annan	3	34 -				
Johnstone, William	Walnutgrove, Lochmaben	6	18 -	M'Allister, Reps. of John, jun.	Isle of Man Moss, Dumfries	2	9 -
Johnstone, William, of Catlins	Glasgow	274	151 -	M'Burnie, J. & W. B.	Annan	10	25 -
Johnstone, Mrs. Andrew	Gibsons, Lockerbie	96	104 10	M'Burnie, James	Laverockhall, Dunscore	50	40 -
Johnstone, Mrs. Grace	Holmfield, Moffat	10	57 -	M'Call, James, of Caitloch	Caitloch, Moniaive	2,502	906 -
Johnstone, Mrs. Jessie	Townfoot, Ecclefechan	6	15 -	M'Call, William Rae	Noblehill, Dumfries	2	27 10
Johnstone, Marion	Dumfries	28	209 10	M'Call, William	Lochmaben	1	6 -
				M'Connel, Frederick, of Robgill	Robgill Tower, Annan	387	563 -
Kean, Mrs.	Langholm	1	107 -	M'Cubbin, Isabella	Pointhead, Penpont	2	18 -
Keay, Mrs. Margaret	Grahamshall, Ecclefechan	28	78 -	M'Cubbin, Margaret and Isabella	Pointhead, Penpont	1	26 -
Kennedy, David, of Castlehill	Castlehill, Kirkmahoe	210	350 -	M'Donald, William Bell, of Rammerscales	Rammerscales, Lockerbie	1,050	1,188 -
Kennedy, James	Clogger, Dumfries	7	115 10	M'Dougall, Richard	Corrie, Lockerbie	7	8 -
Kennedy, James, of Sundaywell	Brandleys, Sanquhar	700	348 -	M'Duff, William	Glencaple, Dumfries	1	36 -
Kennedy, Robert, of Riddings	Riddings, Thornhill	66	56 10	M'Farlan, Rev. James	Manse, Ruthwell, Annan	52	75 -
Kennedy, Robert, of Newlands	Newlands, Kirkmahoe	320	350 -	M'Gill, Alexander	Newton, Dumfries	10	43 10
				M'Gowan, James H.	Ellangowan, Dumfries	40	156 -
Kennedy, Robert, of Dalmakerran	Dalmakerran, Thornhill	360	208 -	M'Gowan, Mrs. Mary	Hightae, Lochmaben	2	8 -
				M'Gregor, Rev. And.	Manse, Johnstone	16	45 -
Kennedy, William, of Shillingland	Northumberland Street, Edinburgh	534	140 -	M'Intosh, George	Boreland, Dumfries	1	1 12
				M'Intosh, William	Frithbie, Annan	3	60 -
Kennedy, William	Lockerbie	1	2 5	M'Kaig, Mrs. Janet	Rosevale, Dumfries	1	210 -
Kennedy, William J.	Sanquhar	133	130 -	M'Kay, John	Wantage, Berkshire	6	17 10
Kennedy, Mrs. Elizabeth	Rosehill Pl., Edinburgh	3	7 5	Mackay, William	Racks, Dumfries	17	28 -
Kennedy, Mrs. Jane, of Kirkland	Kirkland, Thornhill	54	125 -	Mackay, William, and Averill's Heirs	Racks, Dumfries	4	9 10
Kennedy, Mrs. M.	Collin, Dumfries	2	7 -	M'Keane, Robert	Collin, Dumfries	2	5 -
Ker, Hugh	Annan	1	150 -	M'Kelvie, Mrs. Margaret	Cornwall Mo., Dumfries	1	70 -
Kerr, James	Moss-side, Dunscore	23	40 -	M'Kenzie, Rev. C. W.	Manse, Durisdeer	30	45 -
Kerr, John	Warrenhill, Collin	6	31 10	M'Kenzie, Edward, of Newbie	Newbie, Annan	2,929	5,263 8
Kerr, John	Elizafield, Collin	3	80 10	M'Kenzie, Mrs. Agnes	Lakeside, Kirkmahoe	2	17 -
Kershaw, John	Langholm	1	143 10	M'Kie, James, and others	Moat House, Dumfries	9	55 8
Keswick, William, of Beechgrove	Beechgrove, Annan	120	201 12	M'Kie, James	Moat House, Dumfries	4	805 -
Kirkpatrick, Andrew	Drumbreg, Collin	58	157 10	M'Kinnel, James B. A.	Dumfries	4	50 -
Kirkpatrick, James	Thriepmuir, Closeburn	126	45 -	M'Kinnel, John M., of Macmurdoston	North Laurieknowe, Dumfries	425	602 -
Kirkpatrick, Matthew	Woodlands, Lochmaben	2	12 -	M'Kinnon, Mrs. C.	Marchbankwood, Moffat	5	50 -
Kirkpatrick, Roger, of Lagganlees	Glasgow	100	120 -	M'Kitterick, Thomas	Viewfield, Dumfries	4	50 -
				M'Knight, William	Moss Loaning, Dumfries	5	17 10
				M'Knight, Mrs. Margaret	Hightae, Lochmaben	1	1 10
Laidlaw, Rev. James	Wanlockhead, Abington	3	10 -	M'Lean, Campbell	Annan	2	252 -
Lamb, Heirs of C. J., of Cooms	Cooms Ewes, Langholm	3,800	420 -	M'Michael, George, of Moat	Sanquhar	119	184 -

DUMFRIES—continued.

Name of Owner.	Address of Owner.	Estimated Acreage of Property.	Gross Annual Value.	Name of Owner.	Address of Owner.	Estimated Acreage of Property.	Gross Annual Value.
		Acres.	£ s.			Acres.	£ s.
M'Millan, James	Moffat	1	149 —	Morrine, Mrs. Elizabeth	Morrinton, Holywood	45	20 —
M'Millan, John, of Holm	Glencrosh, Moniaive	1,075	370 —	Morrison, Reps. of Alex.	Moffat	3	146 8
M'Millan, Robert	Essexpark, Dumfries	4	56 —	Moses, Thomas	Langholm	2	75 —
M'Millan, Robert, and Trs. of S. J. M'Millan	Maidenbower, Dumfries	39	105 —	Mouncie, Trs. of Mrs.	Moffat	5	222 —
M'Millan, Samuel M'Call, of Corriedoo	Arihoulan, Fort-William	500	195 —	Mundell, Peter, and others	Bogrie, Dumfries	860	324 15
M'Teir, John, of Ladyfield	Netherwood, Dumfries	35	147 —	Munn, Robert, of Whitecroft	Stacksteads, Manchester	330	508 —
M'Turk, Rev. J. W.	Manse, Langholm	62	142 —	Murdoch, Rev. John	Kirkpatrick-Fleming	23	49 —
M'Vicar, Rev. John G.	Manse, Moffat	19	75 —	Murdoch, Walter S., of Dunesslin	Enmore Park, Surrey	184	199 —
M'William, John	Galloway Ho., Dumfries	3	40 —	Murphy, Hugh	Dumfries	1	226 10
Maitland, Lauderdale, of Eccles	York Place, Dumfries	455	607 10	Murray, Heirs of John, of Murraythwaite	Murraythwaite, Ecclefechan	1,356	1,624 10
Malcolm, James, of Williamwood	Royal Circus, Edinburgh	678	547 4	Murray, John	Kirkbeck, Ruthwell, Annan	18	18 —
Malcolm, William E., of Burnfoot	Burnfoot, Langholm	2,115	749 5	Murray, Rev. John	Manse, Morton, Thornhill	25	50 —
Mansfield, Earl of	Comlongan Castle, Annan	14,342	13389 13	Murray, Robert	St. Catherine's, Dumfries	44	87 —
Marchbank, David	Weston, Cherbury, Salop	4	19 10	Murray, Mrs. I. Hay	Waterside, Ecclefechan	5	41 —
Marshall, Thomas	Howes, Annan	63	123 —	Murray, Mrs. Agnes	Moniaive	2	8 —
Martin, John, of Laggan	Over-Laggan	63	80 —	Murray, Mary	St. Catherine's, Dumfries	1	60 —
Martin, John	60 West Scotland Street, Glasgow	10	26 —	Neilson, Mrs., and Robert Nicholson, of Lochbank	Dumfries	59	185 —
Martin, Samuel, of Fraserford	Fraserford, Dunscore	334	195 —	Nelson, Jos. Bryden, and Heirs of John Nelson	Lochmaben	9	25 —
Martin, William, of Dardarroch	Dardarroch, Dunscore	200	359 —	Newall, Trustees of Adam	Dumfries	11	202 —
Martin, Mrs. Sophia	Lochmaben	3	28 —	Newbigging, A. T., and Alex. Cowan	Dumfries	5	16 —
Mather, John Alfred	Nithside, Closeburn	59	90 —	Newbigging, Alex. T.	Dumfries	2	280 5
Mathieson, James & Wm.	Torthorwald	6	28 10	Newton, James Ewan	Linnbank House, Lanark	54	100 5
Maxwell, Francis, of Birkhall	Dunragit, Glenluce	114	130 —	Nicholson, Benjamin	Annan	69	363 8
Maxwell, General George	Kilncleuch, Langholm	3	45 —	Nicholson, John, & Co.	Annan	1	10 —
Maxwell, George, of Broomholm	Broomholm, Langholm	1,886	762 —	Nicholson, Trustees of Thomas	Waterside, Lochmaben	81	79 —
Maxwell, Maxwell H., of Glengaber	The Grove, Dumfries	839	1,117 10	Nicholson, William L., of Dornock	London	136	281 —
Maxwell, Hon. Henry C., of Milnhead	Milnhead, Dumfries	1,470	1,430 16	Nicholson, Mrs. Grace	Gracefield, Dumfries	3	83 —
Maxwell, Heirs of Alex. Harley, of Portrack	Portrack, Dumfries	284	476 —	Nicholson, Mrs. John	Hillside, Annan	19	86 —
Maxwell, James Clerk	Glenlair, Dalbeattie	68	65 —	Nicol, Peter	Scaleridge, Middlebie	10	14 —
Maxwell, Sir John Heron, of Springkell, Bart.	Springkell, Ecclefechan	13,391	8,758 —	Nicol, Mrs. Janet	Thwaite, Ruthwell, Annan	19	16 —
Maxwell, General J. H., of Portrack	Portrack, Dumfries	150	248 —	*North British Railway Company*	Edinburgh (*Railway*)	91	2,909 —
Maxwell, William, junior	Naphtha Works, Dumfries	2	30 —	Ogilvie, Heirs of Augustus George, of Cove	The Cove, Ecclefechan	771	692 8
Maxwell, Sir William, of Cardoness, Bart.	Cardoness, Gatehouse	4	112 —	Osborne, Mrs. Mary	Sanquhar	1	39 10
Maxwell, Mrs. Sarah, of Orchardton	Orchardton, Castle-Douglas	1,025	1,083 5	Otto, Mrs. Susan, and Mrs. Barker	Newark, Sanquhar	596	711 5
Maxwell, Mrs., of Gribton	Gribton, Dumfries	619	1,288 —	Pagan, William	Maxwelltown	37	100 —
Mein, Nicol Alexander	Marsh House, Canonbie	3	62 —	Palmer, William	Annan	34	158 10
Menteith, Rev. John	Manse, Glencairn	17	45 —	Palmer, Mrs. Margaret	Greenhill, Lochmaben	2	8 15
Menzies, Rev. Robert	Manse, Ecclefechan	25	68 10	Park, John	Annfield, Annan	1	14 —
Millar, John O., of Ryecroft	Ryecroft, Dublin	20	54 —	Park, Mrs. William	Holmend, Moffat	4	13 15
Millar, William	Meikleholm, Langholm	5	30 —	Paterson, James, of Longbedholm	Carmacoup, Douglas, Lanark	676	260 —
Milligan, Jacob, of Dempsterton	Dempsterton, Dunscore	83	99 —	Paterson, Rev. C. E.	Manse, Dalton	13	40 —
Milligan, Samuel	Dumfries	1	206 —	Paterson, Representatives of Mrs. Mary	Watchhill, Annan	28	79 —
Milligan, Thomas	Merkland, Dunscore	72	110 —	Paterson, Robert	Dumfries	5	103 —
Milligan, William, sen.	Westpark, Maxwelltown	1	261 —	Paterson, Robert	Liverpool	8	31 —
Milligan, Mrs. Elizabeth	Knowehead, Kirkmahoe	34	40 —	Paterson, Thomas S., of Ironhirst	Liverpool	902	678 —
Mitchell, Rev. J. M.	Manse, Kirkmichael	22	61 —	Paterson, Trs. of Robert	Nunfield, Dumfries	8	690 10
Mitchell, Mrs. Jane	Burnscarth Green, Dumfries	19	105 —	Paterson, William, of Brocklehirst	Nunfield, Dumfries	936	730 —
Moffat, Alexander, of Lochurr	Craig, Dunscore	917	395 —	Paterson, Mrs. M.	Nunfield, Dumfries	40	278 —
Moffat, George	Littlecleuchbrae, Middlebie	7	15 —	Patterson, Edward	Fountainebleau, Dumfries	58	146 —
Moffat, Robert Thomas	Ardnacloich, Moniaive	2	6 —	Paton, Rev. Andrew	Manse, Penpont	8	45 —
Moffat, Thomas	Ardnacloich, Moniaive	3	22 —	Pattie, Andrew	Jocksthorn, Moffat	1	8 10
Moffat and Kirkpatrick-Juxta, Heritors of	Moffat	20	94 —	Pattie, William	Castleyards, Torthorwald	5	16 —
Moffat, Heritors of	Moffat	1	5 —	Pearson, Trustees of Andrew Adam, of Luce	Luce, Hoddam, Annan	951	1,012 —
Moffat Kirk Session	Moffat	5	9 —	Pickering, Mrs. Janet	Skelton, Penrith	13	22 —
Monilaws, Rev. J. J.	Manse, Middlebie	14	63 —	Pool & Nicholson	Annan	1	202 —
Morin, John Anthony, of Allanton	Allanton, Dunscore	595	737 —	Pool, James	Nursery Place, Annan	22	40 —
				Pool, Trustees of William and James	Westcrofthead, Annan	7	33 —

H

DUMFRIES—continued.

Name of Owner.	Address of Owner.	Estimated Acreage of Property.	Gross Annual Value.	Name of Owner.	Address of Owner.	Estimated Acreage of Property.	Gross Annual Value.
		Acres.	£ s.			Acres.	£ s.
Pool, Mrs. Marion	Toppinghall, Annan	50	50 —	Rome, Bryce Moncrieff	21 Doncaster Street, Liverpool	18	30 —
Pool, Mrs. Susannah	Swordwell, Annan	78	80 —	Rome, Robert M.	Langholm	9	33 10
Porteous, Mrs. William	Ecclefechan	6	20 —	Roxburgh, William	Annan	28	60 —
Potter, James	Roucan, Dumfries	137	266 —	Roxburgh, Wm. & Alex.	Annan	8	34 —
Powell, William Frederick, of Scroggs	Manchester	640	792 —	Roxburgh, Mrs. Alex.	Annan	7	16 —
Prophet, Rev. James	Manse, St. Mungo	45	84 —	Rowley, Andrew	Larchhill, Moffat	7	80 —
Proudfoot, James, of Craigieburn	Craigieburn, Moffat	631	453 —	Rutherford, John	Blackburn	14	90 5
Proudfoot, John, of Gateside	Gateside, Wamphray	130	155 —	Rutherford, Mrs.	Violet Bank, Annan	2	30 —
Proudfoot, John	Moffat	2	441 —	Russell, James, of Breconside	Thornhill	382	213 10
Proudfoot, William, of Nethermill	Nethermill, Moffat	96	258 2				
Purdie, William	Lowthertown, Annan	6	27 10	Saffley, John, of Morrinton	Morrinton, Holywood	164	77 —
				Sanquhar, Burgh of	Sanquhar	197	335 —
Queensberry, Marquess of	Kinmount, Annan	13,243	13384 16	Sanquhar United Presbyterian Church (North), Trustees of	Sanquhar	1	20 —
				Sanquhar United Presbyterian Church (South), Trustees of	Sanquhar	1	30 —
Rae, John	Heck, Lochmaben	6	10 10	Saunders, James	Seaforth, Annan	34	242 —
Rae, Matthew, of Newton	Newton, Ecclefechan	239	392 —	Saunders, John	Bottom, Lochmaben	25	30 —
Rae, Robert	Raefield, Sanquhar	5	25 —	Saunders, Heirs of Robert	Cleuchside, Lochmaben	26	15 10
Rae, William	Lockerbie	5	227 —	Saunders, Rev. Robert	Manse, Tundergarth	9	30 —
Ramage, Craufurd Tait	Wallacehall, Closeburn	564	680 10	Scott, Rev. David Lawson	Dumfries	5	60 —
Ramsay, Rev. David O.	Manse, Closeburn	11	45 —	Scott, George	Langholm	7	95 7
Ramsay, Mrs. Peter, of Scotsfield	Scotsfield, Annan	136	80 —	Scott, James	Claygate, Canonbie	2	305 —
Reid, Alexander	Langholm	14	70 —	Scott, John	Langshawbank, Moffat	1	80 —
Reid, Benjamin, of Newton-Reid	Aberdeen	99	200 —	Scott, John	Langholm	1	27 5
				Scott, Mrs., and Mrs. Johnstone	Ewanston, Glencairn	50	228 —
Reid, George	Greystone, Dumfries	4	103 —	Scott, Robert, of Raeburn	Moodlaw	4,500	1,300 —
Reid, Sir John R., Bart.	Greystone, Dumfries	7	34 —	Scott, Walter, & Sons	Dumfries	4	734 —
Reid, Thomas	Moffat	4	11 —	Scott, Lords Walter C. and Charles Thomas	Drumlanrig Castle, Thornhill	32	55 —
Reid & Taylor	Langholm	1	485 4	Scott, Mrs. Margaret, of Watcarrick	Enzieholm, Langholm	1,054	300 —
Reid, William and John	Hallbank, Lockerbie	13	15 —				
Reid, Mary	Barnslaps, Dumfries	2	10 —	Sharpe, William, of Hoddam	Knockhill, Ecclefechan	5,456	5,605 10
Richardson, Andrew	Haggrigg, Lockerbie	9	18 10	Shaw, Charles	London	5	20 8
Richardson, David	Greenhill, Lochmaben	1	6 2	Simpson, Mrs. Harriet, of Dallawoodie	Dallawoodie, Holywood	149	340 —
Richardson, George	Heck, Lochmaben	5	12 —				
Richardson, Heirs of Mrs.	Hightae, Lochmaben	2	22 —	Skelton, James Scott	Greenbank, Annan	2	240 —
Richardson, John	Gilmorecleuchhead, Lochmaben	13	10 10	Skelton, Mrs. J. S.	Greenbank, Annan	9	48 —
Richardson, John	Boghead, Lochmaben	2	7 5	Slater, Mrs. Mary, of Castlebank	Castlebank, Ecclefechan	211	418 10
Richardson, John	Inby Heck, Lochmaben	12	27 —	Sloan, James	Dumfries	1	475 —
Richardson, John	Hightae, Lochmaben	1	8 —	Sloan, Margaret	Penpont	19	50 —
Richardson, John, and Mrs. Dryden	Hightae, Lochmaben	3	21 —	Smith, Alexander, of Upper Glenjan	Upper Glenjan, Moniaive	274	81 —
Richardson, Thomas	Longbank, Dunscore	34	42 —	Smith, Eaglesfield B., of Blackwood	Blackwood, Ecclefechan	268	496 15
Richardson, Thomas	Greenhill, Lochmaben	2	5 —	Smith, Heirs of James	Totness, Longtown	2	5 —
Richardson, Thomas	Dunscore	4	8 10	Smith, Heirs of John	Dumfries	7	62 —
Richardson, William	Middlerow, Dalton	15	25 —	Smith, Henry, of Ingleston	Ipswich	396	366 10
Ritchie, Andrew	Quarrypark, Annan	28	20 —	Smith, John, and others	Lochhill, Moniaive	52	52 —
Robinson, William	Gateshead, Newcastle	3	5 10	Smith, Paulus Æmilius	Allerbeck, Ecclefechan	120	95 —
Robison, Jas. and Robert	Priestholm, Dornock	26	41 —	Smith, Peter, of Newtonairds	Newtonairds, Dumfries	1,164	1,155 —
Robison, Robert	Fairfield, Liverpool	4	14 10				
Robson, John	Gasstoun, Dumfries	7	11 —	Smith, Rev. Thomas	Manse, Ewes, Langholm	30	45 —
Robson, Mary J. H., of Kemyshall	Kemyshall, Kirkmahoe	137	171 15	Smith, Thomas, of Craiglieran	Dalfibble, Kirkmichael	1,513	340 —
Roddick, Robert P. B., of Flosh	Flosh, Kirk-Fleming, Ecclefechan	174	80 —	Smith, William	Moniaive	96	217 10
Rogerson, Alexander, of Girthhead	Girthhead, Moffat	305	250 —	Smith, Mrs. James	Taylorland, Dumfries	1	3 —
Rogerson, Capt. William, of Cleuchheads	Applegarth, Lockerbie	558	565 14	Smith, Mrs. Francis	Lochbank, New Abbey	15	38 —
Rogerson, George, of Pearcebyhall	Dumfries	700	750 —	Smyth, Trustees of Christopher	Dumfries	119	162 10
Rogerson, James	Gateshead, Newcastle	184	212 —	Smyth, Heirs of Thomas Robinson	Dumfries	6	372 —
Rogerson, James Alex., of Gillesbie	Gillesbie, Lockerbie	9284	4,098 5	Society for Propagating Christian Knowledge	Edinburgh	1,283	862 —
Rogerson, John, of Hazelbank	Fingland, Moffat	428	260 —	Solway Junction Railway Company	London (Railway)	98	337 —
Rogerson, Samuel and Joseph, of Broomhillbank	Applegarth, Lockerbie	760	480 —	Sproat, Peter	Mountainhall, Dumfries	34	114 —
				Stearne, Joseph	Dumfries	2	10 —
Rogerson, Trustees of Mr. and Mrs., of Boreland	Boreland, Lockerbie	1,401	747 —	Steel, George	Newington, Annan	73	258 —
Rogerson, William	Muirhouse, Lochmaben	10	30 —	Steel, Joseph, of Kirkwood	Kirkwood, Lockerbie	798	786 3
Rollo, Lord, of Duncrieff	Duncrieff, Moffat	7,220	3,044 —	Steel, William	Lowthertown, Annan	2	8 10

DUMFRIES—continued.

Name of Owner.	Address of Owner.	Estimated Acreage of Property.	Gross Annual Value.	Name of Owner.	Address of Owner.	Estimated Acreage of Property.	Gross Annual Value.
		Acres.	£ s.			Acres.	£ s.
Stevenson, Alexander	Langholm	29	77 10	Villiers, Frederick Ernest	Closeburn Hall, Dumfries	13	80 —
Stevenson, Thomas	Langholm	4	45 5	Veitch, James, of Eliock	Eliock, Sanquhar	5,163	1,693 —
Stewart, Charles, of St. Michael's	Hillside, Lockerbie	266	390 10	Vivers, William	Dornocktown, Annan	2	8 —
Stewart, David W., of Grange	St. Michael's, Lockerbie	852	670 —				
Stewart, Thomas, of Slodahill	Gillenbie, Lockerbie	452	405 —	Walker, Colonel George Gustavus, M.P., of Crawfordton	Crawfordton, Moniaive	7,146	3,478 —
Stewart, Thomas Barker	Auchentaggart, Sanquhar	5	25 —	Walker, John, of Auchencairn	Dalmarnock, Glasgow	68	60 —
Stobo, Robert, of Hallidayhill	Hallidayhill, Dunscore	227	174 —	Wallace, Heirs of James W.	Holywood	28	70 —
Stodart, David	Whitelees, Middlebie	2	11 10	Wallace, Samuel	Auchenbrack, Thornhill	227	262 —
Stodart, Thomas T., of Oliver	Holmshaw, Moffat	1,000	190 —	Waters, Rev. Thomas	Lauder	2	35 10
Stott, Heirs of John, of Netherwood	Netherwood, Dumfries	572	922 —	Watson, David	Farthingwell, Dunscore	63	90 —
Stott, Mrs. Margaret H.	Netherwoodbank, Dumfries	3	30 —	Watson, William	Farthingwell, Holywood	57	129 10
Strathern, Rev. John	Manse, Eskdalemuir	32	45 —	Weild, David	98 London Street, Derby	2	6 10
Sturgeon, William	Dumfries	2	41 —	Weild, Mrs. Margaret	Linden Place, Annan	16	23 —
Swan, Heirs of William	Lochmaben	85	97 10	Weir, Thomas	49 Nelson Square, London	52	40 —
Swan, Robert, of Brae	Lochrutton, Dumfries	262	340 —	Wells, James	Watchhill, Lochmaben	1	4 —
Syme, Robert	Redkirk, Gretna	50	55 —	Wells, Rev. James	Glasgow	2	20 10
				Wells, John Thomson	50 John St., Blackburn	4	14 —
				Welsh, Thomas	Erickstane, Moffat	18	224 —
Tait, James	Bourock, Lochrutton	3	14 10	White, Rev. Robert H.	Manse, Lockerbie	22	49 —
Taylor, James, of Ellisland	Edinburgh	126	230 —	White, Mrs. Eliza, of Minnygapp	Minnygapp, Moffat	742	255 —
Taylor, Thomas C., and John M'K.	Cairnhall, Dunscore	58	100 —	Wight, George	9 Caldmore Road, Walsall	1	6 —
Teenan, James	Newcastle-on-Tyne	5	10 10	Wight, Rev. George	Wamphray, Moffat	82	150 —
Teenan, Michael	Dumfries	20	249 —	Wight, James	Elvanfoot, Abington	25	55 —
Telfer, David	Whiteside, Torthorwald	32	50 —	Wightman, Heirs of Matthew	Northfield, Dumfries	1	16 —
Telfer, George	Hightae, Lochmaben	2	10 —	Wightman, James S., of Courance	Courance, Lockerbie	2,750	1,705 —
Thomson, Archibald	Little Clyde, Moffat	40	49 —	Wightman, John T.	Braehead, Lochrutton	21	72 —
Thomson, James, & others	Leafield, Dumfries	4	24 10	Williamson, Ninian	Croydon, Surrey	2	46 —
Thomson, John, of Milliganton	Milliganton, Dunscore	207	282 —	Williamson, Thomas	Annan	36	61 4
Thomson, John	Newdyke, Annan	8	10 —	Wilson, James	Thornhill	7	21 —
Thomson, John	Cleuchfoot, Langholm	12	81 —	Wilson, John	Burnside, Moffat	2	142 —
Thomson, John	Grovehill, Penpont	32	140 —	Wilson, John, and others	Roundstonefoot, Moffat	882	130 —
Thomson, Trustees of Mrs.	Langholm	10	73 10	Wilson, Thomas J., of Stroquhan	Stroquhan, Dunscore	4,198	2,251 —
Thomson, Wm., & Co.	Dumfries	1	30 —	Wilson, Mrs.	Hightae, Lochmaben	13	30 —
Thomson, Mrs. Janet	Dumfries	18	20 —	Wilson, Mrs. Jane	Paignton, South Devon	3	17 10
Thomson, Mrs. Mary, of Craighaugh	Nether Cassock, Langholm	1,495	415 —	Wood, James	Annan	1	123 —
Thorpe, John	Dumfries	3	93 10	Wood, John	Bowmillholm, Lockerbie	16	27 —
Threshie, Mrs. Jessie, of Mouswald Place	Barnbarroch, Dalbeattie	653	948 —	Wright, James	Ecclefechan	3	12 —
Tod, Representatives of James, of Underwood	Underwood, Lockerbie	456	578 —	Wright, John	Heck, Lockmaben	12	18 —
Tod, William, of Heatheryhaugh	Heatheryhaugh, Moffat	41	130 —	Wright, Thomas	Viewfield, Lochmaben	3	21 10
Turner, Trustees of James, of Mosside	Dumfries	136	132 10	Wright, Walter	Hightae, Lochmaben	2	6 5
Turner, William, of Auchenwrath	Nith House, Dumfries	151	445 —	Wright, William	Lockerbie	1	9 —
Tweedie, Thomas and Gilbert	Annan	1	90 —	Wylie, Trustees of John, of Stapleton	Stapleton, Dornock	1,054	1,706 —
Twentyman, Joseph	Langholm	2	50 —	Wilkin, Herbert	Annan	12	40 —
Tynron, Trustees of Poor of	Tynron, Thornhill	41	51 —	Yorstoun, Morden C., of East Tinwald	East Tinwald, Dumfries	3,330	2,576 —
				Young, Rev. Alex.	Manse, Westerkirk	21	45 —
Underwood, George	Hightae, Lochmaben	2	27 —				
Vallance, Rev. James	Manse, Tinwald	21	55 —	Total Owners of Land of one Acre and upwards		886 676,045	533784 2
Villiers, Trustees for Mrs. Jane Isabella, of Closeburn, wife of Frederick Ernest Villiers, and for Charlotte Marion, Viscountess Cole, wife of Viscount Cole	Closeburn Hall, Dumfries	13,560	11218 16	Total Owners of Lands of less than one Acre in extent		3,291 926	61,727 15
				GRAND TOTAL		4,177 676,971	595511 17

COUNTY OF EDINBURGH.

Population in 1871, including the City of Edinburgh and Town of Leith, - 328,379.
Inhabited Houses, - 27,856.
Number of Parishes, - 32.

Name of Owner.	Address of Owner.	Estimated Acreage of Property.	Gross Annual Value.	Name of Owner.	Address of Owner.	Estimated Acreage of Property.	Gross Annual Value.
		Acres.	£ s.			Acres.	£ s.
Abercorn, Duke of	Duddingston House	1,500	7,400 10	Borthwick, John, of Crookston	Crookston, Stow	5,239	4,366 11
Aberdour, Lord	Dalmahoy	1,467	5,411 10	Borthwick, Thomas	Ratho	1	94 —
Abernethy, Trustees of D.	Penicuik	1	42 10	Boswell, Trustees of J. D., of Wardie	Edinburgh	88	574 —
Abernethy, James	Howgate, Penicuik	25	40 —	Boyd, Trs. of Ebenezer	Eskbank, Dalkeith	1	71 —
Ainslie, David, of Costerton	Costerton, Blackshiels	369	634 15	Boyd, Thomas J.	Midfield House, Lasswade	10	115 10
Ainslie, Mrs. Rachel	Roslin	1	82 —	Brash, Heirs of Peter	Leith	285	1,237 19
Aitchison, Reps. of George	Rosehill, Leadburn	91	60 —	Do. do.	Do. (*Mines*)	—	500 —
Aitchison, John	Mount Vernon	11	910 —	Brash, Richard	Cairnhill, Dunse	4	40 12
Aitchison, Lieut.-Col. W., of Drummore	Drummore, Musselburgh	37	213 —	Bridges, Mrs. James	Bellfield, Musselburgh	5	75 —
Do. do.	Do. (*Mines*)	—	39 10	Brighton Park, Trustees of	Portobello	2	8 —
Aitken, William	Pathhead, Kirknewton	3	13 —	Brodie, David	Liberton	2	90 —
Alexander, George	Gorebridge	43	106 —	Brodie, Rev. W. C.	Lasswade	1	45 —
Alexander, Robert	Greenend	2	45 —	Brown, Curators of Horatio R. F., of Newhall	Newhall, Penicuik	1,635	1,062 8
Alexander, Rev. William Lindsay	Pinkieburn, Musselburgh	12	130 —	Brown, James, of Currie	Currie House, Gorebridge	904	866 —
Alison, Thomas	Dalkeith	2	335 10	Brown, Rev. J. F.	Heriot	23	59 —
Allan, James	Edinburgh	6	34 —	Brown, John	Penicuik	1	19 10
Anderson, David, of Moredun	Moredun, Liberton	194	851 —	Brown, Matthew	Edinburgh	1	41 —
Anderson, John	Fisherrow	2	309 —	Brown, Lieut.-Col. R. J.	Ashley House, Ratho	6	21 —
Anderson, Major-General J. Richard, C.B.	Edinburgh	200	300 —	Brown, William	Lewisvale, Musselburgh	2	82 10
Anderson, W. P.	Dalkeith	6	226 10	Brown, William, Heirs of	Spring Gardens, London Road	5	108 —
Anderson, Mrs. Mary	Bonnington House, Ratho	4	81 —	Brown, Trustees of W. H.	Ashley House, Ratho	251	752 —
Anderson, Mrs. Mary	Oxenford, Dalkeith	4	41 —	Brown, Mrs. Isabella	Carlton Lodge, Murrayfield	1	138 —
Annandale, Heirs of Alexander	Polton Bank, Lasswade	2	85 —	Brown, Mrs. Mary, of Ashley	Ashley House, Ratho	3	55 —
Annandale, A., jun. / Annandale, J. H.	Polton Mill, Lasswade	23	724 10	Bruce, David	Ravenscraft, Gilmerton	1	114 5
Annandale, James H.	Esk Tower, Lasswade	3	95 —	Bruce, George, of West Brook	West Brook, Currie	29	85 —
Arbuthnot, George C., of Mavisbank	Mavisbank, Loanhead	95	648 —	Bruce, Henry	Kinleith Mill, Currie	33	892 —
Archibald, Thomas	Viewbank, Lasswade	66	259 10	Bryce, John	Edinburgh	2	50 —
Auld, Robert	Howden Park, Mid-Calder	64	103 9	Bryce, John	Ratho	2	37 —
				Brydone, Robert	Murrayfield	1	110 —
Baildon, Henry C.	Duncliffe, Murrayfield	1	100 —	Buccleuch and Queensberry, Duke of	Dalkeith Palace	3,532	16216 —
Baillie, William, of Falahill	14 Windsor Street, Edinburgh	961	761 —	Do. do.	Do. (*Mines*)	—	1,479 —
Bain, Trustees of Robert.	Crichtondean, Ford	1	55 10	Do. do.	Do. (*Granton Harbour*)	9	10601 —
Bain, William	Buccleuch Pl., Edinburgh	1	36 —	Buchan, David	Murrayfield	2	168 —
Baird, Sir D., of Newbyth, Bart.	Newbyth, Prestonkirk	751	3,456 12	Buchan, John	Peebles	21	40 15
Do. do.	Do. (*Mines*)	—	400 —	Buchanan, James	Restalrig	2	78 5
Baird, Sir J. G., of Saughtonhall, Bart.	Inch House	340	2,450 —	Bullock, Rev. W. G.	Ratho	3	35 —
Balfour, John, of Balbirnie	Balbirnie, Fife	10	185 —	Burge, Mrs. Margaret	Woodville, Colinton	32	103 —
Bartholomew, James	Duntarvie, Winchburgh	36	50 —	Burton, James C.	Pentland Grove, Roslin	4	64 —
Do.	Do. (*Mines*)	—	100 —	Burton, James Tait, of Toxside	Toxside, Gorebridge	1,240	625 —
Bauchope, Elizabeth	East Brucefield	1	28 5	Cadell, John James	Edinburgh	10	355 —
Belhaven, Trs. of Lord	Wishaw	965	359 10	Calder, Heirs of Thomas	Hillhead, Lasswade	1	155 —
Do. do.	Do. (*Mines*)	—	100 —	Caledonian Railway Company	Glasgow	39	281 —
Bell, Trustees of Mr. & Mrs. C., & Mrs. Dale	Morningside / North Berwick	45	322 9	Do. do.	Do. (*Railway*)	411	37661 —
Bell, Lawrence R.	Ludgate Lodge, Ratho	4	90 10	Callander, Guardians of Henry, of Prestonhall	Prestonhall, Ford	4,869	6,810 —
Bennie, John	Lochend, Ratho	38	125 —	Do. do.	Do. (*Mines*)	—	55 —
Bennie, Mrs. C.	Angle Park, Slateford	2	89 —	Campbell, Alexander, of Cammo	Edinburgh	273	628 —
Beveridge, Rev. J. G.	Inveresk	7	88 10				
Blackburn, James	London	1	11 —	Campbell, A., two-thirds and Campbell, A., junior, one-third	Edinburgh	12	40 —
Blair, George	Eskbank, Dalkeith	2	305 —				
Bonnyrigg Water Company	Bonnyrigg	2	60 —				
Borthwick, Heritors of Parish of	Borthwick	1	6 —				

EDINBURGH—continued.

Name of Owner.	Address of Owner.	Estimated Acreage of Property.	Gross Annual Value.		Name of Owner.	Address of Owner.	Estimated Acreage of Property.	Gross Annual Value.	
		Acres.	£	s.			Acres.	£	s.
Campbell, Sir George, of Succoth, Bart. . .	Garscube House, Glasgow	233	1,649	–	Croall, David . . .	Middlefield, Edinburgh .	29	179	–
Campbell, Heirs of George	Musselburgh . .	3	26	–	Crown, The—War Department	Edinburgh . . .	67	1,614	–
Cardross, Lord . .	107 Belgrave Road, London . . .	76	65	–	Crown, The—Board of Works . . .	Edinburgh . . .	269	243	–
Carmichael, Sir W. H. G., of Durie and Skirling, Bart. . . .	Castle Craig, Dolphinton	732	4,624	–	Cumming, Thomas . .	Dalkeith . . .	1	210	10
Carruthers, D.	Longtown, Cumberland .	822	181	–	Cunyngham, Sir Robert K. A. Dick, of Prestonfield, Bart.	Prestonfield House, Edinburgh . . .	228	1,759	–
Carruthers, Rev. P., and Carruthers, Mrs. M.	Do. (Mines)	–	450	–	Currie, Heritors of Parish of	Currie	1	8	–
Carter, Charles Victor .	Edinburgh . .	1	10	–	Dalhousie, Earl of .	Dalhousie Castle . .	1,419	3,002	2
Cauvin's Hospital, Governors of . . .	Duddingston . .	3	114	–	Do.	Do. (Mines)	–	450	–
Chalmers, Heirs of F. .	Musselburgh . .	2	40	–	Dalkeith, Heritors of Parish of . . .	Dalkeith . . .	2	16	–
Chalmers, Mrs. F. . .	Musselburgh . .	1	57	–	Dalkeith Parliamentary Trustees . . .	Dalkeith . . .	7	249	–
Charles, James . .	Grovend, Lasswade .	6	50	–	Dalkeith Union Poorhouse	Dalkeith . . .	2	130	–
Christie, Braithwaite, of Baberton . . .	Edinburgh . .	320	1,192	10	Dalrymple, Charles, of Newhailes, M.P. . .	Newhailes, Musselburgh	175	693	–
Christie, William . .	Craigend, Liberton .	10	180	–	Darling, Janet and Betsy	Ash Lee, Stow . .	1	45	–
Clapperton, John . .	Gorebridge . . .	22	123	–	Davidson, Lieut.-Col. J. .	Sneinton, Nottingham .	269	155	–
Clapperton, Thomas .	Gorebridge . . .	1	149	–	Davidson, Thomas, of Muirhouse . .	Muirhouse, Cramond .	412	1,216	–
Clarkson, Mrs. J. B. .	Myreside, Edinburgh .	1	140	–	Davidson, William .	Halfway House, West Calder . . .	2	8	–
Cleghorn, Thomas . .	Edinburgh . .	83	140	–	Dawson, Ebenezer .	Dalkeith . . .	4	292	–
Clerk, Sir G. D., of Penicuik, Bart. . .	Penicuik House . .	12,696	8,919	–	Dawson, James . .	Dalkeith . . .	2	145	–
Do. do.	Do. (Mines)	–	2,421	–	Deans, Peter Dods . .	Portobello . . .	1	85	–
Clerk, John . . .	London . . .	1	11	–	Deas, Sir George, Kt. (Lord Deas)	Pittendreich House, Lasswade . . .	36	299	–
Cochrane, Alexander, of Ashkirk . . .	Gort House, Petersham	243	1,173	10	Dewar, Colonel A. C., of Vogrie . . .	Vogrie, Dalkeith . .	1,936	2,898	3
Cochrane, James, of Harburn . . .	Harburn, West Calder .	4,064	1,946	–	Dibb, Thomas T., William Hay, and John William Aikman	Leeds	113	479	11
Cochrane, Annie . .	Edinburgh . .	2	100	–	Dick, Thomas . .	Corstorphine . .	1	28	–
Cockpen, Heritors of Parish of . . .	Cockpen . . .	1	8	–	Dickson, Heirs of D. J. .	Portobello . . .	1	110	–
Coldwell, Mrs. J. A. .	Dambrae, Musselburgh .	1	26	–	Dickson, Trustees of John, of Corstorphine .	Edinburgh . . .	842	2,539	1
Colinton, Heritors of Parish of . . .	Colinton . . .	1	8	–	Dickson, Stair . .	Dalkeith . . .	1	108	–
Colinton Paper Company .	Colinton . . .	2	10	–	Dickson, William . .	Edinburgh . . .	61	159	–
Colt, Mrs. Jane . .	Inveresk House . .	16	160	–	Dixon, Mrs. Eliza . .	Corstorphine . .	2	233	–
Colvin, Rev. W. L. .	Cramond . . .	6	66	10	Dodds, John . .	Stoneypath, Prestonkirk	1,200	309	–
Colvin, Mrs. M. Home, of Torquhan . .	Torquhan, Stow . .	907	978	10	Donaldson, Ann and Elizabeth . .	Newtonloan, Lasswade .	1	27	–
Commercial Bank of Scotland . . .	Dalkeith . . .	1	146	10	Dougal, Mrs. Charlotte, of Ratho . .	Ratho House . .	656	1,731	–
Commissioners of Supply for the County of Edinburgh .	Edinburgh . . .	2	231	–	Douglas, Trustees of Alexander C. .	Dalkeith . . .	1	137	–
Core, Rev. W. G. . .	Carrington . . .	8	43	–	Douglas, James D. S., of Baads	Chilston House, Tunbridge Wells . . .	3,106	1,388	–
Corstorphine, Heritors of Parish of . .	Corstorphine . .	2	16	–	Do. do.	Do. (Mines)	–	366	–
Coutts, James . .	Corstorphine House .	4	105	–	Douglas, Barbara and Agnes . .	Corstorphine . .	2	29	–
Cowan, Alex., & Sons .	Valleyfield, Penicuik .	18	3,387	–	Dove, David . .	Dalkeith . . .	2	117	–
Cowan, Charles, of Loganhouse . . .	Wester Lea, Edinburgh	5,677	1,816	–	Dow, George . .	Gilmerton . . .	2	87	–
Cowan, Captain C. W. .	Penicuik . . .	2	45	–	Downie, Hay . .	Corstorphine . .	1	35	–
Cowan, John, of Beeslack	Beeslack, Penicuik .	50	213	–	Drummond, Trustees of Sir James, of Hawthornden, Bart. .	Hawthornden . .	224	434	–
Cowan, William, of Linburn . . .	Linburn, Ratho . .	126	304	–	Drummond, Lady, of Hawthornden .	Hawthornden . .	258	800	–
Cox, John, of Gorgie .	Murrayfield . .	26	521	–	Duddingston, Heritors of Parish of . .	Duddingston . .	2	16	–
Coxe, Sir James, of Kinnellan, Kt. . .	Murrayfield . .	11	185	–	Dun, John . .	Eskbank, Dalkeith .	1	75	–
Craig, Right Hon. Sir W. Gibson, of Riccarton, Bart. . . .	Riccarton, Hermiston .	1,882	6,037	–	Duncan, Col. F. R., of Firth . . .	Firth House, Roslin .	567	722	5
Craig, Cecilia H. Gibson	Hermiston House . .	5	100	–	Duncan, Rev. Henry .	Crichton . . .	9	50	–
Craigcrook Mortification, Trustees of . . .	Edinburgh . .	334	1,259	–	Duncan, John . .	Edinburgh . . .	29	102	–
Cramond, Heritors of Parish of . .	Cramond . . .	1	8	–	Duncan, William . .	Corstorphine . .	2	29	–
Cranston, G. C. Trotter, of Dewar	Harvieston House, Gorebridge . .	1,652	632	–	Dundas, Sir David, of Beechwood, Bart. .	Beechwood House, Corstorphine . . .	81	355	–
Cranston, Heritors of Parish of . . .	Cranston . . .	1	8	–	Dundas, Robert, of Arniston	Arniston House, Gorebridge . .	10,184	9,549	14
Craufurd, J. R. H., of Craufurdland and Braehead	Craufurdland Castle, Kilmarnock .	60	252	10	Do. do.	Do. (Mines)	–	4,254	–
Craven, William . .	Corstorphine . .	2	134	10	Dundas, Mrs. R. M. .	Craigroyston . .	5	100	–
Crawford, Thomas M. .	Lauriston Castle, Cramond	32	236	–	Dunfermline, Dowager Lady . . .	Colinton House . .	100	536	–
Crichton, Heritors of Parish of . . .	Crichton . . .	1	8	–	Dunlop, David . .	Edinburgh . . .	2	85	–

EDINBURGH—continued.

Name of Owner.	Address of Owner.	Estimated Acreage of Property.	Gross Annual Value.	Name of Owner.	Address of Owner.	Estimated Acreage of Property.	Gross Annual Value.
		Acres.	£ s.			Acres.	£ s.
Dunn, Mrs. Elizabeth, and James Small	Tranent and Edinburgh	2	72 –	Girdwood, William	Corstorphine	3	83 –
Dunsmure, John	London	9	110 –	Glencorse, Heritors of Parish of	Glencorse	1	8 –
Durham, James Gordon	Lasswade	1	37 10	Glendinning, Trustees of George	Overshiel, Mid-Calder	83	176 –
Durham, Mrs. L. D. C., of Polton	Polton House, Lasswade	666	1,738 14	Glover, James	Loanhead	2	214 11
Do. do.	Do. (Mines)	–	300 –	Glover, John	Langhill, Roslin	2	70 –
				Gordon, Edward S.	Edinburgh	2	22 –
Edinburgh Cemetery Company	Edinburgh	9	73 –	Gordon, Captain John, of Cluny	Cluny Castle, Cluny	701	2,116 –
Edinburgh City Parochial Board	Edinburgh	270	2,032 –	Gordon, Rev. Thomas	Newbattle	9	55 –
Edinburgh and District Water Trustees	Edinburgh	243	19828 –	Graham, John, of Muldron	Muldron, West Calder	2,169	264 –
				Do. do.	Do. (Mines)	–	363 –
Edinburgh, County, and District Asylum	Edinburgh	42	160 –	Graham, William	Meadowhead, West Calder	77	90 10
Edinburgh, Lord Provost, Magistrates, and Town Council of	Edinburgh	4	94 –	Graham, William	Campie House, Musselburgh	6	140 –
				Grant, Trustees of Rev. Donald	Edinburgh	48	190 –
Edinburgh Roperie Coy.	Currie	19	643 –	Grant, Rev. John D.	West Calder	25	72 –
Elder, James	Gogar	120	105 –	Do. do.	Do. (Mines)	–	200 –
Elliot, Alexander	Venturefair, Penicuik	1	9 –	Grainger, Trustees of T.	Craig Park, Ratho	69	232 –
Elliot, Heirs of Ralph	Dalkeith	2	141 –	Grainger, Mrs. Thomas	Craig Park, Ratho	10	110 –
Elly, Trustees of Andrew	Musselburgh	5	95 –	Gray, George	Dalkeith	1	222 10
Elphinstone, Lord	Carberry Tower	769	2,580 –	Gray, William	Pottery, Newbigging	3	68 –
Do.	Do. (Mines)	–	1,210 –	Greenhill, Mrs. Margaret, wife of James Greenhill	Edinburgh	145	130 –
Esk Valley Railway Coy.	Edinburgh	2	22 –	Guthrie, Rev. David K.	Liberton	1	45 –
Do. do.	Do. (Railway)	18	767 –				
Fairholm, George K. E., of Old Melrose	Bregenz, Austria	6,200	2,020 –	Halkett, John C., yr. of Cramond	Cramond	6	378 –
Ferguson, Archibald	Liverpool	1	71 –	Hamilton, William	Overtown, Wishaw	933	319 –
Ferguson, Trs. of James	Stenhouse	1	67 –	Handyside, William, of Coruhill	11 Claremont Crescent, Edinburgh	6	42 –
Ferguson, Robert	Millhill House, Musselburgh	3	110 10	Handasyde, Catherine, Handasyde, Mary, and Handasyde, Margaret E.	Portobello	1	126 –
Ferguson, Robert D. O.	Glasgow	3	90 –				
Fettes, Trs. of Sir William, of Comely Bank, Bart.	Edinburgh	331	2,959 11	Hannay, Robert, of Hanley	Hanley, Corstorphine	51	262 –
Fisher, Alexander	Currie	2	140 10	Hardie, Mrs. Jessie, and Mrs. M'Ally	Edinburgh	1	24 7
Fisher, Mrs. Anne	Vanburgh Place, Leith	2	65 –	Hare, Stewart B., of Calderhall	Calderhall, Mid-Calder	2,373	3,107 19
Fleming, Alexander B.	12 Eton Ter., Edinburgh	34	184 –	Do. do.	Do. (Mines)	–	1,074 –
Forbes, William	Auchendinny, Penicuik	1	95 –	Harper, Francis	Springfield, Musselburgh	1	75 –
Ford, William	Holyrood Glass Works	14	259 –	Hatton's Heirs	Hillhead, Lasswade	2	30 –
Forrest, Sir J., of Comiston, Bart.	18 Manor Pl., Edinburgh	500	1,290 –	Hay, Christian	Kingston Grange, Liberton	85	475 10
Forsyth, Rev. James	Aberdeen	5	282 –	Haynes, Mrs. Lilly, wife of J. Haynes	Millford, No. Devon	13	25 –
Foulis, Sir James L., of Colinton, Bart.	Millburn Tower, Ratho	2,804	2,163 14	Henderson, Charles J.	Edinburgh	15	508 –
Fowler, John	Loanhead	3	132 –	Henderson, Rev. John	Roslin	1	29 10
Fraser, Rev. James	West Calder	2	22 –	Herdman, James	Coltbridge House	1	110 –
Free Church of Scotland, Trustees of	Edinburgh	3	24 –	Heriot's Hospital, Governors of	Edinburgh	22	175 –
Frier, Matthew B.	Brotherton, West Calder	120	139 –	Hill, Craig, & Co.	Balerno Bank	1	556 –
Frier, Richard S., of Meikle Catpair	Meikle Catpair, Stow	1,025	800 –	Hill, Trustees of William	Hillwood	234	979 –
Fullarton, Andrew	Edinburgh	1	115 –	Hog, Thomas A., of Newliston	Newliston	146	268 –
Fulton, Andrew, jun.	Woodlands, Duddingston	11	113 –	Hog, Mrs. Helen	Murrayfield	2	95 –
Gardiner, Rev. James	West Colinton House	3	50 –	Hogg, Heirs of John	Edinburgh	4	418 –
Garry, John	Polton Bank	2	25 –	Home, James S.	Musselburgh	1	50 –
Gartshore, John M., of Ravelston	Ravelston House, Blackhall	294	1,388 –	Honeyman, Thomas	Edinburgh	1	100 –
Gavin, William	Leith	1	188 –	Hope, Sir Archibald, of Craighall and Pinkie, Bart.	Pinkie House, Musselburgh	961	3,436 16
Geddes, Roderick	Edinburgh	1	108 –	Hope, James	Bellmont	37	235 –
Gibson, John	Corstorphine	1	45 –	Hope, James	Edinburgh	31	94 –
Gibson, Thomas	Dalkeith	1	63 –	Horne, Rev. R. K. D.	Corstorphine	12	87 –
Gibson, Agnes, Christina, and Janet	Rothesay	190	133 –	Hull, Mrs.	Granton Hotel	2	148 –
Gibsone, Lieut.-Gen. John C. H., of Pentland	Thorn Bank, Leamington	1,474	2,338 –	Hunter, James, of Colzium	Newliston Haugh, Kirkliston	3,000	750 –
Gibsone, Captain John, of Hillend	Narborough, Leicester	274	460 –	Hunter, Robert	Dalhousie Chesters, Lasswade	4	81 10
Giddings, Jacob	Abercorn Gardens	2	210 –	Hutchison, James	Lasswade	1	70 –
Gillespie, David	Kirkton, Fife	1	11 –	Hutchison, Thomas	Duddingston	1	50 –
Gillespie's Hospital, Governors of	Edinburgh	681	955 –	Imrie, Rev. Wm. M.	Penicuik	6	48 –
Gillespie, James	Craigie, Cramond Bridge	100	345 –	Inglis, Charles H. C., of Cramond	Cramond House	637	2,520 –
Gilmour, Walter J. L., of Craigmillar	New Club, Edinburgh	1,690	7,960 –				

EDINBURGH—continued.

Name of Owner.	Address of Owner.	Estimated Acreage of Property.	Gross Annual Value.	Name of Owner.	Address of Owner.	Estimated Acreage of Property.	Gross Annual Value.
		Acres.	£ s.			Acres.	£ s.
Inglis, Harry H.	Edinburgh	1	11 –	Lindsay, James	Dryden Bank, Loanhead	9	110 –
Inglis, Harry M., of Loganbank	Loganbank, Milton Bridge	195	448 1	Lindsay, John	Eskbank, Dalkeith	1	102 –
Inglis, Henry, of Torsonce	Torsonce House, Stow	781	768 10	Liston, Trs. of Mrs. J. R.	Kirknewton	90	248 –
Inglis, Rt. Hon. John, of Glencorse (Lord Justice-General)	30 Abercromby Place, Edinburgh	857	1,603 –	Litster, George	Redhall Mill, Slateford	2	123 –
				Livingstone, Representatives of Allan	Portobello	2	602 –
Inglis, Captain John, of Redhall	Redhall House, Slateford	712	1,937 15	Livingstone, John	Edinburgh	1	102 10
Innes, W. S. Mitchell, of Parsonsgreen	Parsonsgreen, Edinburgh	33	286 –	Livingstone, Josiah	Edinburgh	14	188 –
Inveresk Combination Poorhouse	Inveresk	6	203 –	Lockhart, Sir S. M'Donald, of Lee and Carnwath, Bart.	Carnwath House, Lanark	700	1,327 19
Inveresk, Heritors of Parish of	Musselburgh	1	12 –	Lockhart, Rev. William	Colinton	11	60 –
Irving, Representatives of George, of Newton	Edinburgh	1	11 –	Logan, Eliza H., of Loganlea	Lanark Lodge, Dunse	539	342 –
				Do. do. (Mines)	Do.	–	500 –
				Loganlea Coal Company	West Calder	5	68 –
				Lorimer and Clarke	Gorgie	2	205 –
				Lothian, Marquess of	Newbattle Abbey	4,547	11918 5
				Do. do. (Mines)	Do.	–	6,296 –
Jack, George	Whitehill, Dalkeith	1	51 –	Lothian, Maurice, of St. Catherines	St. Catherines, Liberton	120	628 –
Jacob, Frederick	Wardie Avenue, Edinburgh	2	471 –	Lourie, James	Dalkeith	1	159 –
Jamieson, George A.	Edinburgh	2	110 –	Lowe, William H.	Saughtonhall	12	93 –
Jefferiss, Robert	Dalkeith	1	109 –				
Jeffrey, David, and Jeffrey, John	Edinburgh	5	1,109 –	M'Craw, Trustees of Peter, and M'Craw, Mrs.	Leith	2	68 –
Jockel, Mrs. Catherine	Gogar Mount	27	112 –	M'Dougal, James	Currie	1	50 –
Johnston, David	Cockpen	1	54 –	M'Dougal, Trustees of T.	Eskmills, Penicuik	62	1,472 –
Johnston, George, of Lathrisk	Lathrisk, Falkland	1,500	739 –	M'Kay, Cap. Alexander F., of Blackcastle	36 George Square, Edinburgh	690	593 –
Johnston, Sir William, of Kirkhill, Kt.	Kirkhill House, Gorebridge	40	168 –	M'Kelvie, James	Edinburgh	7	1,240 –
				M'Kenzie, Rev. M.	Lasswade	8	75 –
Keith, George S.	Edinburgh	2	50 –	M'Kinlay, Trustees of D.	Edinburgh	56	246 –
Kelso, Cecilia M.	Ashbrook, Edinburgh	6	225 –	M'Kinlay, Agnes, and M'Kinlay, Jane, of Newlandburn	Newlandburn House, Dalkeith	10	59 10
Kemp, John F.	Musselburgh	1	142 –				
Kennoway, Robert	Polton Farm, Lasswade	1	108 –	M'Kintosh, Janet	Murrayfield	2	62 –
Kerr, Lord Charles L.	Newbattle Abbey	5	12 –	M'Lagan, Peter, of Pumpherston, M.P.	Amondell House	601	906 1
Kerr, Lord Mark R. G.	Newbattle Abbey	4	10 –	M'Laren, Duncan, M.P.	Edinburgh	4	45 17
Kerr, Mrs. Janet G.	Illieston, Kirkliston	300	190 –	M'Laren, James	Gogar Park	23	147 –
Ketchen, Arthur	Loanhead	1	145 –	M'Laren, Peter H.	Beechleigh, Lasswade	2	95 –
Ketchen, Robert	Bonnyrigg	1	19 –	M'Lean, Trs. of Thomas	Nine-mile Burn, Penicuik	2	38 –
Kidd, Mrs. Mary	Mounthooly, Winchburgh	950	140 –	M'Leod, Catherine	Crawford Bank, Lasswade	2	50 –
Do.	Do. (Mines)	–	500 –	M'Millan, The Trustees of Thomas	Musselburgh	34	162 10
King, Heirs of Mrs. Allison	Fernieside, Liberton	4	34 –	M'Murray, William	London	12	70 –
King, J. and A.	West Colinton	4	161 –	M'Nab, John	Inglis Green, Slateford	2	82 –
Kippen, Heirs of Fortunatus	Mid-Calder	3	88 –	M'Neil, Lady Emma, wife of the Rt. Hon. Sir John M'Neil, G.C.B.	Burnhead, Liberton	6	133 –
Kirkland, Mrs., wife of John Kirkland	Dundee	399	289 –	M'Niven, Trustees of Col.	Musselburgh	2	105 –
Kirknewton, Heritors of Parish of	Kirknewton	1	8 –	Macbean, Æneas, of Marchbank	Edinburgh	110	98 –
Kirkwood, Mrs. Jane S.	Edinburgh	1	19 –	Maccal, Thomas S.	Polmont	3	464 –
				Macduff, Rev. Robert C. H.	Ratho	10	54 –
Laing, John	Penicuik	1	33 –	Macfie, Claud, of Gogar Burn	Gogar Burn, Corstorphine	58	343 –
Lamb, John	Rosewell, Lasswade	2	9 –				
Lamb, Mrs. James	Juniper Green	1	23 –	Macfie, David J., of Kilmux	Kilmux House, Kennoway	2,036	1,188 –
Lamond, James	Portobello	1	65 –				
Langhorne, Rev. T.	Musselburgh	8	404 –	Macfie, Robert Andrew, of Dreghorn, M.P.	Dreghorn, Slateford	968	2,156 –
Langwill, Rev. James	Currie	6	51 –				
Lasswade, Heritors of Parish of	Lasswade	2	12 –	Macfie, William, of Clermiston	Clermiston, Corstorphine	124	443 –
Lauder, Sir T. N. Dick, of Fountainhall, Bart.	45 Upper Brook Street, London	714	1,268 –	Macgregor, Rev. M.	Newton	8	50 –
Law, David M.	Roslin	1	85 –	Mackenzie, Alexander K., of Ravelrig	Ravelrig House, Currie	124	351 –
Law, William	Roslin	1	34 –				
Law, William	Hermitage, Murrayfield	2	110 –	Mackie, Trustees of Thomas H.	Edinburgh	6	115 –
Learmonth, Lieut.-Col. Alexander, of Dean, M.P.	93 Eaton Place, London	409	704 –	Magdalene Asylum, Trustees of	Edinburgh	1	180 –
Lee, Alexander	Killochyett, Stow	1	159 –				
Legat, Robert	Eskpark, Musselburgh	15	125 –	Maitland, Sir Alex. C. R. Gibson, of Cliftonhall, Bart., M.P.	Cliftonhall, Ratho	4,505	14246 9
Leitch, William	Routinghill, Blackshiels	2	17 –				
Leslie, James	Edinburgh	2	60 –	Maitland, George F., of Hermand	Stonefield, Inverness	567	1,426 –
Leyden, Trustees of Peter	Dalkeith	3	107 15				
Liberton, Heritors of Parish of	Liberton	1	8 –	Do. do. (Mines)	Do.	–	876 –
Liberton, Parochial Board of	Liberton	1	9 –	Marchbanks, Trustees of William	Pinkhill, Corstorphine	1	27 –

EDINBURGH—continued.

Name of Owner.	Address of Owner.	Estimated Acreage of Property.	Gross Annual Value.	Name of Owner.	Address of Owner.	Estimated Acreage of Property.	Gross Annual Value.
		Acres.	£ s.			Acres.	£ s.
Marr, Mrs. Janet Bathgate, of Alderston	Alderston House, Mid-Calder	665	869 —	Nicolson, Thomas	Nesbit	1	100 —
Marshall, Rev. David	East Calder	1	33 —	Nisbett, John More, of Cairnhill	Drum, Liberton	270	951 —
Marshall, Archibald, and Marshall, John	Easter Newton	1	6 —	Normand, James, junior	Murrayfield	1	198 —
Marshall, Heirs of the late James, of Craigend	Edinburgh	715	708 —	North British Railway Company	Edinburgh	36	397 —
				Do. do.	Do. (Railway and Canal)	873	35634 —
Marshall, John, of Curriehill	Edinburgh	250	912 —	North Esk Reservoir Company	Do.	27	300 —
Martin, James	Reform Street, Dundee	3	269 —				
Martin, John Davie	Brotherton, West Calder	55	79 8				
Martin, Thomas	Edinburgh	1	45 —	Oakbank Oil Company	Kirknewton	1	1,287 —
Mason, Robert, of Belgrave Park	Belgrave Park, Corstorphine	193	793 14	Do. do.	Do. (Mines)	—	300 —
				Ogilvie, Archibald, of Old Liston	Old Liston, Ratho	330	844 —
Mather, Alexander, of Bankhead	Bankhead, Currie	160	461 —	Orman, William	Leith Walk	1	181 —
Maxwell, Trustees of H.	Dean Park, Currie	267	460 —	Ormiston, John	Kames, Ratho	1	12 10
Meikle, James	Wardieburn House	3	108 —	Orphan Hospital, Incorporation of	Edinburgh	31	184 —
Meiklejon, John	Westfield, Dalkeith	3	237 —				
Melville, Viscount	Melville Castle	1,158	3,618 9	Osborne, Walter, of Belstane	Belstane, Mid-Calder	255	220 —
Mercer, Graeme Reid, of Gorthy	Glentulchan, Perth	15	509 —	Oswald, Lady Mary	Inveresk	10	158 —
Mercer, Robert	Portobello	2	80 —				
Merricks, Hezekiah, & Merricks, Trs. of John	Roslin	12	650 —	Park, Representatives of Andrew	Edinburgh	1	11 —
Merricks, Hezekiah	Roslin	4	77 —	Paterson, George M.	Edinburgh	1	58 10
Merricks, Mrs. Isabella	Roslin	1	50 —	Paterson, Hugh	Oak Lodge, Inveresk	1	85 —
Mid-Calder, Heritors of Parish of	Mid-Calder	1	6 —	Paterson, James, of Bankton	Bankton, Mid-Calder	196	250 —
Middlemas, Robert	Edinburgh	6	155 —	Paterson, Richard	Dalkeith	1	65 —
Middleton, James	Manorhead House	1	60 —	Paterson, William, of Catpair	Ettrickhall	325	340 —
Millar, William White, of Dunesk	Edinburgh	12	145 —				
Millar, Heirs of Mrs.	Musselburgh	1	369 —	Paterson, Mrs.	Burnhouse, Portobello	1	65 —
Millar, Mrs. James	Springbank, Musselburgh	1	70 —	Paterson, Helen	Portobello	1	65 —
Miller, Trustees of Robert	Lasswade	2	80 —	Paton, Rev. J. A. H.	Duddingston	10	93 —
Miller, Samuel Christie, of Craigentinny	Craigentinny House	652	5,739 4	Peacock, Peter, Heirs of	Dalkeith	2	278 —
				Pearson, Charles, and others	Edinburgh	1	63 —
Miller, Janet, of Springfield	Edinburgh	82	188 —	Peddie, Heirs of Mary Ann	Annfield, Lasswade	2	48 10
Milne, Vice-Admiral Sir Alexander, G.C.B.	Milne Lodge, Inveresk	36	239 —	Pendreigh, George	Dalhousie	6	333 —
Milne, John	Kevock Tower, Lasswade	1	42 —	Penicuik, Heritors of Parish of	Penicuik	1	12 —
Mitchell, Heirs of Alexander, of Stow	Carolside	9,038	6,308 —	Penicuik Railway Company	Do. (Railway)	36	489 —
				Pennicook, John	Bonnyrigg	1	150 —
Mitchell, Rev. J.	Leith	2	38 —	Philip, John	Bonnyrigg	2	79 —
Mitchell, William	Craigleith House	3	140 —	Pirrie, William	Dalkeith	4	186 5
Moffat, Henry, of Eldin	Edinburgh	23	229 —	Portobello Bowling Club	Portobello	1	15 —
Moffat, W., and others	Edinburgh	1	30 —	Potts, George Honington	Edinburgh	2	72 —
Moffat, Mrs.	Newbigging, Musselburgh	3	167 —	Pow, Trustees of James	Walltower, Penicuik	200	200 —
Monro, Alexander, of Craiglockhart	Craiglockhart, Slateford	38	195 —	Primrose, Trustees of Rachel	Burnbrae, Mid-Calder	844	1,027 —
Montgomery, William	Kelso	1	48 —	Pringle, John	Belgrave Ter., Glasgow	650	547 —
Moray, Earl of	Donibristle House, Fife	138	865 —				
Morrison, Trustees of Sir Alexander, Kt.	Johnsburn, Balerno	10	40 —	Rae, Andrew	Molehall, Lasswade	1	18 —
Morrison, Lady Grace	Balerno Hill	9	60 —	Raeburn, James	Edinburgh	4	17 —
Morton, Earl of	Dalmahoy, Ratho	8,944	9,041 1	Raeburn, Heirs of John Peter	Charlesfield House, Mid-Calder	497	1,338 13
Muir, Rev. John S.	Cockpen	6	56 —				
Muir, William H.	Edinburgh	7	87 10	Do. do.	Do. (Mines)	—	238 —
Muir, Mrs. Ann	Murrayfield	1	140 —	Ramsay, R. B. Wardlaw, of Whitehill	Whitehill, Lasswade	2,963	3,822 4
Muirhead, Trustees of C.	Edinburgh	23	120 —				
Muirhead, James	Edinburgh	7	30 —	Do. do.	Do. (Mines)	—	1,812 —
Munro, Alexander	Musselburgh	2	28 —	Ramsay, William	Johnston	5	135 —
Murdoch, James	Fallhills, Penicuik	6	22 —	Ramsay, Mrs.	London	4	20 10
Mure, David (Lord Mure)	Edinburgh	4	12 —	Ramsay, Mrs., and J. H. Sandilands	London	6	27 —
Murray, Mrs. Marion, wife of R. Murray	Springfield, Penicuik	362	191 —	Rattray, A. Wellwood	Glasgow	135	416 —
Mushet, Robert	Glenarch, Dalkeith	2	68 —	Reid, Heirs of Thomas	Newstead, Leadburn	44	65 —
Mushet, William and Robert	Dalkeith	3	280 —	Reid, Clementina B.	Bonnyrigg	1	160 —
				Renton, Mrs. M.	Oakmount, Lasswade	2	59 —
Mushet, William	Do.	3	47 —	Richardson, Peter	Edinburgh	11	110 —
Musselburgh Harbour Commissioners	Musselburgh (Fisherrow Harbour)	1	172 —	Richardson, Mrs. A. P.	Edinburgh	33	71 —
				Rigg, Trustees of James H., of Tarvit	Tarvit House, Cupar-Fife	27	235 —
Musselburgh, Trustees of, under Estate Act, 1851	Do. do.	145	94 —	Ritchie, Thomas	Bonnyrigg	4	30 —
				Ritchie, William, of Middleton	Middleton, Gorebridge	2,652	3,137 —
Nelson, Robert R.	Loanhead	1	25 —	Robb, James	Gorgie	6	192 —
Nesbitt, Alexander	Joppa	1	129 —	Robb, John	Tyne Castle	2	364 —

EDINBURGH—continued.

Name of Owner.	Address of Owner.	Estimated Acreage of Property.	Gross Annual Value.	Name of Owner.	Address of Owner.	Estimated Acreage of Property.	Gross Annual Value.
		Acres.	£ s.			Acres.	£ s.
Robertson, Adam	Newcalder Paper Mill	3	72 —	Stevenson, James	Edinburgh	2	42 —
Robertson, Heirs of A.	Edinburgh	1	4 —	Stewart, Archibald	London	1	11 —
Robertson, Robert	Bloomiehall, Juniper Green	2	56 —	Stewart, Charles, of Sweethope	Musselburgh	60	435 —
Robertson, Robert	Edinburgh	110	156 —	Stewart, Duncan	Balerno	2	20 —
Robertson, Trustees of R.	Juniper Green	2	70 —	*Stewart's Hospital, Trs. of*	Edinburgh	5	95 —
Robertson, T. R.	Gorgie Lodge	2	130 —	Stewart, Rev. John	Liberton	6	73 —
Rocheid, Curators of C. H. A. F. C. E. J., of Inverleith	Trinity College, Oxford	117	760 —	Stewart, John	Edinburgh	27	188 —
				Stewart, Robert, of Ingliston	Ingliston, Kirkliston	70	284 —
Roman Catholic Church, Trustees of	Dalkeith	1	28 —	Stewart, Isabella	Musselburgh	1	49 —
Romans, John	Edinburgh	7	118 —	Stodart, Thomas } Stodart, Janet }	Walston	511	142 —
Rosebery, Earl of	Dalmeny Park	15,568	8,973 16	Story, John, of Burnhead	Greenburn	821	733 —
Do.	Do. (*Mines*)	—	200 —	Do. do.	Do. (*Mines*)	—	700 —
Ross, David	Poltonhall	3	86 —	*Stow, Heritors of Parish of*	Stow	28	80 —
Ross, Mrs. Daniel	Murrayfield	3	95 —	Strathern, Thomas	Kirkhill, West Calder	17	100 —
Rosslyn, Earl of	Dysart House, Dysart	99	737 —	Stuart, John, of Newmills	Newmills, Currie	97	483 —
Royal College of Physicians, Edinburgh	Edinburgh	4	40 —	Stuart, J. & W.	Musselburgh	4	1,272 —
				Stuart, Elizabeth	Ashfield, Juniper Green	1	42 —
Royal Edinburgh Lunatic Asylum	Edinburgh	38	940 —	Sutherland, Trustees of David	Edinburgh	2	170 —
Royal Infirmary of Edinburgh	Edinburgh	5	200 —	Symington, Robert	Wadingburn, Lasswade	1	66 —
				St. Cuthbert's, Parochial Board of	Edinburgh	10	1,000 —
Sanderson, Matthew	Dovecot Park, Corstorphine	1	42 —	Tait, James	Penicuik	2	151 10
				Tait, William, of Pirn	Australia	200	290 —
Sanderson, Mrs. C.	Burdiehouse	2	27 —	Tait, Mrs. Janet	Lothian Bank	2	38 —
Sclater, James	Townhead, Loanhead	1	84 —	Tait, Mrs. Lucy M.	Pirn, Stow	5	71 10
Sclater, Mrs. Jane	Loanhead	1	31 —	Taylor, James	West Calder	1	100 —
Scott, Andrew	Edinburgh	9	70 —	Taylor, Wm., & Coy.	Leith	6	574 —
Scott, Andrew T. S., of Crosswoodhill	20 Walker St., Edinburgh	350	370 —	*Temple, Heritors of Parish of*	Temple	1	6 —
				Thomas, Rev. David	Howgate U.P. Manse	5	39 —
Scott, Major Francis C., younger, of Malleny	Malleny House, Currie	3,250	3,964 —	Thomson, Alexander, of Glenpark	Glenpark, Currie	33	105 —
Scott, Thomas R.	Musselburgh	1	55 —	Thomson, George, of Burnhouse	Burnhouse, Stow	1,418	1,130 —
Scott, Representatives of Mrs. H. B.	20 Walker St., Edinburgh	510	143 —	Thomson, George J.	Viewfield, Lasswade	5	36 —
Shand, Robert	Morningside	2	102 —	Thomson, James	Dalkeith	51	75 —
Simpson, Andrew	Corstorphine	3	63 —	Thomson, James	Stow	1	145 —
Simpson, James and Peter	Pathhead	1	33 10	Thomson, Rev. John F.	Fala	13	66 —
Sinclair, Alexander	Newlandrigg	2	12 —	Thomson, Laurence Ramsay	Belmont, Dalkeith	2	78 —
Sivwright, Heirs of Catherine, of Southhouse	Edinburgh	497	1,724 —	Thomson, Wm. T., of Bonaly	Bonaly, Colinton	27	206 —
Smart, Charles	Musselburgh	1	282 —	Thomson, Mrs. Isabella	Malleny Bank, Currie	3	22 —
Smart, James	Liberton Park	7	120 —	Thomson, Mrs. J. S.	Musselburgh	3	84 —
Smith, Alexander, of Muirhouse	Muirhouse, Mid-Calder	115	140 12	Thomson, Representatives of Mrs. J.	Bonnyrigg	3	21 —
Smith, Andrew	Willowbrae House, Jock's Lodge	2	85 —	Thornton, Thomas and James	Crofthead	92	127 —
Smith, Archibald	London	1	11 —	Tod, Andrew	Mavisbank, Lasswade	4	105 —
Smith, Rev. George S.	Cranstoun	14	60 —	Tod, James	Eskbank House, Dalkeith	3	75 —
Smith, Glaud, of Blackhill	West Calder	150	110 —	Tod, J. & J.	Dalkeith	1	267 —
Smith, Rev. Henry W.	Kirknewton	3	44 —	Tod, John	Ormisbank, Dalkeith	2	83 —
Smith, James	Edinburgh	19	125 —	Tod, Robert	Clerwood House, Corstorphine	43	264 —
Smith, John	Saughtonhall	12	93 —				
Smith, Robert	West Calder	1	37 —	Tod, Captain R. A. B., of Howden	Howden House, Mid-Calder	231	400 —
Smith, Rev. Theophilus	Temple	14	60 —				
Somervail, David	Beech Park, Lasswade	3	80 —	Tod, Trustees of William	Lasswade	9	762 —
Somerville, Hugh	Dalmore Mill, Milton Bridge	9	701 —	Tod, William	Springfield Mills, Lasswade	13	1,227 —
Somerville, James	Dalkeith	1	323 —				
Spottiswoode, Charlotte	Edinburgh	1	64 10	Torphichen, Lord	Calder House, Mid-Calder	1,880	3,294 —
Stair, Earl of	Oxenford Castle	4,118	3,165 —	Do.	Do. (*Mines*)	—	500 —
Stair, Trustees of John, eighth Earl of	Oxenford Castle	8,384	4,988 —	Torrance, Rev. Alex.	Glencorse	10	55 —
Do. do.	Do. (*Mines*)	—	270 —	Torrance, Archibald P.	Kippilaw, Dalkeith	77	335 —
Stair, Earl of, and Trs. of John, eighth Earl of Stair	Oxenford Castle	1,325	2,359 —	Torrance, William, of Carcant	Hyvots Mill, Liberton	723	310 —
Stark, Trustees of William	Camps, Mid-Calder	47	314 —	Train, John	Edinburgh	2	49 —
Do. do.	Do. (*Mines*)	—	38 —	*Trinity Hospital*	Edinburgh	152	809 —
Steedman, John	Penicuik	1	158 —	Trotter, Richard, of Mortonhall	Mortonhall, Liberton	2,490	6,759 —
Steuart, Archibald	} Edinburgh	4	85 —	Trotter, Col. R. A., of Bush	Bush, Roslin	1,919	2,498 —
Steuart, Charles	}			Do. do.	Do. (*Mines*)	—	500 —
Steuart, James	}			Tytler, James Stuart, of Woodhouselee	67 Queen Street, Edinburgh	556	955 —
Steuart James, junior	}						
Steven, Thomas	Bonnyrigg	10	392 —				

EDINBURGH—continued.—(MUNICIPAL BOROUGH OF EDINBURGH.)

Name of Owner.	Address of Owner.	Estimated Acreage of Property.	Gross Annual Value.	Name of Owner.	Address of Owner.	Estimated Acreage of Property.	Gross Annual Value.
		Acres.	£ s.			Acres.	£ s.
Umpherston, James, & Umpherston, Charles	Elmswood	3	406 —	West Calder, Heritors of Parish of	West Calder	1	8 —
United Presbyterian Congregation	East Calder	1	16 —	West Calder, Parochial Board of	West Calder	2	16 —
				White, Thomas, and Isabella Anderson	Liberton	1	33 —
Veitch, James	Musselburgh	1	100 10	White, William L., of Kellerstain	Kellerstain, Ratho	357	1,352 —
Vere, James C. Hope, of Craigiehall	Blackwood, Lesmahagow	716	2,379 —	Whitelaw, Mrs. C.	Musselburgh	1	185 —
Waddell, Rev. Walter	Borthwick	16	65 —	Wilkie, Archibald, of Ormiston	Ormiston, Kirknewton	1,579	2,289 —
Walker, Alexander	West Calder	5	10 —	Wilkie, James, of Ratho Byres	Edinburgh	69	250 —
Walker, Andrew, of Hartwood	Glasgow	484	644 —	Wilkie, J. and A.	Musselburgh	1	55 —
Do. do.	Do. (Mines)	—	82 —	Wilkie, Trustees of John	Seafield, Roslin	3	34 —
Walker, James, of Dalry	10 Grosvenor Crescent, Edinburgh	1	8 —	Wilson, Alexander	Flowerfield, Loanhead	1	30 —
				Wilson, Trustees of George	Edinburgh	1	20 10
Walker, James Scott	London	10	15 —	Wilson, James	Restalrig House	15	171 —
Walker, Rev. William	Mid-Calder	50	100 —	Wilson, John	Hillhouse, Lamington	3	116 —
Walker, William C., yr. of Bowland	Edinburgh	15	15 —	Wilson, Robert	Dalkeith	2	340 10
Walker, William S., of Bowland	Edinburgh	2,150	1,224 —	Wilson, Thomas, and Robert Stirling	Galashiels	2	34 —
Watson, David	Cramond Bridge	1	57 —	Wilson, William	Broomfield House, Davidson's Mains	17	135 —
Watson, George, of Norton	Norton, Ratho	470	1,381 —	Wilson, Margaret	Olivebank, Musselburgh	26	201 —
Watson, William	Hawthorn Bank, Bonnyrigg	1	75 —	Wood, Alexander	Edinburgh	1	103 —
				Woodward, Major R.	Grove Hill House, Lasswade	2	65 —
Watson's Hospital, Governors of George	Edinburgh	1,189	2,095 —	Wolff, Nicolay de	Inglis Green, Slateford	1	75 —
Watson's Institution, Governors of John	Edinburgh	5	47 —	Wooley, Charles	Dalkeith	1	80 —
Watt, James	Bloomiehall, Juniper Green	2	37 —				
Watt, Robert	Eastmill, Currie	2	41 10	Young, Andrew	Mansfield, Currie	12	32 —
Wauchope, Andrew, of Niddry	Niddry	670	2,594 —	Young, Rt. Hon. George, M.P. (Lord Advocate)	Edinburgh	10	107 10
Do. do.	Do. (Mines)	—	300 —	Young, James, of Kelly	Limefield, West Calder	1,494	1,892 —
Wauchope, Sir J. Don, of Newton Don and Edmonstone, Bart.	Edmonstone House, Liberton	1,350	6,043 —	Do. do.	Do. (Mines)	—	2,266 —
				Young, William	Lasswade	1	48 —
Do. do.	Do. (Mines)	—	267 —	Young, William	Newton Grange	1	18 —
Webster, John	Lasswade	3	106 10	Young's Paraffin Light and Mineral Oil Company (Limited)	West Calder	331	6,580 —
Wedderburn, Sir David, of Ballendean, Bart., M.P.	Edinburgh	9	95 —	Do. do.	Do. (Mines)	—	1,820 —
Welsh, James, and Welsh, Mrs. C.	Middleton Inn Gorebridge	33	44 —				
Welwood, A. A. M., of Meadowbank	Meadowbank, Kirknewton	1,583	1,777 —	Total Owners of Land of one Acre and upwards		696	226,223	535,200 1
Wemyss and March, Earl of	Gosford House, Longniddry	1,504	5,370 —	Total Owners of Lands of less than one Acre in extent		2,541	555	46,403 5
Do. do.	Do. (Mines)	—	200 —				
Wemyss, A. W.	Denbrae, St. Andrews	1	11 —	GRAND TOTAL		3,237	226,778	581,603 6

MUNICIPAL BOROUGH OF EDINBURGH.
Population over 20,000.

Name of Owner.	Address of Owner.	Estimated Acreage of Property.	Gross Annual Value.	Name of Owner.	Address of Owner.	Estimated Acreage of Property.	Gross Annual Value.
		Acres.	£ s.			Acres.	£ s.
Adam, James	19 Claremont Crescent	2	610 —	Baillie, John	Edinburgh	1	264 —
Agnew, Mrs. M. C., of East Warriston	Clifton	41	489 —	Balfour, John M., of Pilrig	Pilrig House, Edinburgh	15	214 —
Aitchison, John, & Co.	South Back of Canongate	1	575 —	Ballantyne & Co.	Causewayside	1	390 —
Aitchison & Sons	77 Queen Street	1	3,109 —	Ballantyne, James	Warriston Lodge, Meadows	3	656 —
Alexander, George	18 Grange Loan	2	1,282 —	Bank of Scotland	Edinburgh	4	2,137 —
Alexander, James	Redbraes	10	303 —	Beattie, William, & Sons	Fountainbridge	1	235 —
Allan, Trs. of William	Hillside Crescent	2	1,453 —	Begg, Trustees of Mrs., of West Warriston	Edinburgh	20	1,423 —
Anderson, James C.	Kilgraston Road	1	420 —	Bell, A. M.	E. Morningside House	4	143 —
Anderson, Jessie	18 Bruntsfield Place	1	110 —	Bertram, George	Sciennes House	2	410 —
				Blackhall, David	Holyrood Terrace	2	386 —
				Blyth, Edward L. I.	2 South Lauder Road	1	170 —
Baillie, Hon. Chas. (Lord Jerviswoode)	Strathearn Road	1	185 —	Bonar, Rev. H.	10 Palmerston Road	1	125 —

EDINBURGH—continued.—(MUNICIPAL BOROUGH OF EDINBURGH.)

Name of Owner.	Address of Owner.	Estimated Acreage of Property.	Gross Annual Value.	Name of Owner.	Address of Owner.	Estimated Acreage of Property.	Gross Annual Value.
		Acres.	£ s.			Acres.	£ s.
Boswell, Alexander	4 Salisbury Road	2	1,584 —	Edinburgh and Leith Brewing Company	212 Canongate	1	703 —
Bremner, Bruce A.	Streatham House, Canaan Lane	5	160 —	Edinburgh and Leith Cemetery Company	Bonnington Road	9	131 —
Brown, Alexander	4 Drumdryan Street	1	651 —	Edinburgh and Leith Gas-Light Company	8 George Street	2	3,419 —
Brown Brothers, & Co.	Rosebank	2	103 —				
Brown, Trustees of J.	14 Spring Gardens	2	117 —	Edinburgh and Leith Joiners' Building Co. (Limited)	25 Cockburn Street	1	584 —
Bryden, Trustees of J.	Spring Gardens	2	149 —				
Bryson, Robert	17 Bruntsfield Place	1	196 —	Edinburgh Cemetery Company	Edinburgh	19	304 —
Buccleuch and Queensberry, Duke of	Dalkeith Palace	4	112 —	Edinburgh City, Lord Provost, Magistrates, and Town Council of	Edinburgh	167	6,983 —
Caledonian Insurance Co.	19 George Street	42	1,561 —	Edinburgh City Improvement Trust, Commissioners of	Edinburgh	3	1,507 —
Caledonian Railway Company	Glasgow	1	913 —	Edinburgh, City and County of	Edinburgh	4	2,380 —
Do. do.	Do. (Railway)	43	9,450 —				
Calton, Incorporated Trades of	Edinburgh	4	116 —	Edinburgh Co-operative Building Co. (Limited)	21 George Street	2	153 —
Campbell, Alexander, of Cammo	6 Charlotte Square	2	1,093 —	Edinburgh Gas-Light Co.	25 Waterloo Place	9	9,319 —
Carfrae, Eliza and Isabella	The Bloom, Canaan Lane	1	55 —	Edinburgh Railway Station Access Company	6 North St. David Street	1	4,464 —
Carrick, James, & Sons	West Dalry	1	207 —				
Chalmers' Hospital, Trustees of	Lauriston	4	661 —	Edinburgh Workmen's Building Improvement Co.	21 Abercromby Place	1	1,285 —
Charlotte Square Gardens, Proprietors of	Edinburgh	2	22 —	Edmonstone, Thomas	Kilgraston Road	2	532 —
Cheyne, Representatives of Mrs., of Lismore	2 Doune Terrace	2	525 —	Eton Terrace Gardens, Proprietors of	Edinburgh	4	44 —
Chisholm, James S. (The Chisholm), of Chisholm	Marchhall Park	1	180 —				
Chisholm, Isabella Scott	19 Bruntsfield Place	4	60 —	Falconer, Mary Jane, and Mrs. Craigie, of Falconhall	Falconhall	20	537 —
City of Edinburgh Brewery Company	Abbey Hill	1	580 —	Ferguson, Davidson, & Co.	Albert Street	3	300 —
Clapperton, John	Spylaw Road	1	140 —	Fergusson, James	Kilgraston Road	2	115 —
Cockburn, John	2 Kilgraston Road	1	150 —	Fettes, Trustees of Sir William, of Comely Bank, Bart.	Fettes College	92	1,241 —
College for Daughters of Ministers of the Established Church of Scotland	Kilgraston Road	2	220 —				
Colville, Arthur	2 St. Andrew Place	2	639 —	Field, Thomas	Hawkhill	4	359 —
Colvin, Rev. Robert	7 Church Hill	1	118 —	Forbes, Colonel J. A.	Aberdeen	1	458 —
Commercial Bank of Scotland	George Street	1	2,804 —	Ford, William	Holyrood Glass Works	2	1,934 —
Cranston, Robert	43 Princes Street	3	2,310 —	Fraser, Patrick Neill	Canonmills Lodge	1	129 —
Crawford, John	Glen Street	2	483 —	Free Church of Scotland, Trustees of	Edinburgh	3	3,062 —
Crichton, G. & M. H.	18 Princes Street	1	117 —	Forsyth, Mrs.	Bell's Mills	6	578 —
Croall, Trustees of John, of Southfield	Southfield	6	3,212 —	Fulton, John	Clinton Road	3	574 —
Crown, The— Board of Manufactures Department Board of Works Department Ordnance Royal Institution		437	25261 —	George Square Gardens, Proprietors of	Edinburgh	5	48 —
				Gibson & Walker	Bonnington Mills	8	328 —
				Gillespie's Hospital, Trs. of	Gillespie Crescent	3	411 —
Cunningham, James	Blackford Road	2	60 —	Gilmour, William and O.	Pleasance	1	522 —
Cunyngham, Sir R. K. A. Dick, of Prestonfield, Bart.	Prestonfield House	11	310 —	Gilmour, W. J. L., of Craigmillar	Inch House	14	2,958 —
				Girdwood, Robert	Tanfield	3	983 —
Currie, William, & Co.	Dalry	1	172 —	Glover, Thomas C.	29 Hope Terrace	1	218 —
Curror, Adam	The Lee, Colinton Road	4	140 —	Gowans, Alexander	3 Viewforth	2	356 —
				Gowans, James	Castle Terrace	3	2,404 —
				Grahame, Barron, of Morphie	12 Hope Terrace	2	200 —
Davidson, Lt.-Col. D. W.	Clinton Road	4	191 —	Greenhill Gardens, Proprietors of	Edinburgh	1	10 —
Deaf and Dumb Institution, Trustees of	Henderson Row	3	100 —	Gregory, Georgina	Canaan Lodge	4	120 —
Deuchar, David	Morningside Park	6	102 —	Greig, D. & J.	Fountainbridge	1	259 —
Donald, Christina	9 Whitehouse Terrace	1	115 —				
Donaldson's Hospital, Governors of	Donaldson's Hospital	21	750 —	Haig, J. R., & others	Lochrin	3	1,974 —
Downie, Laird, & Laing	Haymarket	1	240 —	Haig, Reps. of Mrs.	Viewpark	2	120 —
Drummond Place Gardens, Proprietors of	Edinburgh	2	27 —	Hamilton, Alexander	Clinton Road	2	190 —
Dryden, Adam	31 Minto Street	2	404 —	Hay, William	Water of Leith	1	805 —
Duncan, Mary and Jane	Bellville House	8	33 —	Herdman, J., & Son	Haymarket Mills	1	620 —
				Heriot's Hospital, Governors of	Heriot's Hospital	180	4,770 —
				Hope, John	31 Moray Place	29	1,748 —
Edinburgh Academy, Trs. of	Henderson Row	4	325 —	House of Refuge, Trustees of	Canongate	1	365 —
Edinburgh and District Water Trust	Royal Exchange	1	8,013 —	Hume, Robert	49 Grange Road	3	2,710 —
				Hutchison, Robert	13 Merchiston Avenue	1	888 —

EDINBURGH—continued.—(Municipal Borough of Edinburgh.)

Name of Owner.	Address of Owner.	Estimated Acreage of Property.	Gross Annual Value.	Name of Owner.	Address of Owner.	Estimated Acreage of Property.	Gross Annual Value.
		Acres.	£ s.			Acres.	£
Ingles, Thomas	Onslow House, Eastbourne	1	106 —	O'Connell, Bernard	Beaver Hall	19	267 —
Ivory, Mrs. Robina	St. Roque, Grange Loan	9	190 —	Oman, Creditors of John	76 George Street	1	651 —
				Orman, William	Lover's Lane, Leith Walk	4	573 —
				Orphan Hospital, Governors of	Dean	7	322 —
				Oswald, Lady	Southbank, Canaan Lane	4	140 —
Jamieson, Heirs of Robert	8 South Charlotte Street	4	268 —				
Johnston, D., & Sons	Beaver Bank	4	205 —				
Junner, Trustees of R. G.	1 Northumberland Street	1	149 —	Paterson, John	46 Findhorn Place	1	199 —
				Paterson, John	21 St. Andrew Square	2	105 —
				Patterson, William	10 Queensferry Street	1	1,224 —
				Paton, Chalmers J.	115 Princes Street	1	125 —
Kinghorn, William	Taaphall Lane	2	140 —	Pearson, D. A.	17 Royal Circus	1	371 —
				Peat, Rear-Admiral David	Viewforth House	4	100 —
				Pilrig Model Buildings Association	5 St. Andrew Square	1	537 —
Latta, J., and others	27 Forth Street	8	176 —				
Lauder, Sir Thomas N. Dick, of Fountainhall, Bart.	45 Upper Brook Street, London	68	1,066 —	Queen Street Gardens, East, Proprietors of	Edinburgh	5	54 —
Learmonth, Lieut.-Colonel Alexander, of Dean, M.P.	93 Eaton Place, London	83	2,455 —	Queen Street Gardens, Mid, Proprietors of	Edinburgh	5	46 —
Lithgow, Robert	Stanmore Lodge, Lanark	2	1,078 —	Queen Street Gardens, West, Proprietors of	Edinburgh	7	71 —
Lyon, Alexander	55 Grove Street	1	1,331 —				
M'Dowall, Mrs. Anne Amelia	11 Blackford Road	2	120 —	Raffin, William	Mayfield Street	1	1,162 —
M'Ewan, William	Fountainbridge	15	959 —	Raleigh, Samuel	Park House, Dick Place	8	438 —
M'Gibbon, David	Edgehill House	3	1,109 —	Regent Terrace Gardens, Proprietors of	Edinburgh	13	128 —
M'Gregor, Donald	Royal Hotel, Princes Street	2	2,686 —	Reid, William	Logie Green	9	244 —
M'Gregor, Donald R.	Woodburn, Canaan Lane	10	185 —	Renton, J., junior	4 George Street	2	1,385 —
M'Gregor, W. & D.	40 Grindlay Street	10	1,908 —	Richardson, Robert	16 Bruntsfield Place	2	122 —
M'Kay, David	3 Washington Place	1	440 —	Rigg, Trustees of James H., of Tarvit	Tarvit House, Cupar-Fife	16	240 —
M'Kelvie, James	Haymarket	7	2,150 —	Ritchie, George	46 Pleasance	4	1,046 —
M'Kenzie, William	Hope Park House	1	1,486 —	Roberts, George	Haymarket Terrace	2	1,353 —
M'Laren, Duncan, M.P.	Newington House	35	1,513 —	Rocheid, Curators of Charles H. A. F. C. E. J., of Inverleith	Trinity College, Oxford	96	698 —
MacVicar, Mrs. Isabella	Canaan Park	9	166 —				
Mason, Robert, of Belgrave Park	Belgrave Park, Corstorphine	7	159 —	Roman Catholic Church, Trustees of	Edinburgh	16	2,008 —
Mather, James	South Shields	3	110 —	Rosemount Association	21 Abercromby Place	1	895 —
Melvin, Heirs of Alexander	Edinburgh	1	378 —	Royal Bank of Scotland	St. Andrew Square	2	4,166 —
Menzies, Bernard, & Co.	Caledonian Distillery	6	2,405 —	Royal Company of Archers	Edinburgh	1	70 —
Menzies, W. J.	Canaan Cottage, Grange Loan	4	177 —	Royal Edinburgh Lunatic Asylum, Trustees of	Morningside	12	402 —
Middlemass, Robert	20 W. Preston Street	1	920 —	Royal Infirmary, Trustees of	Royal Infirmary	13	1,437 —
Miller & Co.	London Road	2	140 —	Royal Terrace Gardens, Proprietors of	Edinburgh	10	100 —
Miller, James	16 Hope Terrace	1	860 —				
Milne, James, & Son	Milton House	1	405 —				
Moffat, Henry, of Eldin	5 Mayfield Terrace	3	1,360 —				
Moir, George	12 Gardner's Crescent	1	1,673 —				
Mood, John	Rosehall, Dalkeith Road	1	137 —				
Moray, Earl of	Donibristle, Fife	16	160 —	Scott, J. & T.	10 George Street	1	80 —
Moray Place Gardens, Proprietors of	Moray Place	4	35 —	Scottish Lands & Building Co. (Limited)	6 North St. David Street	5	1,600 —
Moray Place Grounds, Proprietors of	Moray Place	4	43 —	Scottish Vulcanite Co. (Limited)	Viewforth Lane	4	670 —
More, Mrs.	Craigmillar Park	2	451 —	Seater, George	Bonnington Bank House	1	70 —
Morton, William Scott, & Co.	West Dalry	1	110 —	Sime, George	St. Leonard's Hill	1	674 —
Munro, Alexander	Merchiston	2	427 —	Sime, James	Craigmount House, Dick Place	6	524 —
Murdoch, Archd. Burn	Greenhill Lodge	1	195 —	Simpson, James	Hatton Place	1	240 —
Murray, David	Strathearn Road	2	185 —	Simpson, Richard	16 Coates Gardens	4	995 —
				Slater, Andrew	17 Spring Gardens	1	329 —
				Sloan, Thomas	Easter Road	1	414 —
Napier, Trustees of Lady, of Merchiston Castle	Edinburgh	3	250 —	Smith, James	17 Forbes Road	2	357 —
Nelson, Thomas	Arthursley, Dalkeith Rd.	24	182 —	Smith, Thomas	Blandfield, Canonmills	1	70 —
Nelson, William	Salisbury Green	12	206 —	Southern Cemetery Company	Grange	10	155 —
Nelson, Mrs. Margaret	Dalkeith Road	1	110 —	Steel, James	Dalry Road	9	1,626 —
Newington Burying Ground, Trustees of	Newington	2	20 —	Stein, Robert William	49 Raglan Road, Dublin	7	409 —
Nicolson, David	Palace Brewery	3	1,001 —	Stewart's Hospital, Governors of	Dean	6	940 —
North British Railway Company	Edinburgh	20	5,230 —	St. Andrew Square Gardens, Proprietors of	Edinburgh	2	26 —
Do. do.	(Railway and Canal)	91	17969 —	Stuart, R. L.	Moreland Cottage, West Grange Loan	4	135 —
North British Rubber Company	Fountainbridge	5	1,420 —	Syme, James	Millbank House, Grange Loan	15	232 —

EDINBURGH—continued.—(Municipal Borough of LEITH.)

Name of Owner.	Address of Owner.	Estimated Acreage of Property.	Gross Annual Value.	Name of Owner.	Address of Owner.	Estimated Acreage of Property.	Gross Annual Value.
		Acres.	£ s.			Acres.	£ s.
Taylor, John, & Sons	110 Princes Street	1	2,632 —	Watherston, J., & Son	Queensferry Street	17	1,569 —
Trades' Maiden Hospital, Trustees of	Edinburgh	3	347 —	Watson's, George, College Schools, Governors of	Edinburgh	53	1,718 —
Trinity Hospital, Trustees of	Edinburgh	17	232 —	Watson's, John, Institution, Governors of	Dean	10	538 —
Trotter, Richard, of Mortonhall	Mortonhall, Liberton	25	288 —	Western Cemetery Co.	Dean	12	230 —
Tullis, Trustees of W.	35 Gilmore Place	3	864 —	West Princes Street Gardens, Proprietors of	Edinburgh	18	180 —
				White, Burns, & Co.	Bonnington	1	315 —
				White, Thomas	8 St. Anthony Place	1	128 —
University of Edinburgh, Senatus Academicus of	Edinburgh	4	3,566 —				
Usher, Andrew	Blackford Park	2	50 —	Younger, Robert	Croft-an-righ	3	815 —
Usher, Andrew, & Co.	22 West Nicolson Street	1	479 —	Younger, W. & H. J.	Horse Wynd, Canongate	9	3,060 —
Usher, J. & T.	St. Leonards	2	650 —				
Usher, Thomas	18 Lauder Road	1	227 —				
				Total Owners of Land of one Acre and upwards 240		2,558	252967 —
Waddell, Andrew	1 St. David's Terrace	1	1,589 —	Total Owners of Lands of less than one Acre in extent 11,306		1,180	1041364 —
Walker, James, of Dalry	10 Grosvenor Crescent	36	856 —				
Walker, Trustees of Mary, of Drumsheugh	Edinburgh	5	775 —	Grand Total 11,546		3,738	1294331 —
Warrender, Sir George, of Lochend, Bart.	Bruntsfield House	74	908 —				

MUNICIPAL BOROUGH OF LEITH.

Population over 20,000.

Name of Owner.	Address of Owner.	Estimated Acreage of Property.	Gross Annual Value.	Name of Owner.	Address of Owner.	Estimated Acreage of Property.	Gross Annual Value.
		Acres.	£ s.			Acres.	£ s.
Auchinleck, Trs. of J.	Edinburgh	4	305 —	Davidson, Henry, of Muirhouse	Muir House, Cramond	2	243 —
				Dickson, D. S.	Afton Lodge, Ferry Rd.	1	130 —
Balfour, J. M., of Pilrig	Pilrig House	44	661 —	Doig, Charles	Seafield House	8	106 —
Bernard & Co.	Yardheads	1	697 —	Drummond Brothers	Larkfield, Trinity	3	111 —
Bertram, Trs. of James	141 Leith Walk	1	430 —				
Blackie, John	Summerfield	9	271 —				
Bonnington Chemical Co.	Bonnington	12	325 —				
Bonnington Sugar Refining Co.	Breadalbane Street	3	1,425 —	Edinburgh, City of	Edinburgh	8	99 —
Boswell, Trustees of J. D., of Wardie	Edinburgh	42	356 —	Edinburgh Roperie Company	Bath Street	18	1,308 —
Boyd, Trustees of A. B.	The Grove, Trinity	1	100 —	Edinburgh and Leith Gas-Light Company	Baltic Street	2	3,031 —
Building Company, Edinburgh Co-operative	21 George St., Edinburgh	3	371 —	Edinburgh and Leith Glass Company	Salamander Street	5	2,008 —
Building Co., Industrial Co-operative	East Hermitage Place	7	287 —	Episcopal Church, Trs. of	Leith	1	347 —
Caledonian Railway Company	Glasgow (Railway)	29	3,025 —	Field, Thomas	Hawkhill	23	933 —
Callander, Trustees of D.	Bonnington Bridge	1	509 —	Flockhart, William	York Road, Trinity	2	475 —
Carnegy, Anne Grace	Laverockbank House	7	138 —	Forrest, C. L.	Blair Park, Ferry Road	1	100 —
Church of Scotland, Trs. of	Leith	2	869 —	Forsyth, W. F.	Denham Green, Trinity	9	171 —
Clapperton, James	Mavis Bank, Stanley Rd.	1	341 —	Free Church, Trustees of	Leith	2	852 —
Crabbie, John	22 Royal Terrace, Edinburgh	2	1,280 —				
Craig & Rose	172 Leith Walk	1	250 —				
Cranston, Robert	Spring Gardens, Edinburgh	11	110 —	Galloway, James	Stanley Road	11	1,403 —
				Gibson & Walker	Bonnington Steam Mills	19	2,285 —
Crown, The	London	10	3,530 —	Gibson, W. W.	9 Moray Pl., Edinburgh	4	20 —
Cunningham, J. & J.	102 West Bow, Edinburgh	2	765 —	Gillon, John	Wardie House	3	550 —
				Goalen, Rev. W. M.	Star Bank, Trinity	3	186 —
Currie, James	Trinity Cottage, Ferry Road	1	10 —	Gordon, Heirs of Mrs. Catherine	Duke Street, Leith	5	361 —

EDINBURGH—continued.—(MUNICIPAL BOROUGH OF LEITH.)

Name of Owner.	Address of Owner.	Estimated Acreage of Property.	Gross Annual Value.	Name of Owner.	Address of Owner.	Estimated Acreage of Property.	Gross Annual Value.
		Acres.	£ s.			Acres.	£ s.
Haldane, Robert, of Cloanden	17 Charlotte Square, Edinburgh	2	120 —	Orrell, Trustees of John	Liverpool	1	75 —
Hawthorns & Co.	Junction Street	3	876 —				
Hay, James	Links Place	1	175 —				
Hay, John	117 Leith Walk	2	1,516 —	Paterson, D. A.	Restalrig Park	8	233 —
Heriot's Hospital, George	Edinburgh	34	446 —	Pattison, Trustees of W. G., and Mrs.	Russell Place, Trinity	1	152 —
Hill, John	Malta Terrace, Edinburgh	2	232 —	Peddie, D. S.	N. Trinity House, Trinity	2	130 —
Hope, Charlotte and Frances J.	Wardie Lodge, Wardie	7	164 —	Pentland, Young, junior	Newhaven Road	1	370 —
Howkins, John	Wardie	3	190 —	Philip, John	Lasswade	2	334 —
Hunter, James	Broughton Point, Edinburgh	2	1,193 —	Philp, Andrew	Cockburn Hotel, Edinburgh	2	60 —
Hunter, Samuel	223 Leith Walk	1	519 —	Pirrie, Mrs. Jess	Junction Street	2	157 —
Hutton, Peter	223 Leith Walk	1	563 —	*Police Commissioners*	Leith	1	455 —
Hutton & Thomson	144 Leith Walk	2	364 —	Puddicombe's Trustees	Edinburgh	3	80 —
				Pursell, William	Rhind Lodge	3	740 —
Inglis, John	Bonnington Brae	3	883 —				
				Raimes, Blanshard, & Co.	Smith's Place	2	310 —
				Raimes, Richard	Bonnington Park	16	490 —
Johnstone, Heirs of R.	Royal Exchange, Edinburgh	2	266 —	Ranken, Lieut.-Col. G.	Cargilfield	3	341 —
				Rattray, Lieut.-Col. James Clerk, of Craighall	Craighall, Perthshire	21	160 —
Kinghorn, William	Bonnington Villa	1	378 —	Reid, William	Berwick-on-Tweed	1	55 —
Kirk, George	Cassells' Place	1	2,600 —	*Roman Catholic Church, Trustees of*	Leith	1	768 —
Kirkpatrick, John	48 India St., Edinburgh	1	658 —				
Lawson Seed and Nursery Co. (Limited)	George IV. Bridge, Edinburgh	2	37 —	Simpson, Robert	Pilrig Cottages	1	582 —
Leith, Burgh of	Leith	52	125 —	Sinclair, George	191 Leith Walk	1	200 —
Leith Docks and Harbour, Commissioners of	Leith (Docks and Harbour)	68	39630 —	Sligo, A. V. S., and Mrs. Margaret, of Inzievar, Fife	5 Drummond Place, Edinburgh	12	150 —
Leith Industrial Ragged School	Lochend Road	1	175 —	Smith, R. C.	234 Leith Walk	2	330 —
Leith Roperie Company, Retired Partners of	Bath Street	2	233 —	Smith, Rev. William	Ferry Road	1	211 —
				Souter, Anne B. C.	Trinity House, Trinity	4	106 —
Leith, Parochial Board of North	North Junction Street	2	415 —	*Standard Property Investment Co.*	Edinburgh	1	731 —
Leith, Parochial Board of South	Junction Street	2	425 —	Steele, James	Dalry House, Edinburgh	10	811 —
Lindsay, William	Hermitage Hill	7	250 —	Steven, William	Ferry Road	1	90 —
Logan, Elizabeth	Seafield Lodge	1	96 —	Stevenson, Mrs. Isabella	37 Royal Terrace, Edinburgh	1	223 —
Lothian, Marquess of	Newbattle Abbey, Dalkeith	1	494 —	Stewart, William	1 Smith's Place	5	277 —
Low, Mary	Mayfield, Trinity	4	160 —				
Lyell, John G.	Prospect Bank	7	85 —	Taylor, Trustees of James	Edinburgh	1	1,759 —
				Taylor, William, Trustees of	Salamander Street	2	1,316 —
M'Farlane, John	Stead's Place	2	644 —	Thomson, R. V.	Laverock Bank, Trinity	1	70 —
M'Kinlay, D., Trustees of	Upper and Easter Hermitage	11	181 —	Tod, A. & R.	Commercial Street	1	2,389 —
M'Lean & Hope	Timber Bush	1	816 —	*Trinity Hospital*	Edinburgh	105	669 —
Mathieson, George	Clifton Lodge, Wardie	1	129 —				
Mathieson, J. A., and Mrs. Reid's Heirs	203 Hope St., Glasgow	2	440 —	Umpherston & Co.	Bowershall Works	4	670 —
Maxwell, Peter	Trinity Cottage, Trinity	3	120 —				
Melvin, Alexander	Boroughloch Brewery, Edinburgh	1	475 —	Wardlaw, Mrs. John F., and Alice and Margaret	Willowbank, Newhaven	1	197 —
Millar, Richard	Pirniefield	1	241 —	Watt's Hospital	Duke Street	1	329 —
Miller, James, & Sons	121 Constitution Street	1	810 —	Wilson, William	Newhaven Road	1	309 —
Miller, Samuel Christie, of Craigentinny	Craigentinny	15	164 —	Wilson, William	Granton Villa, Granton	39	1,190 —
Milne, John	Trinity Grove, Trinity	5	152 —	Wood, Dr. William, R.N.	London	6	119 —
Mitchell, Houston	Bangholm Bower, Trinity	2	105 —				
Mitchell, John, & Co.	230 Leith Walk	2	160 —				
Moray, Earl of	Donibristle House, Fife	54	380 —	Total Owners of Land of One Acre and upwards		127	956 111,658 —
Morton, Hugh	Stanley Road	4	763 —	Total Owners of Lands of less than One Acre in extent		2,062	270 141,446 —
Neill, John, and others	Lixmount, Trinity	12	278 —				
North British Railway Company	Edinburgh	1	498 —				
Do. do.	Edinburgh (Railway)	26	3,622 —	GRAND TOTAL		2,189	1,226 253,104 —

ELGIN.

Population in 1871, - - - - - - - **43,612.**
Inhabited Houses, - - - - - - - **8,452.**
Number of Parishes, - - - - - - - **22.**

Name of Owner.	Address of Owner.	Estimated Acreage of Property.	Gross Annual Value.
		Acres.	£ s.
Ainslie, Ainslie Douglas, of Blervie	Delgaty Castle, Turriff	3,140	1,896 5
Allan, John	Mills, Bishopmill	3	174 -
Allan, Rev. John	Peterculter, Aberdeen	1	37 17
Alves, Trustees of late Major-General John	Elgin	4	49 -
Anderson, Rev. Alexander	F.C. Manse, Edinkillie	1	27 -
Anderson's Institution, Trustees of	Elgin	9	207 -
Anderson, James	Elgin	2	72 19
Anderson, John	Port-Glasgow	10	48 10
Anderson, John	Spey Cottage, Garmouth	36	101 14
Anderson, Robert	Garmouth	6	29 16
Anderson, Heirs of Thomas	Haughland, Elgin	5	12 10
Anderson, William	Maryhill, Elgin	4	120 -
Badden, Isaac	Lossiemouth	2	42 2
Badenoch, Heirs of James	Garmouth	6	73 15
Bain, Alexander, senior	Forres	8	45 6
Bellie Parish, Heritors of	Bellie	3	3 -
Bennet, Mrs. Margaret	South College St., Elgin	2	245 18
Black, James	Elgin	2	160 10
Bowie, Mrs. Elspet	Lossiemouth	1	7 5
Braco's Mortification, Trs. of	Elgin	8	35 15
Brander, Rev. Alexander	Manse, Duffus (Glebe Lands)	11	40 -
Do. do.	Do.	158	366 5
Brander, George	Garmouth	5	7 -
Brander, Captain James B. D., of Pitgaveny	Pitgaveny House, Elgin	3,121	2,823 18
Brander, Robert	Elgin	9	15 -
Brander, Robert	Rock House, Lossiemouth	4	24 10
Bremner, James	Forres	2	60 16
Bremner, John	Garmouth	2	10 15
Bremner, William	Dunkirk, Urquhart	4	11 15
Brodie, Hugh F. A., of Brodie	Brodie Castle, Forres	4,728	2,172 5
Brodie, James Campbell J., of Lethen	Lethen House, Nairn	1,304	1,120 14
Brown, William	Linkwood, Elgin	29	100 -
Bruce, Charles Lennox Cumming, of Dunphail	Dunphail, Forres	10,518	1,182 10
Caledonian Banking Co.	Inverness	18	47 -
Cameron, Alexander	Highfield House, Elgin	3	118 -
Cameron, Mrs. Janet	Garmouth	5	17 -
Campbell, Heirs of Rev. Augustus	Liverpool	34	70 -
Chadwick, Major Robert, of Binsness	Moy House, Forres	500	55 -
Christie, John	Bloomsbury St., London	1	141 15
Clark, John	Garmouth	1	3 -
Clark, Isabella	Garmouth	2	4 10
Cluny Hill Hydropathic Co.	Forres	8	255 -
Cooper, Alexander	Elgin	2	86 14
Cooper, John Alexander	Spynie, Elgin	19	6 -
Craigen, John	Bulletloan, Forres	2	4 5
Crown, The	London	3	136 -
Culbard, William	North Lodge, Elgin	3	151 15
Cumming, Sir William Gordon Gordon, of Altyre and Gordonstone, Bart.	Altyre House, Forres	36,387	13685 10
Cumming, Mrs. Emily F. Valiant, of Logie	Logie House, Edinkillie	1,625	528 11
Cushny, Rev. Robert	Manse, Bellie	20	50 -
Davidson, Reps. of Thomas	Victoria Place, Forres	3	10 10
Davidson, Mrs. Ann	Batchen Street, Forres	2	78 2
Dean, Heirs of James	Jointure, Leuchars, Urquhart	2	7 -
Dean, Peter	Rothes	1	81 18
Dougal, Mrs. Charlotte, of Balnageath	Ratho Park, Edinburgh	301	728 10
Downie, Trustees of Charles, of Ashfield	Aberdeen	58	72 -
Drainie Parish, Heritors of	Drainie	2	1 10
Drainie, Trustees of Free Church of	Lossiemouth	1	12 -
Duff, Alexander Thomas Wharton, of Orton	Orton House, Fochabers	3,019	1,793 15
Duff, Major Lachlan Duff Gordon, of Drummuir	Drummuir Castle, Keith	5	86 -
Duff, Thomas Duff Gordon, of Hopeman	Drummuir Castle, Keith	552	587 8
Do. do.	Do. (Harbour)	2	72 4
Duffus, James	237 High Street, Elgin	1	29 12
Dunbar, Sir Archibald, of Northfield, Bart.	Duffus House, Elgin	1,828	3,414 8
Dunbar, Mrs. Phœbe Dunbar, of Seapark	Seapark, Kinloss	2,115	773 4
Duncan, Alexander	Wards, Garmouth	1	13 -
Duncan, Capt. John, jun.	Garmouth	2	11 -
Duncan, Robert	Garmouth	2	12 -
Dunn, Rev. Peter	Manse, Speymouth	42	33 -
Dyke and Moy, Heritors of Parish of	Dyke and Moy	2	2 -
Eddie, Rev. John	Institution, Elgin	4	31 10
Elgin Cemetery, Trustees of	Elgin	5	20 -
Elgin, City of	Elgin	93	157 4
Elgin District Lunacy Board	Elgin	5	125 -
Elgin, Guildry Corporation of	Elgin	94	386 18
Elgin, Hospital Master of City of	Elgin	32	91 10
Elgin, Incorporated Trades of	Elgin	43	164 10
Elgin, Kirk-Session of	Elgin	13	33 10
Elgin and Lossiemouth Harbour Company	Lossiemouth (Harbour)	10	750 -
Ferguson, Rev. John	Parsonage, Elgin	25	26 -
Ferguson, Tutors and Curators of Ronald Crawford Munro, of Novar	Novar, Evanton, Ross-shire	3,849	2,494 7
Do. do.	Do. (Harbour)	1	34 16
Ferries, Rev. John	Manse, Edinkillie	10	28 -
Fife, Trustees of Earl of	Innes House, Elgin	40,959	18693 10
Findhorn Railway Company	Forres (Disused Railway)	11	60 -
Forres Cemetery, Directors of	Forres	3	10 -
Forres, Town of	Forres	1,007	846 5

ELGIN—continued.

Name of Owner.	Address of Owner.	Estimated Acreage of Property.	Gross Annual Value.
		Acres.	£ s.
Forster, Mrs. Helen	Findrassie, New Spynie	60	80 –
Forsyth, Trustees of James	Forres	2	7 –
Forsyth, John	Lossiemouth	1	5 –
Forsyth, William	Lhanbryde, Elgin	2	14 –
Forsyth, Jane	Hay Street, Elgin	1	60 –
Forteath, Trs. of G. A., of Newton	Newton House, Alves	243	476 18
Forteath, Mrs. Clementina, of Newton	Elgin	6	105 –
Fraser, Daniel, of Springfield	Springfield, Forres	51	103 –
Fyfe, Heirs of Charles B.	Garmouth Lodge, Surbiton, Surrey	36	85 8
Gatherer, George	Elgin	2	60 –
Geddes, Alexander	Beauly	3	38 9
Geddes, Mrs. Helen Frances	Elgin	1	70 –
Geddie, George	Garmouth	2	19 10
Geddie, James	Kingston	8	35 –
Geddie, James	Garmouth	17	72 15
Geddie, John, senior	Garmouth	6	18 –
Gillan, Trs. of Rev. James	Garmouth	196	172 –
Gordon, Rev. Charles	Manse, St Andrews-Lhanbryde, Elgin	20	35 –
Gordon, Rev. George	Manse, Birnie (*Glebe Lands*)	10	32 –
Do. do.	Do.	6	58 9
Gordon, George	Lossiemouth	2	54 –
Grant, Donald	Grantown, Cromdale	1	31 7
Grant, Sir George M'Pherson, of Ballindalloch, Bart.	Ballindalloch Castle	7,848	2,476 4
Grant, Sir George M'Pherson, of Ballindalloch, Bart., and William Grant, of Wester Elchies	Ballindalloch Castle, (*Undetermined Moor*) Carron Cottage, Craigellachie	2,336	Included in values of Estates.
Grant, Factor *loco tutoris* of Ian Robert James Murray, of Moy	Glenmoriston, Inverness	4,063	1,922 1
Grant, Lieut.-Col. the Hon. James, of Main	Invererne House, Forres	804	743 14
Grant, James & James	Rothes	24	133 15
Grant, Trs. of late James	Elgin	2	250 –
Grant, John	Grantown, Cromdale	1	25 –
Grant, Heirs of Sir Lewis	Forres	1	40 –
Grant, Hon. Lewis Alexander, of Grant	Hopeman Lodge, Elgin	4	65 –
Grant, Robert, of Kincorth	Kincorth House, Forres	457	832 6
Grant, Robert Donald	Thornhill, Forres	235	628 –
Grant, William, of Wester Elchies	Carron Cottage, Craigellachie	20,462	4,940 16
Grant, Georgina H.	Delchaple, Garmouth	18	48 –
Gray, Rev. George	Manse, Rothes	28	49 –
Gray's Hospital, Trustees of	Elgin	3	90 –
Great North of Scotland Railway Company	Aberdeen (*Railway*)	89	3,108 –
Grigor, John	Forres	4	62 –
Grigor, Heirs of William	Elgin	10	118 4
Hay, Robert	Elgin	1	79 17
Highland Railway Company	Inverness (*Railway*)	535	23604 –
Hoyes, Trustees of John	Forres	3	37 5
Hutcheson, Alexander	Forres	2	88 –
Inglis, Archibald	South College, Elgin	7	88 –
Ingram, Rev. George	Manse, Urquhart	5	24 –
Innes, Alexander	Garmouth	3	12 10
Innes, Rev. John Brodie, of Milton Brodie	Milton Brodie, Alves	1,237	1,755 1
James, John	51 Langlands Road, Govan	2	17 –
Jenkins, Mrs. Susan	Forres	3	44 –
Johnston, James	Newmill, Elgin	18	339 17
Keith, Rev. James	Manse, Forres	7	61 –
Kinloss Parish, Heritors of	Kinloss	3	4 10
Kyd, Rev. John	Manse, New Spynie	8	30 –
Kynoch, Robert	Forres	2	154 9
Laing, Heirs of James	Kinloss	3	26 10
Laing's Mortification, Trustees of	Elgin	3	12 10
Larkworthy, Helen Eliza	Elgin	1	50 –
Lawson, Alexander	Braelossie, Elgin	4	55 –
Leith, Major Thomas	Palmercross, Elgin	14	97 10
Leslie, Heirs of Mrs. Catherine	Garmouth	7	33 10
Longmore, John Alexander, of Deanshaugh	56 Melville St., Edinburgh	2	56 –
M'Bey, Peter	Darliston, Elgin	2	45 –
M'Bride, William	Elgin	1	5 –
M'Connachie, James	Lossiemouth	2	112 –
M'Donald, Rev. John	Manse, Dallas	10	15 –
Macduff, Viscount	Innes House, Elgin	1,346	1,251 8
M'Ewan, Rev. John	Manse, Dyke	11	51 –
M'Grigor, Sir Charles R., of Camden Hill, Bart.	12 Hyde Park Street, London	19	96 4
M'Innes, Rev. Duncan	Oban and Cromdale	18	50 –
M'Kay, Rev. David Norris	F. C. Manse, Rafford	4	30 –
M'Kenzie, Alexander	Elgin	1	44 10
Mackie, Rev. James	Manse, Alves	6	31 –
Mackie, Rev. Philip Jervis	Elgin	1	42 –
M'Kissack, Robert, of Ardgye and Roseisle	Ardgye, Alves	4,165	3,291 2
M'Lean, Hugh, of Westfield	Westfield, New Spynie	649	1,195 –
M'Leod, Heirs of D. A.	Dalvey Cottage, Dyke	1	25 –
M'Leod, Norman, of Dalvey	Dalvey, Dyke	1,328	1,357 9
M'Queen, Rev. Hugh Duff	Manse, Grantown, Cromdale	1	20 –
Maitland, Caroline Fuller	Bishopmill, Elgin	2	143 –
Marshall, Alexander	Garmouth	5	13 –
Masson, Rev. Alexander	Manse, Boharm	23	36 –
Miller, Alexander U.	Forres	1	71 18
Milne, Heirs of Alexander	Garmouth	13	20 5
Milne, George	Bauds of Cullen	3	5 –
Milne's Institution, Trustees of	Fochabers	2	150 –
Milne, Heirs of Mrs.	Forres	1	25 10
Milne, Mrs. Christina	Garmouth	2	6 –
Monaghan, Thomas	Garmouth	8	30 –
Moray, Earl of	Darnaway Castle	21,669	9,420 9
Morayshire Railway Co.	Elgin (*Railway*)	136	2,832 –
Morayshire Union Poorhouse, Directors of	Bishopmill	4	120 –
Morrison, George	Elgin	1	156 10
Morrison, Robert	Elgin	9	42 10
Mortimer, Peter, of Inverugie	Inverugie, Duffus	673	973 15
Mustard, John	Lossiemouth	1	6 –
National Bank of Scotland	Edinburgh	1	35 –
New Spynie Parish, Heritors of	New Spynie	1	2 –
Peat, Robert	Forres	1	100 17
Peterkin, James Grant, of Grange	Grange Hall, Forres	1,148	1,676 2
Peterkin, Colonel Peter Grant, of Invererne	Edgefield, Forres	400	675 –
Phimister, Grace	Pans, Elgin	1	30 12
Pirie, Rev. Thomas M.	Manse, Knockando	18	36 –
Riach, Duncan	Forres	1	77 –
Richmond, Duke of	Gordon Castle, Fochabers	12,271	10618 4
Robertson, Alexander	North College, Elgin	16	130 –
Robertson, Andrew	Garmouth	8	16 5

ELGIN—continued.

Name of Owner.	Address of Owner.	Estimated Acreage of Property.	Gross Annual Value.	Name of Owner.	Address of Owner.	Estimated Acreage of Property.	Gross Annual Value.
		Acres.	£ s.			Acres.	£ s.
Robertson, James	Huntly	4	3 —	Tayler, William James, of Glenbarry and Bilboahall	Rothiemay House, Banffshire	103	234 —
Robertson, Heirs of John	Whinnyhall, Garmouth	31	54 12	Taylor, James	Elgin	2	153 10
Robertson, William, of Auchinroath	Auchinroath, Rothes	626	264 2	Thom, William, R.N.	Lossiemouth	2	36 —
Robertson, Jane C.	Elgin	1	34 —	Thomson, Rev. James	Gartly	28	51 12
Roman Catholic Church, Trustees of	Elgin	1	131 —	Thomson, Heirs of Richard	Forres	3	16 10
Ross, George	Findhorn	2	13 —	Tod, Trustees of James Ogilvie, of Findrassie	Findrassie, New Spynie	690	602 2
Rothes Parish, Heritors of	Rothes	1	1 —	Topp, William	Ashgrove, Elgin	28	80 —
Roy, Robert	Chester	20	78 10	Tulloh, Trus. of Robert, of Burgie	Burgie, Forres	2,594	1,290 3
Russell, Alexander	Elgin	1	150 —	Tytler, Charles Edward Fraser, of Sanquhar	Sanquhar, Forres	1,310	1,812 16
Seafield, Earl of	Cullen House	96,721	21138 11				
Seafield, Louisa, Countess Dowager of	Grant Lodge, Elgin	39	195 —	Urquhart, Alexander	Elgin	2	178 1
Shand, Alexander	Garmouth	3	30 9	Urquhart, Alexander	Forres	2	63 8
Shand, James	Garmouth	3	4 5	Urquhart, Lewis C.	Elgin	3	131 10
Shand, Mrs. Margaret	Connagehillock, Garmouth	2	3 —	*Urquhart, Trustees of Free Church of*	Urquhart	1	30 —
Sharp, Adam	Rothes	1	99 15				
Sim, William	Forres	1	62 —				
Sime, James	Elgin	3	25 3				
Sinclair, John	Gallowcrook, Elgin	1	45 —	Walker, George	Forres	1	30 15
Sinclair, William	Clunas, Australia	2	2 —	Watson, A. R., & Co.	Elgin	2	60 —
Skene, James	Garmouth	12	30 —	Watson, William	Forres	1	47 —
Skene, William	Garmouth	13	40 —	Weir, Rev. James	Manse, Drainie	10	30 —
Smith, Andrew	Forres	2	50 —	Williamson, Mrs. Clementina	Bendaugh, Aberdeenshire	31	106 13
Smith, Rev. Robert	Manse, Rafford	10	30 —	Wilson, Heirs of Archibald	Elgin	2	32 6
Smith, Mrs. Lindsay Elizabeth, of Relugas	Emsworth House, Emsworth, Hants	1,034	486 —	Wilson, James T.	Forres	2	100 —
Smyth, Trs. of Alexander	Drumduan, Forres	42	105 —	Winchester, John	Garmouth	11	22 —
Speymouth Parish, Heritors of	Speymouth	1	1 10	Winchester, Mrs. Margaret, and Mrs. Ann Douglas	Garmouth	1	3 10
Steinson, Trustees of Col.	Manse, Gartly	6	19 —	Wiseman, James	Garmouth	2	16 —
Stephen, John	Elgin	32	101 4				
Stephen, Rev. Thomas	Manse of Kinloss	180	503 8				
Do. do.	Do. (*Glebe Lands, &c.*)	5	26 —	Young, Robert	Millbank, Bishopmill	2	92 5
Steuart, Andrew, of Auchlunkart	Auchlunkart House, Keith	483	122 3	Young, William, of Burghead	Fleurs, Elgin	109	412 10
Stewart, Rev. Duncan	Elgin	4	17 —	Do. do.	Do. (*Harbour*)	2	450 —
Stewart, Captain James, of Lesmurdie	Friar's Park, Elgin	149	440 17				
St. Andrews Parish, Heritors of	St. Andrews	2	2 —	Total Owners of Land of one Acre and upwards . . . 251		302,736	167,940 6
St. John's Episcopal Church, Trustees of	Forres	2	46 —	Total Owners of Lands of less than one Acre in extent . . . 2,313		432	35,764 14
Tait, Joseph, of Haughland	Haughland, Elgin	47	100 —	GRAND TOTAL . . . 2,564		303,168	203,705 —

FIFE.

Population in 1871,	160,735.
Inhabited Houses,	27,056.
Number of Parishes,	64.

Name of Owner.	Address of Owner.	Estimated Acreage of Property.	Gross Annual Value.	Name of Owner.	Address of Owner.	Estimated Acreage of Property.	Gross Annual Value.
		Acres.	£ s.			Acres.	£ s.
Abbey, William	Chance Inn, Crail	7	34 –	Anderson, George	St. Andrews	4	91 15
Aberdour, Trs. of Lady	Balmule, Aberdour	514	713 18	Anderson, Henry, of Chapel	Chapel, Kirkcaldy	570	1,368 5
Abbotshall Parish, Heritors of				Anderson, John	Newburgh	1	122 10
Adam, Robert	Kirkcaldy	1	100 –	Anderson, John, of Wards	Pratis, Windygates	185	695 8
Adam, Right Hon. William Patrick, of Blairadam, M.P.	Blairadam, Kinross	1,408	754 5	Anderson, John and Charles	Strathkinness, St. Andrews	25	89 –
				Anderson, Thomas Stuart	Newburgh	5	89 –
				Anderson, Mrs., wife of William Anderson	2 Strathearn Road, Edinburgh	544	697 8
Do. do.	Do. (Minerals)	–	300 –	Anderson, Mrs. Charlotte	Newburgh	1	100 –
Adams, Ord	Hill of Beath, Inverkeithing	12	345 –	Anderson, Mrs. Elizabeth	Leven	3	259 19
Do.	Do. (Minerals)	–	1,335 –	Anderson, Mrs., wife of Rev. David Anderson	Ceres	156	257 –
Adamson, Alexander	Aracan Cottage, Musselburgh	3	12 –	Anderson, Eliza	Cupar	10	56 5
Adamson, Alexander	Burnside, St. Andrews	9	52 15	Andrew, John	North Junction Street, Leith	1	29 –
Adamson, Trustees of Alexander	Burnside, St. Andrews	3	97 –	Angus, Charles	Inverkeithing	4	35 –
				Angus, Mrs. Henry	Aberdeen	1	22 –
Adamson, Trustees of Alexander	South Callange, Cupar	149	316 15	Angus, Mrs. James	London Street, Edinburgh	10	63 15
Adamson, Andrew	Auchtermuchty	3	16 11	Anstruther-Easter Feuars	Anstruther	2	10 –
Adamson, David	Lochgelly	1	18 16	Anstruther-Easter Kirk-Session	Anstruther	8	42 5
Adamson, John Clerk	137 Shield Road, Glasgow	14	162 10	Anstruther-Easter Sea Box Society	Anstruther	556	748 15
Adamson, Heirs of John	Ribbonfield, Crail	77	180 13				
Adamson, Trs. of John	St. Andrews	1	294 –	Anstruther-Easter Trades' Box Society	Anstruther	29	215 –
Adamson, Robert	Blebo Craigs, Cupar	1	22 18				
Adamson, William	Crossgates, Inverkeithing	1	56 12	Anstruther Harbour Commissioners	Anstruther	2	253 –
Addison, John	Lochgelly	1	78 –				
Ainslie, Mrs. James	Inverkeithing	1	10 –	Anstruther, Major-General Philip, of Thirdpart, C.B.	Airth Castle, Stirlingshire	1,433	3,252 2
Aitken, Heirs of Alexander	Thornton, Beath	270	250 –				
Aitken, Andrew	Star, Markinch	1	11 15	Do. do.	Do. (Minerals)	–	250 –
Aitken, David	Kinghorn	52	90 –	Anstruther, Sir Robert, of Balcaskie, Bart., M.P.	Balcaskie, Pittenweem	2,121	5,062 12
Do.	Do. (Minerals)	–	50 –				
Aitken, David	Strathkinness, St. Andrews	2	13 12	Do. do.	Do. (Minerals)	–	53 –
Aitken, Trustees of Henry	Barns, North Queensferry	5	16 –	Anstruther-Wester, Burgh of	Anstruther	30	115 13
Aitken, Robert	Puddledub, Kirkcaldy	1	6 –				
Aitken, William	St. Andrews	2	7 –	Anstruther-Wester Kirk-Session	Anstruther	9	63 13
Aitken, William	Langdyke, Kennoway	2	37 10				
Aitken, Heirs of Mrs.	Strathkinness, St. Andrews	2	15 4	Archbald, Mrs., wife of T. B. Archbald	Nisbetfield, Ladybank	3	89 –
Aitken, Mrs. Janet	Arncroach, Pittenweem	6	28 –				
Aitken, Janet, and Mrs. Wilson, Judicial Factor on Joint Trust Estate of Alexander, James, of Balmule	Hill of Beath, Inverkeithing	350	340 5	Arkley, James, of Kininmonth	Dundee	468	648 15
				Armit, David, of Polduff	Polduff, St. Andrews	75	240 –
				Arngask Kirk-Session	Arngask, Milnathort	36	75 –
	Balmule, Dunfermline	322	458 12	Arnot, Henry	Milesmark, Dunfermline	1	7 10
Alexander, James and Thomas	Dunfermline	2	612 –	Arnot, James M., of Chapel	Chapel, Ladybank	397	637 10
Alexander, Thomas	Dunfermline	1	134 10	Arnot, Mrs. Marion Rae	Lochiehead, Auchtermuchty	84	162 10
Alexander, Mrs. Louisa	Cupar	1	35 –	Arnott, Hugo, of Balcormo	Liverpool	201	478 17
Alison, James	Braeside, Ladybank	3	17 10	Do. do.	Do (Minerals)	–	50 –
Alison, James	Kirkcaldy	1	21 –	Arthur, George	Dunshalt, Auchtermuchty	1	12 –
Allan, Andrew	Union Bank, Glasgow	1	14 11	Arthur, Heirs of James	Falkland	5	26 2
Allan, William, of Hallcroft	Millerfield Place, Edinburgh	225	247 8	Arthur, Thomas	Kettle, Ladybank	22	265 10
Allan, William	Gowkhall, Dunfermline	6	23 –	Arthur, William	Dunshalt, Auchtermuchty	3	16 7
Allan, Mrs., wife of William Allan	Gowkhall, Dunfermline	3	17 10	Arthur, William Forsyth	Kirkcaldy	3	61 7
				Auchtermuchty, Burgh of	Auchtermuchty	29	7 –
Allan, Mrs.	Falkland	4	43 15	Auld, James, junior	Inverkeithing	2	21 15
Amos, Walter	Falkland	9	35 6	Auld, Sarah Janet	Dunfermline	5	13 10
Anderson, Adam	Dunfermline	1	18 3	Aytoun, Major James, of South Lethans	36 Upper Grosvenor Street, London	864	662 –
Anderson, Trs. of Alexander	St. Andrews	15	184 –				
Anderson, David	Cowstrandburn, Dunfermline	6	20 10	Aytoun, James and Robert, of Capeldrae	3 Fettes Row, Edinburgh	671	842 14
Anderson, David	Strathkinness, St. Andrews	2	6 –	Do. do.	Do. (Minerals)	–	775 –
Anderson, Trs. of David	St. Andrews	35	225 4	Aytoun, Roger Sinclair, of Inchdairnie, M.P.	Inchdairnie, Kirkcaldy	3,427	4,457 –
Anderson, George	Pitfirrane, Dunfermline	9	18 10	Do. do.	Do. (Minerals)	–	590 –

FIFE—continued.

Name of Owner.	Address of Owner.	Estimated Acreage of Property.	Gross Annual Value.	Name of Owner.	Address of Owner.	Estimated Acreage of Property.	Gross Annual Value.
		Acres.	£ s.			Acres.	£ s.
Aytoun, Mrs. Eliza, of Purin	Glendevon House, Dollar	484	1,003 2	Bennet, Mrs., wife of James Bennet, and Mrs. Murie, wife of John Murie	Cabbagehall, Leslie	10	240 —
Aytoun, Mrs. Margaret A.	Inchdairnie, Kirkcaldy	815	1,629 8				
				Benny, Robert, of Over Inzievar	Underwood, Denny	178	305 18
Bain, James	St. Andrews	4	60 12	Do. do.	Do. (Minerals)	—	1,731 —
Bain, James, and M'Gregor, John	St. Andrews	3	140 10	Bernard, Mrs. Thomas	Leslie	8	69 10
Bain, Peter	Saline, Dunfermline	1	11 10	Berry, David	Lucklawhill, Leuchars	3	19 18
Baird, William, of Elie	Elie House, Elie	3,120	8,222 10	Berry, John, of Tayfield	Tayfield, Newport	890	2,426 8
Baird, Trustees for William	Elie House, Elie	455	593 10	Berwick, Andrew	Rires, Leuchars	10	39 —
Bairner, Heirs of Alexander	Chance Inn, Cupar	2	12 —	Berwick, Colin	Stravithy Mill, St. Andrews	5	46 17
Baldie, David	Woodside, Largo	4	9 10	Berwick, David	Collairnie, Newburgh	2	7 —
Balfour, Heirs of Charles	Balgonie, Markinch	2,327	4,529 6	Berwick, John	St. Andrews	4	13 10
Do. do.	Do. (Minerals)	—	573 —	Berwick, Mathew	Kettle, Ladybank	1	16 11
Balfour, Major Francis Walter, of Fernie	Fernie Castle, Ladybank	1,725	3,223 18	Berwick, Mrs. James	Freuchie, Ladybank	4	17 6
				Berwick, Mrs. James	St. Andrews	2	9 5
Balfour, Henry, & Company	Leven	12	421 10	Berwick, Mrs. Margaret M.	Elie	2	54 —
Balfour, James	Dunfermline	2	40 —	Berwick, Christian	Lundin Mill, Largo	3	39 —
Balfour, John, of Balbirnie	Balbirnie, Markinch	10,590	14533 15	Bethune, Alexander, of Blebo	Blebo, Cupar	1,355	2,954 19
Do. do.	Do. (Minerals)	—	530 —	Do. do.	Do. (Minerals)	—	40 —
Balfour, John, & Company	Leven	7	356 —	Bethune, Admiral Charles R. D., of Balfour	Balfour, Markinch	1,604	3,613 —
Balfour, Robert F., and Edward Balfour	Balbirnie, Markinch	25	36 —	Bethune, Sir John Trotter, of Kilconquhar, Bart.	Kilconquhar	2,205	5,548 1
Balfour, William	Lingo, St. Andrews	4	15 —	Bethune, Major Robert, of Nydie	St. Andrews	584	990 —
Balfour, William	Ovenstone, Pittenweem	12	64 10	Bethune, William, senior	Star, Markinch	3	22 15
Balfour, Mrs. Henry	Leven Bank, Leven	81	216 6	Bethune, Mrs. Robert	Markinch	2	8 —
Balfour, Trustees of Ann	Carslogie, Cupar	830	1,370 11	Bett, Heirs of James	Kettle, Ladybank	20	64 —
Ballantyne, Heirs of William	Anstruther	5	58 4	Beveridge, Andrew, and Trustees of James Morris	Dunfermline	2	112 —
Ballingal, William	Sweetbank, Markinch	1	67 11				
Ballingall, William	Gauldry, Newport	1	14 10	Beveridge, David	Kettle, Ladybank	2	400 2
Ballingall, Mrs. T. F.	Leven	1	73 3	Beveridge, Trustees of Erskine	Dunfermline	1	152 —
Bank of Scotland	Edinburgh	4	330 10	Beveridge, Erskine, & Co.	Dunfermline	5	1,119 —
Barclay, George	7 Holford Square, Pentonville, London	6	15 5	Beveridge, George	Kirkcaldy	1	195 10
Barclay, Heirs of James	Inverkeithing	1	83 —	Beveridge, Heirs of Henry J.	Kirkcaldy	11	27 —
Barclay, Thomas	Bonville, Cupar	20	132 —	Beveridge, James	Star, Markinch	4	24 5
Bardner, Henry	Dunfermline	2	170 10	Beveridge, James	Dunfermline	1	14 —
Barnet, John	Kirkcaldy	1	100 —	Beveridge, James Adamson, of Brucefield	Edinburgh	140	745 —
Barr, Robert	Inverkeithing	1	37 —				
Barrack, Rev. John	Manse, Falkland	6	42 —	Beveridge, Mathew	Kirkcaldy	8	226 4
Barron, George T. B.	Dunfermline	5	30 —	Beveridge, Michael	Kirkcaldy	8	42 —
Barrowman, Curator for Christian Moir	Saline, Dunfermline	3	49 10	Beveridge, William	Kirkcaldy	18	758 10
Bartholomew, Robert	Inverkeithing	1	76 5	Beveridge, William, of Bonnyton	Dunfermline	40	116 —
Bartholomew, Walter	Auchtertool	3	369 —	Beveridge & Aytoun	Kirkcaldy	3	380 —
Bartholomew, Christina and Jessie	Loups, Dunfermline	90	77 5	Beveridge & Reid	Gallatown, Kirkcaldy	3	49 —
				Beveridge, Mrs. M. E.	Dunfermline	9	136 —
Baxter, Trustees of Edward	Gilston, Largo	1,094	1,959 15	Binney, Edward Wm.	Manchester	1	211 4
Baxter, Rev. William Lang	Manse, Arngask, Milnathort	9	34 15	Binning, John	Glasgow	1	13 —
				Birrell, David	Conland, Falkland	12	54 —
Baxter, Mrs. Elizabeth	Myreside, Falkland	5	20 —	Birrell, David, and J. Marshall	Conland, Falkland / North Wales	229	190 —
Baxter, Lady	Kilmaron Castle, Cupar	1,201	3,287 4				
Bayne, Andrew	Muirhead, Ladybank	15	60 —	Birrell, John	Craigend, Methven	4	15 7
Bayne, James	Drakelands, Ladybank	5	16 —	Birrell, Thomas	Jeaniestown, Ladybank	2	8 15
Bayne, William	Largoward, St. Andrews	4	16 —	Birrell, Thomas	Baintown, Kennoway	2	7 5
Beath, Margaret	Newpark, St. Andrews	9	81 10	Birrell, Heirs of Mrs. Andrew	Freuchie, Ladybank	6	27 9
Beath and Blairadam Colliery Company (Limited)	Beath, Lochgelly	4	154 15				
Beath Kirk-Session	Beath, Lochgelly	3	16 —	Birrell, Mrs. Catherine	Newton, Falkland	2	17 15
Beatson, David	Kirkcaldy	3	135 —	Birrell, Heirs of Mrs. Thomas	Freuchie, Ladybank	11	55 14
Beatson, William	Auchtermuchty	1	14 4				
Beatson, Mrs. Eliza	Burntisland	43	275 15	Bishop Burnett's Mortification, Trustees of	St. Andrews	3	9 2
Begg, Rev. Bruce B.	Manse, Abbotshall, Kirkcaldy	6	83 —	Black, James	Largo	1	61 16
Bell, Alexander	Lathones, St. Andrews	4	17 10	Black, John	8 Nelson Street, Edinburgh	10	72 —
Bell, Andrew Beatson, of Kilduncan	Belmore, Cupar	217	446 14	Black, John	Wemyss	5	55 10
				Black, Robert	Leven	2	170 18
Bell, John Duncanson, of Bankhead	Belville, Gourock	163	166 10	Black, Robert	Baldastard, Largo	4	13 —
				Black, William	Leven	1	53 —
Bell, Rev. William, and others	Gretna	2	4 —	Black, Heirs of Rev. Mr.	Ceres	1	1 7
Bell, William	Muirhead, Ladybank	5	12 —	Black, Mrs. Thomas	Anstruther	1	65 15
Bell, William	Dundee	2	49 —	Black, Mrs. William	Kilconquhar	1	7 5
Bell, Heirs of Mrs. Janet	Ceres	1	27 17	Black, Mrs. William	Dunkeld	2	7 15

FIFE—continued.

Name of Owner.	Address of Owner.	Estimated Acreage of Property.	Gross Annual Value.	Name of Owner.	Address of Owner.	Estimated Acreage of Property.	Gross Annual Value.
		Acres.	£ s.			Acres.	£ s.
Blackwood, Caroline A. M., of Pitreavie	Windsor	1,500	2,194 4	Brown, Mrs. Catherine	Damside, Cupar	15	105 —
Blair, Andrew, & Co.	Pathhead, Kirkcaldy	1	216 —	Brown, Mrs. John, and Robert Kellock	Lundin Mill, Largo	3	8 —
Blair, Mrs., wife of James Blair	11 Dudhope Crescent, Dundee	2	18 —	Brown, Heirs of Mrs. Margaret	New Grange, St. Andrews	120	308 —
Blelloch, David	Dunfermline	1	138 17	Brown, Mrs. Mary	Crossford, Dunfermline	2	21 16
Blyth, Andrew	Newburgh	11	17 15	Brown, Mrs. Mary B.	Tayport	1	15 11
Blyth, Heirs of Charles	Crail	1	46 15	Bruce, George	St. Andrews	2	598 5
Blyth, David, of Leckiebank	Leckiebank, Auchtermuchty	701	770 10	Bruce, Rev. John	24 Saxe-Coburg Place, Edinburgh	197	228 10
Blyth, George	Burnturk, Ladybank	2	13 15	Do. do.	Do. (Minerals)	—	61 —
Blyth, Michael	Kennoway	4	17 —	Bruce, Peter	Cairneyhill, Dunfermline	1	11 10
Blyth, Robert	Craigton, Kinross	7	25 4	Bruce, Hon. Robert Preston, of Spencerfield	Broomhall, Dunfermline	3,243	3,833 7
Blyth, Mrs.	Bottomcraig, Newport	7	20 10	Bruce, Thomas, of Arnot	Kingsdale, Kennoway	21	25 —
Blyth, Mrs. Isabella	Leven	1	59 —	Bruce, Lieut.-Col. W. H. Tyndall, of Falkland	Falkland House, Falkland	7,058	9,992 7
Blyth, Anne	Auchtermuchty	1	28 3	Do. do.	Do. (Minerals)	—	100 —
Boarhill Club	St. Andrews	2	11 16	Bruce, William	Cairneyhill, Dunfermline	5	16 15
Bogie, Trustees of Alexander	Newmill, Cupar	225	676 7	Brunton, Alexander	Inverkeithing	12	57 8
Bogie, David	Saline, Dunfermline	1	3 —	Brunton, Richard	Chance Inn, Cupar	1	2 15
Bogie, Trustees of James	Kinloch, Ladybank	300	589 —	Bryce, Alexander	Peattie Muir, Dunfermline	2	9 —
Bogie, John, of Old Fargie	Balcanquhal, Strathmiglo	131	171 4	Bryden, Rev. Mark T.	Manse, Kirkcaldy	6	85 10
Bogie, Mrs. Alexander	Cupar	246	505 10	Brymer, Ann	Milesmark, Dunfermline	2	11 10
Bogle, Captain Vere W. H., R.N.	Aberdour	2	68 —	Buccleuch and Queensberry, Duke of	Dalkeith Palace	60	15 —
Bonar, Major Henry J. C. Graham, of Greigston	Greigston, Cupar	638	956 13	Buist, Andrew Walker, of Berryhill	Berryhill, Newburgh	372	497 10
Bonella, Rev. David	Blackford, Perth	1	13 8	Buist, George, of Ormiston	Ormiston, Newburgh	395	300 —
Bonella, James	Strathmiglo	6	18 —	Buist, James	Lawpark, St. Andrews	2	50 —
Bonella, John	Foodieash, Cupar	3	22 10	Buist, Rachel	Strathmiglo	1	28 17
Bonella, Mrs. Robert	Auchtermuchty	1	19 6	Burleigh, Lord	Kennet House, Alloa	349	834 10
Bonella, Isabella and Ann	Balcurvie, Windygates	2	16 8	Burns, David, William Burns, and Mrs. Burns	Portobello, Edinburgh, Annesmuir, Ladybank	1	10 —
Bonthrone, Alexander	Newton, Falkland	6	126 —				
Bonthrone, Alexander	Auchtermuchty	3	177 —				
Bonthrone, John	Auchtermuchty	76	472 8				
Bonthrone, Thomas	Coaltown, Markinch	10	34 8	*Burntisland, Burgh of*	Burntisland	25	2,464 4
Bonthrone, Peter	Leven	1	46 3	Burwell, Frederick William	Huntly	6	27 10
Bonthrone, William	Crail	25	140 16	Butchart, Rev. James	Manse, West Anstruther	5	46 —
Bonthrone, Heirs of Mrs. Alexander	Cupar	20	88 10	Buttercase, Robert	Strathkinness, St. Andrews	7	27 —
Bonthrone, Mrs. John	Buckhaven, Leven	1	98 6	Byars, William, junior	Newburgh	1	80 11
Borrie, John	Carnoustie	2	25 10				
Borthwick, Lord	St. Andrews	2	200 —	Cairns, David	Buckhaven, Leven	1	68 10
Boswall, Trustees of Agnes and Elizabeth	Leven	5	100 17	Cairns, Mrs. William	Saline, Dunfermline	1	7 —
				Cairns, Christian	Arncroach, Pittenweem	1	4 —
Boswell, Trustees of John I.	Balmuto, Kirkcaldy	915	1,666 12	Calderhead, John	Cairneyhill, Dunfermline	1	9 10
Boswell, Heirs of Mrs.	Blalowan, Cupar	9	71 —	Cameron, Rev. Andrew	Manse, East Anstruther	13	75 —
Bousie, Trustees of Mrs.	Burntisland	1	156 12	Cameron, James	Balmalcolm, Ladybank	2	6 15
Bowman, John M., of Logie	Logie, Cupar	1,291	1,570 18	Cameron, John	Newburgh	2	100 —
Bowman, William Murray	Crail	14	110 15	*Cameron Kirk-Session*	Cameron, St. Andrews	2	8 4
Boyack, William Spence	Radernie, St. Andrews	6	16 10	Campbell, Rev. Alexander Bell	F.C. Manse, Markinch	1	25 —
Boyd, Rev. A. K. H.	St. Andrews	5	154 5				
Boyd, John	Blebocraigs, Cupar	4	12 —	Campbell, Andrew	Rameldry Bank, Ladybank	2	7 10
Boyd, Lt.-Col. James W.	Burntisland	2	62 —	Campbell, David	Kirkforthar, Markinch	14	33 —
Boyd, Mrs. Margaret, and William Boyd	Brunton, Cupar	9	41 —	Campbell, David Mellis	Star, Markinch	11	47 15
Braid, William	Colinsburgh	1	83 7	Campbell, Douglas	Leven	1	45 —
Brewster, Rev. David	Manse, Kilmany	12	45 —	Campbell, Hon. George, of Edenwood	Government House, Calcutta	245	366 10
Briggs, Trustees of Allan	Prestonhall, Cupar	420	1,225 12				
Briggs, Colonel David, of Strathearly	Strathearly, Largo	656	1,156 5	Campbell, Henry	Lochgelly	1	9 10
				Campbell, James	Balcurvie, Windygates	3	10 10
British Linen Co. Bank	Edinburgh	1	292 15	Campbell, James	Keavil, Dunfermline	1	14 10
Brodie, Rev. James	F.C. Manse, Bow of Fife, Cupar	1	37 11	Campbell, Rev. James	Manse, Balmerino, Newport	22	50 —
Brown, Cunningham	Dunfermline	1	37 10	Campbell, John	Bellfield, Markinch	9	76 3
Brown, David	Crail	65	288 5	Campbell, John	Methill, Leven	7	16 5
Brown, David, and George Brown	Crail, South Quarter, Crail	70	280 10	Campbell, William	Midfield, Carnock, Dunfermline	1	44 15
Brown, George	Westfield, Cupar	4	60 —	Campbell, Mrs. Christopher	Treaton, Markinch	12	30 —
Brown, George	Grange, St. Andrews	3	14 —	Campbell, Mrs. John, sen.	Kirkforthar, Markinch	2	6 17
Brown, James	Newport	4	761 9	Campbell, Isabella	Inverkeithing	1	16 —
Brown, John	Alloa	1	3 —	Cant, James	Orr Bridge, Kirkcaldy	5	151 —
Brown, Rev. John C. C.	Manse, Ceres	10	62 —	*Capeldrae Oil and Coal Co. (Limited)*	Capeldrae, Lochgelly	1	69 —
Brown, John, & Co.	Kirkcaldy	2	188 —	Carmichael, James	Lucklawhill, Leuchars	5	10 —
Brown, Robert	Newport	1	78 —	Carmichael, John	Hawthornvale, Kinross	1	119 18
Brown, Trustees of Walter	Colton, Dunfermline	278	404 13	Carmichael, Thomas, of Easter Craigduckie	33 Spring Gardens, Edinburgh	194	272 10
Brown, William	Lewisvale, Musselburgh	2	36 4				
Brown, Mrs., wife of Rev. R. H. Brown	Kilsyth	2	34 5	Do. do.	Do. (Minerals)	—	75 9

FIFE—continued.

Name of Owner.	Address of Owner.	Estimated Acreage of Property.	Gross Annual Value.	Name of Owner.	Address of Owner.	Estimated Acreage of Property.	Gross Annual Value.
		Acres.	£ s.			Acres.	£ s.
Carron Company	Falkirk	997	1,704 —	Couper, John	St. Andrews	6	63 10
Do.	Do. (Minerals)	—	937 —	Couper, Robert	St. Andrews	1	4 5
Carse, Trustees of Ralph	St. Clairtown, Kirkcaldy	1	157 15	Couper, Mrs. Agnes	St. Andrews	3	10 —
Carstairs, Andrew	Cupar	2	54 10	Couper, Janet	Pittenweem	1	26 —
Carstairs, Andrew	Tongues of Clatto, St. Andrews	3	11 5	Coventry, Andrew, of Pitilloch	29 Moray Place, Edinburgh	251	345 —
Carstairs, Heirs of David	Colinsburgh	1	30 —	Cowan, John	Elie	1	50 —
Carstairs, Mrs. Grace	Sunnybraes, Largo	4	12 6	Craig, Heirs of John	Gauldry, Newport	3	14 5
Carstairs, Heirs of Mrs.	Cupar	26	87 3	Craig, Rev. Robert James	Manse, Dalgety	20	80 —
Carswell, David, of Rathillet	Rathillet, Cupar	756	1,418 10	Craig, Buchanan, Bursary Fund	St. Andrews	5	20 —
Cartwright, Lady Elizabeth, wife of Thomas L. M. Cartwright	Melville House, Ladybank	2,157	3,089 15	Craigie, John	Peattiemuir, Dunfermline	5	24 —
Cathcart, Robert, of Pitcairlie	Pitcairlie, Auchtermuchty	1,050	1,643 6	Craigie, Mrs. Harriet, of Ferrybank	Brighton	95	348 8
Cation, Murdoch	Inverkeithing	1	25 —	Crail, Burgh of	Crail	16	228 10
Chalmers, William	Kirkcaldy	1	131 —	Crail Fishing Box Society	Crail	10	34 —
Chalmers, Mrs. Helen	Crail	6	35 —	Crail Kirk-Session	Crail	9	52 8
Charles, Mrs. John	Chance Inn, Cupar	2	9 —	Crail Sailor's Box Society	Crail	9	28 10
Cheape, Alexander, of Lathockar	Lathockar, St. Andrews	1,188	1,141 16	Crawford, Robert	Cowdenbeath, Lochgelly	4	86 6
Cheape, George Clerk, of Wellfield and Strathtyrum	Wellfield, Strathmiglo	4,230	8,885 —	Crawford, Mrs. Ann	31 Gayfield Square, Edinburgh	47	100 —
				Creich Kirk-Session	Creich, Cupar	4	15 4
				Creighton, David	Holehouse, Tinwald	45	212 4
Chiene, Mrs. William	Kirkwall	9	32 —	Crichton, David	Kingsbarns, St. Andrews	3	75 10
Chisholm, Henry	Lochgelly	1	62 5	Crichton, David	Balcurvie, Windygates	1	8 10
Christie, Heirs of Colonel Charles	Findas, Cupar	98	187 7	Crichton, David Maitland Makgill, of Rankeillour	Bath	943	1,234 5
Christie, Rev. David	Falkland	3	47 18	Crichton, Thomas	Ladybank	2	116 —
Christie, James H. R. Stark, of Teasses	Teasses, Largo	567	779 6	Crichton, Mrs., and Jack, Mrs.	St. Andrews	3	13 18
Christie, John	Cowdenbeath, Lochgelly	1	79 10	Crichton, Helen	Crossgates, Inverkeithing	1	22 —
Christie, Rev. John	Manse, Kilrenny, Anstruther	15	52 12	Crombie, John	Auchtermuchty	4	26 15
				Crombie, Thomas	Auchtermuchty	2	136 —
				Crombie, Mrs. Janet	Cairneyhill, Dunfermline	3	27 16
Christie, Robert, of Durie	Durie, Leven	2,134	4,691 9	Crown, The	London	133	1,276 —
Do. do.	Do. (Minerals)	—	192 10	Cumming, Robert	Elie	14	67 10
Christie, Thomas Stark, of Ballindean	Ballindean, Cupar	145	289 —	Cunningham, George, of Kinsleith	Kinsleith, Cupar	130	305 —
Christie, Mrs. Thomas	Chance Inn, Cupar	3	8 15	Cunningham, Peter Hannay, of Pitarthie	Washington, U.S.	403	666 —
Chrystal, Rev. J. R.	Manse, Cults, Ladybank	7	31 —				
Chrystie, Margaret	Elie Lodge, Elie	4	87 —	Cunningham, Mrs., wife of William Cunningham	Dundee	8	75 5
Clark, George A., of Easter Brucefield	Allanaquoich, Braemar	118	328 10	Cunynghame, Henry L. Dick, of Haltcasses	Rankeillor Hope, Cupar	916	1,032 16
Clark, Trustees of Thomas	Pettycur, Kinghorn	1	44 2	Cupar, Burgh of	Cupar	19	51 5
Clark, William	Ceres	1	20 16	Cupar District Road Trustees	Cupar	1	80 —
Clarkson, Trustee for Mrs. and Family	Halbeath, Dunfermline	5	270 —	Currie, Andrew, of Glassmount	Glassmount, Kirkcaldy	258	612 10
Do. do.	Do. (Minerals)	—	1,476 —	Currie, Thomas	Elie	2	254 5
Cleghorn, H. Francis Clerk, of Stravithy	Stravithy, St. Andrews	1,011	1,517 —	Curror, David, of Wester Craigduckie	India Buildings, Edinburgh	186	225 —
Cleghorn & Young	Rothes, Markinch	6	179 —	Curwen, Lieut. Robert Ewan	St. Andrews	4	215 —
Clydesdale Banking Co.	Glasgow	6	324 10	Cusin, James	Falkland	1	125 —
Cochrane, Rev. James	Manse, Cupar	6	64 10				
Cockburn, Heirs of Wm.	Kennoway	3	35 10				
Collier, Jean	Kinglassie, Kirkcaldy	2	3 8				
Colston, Henry	Haddington	2	3 10				
Colvile, Right Hon. Sir Jas. William, of Craigflower, Kt.	Craigflower, Dunfermline	1,002	2,279 —	Dairsie Kirk-Session	Dairsie, Cupar	6	32 —
				Dale, James	Kirkcaldy	1	170 —
Colville, Alexander, of Hillside	Hillside, Dunfermline	625	437 10	Dalgleish, Trs. of James	Outh, Dunfermline	2,804	1,668 15
Colville, Thos., of Dunduff	Dunduff, Dunfermline	464	411 —	Dalgleish, Captain James Ogilvy, of Woodburne	Woodburne, Ceres	264	812 —
Commercial Bank of Scotland	Edinburgh	2	673 —	Dalgleish, Laurence, of Dalbeath	Athole Crescent, Edinburgh	510	520 —
Commissioners of Supply and Court House Commissioners	Cupar and Dunfermline	2	323 16	Dalgleish, Curator Bonis of Laurence	Sandydub, Dunfermline	293	230 —
Connel, Mrs. James	Burntisland	2	31 —	Dalgleish, Robert, of Tunnygask	Dunfermline	648	381 —
Conolly, Matthew Forster	Anstruther	34	273 10	Dalgleish, Mrs. Archibald Ogilvy	Cupar	9	81 —
Constable, James, of Glencraig	Glencraig, Lochgelly	470	520 —	Dalgleish, Trustees of Mrs. Mary Bayne	Dura, Cupar	218	361 —
Constable, William Briggs, of Benarty	Benarty, Kinross	573	407 —	Dall, William	Kennoway	1	25 —
Cook, Trustees of David	Carphin, Cupar	787	1,300 —	Dalrymple, James	West Meetings, Markinch	6	18 —
Cook, James	Lalathan, Kennoway	12	40 10	Dalzell, General John Melville, of Lingo	Cupar	725	731 10
Cook, James	Lochgelly	1	80 —	Dandie, Andrew	Falkland	2	13 10
Corstorphine, Heirs of Captain Alexander	Kingsbarns, St. Andrews	131	490 12	Darney, Henry	Kinghorn	1	27 18
Coul, John	Lucklawhill, Leuchars	2	12 —	Darsie, George	Anstruther	5	125 10
Coul, Christian	St. Andrews	11	33 6	Davie, John	Dunfermline	2	92 —

FIFE—continued.

Name of Owner.	Address of Owner.	Estimated Acreage of Property.	Gross Annual Value.	Name of Owner.	Address of Owner.	Estimated Acreage of Property.	Gross Annual Value.
		Acres.	£ s.			Acres.	£ s.
Davie, Mrs., wife of James Davie	Kilrie, Kinghorn	11	27 –	Duncan, Andrew	Woodfield, Leuchars	24	75 10
Davidson, Robert	Cupar	12	51 –	Duncan, Rev. Andrew B.	Grey Craigs, Dunfermline	20	50 –
Davidson, Walter	Cairnie, Colinsburgh	37	159 17	Duncan, David	Falkland	21	58 10
Davidson, Rev. William	Manse, Largo	7	51 5	Duncan, Trustees of Henry	Cupar	20	173 10
Davidson, Wm. Gordon, of Southfod	Bogie House, Kirkcaldy	398	816 10	Duncan, James	Prior Muir, St. Andrews	8	39 –
Davidson, Mrs. David	Colinsburgh	3	15 10	Duncan, John	Kennoway	5	59 10
Davidson, Mrs., wife of Robert Davidson	Edinburgh	238	442 16	Duncan, John	Balreavie, Falkland	31	93 10
				Duncan, John	Whitefield, Dunfermline	2	30 –
Deas, Trustees of David	Inverkeithing	1	52 15	Duncan, John	Springhill, Inverkeithing	1	24 –
Deas, Henry	Cairneyhill, Dunfermline	1	11 –	Duncan, John	Saline, Dunfermline	1	9 –
Deas, John	Crossgates, Ladybank	1	23 8	Duncan, John	Peekie, St. Andrews	19	68 8
Dewar, James	Cupar	6	267 –	Duncan, Rev. John	Manse, Abdie, Newburgh	8	58 –
Dewar, John, of Lassodie	Lassodie, Dunfermline	1,047	987 –	Duncan, Rev. John	Manse, Scoonie, Leven	13	108 –
Do. do.	Do. (Minerals)	–	1,100 –	Duncan, Robert, of Kirkmay	Kirkmay, Crail	213	1,215 5
Dewar, Robert	Kelty, Kinross	1	25 17	Duncan, Robert	Freuchie, Ladybank	1	26 –
Dick, Robert	Lochgelly	1	79 –	Duncan, Robert	Leslie	1	103 5
Dick, Robert	Milesmark, Dunfermline	5	55 –	Duncan, Thomas, of Kinkell	Boghall, St. Andrews	871	1,784 15
Dick, Heirs of William Douglas	Montrave, Kennoway	546	755 –	Duncan, William	Cupar	2	51 –
Dick, Mary	Burntisland	20	489 16	Duncan, William	Findas Bank, Cupar	4	11 10
Dingwall, James, of Tarvit Mill	Tarvit Mill, Cupar	126	315 –	Duncan, William	Crail	2	179 12
Dishart, David	Strathkinness, St. Andrews	3	16 –	Duncan, Mrs. Elizabeth	Thornbank, St. Andrews	4	35 10
Dishart, David	Glasgow	2	10 –	Duncan, Mrs. Henry	Kirkcaldy	1	4 10
Dishart, Mrs. Janet	Strathkinness, St. Andrews	3	11 10	Duncan, Agnes	Freuchie, Ladybank	3	25 9
Dobie, Rev. William Jardine	Manse, Kinghorn	8	58 –	Duncanson, James	Cairneyhill, Dunfermline	7	30 2
				Duncanson, John	Burntisland	2	21 10
Dodds, Mrs., wife of Rev. George Dodds	28 Buccleuch Place, Edinburgh	9	80 16	Duncanson, Rev. P. C.	Auchingramont, Hamilton	12	91 17
				Duncanson, Jean	Cairneyhill, Dunfermline	6	23 15
Doig, Charles	Seafield House, Leith	1	20 –	*Dunfermline Building Society*	Dunfermline	2	90 –
Donald, Andrew	Crossford, Dunfermline	2	18 –	*Dunfermline, Burgh of*	Dunfermline	933	1,218 7
Donaldson, David	Innergellie, Anstruther	1	41 10	Do. do.	Do. (Minerals)	–	3,604 –
Donaldson, James	Tayport	1	119 10	*Dunfermline Gas Company*	Dunfermline	1	1,037 –
Donaldson, Thomas	Coalpitden, Ladybank	6	15 10	*Dunfermline Guildry*	Dunfermline	141	504 18
Donaldson, William	Torryburn, Dunfermline	4	26 –	*Dunfermline Parochial Board*	Dunfermline	13	207 10
Dougall, Captain William Heriot Maitland	Scotscraig, Tayport	75	167 5	*Dunfermline Water Trust*	Dunfermline	50	854 –
Dougall, Mrs., wife of Captain William Heriot Maitland Dougall	Scotscraig, Tayport	2,550	2,724 12	*Dunnikier Feuars*	Pathhead Muir, Kirkcaldy	40	105 –
				Dundas, Robert, of Arniston	Arniston House, Gorebridge, Edinburgh	195	248 14
Douglas, John	Cupar	2	184 –	Do. do.	Do. (Minerals)	–	525 –
Douglas, Robert	Kirkcaldy	4	302 12	Durie, Henry	Lizziewells, Ladybank	1	9 –
Douglas, Robert	Newcastle-on-Tyne	2	16 –	Durie, John	Inverkeithing	6	23 17
Douglas, Trs. of Robert	Garvock, Dunfermline	6	13 5	Durie, John, and Currie and Johanna Hutton	Inverkeithing Dunfermline	4	9 –
Douglas, Hon. Mrs., of Strathendry	Strathendry, Leslie	2,080	2,687 12				
Douglas, Mrs. Robert	North Queensferry	4	54 14	Durie, Mrs., wife of Andrew Dewar Durie	Dunfermline	957	843 16
Douglas, Mrs., wife of John Douglas	Lochhead, Dunfermline	232	308 –				
Dow, Rev. John Archibald	Manse, Strathmiglo	6	40 –	*Dysart, Burgh of*	Dysart	135	679 6
Dowie, Alexander	Blebo Craigs, Cupar	5	13 5				
Dowie, James	Letham Feus, Windygates	4	18 –				
Dowie, Meldrum	Blebo Craigs, Cupar	17	53 –	*Earlsferry, Burgh of*	Earlsferry, Elie	15	6 –
Dowie, Mrs. Christian	Kirkcaldy	41	65 –	Easson, James, & Son	Ladybank	1	20 –
Dowie, Mrs. John	Whalleyden, Kennoway	5	12 –	Edgar, Rev. James Pitt	Manse, Dunbog, Newburgh	7	37 –
Dowie, Mrs. Robert	Balgrie, Kennoway	9	21 10				
Downie, Georgina, of Appin	Appin, Argyllshire	345	490 –	Edgar, Rev. Robert	Manse, Newburgh	28	91 7
Drumeldrie School Charity	Orkie, Ladybank	220	401 –	Edie, David	Strathkinness, St. Andrews	6	24 10
Drummond, David	Saline, Dunfermline	1	3 –	Edie, David	Guardbridge, Cupar	14	51 –
Drummond, Trustees of William	Cupar	9	297 –	Edington, Jessie, and Mrs. Margaret Miller	Wemyss, Kirkcaldy	1	94 –
Drummond, Euphemia	Inverkeithing	1	31 –	Edmiston, Heirs of Mrs. Frances	Mount Pleasant, Newburgh	1	46 8
Dryburgh, Mrs., wife of John Dryburgh and Mrs. Lauder, wife of Dewar Lauder	Kininmonth, Cupar St. Nicholas, St. Andrews	19	129 18	Edmiston, Mrs. Janet	Kettlebridge, Ladybank	11	38 –
				Edward, Henry	Saline, Dunfermline	1	13 10
				Edward, William	Saline, Dunfermline	1	14 –
				Elder, James	Charlestown, Dunfermline	2	30 –
Drysdale, John, of Kilrie	Kilrie, Kinghorn	543	1,528 –	Elder, James	Ovenstone Muir, Pittenweem	7	18 –
Drysdale, John	Hillside, Dunfermline	1	5 –	Elder, William	St. Margaret's, Inverkeithing	37	149 –
Drysdale, John James, of Pittenchar	Liverpool	542	1,109 5				
Drysdale, William	Kilrie, Kinghorn	42	20 –	Elder, Mrs. George	Kirkcaldy	2	100 –
Drysdale, Mrs., wife of Adam Drysdale	Steelend, Dunfermline	10	42 10	Elder, Heirs of Mrs. Agnes	Leven	1	30 –
				Elgin, Earl of	Broomhall, Dunfermline	2,663	8,370 4
Duff, J. R.	Dysart	3	30 –	Do.	Do. (Minerals)	–	3,710 –
Dun, Heirs of William	Newburgh	1	94 10	*Elie Parochial Board*	Elie	35	79 –
Duncan, Alexander	Falkland	7	41 5	*Elie Sea Box Society*	Elie	13	54 –

FIFE—*continued.*

Name of Owner.	Address of Owner.	Estimated Acreage of Property.	Gross Annual Value.
		Acres.	£ s.
Erskine, Alexander	Cairneyhill, Dunfermline	3	23 10
Erskine, John	Cairneyhill, Dunfermline	8	36 10
Erskine, Robert	Sunnyside, Dunfermline	3	20 6
Erskine, Rev. Thomas, of Dairsie	Alderley, Cheshire	713	1,774 14
Erskine, Sir Thomas, of Cambo, Bart.	Cambo, St. Andrews	2,937	6,727 4
Erskine, William	Kincardine-on-Forth	6	29 —
Erskine, Lieut. William C. C., of Nether Kinneddar	Nether Kinneddar, Dunfermline	969	880 —
Ewan, Rev. James	Manse, Dunino, St. Andrews	27	70 —
Fairweather, David	16 Arbroath Rd., Forfar	1	4 4
Falkland, Burgh of	Falkland	24	41 10
Falkland Kirk-Session	Falkland	3	12 —
Falkland Parochial Board	Falkland	3	11 14
Farmer, Alexander	Moonzie Mill, Leuchars	5	19 —
Farmer, William	Drumrack, St. Andrews	4	11 —
Farmer, Mrs.	Lebanon, Cupar	1	19 10
Farmer, Heirs of Mrs.	Cupar	12	39 5
Ferguson, George	Burntisland	1	238 15
Ferguson, Trustees of Colonel Robert Munro	Raith, Kirkcaldy	7,195	12337 3
Do. do.	Do. (*Minerals*)	—	1,582 —
Fernie, David Smellon	Dunbeath, Caithness	10	51 17
Fernie & Findlay	Cupar	10	48 —
Fernie, Mrs. John	Kinglassie, Kirkcaldy	6	25 7
Fettes, Trustees of Sir William, of Comely Bank, Bart.	Fettes College, Edinburgh	378	883 5
Fife and Kinross District Lunacy Board	Springfield, Cupar	57	1,005 —
Fife Prison Board	Cupar and Dunfermline	5	292 10
Findlay, James	Inverkeithing	1	12 —
Fisher, Rev. Robert Findlay	Manse, Flisk, Newburgh	6	31 10
Fleming, Peter	St. Andrews	1	116 12
Fleming, William	St. Andrews	2	7 —
Fleming, Mrs. Alexander	Gauldry, Newport	1	16 10
Fleming, Mrs. John	St. Andrews	1	191 10
Fleming, Mrs. Margaret	St. Andrews	9	57 7
Fleming, Jane and Mary	St. Andrews	45	110 —
Foggo, Rev. D. L.	Manse, St. Monance	14	60 —
Forbes, Daniel	132 Hill Street, Glasgow	1	19 —
Forbes, Peter	132 Hill Street, Glasgow	3	14 —
Forbes, Heirs of Thomas	Largoward, St. Andrews	1	1 5
Forbes, William	St. Andrews	7	14 10
Ford, Mrs. David	Auchtermuchty	1	36 15
Forgan, John	Pittenweem	4	23 10
Forrester, William	Drumeldry, Largo	3	25 5
Forrester, Mrs., wife of John Forrester, and Mrs. Kirkcaldy, wife of David Kirkcaldy	Torr-Forret, Cupar	36	65 —
Forrester, Martha	Gladney, Cupar	1	2 15
Forret, Ebenezer	Blebo, Cupar	2	9 10
Forret, Robert	Blebo Craigs, Cupar	11	37 12
Forret, William	Blebo Craigs, Cupar	7	24 —
Forsyth, George	Falkland	3	23 7
Fortune, William Ranken, of Muircambus	Muircambus, Colinsburgh	287	516 —
Fotheringham, Charles S.	Cupar	1	75 —
Fotheringham, John	Orrock, Kirkcaldy	2	28 5
Fotheringham, John	Newburgh	3	11 4
Fotheringham, Mrs. Isabella	Milton, Saline	153	134 5
Foulis, Robert, of Cairnie Lodge	Cairnie Lodge, Cupar	109	252 10
Fowler, George	Lucklawhill, Leuchars	7	28 15
Fowler, James S.	Edinburgh	6	67 —
Fowler, William	Cellardyke, Anstruther	2	19 7
Fowler, William	Lucklawhill, Leuchars	5	18 2
Fowler, Trustees of Janet	St. Andrews	24	147 —
Fraser, Heirs of Rev. Mr.	St. Andrews	2	7 10
Fraser, William	Inverkeithing	5	252 —
Fraser, Mrs. Christian	Tulliebole Mills, Kinross	12	56 6
French, Rev. James	Manse, Dunfermline	5	60 —
Freuchie Feuars	Freuchie, Ladybank	21	8 5
Fyall, Heirs of Robert	St. Andrews	1	17 —
Fyfe, Catherine	Brackmont, Leuchars	7	14 10
Fyffe, George	Cupar	3	22 —
Galletly, David	Burntisland	1	124 18
Galloway, Archibald	Strathmiglo	6	15 —
Gardiner, Jane, Agnes, and Isabella	Auchtermuchty	6	41 18
Garland, Walter	Giffordtown, Ladybank	7	14 10
Geddie, David	Bighty, Kennoway	6	12 —
Geddie, George, and Geddie, James	Freuchie, Ladybank Luthrie, Cupar	4	21 4
Geddie, Mrs. Margaret	Baintown, Kennoway	8	30 —
George Watson's Hospital, Governors of	Edinburgh	464	658 —
Gibb, Alexander	Auchmuty, Markinch	2	16 5
Gibb, David	East Meetings, Markinch	1	16 4
Gibb, James Christie	East Meetings, Markinch	11	37 —
Gibb, William	Newport	1	78 10
Gibb, Mrs. George	Star, Markinch	2	5 10
Gibb, Mrs., wife of William Gibb	Balcurvie, Windygates	3	14 —
Gibson, David	Kirkcaldy	72	269 —
Gibson, Henry	St. Andrews	3	291 10
Gibson, James	Gowkhall, Dunfermline	4	14 10
Gibson, Lawrence	Dunfermline	1	145 5
Gibson, Trustees of James	St. Andrews	1	180 —
Gibson, Trs. of William	St. Andrews	577	1,162 12
Gillespie, David, of Mountquhanie	Mountquhanie, Cupar	3,793	6,571 10
Gillies, David	Crail	5	22 —
Gillies, David	Largo	1	55 10
Gilmour, Allan, of Lundin	Lundin, Largo	2,728	5,243 10
Gilmour, Kenneth	Crossford, Dunfermline	1	14 4
Gilmour, Jane	Kinross	246	320 17
Glasgow, City of	Glasgow	131	250 —
Glasgow, Earl of	Crawfurd Priory, Cupar	5,625	9,024 8
Do. do.	Do. (*Minerals*)	—	60 10
Glass, James	Pleasance, Dunfermline	15	40 12
Glass, Robert	Arlary, Kinross-shire	34	81 —
Glass, William	Cowdenbeath, Lochgelly	1	80 8
Glass, Margaret and Catherine	Balcanquhal, Strathmiglo	161	264 10
Glover, Thomas Craigie	Largo	1	20 —
Goodall, George, of Rennyhill	Rennyhill, Anstruther	143	499 —
Goodall, Heirs of James	Cardenden, Lochgelly	2	24 —
Goodall, Mrs. Thomas	Craigderran, Lochgelly	90	248 10
Goodsir, Rev. Joseph T.	Edinburgh	4	42 —
Gordon, David	Damhead, Milnathort	1	14 —
Gordon, George	St. Andrews	1	170 —
Gourlay, David	Giffordtown, Ladybank	4	12 10
Gourlay, Thomas, of Craigrothie	Craigrothie, Cupar	248	419 —
Gourlay, William	Lucklawhill, Leuchars	3	11 —
Gourlay, Rev. William E. C. A., of Kincraig	Stoke Abbot, Dorsetshire	206	480 —
Gourlay, Mrs. David	Craigrothie, Cupar	1	22 —
Gourlay, Mrs. Robert	Colinsburgh	9	40 10
Govan, Colonel Charles Maitland	Balgove, St. Andrews	18	71 —
Gow, Duncan	Strowan, Blair-Athol	11	16 —
Gow, Mrs. William	Thornton, Lochgelly	19	43 —
Graham, Andrew	Anstruther	2	116 —
Graham, William	Cults, Ladybank	2	28 16
Grainger, Trustees of Thomas	Lochgelly	1	97 16
Grandison, Trustees of James	Pitsoulie, Dunfermline	2	17 10
Grant, John	Marchmont, Inverkeithing	5	65 2
Grant, Rev. Patrick M'Gregor	Manse, Auchterderran	16	76 —
Grant, Mrs. Mary	Durievale, Windygates	69	187 10
Grant, Mrs., wife of J. Grant	West Holden, Durham	13	64 10
Gray, David, of Carngour	Rennyhill, Anstruther	151	249 10

FIFE—continued.

Name of Owner.	Address of Owner.	Estimated Acreage of Property.	Gross Annual Value.	Name of Owner.	Address of Owner.	Estimated Acreage of Property.	Gross Annual Value.
		Acres.	£ s.			Acres.	£ s.
Gray, John	Damside, Cupar	19	54 2	Henderson, Andrew	Inverkeithing	5	64 10
Gray, Mordaunt	Edinburgh	3	204 15	Henderson, Andrew	Tayport	1	21 7
Gray, Mrs. David	Summerfield, Crail	4	10 -	Henderson, Arthur, and John Henderson	Newhouse, Stirling Star, Markinch	5	8 -
Gray, Mrs., wife of Robert Gray	North Shields	3	8 -	Henderson, David	Newburgh	10	242 -
Gray's Prize Fund	St. Andrews	5	23 12	Henderson, David	Dairsie, Cupar	2	12 11
Greenhill, Trustees of Alexander	Burntisland	92	226 -	Henderson, George	Coultra, Cupar	15	41 -
Greenhill, Jane, Margaret, and Wilhelmina	Abernethy	1	81 -	Henderson, Trustees of George	Star, Markinch	1	7 -
Greig, A. O.	Lucklawhill, Leuchars	5	10 10	Henderson, George Wm. Mercer, of Fordel	Fordel, Inverkeithing	1,955	4,533 2
Greig, Alexander	Aberdour	1	26 -	Do. do.	Do. (Minerals)	-	1,310 -
Greig, Heirs of Andrew	St. Clairtown, Kirkcaldy	5	25 10	Henderson, James	Giffordtown, Ladybank	21	64 5
Greig, George, of Balcurvie	Balcurvie, Windygates	132	294 2	Henderson, James	Tayport	1	100 10
Greig, George	Dundee	21	40 -	Henderson, James	Cupar	2	10 6
Greig, Heirs of John	St. Clairtown, Kirkcaldy	1	120 15	Henderson, James, and Littlejohn, David S.	Tayport Dundee	5	107 -
Greig, Peter, & Co.	St. Clairtown, Kirkcaldy	1	85 -	Henderson, John	Giffordtown, Ladybank	4	14 6
Greig, Heirs of Walter	Pathhead, Kirkcaldy	245	405 18	Henderson, John	Star, Markinch	1	2 10
Greig, Heirs of Mrs.	Aberdour	1	88 9	Henderson, Robert	Causewayside, Edinburgh	7	39 9
Grieve, David	Baldinnie, Cupar	4	12 15	Henderson, Robert	Ladybank	1	30 -
Grieve, Robert	Glasgow	40	66 -	Henderson, Robert	Kirkland, Saline	123	172 10
Guild, William, of Lindores	Lindores, Newburgh	460	730 15	Henderson, Robert	Cowhalie, Leuchars	8	27 10
Guland, William	Falkland	2	43 -	Henderson, Robert, and Slater, Andrew	Leith Canongate, Edinburgh	10	140 -
Gulland, Charles	Falkland	16	151 -	Henderson, Stuart	Arncroach, Pittenweem	1	18 -
Gulland, James	Lathones St. Andrews	1	42 5	Henderson, Thomas	Giffordtown, Ladybank	4	7 6
				Henderson, Thomas	Torryburn, Dunfermline	2	43 14
				Henderson, William	Edentown, Ladybank	2	8 15
Haig, John	Cameron Bridge, Windygates	62	1,376 -	Henderson, Heirs of William	Loanfoot, Ladybank	12	60 -
Haig, John, & Co.	Cameron Bridge, Windygates	24	671 2	Henderson, William C.	St. Andrews	17	256 15
Haig, Mrs. Janet, and Barbara Walker	Pitlair, Cupar	2	28 -	Henderson, Wallace, & Co.	Halbeath, Dunfermline	4	123 -
Hain, Thomas, of Balmullo	Balmullo, Leuchars	203	522 -	Henderson, Mrs. Margaret, wife of William Henderson	Blairstruie, Bridge of Earn	5	12 -
Hain, Mary, Isabel, and Catherine	Balmerino, Newport	1	6 4	Henderson, Mrs.	Kettle, Ladybank	6	33 -
Halkerston, Isabella	Kingskettle, Ladybank	8	47 10	Henderson, Mrs.	Newport	12	41 10
Halket, Sir Peter Arthur, of Pitfirrane, Bart.	Pitfirrane, Dunfermline	1,963	3,704 7	Henderson, Mrs., wife of James Henderson	Tayport	5	289 10
Halley, George	Newmills, Dunfermline	2	191 16	Henderson, Mrs., wife of Robert Henderson	Causewayside, Edinburgh	2	22 15
Halley, Mrs. Thomas	Baintown, Kennoway	1	8 12	Henderson, Margaret	Crail	2	12 -
Hallyburton, William	Crail	4	11 -	Henderson, Margaret, and Hardie, Mrs.	Kirkcaldy Wester Balbeigie, Kirkcaldy	92	135 10
Hamilton, Robert	Dunfermline	1	25 -	Do. do.	Do. (Minerals)	-	100 -
Hannay, Major George, of Kingsmuir	Kingsmuir, Pittenweem	1,108	1,169 10	Hendry, Daniel	Kirkcaldy	4	111 10
Hardie, Robert	Dunshalt, Auchtermuchty	2	13 -	Hendry, Daniel and Thomas Meldrum Hendry	Kirkcaldy		
Hardie, Mrs. David	Dunshalt, Auchtermuchty	1	10 -				
Hardie, Heirs of Mrs.	Strathkinness, St. Andrews	8	15 -				
Hardie, Cecilia	Pitlessie, Ladybank	2	58 13	and Mrs. Stewart, wife of Rev. Atholl Stewart	Kirkcaldy Blair Atholl	6	32 2
Harley, David	Cowstrandburn, Dunfermline	5	12 10				
Harley, Jean	147 Sauchiehall Street, Glasgow	2	13 10	Hendry, Thomas Meldrum	Kirkcaldy	4	825 -
Harrower, Heirs of Henry	Dunfermline	3	6 -	Hendry, Whyte, & Strachan	Kirkcaldy	2	662 -
Harrower, Heirs of William	Radernie, St. Andrews	160	205 18	Hepburn, John Buchan, of Clune	Cowes, Isle of Wight	658	655 7
Hastie, Trustees of Alexander	Luscar, Dunfermline	1,590	2,500 12	Herd, Alexander	Cupar	3	42 15
Haxton, William Forsyth	Markinch	1	91 11	Heriot, Frederick Louis Maitland, of Ramornie	Ramornie, Ladybank	1,430	2,115 4
Haxton, Mrs., wife of Rev. James B. Haxton	St. Clairtown, Kirkcaldy	229	614 12	Heron, Robert	Kingston, Dublin	11	48 5
Hay, Edmund Paterson Balfour, of Mugdrum	Mugdrum, Newburgh	785	2,122 19	Heron, Mrs.	Gallatown, Kirkcaldy	1	115 -
Hay, George Bowman	Brunton, Cupar	9	34 10	Hill, Alexander, of Stonywynd	Stonywynd, St. Andrews	151	370 -
Hay, John	Inverkeithing	3	58 10	Hill, James Lumsden	Ladybank	1	295 -
Hay, John D. B., of Morton	Edinburgh	449	205 10	Hillhouse, Rev. James	Manse, Elie	7	65 10
Hay & Robertson	Dunfermline	2	364 10	Hodge, Isabella	Cairneyhill, Dunfermline	1	10 -
Hay, Mrs. George	Crail	1	9 -	Hog, Heirs of Archibald	Bandrum, Dunfermline	257	351 15
Hay, Mrs. Robert	Dunfermline	2	60 -	Hog, Thomas Alexander, of Baldutho	Newliston, Kirkliston	1,320	2,299 16
Hay, Helen and Jane	Leuchars	21	42 -				
Heddle, M. F.	St. Andrews	83	210 -	Hogg, Rev. David N.	Manse, Auchtermuchty	8	77 16
Heggie, Frederick	Kirkcaldy	2	296 10	Hogg, John	Markinch	4	11 10
Heggie, John	Brunton, Cupar	5	21 15	Honeyman, Alexander	13 West Sciennes, Edinburgh	2	7 2
Heggie, Robert	Kirkcaldy	1	336 -				
Heggie, Robert Brownlie	Kirkcaldy	5	515 5	Honeyman, Alexander	Ladybank	61	204 -
Hempseed, David	Torryburn, Dunfermline	1	9 10	Honeyman, Archibald	Castleheggie, Kennoway	3	12 -
Henderson, Adam	Grange, Dunfermline	90	95 -	Honeyman, John	Cupar	2	172 5
Do. do.	Do. (Minerals)	-	119 -	Honeyman, William	Springfield, Cupar	1	8 -

FIFE—continued.

Name of Owner.	Address of Owner.	Estimated Acreage of Property.	Gross Annual Value.	Name of Owner.	Address of Owner.	Estimated Acreage of Property.	Gross Annual Value.
		Acres.	£ s.			Acres.	£ s.
Honeyman, Mrs. Andrew	Springfield, Cupar	3	14 10	Ireland, Mrs., wife of Alex. Ireland	Bannaty, Strathmiglo	288	384 —
Honeyman, Mrs. Janet	Springfield, Cupar	3	11 12	Irvine, Rev. Walter	Manse, Kilconquhar	15	66 —
Honeyman, Mrs. Alison	Star, Markinch	1	8 —	Irvine, Walter Douglas, of Grangemuir	Grangemuir, Pittenweem	2,697	5,297 14
Hood, Robert	Cupar	12	267 7	Isdale, Robert Hawker	Leuchars Lodge, Leuchars	59	124 —
Hope, Sir Archibald, of Craighall, Bart.	Pinkie House, Musselburgh	828	1,000 15				
Hope, Capt. Henry W., of Rankeillour	Luffness, Dunbar	2,509	4,735 12	Jack, Alexander	Pittenweem	1	43 10
Hopetoun, Earl of	Hopetoun House, South Queensferry	941	1,717 17	Jack, Henry	Star, Markinch	4	15 10
Horn, Andrew	Leven	2	24 —	Jackson, Thomas	Kirkcaldy	4	230 4
Horn, Elizabeth and Margaret and David Lawson	Leven Innerleven	3	10 —	Jamieson, John, of Kingask	Kingask, St. Andrews	389	725 —
Horsburgh, Trustees of Andrew	Pittenweem	12	89 5	Jeffrey, John and William Jeffrey	Kirkcaldy Glasgow	7	479 —
Horsburgh, Bethune, of Lochmalony	Lochmalony, Cupar	402	879 18	Jervis, John	Largo	4	17 10
Horsburgh, George	Anstruther	2	8 —	Jobson, William, of Broombrae	Dundee	217	425 —
Houston, David	Lebanon, Cupar	2	9 —	Johnston, Adam	Kingswood, Burntisland	11	211 10
Howieson, John	Cairneyhill, Dunfermline	4	15 10	Johnston, Andrew	Burnturk, Ladybank	2	11 —
Hunt, James, of Navity	53 George Street, Edinburgh	197	492 3	Johnston, Andrew	Gauldry, Newport	2	8 —
				Johnston, Rev. Andrew	Manse, Kinglassie, Kirkcaldy	8	57 —
Hunt, James Alexander, of Logie	Logie, Dunfermline	945	2,588 9	Johnston, George, of Lathrisk and Largo	Lathrisk, Ladybank	10,005	14017 5
Hunt, Trustees of William	Cocklaw, Dunfermline	363	505 4	Johnston, George, of Foxton	Foxton, Cupar	241	570 —
Hunter, Grace	St. Andrews	2	72 10				
Husband, Robert, of Wester Gellet	Wester Gellet, Dunfermline	200	555 —	Johnston, George and James	East Wemyss, Kirkcaldy	2	542 10
Hutchison, James	Coaltown of Balgonie, Markinch	6	16 —	Johnston, James	Kettle, Ladybank	2	47 7
Hutchison, John	Kirkcaldy	5	200 16	Johnston, James, of Kedlock	Upper Mount Street, Dublin	329	599 2
Hutchison, Robert	Kirkcaldy	13	797 —	Johnston, John	Clubstone, Cupar	8	20 —
Hutchison, Heirs of Robert	Kirkforthar, Markinch	10	78 18	Johnston, Robert	Lundin Mill, Largo	5	10 —
Hutchon, Andrew	Crail	26	124 5	Johnston, Rev. Robert	Manse, Leuchars	11	55 —
Hutton, Heirs of Alexander	Kinghorn	1	39 2	Johnston, Rev. Thomas Peter	Manse, Carnbee, Pittenweem	16	63 10
Hutton, George and William and Currie and Johanna Hutton	Inverkeithing Dunfermline	2	77 15	Johnston, Hutchison, & Co.	St. Clairtown, Kirkcaldy	1	237 —
				Johnston, Mrs. Betty	Baldinnie, Cupar	2	7 10
Hutton, Robert	Inverkeithing	1	36 —	Johnston, Mrs., wife of Wm. Johnston	St. Andrews	5	12 —
Hutton, Mrs. John	Saline, Dunfermline	1	36 16	Just, George	Newport	1	103 —
Hutton, Mrs., wife of Alexander Hutton	Cults, Ladybank	25	40 —	Just, Robert	Newport	1	153 —
Hutton, Currie and Johanna	Dunfermline	6	14 10	Just, Rev. Thomas	Kelvedon, Essex	9	328 10
				Kay, Heirs of George	St. Andrews	20	107 4
Inglis, Judicial Factor for James	Bondfield, Cupar	9	53 —	Kay, Robert	Prior Muir, St. Andrews	7	22 10
Inglis, John, of Colluthie	St. Andrews	487	1,226 10	Kay, Mrs., wife of Robert Kay, and Mrs. Moyes, wife of J. Moyes	Kettle, Ladybank	7	47 7
Inglis, John, of Ballenkirk	Markinch	360	559 —				
Inglis, John, of Newington	Newington, Cupar	580	978 —				
Inglis, John John Inglis William Kilgour	Newington, Cupar St. Andrews 22 Warriston Crescent, Edinburgh	246	382 —	Keay, John	Freuchie, Ladybank	2	23 5
				Keddie, Andrew	St. Andrews	4	18 —
				Keir, Allan	Dunfermline	1	101 10
and Robert Thomson	Seggie, Leuchars			Kellie, Earl of	Alloa Park, Alloa	162	331 4
Inglis, Trustees of Thomas	Fairneyhirst, Dunfermline	30	25 —	Kellock, Alexander	Newton, Falkland	2	6 2
Inglis, William	Silverton, Lochgelly	22	50 —	Kellock, John	Lundin Mill, Largo	2	22 —
Inglis, Heirs of William	Balmalcolm, Ladybank	9	26 —	Kellock, Robert, senior	Hatton Law, Largo	2	93 14
Inglis, William, & Co.	Dunfermline	1	305 —	Kellock, Robert, junior	Hatton Law, Largo	6	21 —
Inglis, Mrs. Jane	Crail	190	709 —	Kellock, Mrs. Catherine	Newton, Falkland	3	49 10
Inglis, Ann	Strathendry, Leslie	28	75 8	Kelty, Heirs of Andrew	Perth	2	28 10
Inglis, Helen	Annfield, Lochgelly	2	32 15	*Kemback School Board*	Kemback, Cupar	1	9 —
Ingram, Mrs., wife of David Ingram	Baldinnie, Cupar	3	7 —	Kemp, Andrew	Cowstrandburn, Dunfermline	6	13 —
Innes, Andrew	Kirkcaldy	1	59 6	Ker, William Ferrier, of Middlebank	Loancroft House, Uddingston	160	450 —
Innes, William	Cupar	1	54 10				
Inverkeithing, Burgh of	Inverkeithing	30	107 6	Ker, William Wemyss	Stripeside, Dunfermline	1	36 —
Inverkeithing Sailors' Society	Inverkeithing	3	37 15	Ker, Isabella, Elizabeth, and Alexina	Blackshiels, Edinburgh	485	781 14
Ireland, Alexander, of Bannaty	Bannaty, Strathmiglo	322	367 —	Kermock, James	Ceres	16	44 10
Ireland, David Stevenson	St. Andrews	2	215 —	Kermock, John	Ceres	17	59 7
Ireland, John, of Upper Urquhart	Upper Urquhart, Strathmiglo	177	235 —	Kermock, Elizabeth	Ceres	3	17 —
				Kermock, Euphemia	Ceres	6	35 —
Ireland, John, & Sons	Buckhaven, Leven	1	353 —	Kerr, William	Newport	1	187 10
Ireland, Thomas	Merchiston, Edinburgh	1	329 —	Kerr, Mrs. Eliza	Cupar	9	30 —
Ireland, Thomas	Tanshall, Leslie	3	20 15	Kerr, Mrs., wife of Hugh Kerr	Queensferry Lane, Edinburgh	5	22 —
Ireland, Thomas	Buckhaven, Leven	2	129 —				

L

FIFE—continued.

Name of Owner.	Address of Owner.	Estimated Acreage of Property.	Gross Annual Value.	Name of Owner.	Address of Owner.	Estimated Acreage of Property.	Gross Annual Value.
		Acres.	£ s.			Acres.	£ s.
Ketchen, William Robinson	Elie	1	66 -	Lawson, Andrew	Kirkcaldy	3	78 -
Key, John	Kirkcaldy	20	489 10	Lawson, David	Innerleven, Leven	1	40 5
Kidd, James	Mayfield, Colinsburgh	3	48 -	Lawson, James	Edinburgh	2	13 3
Kidd, John	Kettle, Ladybank	1	8 10	Lawson, John, of Lalathan	Lalathan, Kennoway	118	165 -
Kidd, John	Lucklawhill, Leuchars	3	15 -	Lawson, Thomas, of Carriston	Carriston, Markinch	266	354 -
Kidd, Mrs. Christian	Milton Mill, Anstruther	3	80 10	Lawson, Trs. of William	Pitlethie, Leuchars	203	445 15
Kilgour, Trustees of Alex.	Inverkeithing	12	59 10	Lawson, Mrs. Barbara	Carriston, Markinch	47	92 -
Kilgour, Heirs of Robert	Culross	6	21 -	Leadbetter Brothers	Cupar	1	371 -
Kilgour, William, of Wester Glasslie	22 Warriston Crescent, Edinburgh	220	170 -	Learmonth, Andrew	Crossford, Dunfermline	1	29 2
Kilgour, William	Falkland	4	45 16	Leburn, William Gilmour, of Pitlochie	Gateside, Strathmiglo	477	686 -
Kilgour, Mrs., wife of William Kilgour	22 Warriston Crescent, Edinburgh	128	225 10	Lees, George	St. Andrews	2	70 -
Kilrenny, Burgh of	Kilrenny, Anstruther	14	28 5	Leishman, Alexander	Freuchie, Ladybank	10	70 10
King, George	Pittenweem	3	76 5	Leishman, Mrs., wife of J. Leishman	Freuchie, Ladybank	13	89 12
Kinghorn, Burgh of	Kinghorn	68	327 11	Leitch, Andrew	Ballingry Feus, Lochgelly	1	16 10
Kingsbarns Parochial Board	Kingsbarns, St. Andrews	2	10 12	Leitch, Mrs. Andrew	Largo	1	55 15
Kinnear, Charles, of Kinloch	Kinloch, Ladybank	1,399	2,249 17	Leng, John	Newport	5	176 -
Kinnear, Charles G. Hood	3 South Charlotte Street, Edinburgh	14	14 12	Leny, Mrs. Marion Agatha	30 Great Cumberland Place, London	111	156 5
Kinnear, Henry	Buckhaven, Leven	4	57 15	Leslie, David	Balmullo, Leuchars	1	10 -
Kinnear, John	Redmyre, Largo	9	26 10	*Leslie, Town of*	Leslie	28	53 -
Kirk, William	Hounslow, Middlesex	3	10 -	Leslie, Elizabeth and Euphemia	Largo	1	60 4
Kirk, Mrs. Elizabeth	St. Andrews	2	8 -	Leslie, Margaret	Markinch	2	14 -
Kirk, Mrs. James	Cupar-Muir, Cupar	1	7 -	Leslie, Janet and Margaret	Markinch	4	40 -
Kirk, Mrs. James	Gowkhall, Dunfermline	2	9 10	*Leuchars Parochial Board*	Leuchars	11	47 10
Kirkcaldy, Robert	St. Andrews	2	22 13	Leven and Melville, Earl of	Roehampton, Surrey	1,019	1,761 11
Kirkcaldy, William	Falkland	6	20 -	*Leven and East of Fife Railway Company*	Leven	3	49 13
Kirkcaldy, Burgh of	Kirkcaldy	2	255 -	Do. do.	Do. (*Railway*)	146	6,310 -
Kirkcaldy Combination Poorhouse	Kirkcaldy	4	175 -	*Leven Farina Company*	Leven	3	150 -
Kirkcaldy District Road Trustees	Kirkcaldy	1	65 -	Liddell, Helen	Auchtertool, Kirkcaldy	13	89 10
Kirkcaldy Gaslight Coy.	Kirkcaldy	2	1,096 -	Lindsay, Alexander Kyd, of Balmungo	Balmungo, St. Andrews	85	284 15
Kirkcaldy Harbour Commissioners	Kirkcaldy	1	348 -	Lindsay, David C., of Wormiston	Wormiston, Crail	501	1,542 6
Kirkcaldy and Dysart Water Commissioners	Kirkcaldy	163	2,250 -	Lindsay, George, of Feddinch	Feddinch, St. Andrews	440	749 -
Kirke, Robert, of Greenmount	Greenmount, Burntisland	59	558 7	Lindsay, Sir Coutts T., of Balcarres, Bart.	Balcarres, Colinsburgh	4,672	9,619 7
Kitching, Mrs., wife of M'Laren Kitching	Cupar	5	15 10	Lindsay, Mrs. William	Kettlehill, Ladybank	4	11 -
Knox, Trustees of David	St. Andrews	4	18 10	Lindsay & Anderson	Lilliehill, Dunfermline	14	316 12
Knox's Institution Trustees	Cupar	1	20 -	Littlejohn, David	Carnock, Dunfermline	6	10 -
				Littlejohn, Heirs of Thomas	Carnock, Dunfermline	5	27 8
				Livingston, William	Walkerton, Leslie	13	537 -
Laing, David	Carnbee Muir, Pittenweem	13	15 -	Lloyd, Rev. Fitzroy K.	Pittenweem	25	138 15
Laing, John	Balmalcolm, Ladybank	6	24 -	*Loanfoot Feuars*	Kettle, Ladybank	1	3 7
Laing, Robert	Cowdenbeath, Lochgelly	1	17 10	*Lochgelly Iron Company*	Lochgelly	160	1,374 3
Laing, Thomas	Newton, Falkland	1	9 5	Do. do.	Do. (*Minerals*)	-	63 -
Laing, William	Springfield, Cupar	3	75 5	*Lochore and Capeldrae Cannel Coal Co. (Limited)*	Lochore, Lochgelly	851	1,207 12
Laing, William	St. Andrews	3	9 15	Do. do.	Do. (*Minerals*)	-	650 -
Landale, Andrew, of Pittauchop	Easthall, Cupar	221	540 -	*Lochore Gas Coal Company*	Lochore, Lochgelly	2	91 5
Landale, Andrew	Lochgelly	1	50 12	Lockhart, James	New Gilston, Largo	5	9 -
Landale, David	Binn, Burntisland	12	126 -	Lockhart, John, Robert, & Andrew	Kirkcaldy	2	432 -
Landale, John, of Woodbank	Dunfermline	482	681 -	Lockhart, Ninian, George Douglas, & James	Kirkcaldy	2	945 -
Landale, Robert	15 Royal Circus, Edinburgh	26	30 -	Lockhart, Robert	Kirkcaldy	2	186 -
Landale, Thomas	4 Mayfield Ter., Edinburgh	4	34 14	Lockhart, Robert	Lindores, Newburgh	1	9 3
Landale, Trs. of Thomas	18 Forth St., Edinburgh	4	27 -	Logan, David	Starleyburn, Burntisland	2	52 10
Landale, Mrs., wife of Thomas Landale	4 Mayfield Terrace, Edinburgh	29	213 16	Long, Colonel Samuel, of Earlshall	Bromley Hall, Kent	2,338	2,988 2
Landale, Mrs., wife of Thomas Landale, and David Walker	4 Mayfield Terrace, Edinburgh / Kinclaven	19	222 11	Lorimer, Mrs. Elizabeth	Cupar	15	69 10
				Lornie, Andrew	Kirkcaldy	1	241 5
				Lornie, David	Kirkcaldy	1	331 9
Lassodie Colliery Company	Lassodie, Dunfermline	10	344 6	Lornie, David, & Sons	Pathhead, Kirkcaldy	1	10 -
Laverock, James	Markinch	1	63 7	Lornie, John	Pathhead, Kirkcaldy	1	262 -
Law, George	Star, Markinch	8	19 15	Lothian, John	Newton of Abbotshall, Kirkcaldy	1	17 10
Law, Madeline	Ladybank	1	31 -	Low, David	Leslie	7	129 3
Lawrie, John William	20 South Hanover Street, Edinburgh	8	10 -	Low, General Sir John, of Clatto, K.C.B.	Clatto, St. Andrews	354	686 17
Lawrie, Mrs. Robert	Crossford, Dunfermline	2	17 -	Lowden, Alexander	St. Andrews	1	6 5
Lawson, Adam	Falkland	3	19 5	Lowden, James	St. Andrews	5	27 15
Lawson, Alexander, of Burnturk	Annfield, Ladybank	232	776 15	Lowden, John	St. Andrews	4	17 2
Lawson, Rev. Alexander	Manse, Creich	271	295 10	Lowden, William	Springfield, Cupar	1	24 7

FIFE—continued.

Name of Owner.	Address of Owner.	Estimated Acreage of Property.	Gross Annual Value.	Name of Owner.	Address of Owner.	Estimated Acreage of Property.	Gross Annual Value.
		Acres.	£ s.			Acres.	£ s.
Lowson, Mrs. James	Carnoustie	1	4 12	Mackie, James Wm. Reid	Cupar	1	44 –
Luke, John	Elie	3	123 6	Mackie, Marion, and Mrs. Russell, wife of George Russell	Kincraig, Elie	10	27 6
Luke, Jean	Lucklawhill, Leuchars	8	14 –	Madras Academy Trustees	Cupar	1	108 –
Lumphinnans Iron Company	Lumphinnans, Lochgelly	24	402 –	Madras College	St. Andrews	611	1,304 17
Lumsdaine, Heirs of Rev. F. G. Sandys	Blanerne, Berwickshire	428	1,181 14	Maillardet, Mrs.	Crail	2	35 –
Lumsdaine, Stamford R., of Lathallan	Lathallan, Colinsburgh	1,151	2,139 11	Main, John	Pathhead, Kirkcaldy	1	295 16
Do. do.	Do. (Minerals)	–	444 –	Mair, Joseph	Balcormo, Pittenweem	7	23 –
Lumsden, Andrew	Blebo Craigs, Cupar	10	20 6	Maitland, Captain James, of Lindores	Lindores, Newburgh	302	638 17
Lumsden, Frederick Roome	Newburn, Largo	1	20 16	Makgill, George, of Kemback	Prestbury, Cheltenham	904	1,560 7
Lumsden, James	Freuchie, Ladybank	20	116 18	Makgill, Joanna and Agnes	Stirling	2	60 –
Lumsden, John	Pitmenzies, Auchtermuchty	9	13 –	Malcolm, Alexander	Clayton, Cupar	72	225 –
Lumsden, Thomas	Freuchie, Ladybank	9	764 18	Malcolm, Alexander Greig	Kirkcaldy	2	345 10
Lumsden, Jean	Gowrie, Falkland	8	26 10	Malcolm, James	St. Andrews	2	141 –
Lyell, James Ronaldson	Parkhouse, Falkland	10	50 –	Malcolm, Sir James, of Balbeadie, Bart.	72 Bedford Street, Liverpool	803	1,101 9
Lyell, John	Newburgh	1	83 15	Malcolm, Lady	Kensington, London	388	586 –
Lyell, William R.	Auchtermuchty	3	55 –	Mansfield, Earl of	Scone Palace, Perth	795	638 8
Lyell, Mrs.	Pittenweem	3	73 10	Markinch Combination Poorhouse	Thornton, Kirkcaldy	2	150 –
Lyell, Mrs. Alexander	Newburgh	1	72 –	Markinch Kirk-Session	Markinch	27	64 16
Lyell, Mrs. Euphemia, and John Anderson Millar	Newburgh / Calcutta	1	59 12	Marr, Trs. of Alexander	Lucklawhill, Leuchars	4	14 10
Lyell, Margaret and Christina	Lochty Bank, Auchtermuchty	23	100 13	Marr, Thomas	Greigston, Cupar	4	8 5
Lyon, Joseph	Woodend, Cowdenbeath, Lochgelly	1	25 –	Marshall, John	Dunfermline	1	239 –
				Marshall, Trs. of Walter	Duncrevie, Milnathort	3	5 –
M'Ara, Mrs. Eliza	Kettle, Ladybank	27	95 3	Marshall, Mrs. Jean T., of Conland	Duncrevie, Milnathort	229	245 –
M'Arthur, Peter	Perth	24	40 –	Marshall, Barbara	Freuchie, Ladybank	2	12 –
M'Call, Robert	Radernie, St. Andrews	2	10 18	Marsham, Mrs., wife of R. B. Marsham	Merton College, Oxford	304	997 10
M'Cash, Andrew, of Templehall	Meadowwells, Ladybank	182	274 6	Martin, Trs. of George	Balmaken, Colinsburgh	104	224 3
M'Cash, James	Pitilloch, Falkland	4	14 10	Martin, Eliza	Kinglassie, Kirkcaldy	1	6 10
M'Callum, Mrs. Christian	Inverkeithing	3	19 –	Mason, Andrew	Blebo, Cupar	4	12 –
M'Culloch, Rev. James	West Kirk Manse, Greenock	1	13 –	Mathewson, William	Dunfermline	7	1,124 –
M'Culloch, Thomas	Cowstrandburn, Dunfermline	4	6 –	Mathieson, Kenneth	Dunfermline	1	25 –
M'Dougall, Alexander	Bogside, Culross	5	8 –	Matthew, Alexander	Struthers' Barns, Cupar	15	31 –
M'Dougall, Alexander S.	St. Andrews	5	30 –	Matthew, James	Edinburgh	4	14 10
M'Duff, John	Milton, Markinch	2	14 –	Matthew, Robert	Strathmiglo	2	73 17
M'Farlane, Rev. Patrick	Manse, Pittenweem	5	60 10	Maxwell, Rev. David Skinner	Manse, Monimail, Ladybank	7	46 5
M'Farlane, Thomas	Carhurly, Crail	13	32 –	Maxwell, George	Auchtermuchty	7	81 16
M'Gorian, William	Dunfermline	1	24 18	Meldrum, David Bayne, of Kincaple	Kincaple, St. Andrews	969	2,197 5
M'Gregor, Rev. Alex.	Manse, Inverkeithing	16	73 6	Meldrum, David, of Craigfoodie	Craigfoodie, Cupar	355	1,125 12
M'Gregor, John	St. Andrews	19	1,219 5	Meldrum, David	Moonzie Mill, Leuchars	86	332 2
M'Gregor, John, and M'Intosh, John	St. Andrews	2	36 –	Meldrum, John, of Edenbank	Edenbank, Cupar	359	989 10
M'Intosh, Alexander	Dairsie, Cupar	11	102 16	Meldrum, Robert	Crail	5	33 11
M'Intosh, Robert	Largoward, St. Andrews	3	16 –	Meldrum, Robert, of Pittormie	Pittormie, Cupar	251	697 –
M'Intosh, Heirs of Mrs.	Rosebank, Markinch	1	15 –	Meldrum & Son	Tayport	2	110 –
M'Intosh, Mrs., wife of Alex. M'Intosh	Dairsie, Cupar	2	41 14	Meldrum, Mrs. John	Pitscottie Toll, Cupar	1	28 8
M'Intyre, Allan	St. Andrews	7	26 15	Mellis, Rev. James	F.C. Manse, Arncroach, Pittenweem	1	30 –
M'Kay, William	Pilmuir, Largo	3	16 12	Melville, Alex. Bethune	Blebo Craigs, Cupar	4	7 10
M'Kean, William Blair	Tourville, Inverkeithing	1	59 –	Melville, Alexander M.	Kirkcaldy	8	66 5
M'Knight, Alexander E.	12 London St., Edinburgh	5	14 –	Melville, David	Hazleton Walls, Cupar	3	11 –
M'Laren, Rev. Alexander	Manse, Kemback	12	39 –	Melville, James	Leuchars	2	14 10
M'Laren, Robert	Falkland	3	5 10	Melville, Heirs of James	Torryburn, Dunfermline	1	15 –
M'Laren, Thomas	Hawklymuir, Kirkcaldy	1	168 7	Melville, John	Lucklawhill, Leuchars	8	25 –
M'Lean, Heirs of William	Cowdenbeath, Lochgelly	2	43 10	Melville, John	Inverkeithing	1	10 –
M'Leish, James	Gartmorn Hill, Alloa	8	20 –	Melville, John Whyte, of Bennochy and Strathkinness	Mount Melville, St. Andrews	2,940	6,150 6
M'Leod, Mrs. Agnes, of Burnside	Perth	200	203 –	Melville, Samuel	Lucklawhill, Leuchars	15	35 –
M'Nab, Duncan	Cupar	3	53 16	Melville, Heirs of William	Blebo Craigs, Cupar	3	15 7
M'Naughton, John	Leven	1	57 6	Melville, Trustees of Mrs.	Callange, Cupar	5	13 5
M'Phail, Rev. Archibald C.	Manse, Beath	11	48 –	Methven, David	Largoward, St. Andrews	5	10 –
M'Rae, Colin George	14 Gloucester Place, Edinburgh	4	30 –	Methven, James	Kirkcaldy	4	375 –
M'Rae, Rev. David	Gorbals, Glasgow	77	143 –	Middleton, Mrs., wife of George Middleton	Strathmiglo	5	33 –
M'Ritchie, Thomas Elder, of Denork	Edinburgh	295	549 18	Millar, Andrew	Dunfermline	1	10 –
M'Ritchie, Isabella, and others	Lathones, St. Andrews	441	512 9	Miller, Charles	Newport	1	16 –
Macfie, David Johnston, of Kilmux	Kilmux, Windygates	607	1,138 9	Miller, David	Lindores, Newburgh	1	33 12
Do. do.	Do. (Minerals)	–	110 –	Miller, James Lawson, of Waulkmill	Waulkmill, Dunfermline	199	604 12
Mackie, Archibald	Cupar	4	115 –				
Mackie, James	Freuchie, Ladybank	7	30 10				

FIFE—continued.

Name of Owner.	Address of Owner.	Estimated Acreage of Property.	Gross Annual Value.	Name of Owner.	Address of Owner.	Estimated Acreage of Property.	Gross Annual Value.
		Acres.	£ s.			Acres.	£ s.
Miller, John	Milton, Markinch	3	65 12	Murray, John	Foulhogger, Crail	5	20 —
Miller, John	Inverkeithing	1	16 10	Murray, John	Dysart	3	44 18
Miller, John	Mountquhanie, Cupar	1	6 15	Murray, Rev. John	Manse, Moonzie	20	58 10
Miller, John	Balcurvie, Windygates	1	10 7	Murray, Joseph, of Aytoun	Broomfield House, Hants	1,736	2,384 12
Miller, Thomas	Newburgh	4	10 —	Murray, William	Bondfield, Cupar	1	11 9
Miller, Walter, of Torr	Kedlock, Cupar	123	236 8	Murray, Trs. of William	St. Andrews	2	151 —
Miller, William	Milton, Markinch	1	30 4				
Miller, William M'Gregor	Nookton, Markinch	1	21 —				
Miller, Mrs.	Coal Wynd, Kirkcaldy	1	81 —	Nairn, Michael Barker	Kirkcaldy	1	85 —
Millar, Agnes	Gauldry, Newport	2	7 16	Nairn, Mrs. Catherine	Kirkcaldy	7	2,221 —
Miller Prize Fund	St. Andrews	24	87 14	Nairn, Mrs. Christian	Cupar	15	34 —
Millie, George, of St. Mary's	Kilmaron, Cupar	75	163 —	*National Bank of Scotland*	Edinburgh	2	434 —
Millie, Trustees of Thomas	Dysart	3	234 18	Nelson, James and Henry	Pillars of Hercules, Falkland	12	26 12
Millie, Mrs. William	Pathhead, Kirkcaldy	4	204 15				
Milne, Andrew	Newburgh	3	33 10	Ness, Trs. of Alexander	St. Clairtown, Kirkcaldy	1	86 12
Minto, Earl of	Minto House, Hawick	2,930	2,596 10	Ness, David	Bruntleys, Falkland	1	8 —
Do.	Do. (*Minerals*)	—	2,804 —	Ness, Mrs. James	Viewforth, Largo	1	55 10
Mitchell, Trustees of Archibald	Brighton, Cupar	5	82 12	*Newburgh, Burgh of*	Newburgh	190	270 10
Mitchell, David	Crail	6	32 —	Newton, James	Inverkeithing	4	31 —
Mitchell, David	Muirhead, Ladybank	4	11 —	Newton, Robert Pillans, of Castlandhill	Polmont Bank, Falkirk	275	668 10
Mitchell, John, of Arngask	Arngask, Milnathort	151	380 10	Nicholson, Heirs of Alexander	Cupar	1	61 —
Mitchell, John	Lordscairnie, Cupar	13	252 —	Nicol, Andrew, of Bonnyton	Bonnyton, St. Andrews	306	619 15
Mitchell, Peter	Cairneyhill, Dunfermline	2	9 5	Nicol, Andrew	Cowdenbeath, Lochgelly	1	28 —
Mitchell, Robert	Cupar	3	50 11	Nicol, George	Newburgh	4	32 4
Mitchell, William	11 South Charlotte Street, Edinburgh	6	16 —	Nicol, Heirs of James	Newburgh	1	82 —
Mitchell, Mrs.	Ladyinch, Cupar	11	85 2	Nicol, Thomas	Lawmill, St. Andrews	1	36 —
Mitchell, Mrs. David	Strathkinness, St. Andrews	13	34 10	Nicol, Mrs. David	Baldinnie, Cupar	41	71 10
Mitchell, Mrs. Lillias	Cairneyhill, Dunfermline	6	21 —	Nicolson, Trustees of Alexander	St. Clairtown, Kirkcaldy	1	69 15
Mitchell, Mrs. Elizabeth Jean	Bogside, Kennoway	7	17 —	Nicolson, Andrew	Larennie, Cupar	98	135 —
Mitchell, Margaret	St. Andrews	1	4 10	Nisbet, Charles	Pitfirrane, Dunfermline	10	20 —
Mitchell, Margaret	North Shields	67	85 —	Nisbet, James	Ballomill, Ladybank	9	37 —
Mitchell, Janet and Margaret	Redwells, Lochgelly	58	142 5	Niven, George	Colinsburgh	3	8 —
Moir, James, John, and Aitken	St. Margaret's Stone, Dunfermline	79	206 5	Normand, David	Baltilly, Cupar	19	87 —
				Normand, James, of Whitehill	Dysart	225	546 —
Moir, Mrs. Donald	Cantsdam, Kelty, Kinross	2	8 —	Normand, James, jun.	Kirkcaldy	1	50 —
Moncrieff, Trustees of General George	St. Andrews	3	120 —	Normand, James, & Sons	Dysart	1	1,337 6
				Normand, Creditors of Robert	Kennoway	1	68 —
Monypenny, Rev. James Isaac, of Pitmilly	Hadlow, Kent	2,034	5,698 14	Normand, William James	Dysart	1	83 10
Moon, William	Edenfield, Cupar	33	170 —	*North British Railway Co.*	Edinburgh	48	418 10
Moonzie Kirk-Session	Moonzie, Cupar	8	36 9	Do. do.	Do. (*Railway*)	1,087	46179 —
Moray, Earl of	Darnaway Castle, Forres	7,463	8,735 16				
Do.	Do. (*Minerals*)	—	2,350 —	Oliphant, Major Patrick, of Over Kinneddar	Over Kinneddar, Saline	563	565 10
More, Mrs. David	Kennoway	3	8 —	Oliphant, Philip	Anstruther	2	49 15
Morgan, James, sen.	Saline, Dunfermline	2	17 10	Orford, Peter	Kettlebridge, Ladybank	1	21 15
Morgan, William	Coates, Largo	154	254 —	Orford, Mrs. Janet	Lundin Mill, Largo	2	34 —
Morgan, William	Methil, Leven	1	40 5	Orr, Henry	Dunfermline	2	59 —
Morgan, Mrs. Margaret	Kilconquhar	7	39 5	Oswald, James Townsend, of Dunnikier	Dunnikier, Kirkcaldy	1,623	4,205 18
Morris, Alexander	Dunfermline	1	40 4	Do. do.	Do. (*Minerals*)	—	466 —
Morris, David	Blebo Craigs, Cupar	6	13 5				
Morris, Christian	Kilconquhar	1	10 —				
Morris, Christian	Dunfermline	1	225 5				
Morris, Margaret	St. Andrews	180	257 10				
Morrison, Heirs of Bethune James Walker	Falfield, Cupar	1,146	1,866 8	Page, George	Carmore, Strathmiglo	3	20 10
Morrison, Rev. Peter	Manse, Saline	9	32 —	Page, John	Kintullo, Bridge of Earn	7	29 —
Morrison, Thomas	Dunfermline	1	266 —	Page, Thomas	Dunshalt, Auchtermuchty	6	20 2
Morrison, Catherine H. A. D.	Naughton, Newport	1,591	3,420 17	Page, William	Falkland	10	5 5
Morton, Alexander	Dunfermline	1	106 15	Page, Heirs of William	Falkland	20	151 3
Morton, Earl of	Dalmahoy, Ratho	1,130	2,293 19	Page, Mrs. Catherine	Barrington, Ladybank	7	53 4
Morton, John, of Drunzie	Cupar	8	73 —	Paisley, Rev. John, and Andrew W. Russell	Garelochhead / Parkhill, Newburgh }	198	600 —
Moubray, Captain William H., of Otterstone, R.N.	Otterstone, Aberdour	500	794 —	*Patent Floor Cloth Company* (*Limited*)	Kirkcaldy	3	85 —
Moubray, Jane Laura, Matilda, and Ellen	Cockairney, Aberdour	12	73 —	Paterson, Rev. John	Manse, Torryburn	4	39 —
Moyes, Joseph	St. Andrews	5	10 —	Paterson, Mrs. William	Star, Markinch	1	12 —
Moyes, Mrs. John	Ladybank	4	12 10	Paterson, Frances and Catherine	Trinity, Edinburgh	309	524 —
Moyes, Mrs. Agnes	Ladybank	2	14 10	*Pathhead Established Church, Trustees of*	Denburn, Kirkcaldy	2	60 —
Muckersie, David	Ladybank	1	1 10	Paton, Alexander	Edinburgh	30	56 —
Muckersie, Henry	Balbie, Kirkcaldy	1	194 —	Paton, Joseph N.	Dunfermline	3	47 2
Mudie, David, of Balhousie	Balhousie, Largo	215	307 —	Paton, William	Lochgelly	1	6 17
Murray, David Guthrie	107 Buchanan Street, Glasgow	3	45 —	Paton, Mrs. Agnes	Balcurvie, Windygates	2	6 —

FIFE—continued.

Name of Owner.	Address of Owner.	Estimated Acreage of Property.	Gross Annual Value.	Name of Owner.	Address of Owner.	Estimated Acreage of Property.	Gross Annual Value.
		Acres.	£ s.			Acres.	£ s.
Patrick Yeaman Bursary Fund	St. Andrews	7	32 15	*Ramsay Bursary Fund*	St. Andrews	189	424 10
Patterson, John	St. Andrews	5	170 —	Rankine, James	Auchtermuchty	2	56 15
Paxton, Richard H.	Kirkcaldy	2	114 8	Reddie, John	Dysart	1	36 —
Pearson, George	Inverkeithing	12	36 18	Reddie, Trustees of John	Redhouse, Lochgelly	250	285 —
Pearson, John	Burntisland	1	198 10	Reedie, William	Rameldry, Ladybank	3	29 —
Peat, Admiral David	Viewforth House, Edinburgh	4	25 —	Reekie, Andrew	Kennoway	3	10 —
Peat, Walter	Luthrie, Cupar	5	17 —	Reeve, Trs. of Thomas	Edenpark, Cupar	15	147 10
Peat, Mrs. Helen	Inverkeithing	2	46 —	*Reformed Presbyterian Congregation*	Strathmiglo	2	31 12
Peattie, David & James	Crail	1	6 6	Reid, Andrew	Dunfermline	1	424 —
Peattie, James	Crail	14	47 12	Reid, Henry	Dunfermline	2	544 —
Peattie, Matthew	Craigiewells, St. Monance	7	31 —	Reid, John	Dunfermline	1	62 8
Penman, James	Dysart	2	42 6	Reid, Rev. John	Manse, Crail	10	75 —
Pennel, Rev. James	Manse, Ballingry, Lochgelly	11	50 —	Reid, Robert	Markinch	19	65 —
Pennycook, Rev. Peter	Manse, Carnock, Dunfermline	11	46 —	Reid, Walter	Falkland	18	94 5
				Reid, William	Lochgelly	1	8 —
				Reid, Rev. William	Manse, Kettle, Ladybank	6	31 —
Pentland, John	Craigrothie, Cupar	2	14 —	Reid, Mrs., wife of Walter Reid	Falkland	4	3 10
Peter, H. & T.	Kirkland, Leven	69	1,581 12	Reid, Mrs., wife of John Reid	Bonnington, Dunfermline	70	68 2
Petheram, Henry	Lundin Links, Largo	2	50 —	Reid, Magdalene	Alburnknowe, Markinch	11	173 12
Petrie, William	Buckieburn, Dunfermline	3	18 —	Renton, Rev. John	Auchtermuchty	2	62 10
Petrie, Elspeth	Largoward, St. Andrews	8	26 15	Rettie, Mrs., wife of Middleton Rettie	Dunearn, Burntisland	137	277 8
Philip, James	Crail	5	72 6	Richard, Mrs. Eliza	Aberdeen	41	130 —
Philip, Robert	Cairneyhill, Dunfermline	2	12 10	Rigg, Trs. of James Home	Tarvit, Cupar	2,625	4,260 5
Philp, Alexander	Kennoway	1	9 —	Rigg, Mary and Margaret	Lundin Links, Largo	4	70 —
Philp, Benjamin	Largo	1	45 10	Rintoul, Alexander, junior	Kennoway	1	15 —
Philp, James	Crossford, Dunfermline	1	8 10	Rintoul, James	Gallatown, Kirkcaldy	1	40 —
Philp, Trustees of Robert	Kirkcaldy	1,231	2,979 9	Rintoul, James	Carnbee Muir, Pittenweem	4	10 —
Philp, William	Torr-Forret, Cupar	4	11 —	Rintoul, Robert, of Lahill	Lahill, Largo	754	1,665 12
Philp, William Trail	Edinburgh	8	67 —	Rintoul, Mrs. Janet	Kennoway	3	45 —
Philp, Jean	Cairneyhill, Dunfermline	1	5 10	Ritchie, David	Denbrae, St. Andrews	25	96 10
Pitcairn, Hope, of Kinnaird	Kinnaird, Newburgh	235	560 10	Ritchie, Heirs of James	St. Andrews	11	45 14
Pitcairn, John, of Pitcullo	Pitcullo, Cupar	563	958 10	Ritchie, John	Crail	3	10 10
Pitcairn, Mrs. Agnes	Cunnoquhie, Cupar	561	937 5	Ritchie & Blackie	Tayport	10	672 8
Pitlessie Feuars	Pitlessie, Ladybank	9	2 —	Ritchie, Mrs.	Woodside, Largo	4	9 18
Pittenweem, Burgh of	Pittenweem	109	612 5	Roberts, George	Edinburgh	108	408 —
Pittenweem General Box Society	Pittenweem	4	25 —	Robertson, Alexander	Cameron Bridge, Windygates	2	12 5
Pittenweem Kirk-Session	Pittenweem	27	142 10	Robertson, Charles	Aberdour	2	17 —
Pittenweem Sea Box Society	Pittenweem	79	417 5	Robertson, Charles, senior	Cairneyhill, Dunfermline	6	35 17
Pittenweem Trades Box Society	Pittenweem	23	178 5	Robertson, Donald	Mayfield, Cupar	45	100 —
Playfair, Charles, of Carskerdo	Banchory, Coupar-Angus	520	605 —	Robertson, George L.	Ladybank	1	44 —
Playfair, Major Frederick Lyon	St. Andrews	2	130 —	Robertson, Hugh	Newburgh	5	108 12
Polson, Rev. William	Manse, Wemyss, Kirkcaldy	8	49 10	Robertson, Heirs of James	Dunfermline	1	12 —
				Robertson, John	Comerton, Leuchars	3	41 16
Powrie, James	Reswalli, Forfar	7	62 10	Robertson, John	Kirkcaldy	1	62 —
Pratt, Mrs. Stephen	Kennoway	3	31 7	Robertson, John	Ayr	12	25 —
Prentice, George, of Strathore	Newbigging, Burntisland	652	1,035 13	Robertson, Thomas	Crossford, Dunfermline	2	31 —
Prentice, Heirs of George	Fostertown, Kirkcaldy	6	10 —	Robertson, Mrs. James	Ladybank	3	18 5
Preston, Sir Henry L., of Valleyfield and Lutton, Bart.	Lutton, Lincolnshire	577	662 —	Robertson, Mrs., wife of Henry Robertson	Edengrove, Cupar	5	55 —
				Robertson, Mrs. Jean	Crossgates, Cupar	30	60 15
Preston, Curators of Robert W. P. C.	Valleyfield, Culross	105	178 2	Robertson, Mrs. Isabel	Muirside, Dunfermline	3	14 10
Do. do.	Do. (*Minerals*)	—	71 —	Robertson, Elizabeth	Pitfirrane, Dunfermline	5	11 10
Preston, Mrs. Margaret, of Lumbenny	Scarborough	642	829 —	Robertson, Margaret Turnbull, of Dalladies	Luthermuir, Laurencekirk	626	985 16
				Robin, Rev. John	Manse, Burntisland	6	77 —
Pride, Andrew	Milnwaters, Ladybank	10	40 —	Roddick, Rev. George	Manse, Aberdour	14	92 —
Pride, Heirs of Robert	Woodside, Largo	4	11 —	Rodger, Rev. Mathew	St. Andrews	2	144 4
Pride, Mrs. William	Woodside, Largo	3	8 13	Rodger, Robert M.	Airdrie	16	40 —
Prime Gilt Box Society	Kirkcaldy	7	39 10	Rodger, Thomas	St. Andrews	1	323 —
Proudfoot, Peter	Leuchars	3	27 10	Roger, Mrs. Mary	Kingsbarns, St. Andrews	7	24 10
Pryde, William	Kilmarnock	6	28 5	Rolland, Adam, of Gask	Gask, Dunfermline	466	410 3
Purvis, John, of Kinaldy	Kinaldy, St. Andrews	749	1,321 6	Do. do.	Do. (*Minerals*)	—	211 —
Purdie, Thomas	St. Andrews	4	220 —	Rollo, David	Ladybank	1	11 5
Pyper Bursary Fund	St. Andrews	4	15 —	*Roman Catholic Congregation*	Dunfermline	1	9 —
				Ronald, Heirs of Beveridge	Kirkcaldy	2	293 —
				Rose, Rev. David	Manse, Ferry-Port-on-Craig	14	87 —
Ramsay, David	Cupar	6	23 5	Rose, Rev. James Landale	Manse, Markinch	13	65 5
Ramsay, Joseph	Balmalcolm, Ladybank	19	65 —	Ross, Alexander, of Cruicks	Cruicks, Inverkeithing	93	392 —
Ramsay, Robert Balfour Wardlaw, of Bankhead	Whitehill, Lasswade	368	1,245 —	Ross, David	Inverkeithing	1	25 12
Ramsay, Trs. of Thomas	Letham, Ladybank	1	35 —	Ross, James	Inverkeithing	1	53 —
Ramsay, William	Cupar	20	325 —	Ross, Robert and David	Inverkeithing	1	53 —
Ramsay, Isabella	Inverkeithing	2	10 10	Ross, Heirs of William	Greenside, Largo	272	375 —

FIFE—continued.

Name of Owner.	Address of Owner.	Estimated Acreage of Property.	Gross Annual Value.
		Acres.	£ s.
Ross, Mrs., wife of John Ross	Leven	3	43 5
Rosset, Mrs. Johanna	Kettle, Ladybank	5	17 -
Rosslyn, Earl of	Dysart House, Dysart	3,221	8,449 -
Do. do.	Do. (Minerals)	-	1,224 -
Rothes, Countess of, wife of Hon. G. Waldegrave Leslie	Leslie House, Leslie	3,562	7,343 5
Rowatts & Yooll	Kilrenny, Anstruther	5	225 -
Rowland, Edward	Bonnybank, Kennoway	1	15 10
Roxburgh, John Pirie	Inverkeithing	1	34 10
Roy, James, of Nether Stenton	Springbank, Perth	192	459 -
Roy, Mrs. Janet	Gowkhall, Dunfermline	2	13 14
Roy, John	Auchtermuchty	6	32 15
Rumgay, Robert	Balcanquhal, Strathmiglo	3	13 -
Runciman, Rev. David W.	Manse, Leslie	8	62 -
Russell, Andrew Walker, of Kenly	Parkhill, Newburgh	445	990 6
Russell, Arthur	Cupar	33	195 -
Russell, David, of Hillcairnie	Hillcairnie, Cupar	356	750 -
Russell, David	Ovenstone, Pittenweem	1	40 19
Russell, Henry	Rameldry, Ladybank	2	6 -
Russell, John, of Middlefield	Middlefield, Cupar	125	366 -
Russell, John, of Luthrie Bank	Cupar	344	590 -
Russell, Robert	Kirkcaldy	7	223 -
Russell, Trustees of Robert	Bruckley, Leuchars	200	533 -
Russell, Thomas, of Pitbladdo	Pitbladdo, Cupar	292	539 7
Russell, William	Leslie	14	95 -
Russell, Mrs.	Kenly Green, St. Andrews	17	80 15
Russell, Mrs. Mary	Rameldry, Ladybank	1	50 15
Russell, Mrs. Robert	Kettle, Ladybank	2	41 17
Russell, Jean Burns	Birkenhead	6	35 4
Russell, Margaret	Leslie	10	61 -
Russell, Margaret and Jane	Leslie	1	34 10
Rutherford, Trustees of Janet	Cairnhill, St. Andrews	117	285 10
Sanderson, Mrs. Agnes	Kennoway	2	41 10
Sands, James	Balmalcolm, Ladybank	6	28 -
Sands, Mrs. Robina	Aberdour	2	67 5
Sang, William	Kirkcaldy	11	202 4
Sawers, Mrs. Jessie P.	Edinburgh	4	14 10
Schank, Henry Alexander, of Castlerigg	43 Wilton Crescent, Belgrave Square, London	329	500 -
Scott, Andrew, senior	Innerleith, Ladybank	3	10 8
Scott, Andrew, junior	Innerleith, Ladybank	1	10 7
Scott, Arthur	Dundee	2	11 5
Scott, Arthur and George	Ballingry, Lochgelly	1	9 -
Scott, George, senior	Innerleith, Ladybank	9	18 15
Scott, George	Innerleith, Ladybank	5	10 5
Scott, Heirs of Hugh	Cupar	1	4 10
Scott, John, senior	Inverkeithing	2	47 10
Scott, John, & Sons	Inverkeithing	2	135 -
Scott, Heirs of John	Freuchie, Ladybank	1	94 14
Scott, Robert	8 Greenhill St., Glasgow	2	7 10
Scott, Thomas	Inverkeithing	1	25 -
Scott, Thomas	St. Andrews	2	55 10
Scott, William	Springfield, Cupar	2	17 14
Scott, William	Star, Markinch	1	8 -
Scott & Fyfe	Tayport	2	136 10
Scott, Mrs. Cecilia	Bank Place, Leslie	73	290 2
Scott, Mrs. Sarah	Glasgow	4	36 10
Scott, Isabella and Marjory	Dalgairn, Cupar	107	391 18
Selkirk, Trustees of George	Markinch	6	63 8
Shand, Mrs. Andrew	Lochcraig, Lochgelly	2	13 3
Shepherd, James	Pathhead, Kirkcaldy	41	349 -
Shepherd & Beveridge	Pathhead, Kirkcaldy	2	725 -
Sheppard, Rev. Henry Alexander Graham, of Sauchope	Emsworth, Northampton	654	1,663 8
Sheppard, Mrs. James	37 Castle St., Edinburgh	1	45 16
Sheriff, Andrew	Tealing, Dundee	5	12 -
Sime, James	Ceres	8	32 6
Sime, John	Letham Feus, Windygates	4	18 -
Simpson, Alexander, of New Gilston	Aberdeen	515	544 15
Do. do.	Do. (Minerals)	-	90 -
Simpson, Alexander, David, and Marshall	Auchtermuchty	2	94 2
Simpson, George	Benhar, Whitburn	523	685 -
Simpson, Trustees of George	Brunton, Markinch	344	757 4
Simpson, James, of North Lethans	Cleish, Kinross	343	381 15
Simpson, James	Partick, Glasgow	1	9 -
Simpson, Rev. James	Manse, Dysart	3	44 10
Simpson, Thomas	Morton, Tayport	1	39 10
Sinclair, James	Dander Inn, Carnock, Dunfermline	3	13 10
Skene, William Baillie, of Pitlour	Pitlour, Strathmiglo	2,878	4,219 8
Skinner, Peter	Strathmiglo	3	38 5
Skinner, Robert Peter	Auchtermuchty	2	96 -
Skinner, William	Dairsie, Cupar	7	14 -
Skinner, William	Wester Colzie, Auchtermuchty	38	40 -
Skinner, Mrs. John	Auchtermuchty	2	31 3
Skinner, Mrs.	Balcanquhal, Strathmiglo	12	26 -
Sligo, Mrs. George	Fernwoodlee, Dunfermline	43	95 -
Sligo, Mrs., wife of Archibald Vincent Smith Sligo	Inzievar, Dunfermline	1,547	2,535 7
Do. do.	Do. (Minerals)	-	100 -
Small, John Lumsdaine, of Foodie	St. Andrews	402	1,201 9
Small & Boase	Leven	2	505 -
Smart, John	Falkland	2	7 -
Smart, William	Kinglassie, Kirkcaldy	3	16 -
Smeaton, Trustees of David James	St. Andrews	484	1,087 10
Smith, Andrew	Lucklawhill, Leuchars	5	9 10
Smith, James	Gallatown, Kirkcaldy	1	146 4
Smith, James	Newport	1	60 -
Smith, John	Wellfield, Leuchars	6	16 14
Smith, John Pentland	Carnbee, Pittenweem	9	38 -
Smith, Peter	Windygates	1	47 -
Smith, Robert	Leven	1	114 10
Smith, Robert	Cupar	10	123 6
Smith, Trustees of Robert	Barnbaugh, Cupar	25	70 -
Smith, Thomas	Cupar	1	78 -
Smith, William	Leven	1	118 3
Smith, William	Ceres	2	43 8
Smith, William	Newport	3	198 -
Smith, Heirs of William	Balbaird, Largo	3	24 13
Smith, Trustees of William	St. Andrews	17	68 10
Smith, Anderson, & Co.	Fettykil, Leslie	3	20 -
Smith, Laing, & Co.	Russell Mill, Cupar	13	480 2
Smith, Mrs. Elizabeth	Kinglassie, Kirkcaldy	2	18 -
Smith, Trustees of Mrs.	Arncroach, Pittenweem	9	27 -
Smith, Mrs., wife of John Smith	Gauldry, Newport	2	9 3
Smith, Agnes and Elizabeth	Luthrie, Cupar	4	29 15
Smyth, Mrs. Amelia Gillespie, of Gibliston	Bath	399	849 13
Somerville, Rev. George Reynolds	F.C. Manse, Logie, Cupar	1	18 -
Souter, Mrs., wife of Alex. Souter	Myreside, Leuchars	2	7 10
Speedie, Alexander, of Kinshaldy	Perth	2,200	820 -
Speedie, John	Lochty, Markinch	53	700 -
Speedie, Robert, & Sons	St. Clairtown, Kirkcaldy	2	453 5
Spence, James	Muirside, Crail	5	22 -
Spence, John Thomas	Crieff	5	15 -
Spence, Trs. of Andrew	Guardbridge, Cupar	3	65 15
Spens, Lieut. Nathaniel James, of Craigsanquhar	Craigsanquhar, Cupar	487	1,054 10
Spowart, Thomas, of Broomhead	Broomhead, Dunfermline	240	1,170 8
Do. do.	Do. (Minerals)	-	637 10

FIFE—continued.

Name of Owner.	Address of Owner.	Estimated Acreage of Property.	Gross Annual Value.
		Acres.	£ s.
St. Andrews, City of	St. Andrews	21	244 10
St. Andrews College Hall Co. (*Limited*)	St. Andrews	2	200 –
St. Andrews District Road Trustees	St. Andrews	1	100 –
St. Andrews Kirk-Session	St. Andrews	10	50 –
St. Andrews Parochial Board	St. Andrews	22	136 3
St. Andrews Railway Company	St. Andrews (*Railway*)	32	1,799 –
St. Andrews Sea Box Society	St. Andrews	3	144 15
Stark, David	Kirkcaldy	2	73 12
Stenhouse, Alexander	Dunfermline	1	55 –
Stenhouse, James, of North Fod	North Fod, Dunfermline	593	831 6
Do. do.	Do. (*Minerals*)	–	196 –
Stenhouse, Trustees of James, jun., and Adam Wardlaw, and Adam Low Wardlaw	Cowdenbeath, Lochgelly	420	400 –
Do. do.	Do. (*Minerals*)	–	2,247 –
Stenhouse, William	Star, Markinch	11	30 –
Stenhouse, Mrs. Rebecca	Juniper Green, Edinburgh	5	88 –
Stephen, Andrew Cree, and Rev. W. Cree Stephen	Kincardine-on-Forth } Culross	129	100 –
Stewart, Rev. David	Manse, Kennoway	8	49 10
Stewart, Gavin	Newburgh	1	39 5
Stewart, Rev. William, and Elizabeth Stewart	Burntisland	2	99 –
Stewart, Mrs. Janet Fraser, of St. Fort	St. Fort, Newport	2,664	5,054 13
Stewart, Mrs. Margaret	Kettle	3	47 13
Stewart, Mrs. Robert	Barnyards, Kilconquhar	2	7 5
St. Leonard's Parochial Board	St. Andrews	3	11 5
St. Mary's College	St. Andrews	296	762 –
St. Monance Kirk-Session	St. Monance	2	12 15
St. Monance, Town of	St. Monance	15	186 7
Stocks, John	Kirkcaldy	13	321 4
Stocks, John Thomson	Kirkcaldy	82	861 –
Stoddart, Rev. William, of Pittuncarty	Madderty, Crieff	292	304 –
Storrar, Richard	Rossie, Auchtermuchty	153	189 10
Storrar, Mrs., wife of Alex. Storrar	Craigfoodie, Cupar	9	26 5
Strachan, George	Gilston, Largo	1	8 10
Strachan, James	Chance Inn, Cupar	3	8 4
Strachan, William	Chance Inn, Cupar	2	9 –
Straker, John, of Sherdrum	Willington House, Durham	298	250 –
Strathmiglo Feuars	Strathmiglo	6	23 10
Strathmiglo Parochial Board	Strathmiglo	7	24 –
Strong, Christian	Balmullo, Leuchars	3	23 17
Stuart, Francis Archibald, of Balmerino	Blandford, Dorset	470	1,047 13
Stuart, Mrs. Joseph Gordon	Balgonie, Markinch	10	542 5
Stuart, Mrs., wife of Rev. Atholl Stuart	Blair-Athol	190	402 –
Sutherland, Janet	Kemback Hill, Cupar	2	6 10
Suttie, Mrs. Pitcairn	Leven	2	91 10
Swan, John	Westfield, Leuchars	24	67 15
Swan, Patrick Don, of Springfield	Springfield, Cupar	186	665 10
Swan, Robert	Kelso	4	17 10
Swan Brothers, and Patrick Don Swan	Kirkcaldy	24	2,375 14
Swan, Heirs of Mrs.	Cupar	3	50 –
Swan, Mrs., wife of John Swan	Leslie	5	52 –
Symers, Helen Halliburton, of Kingskettle	Dundee	302	622 2
Tait, John	Lammerlaws, Burntisland	7	436 4
Tait, John	Kirkcaldy	1	185 –
Taylor, James	Starleyhall, Burntisland	8	120 –
Taylor, Rev. James W.	F.C. Manse, Luthrie, Cupar	1	19 –
Taylor, John	Springfield, Cupar	1	19 7
Taylor, John	Cupar	1	105 –
Taylor, Peter	Dunfermline	6	311 –
Taylor, William Alexander	Cupar	1	169 –
Taylor, Mrs. Magdalene	Pittenweem	4	20 –
Telfer, David, of Balgonar	Balgonar, Saline	209	319 9
Telfer, Trustees of Mrs.	Tillyhill, Saline	3	26 16
Terras, Arthur	Balmullo, Leuchars	2	27 –
Terras, James	Kelty, Kinross	1	44 –
Thom, James, of Leden Urquhart	Leden Urquhart, Strathmiglo	164	160 –
Thom, John, of Catochil	Catochil, Strathmiglo	214	150 –
Thomas, James, of Transy	Forthar, Ladybank	197	671 3
Thoms, John	St. Andrews	84	169 –
Thomson, Andrew	Kennoway	2	18 5
Thomson, David	Kinghorn	1	36 10
Thomson, Rev. David	Manse, Forgan, Newport	10	45 5
Thomson, George	Lochgelly	1	37 15
Thomson, James	Cairneyhill, Dunfermline	3	18 5
Thomson, Trustees of James	Orkie Mill, Kettle	216	528 –
Thomson, John	Cairneyhill, Dunfermline	3	15 –
Thomson, John	Strathmiglo	11	64 6
Thomson, Trs. of John	Pathhead, Kirkcaldy	1	40 10
Thomson, John Anstruther, of Charleton	Charleton, Colinsburgh	4,034	7,505 15
Thomson, Robert, of Seggie	Seggie, Leuchars	429	1,274 –
Thomson, Thomas	Gladney, Cupar	3	18 –
Thomson, Thomas	Largoward, St. Andrews	12	28 –
Thomson, Heirs of Thomas	Logie, Cupar	39	99 5
Thomson, William	Kennoway	1	30 15
Thomson, William	Blebo Craigs, Cupar	2	6 2
Thomson, William Christie	Carnock, Dunfermline	1	39 10
Thomson, Mrs. Robert	Smithfield, Crail	1	12 8
Thomson, Mrs. William	Blebo Craigs, Cupar	10	15 –
Thomson, Isabella	Cairneyhill, Dunfermline	2	8 10
Tivendale, Thomas	Largo	1	46 15
Tod, Archibald	Balmalcolm, Ladybank	1	12 –
Tod, George, of Fairfield	London	46	149 5
Tod, William, of Hilton	Hilton, Cupar	197	405 –
Tod, Mrs. James	Strathmiglo	1	34 6
Todd, Rev. Alexander	Manse, Kingsbarns, St. Andrews	13	70 –
Todd, John	Anstruther	3	149 10
Todd, Heirs of Dr. John	Colinsburgh	40	202 6
Tosh, Trustees of Joseph	Overkellie, Pittenweem	253	532 –
Townhill Coal Company	Dunfermline	1	101 –
Traill or Simpson's Charity	St. Andrews	2	9 10
Trevelyan, Mrs.	Glenfarg, Bridge of Earn	369	290 15
Trotter, Heirs of Thomas	Auchtermuchty	1	2 10
Trotter, Mrs. Christian	St. Andrews	12	45 –
Troup, Alexander	Strathmiglo	2	407 –
Tullis, Robert	Rothes, Markinch	11	215 13
Tullis, Robert Landale	Wester Balrymonth, St. Andrews	60	179 5
Tullis, Robert, & Company	Auchmuty, Markinch	35	1,653 16
Tullis, Mrs. Charles	Haughfield, Ladybank	22	82 –
Tullo, Robert C.	Blebo Craigs, Cupar	1	12 –
Turpie, William	Chance Inn, Cupar	4	17 –
Tweeddale, Marquis of	Yester House, Haddington	400	249 15
Do. do.	Do. (*Minerals*)	–	815 15
Union Bank of Scotland	Glasgow	2	221 –
United College	St. Andrews	1,683	3,272 16
United Original Seceders' Synod	Balmullo, Leuchars	3	14 –
University of St. Andrews	St. Andrews	15	178 5
Urquhart, Rev. Alexander	Manse, Newburn, Largo	22	54 –
Waddell, James	Earlsferry, Elie	2	54 12
Waddell, Mrs., wife of James Waddell	Earlsferry, Elie	7	25 –

FIFE—continued.

Name of Owner.	Address of Owner.	Estimated Acreage of Property.	Gross Annual Value.	Name of Owner.	Address of Owner.	Estimated Acreage of Property.	Gross Annual Value.
		Acres.	£ s.			Acres.	£ s.
Walker, David	Strathkinness, St. Andrews	4	18 6	Wemyss, Trustees of Major James	Wemysshall, Cupar	19	63 —
Walker, David	Crossford, Dunfermline	1	9 —	Wemyss, Trs. of Major James; and James Balfour Wemyss	Wemysshall, Cupar	11	45 7
Walker, Harry	Newport	5	180 —				
Walker, Henry West	Auchtermuchty	37	191 2				
Walker, James	Ceres	4	18 10	Wemyss, James Balfour, of Wemysshall	Wemysshall, Cupar	1,490	2,852 8
Walker, John	Newbigging, Ceres	2	14 —				
Walker, Robert Emery	Dunfermline	3	50 —	Wemyss, Trustees of James Hay Erskine	Wemyss Castle, Kirkcaldy	3,457	4,931 8
Walker, Thomas	Dunfermline	4	175 —	Do. do.	Do. (Minerals)	—	5,333 —
Walker, Trs. of Walter	Kingask, Cupar	232	550 —	Wemyss, Randolph G. E., of Wemyss Castle	Wemyss Castle, Kirkcaldy	3,468	7,383 4
Walker, Mrs. John	Falkland	3	39 8				
Walker, Barbara, of Pitlair	Pitlair, Cupar	168	209 13	Do. do.	Do. (Minerals)	—	3,159 —
Walker, Margaret, Agnes, and Euphemia	Kingask, Cupar	1	10 —	Wemyss, Robert	Kirkcaldy	1	363 —
				Wemyss Bursary Fund	St. Andrews	3	11 6
Wallace, Andrew	Dunfermline	1	100 —	West of Fife Coal Co.	Townhill, Dunfermline	2	93 10
Wallace, Rev. Andrew, of Riggs	Oldhamstocks	110	267 —	White, Trs. of Alexander	Leven	1	131 4
				White, James	Kirkcaldy	2	53 —
Wallace, George	Magask, Cupar	4	40 7	White, John	Newburgh	1	31 —
Wallace, George	Blebo Craigs, Cupar	1	4 15	White, John	Lundin Mill, Largo	1	37 15
Wallace, George Johnstone, of Newtonhall	Newtonhall, Markinch	155	275 —	White, John	Ballingry, Lochgelly	1	10 —
				White, Thomas	Tayport	1	83 10
Wallace, James, of Bankhead	Bankhead, Cupar	235	324 —	White, Catherine	Pitlessie, Ladybank	2	52 15
				Whitefield Coal Company	Lathalmond, Dunfermline	1	31 4
Wallace, James	Brake, St. Andrews	2	16 —	Whitelaw, John	Cupar	2	290 —
Wallace, John	Newton, Falkland	2	13 —	Whyte, David, of Cultmill	Edinburgh	76	85 —
Wallace, Robert Agnew, of Rhynd	Rhynd, Dunfermline	141	159 10	Whyte, Michael	Dunfermline	1	108 —
				Wilcot, Heirs of John	Collessie, Ladybank	4	20 15
Wallace, William, of Newton of Collessie	Newton of Collessie, Ladybank	167	334 10	Wilkie, Andrew	Leven	1	26 —
				Wilkie, Heirs of George	Nottingham, Freuchie, Ladybank	4	99 2
Wallace, Mrs. James	Blebo Craigs, Cupar	5	18 10				
Wallace, Mrs. Mary	Denhead, St. Andrews	1	15 5	Wilkie, John	Rameldry, Ladybank	4	10 10
Walls, James	Dunfermline	3	234 —	Wilkie, Robert	Skellyhead, Kennoway	4	11 12
Walls, Lawrence	Inverkeithing	90	143 10	Wilkie, Mrs. James	Rossieden, Auchtermuchty	1	5 —
Walls, Mrs. Helen	Kinghorn	1	70 —				
Wannan, James	Pitscottie, Cupar	1	20 —	Wilkie, Catherine	Cameron, St. Andrews	65	65 —
Watson, Alexander	Pittenweem	2	207 9	Williamson, John	Clunie, Newburgh	7	51 10
Watson, Alexander, & Son	Blebo, Cupar	3	214 —	Williamson, Rev. Robert	Collessie, Ladybank	6	32 —
				Wilson, Alexander, senior	Denhead, St. Andrews	1	17 —
Watson, David	Crossford, Dunfermline	1	30 10	Wilson, Alexander, junior	Denhead, St. Andrews	7	32 10
Watson, John Cobb	Blebo, Cupar	17	899 7	Wilson, David	Touch, Dunfermline	6	175 —
Watson, William	Ceres	11	41 —	Wilson, Trustees of David	Inchrye, Newburgh	1,112	1,591 —
Watson, Heirs of Rev. William Rankine	Manse, Logie, Cupar	135	104 —	Wilson, George	St. Andrews	3	7 —
				Wilson, Henry	Ballingry, Lochgelly	1	21 10
Watson, Mrs. Henry	Lochgelly	1	74 11	Wilson, James	Cowstrandburn, Dunfermline	4	16 10
Watson, Mrs. Mary J.	Cupar	421	490 —				
Watson, Mrs. Helen	Pittenweem	4	41 10	Wilson, John	Hill Park, Bannockburn	170	134 10
Watson's Mortification Trustees	Burntisland	36	67 12	Wilson, Robert	Dunfermline	1	87 10
				Wilson, Heirs of Robert	Auchtermuchty	4	23 16
Watt, Archibald Anderson, of Denmill	Dundee	175	465 —	Wilson, Trs. of Robert	Cupar	188	372 10
				Wilson, Robert Main	Dunfermline	65	190 —
Watt, James, of Lochmill	Dundee	152	115 —	Wilson, Thomas	Newburgh	3	86 —
Webster, Andrew	Edinburgh	8	16 —	Wilson, Trs. of Thomas	Gilliesfaulds, Cupar	27	81 6
Webster, David	Freuchie, Ladybank	3	22 —	Wilson, William	Dunfermline	1	51 —
Webster, George	Crail	12	30 —	Wilson & Son	St. Andrews	2	103 10
Webster, James	Largoward, St. Andrews	29	69 14	Wilson, Mrs. Alexander	Grange, St. Andrews	2	15 8
Webster, James	Crail	4	45 15	Wilson, Mrs. James	Grange, St. Andrews	9	35 10
Webster, Heirs of James	Cupar	2	34 5	Wilson, Mrs. John	Lochgelly	3	9 12
Webster, John	Callange, Cupar	5	13 10	Wilson, Mrs. William	Falkland	1	46 —
Webster, Rev. John	Manse, Cameron, St. Andrews	24	49 10	Wilson, Mrs. Isabella	Dunfermline	3	13 —
				Wilson's Mortification Trustees	St. Andrews	29	105 —
Webster, Thomas	Teuchats, Largo	19	36 10				
Webster, William	Earlsferry, Elie	1	5 —	Wingate, Alexander, of Wester Pitscottie	Millbank, Alloa	255	402 —
Webster, Mrs. Peter	Largoward, St. Andrews	16	34 —	Wise, George	Innerleith, Ladybank	8	14 —
Webster, Margaret, and Sisters	Burnside, Moonzie, Cupar	1	6 10	Wise, Rev. John	Auchtermuchty	15	49 —
				Wise, Helen	Innerleith, Ladybank	7	9 10
Wedderburn, Frederick L. S., of Wedderburn and Birkhill	Birkhill, Cupar	1,456	2,826 17	Wisemann, Robert	Cupar	2	55 15
				Wishart, John	Grange, Burntisland	15	48 —
Wedderburn, Henry S.	Birkhill, Cupar	1	27 —	Woodcock, Alexander, and William Woodcock	Anstruther, St. Andrews	5	126 15
Weir, Mrs. Jane	St. Andrews	3	15 —				
Welch, Charles, of Rumgally	Cupar	544	1,545 17	Woodcock, William	St. Andrews	6	100 —
				Wood's Hospital, Patrons of	Largo	169	409 12
Welch, Rev. Walter	Manse, Auchtertool, Kirkcaldy	7	41 —	Wotherspoon, William, of Hillside	Hillside, Aberdour	173	665 —
				Wright, Rev. Robert	Manse, Dairsie	7	37 —
Welwood, Allan A. M., of Pitliver	Pitliver, Dunfermline	724	1,187 16	Wright, William	Gallatown, Kirkcaldy	3	172 15
Do. do.	Do. (Minerals)	—	500 —	Wright, Heirs of William	Halfields, Kennoway	97	430 17
Wemyss, Alexander Watson, of Denbrae	Denbrae, St. Andrews	318	747 15	Wylie, Andrew, of Prinlaws	Prinlaws, Leslie	141	3,624 —

FIFE—continued.

Name of Owner.	Address of Owner.	Estimated Acreage of Property.	Gross Annual Value.	Name of Owner.	Address of Owner.	Estimated Acreage of Property.	Gross Annual Value.
		Acres.	£ s.			Acres.	£ s.
Yoole, Mrs. Catherine	Ceres, Cupar	5	48 7	Zetland, Earl of	Aske, Richmond, Yorkshire	5,566	8,339 14
Young, Alexander	Cairneyhill, Dunfermline	2	11 5	Do.	Do. (*Minerals*)	–	832 –
Young, David	Grange, Burntisland	6	1,211 10				
Young, George	Cairneyhill, Dunfermline	2	9 15				
Young, James	Kellie Castle, Pittenweem	1	38 5				
Young, Heirs of James	Hawkleymuir, Kirkcaldy	1	67 3				
Young, Robert	Crossford, Dunfermline	1	16 10				
Young, Trs. of Robert	Colinswell, Burntisland	396	1,009 18	Total Owners of Land of one Acre and upwards		1,772	302,846 741,379 10
Young, Heirs of Robert	Leslie	1	43 –	Total Owners of Lands of less than one Acre in extent		8,638	1,517 164,197 17
Young, William	Baincraig, Auchtermuchty	39	72 –				
Young, Curators of Wm.	Burntisland	8	40 –				
Young, Mrs. John	Anstruther	11	83 7				
Young, Isobel	Blebo Craigs, Cupar	8	22 –				
Young & M'Donald	Tayport	2	126 –	GRAND TOTAL		10,410	304,363 905,577 7
Younger, John B. B. C.	Pitlessie, Ladybank	3	67 10				

FORFAR.

Population in 1871, - - - - - - 237,567.
Inhabited Houses, - - - - - - 25,663.
Number of Parishes, - - - - - - 55.

Name of Owner.	Address of Owner.	Estimated Acreage of Property.	Gross Annual Value.	Name of Owner.	Address of Owner.	Estimated Acreage of Property.	Gross Annual Value.
		Acres.	£ s.			Acres.	£ s.
Aberdeen Town and County Bank	Aberdeen	3	897 12	Arkley, Mary Charlotte	Cooksloch, Dunninald, Montrose	4	26 –
Aberdein, Francis, of Keithock	The Mall, Montrose	645	1,803 15	Arkley, Mary, Charlotte, and Mrs. Stansfeld	Do. do.	659	2,255 –
Aberdein, Gordon, & Co.	Montrose	27	1,589 15	Armit, Mrs. Isabella	London	1	435 3
Adam, Harriet Blair	Portobello	8	83 10	Arnott, Heirs of Mrs. Jean	Brechin	1	19 –
Adams, Mrs. Jean	Easter Oathlaw, Forfar	9	66 –	Atherstone, John G.	Hillside, Montrose	1	45 –
Adamson, David	Kirriemuir	1	31 5				
Adamson, William	Forfar	4	114 12				
Addison, Trustees of James, of Hillock	Hillock, Arbroath	5	39 18	Baird, Alexander, of Ury	Ury, Stonehaven	1,150	2,054 10
Admiralty, Lords of	London	1	208 –	Baird, James	Monifieth	16	52 –
Airlie, Earl of	Cortachy Castle, Kirriemuir	65,059	21664 –	Bairnsfather, Peter, of Dumbarrow	St. Andrews	829	1,297 12
Airlie, Earl of, and Dundee Water Commissioners (jointly)	Dundee	338	1,683 8	Balfour, Alexander	Arbroath	7	68 –
				Banks, William	Monifieth	1	102 10
				Barclay, Robert	Inchbrayock, Montrose	1	40 –
Airth, John	Careston, Brechin	3	16 10	Barclay, Thomas	Montrose	2	103 5
Allan, Alexander, and Mrs.	Eassie, Meigle	7	30 –	Barrie, David	Monifieth	1	97 –
Allan, David	Forfar	6	45 –	Batchelor, Alexander	Finhaven, Forfar	1	162 10
Allan, Mary	8 Prior's Road, Forfar	1	42 14	Baxter, Alexander	Broughty Ferry	1	33 –
Alexander, James	Edzell	53	45 –	Baxter, Trustees of Edward, of Kincaldrum	Kincaldrum, Forfar	581	880 –
Alexander, James	Kirriemuir	3	14 –	Baxter, John	Brechin	2	130 –
Alexander, William	Kirriemuir	3	8 –	Baxter, Right Hon. William Edward, of Kincaldrum, M.P.	Dundee	2,097	3,277 7
Alexander, William Maule	School-house, Monikie	2	18 –				
Alison, Representatives of Colin, of Easter Braikie	Easter Braikie, Montrose	410	821 –	Baxter, Rev. William L.	Careston	8	30 10
Alison, George Lloyd	Dundee	5	85 –	Baxter, Mrs. Jean	Hazel Hall, Dundee	15	300 –
Alison, Heirs of John	Rosehill, Montrose	8	36 –	Baxter, Mary Ann, of Balgavies	Dundee	844	1,397 6
Ancient Hospital, Patrons of	Montrose	7	68 4	Beattie, Mrs. Isabella	Renny Place, Montrose	1	25 10
Anderson, Rev. Alexander	Dun Manse, Montrose	7	40 –	Belford, Mrs. Elizabeth	Forfar	1	9 15
Anderson, Alexander	Dundee	126	488 15	Bell, Alexander	Dundee	4	145 –
Anderson, David	Broughty Ferry	2	70 –	Bell, George, of Balconnel	Balconnel, Menmuir	310	332 –
Anderson, David D.	Monifieth	3	45 –	Bell, James H.	Dundee	3	148 –
Anderson, Francis	Brechin	2	10 15	Bell, Peter, of Pitpointie	Pitpointie, Dundee	209	311 –
Anderson, Trustees of G., and others	Back Muir of Liff	26	56 –	Bell, Mrs. Margaret	Dundee	1	90 –
				Berry, Thomas	Rosebank, Forfar	3	31 –
Anderson, Rev. George	Carmyllie	19	46 10	Bertie, David	Edzell, Brechin	2	7 5
Anderson, Rev. James	Kirkden	8	33 –	Bertie, James	Flatnadriegh, Edzell	2	13 –
Anderson, James	Hudson's Bay, North America	2	40 –	Binny, David, senior	Dove Cot Cottage, Forfar	5	51 5
				Binny, James	Gowanbauk Feus, Forfar	3	30 5
Anderson, James	Millfield, Arbroath	50	116 10	Birnie, Trustees of Charles	Montrose	4	265 –
Anderson, Heirs of J. A.	Lochville, Arbroath	2	68 –	Black, David Dakers	Brechin	3	122 5
Anderson, Rev. Mark L.	Menmuir	6	43 –	Borrie, John	Agra Bank, Carnoustie	3	263 3
Anderson, Mrs. Jane	Carnoustie	3	37 –	Bowman, Mrs. John	Liberton, Edinburgh	3	29 2
Anderson, Mrs. John	Seaton, Arbroath	10	96 –	Boyd, John	Letham, Forfar	1	8 –
Anderson, Trs. of Mrs.	Dundee	50	125 –	Boyd, Rev. John	Kirriemuir	5	53 –
Annand, William	Formal, Alyth	16	35 –	Boyd, Rev. William	Mains, Dundee	21	82 10
Annaud, Mrs., Mrs. Brew, and Ann Matthewson	Knowhead, Alyth	90	90 –	*Brechin, Heritors of Parish of*	Brechin	2	– –
Arbroath Harbour Trustees	Arbroath	5	1,236 6	*Brechin Parochial Board*	Brechin	4	42 –
Arbroath Infirmary, Trs. of	Arbroath	1	80 –	*Brechin, Town of*	Brechin	30	356 16
Arbroath Parochial Board	Arbroath	12	27 10	Bremner, James	Carnoustie	7	36 –
Arbroath and St. Vigeans, Parochial Board of	Arbroath	4	240 –	Briggs, Henry Currer	Saltburn by the Sea	6	39 –
				Briggs, William	Arbroath	1	31 10
Arbroath, Town of	Arbroath	38	424 10	Brodie, John Clerk, of Idvies	Edinburgh	1,910	2,559 15
Arbuthnott, Helen Carnegy, of Balnamoon	Balnamoon, Brechin	8,066	5,204 10	*Broughty Ferry Gas Commissioners*	Broughty Ferry	2	579 –
Archer, Trustees of late Andrew	Coupar-Angus	2	38 –	Brown, Alexander	Kirriemuir	4	18 15
Arklay, Robert, of Ethiebeaton	Ethiebeaton, Dundee	392	785 10	Brown, Alexander Johnston	Carnoustie	2	86 15
Arklay, Thomas, of North Grange	North Grange, Dundee	120	275 –	Brown, Rev. George	Newtyle	8	36 –
				Brown, Joseph	Drainside, Letham	1	12 –

FORFAR—continued.

Name of Owner.	Address of Owner.	Estimated Acreage of Property.	Gross Annual Value.		Name of Owner.	Address of Owner.	Estimated Acreage of Property.	Gross Annual Value.	
		Acres.	£	s.			Acres.	£	s.
Bruce, James	Dundee	305	670	–	Coutts, James Alexander Webster	17 Duke St., Edinburgh	41	54	7
Bruce, Robert	Woodfield, Arbroath	9	26	5	Cowan, James	Broughty Ferry	1	104	–
Bruce, William	Panmure Street, Brechin	1	171	12	Cowan, John	Broughty Ferry	12	1,033	5
Buchanan, Rev. Archibald	Logie-Pert	14	46	–	Cox, Thomas Hunter	Dundee	97	460	10
Buick, Mrs. Joanna	Colliston, Arbroath	4	27	–	Craig, Alexander	Forfar	1	44	17
Buist, Alexander Jefferson	Dundee	7	136	–	Craig, Mrs. Elizabeth	Viewmount, Brechin	9	160	6
Burgess, John	Wellington Pl., Montrose	2	161	11	Craik, Alexander	Forfar	4	130	–
Burgess, Samuel	Hillside, Montrose	1	242	5	Craik, Trs. of late James	Forfar	1	127	15
Burness, Trustees of Robert	High Street, Montrose	1	142	12	Craik, James	Forfar	4	11	18
Burness, William, of Auchnacree	Drummond Place, Edinburgh	421	208	–	Craik, J. & A., & Co.	Forfar	7	813	–
Burns, James	East High Street, Forfar	1	75	16	Crammond, Trs. of George	Dundee	1	36	10
Burr, Rev. Peter Lorimer	Manse, Lundie	8	37	–	Crammond, Robert	Christie Lane, Montrose	3	204	14
Butchart, Mrs. Margaret	Dunnichen, Forfar	1	29	3	Crichton, James	Broughty Ferry	1	55	–
Byars, David	Forfar	9	65	10	Crichton, John Thomas, of Woodside	Woodside, Arbroath	23	85	–
					Crichton, Marriage Trustees of John Thomas and Mrs.	Woodside, Arbroath	266	255	–
Cæsar, Rev. James	Manse, Panbride	6	45	–	Crighton, David, of Ardo	Scone, Perth	262	263	–
Caledonian Railway Company	Glasgow (Railway)	572	107267	7	Crow, James	Letham, Forfar	4	10	–
Do. do.	Do.	2	315	17	Cruickshank, Rev. F.	Manse, Lethnot	9	30	–
Cameron, Rev. Thomas A.	Dunnichen, Forfar	7	35	–	Cruikshank, Augustus W., of Langley Park	Langley Park, Montrose	861	2,231	11
Campbell, Sir James, of Stracathro, Kt.	Stracathro, Brechin	3,846	5,901	–	Cumming, James	Arbroath	12	71	4
Camperdown, Earl of	Camperdown House, Dundee	6,770	8,241	9	Cumming, The Family of Mrs., of Auchinreoch	Auchinreoch, Brechin	219	416	5
Cargill & Co.	Dundee	19	737	10	Cumming, Mary Ann and Margaret, of Tulloes	Tulloes Lodge, Cheltenham	1,305	1,466	2
Cargill, Charles, of Ardownie	Ardownie, Alyth	70	28	–	Cunningham, James	Broughty Ferry	4	151	10
Cargill, James, of Easter Craig	Easter Craig, Alyth	201	157	–	Curr, Heirs of William	Dundee	1	60	–
Cargill, John	Forfar	2	203	6	Currie, Trs. of Alexander	Edinburgh	3	15	–
Cargill, Mrs.	Springfield, Brechin	8	274	4	Cushnie, Andrew	Drummond Park, Brechin	30	75	–
Carmichael, John	Baldovan, Dundee	9	69	–	Dalgetty, Mrs. Jean	Caldhame Feus, Forfar	27	39	–
Carmichael, Peter, of Arthurstone	Arthurstone, Meigle	545	1,047	11	Dalgliesh, William Ogilvie	Dundee	21	142	10
Carnegie, Hon. Charles, of Dalgety	Dalgety, Brechin	144	195	1	Dalhousie, Earl of	Brechin Castle	136,602	55601	16
Carnegie, Henry A. F. L., of Boysack	Boysack, Arbroath	3,670	5,171	14	Dall, James	Dall's Lane, Brechin	8	54	–
Carnegie, John	Redhall, Fordoun	1	15	–	Dargie, George	Forthill, Broughty Ferry	1	13	5
Carnegie, John R. S., of Tarrie	Tarrie, Arbroath	1,440	2,982	19	Darling, James Stormonth, of Lednathy	Edinburgh	2,828	511	13
Carnegie, William, of Dunlappie	Dunlappie, Brechin	492	650	–	David, William	Kirriemuir	2	3	–
Carnegy, Patrick A. W., of Lour	Lour, Forfar	4,206	5,024	19	Davidson, Rev. Alexander M.	Manse, Kinnell	26	42	10
Cattanach, Charles	Lunanhead Feus, Forfar	3	9	–	Davidson, Stephen	Broughty Ferry	2	146	–
Cay, Mrs. Jane	Broughty Ferry	1	83	18	De Malahide, Trustees of Lord and Lady, of Simprim	Simprim, Meigle	1,685	2,801	14
Chalmers, Patrick, of Aldbar	Aldbar, Brechin	3,844	3,893	2	Dempster, George H., of Dunnichen	Dunnichen, by Forfar	3,970	4,867	19
Chapel, David	Arbroath	1	70	–	Dick, David	Ravensby, Carnoustie	1	13	15
Chaplin, George C. C., of Colliston	Colliston, Arbroath	723	937	3	Dick, James	Ravensby, Carnoustie	1	6	10
Chree, Rev. Charles	Manse, Lintrathen	7	30	–	Dick, Douglas Drummond, of Pitkerro	Pitkerro, Dundee	349	995	–
Christie, Andrew	Bankhead, Forfar	8	30	–	Dick, Mrs. Margaret, and D. E. Mudie	10 Lauriston Park, Edinburgh	98	200	–
Christie, David	Woodville, Arbroath	4	12	–	Dickson, Trustees of late David, of Clocksbriggs	Clocksbriggs, Forfar	205	393	10
Christie, Rev. John	Manse, Arbirlot	5	42	–	Dickson, James A., of Woodville	Woodville, Arbroath	137	535	10
Christie, William, of Roseville	Roseville, Arbroath	9	159	3	Dickson, John, of Limefield	Limefield, Brechin	37	99	–
Christie, William	Edzell, Brechin	116	100	–	Dickson, John F.	Carnoustie	11	270	–
Clark, David	Little Brechin, Brechin	3	8	–	Dodds, Heirs of Thomas	Baldovie, Dundee	1	31	–
Clark, James, of Loanhead	Loanhead, Alyth	45	75	–	Doig, William	Back Muir of Liff, Dundee	10	20	–
Commissioners of Supply of Forfarshire	Forfarshire	3	180	–	Don, Trustees of James, of Bearshill	Bearshill, Brechin	12	186	10
Comrie, Rev. Alexander	Carnoustie	1	30	–	Don, John	Dundee	2	100	–
Constable, Patrick	Balledgarno, Inchture	424	526	6	Don, Robert	Dundee	5	44	–
Corsar Brothers	Arbroath	2	622	–	Don, William Gilbert	Dundee	1	150	–
Corsar, C. W., and A. J. Lyon, of Seaforth	Seaforth, Arbroath	10	93	5	Don, Trustees of W. G.	Forfar	1	46	1
Corsar, David	Arbroath	4	134	–	Donaldson, Heirs of John	Wellington Place, Montrose	2	71	1
Corsar, David, & Sons	Arbroath	3	1,098	–	*Dorward's House of Refuge*	Montrose	5	140	–
Corsar, James	Arbroath	1	50	–	Dorward, James	Drummitermuth, Letham	9	8	15
Corsar, William H.	Arbroath	6	110	–	Douglas, Trustees of Major Archibald	Broughty Ferry	1	90	–
Couper, Frederick, of Douglasmuir	Edinburgh	142	116	10	Douglas, Robert, of St. Ann's	St. Ann's, Brechin	13	86	2
Couper, George G. D.	Arbroath	2	279	5					
Coutts, Charles	Kirriemuir	2	22	10					

FORFAR—continued.

Name of Owner.	Address of Owner.	Estimated Acreage of Property.	Gross Annual Value.	Name of Owner.	Address of Owner.	Estimated Acreage of Property.	Gross Annual Value.
		Acres.	£ s.			Acres.	£ s.
Douglas, Lieut.-Colonel William, of Brigton	Broughty Ferry	164	409 —	Fleming, Alexander	Frazerfield, Arbroath	10	31 5
Dow, James	Folda, Alyth	3	8 —	Fleming, David	Blacklunans, Blairgowrie	75	150 5
Dow, Heirs of John	High Street, Montrose	1	231 4	Fleming, Rev. James	The Manse, Kettins	7	32 —
Dowall, Charles	Wormyhills, Arbroath	5	206 1	Fleming, Peter, of Dunay	Dunay, Alyth	155	68 —
Downie, Mrs. Alexander	Rosebank, Arbroath	3	12 10	Fleming, William	13 Springfield, Dundee	164	42 10
Drimmie, Daniel, & Co.	Monifieth	118	356 2	Flowerdew, Heirs of William A.	Dundee	1	21 2
Duke, David	Brechin	3	64 19	Fodd, Alexander	6 Prior's Road, Forfar	5	30 6
Duke, David & Robert	Brechin	4	626 17	Foote, Rev. A. L. R.	Brechin	16	124 10
Duke, George	Kirriemuir	353	240 —	Forbes, Thomas	High Street, Arbroath	1	274 1
Duke, James	Kingsmuir Feus, Forfar	4	10 —	Forbes, Ann	Redfield Place, Montrose	3	81 11
Duke, Rev. William	Manse, St. Vigeans, Arbroath	9	51 —	*Forfar, Heritors of Parish of*	Forfar	1	100 —
Duncan, Alexander	Kirriemuir	1	5 —	*Forfar Infirmary*	Forfar	2	50 —
Duncan, Charles	M'Ritch, Lintrathen	20	59 12	*Forfar Parochial Board*	Forfar	5	80 —
Duncan, James	Kirriemuir	8	29 15	*Forfar, The Town of*	Forfar	863	2,199 10
Duncan, John, of Sunnyside	Parkhill, Arbroath	740	1,214 18	*Forfarshire Commissioners of Supply*	Forfar	2	372 —
Duncan, Patrick Geekie	East Memus, Kirriemuir	58	182 —	*Forfarshire Prison Board*	Forfar	1	168 —
Duncan, Trustees of Peter	Broughty Ferry	3	120 10	Forrest, Trustees of late James	Kirriemuir	15	31 10
Duncan, Philip	Little Brechin	1	46 3	Forrest, Trs. of Robert	Kirriemuir	31	189 6
Duncan, Trustees of Mr. and Mrs.	Dalwhirr, Alyth	42	70 —	Forrest, William, of Easter Ogil	Easter Ogil, Kirriemuir	430	592 10
Duncan, Mrs. Martha	Tarbrax, Forfar	1	17 10	Fothringham, Trustees of Captain T. F. S., of Fothringham	Fothringham House, Forfar	8,821	9,512 16
Duncan, Mrs. John	Dundee	1	70 —				
Dundee Burial Board	Dundee	44	15 —	Fothringham, Mrs. M. S., of Tealing	Tealing House, Dundee	3,708	3,887 8
Dundee Harbour Trustees	Dundee	1	50 —				
Dundee Orphan Institution	Dundee	2	224 —	Fowler, Alexander	Carnoustie	2	188 15
Dundee Water Commissioners	Dundee	87	7,944 15	Fowler, John	Carnoustie	3	59 2
Durward, William	Rosebank, Brechin	2	14 —	Fraser, Henry and Douglas	Arbroath	7	200 —
Duthie, Alexander	Carnoustie	1	28 —	Fraser, Trustees of James	Montrose	6	43 19
Duthie, David	Renny Place, Montrose	2	58 —	Fraser, Patrick Allan, of Hospitalfield	Hospitalfield, Arbroath	1,045	1,890 18
				Fraser, Rev. William R.	Manse, Maryton	8	49 —
Eadie, Charles	Fothringham Feus, Forfar	1	10 —	Fridge, Rev. Alexander	Manse, Lunan	7	32 10
East Mill Company	Brechin	33	937 10	Fulton, Robert	High Street, Montrose	1	357 6
Edward, Allan	Dundee	15	310 —	Fyffe, Alexander	Carnoustie	3	12 —
Edward, Charles	Dundee	3	180 —	Fyffe, George	Carnoustie	1	22 5
Edward, James, of Balruddery	Balruddery, Dundee	600	1,364 12	Fyffe, John, of Kingston	Forfar	110	491 —
Edward, Heirs of James	Forfar	8	82 3	Fyffe, Trustees of William, of Newton	Newton, Brechin	270	260 —
Edward, John	Little Brechin	10	25 —	Fyffe, Heirs of Mrs.	Bowriefauld, Letham	5	8 —
Edwards, Mrs. Elizabeth	Kirriemuir	1	4 15				
Edwards, Mrs.	South Muir, Kirriemuir	1	22 10				
Elder, Rev. William	Manse, Tealing	8	35 —	Gall, George	Brechin	2	15 —
Ellis, Mr. and Mrs. West, of Balhall	Balhall, Menmuir	1,209	1,049 —	Gammell, Major Andrew, of Whitewell	Dover Street, London	369	340 —
Erskine, Augustus J. W. H. K., of Dun	Dun, Montrose	1,727	3,571 2	Gardner, Rev. Alexander	Church Street, Brechin	8	85 —
Erskine, James Erskine, of Linlathen	Linlathen, Dundee	1,619	4,447 1	Gardyne, Lieut.-Col. C. G., of Finhaven	Finhaven, Forfar	4,078	4,273 2
Esdaile, Rev. David	Manse, Rescobie	11	45 —	Gardyne, Thomas, M.B., of Middleton	Middleton, Arbroath	1,395	2,130 18
Ewan, Francis Molison	Broughty Ferry	1	70 —	Garland, Trs. of William	Beechwood, Arbroath	93	290 —
Ewan, John	Dundee	696	1,154 3	*Gas Light Company*	Brechin	1	334 15
Ewen, James	Millbank, Forfar	13	144 3	*Gas Light Company*	Kirriemuir	1	130 —
				Gas Light Company	Montrose	1	1,100 10
Fairweather, Brodie, & Co.	Carnoustie	15	213 16	Geekie, Alexander, of Baldowrie	Baldowrie, Coupar-Angus	483	581 15
Fairweather, David	Longhaugh, Brechin	13	87 11	Gellatly, Mitchell, & Co.	Dundee	1	200 —
Fairweather, David	Montrose	1	277 19	Gentle, James	Coupar-Angus	2	35 —
Fairweather, James	Prior's Place, Forfar	3	14 15	Gibb, James	School-house, Kettins	2	10 10
Fairweather, Robert	Kirriemuir	5	11 —	Gibson, Andrew	Ravensby, Carnoustie	1	6 10
Falconer, Alexander	Glasmonies, Letham	5	10 5	Gibson, Trs. of Alexander, of Dunlappie	Dunlappie, Brechin	574	686 —
Falconer, Thomas	Kirriemuir	5	17 5				
Farquhar, Rev. William	5 Cecil Place, Paisley Road, Glasgow	659	1,197 10	Gibson, David	Montrose	5	18 5
Farquharson, Thomas, of Whitehill	Whitehill, Alyth	300	153 10	Gibson, George Soutar	Forfar	2	19 9
				Gibson, James	Forfar	2	18 12
Farquharson, Jean	Letham	1	10 —	Gibson, John	American Muir, Dundee	1	9 —
Feathers, Peter A.	Broughty Ferry	1	208 14	Gibson, William	Broughty Ferry	3	115 —
Fenton, Peter	Templeton, Auchterhouse	1	10 15	Gilroy, Alexander	Dundee	8	212 —
Ferguson, Trs. of John	Banks of Brechin	2	20 —	Gilroy, George	Dundee	13	454 11
Ferguson, John	Redfield, Montrose	10	63 5	*Glamis Trustees*	Glamis	17,034	20566 8
Ferguson, Mrs. Elizabeth	Monifieth	1	134 15	Glass, John	Little Brechin	3	11 —
Fergusson, Robert	Dundee	1	80 —	Glass, Helen	Chapelton of Boysack, Arbroath	4	13 —
Fife, Earl of	Duff House, Aberdeenshire	4,837	5,768 3	Gold, Ann, of Townhead	Montrose	60	76 —
Finlay, William	Broughty Ferry	1	35 —	Gordon, Alexander, of Ashludie	Ashludie, Dundee	198	535 —
Fitchett, William	Little Brechin	5	13 15	Gordon, Alexander, & Co.	Arbroath	3	977 5

FORFAR—continued.

Name of Owner.	Address of Owner.	Estimated Acreage of Property.	Gross Annual Value.	Name of Owner.	Address of Owner.	Estimated Acreage of Property.	Gross Annual Value.
		Acres.	£ s.			Acres.	£ s.
Gordon, Trs. of Harry, of Charleton	Charleton, Montrose	1,056	2,244 15	Hunter, Charles, and Mrs. (jointly)	Forfar	7	55 6
Gordon, Trustees of late James	Kirriemuir	24	174 10	Hunter, James, junior	Dundee	1	30 —
Gordon, John	Dundee	8	115 —	Hunter, Patrick	Kirkton of Lundie, Dundee	9	20 —
Gordon, Samuel	Little Brechin	7	23 —	Hunter, Heirs of William	Kirriemuir	30	75 —
Gordon, Thomas	Lightnie, Lethnot	126	130 —	Hunter, William George, of Burnside	Burnside, Forfar	1,842	2,062 13
Gordon, Mrs. Janet	Exeter	4	71 14	Hunter, Elizabeth, of Polmood	Polmood, Kinnell	209	40 —
Gordon, Mrs. Lockhart	Kettins, Coupar-Angus	6	30 —	Hurry, Trustees of John	Glencoe Park, Forfar	14	38 —
Graham, James	Kirriemuir	2	7 10	Hutcheson, Trustees of James, of Coldside	Coldside, Alyth	70	90 —
Graham, Clementina Stirling, of Duntrune	Duntrune House, Dundee	441	1,365 10	Hutton, Isobel	Forfar	1	85 12
Grant, James	Forfar	4	338 —				
Grant, Rev. Robert	Manse, Stracathro	10	40 10				
Grant, Thomas Macpherson, of Pitforthie, etc.	Edinburgh	4,713	7,082 5	Imrie, William Blair, of Lunan	Lunan, Arbroath	297	746 11
Grant, William	Backhowe, Letham	1	7 —	*Inch Bleaching Company*	Brechin	6	178 —
Grant, Mrs. Ann	Kirriemuir	3	10 —	Inglis, Rev. Robert	F.C. Manse, Edzell	1	25 —
Gray, William	Ravensby, Carnoustie	3	25 10	Innes, Rev. James	Do. Panbride	1	22 —
Gray, William	Broughty Ferry	1	164 5	Inverarity, John D., of Rosemount	Rosemount, Montrose	260	326 —
Gray, Mrs. Alexander	Letham, Forfar	2	10 13	Irons, Alexander	Forfar	3	18 —
Gray, Baroness	Kinfauns Castle, Perth	1,639	2,940 8	Irvine, David	Forfar	4	21 10
Gray, Mrs. Carsina G., of Carsegray	Carsegray, Forfar	3,260	4,849 3				
Greig, Janet	Whitfield Feus, Dundee	8	74 17				
Grewar, John, of Inverharity	Inverharity, Alyth	215	34 10				
Grimond, Joseph	Dundee	6	300 —	Jack, James	Tarbrax, Forfar	1	12 —
Guild, John	Dundee	3	125 —	Jackson, Trustees of late William, of North Balluderon	Kirriemuir	327	273 2
Guild, Robert	Dundee	5	162 —				
Guild, Thomas	Kirriemuir	3	7 —				
Gunn, Rev. W. E. B.	Manse, Montrose	5	71 —	Jackson, Mrs.	Kirriemuir	278	677 17
Guthrie, Trs. of Alexander	Townhead, Brechin	3	83 17	Jameson, George	Broughty Ferry	6	338 —
Guthrie, James	Brechin	2	3 10	Jamieson, George A., as Judicial Factor on Glasswell Trust Estate	Edinburgh	683	904 13
Guthrie, Trustees of James Alexander, of Craigie	Craigie, Dundee	309	979 —				
Guthrie, John, of Guthrie	Guthrie Castle, Arbroath	3,231	5,026 14	Jamieson, James	Crudie, Arbroath	4	18 —
Guthrie, Martin, & Co.	Brechin	2	398 19	Jessiman, George	Dundee	1	145 15
Guthrie, Mrs. Lingard	Taybank, Dundee	1	22 10	Jobson, Ann	Dundee	3	148 —
Guthrie, Clementina and Elizabeth	Townhead, Brechin	2	45 —	Johnston, Rev. Frederick	Manse, Tannadice	10	39 4
				Johnston, Trustees of late George	Kirriemuir	41	95 —
Haldane, Rev. James Ogilvy	Manse, Kingoldrum	15	30 —	Johnston, James, of Lawton	Lawton, Arbroath	255	450 —
Haldane, Robert	Edinburgh	140	426 2				
Halkett, Rev. Andrew	Manse, Brechin	19	80 13	Johnston, Trustees of Catherine William	High Street, Montrose	1	110 1
Hallyburton, Lord John Frederick Gordon	Hallyburton House	5,119	7,048 16				
Hannay, John, of Dennoray	Gavenswood, Banff	551	455 10	Keill, George, of Whitfield	Whitfield, Dundee	183	470 —
Hardie, James	Kirriemuir	8	16 3	Keith, George, of Usan	Usan, Montrose	970	2,261 14
Harrower, George Kerr	Dundee	7	88 —	Kerr, Representatives of late Christopher	Dundee	17	120 —
Hay, Rev. James	Manse, Inverkeillor	4	32 10	Kerr, Peter, of Gallowden	Braikie, Arbroath	40	120 —
Hay, Trs. of late John, of Letham Grange	Letham Grange, Arbroath	2,397	4,758 17	Kerr, Sylvester Rait, of Forthill	Forthill, Dundee	51	302 7
Hay, Trustees of Catherine	Balendoch, Alyth	50	100 —	Kerr, Thomas, of Grange	Grange of Monifieth, Dundee	591	1,313 —
Hean, Mrs. Elizabeth	Dundee	7	25 —				
Henderson, Alexander	Dundee	4	163 —	Kerr, Mrs. Agnes, and others	Nether Finlarg, Dundee	402	430 —
Henderson, Frank	Dundee	10	100 —				
Henderson, George	Brechin	1	8 —	Kinloch, Colonel, of Kilrie	Kilrie, Kirriemuir	2,059	2,732 6
Henderson, George David Clayhills, of Invergowrie	Invergowrie, Dundee	1,742	3,378 4	Kinloch, Sir George, of Kinloch, Bart.	Kinloch, Meigle	1,251	232 5
Henderson, Graham	Forfar	1	29 9	Kinloch, John, of Cairn	Cairn, Kirriemuir	648	659 —
Henderson, James	Dundee	4	20 —	Kinloch, Cecilia	Carnoustie	4	36 10
Henderson, John	Hillside, Montrose	1	133 10	Kinloch, Cecilia, and Mrs. Lingard Guthrie	Carnoustie	295	501 4
Henderson, Mrs. Mary	West Derry, Alyth	64	58 —				
Henry, Isaac Anderson, of Woodend	Woodend, Madderty, Crieff	2	133 12	Kinnear, James	Carcary, Brechin	10	41 10
Herdman, William R. F.	Rattray, Blairgowrie	2	24 18	Kinnear, Joseph	Forfar	1	5 —
Hill, James, of Auchranny	Auchranny, Alyth	100	70 —	Kintore, Earl of	Keith Hall, Aberdeen	1,053	1,562 6
Hill, Peter	Muir of Brechin	8	20 —	*Kirriemuir, Heritors of Parish of*	Kirriemuir	2	66 —
Hird, George	Letham	3	43 18				
Home, Countess of	The Hirsel, Coldstream	5,209	7,356 —	*Kirriemuir, Parochial Board of*	Kirriemuir	9	15 —
Hood, Rev. Alexander O.	Manse, Farnell, Brechin	13	47 15	Knight, William Gray, of Jordanstone	Jordanstone, Meigle	5	6 —
Hood, David	Kirriemuir	2	15 10				
Hood, James	Yeaman Shore, Dundee	1	7 —				
Hood, Rev. John	F.C. Manse, Letham	1	22 —	Kyd, Trustees of Andrew, of Wareslap	Wareslap, Arbroath	24	79 2
Hood, William	Birkhill, Dundee	5	12 —	Kyd, Charles	Caldhame Feus, Forfar	2	6 5
Hood, Mrs. Isabella	Ravensby, Carnoustie	31	101 8	Kyd, David	Carnoustie	2	53 —
Howie, James	Kirriemuir	1	23 —	Kyd, George	Timbergreen, Arbroath	5	30 —
Hunter, Charles	Forfar	13	52 2				

FORFAR—continued.

Name of Owner.	Address of Owner.	Estimated Acreage of Property.	Gross Annual Value.		Name of Owner.	Address of Owner.	Estimated Acreage of Property.	Gross Annual Value.	
		Acres.	£	s.			Acres.	£	s.
Kyd, Trustees of George	Rosebrae, Arbroath	26	161	–	Lyell, Rev. Hugh Arbuthnott	Manse, Auchterhouse	10	49	–
Kyd, Elizabeth	Rosefield, Arbroath	10	119	–	Lyell, Sophia Georgina	Kinnordy, Kirriemuir	866	807	15
Kyd, Margaret	Frazerfield, Arbroath	3	11	10	Lyon, Hugh, of Glenogil	Glenogil, Kirriemuir	2,100	1,471	10
Kyd, Mrs. Marjory	Caldhame Feus, Forfar	1	5	10	Lyon, Major William	32 South Street, London	6,888	1,427	12
Kydd, Margaret	Woodside, Arbroath	3	14	–	M'Bride, Rev. Neil	Manse, Glenisla	20	30	–
Laing, Rev. James M.	Blairduff, Inverurie	3	26	–	M'Culloch, William	Dundee	2	407	10
Laird, Trs. of Col. David, of Strathmartine	Strathmartine, Dundee	1,794	3,883	10	Macdonald, William Kid	Arbroath	8	131	–
Laird, George Wright, of Denfield	Denfield, Arbroath	265	493	–	Macdonald, William Macdonald, of St. Martins	St. Martins, Perthshire	2,801	5,617	10
Laird, James	Carnoustie	3	87	10	M'Donald, William	Dundee	18	70	–
Laird, R. B.	Monifieth	16	101	–	M'Ewen, Trustees of James	Broughty Ferry	2	415	9
Laird, William, & Co.	Forfar	4	402	–	M'Gavin, Robert, of Ballumbie	Ballumbie, Dundee	746	3,104	14
Laird, Ann	Carnoustie	5	18	10	M'Glashan, Alexander, of Peathaugh	Peathaugh, Alyth	44	32	10
Lamb, David	Brechin	1	62	–	M'Glashan, John	Broughty Ferry	1	232	–
Lamb, John	Glencadam, Brechin	27	140	–	M'Ilwraith, Rev. A.	F.C. Manse, Lochlee	1	20	–
Lamb & Scott	Brechin	15	663	3	M'Inroy, William, of The Burn	The Burn, Brechin	23	8	10
L'Amy, John Ramsay, of Dunkenny	Dunkenny, Glamis	475	700	–	M'Intyre, Rev. Malcolm	Manse, Monikie	9	20	–
Langlands, George	Woodside Feus, Arbroath	5	15	–	M'Intyre, W. A.	Craigie Mill, Dundee	6	161	15
Law, Mrs.	Forfar	2	101	13	Mackenzie, James Thomson, of Kintail	Kintail, Ross-shire	7,129	435	–
Lawrence, James	Cumnock, Ayrshire	2	21	–	M'Kenzie, George	Dundee	2	65	–
Leighton, G. D., and Mrs. Soutar, of Cairndrum	Cairndrum, Brechin	292	309	–	M'Kenzie, John, of Nether Alric	Nether Alric, Alyth	500	130	10
Leonard, Peter	Arbroath	7	34	10	M'Kenzie & Reid	Montrose	1	325	–
Leslie, Peter Barty	Ruthven, Meigle	2	26	10	M'Kenzie, Simon and Charles, of Borland	Borland, Alyth	250	105	10
Letham Feuar's Society	Letham	4	37	16	M'Kenzie, Christina	Little Brechin	6	15	15
Lind, John	Fintry Feus, Dundee	1	33	–	Mackie, John, senior	Brechin	1	80	–
Lindsay, Alexander	Little Brechin	41	107	–	Maclagan, Representatives of Mrs. C. A., of Glenquioch	Glenquioch, Kirriemuir	2,216	1,070	14
Lindsay, Rev. David	Manse, Eassie, Meigle	12	47	–	Maclaren, James	Dundee	10	160	10
Lindsay, James, & Co.	Kirriemuir	2	8	10	M'Laren, James, of Balgillo	Balgarrock, Forfar	456	636	13
Lindsay, John	London	3	30	–	Maclean, Dorothea Munro, and Colin Geo. Macrae	14 Gloucester Place, Edinburgh	390	671	14
Lindsay, Stewart	London	5	17	10	M'Nicoll, David, of East Cummock	East Cummock, Alyth	425	146	10
Lindsay, Walter	Little Brechin	5	12	10	M'Nicoll, James	Dalnakebbocks, Alyth	40	47	–
Lindsay, Mrs. Jean	Rossie, Montrose	2	22	18	M'Nicoll, Ann	Holmyrie, Alyth	68	42	10
Lindsay, Mrs. Susan	Kirriemuir	8	14	–	M'Pherson, Rev. John Gordon	Manse, Ruthven, Meigle	28	45	–
Lindsay, Elizabeth	Halfpennyburn, Forfar	55	233	5	Malcolm, Robert	Dundee	5	146	–
Littlejohn, David Stewart	Dundee	17	338	–	Malcolm, William	Murroes, Dundee	1	17	5
Livingston, Trustees of late William	Carnoustie	2	67	1	Mands, James	Forfar	1	15	17
Lorimer, James	21 Hill St., Edinburgh	55	238	10	Mands, William	Forfar	1	4	2
Low, Alexander	Margie, Edzell, Brechin	105	160	–	Marnie, Alexander	Arbroath	8	17	10
Low, Alexander	Dundee	5	206	–	Marnie, Isabella and Charlotte, of Deuchar	Deuchar, Fearn	421	344	10
Low, Trustees of Bishop	Airlie Street, Brechin	8	80	18	Marr, Mrs. John	Forfar	3	53	3
Low, James	Kirriemuir	5	13	15	Marshall, James Scott	Dundee	3	94	–
Low, James F.	Monifieth	6	369	10	Marshall, Rev. William	Coupar-Angus	1	22	–
Low, John	Birkhill, Dundee	2	51	10	Martin, David	Dundee	2	95	–
Low, Trustees of John	Forfar	2	111	8	Martin, George	Kinnettles, Forfar	1	10	–
Low, Rev. Walter	Manse, Lochlee	800	48	–	Martin, James	Carluke, Lanarkshire	4	12	–
Low, William	Kirriemuir	3	15	–	Martin, James	Dundee	1	391	–
Low, Mrs. Margaret	Maryfield, Arbroath	5	15	–	Masson, Mrs. Christina	Little Nursery, Montrose	11	138	3
Lowden, John	Forfar	1	280	–	Mather, Mrs. Alexander	113 High Street, Brechin	1	22	2
Lowson, Andrew, of Elmbank	Elmbank, Arbroath	13	1,994	15	Mather, James	Monifieth	1	14	3
Lowson, Trustees of David, of Springfield	Springfield, Arbroath	37	469	3	Matthew, Trustees of Jas.	Letham	4	14	–
Lowson, Rev. D. R.	Carlisle	6	108	–	Matthewson, David, of Balloch	Balloch, Alyth	69	55	–
Lowson, George, junior	Forfar	1	63	3	Matthewson, David, of Little Kilry	Little Kilry, Alyth	88	185	–
Lowson, James, junior	Forfar	2	147	18	Matthewson, James, of Mid Derry	Mid Derry, Alyth	113	160	–
Lowson, James, younger	Forfar	5	76	10	Maule, Honourable Mrs. Elizabeth, of Fearn	London	6,992	3,639	6
Lowson, John, junior	Forfar	13	666	3	Meffan, Jane	Forfar	19	819	11
Lowson, John, & Son	Forfar	3	770	18	Menzies, Alexander	School-house, Tealing	2	12	–
Lowson, William	Carnoustie	2	74	5	Methven, Thomas Erskine	Broughty Ferry	2	172	7
Luis, John Henry	Dundee	6	280	–	Mill, Charles John	Kirriemuir	2	63	3
Luke, James	Dundee	3	148	–	Millar, John	Kingsmuir, Forfar	3	2	7
Lumgair, Robert	Arbroath	1	151	10	Millar, John	Edinburgh	185	325	–
Lunan, Robert, and William	Damside, Forfar	102	182	6	Millar, Rev. John Primrose	Carnoustie	1	30	–
Lunatic Asylum, Managers of	Montrose	96	870	15					
Lyall, David, of Gallery	Gallery, Montrose	1,576	1,931	11					
Lyall, John	Hillside, Montrose	1	45	–					
Lyell, Alexander, of Gardyne	Gardyne, Arbroath	940	1,057	3					
Lyell, Trustees of late Charles, and others	Kirriemuir	5,728	6,040	9					
Lyell, Sir Charles, of Kinnordy, Bart.	Kinnordy, Kirriemuir	500	706	9					

FORFAR—continued.

Name of Owner.	Address of Owner.	Estimated Acreage of Property.	Gross Annual Value.	Name of Owner.	Address of Owner.	Estimated Acreage of Property.	Gross Annual Value.
		Acres.	£ s.			Acres.	£ s.
Millar, John	Kingsmuir Feus, Forfar	5	6 5	Nicol, Alexander	Letham, Forfar	2	15 11
Millar, Trustees of Patrick	Balbeuchly, Dundee	281	445 –	Nicoll, Trustees of late James	Kinclune, Kirriemuir	505	552 –
Millar, Robert	Dollarbeg, Dollar, Stirling	153	214 –	Nicoll, Rev. James	Manse, Murroes	6	36 –
Millar, Robert	Flowerdale, Balbeggie, Perth	15	42 18	Nicoll, John	Pitruchie, Forfar	15	94 5
Millar, Robert, & Sons	Montrose	11	595 15	Nicoll, Thomas	Dundee	2	70 –
Millar, Mrs. D.	Backmuir of Liff, Dundee	5	12 10	Norrie, Charles, & Sons	Dundee	3	176 –
Millar, Mrs. William, and Mrs. Isabella Martin	Backmuir of Liff, Dundee	5	11 –	Norrie, William H.	Dundee	5	100 –
Milligan, Rev. Peter	Manse, Guthrie	9	45 10	*North British Railway Coy.*	Edinburgh (Railway)	4	640 –
Miln, Alexander, of Milton	Raesmill, Inverkeillor	257	375 –	*Northern Lights, Commissioners of*	Edinburgh	2	90 –
Miln, Alexander Hay, of Woodhill	Woodhill, Carnoustie	404	813 7	Northesk, Earl of	Ethie Castle, Arbroath	4,844	7,761 18
Miln, Robert	Viewfield, Arbroath	5	70 –	Oakenhead, Trustees of Robert	Newington Lane, Brechin	3	45 –
Milne, Alexander, of Kinneries	Kinneries, Arbroath	247	299 –	Ochterlony, Sir Charles M., Bart.	St. Andrews	1,025	1,295 8
Milne, Rev. George Gordon	Manse, Cortachy, Kirriemuir	13	45 –	Ogilvie, Andrew	Dundee	3	100 –
Milne, Trustees of James	Kirriemuir	1	178 6	Ogilvie, David	Kingsmuir Feus, Forfar	3	8 8
Milne, John, of Clacknockater	Clacknockater, Alyth	125	62 –	Ogilvie, Walter	Kirriemuir	3	10 10
Milne, William	Pearsie, Kirriemuir	2	12 –	Ogilvie, Mrs. David	Broughty Ferry	5	114 –
Milne, William	Letham, Forfar	1	5 5	Ogilvy, Donald, of Clova	Balnaboth, Kirriemuir	21,893	3,515 13
Milne, Mrs. Isabella	Forfar	4	122 18	Ogilvy, Trustees of George, of Kirkbuddo	Kirkbuddo, Forfar	1,439	1,523 8
Milne, Magdalene	Little Brechin	15	37 10	Ogilvy, George L., of Newton Mill	Newton Mill, Brechin	78	160 15
Minto, Earl of	Minto, Hawick	3,446	3,308 2	Ogilvy, John, of Inshewan	Edinburgh	2,716	2,244 9
Mitchell, Professor A.	Gowanbank, St. Andrews	14	59 –	Ogilvy, Sir John, of Inverquharity, Bart., M.P.	Baldovan, Dundee	1,431	3,626 4
Mitchell, Alexander	Afflochie, Brechin	2	42 4	Ogilvy, John	Arbroath	2	83 –
Mitchell, David, of Scotston	St. Cyrus, Montrose	467	1,357 3	Ogilvy, Trustees of Peter W., of Ruthven	Ruthven, Meigle	401	580 –
Mitchell, Trustees of George	Banks of Brechin	79	262 17	Ogilvy, Robert	Kirriemuir	5	8 –
Mitchell, Trustees of late James	Affleck, Dundee	452	1,332 6	Ogilvy, Thomas	High Street, Brechin	22	167 10
Mitchell, John	Dundee	1	76 –	Ogilvy, Lieut.-Col. Thos. W., of Ruthven	23 Grafton St., London	6,336	5,734 12
Mitchell, Robert	Dundee	1	115 –	Ogilvy, Mrs. Charles	Eastbank, Brechin	4	90 –
Mitchell, Robert	Leith	1	54 3	Ogilvy, Mrs. C. L. H. Wedderburn	Ranagulzion, Blairgowrie	2,100	224 5
Mitchell, Rev. W. L.	Aberdeen	30	35 –	Ogilvy, Dorothea Maria, of Clova	Clova, Kirriemuir	6	6 –
Mitchell, William	Muirtown of Ballochy, Montrose	17	41 10	Ogilvy, Margaret and Helen	Milnacraig, Alyth	4	8 –
Mitchell, William	Montrose	2	235 10	Orchar, James G.	Dundee	1	95 –
Mitchell, Mrs. Catherine	Carnoustie	1	58 –	Orrock, David	Kirriemuir	3	17 15
Moncur, James	Monifieth	2	180 4	Orrock, David	Broughty Ferry	1	20 –
Monifieth Parochial Board	Broughty Ferry	5	10 –	Oswalds, Guthrie, & Craig	Brechin	1	434 10
Montrose Harbour Trustees	Montrose	7	2,631 5	*Panmure Golf Club*	Monifieth	1	25 –
Montrose, Heritors of Parish of	Montrose	10	250 –	Parker, Mrs. Susan	Aberdeen	1	71 2
Montrose Kirk-Session	Montrose	13	92 –	Paris, Andrew	Carnoustie	4	40 10
Montrose, Town of	Montrose	662	993 –	Paterson, James	March of Gardyne, Letham	41	61 5
Montrose and Bervie Railway Company	Montrose (Railway)	12	145 –	Paterson, James, of Kinnettles	Kinnettles, Forfar	1,183	2,818 8
Moon, James	Dundee	1	94 –	Paterson, James S.	East Seaton, Arbroath	1	153 –
Moonlight, Thomas	Bellevue, Arbroath	9	36 –	Paton, Charles	Carnoustie	1	18 10
Morgan, James	Grange of Conon, Arbroath	354	444 15	Paton, David	Letham, Forfar	1	20 –
Morgan, Representatives of William, of Balbinny	Balbinny, Forfar	358	551 9	Paton, Francis Balfour	Hillside, Montrose	680	603 –
Mount, Trustees of G. D., of South Balluderon	South Balluderon, Dundee	136	280 –	Paton, John G.	Dundee	7	110 10
Morrison, Rev. Peter	Manse, Clova, Kirriemuir	3	15 –	Paton, J. & G.	Montrose	11	1,836 –
Mudie, James	Dundee	4	75 –	Paton, Thomas Bell	Hillside, Montrose	9	130 –
Mudie, John, of Pitmuies	Pitmuies, Arbroath	2,085	3,617 16	Paton, William	American Muir Feus, Dundee	10	33 –
Mudie, Robert Aitken	Dundee	3	125 –	Paton, Mrs. Charles	American Muir Feus, Dundee	1	10 –
Muir, James	Arbroath	6	257 10	Paton, Mrs. Helen	The Mall, Montrose	4	68 –
Munro, Sir Thomas, of Lindertis, Bart.	Lindertis, Kirriemuir	5,702	6,580 8	Patullo, George	Carnoustie	4	51 10
Murray, David	Forfar	2	160 5	Patullo, James, of Persie	Dundee	8	140 –
Murray, Mungo, of Lintrose	Lintrose, Coupar-Angus	992	1,703 1	Patullo, Trustees of John	Newgate House, Arbroath	8	115 –
Murray, Robert	Hillside, Montrose	1	26 –	Pennycook, Trustees of P., of Lochlands	Lochlands, Arbroath	90	335 15
Mustard, William, of Viewbank	Brechin	11	85 –	Petrie, Trs. of late John	Carnoustie	1	16 –
Mustard, Mrs. Elizabeth	Alyth	32	43 –	Philip, George	Letham	3	10 –
Myers, Mrs. John	Hillside, Montrose	3	126 10	Philips, Mrs. David	Cliff House, Arbroath	4	50 –
Myles, John	Forfar	1	210 10	Pierson, James A., of Guynd	Guynd, Arbroath	1,486	2,092 18
Myles, Rev. Thomas	Manse, Aberlemno	11	36 –	Pitcairn, John, as Her. Cr. of John Thomson	Cupar-Fife	6	14 5
Napier, Rodney Barclay	Hillside, Montrose	17	182 9				
Neilson, Alexander	5 Chapel Place, Montrose	2	184 8				
Neish, James, of Laws	Laws, Dundee	1,075	1,876 7				
Neish, William, of Tannadice	Tannadice House, Forfar	889	1,472 19				

FORFAR—continued.

Name of Owner.	Address of Owner.	Estimated Acreage of Property.	Gross Annual Value.	Name of Owner.	Address of Owner.	Estimated Acreage of Property.	Gross Annual Value.
		Acres.	£ s.			Acres.	£ s.
Playfair, Peter, of West Bendochy	West Bendochy, Coupar-Angus	334	260 –	Salmond, James	Carsegownie, Forfar	391	462 10
Police Commissioners	Dundee	36	– –	Salmond, James	Lochshade, Montrose	5	22 –
Popham, Admiral	Cardean House, Meigle	60	23 10	Salmond, Joseph	Arbroath	6	78 –
Porter, James	Lochee, Dundee	1	4 –	Salmond, William, & Sons	Arbroath	2	462 –
Potter, Trs. of William	Forfar	12	29 8	Sandeman, Frank	Dundee	3	130 –
Powrie, James, of Reswallie	Reswallie, Forfar	125	205 –	Scott, David	Brechin	3	52 –
				Scott, George A.	Brechin	1	50 –
Preceptory of Maison Dieu	Brechin	1	20 10	Scott, George, of Renmure	Renmure, Brechin	467	724 –
Presslie, Rev. William	Tarfside, Lochlee	1	11 –	Scott, Robert	Dundee	3	14 –
Proctor, Trs. of James	Kirriemuir	1	30 12	Scott, Rev. Robert	Manse, Craig	8	46 –
Public Park, Curators of	Brechin	8	24 –	Scott, William	Ravensby, Carnoustie	4	12 –
Public Park, Trustees of	Kirriemuir	5	13 –	Scott, Lady, of Balgay	Balgay, Dundee	300	1,328 4
				Scrimgeour, James	Arbroath	2	68 10
				Shanks, Alexander, & Co.	Arbroath	3	280 5
				Shanks, James	Roseley, Arbroath	11	110 –
				Sharp, John	Dundee	7	250 –
Rait, James, of Anniston	Anniston, Arbroath	978	2,743 17	Shaw, David	Edinburgh	154	62 1
Rait, Elizabeth	Broughty Ferry	1	30 –	Shaw, Trustees of Thomas, of Shawfield	Shawfield, Kirriemuir	504	120 –
Ramsay, David, of Wilton	Wilton, Lethnot	151	185 –				
Ramsay, David	Rosebank, Arbroath	4	12 –	Shaw, William, of Finigand	Finigand, Blairgowrie	1,605	314 10
Ramsay, Rev. David O., of Westhall	Closeburn, Thornhill	363	700 –	Sheill, John, of Smithfield	Smithfield, Dundee	612	1,115 12
Ramsay, Trustees of Dr.	Broughty Ferry	6	598 15	Shepherd, George, of Lundie	Lundie, Tarves, Aberdeenshire	1,085	550 –
Ramsay, James	Dundee	5	200 –				
Ramsay, Sir James H., of Bamff, Bart.	Bamff House, Alyth	1,027	1,215 –	Shepherd, John	Herdhill, Kirriemuir	6	15 15
				Sheriff, Charles	Downfield, Dundee	1	21 10
Ramsay, Heirs of James	Dundee	4	12 –	Shiress, William	Brechin	1	83 10
Ramsay, Trustees of late John	American Muir Feus, Dundee	8	62 15	Sim, William, of Lunanbank	Edinburgh	100	261 15
				Simpson, George B.	Dundee	2	125 –
Ramsay, John	Newbigging, Lethnot	143	90 –	Simpson, Rev. James W.	F.C. Manse, Glenisla, Alyth	6	24 –
Rattray, James	Ascreavie, Kirriemuir	1	4 –				
Rattray, John	Templebank, Glamis	7	28 –	Simpson, James	Dundee	7	24 –
Rattray, Peter	Kirriemuir	2	3 10	Simpson, Thomas	Gowanbank Feus, Forfar	7	34 18
Rattray, Thomas	Kirriemuir	5	6 10	Simpson, Thomas, of Newton Bank	Newton Bank, Arbroath	72	147 –
Reid, James	Kirriemuir	1	7 –				
Reid, Trustees of James	Meikle Kenny, Kirriemuir	5	192 8	Sims, David	Banks, Brechin	4	20 –
Reid, Rev. John	Manse, Monikie	9	42 –	Small, James, of Brewlands	Brewlands, Alyth	10,300	1,889 10
Reid, Peter	Dundee	71	150 –				
Reid, Peter	Forfar	1	103 10	Small, John	Coupar-Angus	2	8 –
Reid, Rev. Thomas	Manse, Airlie	7	30 –	Smart, J. & J.	Brechin	3	277 –
Renny, James	Balrenny, Brechin	55	86 5	Smieton, James, & Sons	Carnoustie	20	1,378 17
Renny, Samuel	Jock's Lodge, Arbroath	1	79 18	Smieton, Thomas Anderson	Dundee	3	165 –
Richards & Company	Montrose	6	1,512 10	Smith, Charles	Broughty Ferry	1	65 –
				Smith, Henry	Dundee	3	105 –
Rickards, Peter, of Woodlands	Woodlands, Arbroath	387	592 6	Smith, James	Jeanieswell, Arbroath	4	15 –
Ritchie, Andrew	Colliston, Arbroath	4	16 10	Smith, Trustees of James	Cairnbank, Brechin	304	654 –
Ritchie, George	Forfar	11	46 10	Smith, John	Carnoustie	1	51 7
Ritchie, Patrick	Arbroath	2	58 –	Smith, Trustees of Robert, of Balharry	Balharry, Alyth	5,097	1,097 10
Ritchie, William	Dundee	2	158 –				
Robbie, David	Annfield, Arbroath	7	40 –	Smith's Schools, Trustees of	Andover, Brechin	2	60 –
Roberts, Joseph	Mains of Kincaldrum, Forfar	9	22 –				
				Smith, William	Lochhead Feus, Forfar	1	10 10
Roberts, Trs. of William	Forfar	6	344 17	Smith, Mrs. Ann	Renny Place, Montrose	7	80 10
Robertson, Alexander	Forfar	2	50 –	Smith, Mrs. Janet	Kerrystone Bank, Dundee	3	24 –
Robertson, Charles	Kirriemuir	4	11 –	Smith, Ann	Marywell, Arbroath	1	15 –
Robertson, David S., of Cookston Park	Cookston Park, Brechin	689	1,303 2	Smith, Janet	Kingsmuir Feus, Forfar	1	8 –
				Smith, Mary and Clementina	Kingsmuir Feus, Forfar	4	5 16
Robertson, Hercules J., of Hedderwick (Lord Benholm)	76 Great King Street, Edinburgh	501	1,091 10	Snowie, John	Forfar	3	31 5
				Soote, James	Broughty Ferry	9	210 6
Robertson, Peter	Forfar	5	10 –	Soutar, Robert	Bamph, Bervie	8	23 –
Robertson, William	Dundee	3	128 –	Souter, William	160 East High Street, Forfar	3	18 –
Robertson, William, of Drumfork	Drumfork, Alyth	500	280 10	Southesk, Earl of	Kinnaird Castle, Brechin	22,525	21811 17
Robertson, William	Ravensby, Carnoustie	1	38 5	Souttar, Samuel	Fairmuir, Dundee	2	59 –
Robertson, William	Rosemount, Blairgowrie	1	8 –	Spalding, Charles	Auchterarder	62	171 –
Robertson, Mrs. Ann	Kirriemuir	2	7 5	Spankie, James	Newton of Panbride, Carnoustie	1	25 –
Robertson, Mrs. Janet	Broughty Ferry	1	10 –				
Robertson, Amelia, per Alexander Anderson, Curator Bonis	Herdhill, Kirriemuir	4	15 –	Spied, Henry, of Ardovie	Ardovie, Brechin	1,005	1,291 6
				Spence, Trs. of Andrew	Broughty Ferry	2	166 –
				Spence, Charles	Broughton, Manchester	200	165 –
Rogers, James Samuel	Rose Mill, Dundee	4	109 –	Spence, James	Kirriemuir	6	21 16
Rolland, Louisa, of Abbeythune	Abbeythune, Arbroath	120	308 –	Spence, James	Dundee	6	210 –
Ross, Alexander	Kirriemuir	4	20 –	Stansfeld, Mrs.	Dunninald, Montrose	4	24 –
Ross, Rev. David S.	Manse, Edzell, Brechin	23	47 –	Stark, David	Arbroath	4	10 10
Ross, George	London	2	45 –	Steel, John	Minto, Hawick	2	16 –
Ross, William, & Co.	Montrose	1	263 –	Steel, Ann and Margaret	North Wells, Liff, Dundee	9	22 –
Ruxton, Representatives of David	Chance Inn, Arbroath	4	42 10	Steele, David	Forfar	10	42 10
				Steele, John	Forfar	9	182 17
				Steele, Isabella	Forfar	74	157 17

FORFAR—continued.

Name of Owner.	Address of Owner.	Estimated Acreage of Property.	Gross Annual Value.
		Acres.	£ s.
St. John's Episcopal Congregation	Forfar	1	75 –
Stephen, Alexander	Dundee	4	100 –
Stephen, William	Dundee	4	– –
Stevenson, Rev. Charles F.	Manse, Barry, Carnoustie	6	34 10
Stevenson, Rev. John	Manse, Glamis, Forfar	7	42 –
Stevenson, Rev. Patrick James	Manse, Coupar-Angus	6	15 –
Stevenson, Rev. Patrick	Manse, Inverarity, Forfar	17	45 –
Stevenson, Rev. Robert	Manse, Forfar	9	68 –
Stevenson, Mrs.	Cookston, Brechin	1	25 –
Stewart, John	Church Street, Broughty Ferry	5	348 15
Stewart, John Barclay	Little Brechin	3	7 –
Stewart, John L. D., of Glenogil	Glenogil, Kirriemuir	5,524	510 –
Stewart, Ogilvy, & Co.	Kirriemuir	3	162 –
Stewart, William & David	Broughty Ferry	13	65 –
Stewart, Mrs. Agnes	60 Kemback Street, Dundee	4	12 –
Stewart, Mrs. Ann	Upper Drumgley, Glamis	2	6 –
Stewart, Mrs. Peter	Broughty Ferry	2	12 –
Stirling, Alexander	Broughty Ferry	2	9 –
Stiven, John	Kirriemuir	9	106 5
Stiven, William	Dundee	3	110 –
Strachan, James	Dundee	2	105 10
Strachan, Peter	Fintry Feus, Dundee	1	156 10
Strachan, Robert	Friockhiem	1	24 18
Strachan, Samuel	Brechin	4	80 8
Strang's Mortification, Managers of	Forfar	70	160 5
Strathmore, Earl of	Glamis Castle, Glamis	4,908	2,861 4
Stuart, Francis Archibald, of Balmerino	Balmerino, Fife	145	378 15
Stuart, Rev. Harry	Manse, Oathlaw, Forfar	13	42 –
Stuart, Peter	Broughty Ferry	1	80 –
Sturrock, William	Cailes, Murroes, Dundee	3	16 –
Sturrock, William	Auchterhouse, Dundee	7	23 10
Sturrock, William	Forfar	5	64 6
Sturrock, William	Bents of Turin, Forfar	41	40 –
Sutherland, Mrs. Margaret	Glasgow	1	55 4
Suttie, James	Letham, Forfar	3	12 –
Swinburne, Lieut.-Col. James, of Marcus	Marcus, Forfar	649	528 18
Symers, Helen Hallyburton, of Eassie	St. Helens, Dundee	320	799 –
Tailyour, Thomas Renny, of Borrowfield	Borrowfield, Montrose	557	2,081 7
Tarbat, Alexander	Forfar	5	42 14
Tarbat, John	Over Auchenleish, Alyth	42	17 15
Taylor, Alexander	Letham, Forfar	8	9 5
Taylor, James	Letham Mill, Forfar	8	4 –
Taylor, John	Cupar-Fife	37	65 2
Taylor, Thomas	Broughty Ferry	5	85 –
Taylor, Walter	Dundee	449	605 10
Taylor, Elizabeth	Cupar-Fife	4	36 14
Taylor, Helen	Fettercairn	2	21 –
Taylor, Margaret	Cupar-Fife	3	32 10
Tennent, Charles, & Co.	Glasgow	2	412 –
Thomas, John	Perth	390	765 –
Thomas, Robert, of Noranside	Newtyle	900	871 4
Thoms, Patrick Hunter, of Aberlemno	Dundee	347	525 10
Thoms, Thomas Watt, of Craiksfolds	Dundee	87	125 –
Thoms, Heirs of William	Forfar	15	30 –
Thomson, Andrew	Forfar	3	14 –
Thomson, Rev. Richmond S.	F. C. Manse, Arbirlot, Arbroath	1	25 –
Thomson, William Gordon	Dundee	3	125 –
Thornton, Trustees of late Archibald	Forfar	6	78 8
Thornton, John	Forfar	7	111 17
Thow, Robert, of Turnabrain	Turnabrain, Lochlee	18	14 –
Tosh, William Henderson	Dundee	8	27 –
Trail, Anthony	Dundee	1	80 –
Trinity House	Dundee	2	122 10
Turnbull, Hector	Forthill, Broughty Ferry	2	59 –
Turner, Rev. Duncan	F.C. Manse, Tealing, Dundee	1	25 –
Turner, Rev. Robert	Manse, Kinnettles, Forfar	10	57 –
Urquhart, Daniel	Broughty Ferry	3	125 –
Valentine, Trustees of Mrs.	Letham, Forfar	2	11 –
Waddell, Rev. William	Manse, Fearn, Brechin	10	40 –
Walker, Alexander	Bogside, Kirriemuir	4	13 –
Walker, Alexander	United States of America	2	12 –
Walker, James, of Ravensby	Ravensby, Carnoustie	322	1,045 10
Walker, John	Arbroath	2	215 –
Walker, Joseph	Williesmill Burn, Brechin	10	25 –
Wallace, George	Brechin	1	154 –
Wallace, Robert	Carnoustie	1	19 –
Warden, Alexander	Arbroath	1	8 –
Warden, Alexander J.	Dundee	2	70 –
Waterston, David, of Pitreuchie	Pitreuchie, Forfar	193	969 3
Watson, David Matthew	Bullionfield, Dundee	33	860 12
Watson, James	Kirriemuir	1	58 10
Watson, John	Montrose	5	14 10
Watson, Trs. of Thomas	Forfar	8	35 –
Watson, Agnes, Ann, and Peter	Liff, Dundee	21	103 18
Watt, John A., of Meathie	Meathie, Forfar	436	642 5
Webster, Alexander	12 Christie Lane, Montrose	2	59 16
Webster, Representatives of David	Mill of Balrownie, Brechin	9	34 –
Webster, F. & W.	Arbroath	1	318 15
Webster, James	Kirriemuir	22	120 9
Webster, Trs. of James, of Wester Meathie	Wester Meathie, Forfar	320	668 13
Webster, James, of Balmuir	Balmuir, Dundee	787	2,571 5
Webster, Trs. of James, of Flemington	Flemington, Brechin	417	600 –
Webster, John	Rosemount, Montrose	2	26 10
Webster, Patrick, of Westfield	Westfield, Forfar	156	273 10
Webster, William	Balbirnie House, Brechin	4	23 10
Webster, William	Fintry Feus, Dundee	2	303 –
Wedderburn, Frederick Lewis S., of Wedderburn and Birkhill	Birkhill, Cupar-Fife	1,494	3,529 5
Wedderburn, Mrs. Catherine Maclagan, of Pearsie	Pearsie, Kirriemuir	3,784	1,363 1
Weinberg, Isaac Julius	Dundee	3	200 –
Wells, Trustees of Mrs. Margaret	Forfar	1	54 4
Wharncliffe, Lord	Belmont Castle, Meigle	6,926	9,267 10
Whitson, William	Brechin	1	37 –
Whitton, Andrew, of Couston	Couston, Newtyle	1,402	900 –
Whyte, Archibald	Hayston, Kirriemuir	4	25 –
Whyte, David	Sydney, New South Wales	4	15 –
Whyte, Trustees of Mrs. Isabella	Forfar	2	17 5
Whyte, Mrs. Jane	Fiddes, Fordoun	1	29 10
Whyte, Mrs. Magdalen	Monifieth	2	4 –
Whyte, Robert	Clocksbriggs Feus, Forfar	3	7 –
Whyte, Trustees of William	Forfar	2	270 3
Whyte, William	Letham, Forfar	2	10 –
Wighton, William, of Grange of Barry	Grange of Barry, Dundee	333	764 16
Wilkie, David & John	Kirriemuir	1	200 –

FORFAR—continued.—(MUNICIPAL BOROUGH OF DUNDEE.)

Name of Owner.	Address of Owner.	Estimated Acreage of Property.	Gross Annual Value.	Name of Owner.	Address of Owner.	Estimated Acreage of Property.	Gross Annual Value.
		Acres.	£ s.			Acres.	£ s.
Wilkie, Duncan, of Auchlishie	Auchlishie, Kirriemuir	250	249 —	Young, Heirs of Charles	Pearse Street, Brechin	1	12 15
Wilkie, James, of Tillyarblet	Tillyarblet, Kirriemuir	56	70 —	Young, James	Forfar	6	36 10
Wilkie, John	Cherryfield, Forfar	6	9 12	Young, James	Little Brechin	3	6 10
Will, Adam	Dundee	11	59 10	Young, Rev. James G.	Manse, Monifieth, Dundee	5	52 —
Willocks, James	Little Brechin	3	6 10	Young, Major William Baird, of Ascreavie	Ascreavie, Kirriemuir	661	501 14
Wilson, Trustees of Mr. and Mrs. J. Ure	Carnoustie	1	26 —	Young, Mrs. Martha	Kirriemuir	1	11 —
Wilson, Rev. John	Manse, Liff, Dundee	12	63 16				
Wilson, Mrs. Helen	Woolmanhill, Aberdeen	4	10 15				
Wishart, David	Nebraska, America	1	8 12	Total Owners of Land of one Acre and upwards		971 552,708	655,927 1
Wishart, George	Drumgley, Glamis	2	5 19	Total Owners of Lands of less than one Acre in extent		3,927 1,144	139,654 6
Wishart, Elizabeth	Letham, Forfar	3	9 —				
Works, H.M. Board of	London	3	20 —				
Wyllie, Catherine	5 Poet's Lane, Brechin	3	47 14				
Yeaman, William	Alyth	160	120 —				
Yeaman, Mrs.	Broughty Ferry	11	110 —	GRAND TOTAL		4,898 553,852	795,581 7

MUNICIPAL BOROUGH OF DUNDEE.

Population over 20,000.

Name of Owner.	Address of Owner.	Estimated Acreage of Property.	Gross Annual Value.	Name of Owner.	Address of Owner.	Estimated Acreage of Property.	Gross Annual Value.
		Acres.	£ s.			Acres.	£ s.
Adie, A. & J.	Dundee	1	875 —	Christie, Sinclair	Dundee	1	66 —
Allan, Mrs. William	Letham	1	25 15	Christie, Mrs. Mary and William	Dundee	3	80 15
Anderson, Trustees of Mrs., of Logie	Logie, Dundee	85	214 3	Cleghorn, William	Dundee	5	1,010 12
Angus' Trustees	Dundee	2	232 9	Cleghorn, William, and Robert Blackadder	Dundee	15	357 10
Armitstead, George, & Co.	Dundee	1	1,009 —	Connel, William	Dundee	1	773 15
				Connel, Mrs. A. B.	U.P. Manse, Lochee	1	429 8
				Cowan, James	Dundee	2	691 10
Barrie, David	Dundee	2	214 18	Cox Brothers	Dundee	45	6,575 7
Barrie, George	Dundee	1	43 5	Cox, George A.	Dundee	16	254 —
Barrie, Trustees of George	Dundee	3	13 17	Cox, James	Dundee	31	341 19
Barrie, John	Dundee	1	24 10	Cox, William	Dundee	12	170 —
Baxter Brothers & Co.	Dundee	19	9,530 7	Craigie Yard Warehouses Company	Dundee	1	1,095 —
Baxter, John Boyd	Dundee	2	110 —				
Baxter, John M.	Dundee	2	140 —				
Baxter, Mary Ann, of Balgavies	Ellengowan, Dundee	6	326 15				
Baxter Park, Trustees of	Dundee	37	20 —	Dalgliesh, William Ogilvie	Dundee	12	370 —
Bell, Thomas	Dundee	5	1,226 —	Dingwall, William	Dundee	1	352 13
Black, Alexander	Dundee	1	42 10	Don Brothers, Buist, & Company	Dundee	3	2,423 5
Black, James	Largo, Fife	2	14 1	Donald, James, junior	Dundee	3	75 —
Blair, William	Dundee	2	496 6	Douglas, Andrew	Dundee	1	649 —
Boase, Henry	Dundee	3	720 —	Douglas, Trustees of Major Archibald	Dundee	16	163 16
Boase & Mudie	Dundee	2	467 12	Dundee Cemetery Company	Dundee	5	50 —
Brownlee, William	Dundee	3	1,252 —	Dundee Gas Commissioners	Dundee	10	12500 —
Buchan, Thomas	Dundee	3	1,698 7	Dundee Harbour Trustees	Dundee	112	28067 4
Buchan, Thomas and James Maclaren	Dundee	2	50 —	Dundee Parochial Board	Dundee	14	1,385 —
Burial Board	Dundee	13	— —	Dundee Regiments of Volunteers	Dundee	1	262 10
				Dundee Royal Infirmary	Dundee	8	749 —
Caird, James K.	Dundee	4	1,170 6	Dundee Seal and Whale Fishing Company	Dundee	1	504 —
Caird, John	Dundee	4	509 15	Dundee, Town of	Dundee	23	2,067 8
Caledonian Railway Co.	Glasgow	1	506 5				
Do. do.	Do. (Railway)	26	5,604 —				
Caledonian & North British Railway Companies	Glasgow and Edinburgh	8	227 2				
Carmichael, Peter	Dundee	3	348 15	Easson, Alexander	Affleck, Dundee	1	771 18
Carmichael, James, & Company	Dundee	2	772 —	Edward, Trustees of Alexander	Dundee	8	200 —

FORFAR—continued.—(Municipal Borough of DUNDEE.)

Name of Owner.	Address of Owner.	Estimated Acreage of Property.	Gross Annual Value.	Name of Owner.	Address of Owner.	Estimated Acreage of Property.	Gross Annual Value.
		Acres.	£ s.			Acres.	£ s.
Edward, A. & D., & Company	Dundee	14	3,820 10	M'Grady, Henry	Dundee	2	185 13
Edward, James	Dundee	2	210 —	M'Intosh, Donald. junior	Dundee	2	137 5
Ewan, John	Dundee	2	1,015 15	Malcolm, James, & Sons	Dundee	2	1,040 —
				Malcolm, Ogilvie, & Co.	Dundee	9	2,081 —
				Marshall, James S.	Dundee	1	102 5
				Marshall, Mrs. C.	Dundee	4	202 10
				Martin, David, & Co.	Dundee	2	95 —
				Martin, Trustees of David	Dundee	1	347 10
Fergusson, William, & Sons	Dundee	2	593 1	Maxwell, Alexander	Dundee	3	822 15
Fleming, David Hood	Dundee	4	508 3	Miller, Charles	Dundee	1	549 18
Foggie, Trustees of William	Dundee	1	380 10	Miller, Oliver G.	Dundee	4	3,149 —
Forfarshire Prison Board	Dundee	2	520 —	Miln, Alexander A.	Dundee	15	573 1
Forrester, Alexander	Dundee	7	215 5	Milne, David	Dundee	1	446 9
				Milne, Trustees of David	Dundee	1	90 —
				Milne, John	Dundee	2	1,191 18
				Mitchell & Graham	Dundee	4	373 —
				Mitchell, John	Dundee	2	437 5
Garland's Trustees	Dundee	1	45 —	Moir, John, & Son	Dundee	2	300 —
Gentle, James	Dundee	3	419 —	Moncur, Alexander	Dundee	1	323 —
Gibson, Robertson, & Co.	Dundee	3	1,055 —	Moncur, Alexander, & Son	Dundee	1	302 —
Gilroy Brothers & Co.	Dundee	4	5,638 10	*Morgan Hospital*	Dundee	5	560 —
Gordon, John	Dundee	3	1,408 —	Morison, W. R., & Co.	Dundee	5	1,426 —
Gordon, John, junior	Dundee	5	93 —				
Gourlay Brothers	Dundee	3	1,810 —				
Grimond, A. D.	Dundee	1	120 —	Neish, James, of Laws	Laws, Dundee	3	491 11
Grimond, J. & A. D.	Dundee	14	2,248 —	Neish, William	London	100	503 8
Guthrie, James A.	Dundee	169	295 7	Nicoll, A. & J.	Dundee	1	680 —
Guthrie, Mrs. Lingard	Dundee	20	200 —	*North British Railway Coy.*	Edinburgh	5	224 —
				Ogilvy's Mortification	Dundee	3	200 10
Halley, William, & Sons	Dundee	3	1,088 10				
Halliburton, William	Dundee	1	179 15				
Hamilton, James	Dundee	3	842 17	Parker, Charles, & Son	Dundee	5	806 16
Henderson, Alexander	Dundee	2	854 —	Paterson, James, of Kinnettles	Kinnettles, Dundee	17	1,052 1
Henderson, Henry, & Sons	Dundee	1	854 —	Patullo, George A.	Dundee	1	65 —
Henderson, John, & Sons	Dundee	1	830 —	Pearce Brothers	Dundee	3	725 —
Henderson, Kenneth W.	Dundee	2	170 —	*Police Commissioners*	Dundee	17	2,084 7
High School, Directors of	Dundee	2	300 —				
Hill, George H.	Dundee	1	1,348 10				
Hillbank Spinning Company	Dundee	2	1,100 —	Rankine, William M., of Dudhope	Dudhope, Dundee	337	1,293 19
Hospital Fund	Dundee	15	348 3	Reid, Peter	Dundee	13	313 15
Hunter, David, of Blackness	Blackness, Dundee	98	924 6	Ritchie & Simpson	Dundee	2	1,142 —
Hunter, David, and *Town of Dundee*	Dundee	20	14 —	Robertson, Alexander	Dundee	1	1,273 13
				Robertson, Charles	Perth	1	21 10
				Robertson & Orchar	Dundee	2	547 —
				Roger's Heirs, and R. Nicoll	Dundee	1	872 14
Ireland, George	Dundee	1	696 17	Rollo, David	Dundee	2	171 15
Isdale, Robert Hawker	Dundee	1	877 19	Rollo, George H.	Dundee	1	30 —
Jessiman, George	Dundee	2	1,421 12	Sandeman, Frank	Dundee	9	— —
Johnston, James	Dundee	3	339 —	Scott, J. & W.	Dundee	1	409 15
				Scott, Lady, of Balgay	Balgay, Dundee	85	224 10
				Sharp, John	Dundee	5	1,470 —
Kennedy, John	Dundee	1	821 —	Shaw, Baxter, & Moon	Dundee	2	560 —
Kerr & M'Farlane	Dundee	1	175 —	Sheill, John	Dundee	1	249 7
Kerr, Trustees of Christopher	Dundee	2	107 15	Shepherd, Walter	Dundee	2	230 —
Kinmond, Luke, & Co.	Dundee	3	1,077 5	Small & Boase	Dundee	5	335 —
Kinnear, Fithie, & Co.	Dundee	2	365 —	Smith, Alexander	Dundee	1	373 16
Kirkland, John	Dundee	2	352 —	Smith, Henry, & Company	Dundee	2	1,275 —
Kirkland, William, & Son	Dundee	2	900 —	Stark, Mary A.	Forfar	3	29 17
				Storrier, Brough, & Co.	Dundee	1	250 —
Laing & Sandeman	Dundee	4	1,315 —				
Liddle, William F.	Lochee	1	106 9	Thompson, W. B.	Dundee	1	180 —
Liff and Benvie Parochial Board	Dundee	4	250 —	Thoms, John, of Clepington	St. Andrews	44	282 —
Little Sisters of the Poor	Dundee	5	88 —	Thoms, Patrick H.	Dundee	14	895 19
Lorimer, Henry	Dundee	1	86 10	Thomson Brothers	Dundee	2	369 —
Low, Alexander, & Son	Dundee	4	1,070 4	Thomson, James	Dundee	1	575 11
Low, David	Dundee	1	310 —	Thomson, Trustees of John	Dundee	7	2,297 6
Lowden, Peter	Dundee	1	301 14	Thomson, John W.	Dundee	2	78 10
Lucas, Charles, & Co.	Dundee	1	250 —	Tosh, William H.	Dundee	2	2,202 14
Lunatic Asylum, Directors of	Dundee	17	1,029 10	*Trades Lane Calendering Co.*	Dundee	2	1,583 —

FORFAR—*continued.*—(MUNICIPAL BOROUGH OF DUNDEE.)

Name of Owner.	Address of Owner.	Estimated Acreage of Property.	Gross Annual Value.	Name of Owner.	Address of Owner.	Estimated Acreage of Property.	Gross Annual Value.
		Acres.	£ s.			Acres.	£ s.
Urquhart, Lindsay, & Co.	Dundee	1	305 —	Yeaman, David	Lochee	2	115 5
				Yeaman, James, M.P.	Dundee	2	1,400 10
				Young, Patrick Brown	Lochee	3	98 6
Walker, Harry, & Sons	Dundee	7	— —				
Walker, J. & H.	Dundee	1	749 —				
Watson, Rev. Archibald	Manse, Dundee	7	94 —				
Watson, David	Dundee	4	76 10				
Watson, Peter S.	Lochee	1	46 —	Total Owners of Land of one Acre and upwards		188	1,879 177,134 17
Watt, Thomas	Dundee	1	10 —				
White, James F.	Dundee	1	215 —	Total Owners of Lands of less than one Acre in extent		4,257	263 270,393 4
Whyte, George D.	Dundee	1	341 8				
Worrall, George	Dundee	1	437 —				
Wybrants Brothers	Dundee	1	430 —	GRAND TOTAL		4,445	2,142 447,528 1

HADDINGTON.

Population in 1871,	37,771.
Inhabited Houses,	7,179.
Number of Parishes,	25.

Name of Owner.	Address of Owner.	Estimated Acreage of Property.	Gross Annual Value.
		Acres.	£ s.
Ainslie, David, of Costerton	Costerton, Blackshiels	39	24 5
Ainslie, John Astley, of Huntington	Huntington, Haddington	267	592 —
Ainslie, Robert, of Elvingstone	Elvingstone, Gladsmuir	1,480	3,662 15
Aitchison, Col. William, of Drummore	Drummore, Musselburgh	121	537 15
Do. do.	Do. (Mines)	—	334 11
Aitchison, Jane, of Morham	Alderston, Haddington	285	466 5
Alexander, Trustees of late William	Prestonpans	2	221 15
Alexander, Mrs. Agnes	Dunse	2	12 5
Allan, Alexander	Edinburgh	64	239 8
Allan, Heirs of Thomas, of Bushelhill	Bushelhill, Dunse	801	331 —
Allan, Matilda	Edinburgh	2	8 8
Anderson, Lieut.-Colonel James Warren Hastings, of St. Germains and Bowerhouse	St. Germains, Tranent	1,364	3,593 3
Do. do.	Do. (Mines)	—	200 —
Anderson, John	Ashfield, Dunbar	6	83 —
Anderson, Major-General John Richard, of Whittburgh, C.B.	Whittburgh, Blackshiels	284	700 —
Anderson, William	Ashfield, Dunbar	2	20 —
Annandale, Alexander, of Westbarns	Bielside, Dunbar	101	1,466 14
Annandale, James Hunter, of Westbarns	Polton, Lasswade	93	1,302 16
Arklay, James, of Kingslaw	Kinninmonth, Dundee	70	280 —
Baillie-Cochrane, Alex. Dundas Ross Wisheart, of Lamington and Penston, M.P.	Lamington House, Biggar	1,750	4,244 2
Do. do.	Do. (Mines)	—	600 —
Baird, Sir David, of Newbyth, Bart.	Newbyth, Prestonkirk	2,021	5,098 11
Baird, Robert Bruce, of Pilmuir	Edinburgh	78	175 13
Balfour, Arthur James, of Whittinghame	Whittinghame, Prestonkirk	10,564	10610 15
Bank of Scotland	Edinburgh	1	90 15
Begbie, Trustees of late George	Oatfield, Drem	12	179 2
Bell, Gideon William, of Fortoun	Woll, Hawick	909	1,396 —
Bernard, Thomas	Holme House, Haddington	7	364 10
Blantyre, Lord	Erskine House, Glasgow	2,953	6,420 13
Bourke, Lady Susan Georgiana Broun, of Coalstoun, wife of Hon. Robert Bourke, M.P.	Coalstoun House, Haddington	2,702	4,843 7
British Linen Company Bank	Edinburgh	1	105 —
Brodie, William	Westbarns, Dunbar	17	636 10
Broun, Archibald, of Johnstounburn	Edinburgh	456	827 10
Brown, James	Coldingham	1	38 16
Bruce, Colonel Walter Hamilton Tyndall, of Kingston	Falkland Palace	445	1,247 2
Buchan, Lady Laura, of Upper Keith	London	701	1,330 —
Buchanan, Rev. John Macgregor	Manse, Innerwick, Dunbar	7	52 —
Buchanan, Rev. Robert	Manse, Dunbar	1	52 —
Burn, Trustees of late Thomas	Haddington	2	91 —
Burn, Helen	Glasgow	2	25 —
Burn, Margaret	Glasgow	2	25 —
Burness, James	Edinburgh	10	34 —
Burnet, Heirs of Rev. Thomas	Viewfield, Dunbar	2	55 2
Cadell, Heirs of Hew Francis	Cockenzie	6	73 10
Cadell, Col. Robert, R.A.	Cockenzie	2	12 —
Cæsar, Rev. William	Manse, Tranent	9	91 10
Callander, Guardians of Henry, of Elphinstone	Prestonhall, Dalkeith	919	2,169 10
Do. do.	Do. (Mines)	—	941 3
Campbell, Thos. Buchanan	Edinburgh	2	70 —
Charteris, Hon. Alfred Walter	Gosford, Drem	4	15 6
Charteris, Hon. Frederick	Eccles, Attleburgh	4	15 6
Charteris, Colonel the Hon. Richard	Gosford, Drem	4	15 6
Christie, Alexander	Ormiston	1	20 —
Church of Scotland		2	16 —
Coalston, Henry	Haddington	1	113 11
Cochrane, Thomas	Bootle	1	33 2
Cochrane, Ann	Bootle	1	33 1
Combe, William	Dunbar	3	66 10
Commissioners of Supply of Haddingtonshire	Haddington	1	89 —
Cook, Rev. John	Manse, Haddington	6	70 —
Coullie, Rev. James	Manse, Pencaitland	8	48 —
Craise, Robert	East Linton	1	23 6
Crow, Thomas	Gullane, Drem	3	16 10
Crown, The	(Crown Property)	7	212 2
Cunningham, Heirs of James	Burghdales, Dunbar	3	52 —
Cuthbert, John	Aberlady, Drem	1	26 12
Dale, Mrs. Barbara	Auldhame, North Berwick	1	75 10
Dalgleish, Heirs of Robert	Tranent	1	15 10
Dalrymple, Charles, of Hailes, M.P.	New Hailes, Musselburgh	1,698	4,586 10
Dalrymple, Sir Hew, of North Berwick, Bart.	Leuchie, North Berwick	3,039	8,856 15
Dawson, James	Aberlady	1	11 16
Dawson, Thomas	Tupgill, Middleham	7	46 10
Deans, James	Haddington	2	76 5
Deans, Trustees of late Henry	East Fenton, Drem	7	35 11
Denman, Lady, of Alderston, wife of Lord Denman	Stony Middleton, Sheffield	315	720 —

HADDINGTON—continued.

Name of Owner.	Address of Owner.	Estimated Acreage of Property.	Gross Annual Value.	Name of Owner.	Address of Owner.	Estimated Acreage of Property.	Gross Annual Value.
		Acres.	£ s.			Acres.	£ s.
Dirleton Village Feuars	Dirleton, Drem	4	8 –	Hamilton, Major Sir William, of Preston and Fingalton, Bart.	India	3	25 –
Dods, Trs. of late William	Haddington	1	77 –				
Donoghue, Patrick	Tranent	1	69 1				
Dow, Mrs. Elizabeth	Tranent	1	91 7	Hamilton, Lady Mary, of Biel and Archerfield, wife of Right Hon. R. A. Christopher Nisbet Hamilton	Biel, Dunbar	14,345	24537 9
Drummond, Henry	Edinburgh	2	44 14				
Drummond, Rev. Thomas	Manse, Bolton, Haddington	8	37 15				
Drysdale, Alexander	Castellan, Dunbar	11	140 –				
Drysdale, David, of Congalton	Edinburgh	338	744 12	Hay, Capt. James George Baird, of Belton	Belton, Dunbar	1,042	1,911 1
Dudgeon, Heirs of Ellis	Belhaven, Dunbar	6	169 10	Hay, Major John Charles, of Hopes	Hopes, Haddington	625	357 10
Dun, John, of Gilston	Dalkeith	1,100	818 19				
Dunbar Sailors Society	Dunbar	10	63 –	Hay, Robert James Alexander, of Linplum	Nunraw, Prestonkirk	2,593	3,939 1
Dunbar, Magistrates and Council of Burgh of	Dunbar	2	128 4	Hay, Trustees of late Peter	Gifford Vale, Haddington	17	92 5
Do. do.	Do. (*Harbour*)	1	61 –	Henderson, William	Edinburgh	15	65 –
Duncan, Lady Elizabeth	St. Anns, North Berwick	4	120 –	Hepburn, Sir Thomas Buchan, of Smeaton, Bart.	Smeaton, Prestonkirk	2,772	7,012 14
Dunlop, Robert	Aberlady	1	26 7				
Dunlop, William	New Zealand	1	5 10				
Durie, Robert Hogg	Tranent	2	50 12	Do. do.	Do. (*Mines*)	–	1,500 –
Durie, Trustees of late Mrs. Isabella	Tranent	5	58 15	Herriot, Samuel	Gullane	1	31 15
Durie, Helen	North Berwick	1	125 15	Hislop, John Fowler, of Burnrigg	Castle Park, Prestonpans	96	611 10
				Hislop, Trustees of late Robert	East Windygoul, Tranent	103	428 15
East Lothian Combination Poorhouse, Trustees of	Prestonkirk	4	210 –				
Elcho, Lord	Gosford, Drem	4	15 6	Hope, Capt. Henry Walter, of Luffness	Luffness, Drem	3,201	6,908 3
Elibank, Lord	Darnhall, Peebles	1,863	5,564 17	Hope, Jessie Ann	Edinburgh	5	37 2
Elly, Trustees of late Andrew	Beggarsbush, Musselburgh	3	27 10	Hopetoun, Earl of	Hopetoun House, Linlithgow	7,967	15369 15
Elphinstone, Lord	Carberry Tower, Musselburgh	384	909 12	Do. do.	Do. (*Mines*)	–	128 –
Do. do.	Do. (*Mines*)	–	551 3	Houston, Colonel Alexander, of Clerkington	Clerkington House, Haddington	5,148	2,267 15
				Howden, Thomas	Maitlandfield, Haddington	14	95 –
Farquharson, Francis	Haddington	2	185 –	Howden, Thomas, junior	Maitlandfield, Haddington	4	72 –
Ferme, John	Haddington	2	188 –	Howden, Christina	St. Laurence House, Haddington	4	22 –
Fletcher, Andrew, of Salton	Saltonhall, Tranent	3,928	6,456 13	Howden, Helen	Ormiston, Tranent	2	25 14
Ford, William	Edinburgh	2	64 –	Howden, Jane	St. Laurence House, Haddington	4	22 –
Forrester, James	Cottyburn, Haddington	2	21 –				
Forrest, John Martine, of Morhambank	Morhambank, Haddington	173	267 10	Hume, John Kippen	India	5	60 –
Forrest, Anne	Tynebank, Haddington	9	80 –	Hunter, James	Prora, Drem	1	43 5
Fowler, William	Dunrobin, Golspie	4	44 3	Hunter, James William, of Thurston	Thurston, Dunbar	6,492	5,713 18
Fowler, John, & Company	Prestonpans	8	632 –	Hunter, William	Edinburgh	7	65 –
France, Peter, of Seafield	Seafield, Dunbar	75	487 10	Huntly, Robert	Dunbar	1	23 –
Free Church of Scotland		3	30 –	Hutchison, Heirs of Mrs. Emma	Tranent	2	28 –
Gillie, Thomas	East Linton, Prestonkirk	1	20 10	Inglis, George	Tranent	2	29 17
Gifford Kirk-Session	Gifford, Haddington	17	43 15	Innes, Alexander Mitchell, of Eastbarns	Ayton Castle	527	2,415 –
Gifford Village Feuars	Gifford, Haddington	53	129 7				
Goldie, Robert George Middleton	Edinburgh	2	42 –	Innes, Thomas Shairp Mitchell, of Phantassie	Phantassie, Prestonkirk	749	2,483 –
Gourlay, Trustees of late David	Gourlayfield, Haddington	5	42 –				
Grainger, Adam	Oldhamstocks	2	10 –	Kedzlie, Heirs of Henry Turnbull	Tranent	3	68 10
Greenfield, Archibald	Prestonpans	11	59 1				
Grieve, Charles Cassils	Bank Park, Tranent	15	107 12	Keith, Rev. William Alexander, of Pogbie	Burham, Rochester, Kent	545	470 6
Grieve, John	Bank Park, Tranent	15	107 12				
Grieve, Mrs. Margaret	Bank Park, Tranent	1	45 –	Kellie, Robert	Haddington	1	238 6
				Kelly, James	India	2	10 –
				Kerr, Rev. Samuel	Manse, Gifford	13	55 –
				Ker, Alexina C. E., of Westmains	Edinburgh	134	103 14
Haddington, Earl of	Tynninghame, Haddington	8,302	13678 10	Ker, Elizabeth M. C., of Westmains	Edinburgh	133	103 13
Haddington, Magistrates and Council of Burgh of	Haddington	11	415 6	Ker, Isabella C. J., of Westmains	Edinburgh	133	103 13
Haddington Parochial Board	Haddington	1	29 10				
Haddingtonshire Lunacy Board	Haddington	13	389 –	Kinloch, Sir David, of Gilmerton, Bart.	Gilmerton, Drem	2,846	7,673 3
Haldane, Isabella	Haddington	2	53 –	Kirkwood, James	Dunbar	2	68 13
Hall, Sir James, of Dunglass, Bart.	Dunglass, Cockburnspath	887	2,158 2	Kirkwood, Thomas	Dunbar	1	100 13
				Knox, Thomas Dobie	Belhaven	1	19 –
Halliday, Thomas	Haddington	1	73 10	Knox, Mrs. Mary	Nungate, Haddington	1	14 –

HADDINGTON—continued.

Name of Owner.	Address of Owner.	Estimated Acreage of Property.	Gross Annual Value.
		Acres.	£ s.
Laidlay, John Watson, of Seacliffe	Seacliffe, North Berwick	720	2,075 17
Lamb, Peter	America	1	58 10
Lamb, Representatives of John	Gullane, Drem	4	46 —
Lauder, Sir Thomas N. Dick, of Fountainhall, Bart.	The Grange House, Edinburgh	600	1,099 19
Do. do.	Do. (Mines)	—	174 7
Lauderdale, Earl of	Thirlstane Castle, Lauder	75	482 13
Lawrie, Charles	East Linton	1	54 —
Lawson, Mrs. Jane	Westbarns	2	103 5
Logie, Rev. William	Manse, Dirleton, Drem	16	55 —
M'Douall, James, of Bankton	Logan, Stranraer	143	460 —
M'Laren, Rev. David	Manse, Humbie, Upper Keith	6	45 —
M'Niven, David, senior	Haddington	6	48 —
M'Watt, Rev. James	Manse, Salton, Tranent	6	39 —
Marjoribanks, Rev. George	Manse, Stenton, Prestonkirk	11	54 10
Marjoribanks, Rev. Thomas Stirling	Manse, Garvald, Prestonkirk	18	52 —
Meikleham, David Stewart	Muirfield, Drem	36	233 —
Mellis, James	Prestonpans	1	100 —
Menzies, Rev. William	Manse, Gladsmuir	7	21 —
Miller, William, of Barneyhill, M.P.	Manderston, Dunse	172	923 4
Mitchell, Rev. Thomas	Manse, Oldhamstocks, Cockburnspath	15	72 10
Mitchell, Mrs. Euphemia	Aberlady	1	28 10
More, James, of Monkrigg	Haddington	329	1,454 12
Murray, Thomas Graham	Edinburgh	5	16 17
Nelson, Trustees of late Charles	Summerfield, Dunbar	54	220 —
Newton, Captain William Drummond Ogilvie Hay, of Newton	Newtonhall, Haddington	2,857	2,818 —
Nimmo, Mrs. Margaret	Tranent	1	92 16
Nisbet, George	Tranent	3	150 18
Nisbet, Trustees of late William Hamilton, of Beil	Beil, Dunbar	2,321	4,003 7
Nisbet, Mrs. Agnes	Tranent	3	12 2
North Berwick Feuars	North Berwick	15	12 —
North Berwick, Magistrates and Council of Burgh of	North Berwick	25	85 10
North Berwick Water Company	North Berwick (Waterworks)	3	60 —
North British Railway Company	Edinburgh (Railway)	414	16871 —
Do. do.	Do.	22	101 3
Oag, Ann	Rosebank, Dunbar	14	107 7
Ogilvie, Mrs. Alexina, of Soutra Mains, wife of William Ogilvie of Chesters	Chesters, Jedburgh	1,269	825 —
Orr, Mrs. Marion	Uddingston	2	160 —
Pape, Trustees of late George	Riggonhead, Tranent	299	847 14
Park, William Robert, of Blegbie	Abbots Meadow, Melrose	839	868 4
Parlane, Rev. William	U.P. Manse, Tranent	4	34 5
Paterson, Adam, of Nether Brotherstone	Edinburgh	175	200 —
Paterson, Trustees of Rev. John	Haddington	1	93 12
Pearson, Charles	Edinburgh	4	26 —
Peffers, Heirs of Alexander	Haddington	1	102 10
Pennycook, Mrs. Jean	Leith	1	18 8
Petticrew, James	Prestonpans	3	108 —
Polson, John, of Tranent	West Mount, Paisley	648	2,038 10
Do. do.	Do. (Mines)	—	300 —
Polwarth, Lord	Mertoun House, St. Boswells	1,848	2,361 6
Porteous, Rev. James	Manse, Prestonkirk	11	60 —
Prestonpans Incorporation of Sailors	Prestonpans	13	55 —
Pringle, Heirs of Andrew	East Linton, Prestonkirk	7	40 —
Punton, Peter	Aberlady Mains, Drem	1	45 10
Purves, Lieutenant-Colonel William	Edenholm, Dunbar	4	70 —
Purves, Trustees of late George	Newhouse, Dunbar	36	238 —
Quarton, John	Kirkcaldy	2	50 10
Rait, George Thomas	London	5	28 —
Reid, Adam Johnston	Rentonhall, Haddington	69	117 16
Reid, David Montgomery	Rentonhall, Haddington	69	117 17
Reid, Mrs. Jemima	Aberlady	3	46 7
Rennie, William, of Winterfield	Oxwell Mains, Dunbar	125	531 1
Riddell, Jane	Edinburgh	3	55 10
Ritchie, Rev. Adam Inch	Manse, Whitekirk, Prestonkirk	8	50 —
Robertson, James, of Tranent	Clydeside House, Renfrew	648	2,038 10
Do. do.	Do. (Mines)	—	300 —
Robertson, Rev. James	Manse, Whittinghame, Prestonkirk	8	54 —
Robertson, William	Glasgow	1	179 4
Ross, Rev. William	Manse, Haddington	7	58 15
Roughead, David	Haddington	8	234 19
Roxburghe, Duke of	Floors Castle, Kelso	3,863	6,281 8
Rutherford, Mrs. Alison	Edinburgh	3	75 13
Ruthven, Lady	Winton Castle, Tranent	2,875	4,662 10
Do.	Do. (Mines)	—	582 6
Sanderson, Mrs. Jean	Prestonpans	1	31 —
Schaw's Hospital, Trustees of	Edinburgh	174	723 9
Do. do.	Do. (Mines)	—	140 6
Scott, Alexander	Hopetoun House, South Queensferry	1	48 —
Scott, George	Galashiels	20	86 4
Scott, Peter	Bonehill, Paddock, Tamworth	2	12 10
Shaw, Mrs. Charlotte, wife of James Shaw	Haddington	3	32 —
Sheriff, Christina	East Linton, Prestonkirk	1	23 5
Simpson, George	Edinburgh	3	25 14
Simpson, Joseph Tait	Edinburgh	3	25 14
Simpson, Heirs of Walter	Dunbar	1	30 —
Simpson, Mary	Tranent	3	25 14
Sinclair, George Lewis	Manor House, Belhaven	6	68 14
Sinclair, John	East Linton, Prestonkirk	1	58 10
Sinclair, John	Abbey Lands, Dunbar	4	54 —
Sinclair, Sir Robert C., of Stevenson, Bart.	Achvarasdale Lodge, Thurso	473	1,041 10
Sinclair, Lord	Herdmanstone, Haddington	545	1,148 15
Sivess, Adam	East Linton	1	25 —
Smellie, Trustees of late Rev. James	Belhaven, Dunbar	3	62 8
Society for Propagating Christian Knowledge	Edinburgh	820	1,185 —
Sprott, Rev. George Washington	Manse, North Berwick	8	65 10
Sprot, James, of Spott	Spott House, Dunbar	1,138	1,873 15
Stair, Earl of	Oxenford Castle, Ford	88	110 —
Stenton Village Feuars	Stenton, Prestonkirk	1	— 10
Stiel's Hospital, Trustees of	Meadowmill, Tranent	11	87 —

HADDINGTON—continued.

Name of Owner.	Address of Owner.	Estimated Acreage of Property.	Gross Annual Value.	Name of Owner.	Address of Owner.	Estimated Acreage of Property.	Gross Annual Value.
		Acres.	£ s.			Acres.	£ s.
Stephenson, William	Heathery Hall, Haddington	13	122 —	United Presbyterian Church	. . . .	2	22 —
Stirling, Charles, senior	Kirkintilloch	3	38 16	Vetch, Heirs of Lieut.-Col. George Anderson, of Caponflat	Hawthornbank, Haddington	107	511 2
Stirling, Mrs. Mary, wife of Charles Stirling, sen.	Kirkintilloch	3	38 15				
Storie, Francis	East Linton, Prestonkirk	3	47 1				
Storie, John	East Linton, Prestonkirk	1	159 18				
Storie, William	East Linton, Prestonkirk	3	78 15	Warrender, Sir George, of Lochend, Bart.	Bruntsfield House, Edinburgh	1,089	3,988 12
Struthers, Rev. John	Manse, Prestonpans	8	82 13	Watson's Hospital, Governors of	Edinburgh	95	300 9
Stuart, Alexander Charles, of Eaglescairnie	Eaglescairnie, Haddington	465	626 17				
Stuart, Rev. James	F.C. Manse, Gifford	1	20 —	Watson, James	Linlithgow	4	154 19
Suttie, Sir George Grant, of Prestongrange and Balgone, Bart.	Balgone, Drem	8,788	9,763 1	Watson, James	Edinburgh	3	37 —
				Watson, William	Haddington	2	152 14
Do. do.	Do. (Mines)	—	1,195 6	Welch, Trustees of late Matthew	Cockenzie	2	32 5
Suttie, Major George Grant	Balgone, Drem	4	15 6	Wemyss and March, Earl of	Gosford, Drem	10,136	22302 3
Suttie, Major James Grant, younger of Prestongrange	Mains, Chirnside	3	15 —	Do. do.	Do. (Mines)	—	226 9
				Whitelaw, Rev. John M.	Manse, Athelstaneford, Drem	6	40 15
Suttie, Robert Grant	Balgone, Drem	4	15 6	White, Heirs of Mrs. Mary	Belhaven, Dunbar	1	110 16
Swinton, Peter Burn	Holyn Bank, Gifford	2	45 10	Wilkie, James	Ratho Byres	4	58 —
Sydserff, Thomas Buchan, of Ruchlaw	Ruchlaw, Prestonkirk	2,200	1,700 16	Wilkie, Heirs of William	Haddington	7	215 8
Syme, George, of Northfield	Northfield, Prestonpans	111	537 7	Wilkie, Mary Emelia Lockhart	Edinburgh	3	60 —
				Wilkie, Marion	Haddington	8	33 —
Tainsh, Rev. John Grant	Manse, Morham, Haddington	6	39 —	Williamson, Rev. William Taylor	Manse, Ormiston, Tranent	10	80 12
				Williamson, William	Tranent	4	56 12
Tait, Rev. James Hill	Manse, Aberlady, Drem	12	95 —	Wilson, Andrew	Tranent	1	113 10
Tait, Robert	Aberlady, Drem	1	38 —	Wilson, John	Tranent	4	69 16
Tait, Robert	Gullane, Drem	1	36 19	Wilson, John	Haddington	1	122 5
Talbot, Christopher Rice Mansel, of Milton, M.P.	3 Cavendish Square, London	186	370 —	Wilson, Robert	Tranent	20	200 14
				Wilson, William	Ormiston, Tranent	2	22 10
Tawse, John, of Bughtknowe	Edinburgh	441	529 10	Wood, John Andrew, of Woodcote	Edinburgh	369	701 11
Tawse, John Wardrobe, of Stobshiel	Edinburgh	1,169	474 12				
Taylor, John Banks	Seton West Mains, Prestonpans	7	90 —	Young, Trustees of late George	Haddington	5	196 —
Thomson, Rev. Arthur	F.C. Manse, Pilmuir, Haddington	2	23 —	Youngson, Thomas Alexander William Andrew	Aberdeen	6	19 10
Thomson, John, of East Craig	Dirleton, Drem	250	621 —	Yule, Sir George Udny, K.C.S.I.	Beechhill, Haddington	15	92 —
Thomson, John	East Linton, Prestonkirk	1	40 10	Yule, John	Yarmouth	2	66 4
Thomson, Rev. Robert Burns	Manse, Spott, Dunbar	8	53 —	Yule, Thomas	Haddington	2	66 5
Tinto, Patrick	Longniddry	2	6 6	Yule, Ann	Haddington	2	66 4
Todrick, Trustees of late Archibald	Haddington	3	131 15	Total Owners of Land of one Acre and upwards 320		171,431	316,324 3
Todrick, Thomas	Tenterfield, Haddington	5	82 —	Total Owners of Lands of less than one Acre in extent 1,191		308	32,885 14
Trevelyan, Arthur, of Tyneholm	Tyneholm, Tranent	693	1,821 5				
Tweeddale, Marquis of	Yester House, Haddington	20,486	11485 4	GRAND TOTAL . . . 1,511		171,739	349,209 17

INVERNESS.

Population in 1871, - - - - - - **87,531.**
Inhabited Houses, - - - - - - **16,575.**
Number of Parishes, - - - - - - **36.**

Name of Owner.	Address of Owner.	Estimated Acreage of Property.	Gross Annual Value.		Name of Owner.	Address of Owner.	Estimated Acreage of Property.	Gross Annual Value.	
		Acres.	£	s.			Acres.	£	s.
Abinger, Lord	Inverlochy Castle, Fort-William	39,414	4,346	11	Cowan, Mrs. Agnes	Beaufort Villa, Inverness	2	45	–
Anderson, James	Inverness	7	55	–	Crown, The	.	1	366	–
Ansdell, Richard, of Moy	Moy, Kingussie	3,000	250	–	Do.	(Fishings)	–	35	–
Arbuckle, Murdo	North Uist, Lochmaddy	1	10	–	Cunningham, John C., of Foyers	Foyers, Gorthlech	22,506	2,466	–
Archibald, George	Hillhead, Ardersier	714	504	–	Dallas, Alexander Grant, of Dunain	Dunain House, Inverness	1,215	490	–
Astley, Trustees of late F. D. P., of Arisaig	Arisaig House, Fort-William	27,960	2,232	–	Darroch, Rev. John	Manse of Portree	500	80	–
					Davidson, Rev. Alexander	F.C. Manse, Harris	1	12	–
Baillie, Evan, of Dochfour	Dochfour, Inverness	141,148	15931	4	Davidson, Donald	Drummond Park, Inverness	33	1,059	–
Baillie, Evan M., and W. M. Baillie	Bristol	150	200	–	Davidson, Hugh, of Cantry	Cantry House, Cawdor	3,228	1,934	9
Baillie, Right Hon. Henry James, of Letterfinlay	Redcastle, Inverness	5,447	762	10	Davidson, James	Inverness	1	35	–
Baillie, John B., of Leys	Leys Castle, Inverness	2,142	1,682	10	Davidson, Robert	Mayfield, Inverness	4	82	10
Baird, Alexander, of Urie	Urie House, Stonehaven; and Inshes House, Inverness	1,662	2,216	12	Dores, Free Church Congregation of	Dores, Inverness	1	16	–
					Dougall, Andrew	Strawberryhill, Inverness	1	60	–
Baird, James, of Knoydart	Inverie, Fort-Augustus	60,000	4,033	–	Douglas, John	Drummond, Inverness	2	25	–
Barclay, Alexander	Drummond, Inverness	3	9	–	Duff, Georgina Huntly, of Muirtown	Muirtown, Inverness	985	922	–
Beatson, Rev. Henry	Barra Manse, Lochmaddy	145	50	–	Duirinish, Minister and Kirk-Session of	Duirinish, Skye	4	12	–
Belford's Hospital	Fort-William	8,001	1,226	3	Dunlop, Alexander, of Cairnduff	Priory Lodge, Largs; and Dalwhinnie, Kingussie	1,313	107	10
Black, George	Inverness	3	209	–
Blackburn, Hugh, of Roshven	Roshven, Fort-William	5,000	320	–	Dunmore, Earl of	South Harris; and Dunmore Park, Stirling	60,000	2,339	3
Biscoe, Thomas P. B., of Newton	Kingillie, Kirkhill	2,349	1,831	–	Eden, Right Rev. Robert	Hedgefield House, Inverness	8	190	–
Bunbury, Major William D.	Willowbank, Inverness	4	95	–	Ellice, Edward, of Glenquoich, M.P.	Glengarry, Fort-Augustus	99,545	6,721	5
Burnett, Newell, of Kyllachy	Kyllachy, Moy	3,015	471	10	Episcopal Church of Scotland	Kinlochmoidart, Strontian	6	16	–
Caledonian Canal Commissioners	Inverness	91	265	10	Eyre, Most Rev. Charles	248 West George Street, Glasgow	14	47	7
Do. do.	Do. (Canal)	1,129	947	–
Cameron, Archibald H. F., of Lakefield	Lakefield, Glen Urquhart	2,200	482	10	Falconer, James	Island Bank, Inverness	2	277	12
Cameron, Donald, of Clunes	Clunes, Kirkhill	283	606	10	Forbes, Arthur, of Culloden	Culloden House, Inverness	3,644	3,903	15
Cameron, Donald, of Lochiel, M.P.	Achnacarry Castle, Fort-William	109,574	7,830	–	Forbes, Duncan George, of Millburn	Millburn, Inverness	92	470	15
Cameron, Rev. Donald	Manse of Kilmorack, Beauly	20	42	–	Forsyth, Rev. William	Manse of Abernethy	30	39	–
Cameron, Duncan	Kingussie	2	127	10	Fowler, John, of Braemore	Glenmazeran, Moy	7,618	760	–
Cameron, Duncan, of Inverailort	Inverailort, Fort-William	10,000	620	–	Fraser, Alexander	Inverness	3	537	10
Cameron, Rev. John	Manse of Urquhart	9	40	–	Fraser, Rev. Alexander	F.C. Manse of Kirkhill, Beauly	2	25	–
Cameron, Ann	Fort-William, Inverness	3	12	–	Fraser, Hon. Alexander E.	Beaufort Castle, Beauly	20	18	–
Campbell, James	Clachnaharry of Dunain, Inverness	1	2	–	Fraser, Alexander William	Culduthel Road, Inverness	4	22	–
Campbell, William	Mill of Tore, Inverness	10	10	–	Fraser, Andrew	Inverness	2	27	10
Campbell, Mrs. Christina Cameron, of Fassifern	Callart House, Fort-William	74,000	4,827	10	Fraser, Archibald T. F., of Abertarff	The Crown, Inverness	20,063	2,247	–
Campbell, Mrs. Charlotte W.	Devon Cottage, Inverness	5	220	10	Fraser, Archibald T. F.	Claypotts, Inverness	1	4	–
Campbell, Mary Ann	Corran, Glenelg	1	22	–	Fraser, Captain Charles E.	Heatherley, Inverness	7	115	–
Carruthers, Walter	Gordonville, Inverness	6	170	10	Fraser, Colonel Hastings, of Ardachy	Ardachy, Fort-Augustus	3,000	338	10
Cawdor, Earl of	Cawdor Castle, Nairn	3,943	1,738	–	Fraser, Hugh, of Auchnagairn	Auchnagairn House, Kirkhill	500	812	–
Chisholm, James S. (The Chisholm), of Chisholm	March Hall, Edinburgh	94,328	6,565	10	Fraser, Hugh	Errogie, Gorthleck	14	11	–
Chisholm-Batten, Edmund, of Aigas	Aigas, Beauly	1,593	675	–	Fraser, James	Ashton, Inverness	1	37	10
					Fraser, James, junior	Bellevue, Inverness	3	70	–
Commissioners of Supply for Inverness-shire	Inverness	4	233	–	Fraser, James George	Merlewood, Inverness	5	65	–

O

INVERNESS—continued.

Name of Owner.	Address of Owner.	Estimated Acreage of Property.	Gross Annual Value.	Name of Owner.	Address of Owner.	Estimated Acreage of Property.	Gross Annual Value.
		Acres.	£ s.			Acres.	£ s.
Fraser, John, of Bunchrew	Bunchrew, Inverness	978	705 -	Johnstone, Rev. David	Waternish Manse, Portree	4	22 -
Fraser, John	Dores Road, Inverness	1	55 -				
Fraser, Rev. John	Manse of Petty, Inverness	12	42 -	Kilmalie Parish, Heritors of	Fort-William	2	13 -
Fraser, Captain John, of Farraline	Farraline, Gorthleck	10,306	2,208 16	Kilmuir, Free Church Congregation of	Kilmuir, Portree	2	15 -
Fraser, Robert A.	Claypotts, Inverness	1	4 -	Kinmont, William G.	Melrose	1	39 -
Fraser, Roderick	Culneilan, Inverness	1	35 -				
Fraser, Heirs of Simon	Inverness	2	187 -				
Fraser, Rev. Thomas	Manse of Croy	12	41 17	Lamond, Rev. Joseph	F.C. Manse, Snizort	2	24 -
Fraser, William, of Kilmuir	Kilmuir, Portree	46,142	6,250 -	Livesey, John James	Broadstone, Inverness	2	28 -
Fraser, William Alexander	Viewville, Glen Urquhart	2	20 -	Lovat, Lord	Beaufort Castle, Beauly	161,574	28148 -
Fraser, Mrs. Barbara, of Ballindown	Ballindown, Beauly	279	310 -	Lovat, The Master of	Do. do.	444	71 10
Fraser, Mrs. Jane Ann, of Reelick	Reelick, Kirkhill	2,150	929 18	Macainsh, Peter	Woodburn, Crieff	180	10 -
Fraser-Mackintosh, Chas., of Drummond	Inverness	390	911 -	Macallister, Alexander, of Strathaird	Strathaird, Broadford	13,000	957 9
Fletcher, Rev. John	F.C. Manse, Bracadale	2	18 -	Macandrew, Henry C.	Midmills, Inverness	9	64 -
Galbraith, Rev. Angus	F.C. Manse, Raasay, Strome Ferry	1	18 -	Macbean, Col. William, of Tomatin	Tomatin House, Moy	2,264	385 9
Gollan, John G., of Gollanfield	Gollanfield, Ardersier	906	864 14	MacCallum, Rev. Duncan	Manse of Duirinish, Dunvegan	600	50 -
Gordon, John, of Cluny	Cluny Castle, Aberdeen; and South Uist, Lochmaddy	84,404	8,954 -	MacCaskill, Norman	Carbost, Portree	3	12 -
				MacCaskill, Mrs. Janet H.	Portree	1	18 -
Grant, Donald	Craigellachie Cottage, Aviemore	2	40 -	MacColl, Rev. Alexander	F.C. Manse, Fort-Augustus	3	25 -
Grant, Duncan, of Bught	Bught, Inverness	220	322 -	Maccormack, Donald	Arisaig	2	11 -
Grant, Sir George Macpherson, of Ballindalloch, Bart.	Ballindalloch Castle	103,372	5,454 -	Macdonald, Rev. Alexander	Stenscholl Manse, Portree	12	16 -
				Macdonald, Alexander, of Lyndale	Lyndale House, Portree	5,000	465 -
Grant, Rev. John	Manse of Rothiemurchus	5	15 -	Macdonald, Capt. Allan, of Waternish	Waternish, Portree	5,755	1,106 4
Grant, John	Dunean Cottage, Inverness	225	225 -	Macdonald, Rev. Donald	Hillpark, Inverness	5	69 -
				Macdonald, Rev. Donald	Manse of Alvie, Kingussie	20	40 -
Grant, Trustees of late J. M., of Glenmorriston	Glenmorriston	74,646	4,954 17	Macdonald, Donald P.	Fort-William	2	110 -
Grant, Sir John Peter, of Rothiemurchus, K.C.B.	Government House, Jamaica	24,457	2,290 15	Macdonald, Duncan	Culduthel Road, Inverness	1	20 -
				Macdonald, Harry, of Treaslane	Viewfield, Portree	3,001	250 -
Grant, Robert	Inverness	2	8 -	Macdonald, Rev. Hugh	Bernera Manse, Lochmaddy	3	16 -
Grant, Thomas Macpherson	Coull, Kingussie	36	10 10	Macdonald, Rev. James	Manse of Daviot	29	44 -
Grant, Rev. William	Manse of Duthil, Carrbridge	6	25 10	Macdonald, James	Drummond	1	16 5
Gray, Thomas R.	Spean Lodge, Kingussie	2	50 -	Macdonald, Right Rev. John	Aberdeen	9	10 -
Great North of Scotland Railway Company	Aberdeen (Railway)	63	1,618 -	Macdonald, John Andrew, of Glenaladale	Glenfinnan House, Fort-William	24,000	1,550 -
Gregory, Alexander A.	Inverness	4	20 -	Macdonald, Lauchlan, of Skeabost	Skeabost House, Portree	6,289	711 9
Guthrie, Trustees of late James A., of Craigie	Flichity, Inverness	6,000	1,501 10	Macdonald, Lord	Armadale Castle, Skye	129,919	11613 15
				Macdonald, Rev. Norman	F.C. Manse, Kincraig	1	25 -
Harrison, Mrs. Robina R.	Woodfield Cottage, Inverness	1	55 -	Macdonald, Rear-Admiral Reginald J. J. G., Chief of Clanranald	Castle Tirim, Strontian	20	5 -
Hay, Alexander Penrose	Riverdale, Inverness	4	65 -	Macdonald, Roderick	Balgown, Laggan	1	5 -
Highland Railway Company	Inverness	2	1,596 -	Macdonald, Rev. William	F.C. Manse, Cuilchenna	2	20 -
Do. do.	Do. (Railway)	505	25624 -	Macdonell, Eneas R., of Morar	Morar, Arisaig	3,000	670 14
Howard, Lord, of Glossop	Dorline House, Strontian	8,800	809 2				
Inglis, George	Ballifeary, Inverness	3	95 -	Macdonell, Elizabeth and Marjory	Milnfield, Inverness	14	156 -
Inglis, Colonel Hugh, of Kingsmills	Kingsmills, Inverness	49	226 16	Macfadzean, Rev. Donald	Manse of Laggan, Kingussie	34	59 5
Innes, Charles	Bruar, Inverness	2	67 -	MacGillivray, Neil John, of Dunmaglass	Dunmaglass, Inverness	4,000	392 -
Innes, Thomas G. Rose, of Bunachton	Netherdale, Banff	2,291	285 -	Macgregor, Duncan	Petty, Inverness	1	10 -
Inverness Cathedral Trustees	Inverness	2	80 -	Macgregor, Roderick	Braerannoch, Inverness	3	60 -
Inverness Cemetery Company	Inverness	21	100 -	Macgregor, William	Drummond, Inverness	1	5 -
Inverness District Lunacy Board	Inverness	170	950 -	MacInnes, Rev. Joseph	Arisaig Manse	2	16 -
				MacIntyre, Rev. Malcolm	Manse, Fort-Augustus	52	85 -
Inverness Gas and Water Company	Inverness	5	2,268 12	Mackay, Charles	Culduthel Road, Inverness	2	133 8
				Mackay, Duncan	Inverness	2	155 10
Inverness Harbour Trustees	Inverness (Harbour)	1	973 5	Mackay, Donald	Kiltarlity, Beauly	2	8 -
Inverness Kirk-Session	Inverness	35	219 2	Mackay, George G., of Raasay	Raasay House, Strome Ferry	17,551	2,770 15
Inverness Parochial Board	Inverness	6	250 -				
Inverness Public Park Company	Inverness	10	60 -	Mackay, Robert	Inverness	2	168 -
				Mackay, Mrs. Margaret	Woodfield, Inverness	3	70 -
Inverness Royal Academy	Inverness	2	80 -	Mackenzie, Rev. Alexander	F.C. Manse, Broadford	1	20 -
Inverness Royal Infirmary, Trustees of	Inverness	5	150 -	Mackenzie, Colin Lyon	Sunnyside, Inverness	9	425 -
Inverness, Town of	Inverness	129	1,292 10	Mackenzie, Rev. David	Drummond Road, Inverness	2	89 10

INVERNESS—continued.

Name of Owner.	Address of Owner.	Estimated Acreage of Property.	Gross Annual Value.	Name of Owner.	Address of Owner.	Estimated Acreage of Property.	Gross Annual Value.
		Acres.	£ s.			Acres.	£ s.
Mackenzie, Rev. Ewen	Manse of Kirkhill	10	50 —	Moy, Free Church Congregation of	Moy, Inverness	1	18 —
Mackenzie, Rev. Kenneth A.	Manse of Kingussie	40	95 —	Munro, Rev. Daniel	Insh, Kingussie	2	12 —
Mackenzie, John	Eileanach, Inverness	2	464 10	Murray, Capt. Peter	Roseheath Cottage, Inverness	1	20 —
Mackenzie, Rev. John	Manse of Kilmuir, Portree	35	40 —				
Mackenzie, Rev. Roderick	F.C. Manse, Tarbert, Harris	1	20 —				
Mackinnon, Rev. Donald	Kilbride, Broadford	44	27 6	Newton & Cargill	Telford Street, Inverness	4	169 10
Mackintosh, Alexander Æ. (The Mackintosh), of Mackintosh	Moy Hall, Inverness	124,181	12816 —	Nicol & Company	Holm Mills, Inverness	6	204 —
				Noble, John	Inverness	2	127 —
Mackintosh, Angus, of Holme	Holme House, Inverness	8,395	1,612 10	Northern Lighthouses, Commissioners of	Edinburgh	99	195 —
Mackintosh, Eneas, of Balnespick	Balnespick, Moy	9,500	879 —	Northern Meeting Trustees	Inverness	4	318 10
Mackintosh, Eneas, of Dalmigavie	Inverness	7,000	489 —	Ogilvy, Thomas, of Corriemony	Corriemony, Drumnadrochit	10,856	1,085 6
Mackintosh, Eneas W., of Raigmore, M.P.	Raigmore, Inverness	6,556	4,368 —	Orde, Sir John P., of Kilmory, Bart.	Kilmory, Lochgilphead; and North Uist, Lochmaddy	81,099	4,975 1
Mackintosh, Capt. James E. A., of Farr	Farr, Inverness	4,500	935 4				
Mackintosh Trust	Inverness	133	925 —				
Mackintosh, Robert	Kilmuir, Portree	1	7 —	Paterson, William	Larkfield, Inverness	2	50 —
Maclean, Rev. Charles	Manse of Harris, Stornoway	192	33 —	Patillo, Alexander	Inverness	1	35 —
Maclean, Rev. Donald	Trumisgarry Manse, Lochmaddy	4	12 —				
Maclean, John	Glen Uig, Strontian	2,200	214 9	Ramsden, Sir John W., of Byrom Hall, Bart., M.P.	Ardverikie, Laggan; and Byrom Hall, Yorkshire	60,400	6,131 6
Macleod, Rev. Adam G.	F.C. Manse, Croy	1	20 —				
Macleod, Reps. of late Gordon, of Lochbay	Lochbay, Skye	2,300	284 —	Reid, Rev. Thomas	F.C. Manse, Portree	1	20 —
Macleod, Kenneth R., of Greshernish	Greshernish, Portree	15,550	1,516 6	Richmond, Duke of	Kinrara, Aviemore	27,409	1,182 5
				Robertson, Alexander I.	Aultnaskiah, Inverness	42	127 5
Macleod, Right Hon. Sir John Macpherson, of Glendale, K.C.S.I.	1 Stanhope Street, Hyde Park, London; and Glendale, Dunvegan	35,022	1,257 12	Robertson, George	Longman Rd., Inverness	1	69 —
				Robertson, Joseph	Ness Bank, Inverness	41	65 —
				Robertson, William, of Kinlochmoidart	Kinlochmoidart, Strontian	9,349	1,007 10
Macleod, Norman, of Macleod	Dunvegan Castle, Skye	141,679	8,464 —	Roman Catholic Church, Trustees of	Arisaig	1	10 18
Macleod, Rev. Norman	F.C. Manse, North Uist, Lochmaddy	2	20 —	Roman Catholic Church, Trustees of	Mingry, Moidart	6	13 —
Macnaughton, Rev. James	Manse of Dores, Inverness	25	48 —	Rose, Hugh	Inverness	7	691 10
Macneil, Rev. Archibald	Manse of Sleat, Broadford	14	30 —	Rose, Rev. Hugh Francis, of Holme	Holme, Croy	1,137	435 9
Macniven, Heirs of Mrs.	Porterfield, Inverness	2	47 —	Ross, Alexander	Inverness	2	65 —
Macphail, Rev. John S.	F.C. Manse of Sleat, Broadford	1	20 —	Ross, Rev. David	Manse of Kiltarlity, Beauly	62	90 —
Macpherson, Angus Jas.	Inverness	12	108 —	Ross, Rev. Ewen	Manse of Ardersier	18	33 —
Macpherson, Col. David Edward, of Belleville	Belleville House, Kingussie	26,773	3,200 14	Ross, James	Island Bank, Inverness	2	45 —
Macpherson, Ewen, of Cluny (Cluny Macpherson)	Cluny Castle, Kingussie	42,000	4,250 13	Ross, Col. Patrick Robertson, of Glenmoidart	Glenmoidart, Strontian	2,300	290 —
				Rule, William Taylor	The Camp, Inverness	12	65 —
Macpherson, Major Lachlan, of Glentruim	Glentruim House, Kingussie	21,000	2,350 —				
Macpherson, Norman, of Eig	6 Duke St., Edinburgh	7,159	899 16	Saunders, Charles	Barnoch, Glen Urquhart	3	35 —
				Scott, Edward H., of Ardvourlie Castle	Ardvourlie Castle, Harris, Stornoway	59,125	3,271 9
Macrae, Rev. Angus	F.C. Manse, Glen Urquhart, Drumnadrochit	1	20 —	Seafield, Earl of	Balmacaan, Glen Urquhart	160,224	16478 —
Macrae, Rev. John	Manse of Glenelg	340	125 —	Shaw, Rev. Dugald	F.C. Manse, Laggan	2	22 —
Macrae, Rev. John	F.C. Manse, Dunvegan	2	19 —	Simpson, Rev. Donald M.	Manse of Moy, Inverness	33	43 —
Macrae, Rev. John A.	North Uist, Lochmaddy	200	35 —	Simpson, James	Maryfield, Inverness	2	35 —
Malkin, Arthur Thomas, of Corrybrough	Corrybrough, Tomatin	6,900	625 —	Simpson, William	Springfield, Inverness	7	218 —
				Simpson, Mrs. Elizabeth H.	Millburn, Inverness	1	75 —
Marjoribanks, Sir Dudley Coutts, of Guisachan, Bart.	Guisachan, Beauly	19,186	1,097 —	Sinclair, Rev. John	Manse of Small Isles, Eig, Arisaig	100	50 —
Marshall, John, of Flemington	11 York Place, Edinburgh	220	266 —	Skene, Lawrence	Portree	2	60 —
				Smith, Mrs. Margaret	Ardersier	1	12 —
Martin, Rev. Angus	Manse of Snizort, Portree	30	40 —	Smithson, Samuel, of Faillie	Lentran House, Inverness	7,160	1,067 —
Martin, Nicol, of Glendale	Glendale, Dunvegan	5,000	501 15	Spinks, Charles	Millburn, Inverness	3	187 10
Mather, Miles Edward	Glendruidh, Inverness	3	81 —	Stewart, Rev. Alexander	Ballachulish Manse, Fort-William	4	16 —
Matheson, Alexander, of Ardross, M.P.	Ardross Castle, Alness	230	2,141 5	Stewart, Archibald, of Ensey	Ensey, Harris, Stornoway	2,600	300 —
Merry, James, of Belladrum, M.P.	Belladrum, Beauly	5,466	1,976 5	Stewart, Charles, of Brin	Brin House, Inverness	5,330	1,780 —
Miller, Mrs. Lydia	Old Drummond, Inverness	3	165 10	Stewart, Rev. Charles	F.C. Manse, Fort-William	3	25 —
Mitchell, Joseph	Viewhill, Inverness	4	259 —	Strother, Alexander	Academy St., Inverness	2	185 —
Moray, Earl of	Castle Stuart, Petty	7,035	5,171 —	Studd, Major-Gen. Edward M., of Banchor	Banchor, Moy	2,903	220 —
Morrison, Rev. Roderick	Bracadale Manse, Portree	35	40 —	Sutherland, Rev. Donald	F.C. Manse, Gaerlochy, Fort-William	1	15 —
Morrison, William	Birchwood, Inverness	2	59 —				

INVERNESS—continued.

Name of Owner.	Address of Owner.	Estimated Acreage of Property	Gross Annual Value.	Name of Owner.	Address of Owner.	Estimated Acreage of Property.	Gross Annual Value.
		Acres.	£ s.			Acres.	£ s.
Swinburne, Capt. Thomas A., of Eilean Shona, R.N.	Eilean Shona, Strontian	1,000	165 –	Walker, Fountaine, of Ness Castle	Ness Castle, Inverness	836	405 –
Sutherland, Colonel Robert M., C.B.	Huntly Lodge, Inverness	1	70 –	Walker, Colonel George G., of Loch Treig, M.P.	Banks of Cluden, Dumfries; and Loch Treig, Kingussie	70,940	3,341 12
Trustees of Dr. Bell's Institution	Inverness	2	60 –	*War Department*	London	250	566 16
Tytler, Colonel William Fraser, of Aldourie	Aldourie, Inverness	15,978	3,150 10	Waterston, Charles	Oaklands, Inverness	10	110 –
				Wedderspoon, James	Croy	1	10 –
Urquhart, David	Ness View Villa, Inverness	2	70 –	White, Henry W., of Monar	Lentran, Kirkhill	510	624 16
				Total Owners of Land of one Acre and upwards		292 2,589,152	322,360 –
				Total Owners of Lands of less than one Acre in extent		1,575 256	39,488 5
Walker, E. C. Sutherland, of Aberarder	Aberarder, Inverness	5,000	684 10	GRAND TOTAL		1,867 2,589,408	361,848 5

KINCARDINE.

Population in 1871, - - - - - - - 34,630.
Inhabited Houses, - - - - - - 6,661.
Number of Parishes, - - - - - - 21.

Name of Owner.	Address of Owner.	Estimated Acreage of Property.	Gross Annual Value.	Name of Owner.	Address of Owner.	Estimated Acreage of Property.	Gross Annual Value.
		Acres.	£ s.			Acres.	£ s.
Aberdeen, City of	Aberdeen	78	799 8	Crombie, Alexander, of Thornton	Thornton Castle, Laurencekirk	2,755	3,537 13
Aberdeen, Harbour Commissioners of	Aberdeen	17	986 —	Crown, The		9	339 —
Aberdeen, Synod of	Aberdeen	331	600 7	Do.	(Fishings)	—	1,657 4
Aberdeen Town and County Bank	Aberdeen	39	125 —	Cushny, Alexander	Banchory	3	55 —
Aberdeen, University of	Aberdeen	1,010	1,127 9				
Aberdeen, Water Commissioners of	Aberdeen	10	1,528 —	Dallas, Alexander	Drumlithie	16	55 —
Airth, William	Primrosehill, Fettercairn	48	79 —	Davidson, James, of Balnagask	Balnagask House, Nigg, Aberdeen	495	1,190 4
Alexander, John	West Caldhame, Marykirk	28	47 —	Davidson, Patrick, of Inchmarlo	Inchmarlo House, Banchory	985	895 14
Anderson, William	Luthermuir, Marykirk	13	19 —	Deeside Railway Company	Aberdeen (Railway)	94	2,224 —
Anderson, Rev. William	Manse, Fettercairn	7	50 —	De Virte, Baroness	Benholm Castle, Bervie	728	1,096 8
Arbuthnott, Viscount	Arbuthnott House, Fordoun	13,560	13036 9	Dickson, David	Laurencekirk	5	180 —
Avery, John, of Cairngrassie	Crown Street, Aberdeen	145	228 5	Dickson, James	Caldhame, Laurencekirk	8	15 —
Arbutknott, Major-Gen. the Hon. William, of Hatton	Hatton, Marykirk	633	885 1	Donald, George	Westerton, Maryculter, Aberdeen	30	50 —
				Donald, John	Kemnay, Aberdeen	61	40 —
				Donald, Mrs. Jean	Bishopton, Banchory-Devenick, Aberdeen	14	20 —
				Donaldson's Hospital, Trustees of	Edinburgh	3,821	4,267 13
Baird, Alexander, of Urie	Urie House, Stonehaven	4,500	4,247 6	Donaldson, Trustees of William	Beltcraigs, Stonehaven	160	96 —
Baker Incorporation of Aberdeen	Aberdeen	520	1,190 14	Douglas, Robert	St. Ann's Cottage, Brechin	21	84 18
Banchory-Devenick, Heritors of Parish of	Banchory-Devenick	1	6 —	Douglass, John Sholto, of Tilquhillie	Invery House, Banchory	1,808	1,015 7
Banchory-Ternan, Heritors of Parish of	Banchory-Ternan	1	5 —	Duff, Robert William, of Fetteresso, M.P.	Fetteresso Castle, Stonehaven	8,722	4,536 18
Bannerman, Sir Alexander, of Elsick, Bart.	Crimmonmogate, Aberdeen	500	702 11	Duff, Mrs. Thomas Fraser	Paris	122	47 10
Berry, James	Banchory	2	81 —	Duguid, Peter, of Auchlunies	Auchlunies House, Maryculter, Aberdeen	601	419 8
Birnie, John Birnie Leslie of Redcraigs	Gloucester Place, Edinburgh	200	394 19	Duguid, Peter, of Cammachmore	Fonthill Place, Aberdeen	247	368 15
Blaikie, John	Cameron Street, Stonehaven	2	45 —	Duguid, William, of Fawsyde	Fawsyde House, Bervie	220	405 —
Boswell, Mrs. Margaret Irvine, of Kingcausie	Kingcausie House, Maryculter	1,889	1,583 7	Duirs, Rev. James	Manse, Durris, Aberdeen	28	39 —
Brown, Andrew	Dundee	2	9 —	Duncan, John, of Parkhill	Parkhill House, Arbroath	63	103 —
Bruce, Rev. William	Manse, Portlethen, Aberdeen	10	26 —	Duncan, Trustees of John	Cameron St., Stonehaven	5	185 7
Buchan, Rev. Charles F.	Manse, Fordoun	5	41 —	Eddie, Mrs. Jean	Roadside, Kinneff, Bervie	3	5 —
Burness, Fanny and Elizabeth	Auchinblae, Fordoun	1	75 —	Edmond, Francis	Aberdeen	170	654 5
Burnett, James Cumine, of Monboddo	Monboddo House, Fordoun	3,013	2,542 8	Edmond, James	Banchory	2	45 —
Burnett, Sir James Horn, of Leys, Bart.	Crathes Castle, Banchory	12,025	5,006 14	Elphinstone, Lady William G. Osborne, of Kinneff	Tulliallan, Kincardine-on-Forth	3,030	3,470 8
Burnett, Robert, yr. of Crathes	Corsee House, Banchory	2	53 —	Erskine, Trustees of Henry	Laurencekirk	1	184 1
				Ewan, Alexander	Banchory	1	119 —
				Fairweather, Rev. Robert	Manse, Nigg, Aberdeen	40	98 —
Caledonian Railway Company	Glasgow (Railway)	344	31322 —	Falconer, Robert	Stonehaven	3	82 10
Campbell, Alexander D., of Blackhall	Blackhall Castle, Banchory	3,382	1,524 11	Falconer, Robert	Buckiesmill, Glenbervie, Stonehaven	53	55 —
Carnegie, John, of Redhall	Redhall House, Fordoun	810	1,464 7	Farquhar, Arthur	6 Bon-Accord Square, Aberdeen	42	32 10
Clark, James	Stoneyroo, Fordoun	32	26 —	Farquhar, James, of Hallgreen	Hallgreen Castle, Bervie	1,464	2,388 18
Cochran, James	Belmont, Stonehaven	2	65 —	Farrell, Michael, of Davo	Woodburnden, Laurencekirk	1,349	1,280 14
Cowie, James	Sundridge Hall, Bromley, London	40	93 10	Ferguson, Mrs. Jane, of Altens	Altens, Aberdeen	481	746 16
Cranstoun, Lady, of Benholm	Duncroft House, St. John's Wood, London	733	556 5				

KINCARDINE—continued.

Name of Owner.	Address of Owner.	Estimated Acreage of Property.	Gross Annual Value.	Name of Owner.	Address of Owner.	Estimated Acreage of Property.	Gross Annual Value.
		Acres.	£ s.			Acres.	£ s.
Fergusson, Rev. David Scott	Free Manse, Banchory	3	24 —	Leslie, Trustees of Alexander	Birkwood, Banchory	4	40 —
Fetteresso, Heritors of Parish of	Fetteresso	2	7 —				
Forbes, Heirs of Sir John H. Stuart, of Pitsligo, Bart.	Fettercairn House, Laurencekirk	5,007	4,056 18	M'Clure, Rev. James Campbell	Manse, Marykirk, Montrose	6	32 —
Forbes, William Forbes, of Castleton	Lochcote House, Bathgate	590	496 17	Macdonald, Mrs. Jessie	Shannaburn, Maryculter, Aberdeen	41	115 —
Forbes, Wm. Nathanael, of Dunnottar	Dunnottar House, Stonehaven	6,528	5,493 12	M'Hardy, James	Bellfield, Banchory	7	40 —
Fordyce, William Dingwall, of Brucklay, M.P.	Brucklay Castle, Aberdeen	46	1,091 —	M'Inroy, Lieut.-Col. William, of The Burn	The Burn, Brechin	4,988	3,182 8
Forrest, Trustees of Alexander, of Tulloch	Tulloch, Laurencekirk	969	765 —	M'Kenzie, William	Banchory	1	35 —
Fraser, Trustees of Col. Wm., of Balmakewan	Balmakewan House, Montrose	865	822 —	Mackintosh, Rev. Thomas	Manse, St. Cyrus, Montrose	5	15 —
Fraser, Mrs. Jane	Banchory	2	20 —	M'Lean, Rev. Alexander	Manse, Strachan, Banchory	6	40 —
				Master of Mortifications, Aberdeen	Aberdeen	2	31 —
				Mavor, Robert, of Newpark	Church Street, Aberdeen	14	32 —
Gammell, Major Andrew, of Drumtochty	Drumtochty Castle, Fordoun	4,823	2,224 9	Mearns, Rev. William	Manse, Kinneff, Bervie	8	48 —
Gibb, James Gilchrist	Bervie	2	150 —	Melville, Rev. Charles Nairn Barker	Manse, Maryculter, Aberdeen	12	40 —
Gibbon, Alexander, of Johnston	Johnston Lodge, Laurencekirk	774	1,811 10	Michell, John, of Glassel	Glassel House, Banchory	565	263 10
Gilfillan, Rev. George	Paradise Row, Dundee	2	40 —	Middleton, James	Invery Cottage, Banchory	4	20 —
Gladstone, Sir Thomas, of Fasque, Bart.	Fasque House, Laurencekirk	45,062	9,174 10	Miller, John, of Drumlithie, M.P.	2 Melville Crescent, Edinburgh	2,750	3,352 15
Glegg, Rev. John	Manse, Bervie	6	52 10	Milne, Trustees of John, of Muchalls	Muchalls Castle, Stonehaven	2,196	3,303 8
Gordon, Heirs of Arthur Forbes, of Rayne	16 Rutland Square, Edinburgh	5	35 —	Mitchell, Adam, of Heathcot	Heathcot House, Maryculter, Aberdeen	295	674 15
Gordon's Hospital, Governors of	Aberdeen	89	83 16	Mitchell, Rev. James	Manse, Garvock, Laurencekirk	12	40 —
Gordon, Rev. William	Manse, Glenbervie, Fordoun	8	40 —	Molison, Trs. of James, of Craigshaw	Balnagask, Aberdeen	119	334 6
Gordon, William Cosmo, of Maryculter	Fyvie Castle, Aberdeen	1,340	906 17	Monro, George, of Berryhill	Edinburgh	107	374 10
Graham, Janet, of Kirkside	Kirkside House, Montrose	499	1,733 9	*Montrose and Bervie Railway Company*	Stonehaven (Railway)	65	960 —
Grahame, Barron, of Morphie	Bowbutts House, Kinghorn	1,175	2,730 11	*Montrose, Town of*	Montrose	397	500 —
Grant, Captain Frederick Grant Forsyth, of Ecclesgreig	Ecclesgreig House, Montrose	1,284	2,033 14	Morice, Rev. William David, of Tullos	Vicarage, Longridge-Deverill, Wilts	453	634 5
				Morrison, Rev. Charles	Manse, Laurencekirk	22	61 —
				Murray, Sir Patrick Keith, of Ochtertyre, Bart.	Ochtertyre, Crieff	2,248	2,891 3
Harvey, Trustees of William, of Bellfield	Bellfield, Kinneff, Bervie	333	460 —	Myers, Rev. Alexander Smart	Manse, Benholm, Bervie	8	42 —
Hector, Heirs of James	Fernyflatt, Kinneff, Bervie	330	507 —				
Hepburn, Heirs of William Rickart, of Rickarton	Rickarton House, Stonehaven	5,400	2,624 10				
Hogarth, Hugh	Stonehaven	9	93 —	Nicol, Trustees of James Dyce, of Ballogie	Ballogie House, Aberdeen	2,350	3,402 2
Hutchison, Rev. George	Manse, Banchory	7	40 —	Nicolson, James Badenach, of Arthurhouse	Glenbervie House, Fordoun	1,161	727 2
Hutchison, Heirs of Mrs.	Woodfield, Banchory	1	35 —	Nicolson, Mrs. Badenach, of Glenbervie	Glenbervie House, Fordoun	8,481	3,919 17
Innes, Alex., of Raemoir	Raemoir House, Banchory	4,750	2,847 9	*North of Scotland Bank*	Aberdeen	1	148 —
Inverbervie, Town of	Bervie	54	141 14	*Northern Lights, Commissioners of*	Edinburgh	10	35 —
Jack, James	Stonehaven	1	118 5				
Johnston, David, of Kair	Kair House, Fordoun	871	1,315 12				
				Ogston, Alexander Milne, of Ardoe	Ardoe House, Aberdeen	944	1,216 9
Keith, Trs. of William, of Mill, of Muchalls	Union Street, Aberdeen	114	386 1	Orr, John H. E., of Brigton	Brigton House, St. Cyrus, Montrose	232	531 14
Kerr, George	Laidlestone, Glenbervie, Fordoun	45	25 2				
Kilgour, Alexander, of Loirston	Loirston House, Nigg, Aberdeen	676	1,762 6	Paterson, James	Burnhead, Garvock, Laurencekirk	7	15 —
Kinloch, Alexander John, of Park	Park House, Aberdeen	4,532	2,995 1	Paul, William	Aberdeen	1	35 —
Kinnear, John	Laurencekirk	2	70 16	Paul, Rev. William	Manse, Banchory-Devenick, Aberdeen	9	47 —
Kintore, Earl of	Keithhall, Aberdeen	17,370	16908 19				
Knox, David	Keith Lodge, Stonehaven	2	45 —	Pirie, Rev. W. R., and the Representatives of Col. Munro of Findon	Findon, Aberdeen	360	692 14
				Philip, Rev. John	F.C. Manse, Fordoun	1	25 —
Laurencekirk, Heritors of Parish of	Laurencekirk	1	3 —	*Poorhouse Combination*	Stonehaven	3	150 —
Law, John	Caldhame, Laurencekirk	1	17 —	Porteous, Trustees of Alexander, of Lauriston	Lauriston Castle, St. Cyrus, Montrose	3,437	5,534 6
Logie, Joseph	India Lane, Montrose	5	11 —				

KINCARDINE—continued.

Name of Owner.	Address of Owner.	Estimated Acreage of Property.	Gross Annual Value.	Name of Owner.	Address of Owner.	Estimated Acreage of Property.	Gross Annual Value.
		Acres.	£ s.			Acres.	£ s.
Ramsay, Sir Alexander, of Balmain, Bart.	Cheltenham	4,028	3,571 1	Swan, Rev. Thomas	U.P. Manse, Luthermuir, Laurencekirk	6	24 -
Ramsay, Thomas Burnett, of Arbeadie	Banchory Lodge, Banchory	1,800	1,843 9	Symmers, Alexander Anderson, of Cookney	Glenburnie Cottage, Aberdeen	353	383 16
Ramsay, Mrs. Anne	Lerrachmore Cottage, Banchory	1	30 -	Symmers, George Symmers Anderson, of Elrick	Glenburnie Cottage, Aberdeen	251	242 5
Scott, Hercules, of Brotherton	Brotherton Castle, Bervie	3,912	5,388 6	Taylor, Alexander	Cushnie, Fordoun	258	362 -
Scott, Mrs. Fanny Fitzmaurice, of Commieston	Commieston, Edinburgh	953	1,823 6	Taylor, George, of Kirktonhill	Kirktonhill House, Montrose	2,489	2,505 11
Scott, Lady Harriet Anne	The Villa, Laurencekirk	9	86 -	Taylor, Rev. James	Manse, Cookney, Stonehaven	4	20 -
Shand, Robert Shand Kynoch, of Hillside	Hillside House, Aberdeen	540	749 2	Taylor, Mrs. Rosa Ann, of Portlethen	Portlethen, Aberdeen	831	1,095 9
Shirres, William	The Parsonage, Banchory	2	40 -	Thomson, John Watt	Stonehaven	1	148 -
Silver, Rev. Alexander	Manse, Dunnottar, Stonehaven	8	38 10	Thurburn, Henry	43 Russell Road, Kensington, London	3	30 -
Sim, William	Banchory	2	75 -	Tough, Alexander	Arbeadie, Banchory	1	20 -
Smith, Lewis	Marybank, Maryculter, Aberdeen	8	46 10	Towns, John, of Leithfield	Leithfield House, Fordoun	546	546 -
Spark, Thomas Spark Sinclair	Fernbank, Banchory	1	24 -	Trew, Henry	Grove Cottage, Banchory	4	24 -
Spence, Rev. Robert Moir	Manse, Arbuthnott, Bervie	7	39 -	Turnbull, Margaret Robertson, of Dalladies	Dalladies, Fettercairn, Laurencekirk	253	280 -
Stewart, Alexander	Wedderhill, Stonehaven	222	90 -				
Stewart, John, of Banchory	Banchory House, Aberdeen	1,571	2,888 -	Walker, John	Stonehaven	1	51 -
				Walker, Rev. William	Parsonage, Laurencekirk	4	35 -
Stewart, Trustees of William, of Hilton	Hilton, Kinneff, Bervie	109	241 10	Watt, Rev. John	Manse, Fetteresso, Stonehaven	10	43 10
Stewart, Trustees of William and John	Cotbank, Kinneff, Bervie	140	227 -				
Stonehaven Harbour, Trustees of	Stonehaven (Harbour)	6	250 -	Young, James, of Durris	Durris House, Aberdeen	16,659	10140 -
Strain, Right Rev. John, and others, as Trustees for Blairs' College	Maryculter, Aberdeen	1,140	950 5	Total Owners of Land of one Acre and upwards	195	244,396	236,021 17
Strain, Right Rev. John, and others, as Trustees for Estate of Charlestown	Aberdeen	742	752 17	Total Owners of Lands of less than one Acre in extent	1,189	189	17,370 15
Stuart, Alexander, of Inchbreck	Laithers House, Turriff	1,009	479 -	GRAND TOTAL	1,384	244,585	253,392 12

KINROSS.

Population in 1871, - - - - - - - **7,198.**
Inhabited Houses, - - - - - - - **1,517.**
Number of Parishes, - - - - - - - **7.**

Name of Owner.	Address of Owner.	Estimated Acreage of Property.	Gross Annual Value.	Name of Owner.	Address of Owner.	Estimated Acreage of Property.	Gross Annual Value.
		Acres.	£ s.			Acres.	£ s.
Abercrombie, Barbara, Agnes, and Harriet	7 Doune Terrace, Edinburgh	716	227 15	Brown, Mrs. Ann . . and Mrs. Brown, wife of William Brown	Gairney Cottage, Kinross . . . Kelso . . .	60	130 --
Adam, Right Hon. William Patrick, of Blairadam, M.P. . . .	Blairadam, Kinross .	2,869	2,985 --	Bruce, Colonel Robert, of Glendeuglie . .	Glendeuglie, Milnathort	45	80 10
Do. do.	Do. (*Minerals*)	--	100 --	Bruce, Thomas, of Arnot	Kingsdale, Kennoway .	853	1,134 --
Anderson, James . .	Hallhill, Kinross . .	19	55 5	Buchan, Thomas . .	Dundee . . .	2	13 6
Arnott, David . .	Portmoak, Kinross .	200	230 --	Buchanan, James . .	215 Piccadilly, London .	20	50 --
Arnott, Trustees of G. A. Walker . . .	Holeton and Newlands .	681	647 --	Buchanan, Mrs. Ann .	Scotlandwell, Kinross .	15	25 10
Arnott, Trustees of G. A. Walker; . . Mrs. Dougall, wife of Rev. James Dougall; Mrs. Glegg, wife of Robert Glegg; . . Williamina Hogg; and James Walker .	Holeton and Newlands Stoneykirk, Stranraer Edinburgh . . Edinburgh . . Edinburgh . .	120	16 --	Cairns, Robert and William Dun	Roscobie, Dunfermline Kinnesswood, Kinross	10	5 --
				Campbell, William . .	Mawbank, Milnathort .	4	14 --
				Carmichael, John . .	Hawthornvale, Kinross .	6	24 10
				Cation, Robert . .	Hopefield, Milnathort .	5	18 --
Arnott, John . . .	Easter Bowhouse . .	40	86 --	Chapman, Mrs. Margaret	Milnathort . . .	2	17 10
Arnott, Robert . .	Milnathort . . .	2	14 5	Christie, John, of Braughty . . .	Cowden Castle, Dollar .	616	367 --
Arnott, Elizabeth, and Mrs. Beath, wife of James Beath . .	Kinnesswood, Kinross Glenvale, Kinross .	23	26 10	Constable, William Briggs, of Benarty . . .	Benarty, Kinross . .	60	104 --
				Cook, Trustees of Archibald . . .	Mid-Bowhouse, Leslie .	105	181 13
				Coventry, Alexander .	Duncrevie, Milnathort .	9	26 --
Barclay, Heirs of Arthur Hay, of Paris . .	Paris House, Milnathort	488	475 17	Coventry, Trustees of Captain George Andrew, of Shanwell .	Shanwell, Milnathort .	260	396 --
Barclay, John . .	Scotlandwell, Kinross .	5	19 19	Crawford, Andrew .	Stirling . . .	8	12 --
Barclay, Robert . .	Heatheryford, Kinross .	7	25 15	Crawford, James . .	Drum of Tullibole, Kinross . . .	11	17 --
Barclay, Isabella . .	Leslie	3	9 10				
Beath, David . .	Harelaw, Kinross . .	38	55 --	Crawford, Robert . .	Drum of Tullibole, Kinross . . .	10	22 --
Beath, David . .	Auchmuir, Leslie . .	5	25 10				
Beattie, William, of Craigton	13 Upper Berkeley St., London . . .	224	253 10	Curror, John, of Nivingston . . .	Comiston, Lothianburn .	235	529 --
Bennet, William . .	Drum of Tullibole, Kinross . . .	13	24 10				
Bennet, Mrs. Agnes .	South Bogside, Lochgelly	3	22 --	Davidson, James . .	Blackford, Perth . .	7	8 --
Bethune, William . .	Craigow, Milnathort .	316	243 18	Dawson, John Ramage, of Wester Balado .	Linlithgow . . .	500	530 --
Beveridge, James . .	Middle Balado, Kinross	322	390 --	Deas, Alexander . .	Damhead, Milnathort .	3	13 --
Beveridge, John . .	Kinneston, Leslie . .	715	775 --	Deas, William, junior .	Damhead, Milnathort .	3	6 --
Beveridge, John, Mrs. Janet Birrell, Robert Cairns, William Dun, and Hector Monro .	Bishophill, Kinross .	380	80 --	Dempster, Heirs of James	Tillyochie, Kinross .	184	305 --
				Dick, David . . .	Damhead, Milnathort .	9	22 --
Beveridge, Mrs. William .	Drum of Tullibole, Kinross . . .	10	34 10	Donald, Mrs., wife of John Donald . .	Denhead, Denlugas .	4	9 --
Beveridge, Mrs., wife of J. K. Beveridge . .	Drum of Tullibole, Kinross . . .	5	15 --	Dougall, Mrs., wife of Rev. James Dougall .	Stoneykirk, Stranraer .	20	48 10
Beveridge, Mrs. . .	The Well, Milnathort .	4	33 --	Dougall, Mrs., wife of Rev. James Dougall; . Mrs. Glegg, wife of Robert Glegg; and Williamina Hogg .	Stoneykirk, Stranraer Edinburgh . .	324	391 --
Beveridge, Janet . .	The Elms, Kirkcaldy .	7	14 --				
Bickerton, Heirs of David	Browheads, Kinross .	10	20 --				
Bickerton, Mrs. Grace .	Kinnesswood, Kinross .	2	11 17				
Birrell, Mrs. Janet . .	Kinnesswood, Kinross .	41	134 1				
Black, David, of Tillywhally . . .	Limerick . . .	169	314 --	Douie, Mrs., wife of James L. Douie . . .	Moira, Belfast . .	341	409 14
Black, Mrs., wife of Charles Black . .	Drum of Tullibole, Kinross . . .	14	34 --	Dow, William . .	Gallahill, Kinross . .	8	14 --
				Dowie, William . .	Kirkcaldy . . .	5	10 10
Blackwood, Mrs. James .	Cupar	2	65 --	Dowie, Jeanie L. . .	Crook of Devon, Kinross	29	73 17
Bogie, George . .	Gairneybridge, Kinross .	110	155 --	Drummond, James . .	Scotlandwell, Kinross .	4	13 6
British Linen Company Bank	Edinburgh . . .	2	98 10	Drummond, William .	23 Nassau Street, London . . .	13	22 --
Brough, John . .	Kinross . . .	2	108 10				
Brown, Trustees of Walter	Netherhall, Kinross .	142	306 10	Drysdale, David . .	Milnathort . . .	10	34 10
Brown, William . .	Kelso	5	30 --	Dumble, James Wilson .	Lochend, Kinross . .	79	132 10
Brown, Mrs. Ann . .	Gairney Cottage, Kinross	31	35 --	Dun, William . .	Kinnesswood, Kinross .	102	148 10

KINROSS—continued.

Name of Owner.	Address of Owner.	Estimated Acreage of Property.	Gross Annual Value.	Name of Owner.	Address of Owner.	Estimated Acreage of Property.	Gross Annual Value.
		Acres.	£ s			Acres.	£ s
Duncan, Andrew	Milnathort	4	35 –	Hutton, Robert	Higham, Newburgh	1	5 10
Duncan, John Scarlett, of Vane	6 Lombard Street, London	292	166 –	Hutton, Mrs., wife of Alexander Hutton	Cults, Ladybank	100	170 –
Duncan, Mrs. Helen	2 Bank Place, Leith	30	66 –				
				Ireland, Thomas	Scotlandwell, Kinross	2	8 –
Elder, Alexander	Newhill, Milnathort	170	195 –				
Elder, Mrs., wife of Robert Elder	Reidiehill, Auchtermuchty	4	14 5	Keay, Alexander, of Butterwell	Butterwell, Kinross	128	168 –
Ewing, John	Hattonburn, Milnathort	90	116 –	Kerr, James, of Lathro	Burntisland	140	297 –
				Kidston, Archibald Glen	Cambuslang, Glasgow	500	521 3
				Kinross Feuars	Kinross	6	15 –
Fergus, John	Wood of Coldrain, Kinross	210	260 –				
Ferguson, Rev. William	Manse, Fossoway	9	45 –	Laing, James	Cuthil Muir, Milnathort	2	10 –
Field, Rev. Edward Burch, of Moreland	43 Moray Place, Edinburgh	295	380 –	Laing, Janet; and Mrs. Small, wife of Andrew Small	Balgedie, Kinross	293	248 15
Finlay, James	Blalowan, Leslie	7	26 –	Laird, Hugh	Kinross	2	22 12
Flockhart, Heirs of William	Annocroich and Easter Coldrain, Kinross	493	695 –	Lamont, Charles, of Eastbank	Barns House, Kinross	214	350 –
Forfar, Alexander, of Seggiebank	Seggiebank, Milnathort	548	521 12	Lansdowne, Marchioness Dowager of	Baleave and Craighead, Kinross	1,348	786 10
Forgan, James, of Blairhead	Largo	61	127 –	Lawrie, John	Wester Blair, Milnathort	90	34 –
Fraser, William, of Ledlanet	Ledlanet, Milnathort	350	330 –	Layton, Trustees of Mrs.	Kinross	2	59 11
Fraser, William	Tullibole Mill, Kinross	270	380 –	Leslie, Andrew	36 Highbury Hill, London	1	13 –
				Liddall, William, of Kilduff	13 Buckingham Terrace, Edinburgh	485	500 –
				Little, Rev. Walter	Orwell Manse, Milnathort	11	50 –
				Little, Mrs., wife of Rev. Walter Little	Orwell Manse, Milnathort	276	226 10
Gentle, Mary Wemyss	Baberton House, Edinburgh	450	313 –	Livingston, James	Balgedie, Kinross	6	18 10
Gibson, James, of Bankhead	Dollar	296	247 –				
Gibson, William	Gartwhenzean, Dollar	8	41 11				
Gibson, Heirs of William	Westruther, Lauder	646	431 –	M'Ara, Duncan	Rumbling Bridge Hotel, Dollar	10	27 –
Glass, Alexander	Shuttlefold, Milnathort	24	45 –				
Glass, Robert, of Arlary	Arlary, Milnathort	362	806 –	M'Callum, Mrs., wife of Alexander M'Callum	Baulk of Struie, Bridge of Earn	4	16 –
Gray, Heirs of Alexander	Kinross	1	30 7	M'Culloch, Archibald	Kinross	4	68 10
Gray, Mrs. Helen	Kinross	3	28 10	M'Culloch, John	Aberdour	3	92 6
Greig, John, of Tillyrie	Coltness, Wishaw	151	371 15	M'Donald, Alexander, Mrs. Agnes Shoolbraid, and Peter Taylor	Kinnesswood, Kinross	34	34 –
Greig, Mrs., Wife of George Greig; William M'William; and Heirs of George Robertson	Muirs, Kinross	6	18 10	M'Donald, Mrs. Jane	6 Simon Square, Edinburgh	1	4 –
Greig, Mrs. Agnes Helen	5 Coates Place, Edinburgh	68	65 –	M'Dougall, John, of Findaty	Longadale, Lochgilphead	290	330 –
Greig, Mrs. Jean B.	Briglands, Kinross	160	219 15	M'Gill, Heirs of Mrs. Janet	Milnathort	38	170 15
				M'Kenzie, David Lyall	7 North-West Circus Place, Edinburgh	90	30 –
Haig, Alexander	Drum of Tullibole, Kinross	10	15 –	M'William, William	Scotlandwell, Kinross	5	17 5
Haig, James Richard	Blairhill, Dollar	1,690	2,644 7	Mailer, Alexander, of Springhall	Springhall, Milnathort	251	276 –
Haig, William James	Dollar	17	61 8	Maitland, Henry	Muirs, Kinross	2	14 7
Haxton, James, John, Isabella, Janet, and Margaret	Balgedie, Kinross	18	30 –	Malcolm, Heirs of Andrew	Scotlandwell, Kinross	6	22 10
Hay, James	Scotlandwell, Kinross	7	23 –	Malcolm, David	Kinross	1	8 –
Hay, Mary	Scotlandwell, Kinross	5	13 5	Malcolm, Robert Butter	Perth	7	21 15
Hayfield Mortification Trs.	Kinross	19	55 –	Marshall, Trs. of Walter	Duncrevie, Milnathort	368	479 15
Heggie, Andrew	Kilmagadwood, Kinross	10	14 –	Martin, Trustees of George	Tarhill, Kinross	151	201 –
Henderson, George, of Turfhills	Turfhills, Kinross	435	759 –	Martin, James	Carluke	290	275 14
Henderson, Heirs of Robert	Kinross	1	7 –	Menzies, John, of Craigfarg	Inch, Kincardine-on-Forth	155	120 –
Henderson, William	Blairstruie, Path of Condie	3	31 10	Millar, Robert, of Easter Blair	Easter Blair, Milnathort	100	85 –
Henry, Mrs., wife of Isaac A. Henry; and Mrs. Agnes Weighton	Trinity, Edinburgh; Broughty Ferry	155	211 10	Miller, William	Tullibole Muir, Kinross	3	12 5
				Miller, Margaret and Lillias	Drum of Tullibole	11	17 –
Horn, John, of Thomanean	Thomanean, Milnathort	1,431	2,110 2	*Milnathort Wool Spinning Company*	Milnathort	3	300 –
Houston, Heirs of Mrs. Jessie	Kinross	1	75 –	Mitchell, Robert	Golland, Kinross	470	485 –
Hoy, James	Scotlandwell, Kinross	5	17 16	Moncreiff, Lord (Lord Justice-Clerk)	Edinburgh	253	386 –
Hugh, James	4 Great Hamilton Street, Glasgow	2	44 4	Moncrieff, Rev. William S.	14 George Square, Edinburgh	125	155 10
Hunter, William	Fossoway, Kinross	16	27 –	Monro, Hector	Edinburgh	94	209 10
Hutton, James, of Waulkmill	Waulkmill, Milnathort	270	440 –	Montgomery, Sir Graham G., of Stanhope, Bart.	Stobo House, Peebles	2,336	3,129 15

P

KINROSS—continued.

Name of Owner.	Address of Owner.	Estimated Acreage of Property.	Gross Annual Value.	Name of Owner.	Address of Owner.	Estimated Acreage of Property.	Gross Annual Value.
		Acres.	£ s.			Acres.	£ s.
Montgomery, Sir Graham Graham, Bart., John Storer, and Ann Wilson	Bishophill, Kinross	20	8 —	Simpson, James, of Mawcarse	Mawcarse, Milnathort	370	537 —
Montgomery, Thomas H.	Hattonburn, Milnathort	335	662 —	Simpson, James	Duncrevie, Milnathort	2	16 —
Mood, John, of Hatchbank	Newington, Edinburgh	291	348 —	Skene, William Baillie, of Pitlour	Pitlour, Strathmiglo	537	483 —
More, Mrs., wife of James More	Balgedie, Kinross	2	12 —	Skinner, Peter, of Drunzie	Strathmiglo	124	155 —
Morgan, Andrew	Broomhill, Kinross	8	13 10	Small, Andrew	Balgedie, Kinross	9	34 10
Morgan, George	17 King Street, Stirling	3	10 —	Small, Rev. Robert	Southend, Campbelton	3	10 10
Morgan, John	Carnbo, Kinross	2	39 16	Small, Margaret	Kinnesswood, Kinross	3	12 —
Morgan, John	Shanwell, Milnathort	1	11 7	Speed, Mrs., wife of George Speed	Broomhill, Kinross	4	8 —
Morgan, Robert, of Claysike	Newburgh	92	100 —	Spowart, Thomas, of Bellfield	Broomhead, Dunfermline	265	415 5
Morison, John	Milnathort	2	23 —	Steedman, Alexander	Kinross	2	50 10
Morison, John Brown Brown, of Finderlie	Murie House, Errol	164	426 10	Steedman, James, of Fruix	Fruix, Kinross	116	191 —
Morison, Isobel	Milnathort	7	60 5	Steele, Rev. John	Manse, Portmoak	13	38 —
Morrison, Robert	Rashiefold, Milnathort	19	46 10	Stenhouse, Trustees of James, junior	Wester Cleish, Kinross	134	112 —
Morton, Mrs., wife of John Morton, of Drunzie	Cupar	111	170 —	Stobie, Catherine and Helen	Balgedie, Kinross	259	263 15
				Stocks, James	Kinross	1	129 10
				Stocks, James	Blairathort, Milnathort	157	130 —
				Stocks, Lawrence	54 Albert St., Glasgow	3	16 8
Niven, James	West Plains, Bridge of Earn	142	78 —	Stocks, Mrs. Anne	Milnathort	1	10 10
				Storer, John	Glasgow	11	10 —
Niven, Mrs., wife of James Niven and Mrs. Thomson, wife of Hugh Thomson	West Plains, Bridge of Earn Redfordneuk, Milnathort	60	64 —	Sutherland, Mrs., wife of Duncan Sutherland	Inverness	1	10 10
				Syme, David, of Warrock	Kinross	1,168	837 —
Northampton, Marquess of	Castle Ashby, Northampton	864	1,244 4				
Do. do.	Do. (Minerals)	—	200 —	Tainsh, Elizabeth, Isabella, Marion, and Mary	Scotlandwell, Kinross	2	13 15
North British Railway Co.	Edinburgh (Railway)	65	3,484 —	Thomson, Andrew, of Gelvan	11 Northumberland St., Edinburgh	196	182 —
Oliphant, Capt. Lawrence James, of Auchtenny	Condie, Bridge of Earn	1,210	621 —	Thomson, David	Cockamy, Milnathort	20	105 12
Orwell Parochial Board	Milnathort	35	65 —	Thomson, Rev. Peter	1 William St., Stepney, London	51	83 —
				Tod, Alexander	Middleton, Milnathort	3	9 —
				Tod, David	Milnathort	1	2 15
Palmer, Rev. James Nelson	Bembridge, Isle of Wight	360	325 10	Tod, Heirs of George, of East Brackley	Lochran, Kinross	418	390 —
Paterson, David	Lochend, Kinross	7	12 —				
Paton, Jas., of Lethangie	Tillicoultry	209	472 —	Tod, Thomas	Findaty, Kinross	47	100 —
Paxton, Mrs., wife of Hugh Paxton	Arlary, Milnathort	3	9 —	Tod, Heirs of Mrs. Margaret	West Brackley, Kinross	355	424 10
Peat, Admiral David, of Seggie	Viewforth House, Edinburgh	583	795 —				
Peat, John	Manor, Stirling	23	48 5	Vale of Devon Railway Co.	Tillicoultry (Railway)	35	692 —
Peters, Rev. William	Kinross	13	66 10				
Prentice, Robert Russell, of Hoarlawhill	Skeddoway, Kirkcaldy	301	387 —	Walker, James, of Dalry	10 Grosvenor Crescent, Edinburgh	736	606 —
				Weighton, John	Pickletillum, Alyth	12	22 —
Readdie, John, of Cuthill	Perth	330	455 —	Whyte, Andrew	Duncrevie, Milnathort	5	34 15
Reid, George, of Tillyrie	Tillyrie, Milnathort	336	269 —	Whyte, John	Milnathort	4	40 16
Reid, William, of Hardiston	Hardiston, Kinross	240	246 5	Wilson, David	Scotlandwell, Kinross	5	17 —
				Wilson, John	Hill Park, Bannockburn	229	226 4
Richmond, Thomas, of Colliston	Hilton, Perth	435	417 —	Wilson, Thomas	Scotlandwell, Kinross	5	18 2
Ritchie, Thomas, senior	Scotlandwell, Kinross	4	22 11	Wilson, Right Rev. William S.	Ayr	317	425 —
Ritchie, Thomas, junior	Scotlandwell, Kinross	6	47 10	Wilson, Ann	Newlands Feus, Kinross	12	20 10
Robertson, Henry	Milnathort	25	71 —	Wylie, Robert	Trinity-Gask, Auchterarder	8	18 —
Robertson, Heirs of Rev. James	Kinross	4	7 —				
Robertson, Trustees of James	Touchie, Kinross	535	375 —	Young, David	Balgedie, Kinross	105	143 15
Robertson, Peter	Braefoot, Kinross	39	42 —	Young, Harry, of Cleish	Cleish Castle, Kinross	1,910	1,979 10
Ross, Rev. Charles	Manse, Cleish, Kinross	9	40 —	Young, James, of Hallhill	Ayr	140	155 —
Russell, David	Parkhall, Linlithgow	2	13 12	Young, John, as Trustee	Perth	24	10 —
Russell, George	Collins & Co., Glasgow	3	14 14				
Rutherford, Grace	Milnathort	2	46 —				
Scott, Donald	Crook of Devon, Kinross	15	22 10	Total Owners of Land of one Acre and upwards		257	44,802	58,361 4
Seton, Christopher, of Wester Coldrain	Falkland	293	338 10	Total Owners of Lands of less than one Acre in extent		468	86	6,110 10
Sim, David, of Netherton	Muthill, Perth	82	120 —					
Simson, Mrs., wife of Robert Simson	Blairathort, Milnathort	146	220 —	GRAND TOTAL		725	44,888	64,471 14

KIRKCUDBRIGHT.

Population in 1871,	41,859.
Inhabited Houses,	7,457.
Number of Parishes,	28.

Name of Owner.	Address of Owner.	Estimated Acreage of Property.	Gross Annual Value.	Name of Owner.	Address of Owner.	Estimated Acreage of Property.	Gross Annual Value.
		Acres.	£ s.			Acres.	£ s.
Abercromby, Sir Robert John, of Birkenbog and Forglen, Bart.	Forglen House, Turriff	1,339	1,857 16	Black, Captain Archibald, of Kilmichael	Kilmichael, Castle-Douglas	86	196 8
Adamson, John William Mackie, of Balmangan	2 Seton Place, Grange, Edinburgh	289	354 5	Blackett, Lieut.-Colonel Christopher Edward, of Arbigland	Arbigland, Kirkbean	1,453	2,291 17
Adamson, Samuel, of Drumclyer	Terraughty, Dumfries	1,400	1,044 —	Blair, Hugh, of Auchenreoch	15 Randolph Crescent, Edinburgh	266	255 —
Affleck, James and William, of Auchengibbert	Auchengibbert, Crocketford	471	580 17	Blair, Rev. Samuel	Manse of Dalry, Galloway	15	38 —
Affleck, Joseph, of Northpark	Northpark, Lochfoot	90	120 —	Borthwick, Alexander, Richard, Janet, Georgina, and Andrewina, of Drungans	Dumfries	635	72 —
Affleck, Mrs. Margaret, of Over Linkins	Over Linkins, Castle-Douglas	396	126 —	Bowman, Mrs. Elizabeth	Craighead, Dalry, Galloway	15	26 —
Aglionby, Charles, of Rotchell	Virginia, America	140	345 10	Bowstead, Trustees of Mrs. Jane	Castle-Douglas	1,148	1,322 17
Airey, Trustees of late Mrs. Emily	Castle-Douglas	664	952 11	Brown, Rev. George	F.C. Manse, Castle-Douglas	3	36 —
Aitken, James, of East Auchensheen	East Auchensheen, Dalbeattie	37	33 —	Brown, James, of Park	Drummuckloch, Gatehouse	21	50 —
Aitken, John, of West Auchensheen	West Auchensheen, Dalbeattie	56	109 8	Brown, John, of Knockmulloch	4 Rutland Street, Hampstead Road, London	150	218 —
Alexander, James, of Corriedow	Miltonpark, Dalry, Galloway	724	180 —	Brown, John Gordon	Lochanhead, Dumfries	15	56 —
Alexander, William, of Mackilston	Glenhowl, Dalry, Galloway	2,184	640 —	Brown, Samuel	High Street, Dalbeattie	1	60 18
Allan, John, of Largs	Bankend House, Cumnock	272	405 —	Brown, Heirs of William	Craigmullen, Kirkcudbright	22	105 8
Anderson, James, of Killylour	Killylour, Shawhead	501	340 —	Browne, Trustees of late Alexander, of Langlands	Langlands, Twynholm	136	157 15
Anderson, James Simpson	Dalry, Galloway	12	22 —	Bruce, Thomas Rae, of Slogary	Slogary, New Galloway	1,863	611 —
Anderson, William	20 Pavement, York	18	138 15	Buccleuch and Queensberry, Duke of	Drumlanrig Castle, Thornhill	1,000	100 —
Arbuckle, Trustees of late Robert, of Auchenhay	Auchenhay, Borgue, Kirkcudbright	323	328 —	Burnside, Mrs. Elizabeth	45 Buccleuch Street, Dumfries	70	25 —
Armstrong, Thomas	Hillhead, Crocketford	19	25 —	Byrne, John William, of Elshieshields	Elsie House, South Norwood Park, Surrey	454	140 —
Bairden, Thomas	New-Abbey			Caird, Andrew	Abbeybank, New-Abbey	9	40 —
Mrs. Catherine Thomson and Mrs. Mary Smith, of Barr	Clouden, Shawhead / Maxwelltown	239	255 —	Caird, James, of Cassencary	Cassencary, Creetown	2,036	1,296 14
Balmaclellan School, Trustees of	Balmaclellan, Galloway	85	95 —	Caird, John	St. Cuthbert's Cottage, Kirkcudbright	3	45 —
Barbour, William, of Barlay	Barlay, New Galloway	2,120	1,109 —	Caldow, Rev. John A., and Mrs. Janet Grierson	Torpenhow, Aspatria, and Melrose	2	205 —
Barbour, William	Dunmuir House, Castle-Douglas	1	47 —	Caldow, Rev. John A., and Heirs of Mrs. Barbara Hope	Torpenhow, Aspatria, and Glasgow	9	97 —
Barclay, William	Mark, Twynholm	18	22 12				
Barker, David, of Woodland	Woodland, Dumfries	32	134 —	Callander, Robert and William	Minnigaff, Newton-Stewart	1	72 —
Barry, William	Glencroft, Twynholm	14	30 —	Campbell, Trustees of John, of Lochfield	249 West George Street, Glasgow	157	426 —
Beattie, James, of Crochmore	Newton, Dunscore, Dumfries	300	297 —	Campbell, Samuel, of Tonguecroft	Rattra, Kirkcudbright	79	95 —
Beattie, Robert, of Poundland	Poundland, Parton, Castle-Douglas	610	230 —	Campbell, Thomas Walton, of Waltonpark	Waltonpark, Dalbeattie	1,100	1,113 19
Bell, John, of Castlecreavie	Edinburgh	314	270 —	Campbell, Mrs. Isabella	60 North Castle Street, Edinburgh	1	27 2
Bell, John, of Dunjop	Hillowton, Castle-Douglas	235	349 10	Candlish, Rev. John M'Kay	Manse of Carsphairn, Galloway	21	79 —
Bell, William, of Gribdae	Balgreddan, Kirkcudbright	327	299 —	Carlaverock, Kirk-Session of	Dumfries	1,367	872 6
Bell, Mrs. Jane, of Hillowton	Hillowton, Castle-Douglas	550	843 —	Carnegie, Trustees of Mrs. Mary, of Barnshalloch	Barnshalloch, New Galloway	547	331 —
Berwick, Mrs. Janet, of Whiteside	Allanbank, Dumfries	325	263 —	Carruthers, Heirs of James, of Craig	Craig, New Galloway	522	269 —
Biggar, Thomas, of Chapelton	Chapelton, Dalbeattie	202	394 16				
Birney, John, of Glenswinton	Oakley Park, Downpatrick, Ireland	2,855	1,411 —				

KIRKCUDBRIGHT—continued.

Name of Owner.	Address of Owner.	Estimated Acreage of Property.	Gross Annual Value.	Name of Owner.	Address of Owner.	Estimated Acreage of Property.	Gross Annual Value.
		Acres.	£ s.			Acres.	£ s.
Carruthers, Robert, of Crocketford	Crocketford, Dumfries	144	167 —	Cunningham, Alexander, of Nether Linkins	Underwood, Ringford	519	196 —
Carruthers, Mrs. Margaret, of Durhamhill	Durhamhill, Dalbeattie	110	226 6	Cupar Madras Academy, Trustees of	Cupar-Fife	521	674 10
Carsewell, James	Barhill, Dalbeattie	3	73 —				
Carsewell, Robert	Palnackie, Dalbeattie	2	36 5				
Carson, James	Underhill Cottage, Castle-Douglas	3	25 —	Davidson, James, of Summerville	Summerville, Dumfries	25	121 —
Carter, Mrs. Barbara, of Castlehill	Dalbeattie	133	138 10	Dick, David, of Moorbrock	4 Barns Terrace, Ayr	2,000	320 —
Carter, Mrs. Catherine, of Netheryett	Kirkpatrick-Durham, Dalbeattie	12	47 10	Dick, Thomas Boyd, of Barncalzie	Blackpark, Crocketford	876	862 5
Castle-Douglas Free Church, Trustees of	Castle-Douglas	1	80 —	Dickson, Adam, of Pearmount	Pearmount, Dumfries	51	138 —
Castle-Douglas, Town Council of	Castle-Douglas	9	131 —	Dickson, John, Thomas Goldie, Walter George, James Gilchrist, George William, David Scott, and Helen, of Minniebuie	Minniebuie, Corsock, Dalbeattie	2,664	761 10
Cathcart, Colonel The Honble. Augustus Murray, of Brockloch	Spennithorne, Bedale, Yorkshire	1,000	335 —	Dickson, Rev. John Inches	Manse of Kirkbean	13	41 10
Cathcart, Mrs. Jean Macadam, of Craigengillan	Berbeth House, Dalmellington	39,889	5,674 5	Dickson, Thomas, of Crochmore, etc.	Drumcruil, Thornhill, Dumfries	474	461 —
Do. do.	Do. (Lead Mines)	—	58 3	Dinwoodie, Thomas, of Kirkland	Dryburgh, Castle-Douglas	57	100 —
Cavet, Trustees of late James, of Little Larg	Little Larg, Crocketford	193	130 —	Dobie, Andrew	Rockpark, Castle-Douglas	3	68 —
Chalmers, Archibald, of Kipp	Kipp, Dalbeattie	165	195 —	Douglas, Mary Rorrison, and Jane Newall Douglas	New Galloway	5	10 —
Champion, Trustees of late Rev. John, of Barwhillanty	Edale, Hope, Sheffield	1,772	1,482 12	Downie, Rev. William	New-Abbey, Dumfries	7	56 —
Charters, Mrs. Jane	Kirkpatrick-Durham, Dalbeattie	4	16 —	Drew, James, of Craigencallie	Doonhill, Newton-Stewart	4,000	358 10
Clark, James, of Dunmuir	Dunmuir, Castle-Douglas	45	134 —	Drew, Representatives of William, of Craigneuk	Glasgow	254	60 —
Clark, James, of Bush	Bush of Killylour, Shawhead, Dumfries	113	174 5	Dudgeon, Henry Hepburn, of Woodhead	Woodhead, Dumfries	610	185 —
Clark, John Gilchrist, of Speddoch	Dabton, Thornhill	1,484	786 —	Dudgeon, Patrick, of Cargen	Cargen, Dumfries	871	1,631 1
Clark, Maxwell, of Little Culmain	Little Culmain, Crocketford	194	203 —	Dumfries and Maxwelltown Waterworks Trust	Dumfries	1	115 —
Cleland, Andrew, of Deanston	18 Shakespeare Street, Nottingham	163	156 —	Dumfries, Magistrates and Town Council of	Dumfries	3	476 8
Coltart, Alexander and Robert	Palnackie			Dun, George, of Brandedleys	Brooklands, Crocketford	58	58 10
John Coltart	Glasgow	182	354 16	Dunbar, Robert Lennox, of Machermore	5 Brompton Sq., London	1,013	1,338 8
and Mrs. Mary Edgar, of Threave Mains	Whitehaven			Do. do.	Do. (Mines)	—	15 —
Coltart, Marion and Elizabeth	Haugh of Urr, Dalbeattie	1	23 5	Duncan, Trustees of late Alexander, of Ernmenzie	Edinburgh	160	230 —
Colvin, Rev. John	Manse of Kirkmabreck, Creetown	28	75 —	Duncan, Thomas, of East Glenarm	Belmont, Otley, Yorkshire	243	405 —
Do. do.	Do. (Quarry)	—	105 18	Dunlop, Mrs. Eliza Esther Murray, of Corsock	Corsock House, Dalbeattie	12,774	5,213 1
Commissioners of Supply	Kirkcudbright	2	96 10				
Comrie, James, of Gategill	Gategill, Gatehouse	891	851 —				
Connell, Mrs. Helen	Moat of Troqueer, Dumfries	20	105 —	Eccles, James, of Larg	Springwell House, Blackburn	864	730 —
Cook, Rev. George	Manse of Borgue, Kirkcudbright	26	81 —	Edgar, Rev. Andrew	Manse of Tongland, Kirkcudbright	10	52 —
Copland, Charles, of Colliston	Blackwood, Dumfries	714	372 5	Edinburgh, Town Council of, as Trustees of late William Lennie	City Chambers, Edinburgh	190	167 13
Do. do.	Do. (Quarry)	—	50 —	Elliot, John, junior	Maidenholm, Dalbeattie	3	73 7
Copland, John	Mount Sydney, Dumfries	48	77 —	Ewart, John, of Shenrick	Shenrick, Crocketford	142	100 10
Corrie, John, of Senwick	Senwick, Kirkcudbright	1,062	1,155 19				
Corson, Rev. William, of Blackmark	Manse of Girvan	381	75 —				
Cowan, David	Dalry, Galloway	1	117 —	Ferguson, John Chrystal	Castle St., Kirkcudbright	1	90 10
Cowan, John and Janet, of Dildawn	Dildawn, Castle-Douglas	221	416 —	Ferguson, Robert Cutlar, of Craigdarroch	Craigdarroch, Moniaive	1,539	1,707 7
Cowan, Rev. Samuel	Manse of Kelton, Castle-Douglas	17	54 —	Ferguson, Robert Don Gillon, of Isle	31 Chester Street, Edinburgh	4	11 —
Craig, Mrs. Janet, of Valleyfield	Valleyfield, Castle-Douglas	52	72 10	Ferguson, Margaret Crosbie, Mrs. Helen Ferguson, and Mrs. Nicholas Primrose	Dumfries	8	73 5
Craig, James, of Gateside	Maxwelltown, Dumfries	91	156 19				
Craig, Joseph, of Three Crofts	Three Crofts, Lochfoot	177	166 —	Ferguson, John, of Kilquhanity	Kilquhanity, Dalbeattie	737	750 —
Craig, William, of Milnthird	Milnthird, Castle-Douglas	227	195 —	Finlay, James	78 South Street, Prince's Park, Liverpool	62	85 —
Cuninghame, Richard Dunning Barré, of Hensol	Hensol, Castle-Douglas	2,886	1,983 —	Finlay, Children of late James, of East Logan	Castle-Douglas	262	491 8

KIRKCUDBRIGHT—continued.

Name of Owner.	Address of Owner.	Estimated Acreage of Property.	Gross Annual Value.	Name of Owner.	Address of Owner.	Estimated Acreage of Property.	Gross Annual Value.
		Acres.	£ s.			Acres.	£ s.
Fisher, William	35 Port-Dundas Road, Glasgow	5	14 –	Halliday, Capt. David, of Chapmanton, 11th Regiment	Glasgow	267	415 –
Forbes, William, of Callendar	Callendar House, Falkirk	40,445	7,639 11	Halliday, Mrs. Marion, of Mulloch	Balcary House, Auchencairn	451	619 5
Forrest, James, of Brockloch	Kirriemuir	307	237 –	Hamilton, George	Ardendee, Kirkcudbright	4	67 –
Forrester, William, of Blaiket	Arngibbon, Kippen, Stirling	1,035	1,122 10	Hamilton, John Craik	Arundel, Maxwelltown	1	50 –
				Hamilton, William Charles Stewart, of Craighlaw	Craighlaw, Kirkcowan	152	185 –
Forsyth, Heirs of Philip, of Nithside	Nithside, Dumfries	72	213 10	Do. do.	Do. (Mines)	–	20 –
Foulds, Samuel	Greenock	4	13 10	Hamilton, Mrs. Janet	Newhouse, Beeswing, Dumfries	15	13 10
Fraser, Rev. James	Manse of Colvend, Dalbeattie	12	50 –	Hannah, Mrs. Grace	Blackloch, Kirkpatrick-Durham, Dalbeattie	3	9 6
				Hannah, William Couper	Calcutta	3	60 –
				Hannay, Major Frederick Rainsford, of Kirkdale	Kirkdale, Gatehouse	3,938	2,140 10
Galloway, Earl of	Galloway House, Garliestown	55,981	7,333 12	Do. do.	Do. (Quarry)	–	45 –
Geddes, David, of Bellrigg	23 Norton St., Liverpool	54	98 –	Hannay, James Lennox, of Lincluden	67 Queen's Gardens, Bayswater, London	2,848	1,700 17
Gibson, James	Haugh of Urr, Dalbeattie	1	10 10				
Gillespie, Rev. James Ewer	Manse of Kirkgunzeon	11	36 –	Hannay, John, of Barbey	Mill of Borgue, Kirkcudbright	110	202 –
Gillespie, William, of Little Culloch	Scroggiehill, Castle-Douglas	280	280 –	Hannay, Robert, of Rusko	Springfield, Ulverstone	2,390	1,068 10
Gillespie, Mrs. Susan, of Park	Craignair St., Dalbeattie	91	85 –	Hannay, Mary, Elizabeth, and Robina	Flowerbank, Creebridge, Newton-Stewart	1	20 –
Glasgow and South-Western Railway Company	Glasgow (Railway)	308	24981 –	Henderson, James, of Burnbrae	Burnbrae, Crocketford	211	209 6
Good, John	Dalry, Galloway	1	24 17	Heron, James, of Duncow	Duncow, Dumfries	556	605 11
Good, William	Dalry, Galloway	3	33 10	Heron, Captain John Maxwell, of Heron	25 Hans Place, London	12,300	3,452 8
Goodall, John	Laurieknowe, Maxwelltown	16	136 6	Herries, Alexander Young, of Spottes	Spottes, Dalbeattie	987	920 10
Gordon, Rev. Alexander	St. Peter's, Dalbeattie	4	88 10	Herries, Lord	Everingham Park, Yorkshire	3,423	885 15
Gordon, David Alexander, of Culvennan	Greenlaw House, Castle-Douglas	1,067	1,689 4				
Do. do.	Do. (Quarry)	–	20 –	Hill, David	King Street, Castle-Douglas	2	14 –
Gordon, David Hutchison, of Larglanglee	Kirkcudbright	532	266 15	Hilton, Henry, of Fairgirth	Harpurhey Cottage, Harpurhey, Manchester	3,551	1,438 18
Gordon, Robert Macartney, of Rattra	Ellenbank, Kirkcudbright	1,124	636 –	Hoggan, Rev. Charles Adam, of Stranfasket	Stranfasket, New Galloway	1,353	284 10
Gordon, Sir Robert G., of Letterfourie, Bart.	Letterfourie, Buckie	460	437 10	Hood, Mrs. Jane	Newhouse, Beeswing, Dumfries	15	13 10
Gordon, Sir William, of Earlston, Bart.	Earlston, Kirkcudbright	765	1,179 8	Hope, Robert, of Summerhill	11 Cumberland Terrace, Regent's Park, London	100	313 –
Gordon, William, of Threave	Threave House, Castle-Douglas	1,408	2,024 13	Houston, Mrs. Mary	Bridgend of Kildarroch, Borgue, Kirkcudbright	1	10 –
Gordon, William, of Trostrie	Barstibly, Ringford	328	190 –	Howat, Robert Kirkpatrick, of Mabie	Mabie, Dumfries	2,566	2,139 15
Gordon, Heirs of William R., of Campbelton	Redbraes House, Edinburgh	627	631 10	Hughan, Thomas, of Airds	9 West Eaton Place, London	6,605	1,607 7
Gordon, Hon. Mrs. Louisa Gordon Bellamy, of Kenmure	Kenmure Castle, New Galloway	14,093	4,229 18	Hume, Archibald, of Auchendolly	Auchendolly, Dalbeattie	1,850	1,936 15
Gordon, Mrs. Margaret Macadam, of Craigadam	Craigadam, Dalbeattie	717	395 8	Hunter, George, of Lanecroft	Lanecroft, Beeswing, Dumfries	130	100 –
Graham, Rev. William	Manse, Maxwelltown	1	38 –	Hunter, William, of Holmpark	Holmpark, Creetown	42	95 –
Grant, Captain George, of Barholm	Barholm House, Creetown	2,083	1,561 6	Hutchison, Graham, of Balmaghie	Balmaghie House, Castle-Douglas	3,113	2,826 5
Grant, Rev. James Robb	Manse of Buittle, Castle-Douglas	26	50 –	Hutchison, John William, of Edingham	Balmaghie House, Castle-Douglas	1,542	1,593 18
Gray, Thomas Rawson, of King's Grange	King's Grange, Dalbeattie	509	845 –	Hutton, James	Townhead of Glengaber, Holywood, Dumfries	2	124 16
Grierson, James, of Furmiston	Morton Mains, Thornhill	1,270	197 –	Hyslop, Trustees of late Colonel Archibald Geddes, of Lotus	Lotus, Beeswing, Dumfries	432	370 –
Grierson, John	Gordon Street, Dumfries	1	192 17				
Grierson, Trustee of late William	Nottingham Cot., Castle-Douglas	1	67 –	Hyslop, John, of Southpark	Southpark, Lochfoot	65	70 10
Grieve, Mrs. Elizabeth, of Minnidow	Minnidow, Dalbeattie	99	109 10	Hyslop, Trustees of late Thomas, of Woodpark	Woodpark, Dalbeattie	85	76 10
Guthrie, Trustees of late George, of Meikle Ernambrie	Rephad, Stranraer	578	891 –	Hyslop, William, of Knockwalloch	Knockwalloch, Dalbeattie	127	120 –
Haining, Mrs. Mary	Midrigg, Shawhead	22	37 14				
Halbert, John Potts, and Agnew Black Bogie	Annan	26	26 –	Imrie, George James, of Springfield	Springfield, Castle-Douglas	24	60 10
				Irongray, The Poor of	Shawhead, Dumfries	4	5 5
Hall, Trustees of Mrs. Charlotte	Castle-Douglas	526	714 4	Irving, Robert Nasmyth, of Bonshaw	Bonshaw Tower, Ecclefechan	284	320 –
Halliday, Archibald	Townend, Kirkcudbright	1	24 5				

KIRKCUDBRIGHT—continued.

Name of Owner.	Address of Owner.	Estimated Acreage of Property.	Gross Annual Value.	Name of Owner.	Address of Owner.	Estimated Acreage of Property.	Gross Annual Value.
		Acres.	£ s.			Acres.	£ s.
Irving, Thomas, of Curriestanes	51 Bury New Road, Manchester	127	342 —	Laurie, Rowland Craig, of Redcastle	Myra Castle, Downpatrick, Ireland	1,219	1,629 2
Irving, Mrs. Margaret, of Barwhinnock	Barwhinnock, Twynholm	782	1,084 8	Laurie, Thomas, of Locharthur	Locharthur, Beeswing, Dumfries	354	217 —
				Laurie, William Kennedy, of Woodhall	Woodhall, Laurieston, Castle-Douglas	6,569	2,276 13
Jack, Rev. Hugh Morton	Manse of Girthon, Gatehouse	26	65 —	Lawson, James, of Culgruff	Blackburn, Lancashire	268	546 12
Jackson, Janet, of Newton	Newton, Dumfries	17	88 —	Learmont, Thomas	Welldale, Maxwelltown	6	36 —
Johnston, Colonel George, of Balcary	Balcary, Auchencairn	513	465 13	Leny, William Macalpine, of Dalswinton	Dalswinton, Dumfries	1,219	167 —
Johnston, James, of The Hill	The Hill, Creetown	11	91 15	Lidderdale, James	Lochbank, Castle-Douglas	3	53 —
Johnston, Lieut.-General Thomas Henry, of Carnsalloch	Carlinwark, Castle-Douglas	765	688 —	Lindsay, Hugh	Tain, Ross-shire	1	16 —
				Lindsay, James	Islecroft, Dalbeattie	1	45 —
Johnstone, James	Hermitage Croft, Dalbeattie	1	14 10	Livingston, Alexander, of Grobdale	Glenlochar, Castle-Douglas	1,016	140 —
Johnstone, John and Thomas Johnstone, of Waterside	Dumfries Waterside, Terregles, Dumfries	59	85 —	Locke, Robert, and Trustees of late James Locke	39 Regent Park Square, Queen's Park, Glasgow	4	38 —
				Locke, William	Crossmichael Village, Castle-Douglas	1	26 19
Johnstone, Rev. Michael Shaw Stewart	Manse of Minnigaff, Newton-Stewart	17	59 —	Loudon, John, of Clonyard	Clonyard, Dalbeattie	475	474 —
Johnstone, Robert, of Netherhall	Netherhall, Castle-Douglas	156	216 —	Lowden, William Muirhead Herries	Haugh of Urr, Dalbeattie	1	16 7
Johnstone, Rev. Thomas	Manse of Anwoth, Gatehouse	8	44 —				
Johnstone, Major Walter Gracie Farquhar, of Garroch	George Street, Dumfries	168	408 3	M'Burnie, Joseph, of Oakbank	Oakbank, Shawhead, Dumfries	64	83 5
Jones, Trustees of late George Charles, of Brooklands	Brooklands, Crocketford	202	342 —	M'Burnie, Samuel and Thomas, of Knockshinnoch	Knockshinnoch and Meikle Barncleugh, Shawhead	169	197 10
				M'Call, James, of Caitloch	Caitloch, Moniaive	350	100 —
				M'Cartney, George	St. Ninian's Place, Castle-Douglas	2	72 2
Kay, Duncan James, of Drumpark	Drumpark, Dumfries	874	761 5	M'Cartney, George, of Holehouse	Holehouse, Springholm, Dalbeattie	108	134 —
Kennedy, Alexander William Maxwell Clark, of Knockgray	14 Princes Gardens, Princes Gate, London	3,609	1,072 —	M'Cartney, John, of Barlocco	Dundrennan Cottage, Kirkcudbright	333	280 —
Kennedy, John Lawson, of Knocknalling	Knocknalling, Dalry, Galloway	2,646	1,014 10	M'Cartney, Robert, of Kirklandhill	Church Stretton, Salop	30	61 —
Kenworthy, John	Ashton Villa, Tongland, Kirkcudbright	2	26 —	M'Caw, Robert, of Wellhill	Wellhill, Kirkpatrick-Durham, Dalbeattie	135	88 3
Ker, Trustees of late Robert, of Argrennan	Argrennan, Castle-Douglas	959	1,265 —	M'Clellan, Mary	Ringanwhy, Castle-Douglas	6	24 —
Kerr, Trustees of late Alex., of Scroggiehill	Scroggiehill, Castle-Douglas	496	788 —	M'Clymont, William, of Kirkland	Kirkland, Castle-Douglas	39	69 10
Kerr, Samuel	The Grove, Castle-Douglas	4	31 —	M'Culloch, Alexander, of Glen	Kirkclaugh, Gatehouse	4,348	1,266 15
Kinna, James	Masonfield, Newton-Stewart	4	109 15	Do. do.	Do. (Mines)	—	50 —
Kirk, Mrs. Jane, of Drumstinshall	Drumstinshall, Dumfries	636	644 —	M'Culloch, Trustees of late Henry, and Representatives of Mrs. Margaret Cameron Mouat	Kirkmabreck, Creetown	3,077	842 6
Kirkconnell, Thomas, of Westpark	Beeswing, Dumfries	19	30 —	Do. do.	Do. (Quarry)	—	40 —
Kirkcudbright, Magistrates and Town Council of	Kirkcudbright	417	907 9	M'Culloch, Walter, of Ardwall	Ardwall, Gatehouse	4,275	3,064 8
Kirkcudbright Poorhouse Combination of Parishes	Kirkcudbright	2	120 —	M'Dermid, Rev. John, of Maryland	15 Cumberland Street, Glasgow	14	40 —
Kirkpatrick, George	Haugh of Urr, Dalbeattie	1	6 —	M'Douall, James, of Logan	Logan, Stranraer	2,600	1,346 3
Kirkpatrick, John, of Bogrie	Deanside, Lochrutton, Dumfries	210	282 —	M'Dowall, Andrew	Girdstingwood House, Kirkcudbright	74	151 10
Kirwan, Mrs. Matilda Elizabeth Maitland, of Gelston	Gelston Castle, Castle-Douglas	5,080	3,967 8	M'Dowall, James, of Auchnabony	Auchnabony, Kirkcudbright	70	75 —
Kissock, Mrs. Jessie Gillespie, of West Glenarm	Heathview, Tipperary, Ireland	125	150 —	M'Dowall, John, of Girdstingwood	Girdstingwood House, Kirkcudbright	320	325 —
Kissock, Margaret, of Thorn	Thorn, Kirkcudbright	34	42 10	M'Duff, Agnes	Lochhouseshank, Dalbeattie	23	48 —
Knox, Robert	Burnside of Culshan, Dalbeattie	8	18 —	M'Ewan, Robert	Cheshunt, Waltham Cross, Herts	1	3 —
				Macfarlane, Rev. Walter	Manse of Troqueer, Dumfries	13	75 —
Laidlaw, Rev. Andrew	Manse of Kirkpatrick-Durham, Dalbeattie	7	35 —	M'Gowan, Mrs. Isabella, and Anna and Margaret Murray	New Galloway	3	35 —
Laing, Heirs of Robert	Kindar Lodge, New-Abbey	3	125 —	M'Gurk, John	William Street, Dalbeattie	4	32 —

KIRKCUDBRIGHT—continued.

Name of Owner.	Address of Owner.	Estimated Acreage of Property.	Gross Annual Value.	Name of Owner.	Address of Owner.	Estimated Acreage of Property.	Gross Annual Value.
		Acres.	£ s.			Acres.	£ s.
Mackenzie, Edward, of Auchenskeoch	Fawley Court, Henley-on-Thames	6,364	2,905 5	Maxwell, Alexander, Samuel Bryce Elton, and John	Stakeford, Maxwelltown	2	115 –
M'Keur, Mrs. Ann	King Street, Castle-Douglas	2	111 –	Maxwell, Francis, of Gribton	Dunragit, Glenluce	936	647 –
M'Keur, Mrs. Ann, and Janet Broadfoot, of Bearlochan	Castle-Douglas	105	174 10	Maxwell, Frederick Henry Constable, of Terregles	Terregles, Dumfries	15,803	12109 12
M'Kie, George, of Dunjarg	Dunjarg, Castle-Douglas	33	115 –	Maxwell, James Clerk, of Glenlair	Glenlair, Dalbeattie	1,906	1,233 10
M'Kie, James, William, Thomas, and Jessie	Moat House, Dumfries	3	44 –	Maxwell, John	Lochside, Colvend, Dalbeattie	1	11 –
Mackie, Trustees of late Ivie, of Auchencairn	Auchencairn House, Castle-Douglas	3,284	4,210 14	Maxwell, Maxwell Hyslop, of Glengaber	The Grove, Dumfries	400	578 –
Mackie, Trustees of late James, of Bargaly	Ernespie, Castle-Douglas	10,850	2,532 10	Maxwell, Robert, of Breoch	Terregles Banks, Dumfries	389	473 5
M'Kinnel, John, of Macmurdostown	Laurieknowe, Maxwelltown	123	166 –	Maxwell, Trustees of late Wellwood, of Glenlee	Glenlee, New Galloway	15,090	2,736 –
M'Kinnel, Mrs. Agnes, of Macmurdostown	Laurieknowe, Maxwelltown	170	200 –	Maxwell, Wellwood, of Kirkennan	Munches, Dalbeattie	510	421 10
M'Kinnell, John, of Over Arkland	Over Arkland, Castle-Douglas	70	75 –	Maxwell, Wellwood Herries, of Munches, M.P.	Munches, Dalbeattie	4,597	4,728 14
M'Lellan, Mrs. Frances Sophia, of Marks	Kirkcudbright	364	463 10	Do. do.	Do. (Quarries)	–	420 1
M'Master, Maxwell	Borgue Academy, Kirkcudbright	1	12 10	Maxwell, Sir William, of Cardoness, Bart.	Cardoness, Gatehouse	6,381	2,136 4
M'Michan, Trustees of Mrs. Helen M'Morrin, of Corbieton	Corbieton, Castle-Douglas	423	971 –	Maxwell, Agnes, of Westhill	Munches, Dalbeattie	122	170 –
Macmillan, David, of Drumanister	Balmaclellan, New Galloway	300	130 –	Maxwell, Mrs. Mary, of Carruchan	Carruchan, Dumfries	271	570 5
M'Millan, John, of Holm	Glencrosh, Moniaive	3,322	900 –	Maxwell, Margaret Heron	Creebridge House, Newton-Stewart	10	76 –
M'Millan, William, of Chapel	Chapel, Ringford	209	297 –	Maxwell, Mrs. Sarah, of Orchardton	Orchardton, Castle-Douglas	3,495	2,020 16
Macmillan, Wm. M'Call, of Lamloch	Lamloch, Carsphairn, Galloway	1,200	200 12	Millar, Archibald	New-Abbey	2	15 –
M'Millan, Elspeth, of Maryholm	Maryholm, Dumfries	50	172 –	Millar, James, of Priestlands	Priestlands, Dumfries	186	450 10
M'Murdo, Admiral Archibald, of Cargenholm	Cargenholm, Dumfries	12	76 –	Milligan, Rev. John	Manse of Twynholm	37	86 10
M'Murdo, Mrs. Emily, of Mavisgrove	Mavisgrove, Dumfries	92	257 –	Milligan, Trustees of late John, of Barmoffity	Barmoffity, Dalbeattie	212	291 –
M'Neil, Rev. Patrick	F.C. Manse, Auchencairn	5	26 –	Milligan, William	Westpark, Maxwelltown	1	67 –
M'Neillie, Captain William, of Castlehill	Castlehill, Dumfries	373	406 12	Mitchell, Houston, of Port Mary	Bangholm Bower, Trinity Road, Edinburgh	342	538 10
M'Noe, Trustees of late James	Barbush, Troqueer	6	40 5	Mitchell, John, of Westland	New Zealand	271	120 –
Macpherson, Alexander	City Chambers, Edinburgh	2	15 –	Moffat, James, of Ken Ervie	Castle-Douglas	473	325 –
M'Queen, James, of Crofts	Crofts, Dalbeattie	3,422	1,151 8	Monteath, Mrs. Mary, of Ryedale	Enclosure House, Stirling	38	157 4
M'Turk, John, of Knocksting	Cranoe, Market Harboro', Leicester	775	135 –	Moore, John Carrick, of Corsewall	Corsewall, Stranraer	3,515	2,132 10
M'Turk, Mrs. Elizabeth	Ullioch, Castle-Douglas	10	29 –	Moore, Rev. William	Manse of Lochrutton	11	39 –
M'William, Heirs of George	Wigan	1	45 –	Moray, Earl of	Darnaway Castle, Forres	339	345 –
M'William, James and Robert, of Garrochar	Lewis Street, Stranraer } Elm Row, Edinburgh	544	592 11	Murdoch, James, of Drumwhirn	Drumwhirn, Corsock, Dalbeattie	1,161	250 15
M'William, John, and James Milligan M'William	King Street, Castle-Douglas	1	52 12	Murdoch, John	Balmoral Cottage, Castle-Douglas	1	80 10
M'William, Mrs. Agnes, of Easthill	Grennan, Dalry, Galloway	55	75 –	Mure, Heirs of James Ochterlony Lockhart, of Livingston	Livingston, Castle-Douglas	1,240	1,056 –
Maitland, David, of Compstone	Compstone, Kirkcudbright	2,304	2,145 7	Murphy, Samuel, of Kirkbride	Kirkbride, Kirkcudbright	338	170 –
Maitland, Heirs of late David, of Valleyfield	Valleyfield, Ringford	540	817 –	Murray, Benjamin Rigby, of Parton	Parton Place, Castle-Douglas	1,256	1,217 6
Maitland, Heirs of late James, of Barnbachle	Kells, New Galloway	347	296 –	Murray, Rev. George, of Troquhain	Balmaclellan Manse, New Galloway	2,412	833 5
Maitland, John, of Barcaple	3 Ainslie Place, Edinburgh	231	463 –	Neilson, James	Meikleyett, Tongland, Kirkcudbright	7	33 –
Maitland, William Fuller, of High Barcaple	Stanstead, Bishop-Stortford	464	348 15	Neilson, Walter Montgomerie, of Queenshill	Queenshill, Ringford	1,822	1,558 16
Maitland, Catherine, and Helen Goldie, of Chipperkyle	Chipperkyle, Dalbeattie	179	204 –	New-Abbey, Kirk-Session of	New-Abbey	214	193 10
Maitland, Elizabeth Agnes	Fludha Cottage, Kirkcudbright	2	34 –	Newall, Ann	New-Abbey	5	20 –
Maitland, Mrs. Margaret, of Compstone	Compstone, Kirkcudbright	5	95 –	Newall, Mrs. Marion, of Goldielea	Goldielea, Dumfries	447	883 –
Martin, William	Kelton, Dumfries	2	16 15	Newall, Heirs of Nicholas (spinster)	Craigend, New-Abbey	300	77 10
Martin, Mrs. Elizabeth	Queen St., Castle-Douglas	2	104 17	Nicholson, Heirs of John, of Arkland	Castle-Douglas	175	186 15
				Nicol, Rev. Thomas	Manse of Kells, New Galloway	12	34 –

KIRKCUDBRIGHT—continued.

Name of Owner.	Address of Owner.	Estimated Acreage of Property.	Gross Annual Value.	Name of Owner.	Address of Owner.	Estimated Acreage of Property.	Gross Annual Value.
		Acres.	£ s.			Acres.	£ s.
Oswald, Richard Alexander, of Auchincruive	Auchincruive, Ayr	24,160	16184 17	Selkirk, Earl of	St. Mary's Isle, Kirkcudbright	20,823	19749 10
Otto, Mrs. Susan, and Mrs. Margaret C. Barker	Newark, Sanquhar ⎫ Woodland, Dumfries ⎭	50	51 —	Do. do. Shaw, Trustees of late Ebenezer, of Drumrash	Do. (Mines) Wigtown	— 683	20 — 367 10
Ovens, Walter, of Torr	Lynwood, Galashiels	700	597 —	Skinner, William, of Corra	31 Great King Street, Edinburgh	250	445 5
				Skirving, Adam, of Croys	Croys, Dalbeattie	727	938 3
Pagan, George Hair	Cupar-Fife	5	34 —	Sloan, Alexander, John, and Robert, of Barbain	Barbain, Dalbeattie	110	50 —
Paterson, James	Drumwhannie, Beeswing	13	27 —	Sloan, James, of Waterside	Brighton	106	130 —
Paterson, John, of Milton	Craigdarroch, Sanquhar	454	510 —	Sloan, James, of Barbeth	Dumfries	803	259 2
Paterson, Trustees of late Robert, of Nunfield	Nunfield, Dumfries	45	105 —	Sloan, Trustees of John Cumming	Ironshinnie, Dalbeattie	178	236 2
Paterson, Mrs. Isabella, of Airrieland	Castle-Douglas	820	550 —	Smith, James, of South Carleton	Roberton, Borgue, Kirkcudbright	127	167 16
Paterson, Jessie	Albyn House, Dalry, Galloway	1	26 —	Smith, James, and Mrs. Janet Murphy	Cairnyard, Beeswing, ⎫ Dumfries Foremannoch, Lochrutton ⎭	291	348 —
Pattullo, Rev. Henry Alexander	Manse of Parton, Castle-Douglas	18	60 —				
Payne, John	King Street, Castle-Douglas	2	222 10	Smith, John	Chelsea Barracks, London	2	22 —
Platt, Trustees of late William Wright, of Kirkennan	Kirkennan, Dalbeattie	12	115 —	Smith, Robert	Southpark, Springholm, Dalbeattie	12	16 —
Portpatrick Railway Coy.	Stranraer (*Railway*)	247	5,094 —	Smith, Thomas Ferguson	Millbrae, Maxwelltown	1	60 —
Primrose, Alexander and William, of Palmerston	Kirkhouse, Kirkbean, and Ingliston, New Abbey	13	125 —	Smith, Nicholas (spinster)	Low Lochbank, New-Abbey	4	10 —
Primrose, William	Primrosehill, Maxwelltown	2	60 —	Society for Propagating Christian Knowledge	Edinburgh	737	791 6
Pringle, Andrew, of Borgue	Borgue, Kirkcudbright	1,327	1,628 —	Spalding, Augustus Frederick Montagu, of Holme	24 Charles Street, Berkeley Square, London	3,785	4,259 —
Proudfoot, Heirs of James	America	3	11 —				
Purdie, Nathaniel	Slatehole, Rhonehouse, Castle-Douglas	1	10 12	Sproat, David, of Standingstone	Kirkcudbright	191	200 —
				Sproat, John	Landis, New-Abbey	15	29 —
Rae, Jane, of Park	Park, Dumfries	45	148 5	Sproat, Mrs. Jean, of Auchengassell	Auchengassell, Twynholm	429	323 —
Rain, William, of Miefield	Kempleton, Twynholm	851	265 5	Sproat, Mrs. Mary	High St., Kirkcudbright	3	48 —
Ramsay, Trustees of John, of Dallash	Coulby Manor, Yorkshire	566	339 10	Starke, James, of Troqueerholm	Troqueerholm, Dumfries	46	172 —
Rawlin, Thomas, of Little Furthhead	Little Furthhead, Dalbeattie	139	157 —	Stephen, Rev. James Innes	Manse of Terregles, Dumfries	13	45 10
Renny, William John, of Danevale	Danevale Park, Castle-Douglas	610	1,036 —	Stevenson, Rev. Thomas	Manse of Balmaghie, Castle-Douglas	18	57 —
Rhenius, Rev. Josiah	F.C. Manse, Tongland, Kirkcudbright	3	32 10	Stewart, Horatio Granville Murray, of Broughton	Cally, Gatehouse	45,867	14615 16
Richardson, Christopher Pringle	Castle-Douglas	1	35 2	Do. do. Stewart, James, of Cairnsmore	Do. (*Mines*) Cairnsmore, Newton-Stewart	— 5,625	20 — 1,605 17
Richardson, William, of Slongaber	44 Dick Place, Edinburgh	1,000	431 —	Stewart, Rev. John Douglas	Manse of Crossmichael, Castle-Douglas	23	55 —
Riddick, John	Ashleybank, Castle-Douglas	3	46 —	Stewart, Mark John, younger, of Southwick	Ardwell, Stranraer	10	12 —
Robinson, Rev. George, of Almorness	Almorness, Dalbeattie	1,825	1,321 3	Stewart, Mark Sprot, of Southwick	Southwick, Dumfries	2,310	1,939 —
Robson, Robert, of Nether Barncleugh	Nether Barncleugh, Shawhead	222	230 —	Stewart, Patrick	Walltrees, Twynholm	6	12 —
Rutherford, John	Copland Street, Dalbeattie	1	99 8	Stewart, William, of Shambellie	Shambellie, New-Abbey	2,468	1,517 18
				Strong, John, of Barlochan	4 Chapel Walks, Liverpool	377	617 —
				Swan, Robert, of Brae	Brae, Lochrutton, Dumfries	1,243	1,173 —
Sanders, John	New Zealand	5	26 5	Symons, John	Irish Street, Dumfries	5	73 10
Sanderson, Captain Archibald Christie, of Glenlaggan	Glenlaggan, Castle-Douglas	1,400	650 16				
Sandilands, Rev. John Macrae	Manse of Urr, Dalbeattie	15	55 —	Tayleur, Edward, of Dalscairth	Dalscairth, Dumfries	575	617 —
Scot, Thomas Goldie, of Craigmuie	Craigmuie, Moniaive	1,592	564 10	Thomson, Rev. James	Manse of Rerwick, Kirkcudbright	15	50 —
Scott, John Lindsay, of Mollance	Mollance, Castle-Douglas	493	976 —	Thomson, Trustees of late James, of Hazlefield	Hazlefield, Auchencairn	682	631 9
Scott, Samuel, of Auchenfranco	12 Watling Street, Manchester	584	785 10	Thomson, John, of Milton Mains	Milton Mains, Crocketford	97	97 —
Scott, Walter, of Broomlands	Broomlands, Dumfries	19	192 —	Thomson, Robert, of Rigghead	Rigghead, Shawhead	104	147 —
Scott, Walter, & Sons	Troqueer Mills, Maxwelltown	6	714 —	Threshie, Mrs. Jessie, of Barnbarroch	Barnbarroch, Dalbeattie	912	525 6
Seaton, Robert, Agnes, Jane, Margaret, and Lucy	New-Abbey	4	40 4	Trueman, Mrs. Penelope Susan, of Torrs	Oakwell, Canterbury	427	586 1
				Turnbull, John	Minto Cottage, Twynholm	11	12 —

KIRKCUDBRIGHT—continued.

Name of Owner.	Address of Owner.	Estimated Acreage of Property.	Gross Annual Value.	Name of Owner.	Address of Owner.	Estimated Acreage of Property.	Gross Annual Value.
		Acres.	£ s.			Acres.	£ s.
Underwood, Rev. John	Kirkcudbright	9	71 5	Wilson, John, of Burnbrae	Burnbrae, Castle-Douglas	41	54 18
Underwood, Rev. Thomas	Manse of Irongray, Dumfries	12	47 10	Wilson, Samuel	Orchardton Mains, Palnackie, Dalbeattie	2	141 10
				Witham, Robert Maxwell, of Kirkconnell	Kirkconnell, Dumfries	2,974	2,739 9
Walker, Lieut.-Col. Geo. G., of Crawfordton, M.P.	Crawfordton House, Thornhill	353	64 —	Wood, William, of Culshan	Springholm, Dalbeattie	127	184 7
Walker, James, of Conchieton	Conchieton, Kirkcudbright	185	237 —	Wright, William and John, of Bonerick	Bonerick, Shawhead	159	187 —
Walker, John	Moat of Urr, Dalbeattie	1	3 —				
Wallace, John	The Grange, Eden Hall, Penrith	3	30 —	Yorstoun, Mrs. Emma Grierson, of Ballingear	Ballingear, New Galloway	1,476	695 5
Wark, Rev. David	Manse of Auchencairn	6	23 —	Young, Right Hon. George, M.P.	28 Moray Place, Edinburgh	207	198 10
Welsh, Trustees of James, of Furthhead	Dumfries	342	505 —	Young, Major Thomas, of Lincluden	Lincluden House, Dumfries	1,318	1,212 8
Welsh, James, of Skaar	M'Naughton, Shawhead	1,041	340 7	Young, Mrs. Marion, of Rosefield	Rosefield, Maxwelltown	7	90 —
Welsh, Mrs. Helen, of Town of Urr	Town of Urr, Dalbeattie	48	80 —				
Whigham, James, of Margreig	4 Craven Terrace, Ealing, London	800	140 —				
Wightman, John, of Breconside	Armannoch, Lochrutton	891	569 10	Total Owners of Land of one Acre and upwards 478		571,524	329,304 9
Wightman, John Thomson, of Head	Head, Lochfoot	86	90 —	Total Owners of Lands of less than one Acre in extent 1,908		426	31,655 18
Wightman, Mrs. Barbara, of Foremannoch	Armannoch, Lochrutton	89	113 —				
Wilson, Rev. James S.	Manse of New-Abbey	13	67 10	GRAND TOTAL . . . 2,386		571,950	360,960 7

LANARK.

Population in 1871,	**765,339.**
Inhabited Houses,	**47,962.**
Number of Parishes,	**41.**

Name of Owner.	Address of Owner.	Estimated Acreage of Property.	Gross Annual Value.	Name of Owner	Address of Owner.	Estimated Acreage of Property.	Gross Annual Value.
		Acres.	£ s.			Acres.	£ s.
Adam, James	Millerston, Glasgow	1	20 15	Alston, John	Breckonhill, Hamilton	30	42 –
Adam, John	Larchgrove, Shettleston	25	142 –	Alston, John P., of Muirburn	Muirburn, Hamilton	666	1,337 –
Adam, William	Airdrie	4	143 5	Alston, Robert	Loudonhill, Darvel	99	180 –
Do.	Do. (*Minerals*)	–	150 –	Alston, Robert L.	West Hartlepool	92	202 –
Addie, Alexander, of Braidhurst	Braidhurst, Motherwell	248	675 –	Alston, Robert L.	14 Van Mildert Terrace, Stockton-on-Tees	183	220 –
Addie, John	Newarthill	10	76 –				
Addie, Robert	Langloan, Coatbridge	4	135 –	Alston, William, of Stockbriggs	Stockbriggs, Lesmahagow	2,570	1,500 –
Addie, Robert, & Sons	Langloan, Monkland	465	4,811 –	Do. do. (*Minerals*)		–	289 –
Do. do. (*Minerals*)		–	40 –	Anderson, George	Springfield, Blantyre	234	318 –
Affleck, James	9 Ravensworth Terrace, Newcastle-on-Tyne	3	24 –	Anderson, John	Hosnet, Strathaven	40	50 –
Aikman, Alexander	Hollandbush, Hamilton	1	132 –	Anderson, Rev. John	Culter, Biggar	11	63 –
Aikman, Alexander	Ivy Grove, Hamilton	6	524 –	Anderson, James W.	Kincaid House, Campsie (*Vacant Ground*)	11	150 –
Aikman, G. R., of Ross	Hamilton	1,020	1,386 –	Anderson, Trs. of James	Airdrie	3	120 15
Aitken, David	Carnwath	2	8 –	Anderson & Waugh	Holehouse, Slamannan	101	40 –
Aitken, James	2 Claremont Terrace, Glasgow	12	111 –	Anderson, William	Simsonland, Hamilton	1	7 –
Aitken and Mansell	Whiteinch, Glasgow	5	1,122 12	Anderson, Rev. William	Prospect House, Uddingston	2	50 –
Aitken, Robert C.	2 Claremont Ter., Glasgow (*Vacant Ground*)	1	5 –	Andrews, Henry	Crawforddyke St., Carluke	10	15 –
Aitken, Trs. of William	Chapel, Wishaw	101	302 –	Andrews, Mrs. Mary	Crawforddyke St., Carluke	20	25 –
Aitkenhead, James, and others	Rutherglen	3	9 –	Annan, William	Lanark	9	91 –
Aitkenhead, Heirs of William	Rutherglen	5	253 –	Anstruther, Sir Windham C. J. Carmichael, of that Ilk, Bart.	Westraw House, Lanark	13,624	9,228 –
Aitchieson, Mrs. Christina	Springbank, Bothwell	1	40 –	Do. do. (*Minerals*)	Do.	–	722 –
Aiton, Trustees of Mrs. Mary S.	22 Abercromby Place, Edinburgh	10	48 –	Archibald, George	Quothquan, Biggar	3	7 –
Airdrie and Coatbridge Water Company	Airdrie	144	921 –	Archibald, Rev. Robert	New Monkland	13	40 –
Airdrie Gas Company	Airdrie	1	700 –	Armour, Andrew	South Cairnduff, Strathaven	63	40 –
Airdrie Iron Company	Airdrie	1	100 –	Armour, John and Robert	South Cairnduff, Strathaven	63	80 –
Alexander, Alexander John	Airdrie House, Airdrie	798	1,399 6	Armour, King, & Gray	Rutherglen	1	333 –
Do. do. (*Minerals*)	Do.	–	2,170 15	Armour, Robert	Waterside, Carmunnock	85	254 –
Alexander, Archibald, of Boydston	Ardrossan	1,509	476 –	Arnot, James C.	121 Douglas Street, Glasgow	15	82 –
Alexander, Charles S.	84 South Bridge, Edinburgh	1	252 –	Arnot, Thomas L.	Laurelbank, Partick	1	120 –
Alexander, George	Dowanhill Gardens, Glasgow	1	205 –	Arthur, John	80 Argyle Street, Glasgow	2	90 –
Alexander, James	19 Argyle St., Glasgow	5	56 –	Arthur, William	Woodlea, Bothwell	1	80 –
Alexander, John	Dowanhill, Glasgow	1	145 –	Austine & Co.	Hamilton	8	347 –
Alexander, William, and Mrs. Janet	Nerston, East Kilbride	39	97 –	Austine, John	Almada Street, Hamilton	1	89 –
Alexander, Mrs. Janet	Nerston, East Kilbride	53	101 –	Ayton, James	Forth Mains, Carnwath	38	30 –
Alexander, Mrs. Jean	Forth, Carnwath	30	19 –				
Allan, Alexander	Hillhead, Carluke	41	72 –				
Allan, Elizabeth H.	Westmains, Stonehouse	22	41 –	Baillie-Cochrane, A. D. R. W., of Lamington, M.P.	Lamington House, Biggar	10,833	5,539 –
Allan, Trustees of James	Rutherglen	5	389 –	Do. do. (*Minerals*)		–	788 –
Allan, John	Burnbank Cot., Carluke	108	76 –	Baillie, James William, of Culterallers	Arundel Villa, Croydon, Surrey	4,510	1,826 –
Allan, Trustees of John B., of Eddlewood	St. Paul's Churchyard, London	450	732 –	Baillie, Heirs of John	Cuparhead, Coatbridge	12	15 –
Allan, Thomas	Maryhill Road, Glasgow	2	80 –	Baillie, John M.	15 Northumberland St., Edinburgh	138	184 –
Allan, Janet	29 Bartholomew Street, Glasgow	37	34 –	Baillie, William A.	177 Buchanan Street, Glasgow	83	31 10
Allan, Mrs. Jean	Burnbank, Carluke	1	14 –	Do. do. (*Minerals*)		–	228 19
Allison, Alexander	Hill of Kilncadzow, Carluke	75	150 –	Baillie, William H.	43 Norfolk Sq., London	178	260 –
Allison, Trs. of Joseph	Hillhead, Strathaven	40	131 –	Baillie, Trustees of late Dowager Lady Mary	Maryhill	99	165 –
Allison, Thomas	Over Letham, Strathaven	196	310 –	Baird, Archibald	Rutherglen	1	122 –
Allison, William	Dunavon, Strathaven	188	281 –	Baird, James	Kirkmuirhill, Lesmahagow	1	15 –
Alston, George, of Craighead	Craighead, Hamilton	167	412 –				

LANARK—continued.

Name of Owner.	Address of Owner.	Estimated Acreage of Property.	Gross Annual Value.		Name of Owner.	Address of Owner.	Estimated Acreage of Property.	Gross Annual Value.
		Acres.	£ s.				Acres.	£ s.
Baird, Heirs of John	Lochwood, Old Monkland	662	1,206 –		Blantyre, Lord	Erskine House, Renfrew	835	510 –
Do. do.	Do. (*Minerals*)	–	400 –		Do.	Do. (*Minerals*)	–	225 –
Baird, Matthew	High Cross, Carluke	16	37 –		*Blantyre Bowling Club*	Pildacre, Blantyre	1	12 –
Baird, William, & Co.	Gartsherrie, Coatbridge	1,152	8,418 –		*Blochairn Iron Company*	182 Hope St., Glasgow	37	80 –
Do. do.	Do. (*Minerals*)	–	4,254 7		Boe, David	Quothquan, Biggar	3	4 –
Baker, Joseph	Woodside, Coatbridge	2	80 –		Bogue, Robert A.	Beechhill, Govan	1	65 –
Ballantyne, John	Fiddlersbridgebar, Carluke	20	15 –		*Botanic Gardens, Proprietors of*	106 St. Vincent Street, Glasgow	24	206 –
Ballantyne, William	Lanark	1	16 –		*Bothwell Free Church, Trustees of*	Bothwell	1	65 –
Bank of Scotland	Edinburgh	1	50 –		Bowie, Thomas	33 Wellgate St., Lanark	3	179 –
Bankier, Robert	Stepps, Cadder	1	54 8		Boyd, James B.	Mayflatt, Hamilton	72	100 –
Bannatyne, Andrew, jun.	Wellhall Road, Hamilton	1	55 –		Boyd, James C.	Burton Villa, Wrexham	1	322 –
Bannatyne, Mrs. Margaret	Millheugh, Blantyre	144	389 –		Boyd, John	149 St. Vincent Street, Glasgow	20	50 –
Bannerman, Walter	85 Hope Street, Glasgow	158	222 –					
Barclay, Curle, & Co.	Whiteinch, Glasgow	15	2,436 19		Boyd, Mrs. Mary	Raploch Croft, Larkhall	6	30 –
Barony Parochial Board	38 Cochran St., Glasgow	36	1,637 –		*Braehead U.P. Church, Trustees of*	Carnwath	33	25 –
Barr, James	Clydeside, Uddingston	76	852 –					
Do.	Do. (*Minerals*)	–	150 –		Brand, Harvey, & Co.	37 New Broad Street, London	10	43 18
Barr, William	Uddingston	1	204 –					
Barr, Mrs Ann	Carnarvon Street, Glasgow	155	300 5		Brand, Robert	Laigh Coats, Coatbridge	6	425 –
Barr, Marion and Mary	Moat, Lesmahagow	222	233 –		Brander, Rev. James	Clarkston, New Monkland	6	33 10
Barnhill, Mrs. Janet	Jackton, East Kilbride	4	19 –		Breckonridge, Samuel	Biggar	1	5 –
Barrie, Trustees of John	Bushelhead, Carluke	1	22 –		Breeze, James	Balgray Tower, Springburn	12	296 –
Barrow, Fred. Augustus.	Viewpark, Partick	1	72 –		*British Linen Co. Bank*	Edinburgh	1	105 –
Barrowman, James	Marchbank Cottage, Bo'ness	1	171 –		Brown, Alexander	Mayfield, Biggar	2	23 –
Battismains Mortification	Lanark	19	52 –		Brown, Archibald	Flatt, Glassford	9	20 –
Baxter, James	Summerhill, Lesmahagow	1	10 –		Brown, James, junior	The Orchard, Carluke	297	478 –
Baxter, John	Blackwood, Lesmahagow	1	66 –		Do. do.	Do. (*Minerals*)	–	160 –
Begg, Hugh A.	103 Hutcheson Street, Glasgow	14	30 –		Brown, James	Govanpark, Glasgow	1	140 –
Belch, John	9 Stobcross Street, Glasgow	69	264 –		Brown, James Thomas, of Auchlochan	Auchlochan, Lesmahagow	3,100	1,718 –
					Do. do.	Do. (*Minerals*)	–	761 –
Belhaven, Trustees of Lord	Wishaw	2,078	4,674 –		Brown, John	Brandon Grove, Helensburgh	719	982 –
Do. do.	Do. (*Minerals*)	–	19521 –		Do.	Do. (*Minerals*)	–	5 –
Bell, Andrew	Westerhouse, Wishaw	400	180 –		Brown, John	Dykehead, Shotts	1	10 –
Bell, Benjamin B.	17 Gordon St., Glasgow	816	190 –		Brown, John	High Street, Carluke	1	75 –
Do.	Do. (*Minerals*)	–	161 –		Brown, John	Whitecleugh, Carstairs, Lanark	2	65 –
Bell, John	Glasgow Pottery, Glasgow	4	150 –					
Bell, Rev. John	Pettinain, Lanark	9	48 –		Brown, Peter	Biggar	6	89 –
Bell, Trustees of John	Cambusnethan, Wishaw	1	356 –		Brown, Thomas, of Lanfine	Lanfine, Newmills	1,161	345 –
Bell, Robert	Wishaw	2	265 –		Do. do.	Do. (*Minerals*)	–	35 –
Bellahouston Bowling Club	3 Rutland Pl., Glasgow	2	80 –		Brown, Thomas	Newton, Strathaven	44	95 –
Benhar Coal Company	144 St. Vincent Street, Glasgow	130	244 –		Brown, Thomas	Skellyton, Larkhall	55	64 –
					Brown, Thomas	Brisbane House, Govan	1	140 –
Bertram, William, of Kersewell	Kersewell, Carnwath	5,863	2,893 –		Brown, William	Chapelhall, Airdrie	1	98 –
					Brown, William	Rankin's Row, Carstairs	3	10 –
Bickers, James, and others	66 S. Portland St., Glasgow (*Vacant Ground*)	5	9 –		Brown, William	Caldwell, Biggar	35	25 –
Biggar, Kirk-Session of	Biggar	5	9 –		Brown, William	Lanark	2	24 –
Biggar U.P. Church, Trs. of	Moat Park	1	18 –		Brown, William	Port-Dundas, Glasgow	5	160 –
Binnie, Thomas	152 W. George St., Glasgow (*Vacant Ground*)	6	359 –		Brown, Trustees of Mrs. Elizabeth	Biggar	278	300 –
Binnie, Trs. of Thomas	234 Buchanan Street, Glasgow	1	205 –		Brown, Mrs. Marion	Kirkmuirhill, Lesmahagow	5	9 –
Binnie, Mrs. Mary	Sandyhills, Shettleston	4	24 –		Brown, Alexandrina L.	Kirkmuirhill, Lesmahagow	5	86 –
Binning, Robert, & Son	16 Bothwell St., Glasgow	4	405 –		Brownlie, Alexander and Robert	Carluke	1	25 –
Birrell, Trs. of Gen. David	Dumbroxhill, Lesmahagow	1,350	376 –		Brownlie, Archibald	Barrhead	63	413 –
Black, James	Newmills, Shotts	20	63 –		Brownlie, James	Bilboa Street, Strathaven	111	228 –
Black, Trustees of James	Glasgow	1	259 10		Brownlie, James	Headlesscross, Cambusnethan	600	148 –
Black, John	Lea Cottage, Cambuslang	1	35 –					
Black, John	Ohio, U.S.	35	36 –		Brownlie, John	Bilboa St., Strathaven	3	14 –
Black, Rev. Peter C.	Old Monkland	6	58 –		Brownlie, John	Garion Mills, Wishaw	2	48 –
Black, Robert	Miltonbank, Bishopbriggs	1	97 –		Brownlie, Matthew	Back Road, Strathaven	1	64 –
Black & Steel	86 West Regent Street, Glasgow	112	285 –		Brownlie, Thomas, of Goodsburn	Goodsburn, Strathaven	66	183 –
Black, Reps. of William	Whiterigg, New Monkland	252	357 –		Bruce, Rev. Robert S.	U.P. Manse, Wishaw	1	20 –
Do. do.	Do. (*Minerals*)	–	804 3		Bruce, William	10 Carrington St., Glasgow	36	72 –
Black & Sons, William	Whiterigg, New Monkland	3	209 4		Brunton, Mrs. Isabella	Greenwell, Carnwath	38	15 –
					Bryden, James	Newfoundland	2	101 –
Black, Agnes and Jessie	Heatheryknowe, Baillieston	344	694 –		Buccleuch and Queensberry, Duke of	Dalkeith Palace	9,091	1,544 –
Do. do.	Do. (*Minerals*)	–	850 –		Buchanan, Andrew	Greenfield Ho., Shettleston	2	164 –
Blair, Andrew, & Co.	45 Walker St., Maryhill	4	292 –		Buchanan, Col. D. C. R. C., of Drumpellier	Drumpellier, Coatbridge	8,549	8,693 12
Blair, John	Summerlee House, Thornliebank	2	29 10		Do. do.	Do. (*Minerals*)	–	15180 9

LANARK—*continued.*

Name of Owner.	Address of Owner.	Estimated Acreage of Property.	Gross Annual Value.
		Acres.	£ s.
Buchanan, James	7 Sommerville Place, Glasgow	57	140 –
Buchanan, Thomas G., of Wellshot	Wellshot, Cambuslang	438	1,496 10
Do. do.	Do. (*Minerals*)	–	2,687 5
Buist, Jane and Isabella	Union Street, Hamilton	2	80 –
Bunting, Thomas	Bankhouse, Lesmahagow	1	10 –
Burdon, Rev. James A.	Crawford, Abington	12	46 –
Burns, Alexander W.	19 Melville St., Portobello	20	25 –
Burns, James C., of Glenlee	Glenlee, Hamilton	30	226 –
Burns, John	Maxwellton, E. Kilbride	3	12 –
Burns, Michael	11 Torphichen St., Edinburgh	30	20 –
Burns, William	Kirkmuirhill, Lesmahagow	6	12 –
Burton, Thomas	Hawksland, Lesmahagow	15	40 –
Burton, William	Burnhead, Lesmahagow	38	29 –
Building Society, No. 3	Larkhall	2	245 –
Building Society, No. 7	57 Lockhart St., Stonehouse	2	108 –
Building Society, No. 8	2 Camnethan St., Stonehouse	3	120 –
Building Society, No. 9	25 Kirk St., Stonehouse	2	115 –
Building Society, No. 10	Green Street, Stonehouse	2	87 –
Building Society, No. 11	Green Street, Stonehouse	1	64 –
Busby Railway Company	Glasgow (*Railway*)	66	2,217 –
Buttery, Alexander W.	Chapelhall, Airdrie	33	27 –
Cadzow, William	Craighead, Carluke	151	85 –
Cairns, John	Hamilton	101	65 –
Cairns, John, James, Mary, and Marion	Dalserf	1	15 –
Cairns, Moses, & Co.	Broomloan, Govan	1	320 –
Caledonian Railway Company	Glasgow (*Railway*) Do. (*Canals*)	2,505} 254}	209033 –
Do. do.	Do.	10	3,058 –
Caledonian and Glasgow and South-Western Joint Railway Co.	Glasgow	25	289 –
Do. do.	Do. (*Railway*)	71	3,809 –
Callan, James	Turfholm, Lesmahagow	3	18 –
Canfield, Thomas	London St., Larkhall	10	20 –
Cambuslang Water Commissioners	Cambuslang	5	142 –
Cambusnethan Curling Club	Wishaw	3	1 –
Campbell, Alexander	Killbank, Lanark	214	230 –
Campbell & Alexander	Rutherglen	1	195 –
Campbell, Duncan	Abbeygreen, Lesmahagow	1	18 –
Campbell, Sir George, of Succoth, Bart.	Garscube House, Glasgow	253	570 10
Campbell, John, of Possil	Villa Como, Torquay	643	1,530 –
Do. do.	Do. (*Minerals*)	–	50 –
Campbell, Joseph	Millerston, Glasgow	2	37 10
Campbell, Mrs. Elizabeth	Flemington, Strathaven	1	8 –
Campbell, Mrs. Flora	Floral Bank, Gourock	2	22 –
Cardowan Trustees—per M'Leod & Ralston	205 St. Vincent Street, Glasgow	111	100 –
Do. do.	Do. (*Minerals*)	–	100 –
Carluke Free Church, Trs. of	Carluke	2	14 –
Carmichael, Daniel	Greenshield House, Carnwath	70	60 –
Carmichael, John	Gillbank, Carluke	64	60 –
Carmichael, M. T., of Eastend	Carmichael, Lanark	2,125	2,058 –
Carmichael, Richard	King's Inn, Carnwath	190	120 –
Carmichael, William	Biggar	1	22 –
Carrick, James	Maryhill	1	359 –
Carron Company	Falkirk (*Minerals*)	–	1,827 16
Cassells, Alexander, James, and Janet	Bannatyne St., Lanark	5	18 –
Catterson, Mrs. Louisa, of Birkcleugh	Birkcleugh, Abington	6,870	1,562 –
Cemetery Company, Craigton	116 St. Vincent Street, Glasgow	29	67 15
Cemetery Company, New	Bent Road, Hamilton	7	12 –
Chancellor, John G., of Shieldhill	Shieldhill, Biggar	1,500	1,986 –
Chapman, Gavin	Bellshill	9	75 –
Chapman, James	Commonside, Airdrie	4	78 15
Chapman, Thomas	Commonhead, Airdrie	140	355 6
Do.	Do. (*Minerals*)	–	268 –
Charity, The Sisters of	Smylum, Lanark	135	249 –
Cherrie & Clark	Airdrie	2	44 5
Christison, Rev. John	Biggar	13	83 –
Christie, George F.	Mount Vernon, Old Monkland	1	50 –
Christie, John, of Milnwood	Cowden House, Dollar	520	756 –
Christie, Thomas C., of Bedlay	Bedlay, Cadder	910	1,224 6
Do. do.	Do. (*Minerals*)	–	226 17
Christie, Mrs. Marion	Catherine's Croft, Lanark	2	28 –
City of Glasgow Bank	Glasgow	33	1,947 5
Clark, Daniel	7 Walworth Terrace, Glasgow	11	21 –
Do.	Do. (*Minerals*)	–	23 –
Clark, George W.	Dumbreck Villa, Glasgow	6	105 –
Clark, James, of Crossbasket	Crossbasket, East Kilbride	27	260 –
Clark, John, of Kirkland Park	4 Inverleith Row, Edinburgh	238	697 –
Do. do.	Do. (*Minerals*)	–	9 14
Clark, John	Hazelbankbraes, Lanark	3	16 –
Clark, Richard and Agnes	Union Hotel, Lanark	9	16 –
Clark, Trustees of William Towers	Wester Moffat, Shotts	403	984 6
Do. do.	Do. (*Minerals*)	–	500 –
Clelland Trustees	Clelland, Motherwell	1,465	1,422 –
Do.	Do. (*Minerals*)	–	5,130 –
Clelland, James	Beechmont Cott., Bishopbriggs	38	47 10
Clelland, Mrs. Barbara M'Caig	Lochgilphead	144	526 17
Do. do.	Do. (*Minerals*)	–	1,221 17
Clelland, Trs. of William	Bloomgate, Lanark	1	31 –
Clelland, Trustees of Mrs. Christina	Glasgow	19	54 –
Clow, Andrew	15 Otago St., Glasgow	1	65 –
Clyde Navigation Trustees	16 Robertson Street, Glasgow	99	3,629 10
Do. do.	Do. (*Quays, &c.*)	8	5,761 –
Clyde Paper Company	Rutherglen	9	1,247 –
Clydesdale Iron Company	Milnwood, Bellshill	11	621 –
Coatbridge Gas Company	Coatbridge	2	1,790 –
Coatbridge Oil Company	Kirkwood, Coatbridge	8	2,999 –
Coatbridge Tin Plate Co.	Laigh Coates, Coatbridge	8	1,017 –
Coats, James (a minor)	Whitehill, East Kilbride	62	180 –
Coats, James	Whitehill, East Kilbride	203	320 –
Coats, James, jun. and sen.	East Kilbride	78	150 –
Coats, John	Newhouse, Blantyre	18	35 –
Coats, John	Blantyre Farm, Blantyre	11	9 –
Coats, John	121 Bath Street, Glasgow	122	262 –
Coats, Thomas James and Thomas G.	Draffan, Lesmahagow	2	190 –
Coats, William	Blantyre Farm, Blantyre	63	134 –
Coats, Mrs. Elizabeth	Stonefield, Blantyre	3	101 –
Cochran, Robert	7 Crown Circus, Partick	2	300 –
Cochrane, Alexander	Water Road, Barrhead	160	177 –
Cochrane & Brand	Hamilton	4	81 –
Cochrane, John	Struther, Strathaven	30	90 –
Cochrane, John	Over Brownside, Strathaven	61	110 –
Cochrane, John	Strathaven	138	139 –
Cochrane, Trustees of John	Kirk Street, Strathaven	10	46 –
Cochrane, John R.	Calderbank, Blantyre	39	182 –
Cochrane, Thomas	Waterside, Strathaven	120	250 –
Cochrane, William	Easthouse, Newcastle-on-Tyne	64	100 –
Colebrooke, Sir Thomas E., of Crawford, Bart., M.P.	Abington House, Abington	29,604	9,282 –
Collins, Edward	North Balgray, Glasgow	4	100 –
Collins & Sons, Edward	Kelvindale, Glasgow	10	1,360 –
Colquhoun, Trustees of Archibald	Reddriepark, Hogganfield	38	217 10
Colquhoun, Hugh	Anchorage, Bothwell	9	132 –
Colquhoun, Rev. John E. C.	Killermont, Cadder	915	1,038 18
Do. do.	Do. (*Minerals*)	–	350 –
Colquhoun, William C., of Clathick	Clathick, Crieff	290	293 2
Colville, David	251 Bath Street, Glasgow	11	660 –

LANARK—continued.

Name of Owner.	Address of Owner.	Estimated Acreage of Property.	Gross Annual Value.	Name of Owner.	Address of Owner.	Estimated Acreage of Property.	Gross Annual Value.
		Acres.	£ s.			Acres.	£ s.
Collyer, William D., of Cormiston	Cormiston, Biggar	400	518 –	Cunninghame, Sir William J. Montgomery, of Corsehill and Kirktonholme, Bart.	Glenmore House, Maybole	161	152 10
Colt, Trustees of John H.	Gartsherrie	1,416	2,397 12				
Do. do.	Do. (Minerals)	–	4,023 10	Do. do.	Do. (Minerals)	–	149 –
Colthart, Mrs. Marion	Abington	1	28 –	Curr, James	Rigghead, Strathaven	53	105 –
Coltness Iron Company	Newmains, Wishaw	700	768 –	Curr, William	Peddies Cottage, Cathcart	126	148 –
Commercial Bank of Scotland	Edinburgh	3	67 –	Currie, William	Strathaven	8	73 –
Commissioners for the repression of Juvenile Delinquency in Glasgow	67 West Regent Street, Glasgow	59	665 –	Currie, Catherine, Margaret, and Jane	Trynlaw, Strathaven	91	160 –
Commissioners of Supply	Almada Street, Hamilton	14	1,311 –	Cuthill, Mrs. Catherine	Bothwell Road, Hamilton	2	364 –
Community of the Good Shepherd	Dalbeith	10	165 –	Dalbeith Cemetery Trustees	178 St. Vincent Street, Glasgow	2	13 19
Connall, William, junior	Coldstream, Carluke	57	57 –	Dalgleish & Sons, William	Rutherglen	1	219 –
Connall & Co.	81 St. Vincent Street, Glasgow	4	1,220 –	Dalserf Coal Company	88 Great Clyde Street, Glasgow	17	510 –
Connell & Co., Charles	Scotstown, Glasgow	10	968 –	Dalziel & Dempster	Langlands, Glasgow	13	148 –
Connor, Rev. David Muir	Biggar	1	19 –	Darling, John, of Forth	178 St. Vincent Street, Glasgow	678	380 –
Connor, James	Airdrie	4	167 11	Do. do.	Do. (Minerals)	–	600 –
Convalescent Home, Managers of	157 Hope St., Glasgow	83	161 6	Darling, Trs. of William	Carnwath	844	2,912 –
Cook, William, junior	Rosebank, Cambuslang	4	118 –	Davie, James	Kirkshaws, Coatbridge	3	10 –
Cook, Mrs. Janet	Biggar	1	80 –	Davidson, Trs. of James	Glasgow	56	150 15
Cooper, Reps. of John	Green Street, Bothwell	1	59 –	Do. do.	Do. (Minerals)	–	300 –
Cooper, Robert G.	Braehead, Larkhall	20	106 –	Davidson, Hugh	Lanark	3	61 –
Cooper, Grace	Newbridgend, Carluke	1	8 –	Davidson, Robert	Bellshill	1	16 –
Corbett, Thomas	85 Gracechurch Street, London	4	1,161 7	Davidson, William	Littlehill, Cadder	105	439 17
Core, William	Carmichael, Lanark	3	16 –	Davidson, William Jas., of Ruchill	22 South Frederick Street, Glasgow	249	641 –
Core, William	Wiston, Abington	2	12 –	Do. do.	Do. (Minerals)	–	300 –
Corporation Gas Company	42 Virginia St., Glasgow	4	135 10	Davidson, Mrs. Grace	Bellfield, Lesmahagow	45	22 –
Cowan, Rev. James	Manse, Abington	11	44 –	Do. do.	Do. (Minerals)	–	58 –
Craig, Allan	Kirkton, Blantyre	1	129 –	Dawson, Thomas, of Meadowbank	Meadowbank, Uddingston	10	92 –
Craig, Archibald	Birdsfield, Blantyre	77	250 –				
Craig, James, junior	Westfield Ter., Partick	1	45 –	Deans, Alexander	Braehead, Carnwath	1	26 –
Craig, John	Udston, Hamilton	115	209 –	Deas, Sir George, Kt. (Lord Deas)	Pittendreich House, Lasswade	340	273 –
Craig, Robert	16 Virginia St., Glasgow	4	15 –				
Craig, Robert	Bellshill	1	61 –	Do. do.	Do. (Minerals)	–	1,739 –
Craig, Robert	Newbattle Mills, Dalkeith	8	792 –	Deas, Francis	9 St. Colme Street, Edinburgh	110	95 –
Craig, Robert and Margaret	Maryhill, Glasgow	220	299 15	Denholm, Robert	Greenhill, Shotts	387	397 –
Do. do.	Do. (Minerals)	–	81 4	Do.	Do. (Minerals)	–	1,038 –
Craig, William	24 St. Vincent Crescent, Glasgow	216	320 –	Denholm, William	Rutherglen	5	62 –
Do.	Do. (Minerals)	–	400 –	Dick, Trs. of Alexander	Hope Street, Glasgow	105	185 –
Craig, Mrs. Jemima	Biggar	20	28 –	Do. do.	Do. (Minerals)	–	300 –
Craig, Susan and Mary	Springbank, Strathaven	4	28 –	Dick, Alexander	Airdrie	1	795 5
Cranston, C. E. H. Edmondstoune, of Corehouse	Corehouse, Lanark	2,860	1,893 –	Dick, James	High Street, Carluke	1	66 –
				Dick, John	Cliftonhill, Coatbridge	1	165 –
Crawford, James	Meikledripps, Busby	38	28 –	Dick, John	Airdrie	2	107 15
Crawford, James C.	Overton, Strathaven	165	456 –	Dick, Matthew	75 Hill Street, Glasgow	115	258 –
Crawford, John	Thinacres, Hamilton	31	45 –	Do.	Do. (Minerals)	–	50 –
Crawford, John	Langlands, East Kilbride	110	154 –	Dick, William	Chapel Street, Carluke	4	40 –
Crawford, John	Faulds, Baillieston	4	26 –	Dickson, A. & Archibald	11 Royal Circus, Edinburgh	20	35 –
Crawford, Heirs of John	Strathaven	82	135 –	Dickson, Alexander, of Hartree	11 Royal Circus, Edinburgh	1,416	1,323 –
Crawford, Robert	Aitkenfin, East Kilbride	95	100 –	Dickson, James	Wiston, Biggar	8	16 –
Crawford, William	Shawton, Glassford	205	259 –	Dickson, James A.	Eastfield, Biggar	7	24 –
Crawfurd, William S. S., of Milton	91 Eaton Square, London	1,267	2,406 9	Dickson, John	Priorhill, Lesmahagow	20	40 –
Do. do.	Do. (Minerals)	–	1,671 –	Dickson, John	Newfield, Blantyre	28	83 –
Crichton, Heirs of David	Coatbridge	6	10 10	Do.	Do. (Minerals)	–	35 –
Cringan, Robert	Clyde Street, Carluke	85	56 –	Dickson, John R.	144 Bath St., Glasgow	225	139 –
Cross, Alexander	9 Rumford St., Liverpool	70	300 –	Dickson, William G.	Westfield, Partick	2	150 –
Cross, David	51 Argyle St., Glasgow	9	26 –	Dixon, Peter W.	19 Elmbank Crescent, Glasgow	15	72 –
Crosser, Mrs. Elizabeth	Carluke	1	8 –				
Crown, The	(Government Property)	45	820 –	Do.	Do. (Minerals)	–	147 –
Cruden, George R.	Wellhouse, Shettleston	145	490 –	Dixon, William, of Govan	Govan, Glasgow	276	772 13
Cruickshanks, Low, & Co.	Cornwall Street, Glasgow	2	540 –	Dixon, Trs. of William	Govan, Glasgow	1,642	7,430 –
Cullen, James	Baillieston	1	150 –	Do. do.	Do. (Minerals)	–	9,066 –
Cullen, Matthew	Bellshill	2	127 –	Dobie, Lockhart	69 Hallcraig Street, Airdrie	5	416 14
Cumming, Melville, & Houston	Caldervale, New Monkland	10	399 10	Dobie, Thomas	Whitehill, Lanark	1	45 –
Cumming, Thomas	Gilmerton, Strathaven	3	13 –	Dobie, Mrs. Elizabeth	Eastercraigannet, Denny	10	22 –
Cunningham, Heirs of Alexander	Woodhead, Bothwell	15	139 –	Donald, Alexander	Ford, New Monkland	5	50 –
				Donald, Trs. of David	Glasgow	2	24 –
Cunningham, James	Netherton House, Pollokshields	437	568 –	Donald, James	Waterside, Lesmahagow	22	44 –
				Donald, Robert	Holm Forge, Motherwell	2	136 –
Cunningham, Mrs. Elizabeth	Summerhill, Wishaw	4	4 –	Donald, Robert	Spittal, Penicuik	15	46 –

LANARK—continued.

Name of Owner.	Address of Owner.	Estimated Acreage of Property.	Gross Annual Value.		Name of Owner.	Address of Owner.	Estimated Acreage of Property.	Gross Annual Value.	
		Acres.	£	s.			Acres.	£	s.
Donald, William	Westlinbank, Strathaven	14	36	–	Easton, Mrs. Jean	Knowehead, Whitburn	12	20	–
Donaldson, Rev. Alexander W.	U.P. Manse, Strathaven	2	25	–	Edgar, Mrs. Margaret	Carmunnock	4	52	–
Dougall, Daniel	Strathaven	20	55	–	Edmiston, Hugh F.	Yoker Mains, Partick	82	215	–
Dougall, James	Netherfauld House, Lesmahagow	55	60	–	Eglinton and Winton, Earl of	Eglinton Castle, Irvine	5,866	4,097	–
Douglas, James C.	15 Howard Place, Edinburgh	1,256	249	–	Elder, John	Westeryardhouses, Carnwath	81	52	–
Douglas, James D. S., of Baads and Craigs	Chilston House, Tunbridge Wells	2,190	752	–	Elder, John, & Co.	Fairfield, Glasgow	69	5,655	–
Do. do.	Do. (Minerals)	–	2,543	–	Ellis, Thomas	Coatbridge	4	877	–
Douglas, John	Auchmeddon, Lesmahagow	120	75	–	Elphinstone, Lord	Carberry Tower, Musselburgh	678	1,191	3
Do.	Do. (Minerals)	–	100	–	Do.	Do. (Minerals)	–	1,100	18
Douglas, Trs. of Robert, of Orbiston	Orbiston, Bellshill	651	1,284	–	English and Scottish Law Life Assurance Association	105 St. Vincent Street, Glasgow	2	55	–
Do. do.	Do. (Minerals)	–	1,067	–	Espie, George	6 Rutland Square, Edinburgh	19	61	–
Douglas, Rev. Sholto D. C.	Douglas Support, Old Monkland	1,393	1,814	–	Ewart, Robert William, of Allershaw	Allershaw	8,485	1,575	–
Do. do.	Do. (Minerals)	–	6,429	3	Ewing, George	Yoker, by Glasgow	4	39	–
Douglas, Trs. of General Sir T. M., K.C.B.	Lesmahagow	825	1,091	–	Ewing, James	Roadmeetings, Carluke	4	6	–
Downie, James	Kirkfieldbank, Lanark	4	100	–	Ewing, William	Roadmeetings, Carluke	3	5	–
Downs, Rev. John	East Kilbride	7	82	–					
Do.	Do. (Minerals)	–	256	14	Fairless, William D.	Kirklands, Bothwell	8	422	–
Dreghorn, Heirs of Allan	Govan, Glasgow	2	565	–	Fairley, Matthew	Forefaulds, East Kilbride	60	80	–
Drumclog School Committee	Strathaven	1	6	–					
Drysdale, Trustees of Mrs. Mary	Jerviston, Motherwell (Minerals)	–	250	–	Fairley, Samuel	48 Oswald Street, Glasgow	1	85	–
Dubs and Co.	Little Govan, Glasgow	8	2,376	–	Farie, James, of Farme	Farme, Rutherglen	295	1,602	10
Duff, Alexander	Bothwell	1	105	–	Do. do.	Do. (Minerals)	–	1,536	16
Duncan, Robert	Partick, Glasgow	2	336	–	Farie, James, junior	Farme, Rutherglen	2	5	–
Duncan, Trustees of Mrs. Mary	48 Gordon St., Glasgow	4	193	10	Ferguson, David	Brae, Strathaven	40	80	–
Duncanson, John	28 Raglan St., Glasgow	1	100	–	Ferguson, Representatives of James	Auchinheath, Lesmahagow	16	102	–
Dunlop, Alexander	Priory Lodge, Largs	92	252	–	Ferguson, Trs. of James	Auchinheath, Lesmahagow	3,800	1,761	–
Dunlop, Alex. Graham, and others	Gairbraid, Glasgow	204	342	19					
Dunlop, Colin, & Co.	Quarter, Hamilton	72	2,075	–	Ferguson, James	Marylands, Glasgow	3	90	–
Dunlop, Colin R.	Quarter, Hamilton	40	221	–	Ferguson, John, & Co.	Omoa, Motherwell	13	570	–
Do.	Do. (Minerals)	–	500	–	Ferguson, John	Larchfield, Partick	2	120	–
Dunlop, James, & Co.	Clyde Iron Works, Tollcross	126	2,905	8	Ferguson, Mrs. Ellen	Auchinheath, Lesmahagow	45	190	–
Do. do.	Do. (Minerals)	–	1,550	–	Ferrie, Joseph	197 Crown Street, Glasgow	99	327	–
Dunlop, James	Tollcross	250	851	–					
Do.	Do. (Minerals)	–	150	–	Findlay, John	Woodlands Road, Glasgow	1	1,629	–
Dunn Brothers	Braehead, Old Monkland	12	266	–	Findlay, John, of Boturich	Boturich Castle, Alexandria	146	663	17
Dunn, Rev. James	Manse, Stonehouse	9	47	–	Do. do.	Do. (Minerals)	–	600	–
Dunn, John	Kennedies, Hamilton	90	155	–	Finlay, Alex. & Robert	Mainhill, Baillieston, (Minerals)	–	500	–
Dunn, William	193 High Street, Glasgow	2	101	–	Finlay, Alexander	Springhill, Old Monkland	50	123	–
Dunn, William Laurie	Mount Vernon, Tollcross	3	100	–	Finlay, James, & Co.	Catrine Works, Ayrshire	27	21	–
Dunsmore, James F.	Gaindykehead, Airdrie	50	50	–	Finlay, Robert	Springhill, Old Monkland	35	88	–
Dyce, John N.	Castlebank, Lanark	62	84	–					
Dykes, Andrew	North Kirkwood, Strathaven	282	407	–	Finlay, William	Brackenbrae, Bishopbriggs	60	150	–
Dykes, Andrew	5 Hamilton Crescent, Glasgow	73	84	–	Do.	Do. (Minerals)	–	300	–
Dykes, Andrew, junior	St. Bride's Chapel, Strathaven	32	55	–	Fisher & Watt	194 West George Street, Glasgow	78	447	10
Dykes, Andrew	Bent, Lesmahagow	93	93	–	Fleming, Alexander	10 Royal Circus, Glasgow	168	189	14
Dykes, James	Fieldhead, Strathaven	69	90	–	Fleming, Andrew	Rutherglen	3	150	–
Dykes, James	Hairlaw, East Kilbride	30	50	–	Fleming, Hon. Cornwallis	Cumbernauld House, Glasgow	3	12	–
Dykes, John	Westpark, Strathaven	52	130	–					
Dykes, Trustees of John	Auchingramont, Hamilton	5	146	–	Fleming, John B., of Nook	Nook, East Kilbride	104	328	–
Dykes, Robert	Priestgill, Strathaven	84	147	–	Fleming, John G.	155 Bath Street, Glasgow	144	210	–
Dykes, Robert	Middlehouse, Carluke	134	160	–					
Dykes, Thomas	Whitelaw, Strathaven	120	100	–	Fleming, James	Cauldcoats, Strathaven	11	35	–
Dykes, Thomas	Hamilton	118	289	–	Fleming, James	Castleton, Carmunnock	5	16	–
Dykes, William	Hazlebank, Strathaven	174	200	–	Fleming, John	Meadowbank Cottage, Strathaven	43	116	–
Dykes, William	South Newton, Strathaven	30	90	–	Fleming, Robert	Easter Overmilton, East Kilbride	70	105	–
Dykes, William A.	Hamilton	3	117	–					
Dykes, Mrs. Jean	Woodview, Hamilton	100	208	–	Fleming, Mrs. Jane	Kirk Street, Strathaven	2	55	–
Dymock, John	Westyardhouses, Carnwath	80	36	–	Flowers, Thomas G.	1 Athole Crescent, Edinburgh	264	100	–
Eadie & Spencer	Dalmarnock Bridge, Rutherglen	4	845	–					

LANARK—continued.

Name of Owner.	Address of Owner.	Estimated Acreage of Property.	Gross Annual Value.	Name of Owner.	Address of Owner.	Estimated Acreage of Property.	Gross Annual Value.
		Acres.	£ s.			Acres.	£ s.
Forbes, Rev. John	Symington, Biggar	13	35 –	Gilchrist, William	High Street, Carluke	60	278 –
Forrest, Archibald	Windales, Symington, Biggar	62	98 –	Gilchrist, William	Milncroft, Shettleston	4	125 17
Forrest, David	Treesbanks, Shotts	900	510 –	Gillespie, John	81 George St., Edinburgh	1	3 –
Forrest, John C.	Hamilton	200	449 –	Gillespie, Robert	Springhill, Douglas	30	149 –
Do.	Do. (*Minerals*)	–	10 –	Gillespie, William H.	30 Dublin Street, Edinburgh	230	186 –
Forrest, Peter	Shotts	728	603 –				
Forrest, Robert & A.	Calderhead, Shotts	210	260 –	Gillon, Alexander	123 John Street, Glasgow	1	133 –
Forrest, Trs. of William	Hamilton	5	50 –	Gillon, Robert	Langloan, Old Monkland	1	483 –
Do. do.	Do. (*Minerals*)	–	1,011 –	*Gilmerton School Trustees*	Gilmerton, Strathaven	4	10 –
Forrest, William	High Street, Carluke	25	92 –	Gilmour, Alexander	Windmill Road, Hamilton	11	30 –
Do.	Do. (*Minerals*)	–	10 –	Gilmour, Arthur	Crosshill, East Kilbride	101	154 –
Forrest, William	Nemphlar, Lanark	10	28 –	Gilmour, Hugh	Fieldhead, East Kilbride	93	109 –
Forrest, William	Douglas	2	21 –	Gilmour, John M'Ghie	Windmill Road, Hamilton	1	73 –
Forrest, William	Hamilton	243	384 –	*Glasgow Board of Police*	70 Bell Street, Glasgow	9	100 –
Do.	Do. (*Minerals*)	–	30 –	*Glasgow, City of*	Glasgow	34	312 12
Forrest, Trs. of William	Airdrie	72	133 10	*Glasgow, College of*	Glasgow	420	553 18
Forrest, Mrs. Janet C., senior	Hamilton	5	40 –	*Glasgow Industrial Schools*	74 Royal Bank Place, Glasgow	16	400 –
Forrester, Robert	12 Dixon St., Glasgow	40	401 8	*Glasgow Iron Company*	166 St. Vincent Street, Glasgow	27	6,141 –
Forsyth, Mrs. Elizabeth	Flowerhill, Airdrie	5	71 15	*Glasgow Plate-Glass Co.*	Firhill Road, Glasgow	3	275 –
Foster & Main	Whitehill, Lanark	2	11 –	*Glasgow, University of*	Gilmorehill, Glasgow	4	240 –
Frame, Mrs. Margaret	Newmains, Wishaw	1	6 –	*Glasgow Water Commissioners*	Miller Street, Glasgow	21	61 –
Fraser, Robert	Callagreen, Carluke	101	111 –	Glen, Thomas	Thornhill House, Paisley	235	386 –
Frederick, Thomas	Carluke	105	108 –	Goff, Bruce	Lindens, Bothwell	4	71 –
French, Thomas	North Garngower, Lesmahagow	140	116 –	Gold, John and Alexander	Hairleshill, Wishaw	10	36 –
Frew, John, & Company	Burnbank, Hamilton	1	97 –	Goodall & Smellie	209 St. Vincent Street, Glasgow	7	21 –
Frew, John, & Company	Parkburn, Cadder	2	80 –	Goodfellow, Alexander	Crawford, Abington	110	86 –
Gairns, John	Kirklawhill, Skirling	11	116 –	Goodwin, James, & Co.	Motherwell	2	75 –
Galbraith, Robert	Greenhead, Govan	31	243 –	Goodwin, John	Clydeview, Motherwell	1	40 –
Galbraith, Heirs of William	Govan	110	138 –	Goodwin, John	Hazelwood, Govan	5	95 –
Gall, William	Stonebyres, Lanark	3	11 –	Gordon, Rev. Charles	Manse, Douglas	2	27 –
Gall, Mrs. Agnes	Abbeygreen, Lesmahagow	50	76 –	Gordon, John, of Aikenhead	Aikenhead, Cathcart	464	1,220 –
Galloway, R., & Company	Tarbrax, Carnwath	1	236 –	Gordon, Trustees of late Sir J.W., Bart., K.C.B., of Harperfield	Harperfield, Lesmahagow	275	217 –
Galloway, Trustees of James and John	132 St. Vincent Street, Glasgow	84	132 11				
Do. do.	Do. (*Minerals*)	–	1,257 19	*Govan Forge Company*	Greenhaugh, Glasgow	2	650 –
Gardiner, James	Campbeltown	90	430 –	*Govan Parochial Board*	Merryflats, Glasgow	24	1,680 –
Do.	Do. (*Minerals*)	–	859 –	Govan, William	15 Renfield Street, Glasgow	2	290 –
Gardner, John	Newmains, Blantyre	48	180 –	Gow, David, and others	Silverwells, Bothwell	2	180 –
Gardner, William	Auchinraith, Blantyre	88	180 –	Græme, Trustees of Robert, of Wellhall	Wellhall, Hamilton	66	158 –
Do.	Do. (*Minerals*)	–	223 –				
Garnkirk Coal Company	Garnkirk	19	979 –	Graham, Adam	Thornwood, Partick	27	263 10
Garroway, James A.	Nerston, East Kilbride	13	47 –	Graham, Trustees of Alexander	187 West George Street, Glasgow	1,045	2,570 –
Garroway, Robert	Rosemount, Parkhead	3	65 –				
Gartness Iron and Steel Company	Gartness, Motherwell	12	182 10	Graham, Adam and J.	187 West George Street, Glasgow	66	122 –
Gartshore, Alexander	Maryburgh, New Monkland	30	45 –	Graham, Andrew Lang, and others	187 West George Street, Glasgow (*Vacant Ground*)	12	20 –
Gebbie, Francis	39 Albany Street, Edinburgh	148	163 –				
Gebbie, James	Strathaven	235	690 –	Graham, George	28 East John Street, Glasgow	1	38 –
Gebbie, John, of Netherfield	Netherfield House, Strathaven	130	165 –	Graham, John	Muldron, Whitburn	252	28 –
Gebbie, Helen and Mary	Netherfield House, Strathaven	2	6 –	Graham, John	Kittochside, East Kilbride	140	252 –
Gerard, Archibald, of Rochsoles	Rochsoles, New Monkland	1,141	929 –	Graham, John G. B., of Fereneze	Limekilns, East Kilbride	971	2,807 –
Do. do.	Do. (*Minerals*)	–	3,234 2	Graham, Trs. of Robert	Lambhill, Glasgow	51	154 19
Gibb, John, & Son	Lambhill, Glasgow	6	160 –	Graham, William	Lambhill, Glasgow	88	107 15
Gibson, Alexander	Biggar	2	60 –	Granger, Trustees of John	Balgreen, Strathaven	5	62 –
Gibson, Trs. of Alexander	St. Patrick's, Lanark	3	94 –	Granger, Janet	Broomknowe, Cambuslang	14	20 –
Gibson, Trustees of James and Mrs. Elizabeth	Glasgow	3	180 15				
Gibson, Thomas, of Toftcombs	Toftcombs, Biggar	1,341	1,134 –	Granger, Mary Semple	Broomknowe, Cambuslang	14	56 –
Gibson, Mrs.	Rosemount, Carluke	3	12 –	Grant, Alexander	Lamb Street, Hamilton	2	159 –
Gibson, Christina, Janet, and Agnes	Rothesay	675	349 –	Gray, Hubert M. M.	Gartloch, Cadder	347	480 14
Gibson, Jane	Clydesdale Cot., Lanark	3	7 –	Gray, John, & Company	Uddingston	4	200 –
Gilchrist, Archibald	Woodend, Carluke	1	6 –	Gray, Trustees of Rev. J. H.	Largo, Fife	215	693 –
Gilchrist, James, of Gillfoot	Gillfoot, Carluke	465	415 –	Do. do.	Do. (*Minerals*)	–	12 10
Gilchrist, James	Bellshill Road, Bellshill	1	24 –	Gray, John R.	Rutherglen	2	47 –
Gilchrist, Matthew	Drumgelloch, New Monkland	2	16 –	Gray, Robert	Hillmuir, Carstairs, Lanark	2	5 –

LANARK—continued.

Name of Owner.	Address of Owner.	Estimated Acreage of Property.	Gross Annual Value.	Name of Owner.	Address of Owner.	Estimated Acreage of Property.	Gross Annual Value.
		Acres.	£ s.			Acres.	£ s.
Gray, Robert	Ravenstruther, Carstairs, Lanark	15	12 –	Hamilton, Robert	335 Paisley Road, Glasgow	49	75 –
Gray, Robert, & Co.	Shettleston (Minerals)	–	371 16	Hamilton, Robert	Shawton, Glassford	191	211 –
Gray, Thomas	100 Bellgrove Street, Glasgow	1	4 –	Hamilton, Robert	Holms of Chryston, Moodiesburn	358	595 –
Gray & Wyllie	Cliftonhill Ironworks, Coatbridge	2	600 –	Do. do.	Do. (Minerals)	–	114 –
Gray, Mrs. Margaret	Bellshill	2	29 –	Hamilton, Robert	Airdrie	2	197 –
Greenshields, John B., of Kerse	Kerse, Lesmahagow	699	524 –	Hamilton, Thomas	Shawtonhill, Glassford	116	135 –
Greenshields, William	Willands, Carluke	4	50 –	Hamilton, Thomas	Heathland, Carnwath	24	75 –
Greig, Joseph	Drumboy Lodge, East Kilbride	27	37 –	Do. do.	Do. (Minerals)	–	200 –
Greig, Mrs. Marion	Longfaugh, Hamilton	14	15 –	Hamilton, Thomas	Lampits, Carnwath	77	113 –
Grierson, Heirs of James	Oggs Castle, Carnwath	109	139 –	Hamilton, Water Commissioners of	Hamilton	35	300 –
Grierson, Heirs of John	Townhead, Strathaven	9	42 –	Hamilton, Thomas, and Wharrie, Thos.	Browshot, Carnwath	97	53 –
Grossart, William	Newmains, Carstairs, Lanark	127	70 –	Hamilton, William	Strutherhead, Strathaven	175	206 –
				Hamilton, William	Peelhill, Strathaven	40	55 –
				Hamilton, William	Carlindean, Carnwath	15	37 –
				Hamilton, William	Bellshill	1	176 –
Haddow, John	Galla Lodge, Greenock	270	156 –	Hamilton, William	Poplarhill Orchard, Carluke	1	10 –
Haddington, Earl of	Tyninghame House, Prestonkirk	501	588 –	Hamilton, William	Brackenhill, Carluke	194	170 –
Hagart, Major-General Charles, of Bantaskine	Bantaskine, Falkirk	323	388 –	Hamilton, Captain W. H. M'Neil, of Raploch	Raploch, Larkhall	2,282	1,905 –
Hair, William	16 Hope Street, Glasgow	1	25 –	Do. do.	Do. (Minerals)	–	854 –
Halliday, Mrs. Margaret	Strawfrank, Carstairs, Lanark	10	32 –	Hamilton, Mrs. Jane	Rogerton, East Kilbride	3	23 –
Hamilton Academy	Hamilton	2	30 –	Hamilton, Mrs. Jane and Mary	Coldstream, Strathaven	80	187 –
Hamilton, Adam	Whiteshaw, Strathaven	30	60 –	Hamilton, Mrs. Jane	Strathaven	40	99 –
Hamilton, Andrew	East Drumclog, Strathaven	518	240 –	Hamilton, Mrs. Martha	Lawmuir, Carluke	9	10 –
Hamilton, Andrew	Springbank, Lesmahagow	142	119 –	Hamilton, Anne	Woodlands, Hamilton	8	155 –
Hamilton, Alexander	Hill, Hamilton	38	40 –	Harper, Arch. & James	570 Gallowgate Street, Glasgow	9	40 –
Hamilton, Archibald	Ryelandside, Strathaven	125	182 –	Harrington, Robert E. S., of Crutherland	Crutherland, East Kilbride	197	268 –
Hamilton, Burgh of	Hamilton	34	337 –	Harvey, Mrs. Jane	Brook Villa, Manchester	61	68 –
Hamilton Combination Poorhouse	Bothwell Road, Hamilton	2	305 –	Harvey, Trustees of Mrs. Janet	Wishaw	277	120 –
Hamilton, David	Gateside, Lesmahagow	51	33 –	Do. do.	Do. (Minerals)	–	12 –
Hamilton, Trustees of Duke of	Hamilton Palace, Hamilton	45,731	38441 –	Harvey, Mrs. Mary	Roseneath, Helensburgh	4	18 –
Do. do.	Do. (Minerals)	–	56920 14	Harvie, George	High Street, Carluke	1	39 –
Hamilton, Gavin	Auldton, Lesmahagow	180	225 –	Harvie, William, of Brownlie	Brownlie, Carluke	220	237 –
Hamilton, George	Easterseat, Carluke	50	61 –	Do. do.	Do. (Minerals)	–	2,173 –
Hamilton, Reps. of George	Strathaven	76	200 –	Hastie, Alexander	Townhead Farm, Carluke	1	16 –
Hamilton, Hugh	Greenhill of Cairnduff, Strathaven	10	35 –	Hastie, James	Market Place, Carluke	1	70 –
Hamilton, Hugh	Fauldshead, Renfrew	101	90 –	Hastie, Robert & John	Mid-Breckonridge, Strathaven	183	180 –
Hamilton, James	Strathaven	70	203 –	Hastie, Thomas	Craig Mills, Strathaven	130	154 –
Hamilton, James	Bogside, Stonehouse	113	120 –	Hay, Merricks, & Co.	Powder Mills, Roslin	12	20 –
Hamilton, James	Derwent Cottage, Crosshill, Glasgow	28	85 –	Haywood Gas-Coal Company	Haywood, Carnwath	334	970 –
Hamilton, James	Millbank, Douglas	9	82 –	Henderson, Alexander	Quothquan, Biggar	1	6 –
Hamilton, James	Threshold, East Kilbride	7	13 –	Henderson & Dimmack	Langloan, Coatbridge	6	837 –
Hamilton, James A.	Whiteshawgate, Strathaven	176	315 –	Henderson, John	Westbank, Partick	2	120 –
				Henderson, John	Sandyhills, Shettleston	5	57 10
Hamilton, Trustees of James C., of Dalserf	Dalserf, Larkhall	3,200	1,860 –	Henderson, Trustees of William	Shawburn, Hamilton	3	295 –
Do. do.	Do. (Minerals)	–	2,871 –	Henderson, Jessie	Sandyhills, Shettleston	26	47 –
Hamilton, James Dunlop	60 George Sq., Glasgow	154	256 –	Hendrie, John	Kirkwood, Coatbridge	85	756 –
Hamilton, Captain James S., of Fairholm	Fairholm, Hamilton	817	1,157 –	Do.	Do. (Minerals)	–	650 –
Do. do.	Do. (Minerals)	–	1,379 –	Hendry, Alexander	Langside, Glasgow	88	52 –
Hamilton, John	Woodhead, Crosshands, Ayrshire	151	206 –	Do.	Do. (Minerals)	–	13 –
				Hendry, Alexander	Langacre, Salisbury, Shotts	26	21 –
Hamilton, John	Lawmuir, Carluke	106	40 –	Hepburn, John	Greenwell, Carnwath	20	20 –
Hamilton, John	97 Wellgate, Lanark	2	33 –	Herbertson, Mrs. Helen	Rosebank, Bothwell	2	213 –
Hamilton, John	Longridge, Stonehouse	204	160 –	Heys, Simeon and Susan	17 Lower Hanover Street, Sheffield	111	50 –
Hamilton, John	Bottom, Chapelton	279	35 –				
Hamilton, John	60 George Sq., Glasgow	28	70 –	Higgans, William	Murdiston, Clelland, Motherwell	50	75 –
Do. do.	Do. (Minerals)	–	148 3	Hill, Trustees of Abram	5 Dixon Street, Glasgow (Vacant Ground)	2	6 –
Hamilton, John G. C., of Dalzell, M.P.	Dalzell, Motherwell	2,460	4,180 –	Hill, Alexander B.	Daviesdykes, Wishaw	85	66 –
Do. do.	Do. (Minerals)	–	10779 –	Do. do.	Do. (Minerals)	–	50 –
Hamilton, M'Culloch, & Company	88 Great Clyde Street, Glasgow	7	262 –	Hill, Heirs of James	North Castle Street, Edinburgh	326	413 13
Hamilton, Robert	West Breckonridge, Strathaven	292	360 –	Do. do.	Do. (Minerals)	–	418 10
Hamilton, Robert	High Brownside, Strathaven	105	201 –	Hill, John	Kirk Road, Carluke	1	7 –
				Hill, John	Coatbridge	2	527 –

LANARK—continued.

Name of Owner.	Address of Owner.	Estimated Acreage of Property.	Gross Annual Value.	Name of Owner.	Address of Owner.	Estimated Acreage of Property.	Gross Annual Value.
		Acres.	£ s.			Acres.	£ s.
Hill, William Henry, of Barlanerk	Shettleston	25	125 –	Inglis, James	Uphall, Linlithgowshire	123	80 –
				Do. (Minerals)		–	50 –
Hinshaw, Trustees of John	Ballgreen, Hamilton	4	112 –	Inglis, Trs. of William	East Hassockridge, Shotts	66	55 –
Hinshelwood, John	Ibrox, Glasgow	138	2,343 19				
Do. do.	Do. (Minerals)	–	2,694 14	Do. do.	Do. (Minerals)	–	50 –
Hogg, John	Whitefield, Cambuslang	2	234 –	Inglis, Mrs. Elizabeth	Stanley Cottage, New Monkland	4	309 15
Hoggan, Rev. James	Covington, Biggar	14	45 –				
Holmes & Allan	Cornsilloch, Dalserf	1	42 –	Irvine, William	Mansefield, Lanark	23	101 –
Holmes, Archibald C.	Hope Park, Partick	1	160 –				
Holmes, James	Cornsilloch, Dalserf	22	100 –				
Home, Hon. George D.	Douglas	3	10 –	Jack, James	Mains Park, Uddingston	5	43 –
Home, Hon. William S. D.	Douglas	3	15 –	Jack, John	Newarthill, Motherwell	53	48 –
Home, Countess of	Bothwell Castle, Bothwell	61,943	24770 –	Jack, Robert	Dykehead, Strathaven	63	80 –
Do. do.	Do. (Minerals)	–	4,716 –	Jack, Robert	Hall of Kype, Strathaven	81	167 –
Hood, William	25 Merkland St., Partick	13	18 –	Jack, Robert	North Gyle, Corstorphine	54	30 –
Hope, Alexander P.	Bordlands, Noblehouse	6	15 –	Jack, William	Newarthill, Motherwell	1	63 –
Hope, George, of Sunwick	Bordlands, Noblehouse	85	94 –	Jack, William	Hutchland, Lesmahagow	8	41 –
Hopetoun, Earl of	Hopetoun House, South Queensferry	19,180	3,246 –	Jackson, Andrew	Spittal, Cambuslang	72	104 15
				Jackson, Andrew and Thomas	Cambuslang	14	100 –
Do. do.	Do. (Minerals)	–	2,246 –	Jackson, James	East Newton Cottage, Strathaven	48	55 –
Houldsworth, James, of Coltness	Coltness, Wishaw	3,717	11498 –				
Do. do.	Do. (Minerals)	–	21239 –	Jackson, John	Spittalhill, Cambuslang	127	194 –
Houldsworth & Company	124 St. Vincent Street, Glasgow	43	647 –	Jackson, John	Barnhill, Blantyre	132	333 –
				Do. do.	Do. (Minerals)	–	173 –
Houston, Rev. James R.	Grace Street, Carluke	2	32 –	Jackson, John W.	Hallhill, Glassford	210	500 –
Houston, Trustees of John	Glasgow	96	497 19	Jackson, John M. W.	5 Hill Street, Edinburgh	563	420 –
Houston, William	45 John Street, Glasgow	10	26 –	Do. do.	Do. (Minerals)	–	14 –
Howieson, Trs. of James	Lanark	1,100	454 –	Jackson, Trs. of Robert	Bardykes, Blantyre	127	236 –
Howieson, John, junior	Uddingston	2	75 –	Jackson, Thomas	Spittalhill, Cambuslang	85	120 –
Howieson, Stephen Y.	Lanark	345	326 –	Jackson, Thomas	Coates, Coatbridge	5	1,417 –
				Jackson, Thomas	Croftfoot, Blantyre	60	60 –
Howieson, Mrs. Anne	2 Greenhill Bank, Edinburgh	10	95 –	Jackson, William	East Newton Cottage, Strathaven	50	90 –
Howieson, Louisa G. and Elizabeth E.	1 Fern Bank, Cheltenham	80	157 –	Jackson, William	Craigthorn, Glassford	106	55 –
Hozier, James, of Mauldslie	Mauldslie, Carluke	517	1,350 4	Jackson, William E.	3 Bellgrove Terrace, Newcastle-on-Tyne	2	788 –
Do. do.	Do. (Minerals)	–	558 18				
Hozier, Colonel W. W., of Tannochside	St. Enoch's Hall, Bellshill	655	755 –	Jackson, Mrs. Janet	Spittal, Cambuslang	49	91 –
				Do. do.	Do. (Minerals)	–	8 –
Do. do.	Do. (Minerals)	–	4,032 –	Jackson, Marion	Hallhill, Glassford	7	37 –
Hunter, Alexander	Covington, Biggar	2	10 –	Jackson, Marion	Letham, Strathaven	381	260 –
Hunter, David	Yieldshields, Carluke	1	7 –	Jackson, Mary	Cowleybank, Biggar	1	20 –
Hunter, James, junior	Rhindsdale, Baillieston	15	153 –	Jamieson, William	Tofts, Strathaven	30	148 –
Hunter, John	Tailend, Bathgate	2	86 –	Jardine, George C.	10 Shaftesbury Terrace, Glasgow	76	304 –
Hunter, John E.	14 Walmer Crescent, Glasgow	520	308 –	Jardine, James	North Whitelawburn, Largs	32	50 –
Hunter, John R. S.	Dales, Carluke	1	36 –	Jarvie, Heirs of James	25 Bath Street, Glasgow	63	89 –
Hunter, Moses, & Co.	19 Macfarlane Street, Glasgow	4	170 –	Jeffrey, Rev. Hugh	Stevenston, Holytown	3	22 –
Hunter, Peter	Stobwood, Carnwath	8	11 –	Jeffrey, James	8 Elmbank Crescent, Glasgow	308	142 7
Hunter, Mrs. Margaret	Abington	1	16 –	Do.	Do. (Minerals)	–	223 1
Hutcheson, Alexander	Dunclutha, Bothwell	4	140 –	Jeffrey, John	193 St. Vincent Street, Glasgow	260	262 –
Hutcheson, Alexander, and Rev. R. P.	St. Thomas' Rectory, Winchester	78	434 –	Do.	Do. (Minerals)	–	179 6
Hutcheson, Trustees of Graham	63 St. Vincent Street, Glasgow	42	242 10	Jeffrey, Robert, & Sons	110 Brunswick Street, Glasgow	5	417 10
Hutcheson, James	Hamilton Street, Govan, Glasgow	1	978 19	Johnstone, Alexander	Chapelside, Wishaw	73	186 –
				Johnstone, John A.	Archbank, Moffat	1,426	440 –
Hutcheson, Trustees of James	Woodside	110	228 –	Johnstone, Exrs. of John	Mucroft, Cadder	303	322 –
Do. do.	Do. (Minerals)	–	1,066 –	Johnstone, J. J. Hope, of Annandale	Raehills, Moffat	1,287	352 –
Hutcheson, Joseph	Woodside, Dalserf	6	17 –	Johnstone, John Y.	Port Natal	2	22 –
Hutcheson, Trustees of Joseph	Woodside, Dalserf	330	477 –	Johnstone, Rev. James S.	Kirkhill, Cambuslang	6	65 –
Hutcheson Hospital	Ingram Street, Glasgow	41	649 7	Johnstone, Robert	Bothwell Ter., Glasgow	1	3 –
Hutcheson, Peter & Joseph	Hamilton Street, Govan, Glasgow	2	665 –	Johnstone, Thomas	Stevenston, Holytown	1	220 –
				Johnstone, Thomas	6 Rose Street, Glasgow	1	52 –
Hutton, Rev. Robert S.	Cambusnethan, Wishaw	6	50 –	Johnstone, Thomas	Holytown	1	53 15
				Johnstone, William	9 Royal Ter., Edinburgh	1,821	436 –
				Johnstone, William	Blackhill, Springburn	52	120 9
				Johnstone, William	Easter Cleddans, Cadder	33	115 –
Inch, John	Westmains, Liberton, Edinburgh	1	66 –	Johnstone, Jeanie	Orchard Farm, Thornliebank	3	16 –
Industrial Building Company	Lenzie, Cadder	11	150 –	Jolly, Trustees of William	Stevenson, Bothwell	405	452 –
Inglis, Anthony	Broomhill, Partick	4	240 –	Do. do.	Do. (Minerals)	–	1,373 –
Inglis, Cornelius, of Verehills	Verehills, Lesmahagow	1,095	954 –	Jones & Wilson	Burnbank, Coatbridge	1	112 –
Inglis, Charles Craigie Halkett, of Cramond	Cramond, Edinburgh	2,249	1,357 –	Kay, Alexander	Cornhill, Biggar	833	388 –
Do. do.	Do. (Minerals)	–	2,020 –	Do.	Do. (Minerals)	–	26 –

R

LANARK—continued.

Name of Owner.	Address of Owner.	Estimated Acreage of Property.	Gross Annual Value.	Name of Owner.	Address of Owner.	Estimated Acreage of Property.	Gross Annual Value.
		Acres.	£ s.			Acres.	£ s.
Kay, Thomas	Partick, Glasgow	1	90 —	Leiper, John	St. Lawrence Chapel, Glassford	79	90 —
Kaye, Robert	Millbrae, Cadder	140	329 5	Leiper, John	Bankend, Crossford	25	69 —
Kello, Mrs. Jane	Biggar	1	3 —	Leiper, John	Laigh Unthank, Strathaven	72	150 —
Kelvinside Estate Proprietors	158 St. Vincent Street, Glasgow	342	885 17	Leiper, Mrs. Janet	Crofthead, Strathaven	60	95 —
Do. do.	Do. (Minerals)	—	2,958 2	Leishman, Rev. Matthew	Govan, Glasgow	63	286 —
Kemp, Trustees of James	Hamilton	264	294 —	Lennox, John	West Drumloch, Glassford	30	35 —
Kennedy, Hugh	Partick, Glasgow	2	1,554 —	Lennox, Walter W.	Cadzow Street, Hamilton	1	105 —
Kennedy, Trustees of Peter	Glasgow	3	106 —	Lewars, Heirs of William	Almada Street, Hamilton	3	155 —
Ker, Robert, of Auchinwraith	Auchinwraith, Hamilton	96	285 —	Liddell, Trustees of Peter	62 Frederick Street, Glasgow	98	96 —
Kerr, John G. D.	Baronald, Lanark	100	240 —	Lidgerwood, William V.			
Kerr, Robert M.	West Regent St., Glasgow	9	4 —	V.	Whifflet, Coatbridge	2	250 —
Kidston, John P.	Cairns, Cambuslang	34	262 —	Lindsay, Charles	Ridgepark, Lanark	10	120 —
King, Trustees of James	Hamilton	1	373 —	Lindsay, James	Ryeland, Strathaven	48	100 —
King, John	17 Blythswood Square, Glasgow	260	388 14	Lindsay, Heirs of John	Bellfield, Lanark	26	74 —
King, John	Tyrefield, Hillhead, Glasgow	39	110 —	Lindsay, Robert	Stonefield, Blantyre	1	60 —
King, William	Merry Street, Motherwell	2	1,199 —	Lindsay, William	Cambusnethan, Wishaw	1	10 —
King, Mrs. Ellen	Parkhall, Stonehouse	2	37 —	Lindsay, Mrs. Catherine	Clydesdale Cottage, Lanark	1	87 —
King, Mary Anne	Laurelbank, Hillhead	1	250 —	Liberton, Parochial Board of	Liberton, Carnwath	2	7 —
Kippen, Durham	121 Wellington Street, Glasgow	417	1,926 —	Linton, John	Eastfield, Symington, Biggar	1	82 —
Kirkhope, James, senior	Roadmeetings, Carluke	8	15 —	Lithgow, Robert, of Stanmore	Stanmore, Lanark	155	248 —
Kirkland, Andrew	Windmillhill, Motherwell	1	90 —	Little, John M.	Blackheath, Kent	93	212 —
Kirkland, James	Rosebank, Cadder	1	70 —	Little, Rev. Thomas	Clydeview, Lanark	8	11 —
Kirkland, William	Bournanflatt, Larkhall	4	18 —	Livey, Alexander	New Stevenston, Holytown	3	20 —
Kirkpatrick, Alexander, of Allanshaw	Allanshaw, Hamilton	181	506 —	Livingstone, James	Rawyards, New Monkland	1	204 15
Kirkwood, William T.	Woolfcrooks, Douglas	98	150 —	Livingstone, Robert	Wishaw	4	29 —
Laidlaw, David	Dowanhill, Glasgow	1	200 —	Lochhead, William	7 Belmont Crescent, Glasgow	7	1,171 10
Laing, Rev. James	Smithyhill, Lesmahagow	1	36 —	Lockhart, Allan E., of Cleghorn	Borthwickbrae, Hawick	2,280	2,554 —
Laing, William	Rutherglen	2	96 —	Lockhart, A. E., and others	Lanark	1	250 —
Lamb, George, and others	Hillhead, Glasgow	4	448 12	Lockhart, James	Midtown, Lanark	22	40 —
Lamb, John	Carmichael, Lanark	137	110 —	Lockhart, James S., of Castlehill	Castlehill, Carluke	4,422	5,250 —
Lamb, Heirs of Mrs. Lydia	Carluke	4	15 —	Do. do.	Do. (Minerals)	—	2,183 —
Lamberton, Hugh	Balgraybank, Springburn	15	92 —	Lockhart, Rev. Lawrence	Milton Lockhart, Carluke	1,059	1,884 —
Lambie, Andrew	Birkhill, Lesmahagow	50	57 —	Do. do.	Do. (Minerals)	—	698 —
Lambie, James	Overton, Strathaven	5	18 —	Lockhart, Sir Simon Macdonald, of Lee and Carnwath, Bart.	Lee Castle, Lanark	31,556	21050 —
Lambie, William	Hallburn, Strathaven	88	138 —	Do. do.	Do. (Minerals)	—	869 —
Lamont, John Henry, of Ardlamont	Ardlamont, Argyllshire	746	863 —	Lockhart, William	Nemphlar, Lanark	86	154 —
Do. do.	Do. (Minerals)	—	1,050 —	Lockhart, Janet, Elizabeth, and Agnes	Halltown, Lanark	20	26 —
Lanark Burgh Hospital	Lanark	31	79 —	Logan, Abraham, of Burnhouses	Caverton Mill, Kelso	171	102 —
Lanark, Heritors of Parish of	Lanark	6	36 —	Logan, Edward Orr	Lanark	27	111 —
Lanark, Magistrates and Town Council of	Lanark	544	528 —	Logan, James	Eastshields, Carnwath	800	386 —
Lang, John	Crown Gardens, Glasgow	5	112 —	Logan, Robert	Braehead House, Carluke	390	354 —
Lang, Thomas	Crossford, Lanark	35	135 —	Logan, Eliza H.	Dunse	418	910 —
Lang, William	Crosspark, Glasgow	4	122 —	London and Glasgow Engineering Company	Lancefield Street, Glasgow	10	3,000 —
Larkhall Building Society	Larkhall	2	79 —	Long, John	Uddingston	1	52 —
Larkhall, Parochial Board of	Larkhall	2	10 —	Longmore, Captain Arthur	Hamilton	2	100 —
Laurie, Rev. Alexander	13 Comely Bank, Edinburgh	5	16 —	Lorraine, Trustees of Walter S.	Loaningdale House, Biggar	46	177 —
Law, Duncan, & Co.	Shettleston	2	130 —	Loudon, Gavin	Strathaven	3	41 —
Law, Heirs of Robert	Victoria Place, Airdrie	2	217 10	Loudon, Rev. Joseph	Manse, Dalziel	9	60 —
Lawcock, Gavin	Burnside, Glassford	62	150 —	Love, John	Burnside, Rutherglen	89	151 —
Lawrie, Gavin	Haggs, Glassford	1	12 —	Lynch, John	Reddrievale, Cumbernauld Road, Glasgow	3	102 —
Lawrie, Rev. John	Liberton, Carnwath	11	38 —	Lyon, John	Langlands, East Kilbride	60	105 —
Lawrie, James G.	241 West George Street, Glasgow	10	850 —	Lyon, Peter	Rutherglen	6	60 —
Lawson, David	East Toftcombs, Biggar	3	11 —	M'Adam, Rev. Thomas	Chryston, Cadder	1	40 —
Lawson, Margaret	Walston, Biggar	8	21 —	M'Alpine, Trustees of Angus	180 St. Vincent Street, Glasgow	18	128 5
Leadbetter, James G.	Hillside, Bothwell	122	400 —	M'Alpine, Agnes	Muirhead, Cadder	18	63 14
Leadbetter, Thomas	Alderbank, Bothwell	7	135 —	M'Ara, Trustees of Peter	22 Dundas St., Glasgow	86	323 15
Lean, Samuel	Westside, Lesmahagow	38	30 —	M'Ausland, Alexander	Gartcraig House, Shettleston	100	120 —
Leck, Henry	34 Gordon St., Glasgow	30	700 —				
Leggat, James	Broadlees, Glassford	32	56 —				
Leggate, Arthur	Springfield Place, Uddingston	4	23 —				
Leggate, James	Royal Navy, Cork	1	49 —				
Leggate, James	Burnbank, Strathaven	96	70 —				
Leggate, William	Carliebog, Strathaven	21	16 —				
Leiper, Andrew	Newark, Glassford	63	130 —				
Leiper, Rev. John	Manse, Chapelton, Glassford	152	184 —	M'Bride, William, & Co.	Greenfields, Shettleston	1	115 —

LANARK—continued.

Name of Owner.	Address of Owner.	Estimated Acreage of Property.	Gross Annual Value.	Name of Owner.	Address of Owner.	Estimated Acreage of Property.	Gross Annual Value.
		Acres.	£ s.			Acres.	£ s.
M'Call, Henry	Daldowie, Tollcross	179	437 –	M'Lean, Mrs. Margaret	Burnhead, Larkhall	8	34 –
M'Call, Executors of James	7 West Regent Street, Glasgow	28	300 –	M'Lellan, George, & Co.	49 Robertson Street, Glasgow	2	270 –
M'Call, Mrs. Anna	Daldowie, Tollcross	19	180 –	M'Lellan, Peter & Walter	Trongate, Glasgow	24	460 –
M'Callum, Donald	Over Tweedieside, Strathaven	54	60 –	M'Nab, John	Dumbreck Priory, Glasgow	2	106 –
M'Callum, George	Rosebank, Cambuslang	2	65 –	M'Nair, James S.—per Donald Fisher, Curator Bonis	194 West George Street, Glasgow	232	453 –
M'Clymont, Alexander	Viewfield, Partick	1	85 –				
M'Conville, Mrs. Christina	27 Elmbank Place, Glasgow	5	400 –	Do. do.	Do. (Minerals)	–	200 –
M'Craw, Archibald	Partick, Glasgow	1	1,031 –	M'Naught, Norman D.	Union Street, Hamilton	2	85 –
M'Creath, James	138 West George Street, Glasgow	67	92 –	M'Naughton, Rev. Allan	Lesmahagow	6	67 –
				M'Neal, Frederick H.	Westquarter, Lenzie, Cadder	171	268 –
M'Culloch, John	West Muckroft, Cadder	68	110 –				
M'Donald, Alexander	Holytown	5	77 7	M'Neil Street Building Society	Larkhall	8	432 –
M'Donald, Reps. of John	Freelandbank, New Monkland	1	32 –	M'Pherson, John	Blantyre Farm, Blantyre	73	306 –
M'Dowall, John S.	Burnside, Rutherglen	1	120 –	M'Pherson, William	Bridgeway House, London	440	701 –
M'Farlane, Rev. Duncan	Walston, Biggar	11	40 –	M'Queen, Arthur James, of Hardington	Hardington House, Biggar	1,216	1,089 –
M'Farlane, George, junior	18 Elmbank Crescent, Glasgow	4	424 2				
M'Farlane, James	Stonefield, Blantyre	1	130 –	M'Queen, William	Shotts	20	35 –
M'Farlane, Rev. John T.	Miller Street, Hamilton	1	45 –	M'Rae, Mrs. Marion	Knowenock, Lesmahagow	2	22 –
M'Farlane, Walter, & Co.	46 Washington Street, Glasgow	100	1,094 –	M'Vicar, Rev. John G. C.	Moffat	140	45 –
				Mack, James	Baillieston	34	162 –
Do. do.	Do. (Minerals)	–	86 –	Mack, Trs. of Mrs. Janet	Bellside, Shotts	130	178 –
M'George & Galloway	91 West Regent Street, Glasgow	4	50 –	Mack, Jane	Springfield, Airdrie	5	31 10
				Mackenzie, John Ord, of Dolphinton	7 Royal Circus, Edinburgh	2,817	2,080 –
M'Ghie, David	Auchren, Lesmahagow	180	184 –				
M'Ghie, Henry	Shettleston, Glasgow	4	192 –	Mackenzie, Walter H.	7 Royal Circus, Edinburgh	2	10 –
M'Ghie, Robert	Trows, Lesmahagow	150	268 –				
M'Ghie, Thomas	Bishopbents, Carluke	22	31 –	Mackie, Andrew	Whiteside, Lesmahagow	49	54 –
M'Ghie, William	Southinch, Bathgate	25	20 –	Magdalene Asylum	Maryhill, Glasgow	4	400 –
M'Ghie, Trustees of James	Lesmahagow	75	98 –	Main, James	12 Argyle Street, Glasgow	3	95 –
M'Gown, Margaret	Cardowan, Springburn, Glasgow	8	45 –	Mair, Robert	Lanark (Minerals)	–	46 –
M'Gown, William	Gartochan, Alexandria	34	67 –	Maitland, Mrs. Agnes, and others	Heriot Row, Kirkintilloch	63	50 –
M'Gregor, Heirs of Andrew	41 West George Street, Glasgow	34	145 –	Marchbank, William	Devonburn, Lesmahagow	6	10 –
				Marr, James	Oxhill, Dumbarton	1	48 –
M'Gregor, James	156 West George Street, Glasgow	2	150 –	Marr, Heirs of John	Markgreen, Lanark	32	185 –
				Marr, Mrs. Christina	Markgreen, Lanark	14	41 –
M'Gregor, Mrs. Jeanie	172 New City Road, Glasgow	44	60 –	Marshall, James	Newhouse, Holytown	264	328 –
				Do. do.	Do. (Minerals)	–	59 –
M'Haffie, Alexander	48 Lansdowne Place, Brighton	46	160 –	Marshall, James	Goodockhill, Holytown	255	167 –
M'Haffie, William	Tranmere Park, Cheshire	18	144 –	Marshall, James	Glentore, Airdrie	83	110 –
M'Ilquham, Trustees of Walter	166 St. Vincent Place, Glasgow	154	240 –	Marshall, Trs. of James	140 St. Vincent Street, Glasgow	4	20 –
M'Intosh, Donald	Dykehead, Shotts	1	91 –	Marshall, John, of Machan	Machan, Larkhall	487	721 –
M'Intosh, Rev. Joseph	Airdrie	3	115 –	Do. do.	Do. (Minerals)	–	55 –
M'Ivor, Daniel, and Mrs. Janet	Westend, Lanark	7	120 –	Marshall, John, of Chapelton	63 Hamilton Drive, Glasgow	1,567	1,101 –
M'Kay, Joseph	Biggar	16	7 –	Marshall, John, jun.	168 St. Vincent Street, Glasgow	1	85 –
M'Kechnie, Daniel W.	Royal Exchange, Glasgow	7	94 –	Marshall, John	Dunsyston, Chapelhall, Airdrie	150	95 –
M'Kellar, Stevenson, & Galbraith	Sheepmount, Glasgow	3	10 –	Marshall, John	Caldergrove, Blantyre	45	230 –
M'Kenzie, Donald	Motherwell	2	53 –	Marshall, Representatives of John	Greenhill, Cadder	49	54 –
M'Kenzie, James	24 Stockwell Street, Glasgow	209	260 –	Martin, Hugh, & Sons	Coatbridge	2	309 –
M'Kenzie, John M.	Distillery, Wishaw	2	463 –	Martin, Hugh	Coatbridge	2	331 –
M'Kinnell & Dyer	Carluke	2	29 –	Martin, James	Kirkton Street, Carluke	32	187 –
M'Kinnell, Hugh	Carluke	2	30 –	Martin, Trustees of John	Coatbridge	2	518 –
M'Kirdy, John G., of Birkwood	Birkwood, Lesmahagow	1,250	1,170 –	Martin, William	Springrove, Cumbernauld Road, Glasgow	27	173 –
M'Kirdy, Major David E., junior	Lesmahagow	70	140 –	Martin, William	Greenhill, Strathaven	217	88 –
M'Lachlan, Henry	Coatbridge	2	82 –	Martin, Mrs. Jane	Westdyke, Strathaven	64	85 –
M'Lae, Alexander, of Cathkin	Cathkin, Carmunnock	894	1,696 –	Mason, Eadie, & Co.	Broomloan, Govan	2	300 –
				Mason, Alexander	Commonhead, Airdrie	57	91 –
Do. do.	Do. (Minerals)	–	75 –	Mason, James	Dungeon Hill, Old Monkland	63	98 –
M'Lean, Rev. Alexander H.	Carnwath	10	55 –	Do.	Do. (Minerals)	–	650 –
M'Lean, John	27 India Street, Glasgow	4	540 –	Mason, James, jun., and others	158 Buchanan Street, Glasgow	135	15 –
M'Lean, Joseph	Haughhead, Govan	5	50 –	Mason, Trustees of James	Cairnduff, Strathaven	126	200 –
M'Lean, William	Shields, by Renfrew	175	554 –	Mason, Robert	158 Buchanan Street, Glasgow	319	114 –
M'Lean, William	188 West Regent Street, Glasgow	1	50 –	Mather, Heirs of James	Langbank, Port-Glasgow	216	340 –
M'Lean, Trustees of William	Plantation, Glasgow (Vacant Ground)	25	75 –	Mather, Reston	Provanhall, Glasgow	80	135 –
				Do.	Do. (Minerals)	–	150 –

131

LANARK—continued.

Name of Owner.	Address of Owner.	Estimated Acreage of Property.	Gross Annual Value.		Name of Owner.	Address of Owner.	Estimated Acreage of Property.	Gross Annual Value.	
		Acres.	£	s.			Acres.	£	s.
Mather, Reston & Robert	Provanhall, Glasgow	130	345	–	Montgomery, John Basil Hamilton, of Newton	Peebles	418	1,160	–
Do. do.	Do. (Minerals)	–	55	–	Do. do.	Do. (Minerals)	–	800	–
Mather, William	Waterfoot, Busby	378	391	–	Montgomery, Mrs. Helen M.	Broughty Ferry	33	126	18
Mathieson, John	Eastfield, Rutherglen	12	605	–	Moodie, Robert	198 West George Street, Glasgow	3	125	–
Maule, Trustees of Rev. Thomas	4 Dunmore Pl., Glasgow	2	387	–	Moore, John W., of Greenhall	Greenhall, Blantyre	332	628	–
Maxwell, John, of Baillieston	Baillieston	157	653	–	Do. do.	Do. (Minerals)	–	158	–
Do. do.	Do. (Minerals)	–	700	–	Morton, Charles Macdonald, of Largie	Largie Castle, Argyllshire	166	148	–
Maxwell & Moore	Partick, Glasgow	3	330	–	Morrison, Alexander	Townhead, Strathaven	25	50	–
Maxwell & Turner	Hamilton	2	544	–	Morrison, James	Corneygroats, Strathaven	7	18	–
Maxwell, Sir William, of Calderwood, Bart.	Calderwood, Hamilton	6	15	–	Morrison, John	Govan, Glasgow	1	171	–
Maxwell, Sir William Stirling, of Pollok and Keir, Bart.	Keir House, Dunblane	5,691	8,741	–	Morrison, John	Canada	60	185	–
					Morrison, Robert	Rosebank, Edinburgh	3	20	–
Do. do.	Do. (Minerals)	–	3,231	–	Morrison, Thomas	Crossbank, Crossford	16	13	–
Maxwell, Trs. of late Sir William Alexander, Bart.	Calderwood, Hamilton	1,393	2,309	–	Morrison, William	Lanark	2	37	–
					Morton, Archibald	Strathaven	76	115	–
Do. do.	Do. (Minerals)	–	142	–	Morton, George	Thorniebank, Carluke	11	71	–
Meek, John, of Fortisset	Hamilton	1,701	958	–	Morton, Hugh	Eastdykes, Strathaven	81	150	–
Do. do.	Do. (Minerals)	–	2,386	–	Morton, Trustees of James	Strathaven	36	71	–
Meiklam, Trustees of James, of Carnbroe	Carnbroe, Bothwell	1,019	1,659	–	Morton, John	Nether Abington, Abington	75	160	–
Do. do.	Do. (Minerals)	–	2,435	–	Morton, Trs. of Mrs. Jane	Burnhead, Strathaven	28	40	–
Mcikle, John	Newcastle-on-Tyne	28	46	–	Mossend Iron Co.	Mossend, Bellshill	3	2,790	–
Meikle, Executors of John	Littlekype, Strathaven	38	45	–	Mossman, Hugh, of Auchtyfardle	11 Chalmers Street, Edinburgh	750	1,607	–
Meikle, Robert	Bogside Cottage, Douglas	6	63	–	Motherwell Combination Poorhouse	Park Street, Motherwell	2	247	–
Meikle, Thomas	High Dykes, Strathaven	88	80	–	Motherwell, Gavin Black	Airdrie	150	167	2
Melrose, Peter	Biggar	105	145	–	Do. do.	Do. (Minerals)	–	250	–
Memes, Mrs. Ann	Hamilton	1	120	–	Motherwell, John	Rawyards, Airdrie	160	265	10
Menzies, Representatives of Andrew, of Balornock	Balornock, Glasgow	90	200	–	Do. do.	Do. (Minerals)	–	50	–
Menzies, William	5 Allison St., Glasgow	4	2,327	10	Motherwell Water Commissioners	Motherwell	6	25	–
Menzies, Mrs. Barbara	Bellfield, Abington	68	156	–	Motherwell, William	Airdrie	10	388	5
Merry & Cunninghame (Limited)	127 St. Vincent Street, Glasgow	6	4,280	–	Muir, Alexander	Woodlands Park, Manchester	6	27	–
Middleton, David	Bothwell	1	85	–	Muir, John	Bonnyhill, Kilmarnock	88	70	–
Miller & Anderson	Dundyvan, Coatbridge	3	425	–	Muir, Michael	Milton Bank, Carluke	1	43	–
Miller, Archibald	Nerston Mill, East Kilbride	6	17	–	Muir, Heirs of Richard	Carluke	2	17	–
Miller, David C.	Avonbank, Larkhall	17	470	–	Muir, Robert	Lanark	56	81	–
Miller, George	Wingfield, Bothwell	2	60	–	Muir, Thomas	Whitehill, Lanark	7	55	–
Miller, George John, of Frankfield	Frankfield, Shettleston	804	1,943	–	Muir, Thomas	24 York Terrace, Regent Park, London	7	120	–
Do. do.	Do. (Minerals)	–	474	4	Muir, William	Gilbertfield, Cambuslang	2	11	–
Miller, Trustees of Henry	Biggar	138	234	–	Muir, Mrs. Helen	Strathaven	2	30	–
Miller, James	Strathaven	86	270	–	Muir, Mary and Isabella	Lanark	1	4	–
Miller, James	Mosside, Ayr	15	32	–	Muir, Mary and Isabella, Margaret and Mrs. Jessie Walker, wife of William Walker	13 Montpelier Terrace, Liverpool	76	251	–
Miller, James	Tackhouse, Strathaven	74	70	–					
Miller, James	Loudon Street, Larkhall	2	365	–					
Miller, James	Rosebank, Cambuslang	1	237	15					
Miller, James	Coatbridge	1	30	–	Muir, John	Dowanside, Glasgow	1	120	–
Miller, Trustees of John	Pollockshields, Glasgow	190	166	–	Muirhead, Henry	Bushyhill, Cambuslang	79	653	–
Miller, Rev. Peter G.	F.C. Manse, Wishaw	1	46	–	Muirhead, William	Clayslap, New Monkland	18	30	–
Miller, Thomas P.	Rosebank, Cambuslang	5	442	–	Muirhead, Emily G., of Bredisholm	Bredisholm, Motherwell	1,077	2,149	–
Miller, William	High Dykes, Strathaven	174	100	–					
Miller, William, & Son	54 Gordon St., Glasgow	17	8	–	Do. do.	Do. (Minerals)	–	5,471	5
Miller, Mrs. Janet	Croftfoot, Blantyre	13	85	–	Murdoch, James Finlay	Hallside, Cambuslang	10	92	–
Miller, Janet	Park, Blantyre	63	70	–	Murdoch, John	10 Annfield Terrace, Partick	2	24	–
Do.	Do. (Minerals)	–	6	–					
Mirrlees, James B.	Redlands, Glasgow	24	315	–	Murdoch, Neil	Ashleypark, Bothwell	2	110	–
Mitchell, Andrew & Alexander O.	160 West George Street, Glasgow	1	3	–	Murdoch, Robert	Hallside, Cambuslang	83	288	–
Mitchell, Andrew	4 Claremont Terrace, Glasgow	420	370	–	Murdoch & Rodger	107 West Regent Street, Glasgow	575	233	–
					Murdoch, Mrs. Christina	East Haughhead, Uddingston	46	110	–
Mitchell, Alexander	Ardenclutha, Hamilton	2	100	–	Murray & Co.	Rutherglen	8	780	–
Mitchell, Alexander M.	Dunrowan-Lenzie, Cadder	2	65	–	Murray, James	Rutherglen	3	46	–
Mitchell, James	Boghead, Lesmahagow	2	14	–	Murray, James W.	19 Young St., Edinburgh	760	303	–
Mitchell, Thomas	Glenbank, Cadder	1	58	–	Do. do.	Do. (Minerals)	–	46	–
Mitchell, William G., of Carwood	Carwood, Biggar	1,525	1,413	–	Murray, John, sen.	Maryhill Road, Glasgow	4	277	–
Mitchell, William J.	Currie, Edinburgh	245	148	–	Murray, John L., of Heavyside	Heavyside, Biggar	409	518	–
Mitchell, Trs. of Mrs. Anne	Dykehead, Stonehouse	159	261	–	Murray, Robert G.	Spittall, Biggar	265	319	–
Moncrieff, Hope Margaret	Lanark	4	70	–	Murray, Robert Simpson	Rutherglen	2	150	–
Monkland Iron and Coal Company (Limited)	Calderbank, Airdrie	35	5,908	–	Murray, Mrs. Janet	Crawford, Abington	120	49	–
					Murray, Mrs. Jane	Bloomgate, Lanark	2	78	–
Monteith, Robert, of Carstairs	Carstairs House, Lanark	5,581	8,963	–	Muter, Thomas and John	Pleasance, Larkhall	1	13	–

LANARK—continued.

Name of Owner.	Address of Owner.	Estimated Acreage of Property.	Gross Annual Value.		Name of Owner.	Address of Owner.	Estimated Acreage of Property.	Gross Annual Value.	
		Acres.	£	s.			Acres.	£	s.
Naismith, John	Union Street, Hamilton	1	87	–	Paterson, John	East Kilbride	126	121	–
Naismith, John, and others	Hamilton	35	135	–	Paterson, Johnstone	Braehead, Airdrie	5	107	3
Naismith, James	Coatshill, Blantyre	85	292	–	Paterson, Matthew	East Kilbride	126	73	–
Naismith, Trustees of John	Drumloch, Glassford	398	282	–	Paterson, Rev. Robert	Manse, Glassford	10	72	–
Do. do.	Do. (Minerals)	–	28	–	Paterson, Robert	Holytown	7	198	–
Napier, John	Govan	11	220	–	Paterson, Robert	53 Hutcheson Street, Glasgow	2	19	–
Napier, John S.	Letham, Strathaven	700	646	–					
Napier, Robert	127 Lancefield Street, Glasgow	18	3,850	–	Paterson, Robert, of Birthwood	Birthwood, Biggar	1,500	289	–
National Heritable Property Association	71 W. Nile St., Glasgow	13	227	–	Paterson, Thomas, of Simsonland	Simsonland, Hamilton	90	135	–
Nelson, James	Hillendbraes, Lesmahagow	2	13	–	Paterson, Captain Thomas	Kenmure House, Bishopbriggs	2	70	–
Nelson, James	Biggar Park, Biggar	348	625	–	Paterson, Thomas Lucas, of Dowanhill	Dowanhill, Glasgow	118	7,188	–
Nelson, William	Bellshill	1	61	–	Do. do.	Do. (Quarry)	–	50	–
Nelson, Trs. of William	West Regent Street, Glasgow	43	185	–	Paterson, William	Howlands, Carluke	1	10	–
Newarthill U.P. Church	Motherwell	1	17	–	Paterson, William	Glengonner, Biggar	378	149	–
Newbigging, Heirs of James	Lanark	202	193	–	Paterson, William	Laigh Huntlawridge, East Kilbride	210	122	–
Do. do.	Do. (Minerals)	–	150	–	Paterson, William	Knowenoblehill, Shotts	40	52	–
New Monkland, Parochial Board of	Airdrie	2	116	–	Paton, Samuel	Lamington, Biggar	8	13	–
Newton, James E.	Linnville, Lanark	1	25	–	Patrick, John	23 St Leonard Street, Lanark	4	8	–
Nimmo, Mrs. Jane	9 Bernard Terrace, Edinburgh	46	38	–	Paul, John, of Cambuswallace	Cambuswallace, Biggar	71	183	–
Nisbet, Alexander	Govan Place, Hareshaw, Shotts	34	34	–	Pearson, Trustees of Andrew A.	Edinburgh	473	302	–
Nisbet, John More, of Cairnhill	Cairnhill House, Airdrie	1,326	1,673	9	Pearson, Margaret M.	Southborough, Tunbridge Wells	4	140	–
Do.	Do. (Minerals)	–	2,796	8	Peat, John G. and Mrs. Jeanie	Auchingramont, Hamilton	1	90	–
North British Oil & Candle Company	48 Dundas Street, Glasgow	8	1,040	–	Pender, John	Springhill, Shotts	15	40	–
North British Railway Co.	Edinburgh (Railway)	588	39838	–	Do.	Do. (Minerals)	–	20	–
Do. do.	Do.	7	595	–	Perrott, Heirs of John	Maryhill	9	89	–
					Do. do.	Do. (Minerals)	–	30	–
Old Monkland, Parochial Board of	Old Monkland	6	540	–	Peterkin, William	148 Broomielaw, Glasgow	11	12	–
Original Secession Church, Managers of	Carluke	1	21	–	Pettigrew, James	Braehead, Shotts	4	72	–
Orr, James	Blythswood Square, Glasgow	223	44	–	Pettigrew, William V.	Colebrooke Lodge, Upper Norwood, London	21	103	5
Orr, James	Shotts, Whitburn	200	140	–	Phillips, Thomas	Coatbridge	1	246	–
Orr, John	Bogend, Whitburn	101	65	–	Pickering, John, & Son	Wishaw	4	300	–
Orr, Thomas	Baads, Whitburn	84	52	–	Pinkerton, John	Hogganfield, Glasgow	103	425	–
Orr, Mrs. Margaret	Fieldhead, East Kilbride	4	8	–	Pinkerton, Janet	Rutherglen	5	66	–
Osborne, Robert	Thornton Hall, East Kilbride	96	249	–	Pollock, Alexander	Brigbrae, Bellshill	7	110	–
Do.	Do. (Minerals)	–	300	–	Pollock, Allan	Lismany, Ballinasloe, Ireland	50	100	–
Oswald, James G., of Scotston	Scotston, Glasgow	432	1,470	10	Do.	Do. (Minerals)	–	328	17
Do. do.	Do. (Minerals)	–	119	10	Pollock, Andrew	South Linnridge, Holytown	3	43	–
Ovens, William	Biggar	15	62	–	Do.	Do. (Minerals)	–	200	–
					Pollock, Andrew	Holytown	6	85	–
					Pollock, George	Rhindsmuir, Baillieston	165	481	–
Padkin, Alexander	Wiston, Biggar	4	3	–	Pollock, James	Nerston, East Kilbride	2	15	–
Pagan, Rev. John	Bothwell	8	84	–	Pollock, John	Blackhouse, Mearns	164	210	–
Pagan, Agnes, Jane, and Margaret	63 Kelvingrove Street, Glasgow	206	187	–	Pollock, John	Old Kilpatrick	122	165	–
Pairman, Adam	Biggar	1	102	–	Pollock, Mrs. Jane	Peats Cottage, Bellshill	3	44	–
Panton, James Alex., of Garthamlock	38 Gordon Square, London, W.C.	183	716	–	Pollock, Mrs. Janet	Hamilton	8	30	–
Do. do.	Do. (Minerals)	–	600	–	Do. do.	Do. (Minerals)	–	15	–
Park, John	1 Thomas St., Edinburgh	485	156	–	Pollok, Morris	Govan Factory, Glasgow	10	864	5
Park, Rev. John	Cadder	10	42	–	Potter, Lewis, of Udston	Udston, Hamilton	356	991	–
Park, Rev. John and William	Cadder	35	47	–	Do. do.	Do. (Minerals)	–	2,345	–
Parker, Mrs. Eliza	Grange, Bothwell	3	85	–	Poynter, John E., of Clydeneuch	72 Great Clyde Street, Glasgow	20	258	–
Partick & Hillhead Gas Co.	Hillhead	1	60	–	Prentice, John	21 Lyndoch Street, Greenock	34	40	–
Paterson, Adam	Springhall, Rutherglen	37	200	–	Prentice, William	Carnwath	15	21	–
Paterson, Alexander, of Carmacoup	Crossburn House, Douglas	1,150	958	–	Prentice, Elizabeth	104 York Place, Manchester	2	23	–
Paterson, Gavin	Bent Road, Hamilton	2	600	–	Proudfoot, John, & James Scott	33 Lynedoch St., and 1 Woodside Pl., Glasgow	323	1,047	7
Paterson, James	Lamlash, Arran	180	468	–	Provan, Charles	Roadmeetings, Carluke	1	7	–
Do.	Do. (Minerals)	–	75	–	Provan, Reps. of John	North Broomknowe, Moodiesburn	1	48	14
Paterson, James	Knowenoblehill, Shotts	100	148	–	Provanhall Coal Company	30 Oswald St., Glasgow	25	989	–
Do.	Do. (Minerals)	–	770	–	Purdie, Alexander	Lesmahagow	4	15	–
Paterson, James	Over Abington, Abington	28	25	–	Purdie, Peter & George	Bellevue, Glasgow	2	120	–
Paterson, James Henry	Forthbank, Cadder	1	58	–					
Paterson, Rev. James	Culter, Biggar	1	17	–	Quinton, James	Wishaw	1	36	8
Paterson, John	North Torfoot, Strathaven	179	176	–					

LANARK—continued.

Name of Owner.	Address of Owner.	Estimated Acreage of Property.	Gross Annual Value.	Name of Owner.	Address of Owner.	Estimated Acreage of Property.	Gross Annual Value.
		Acres.	£ s.			Acres.	£ s.
Rae, Rev. Robert R.	Manse, Strathaven	10	44 —	Riddell, John	Strathaven	56	73 —
Rankin, Gavin	West Myvot, New Monkland	81	112 —	Riddell, John	Bankfield, Chapelton	67	67 —
Rankin, James	High Street, Carluke	1	124 —	Riddell, William	Wellgreen, Glassford	112	120 —
Rankin, James	Lanark	3	10 —	Rintoul, Peter	Bothwell Bank, Bothwell	75	274 —
Rankin, John	Airdrie	3	486 10	Rintoul, Robert, junior	Fairfield Lodge, Bothwell	1	96 —
Rankin, Gavin and Walter	West Myvot, New Monkland	126	165 —	Risk, John, & Co.	Maryhill, Glasgow	1	120 —
Rankin, Reps. of James Thomson	Airdrie	190	194 —	Risk, Mrs. Catherine	Provanmill, Glasgow	4	162 —
Rankin, Patrick	Garngibbock, Airdrie	565	432 5	Ritchie, Arthur, of Middleton	Middleton, Liverpool	1,973	364 —
Do.	Do. (Minerals)	—	573 —	Ritchie, Robert	Southlee, Liberton, Biggar	1	4 —
Rankin, Patrick, junior	Airdrie	185	350 —	Robb, Archibald	Galla Lodge, Biggar	11	27 —
Do. do.	Do. (Minerals)	—	100 —	Roberton, James, of Lauchope	Lauchope, Bothwell	359	502 —
Rankin, Patrick	Airdrie	189	159 —	Robertson, Andrew, & Sons	Clydebank, Rutherglen	1	175 —
Do.	Do. (Minerals)	—	120 —	Robertson, Rev. Anselm	Tollcross	33	182 —
Rankin, Patrick, of Auchingray	Auchingray, Airdrie	4,365	3,196 10	Robertson, Andrew Carrick, John, and others	116 St. Vincent St., Glasgow (Vacant Ground)	21	25 10
Do.	Do. (Minerals)	—	2,079 —	Robertson, David S., of Lawhead	1 North Manor Place, Edinburgh	4,170	2,096 —
Rankin, Rev. Robert	Manse, Lamington, Biggar	12	47 —	Do. do.	Do. (Minerals)	—	961 —
Rankin & Shaw	Airdrie	8	95 10	Robertson, James	Biggar	20	71 —
Rankin, Walter	West Myvot, Airdrie	100	150 10	Do.	Do. (Minerals)	—	454 —
Raploch Building Society	Larkhall	5	246 —	Robertson, James	76 Main Street, Maryhill	2	802 13
Readman, George	28 Woodside Place, Glasgow	7	300 —	Robertson, John M'Millan	Crosshill, Glasgow	4	1,535 —
Reformed Presbyterian Congregation	Wishaw	1	30 —	Robertson, John	24 West Lauriston Place, Edinburgh	4	13 —
Reid, Alexander	Govan	4	938 —	Robertson, John	Rogerfield, Old Monkland	4	23 —
Reid, Archibald	Dalziel Colliery, Motherwell	2	74 —	Robertson, John	Blairbeth, Rutherglen	45	165 —
Reid, Francis Robertson	Gallowflatt, Rutherglen	70	458 —	Robertson, John	Meadowbank, Airdrie	3	204 16
Reid, Francis and James Robertson	Rutherglen (Minerals)	—	4,365 16	Robertson, Trs. of Robert	Whitefield	37	186 10
Reid, Hugh	Meadowbank, Tollcross	2	26 —	Robertson, Mary	Lauchope, Bellshill	3	145 —
Reid, Trustees of James	Calderbank, Baillieston	100	200 —	Robin, Robert and Sarah	Castlehill, Hamilton	5	232 —
Reid, James	Berridale, Helensburgh	325	318 —	Robinson, Robert	Whiteinch, Glasgow	8	733 —
Reid, James	Lawside, East Kilbride	83	201 —	Rochsolloch Iron Company	Airdrie	7	475 —
Reid, Trustees of James	Maryhill, Glasgow	131	868 13	Rodger, David	West Regent Street, Glasgow	3	6 —
Do. do.	Do. (Minerals)	—	300 —	Rollo, Archibald	Sunbury House, Edinburgh	190	185 —
Reid, Trustees of James	St. Vincent St., Glasgow	102	309 19	Roman Catholic Congregation, Trustees of	Bannatyne St., Lanark	9	70 —
Reid, James Robertson	Woodburn, Rutherglen	11	489 —	Rorison, Rev. William P.	Larkhall	10	75 —
Reid, John, of Nellfield	Nellfield, Carluke	280	208 —	Ross, Sir C. W. A., of Balnagown, Bart.	Balnagown Castle, Tain	1,421	1,511 —
Reid, John	Newton, Wiston, Biggar	15	48 —	Ross, William	1 Royal Bank Place, Glasgow	50	348 —
Reid, Trustees of John	8 Westmuir Street, Parkhead	7	112 —	Ross, Mrs. Jane	19 Union Street, Larkhall	1	4 —
Reid, John	Castlehill, Carmunnock	44	92 —	Ross, Janet, Mary, and Ann	Whitehill, Lanark	5	12 —
Reid, John	Peel Park, East Kilbride	105	164 —	Rowan, Michael	10 Lansdowne Crescent, Glasgow	1	930 —
Reid, John	Kittochside, East Kilbride	83	234 —	Rowan, Trs. of George	Govan, Glasgow	122	387 —
Do.	Carluke (Minerals)	—	225 —	Rowatt, Thomas	Bonnanhill, Strathaven	279	315 —
Reid, John	Calderbank, Baillieston	80	230 —	Royal Asylum for Lunatics, Directors of	40 West George Street, Glasgow	66	1,425 —
Do.	Do. (Minerals)	—	725 —	Russell, Alexander	Biggar	1	4 —
Reid, Trustees of John	West Calder	200	125 —	Russell, Andrew	Causewayend, Airdrie	160	143 —
Reid, Thomas	Govan, Glasgow	10	195 —	Russell, Archibald	69 Great Clyde Street, Glasgow	9	580 —
Reid, Walter W. W.	3 Burnbank Place, Glasgow	4	16 10	Russell, Archibald	Rutherglen	4	120 —
Reid, William	Craighall, East Kilbride	33	68 —	Russell, George	High Street, Carluke	1	16 —
Reid, William	Kittochside, East Kilbride	129	250 —	Russell, James	Rutherglen	3	31 —
Reid, William	Castlehill, East Kilbride	121	316 —	Russell, James	Burnbank, Shotts	224	145 —
Reid, Mrs. Jane	Peel Park, Busby	184	171 —	Russell, James, senior	Windmillhill, Motherwell	3	520 —
Do.	Do. (Minerals)	—	20 —	Russell, John	Burnbrae, Blantyre	15	56 —
Reid, Anna	12 Gladstone Terrace, Edinburgh	3	14 —	Russell, Peter	Westerhinds, Baillieston	4	27 —
Reid, Fanny	Motherwell	2	8 —	Russell, Stephen	Bellabra, East Kilbride	10	22 —
Renton, Alexander	Crawfordjohn, Abington	1	31 —	Russell, Thomas	14 India Street, Glasgow	11	33 —
Renton, Rev. George C.	Manse, Dunsyre, Noblehouse	14	40 —	Russell, Mrs. Mary	Merry Street, Motherwell	2	16 —
Renton, John	Craigton, Glasgow	35	32 —	Rutherglen, Burgh of	Rutherglen	102	651 —
Renwick, Mrs. Agnes, and Sons	Maryhill, Glasgow	3	41 —	Ruthven, Lady	Winton Castle, Tranent	30	136 —
Reston, Alexander	Airdrie	1	43 15				
Richardson, George, & Sons	5 King Street, Tradeston, Glasgow	2	17 12	Saidler, Andrew	St. Leonard's Cottage, Lanark	7	22 —
Richardson, Thomas, David, & John	Wilson Street, Glasgow	50	136 —	Saidler, Trustees of Mrs. Elizabeth	St. Leonard's Cottage, Lanark	42	60 —
Do. do.	Do. (Minerals)	—	549 8	Salmon, Jane, and others	Annfield, Airdrie	1	17 10
Riddell, John	Todshill Street, Strathaven	5	32 —	Salmond, James	4 Scotia Street, New City Road, Glasgow	1	3 —

LANARK—continued.

Name of Owner.	Address of Owner.	Estimated Acreage of Property.	Gross Annual Value. £ s.
Samuel, Trustees of James	132 St. Vincent Street, Glasgow	63	168 –
Sandford, John	Broomlea, Cambuslang	1	60 –
Sandylands, Gavin, of Glendevon	Glendevon, Lesmahagow	176	159 –
Sawyers, John	Parkfoot, Whitburn	13	25 –
Sawyers, William	Wellsley, Whitburn	66	42 –
Scott, David	Lenzie, Cadder	2	10 –
Scott, Gavin	Barrochan, Renfrewshire	2	5 –
Scott, Trustees of George	Blantyre Farm, Blantyre	517	1,042 –
Scott & Gibson	Firhill Road, Glasgow	1	80 –
Scott, Rev. James H.	Bonkle, Wishaw	1	24 –
Scott, John	Springfield, Uddingston	2	156 –
Scott, John Baird	Lenzie, Cadder	179	202 –
Scott, Ralph E.	Melville St., Edinburgh	130	104 –
Scott, Robert	Greenoakhill, Tollcross	114	382 –
Scott, Thomas	Priestfield, Blantyre	77	100 –
Do.	Do. (*Minerals*)	–	203 –
Scott, Thomas	Croftbank, Uddingston	66	165 –
Scott, William	Uddingston	5	8 –
Scott, William, junior	Strathaven	70	162 –
Scott, William	Gowanglen, Carluke	2	44 –
Scott, William	3 Duncan St., Glasgow	40	66 –
Scott, William	Rutherglen	2	114 –
Scott, William	Craigmuir, Strathaven	34	65 –
Scott, Mrs. Agnes	Blantyre	101	255 –
Scott, Mrs. Isabella	Unthank, Bellshill	1	52 –
Scott, Mrs. Jane	Omoa, Motherwell	10	86 –
Scottish Provident Insurance Company	Edinburgh	3	6 –
Scoullar, Heirs of Joseph	Phillipshill Mill, East Kilbride	3	40 –
Seath, Thomas Bollen	Rutherglen	4	234 –
Secession Church, Managers of	Shotts	1	12 –
Selkirk, Andrew C.	Kirkston Street, Carluke	150	309 –
Do.	Do. (*Minerals*)	–	30 –
Selkirk, Isaac	Priesthill, East Kilbride	3	20 –
Semple, Alexander	Burn, Glassford	44	70 –
Semple, Alexander	Hairlaw, Glassford	32	53 –
Semple, Andrew	East Coldstream, Strathaven	76	160 –
Semple, Archibald	Ardgillion, Old Scone, Perth	110	165 –
Semple, James, of Overton	Overton, Strathaven	999	772 –
Semple, James	Hareshead, Strathaven	145	142 –
Semple, Heirs of James	Low Brownsmuir, Glassford	97	108 –
Semple, John	Westfield, Strathaven	65	150 –
Semple, John	Kirk Street, Strathaven	27	66 –
Semple, John	Hareshawhead, Strathaven	26	45 –
Semple, John	Heads, Glassford	300	468 –
Semple, Thomas	Farnhall, Brechin, Forfarshire	131	176 –
Semple, William and John	South Townend, Strathaven	2	86 –
Semple, William	Strathaven	17	35 –
Semple, William	High Coldstream, Strathaven	52	80 –
Semple, William, junior	Southshields, Glassford	32	60 –
Semple, William	High Burn, Glassford	37	70 –
Semple, William	Boghall, Glassford	2	16 –
Semple, William	Greenrig, Lesmahagow	100	130 –
Semple, Mrs. Mary	Castlemains, Strathaven	5	20 –
Semple, Janet	Strathaven	160	142 –
Service, Robert	Greenwood, Govan	1	90 –
Shand, Mrs. Emily	Lanark	13	46 –
Shanks, Trustees of David	Harmon Cottage, Uddingston	2	59 –
Shanks, James	Whinrigg, Airdrie	2	6 5
Shanks, John	Riggend, Airdrie	1	19 –
Shanks, John	Luckenhill, Airdrie	59	110 –
Shanks, William	Millerston, Glasgow	2	6 5
Shaw, Andrew	Crosshouse, E. Kilbride	97	152 –
Shaw, David	Lesmahagow	1	26 –
Shaw, James	Staylees, Airdrie	67	32 10
Shaw, James	Springbank, Glasgow	2	170 –
Shaw, John	Kirkwood, Coatbridge	25	40 –
Shaw, Trustees of John	Airdrie	50	189 10
Shaw, John	Mount Vernon, Tollcross	1	50 –
Shaw, John, & Company	Ironworks, Maryhill	7	320 –
Shaw, William	Elmwood, Bothwell	12	201 –
Shaw, Robert	Thornhill, Blantyre	4	95 –
Shearer, James	Hall, Muirkirk	9	25 –
Shearer, Wm. and Mrs. Jemima	Porterswell, Uddingston	21	230 –
Shettleston Church, Managers of	Shettleston	3	40 –
Shotts Free Church, Trustees of	Dykehead, Shotts	3	24 –
Shotts Iron Company	Shotts	1,012	5,312 –
Simpson, Andrew	83 Cubie Street, Glasgow	2	191 –
Simpson, Alexander G., of Carfin	Carfin, Motherwell	300	592 –
Simpson, Bruce, & Broom	170 Hope Street, Glasgow	42	137 –
Simpson, Dundas	Monkland Villa, Airdrie	51	144 –
Sinclair, George	John Street, Hamilton	2	115 –
Sligo, Mrs. Margaret Smith, wife of Arch. Vincent Smith Sligo, of Inzievar	Inzievar, Dunfermline	603	2,717 6
Do.	Do. (*Minerals*)	–	346 15
Smellie, Gavin	Viewhill, Bellshill	5	108 –
Smellie, George	Partick, Glasgow	6	18 –
Smellie, John, senior	West Merryston, Old Monkland	4	146 –
Smellie, Thomas D.	209 St. Vincent Street, Glasgow	9	15 10
Smith, Andrew	Braehead, Carnwath	44	15 –
Smith, David	Braehead, Carnwath	1	5 –
Smith, Rev. David	Wiston, Biggar	20	74 –
Smith, Francis	13 Park Terrace, Glasgow	1	24 18
Smith, James, & Son	8 Whitehill Street, Denniston, Glasgow	2	71 –
Smith, John	Grindstonefaulds, Hamilton	24	20 –
Smith, John	Birkhill, Lesmahagow	517	365 –
Smith, John	Carluke	23	35 –
Do.	Do. (*Minerals*)	–	5 –
Smith, John	Dolphinton, Noblehouse	5	12 –
Smith & M'Lean	Mavisbank, Glasgow	7	1,585 –
Smith, Thomas	Hareshaw, Strathaven	29	50 –
Smith, Rev. William	Manse, Douglas	220	158 –
Smith, William	Townhead, Newmills	1,500	170 –
Smith, Mrs. Barbara	Hawthornden House, Reddrie	1	118 –
Smith, Mrs. Susan Emma	Jordanhill, Glasgow	38	257 10
Do. do.	Do. (*Minerals*)	–	100 –
Smith, Mary	Eastgate Carmichael, Lanark	7	23 –
Smith, Augusta Charlotte	Bothwell Road, Hamilton	2	247 –
Sneddon, D. & J.	149 West George Street, Glasgow	1	304 –
Sneddon, James	149 West George Street, Glasgow	4	50 10
Society for Propagating Christian Knowledge	Edinburgh	2,188	1,590 –
Somervell, Graham, of Sorn	Sorn Castle, Mauchline	218	799 –
Sommerville, Alexander	Rosehill, Lesmahagow	25	43 –
Sommerville, David H.	Sandyford, Glasgow	310	166 –
Sommerville, James	3 Regent Park Square, Glasgow	4	13 –
Sommerville, James	Sommerville Place, Carluke	190	69 –
Sommerville, James	Lanark	55	79 –
Sommerville, John	Strawfrank, Carstairs, Lanark	34	43 –
Sommerville, John	Wampherflatt, Lanark	112	170 –
Sommerville, Robert	Cormiston, Biggar	370	466 –
Sommerville, Samuel	17 Hart Street, Edinburgh	472	465 –
Sommerville, Thomas	Nemphlar, Lanark	2	22 –
Sommerville, Walter	Gosforth, Cumberland	376	293 –
Do. do.	Do. (*Minerals*)	–	100 –
Sommerville, William	Bannatyne Street, Lanark	8	30 –
Sommerville, William	Covanhill, Carstairs, Lanark	185	191 –

LANARK—continued.

Name of Owner.	Address of Owner.	Estimated Acreage of Property.	Gross Annual Value.	Name of Owner.	Address of Owner.	Estimated Acreage of Property.	Gross Annual Value.
		Acres.	£ s.			Acres.	£ s.
Sommerville, William	Windales, Crosshill, Glasgow	228	275 —	Stewart, John	Sykehead, Strathaven	23	54 —
Sommerville, Mrs. Martha	Greenfield, Carnwath	6	15 —	Stewart, Michael J. S.	Holmhead, Abington	210	110 —
Speirs, Alexander A.	Elderslie, Paisley	206	640 —	Stewart, Robert	Raws, Strathaven	78	95 —
Spence, George	Craighead, Carluke	70	33 —	Stewart, Robert	Priestgill, Strathaven	49	85 —
Spencer, Andrew	13 Dixon Street, Glasgow	2	271 —	Stewart, Robert	Haghill, Glasgow	45	186 13
Spencer, James	Airdrie	1	50 —	Stewart, Trs. of Robert, of Murdoston	Glasgow	1,760	1,783 —
Spencer, John	Coates, Coatbridge	3	690 —	Do. do.	Do. (Minerals)	—	1,050 —
Spittall, Robert	Tollcross	2	48 —	Stewart, Robert, of Brownlie	Brownlie, Carluke	102	412 —
Sprott, Trustees of Alexander	Edinburgh	1,792	1,977 —	Do. do.	Do. (Minerals)	—	270 —
Do. do.	Do. (Minerals)	—	1,043 3	Stewart, Walter	Haghill, Glasgow	55	119 5
Sprott, Representatives of Mark	Edinburgh	103	177 —	Stewart, William	Crawforddyke Street, Carluke	2	57 —
Stainton, Josephine	Biggarshiels, Biggar	1,326	1,138 —	Stewart, William L.	Kirkfield, Bothwell	1	135 —
Stanrigg Oil Company	65 Jamaica Street, Glasgow	6	600 —	Stewart, Wilson, & Co.	Rutherglen	3	606 —
Stark, James	21 Rutland Street, Edinburgh	550	356 —	Stewart, Mrs. Janet	Braeheadmains, Carnwath	19	18 —
Stark, James	Braehead, Carnwath	1	11 —	Stewart, Christina Anne, of Torrance	East Kilbride	2,274	2,671 —
Steel, Alexander	Tarbrax, Shotts	1	8 —	Do. do.	Do. (Minerals)	—	10 —
Steel, David	Teathes, Lanark	174	142 —	Stirling, Alexander	East Nerston, East Kilbride	54	91 —
Steel, Ebenezer	4 Annfield Terrace, Partick	15	22 —	Stirling, Charles C. Graham	Craigbarnet House, Campsie	90	108 —
Steel, Gavin	Hillpark, Bothwell	5	131 —	Stirling, John	Coatbridge	1	46 —
Steel, Gavin, of Holmhead	Holmhead, Lanark	323	677 —	Stobo, Thomas	2 Strathearn Place, Glasgow	2	360 —
Steel, John	103 St. Vincent Street, Glasgow	16	252 —	Storrie, Alexander	Whiteinch, Glasgow	2	44 —
Steel, John	Summerside, Wishaw	110	91 —	Storrie, William	East Badallan, Whitburn	80	50 —
Steel, John	Kepplehill, Wishaw	378	91 —	Story, Rev. Alexander R.	Carmunnock	10	54 —
Steel, John, senior	Skellyhill, Lesmahagow	182	156 —	Storry, John	33 Regent Park Square, Glasgow	94	70 —
Steel, John	Biggar	7	60 —	Strachan, William	Blacklaw, East Kilbride	285	76 —
Steel, Robert	Bo'ness	240	150 —	Strain, Hugh	Grahamshill, Airdrie	1	55 —
Steel, Trustees of Robert	St. Vincent Street, Glasgow	1,419	785 —	Strang, Andrew	Causewayhead, East Kilbride	42	110 —
Steel, Thomas	Newtonhead, Douglas	130	101 —	Strang, George	13 Carlton Place, Glasgow	189	109 10
Steel, Thomas	Aikmanhill, Lesmahagow	1	30 —	Strang, James	Millhouse, East Kilbride	89	130 —
Steel, Heirs of William	Greathill, Strathaven	2	10 —	Strang, John, senior	Bethern, East Kilbride	51	85 —
Steel, William	Woodburn, Blantyre	1	60 —	Strang, William	Auldhouse, East Kilbride	54	158 —
Steel, William	Liquo, Stane, Shotts	95	67 —	Strang, William & Gavin	Letham, Strathaven	5	39 —
Steel, William	Reddochbraes, Lesmahagow	57	50 —	Strathaven (First) U. P. Church	Strathaven	2	10 —
Steel, Mrs. Mary P.	Carluke	3	53 —	Struthers, Heirs of Gavin	Overfield, Strathaven	295	469 —
Steel, Jane S. A. M.	Waygateshaw, Carluke	670	490 —	Struthers, James	Drumloch, Glassford	30	35 —
Do.	Do. (Minerals)	—	882 —	Struthers, James, of Avonholm	Avonholm, Westquarter	794	576 —
Stein, John, of Kirkfield	Kirkfield, Lanark	378	499 —	Struthers, James	Chantinghall, Hamilton	6	75 —
Stephen, Alexander, & Sons	Linthouse, Glasgow	32	4,263 —	Struthers, James	Kilncadzow, Carluke	1	9 —
Steuart, Sir H. J. Seton, of Touch-Seton and Allanton, Bart.	Touch House, Stirling	2,673	1,879 —	Struthers, Thomas	Avon Villa, Pollockshields	2	941 10
Do. do.	Do. (Minerals)	—	2,197 —	Struthers, William	Laigh, Walkerdyke, Strathaven	90	143 —
Steven, Allan	Clincart, Cathcart	15	70 —	Struthers, Rev. William	Carstairs, Lanark	18	65 —
Steven, Robert	Newlands, East Kilbride	82	89 —	Struthers, Ellen and Elizabeth	Cullen Park, Strathaven	5	40 —
Steven, William	High Street, Lanark	5	16 —	Swan, junior, & Aitken	Maryhill, Glasgow	3	42 —
Steven, Elizabeth and Grace	Govan	270	981 15	Swan, Alexander	Leadhills, Abington	8	12 —
Stevenson, James	411 Edgeware Road, London	40	112 —	Swan, David	Maryhill, Glasgow	2	130 —
Stevenson, Mark	Birdston, Cadder	58	90 —	Swan, David, junior, & Co.	Maryhill, Glasgow	3	100 —
Stevenson, Rev. Robert J.	Dolphinton, Noblehouse	294	192 —	Swan, J. & R.	Maryhill, Glasgow	2	80 —
Stevenson, Rev. William F.	Rutherglen	6	63 —	Swan, James	Flemington, Strathaven	4	11 —
Stevenson, Mrs. Margaret	Braidwood, Carluke	38	98 —	Swan, James	Collierhall, Douglas	12	16 —
Stewart, Alexander	Burnbank Road, Hamilton	7	490 —	Swan, William	Maryhill, Glasgow	6	60 —
Stewart, Andrew & James	Cliftonhill, Coatbridge	5	850 —	Swan, Elizabeth	Dovecotedubbs, Lanark	2	19 —
Stewart, Basil	Orcharddell, Lanark	12	42 —	Sword, Alexander	13 Queen's Crescent, Glasgow	119	100 —
Stewart, Archibald	Leigham Avenue, Streatham	905	560 —	Symington, Andrew J.	Nyeholm House, Govan	1	80 —
Do. do.	Do. (Minerals)	—	350 —	Symington, James	Lanark	8	61 —
Stewart, George	Easter Stobwood, Carnwath	40	35 —	Symington, Walter and Mrs. Isabella Gordon	North House, Horndean, Hants Newburgh, Fife	95	123 —
Stewart, Rev. James	Hawick	6	42 —				
Do. do.	Do. (Minerals)	—	60 —	Tainsh, John, senior	Quarryhall, Hamilton	48	772 —
Stewart, James Reid, of Calderpark	Baillieston	154	495 —	Tait, Jessie	24 Pollock St., Glasgow	6	30 —
Do. do.	Do. (Minerals)	—	1,012 4	Taylor, Joseph Macintyre	180 St. Vincent Street, Glasgow	3	120 —
Stewart, James Stirling	Castlemilk, Carmunnock	2,137	3,260 —	Templeton, John	Bogside, Larkhall	11	45 —

LANARK—continued.

Name of Owner.	Address of Owner.	Estimated Acreage of Property.	Gross Annual Value.	Name of Owner.	Address of Owner.	Estimated Acreage of Property.	Gross Annual Value.
		Acres.	£ s.			Acres.	£ s.
Templeton, William	Crossford	25	30 —	Tudhope, William	Coatbridge	2	781 —
Tennant, Trustees of James Tovey, of Pool—per Hugh Blair, *Curator Bonis*	7 York Place, Edinburgh	1,238	792 —	Tudhope, Mrs. Janet	High Dykes, Strathaven	14	24 —
				Turnbull, John	Cumbernauld Road, Glasgow	52	142 —
Do. do.	Do. (*Minerals*)	—	508 —	Do.	Do. (*Minerals*)	—	45 —
Tennent, Hugh, junior	Eastfield, Rutherglen	4	13 —	Turnbull, Robert	Regent Square, Lenzie, Glasgow	4	208 —
Tennent, Robert B.	Laigh Coates, Coatbridge	4	1,002 —	Turnbull, William	Smithycroft, Shettleston	40	112 10
Tennent, Thomas, of Ryeland	Strathaven	404	723 —	Tweddale, John	Warrenhill, Carmichael	200	338 —
Tennent, Mrs. Margaret	Carstairs, Lanark	7	9 —	Uddingston Oil Company	Bredisholm, Uddingston	13	1,076 —
Tennent, Mrs. Marion	Clydegrove, Crossford	80	74 —	United Kingdom Insurance Co.	161 Hope Street, Glasgow	1	154 —
Thom, John & Robert	Uddingston	1	89 —	Ure, Robert	East Kilbride	3	82 —
Thomas, Charles	32 John Street, Glasgow	82	145 13	Urquhart, John, of Fairhill	Auchingramont, Hamilton	81	457 —
Thomson, Andrew	Commongreen, Strathaven	12	45 —	Urquhart, Representatives of Robert	Glasgow	65	171 —
Thomson, Andrew	Birniehill, Shotts	75	37 —				
Do.	Do. (*Minerals*)	—	35 —	Vallance, Alexander	Greathill, Strathaven	94	194 —
Thomson, Daniel A. V.	Bothwell Street, Glasgow	62	130 —	Vallance, Heirs of Alexander	Strathaven	6	47 —
Thomson, David	Royal Bank, Biggar	13	81 —	Vallance, Trustees of Jas.	Rutherglen	7	82 —
Thomson, Trustees of Thomas	Hamilton	2	224 —	Vallance, John	Biggar	3	49 —
Thomson, James	Stonehouse	1	31 —	Vallance, Mrs. Agnes	Main Street, Biggar	42	62 —
Thomson, James	Knocknaha, Campbeltown	85	62 —	Vary, Rev. John	Carmichael, Lanark	10	42 —
Do.	Do. (*Minerals*)	—	150 —	Vassie, John	North Vennel, Lanark	2	24 —
Thomson, James	37 Moray Place, Edinburgh	540	190 —	Vassie, John	Croftonhill, Lesmahagow	11	334 —
Thomson, James	Wilderhaugh, Galashiels	185	100 —	Vere, William Edward Hope, of Blackwood	Blackwood, Lesmahagow	6,863	5,522 —
Thomson, James	Cumnock	4	52 —	Do. do.	Do. (*Minerals*)	—	5,781 —
Thomson, Representatives of James	Hill, Lesmahagow	24	30 —				
Thomson, John	110 North Frederick Street, Glasgow	43	61 —	Waddell, James	Post Office Box 373, Glasgow	210	163 —
Thomson, Representatives of John	Annfield Cottage	4	136 —	Waddell, James	Crawfordwalls, Carluke	4	15 —
Thomson, John	Avonhead, Airdrie	267	48 —	Waddell, James	Stonefield, Rothesay	221	516 10
Do.	Do. (*Minerals*)	—	650 —	Do.	Do. (*Minerals*)	—	200 —
Thomson, Mrs. Marjory	Abbots Heyes, Chester	80	175 —	Waddell, James	Whinhall, Airdrie	100	196 —
Thomson, Matthew	Law, Stonehouse	44	38 —	Do.	Do. (*Minerals*)	—	33 —
Thomson Mortification	Lanark	6	20 —	Waddell, James	Airdriehill, Airdrie	91	121 —
Thomson's Mortification, Trustees of	Lanark	1	5 —	Do.	Do. (*Minerals*)	—	150 —
Thomson, Robert	Stanemains, Shotts	16	10 —	Waddell, James, and Mrs. Euphemia	West Regent Street, Glasgow	170	316 —
Thomson, Robert	300 Duke Street, Glasgow	90	145 —	Do. do.	Do. (*Minerals*)	—	100 —
Thomson, Robert	Dalshannon, Airdrie	18	39 —	Waddell, John	Windmillhill, Motherwell	2	50 —
Thomson, Robert	Clarkston, Airdrie	1	35 6	Waddell, John A.	10 Moray Pl., Glasgow	57	80 —
Thomson, Samuel	Merry Street, Motherwell	7	272 —	Waddell, John Craig	Rosemount, Airdrie	5	404 —
Thomson, Thomas	Rosehall, Shotts	41	109 —	Waddell, John M.	Lauderbarns, Lauder	2	41 —
Do.	Do. (*Minerals*)	—	65 —	Waddell, Matthew	Medrox, Airdrie	95	150 —
Thomson, William	F.C. School, Dalbeattie	1	40 —	Waddell, William	20 Royal Circus, Edinburgh	883	627 —
Thomson, William	Larkhall	1	55 —	Do.	Do. (*Minerals*)	—	250 —
Thomson, William	Burnside Orchard, Carluke	1	8 —	Waddell, Mrs. Euphemia	3 Annfield Pl., Glasgow	114	100 —
Thomson, Rev. William	Lochanbank, Lesmahagow	2	30 —	Waddell, Mrs. Georgina P. C.	Balquhatston, Slamannan	295	175 10
Thomson, Mrs. Elizabeth	Lesmahagow	7	12 —	Waddell, Agnes	Crofthill, Airdrie	1	22 10
Thomson, Mrs. Margaret	Hillside, Lesmahagow	591	310 —	Walker, Alexander	Larkhall	3	478 —
Thomson, Mrs. Janet	Blackhill, Shotts	15	10 —	Walker, Andrew, senior, and Andrew, junior	Richmond St., Glasgow	5	12 —
Thomson, Mrs. Mary, and others	Pollokshields, Glasgow	27	132 —	Walker & Company	New Lanark, Lanark	274	2,318 —
Thomson, Janet, Agnes, and Grace	Windmill Road, Hamilton	114	150 —	Walker, John	Partick, Glasgow	3	251 —
Thomson, Elizabeth, Rachel, and Marion	Hillhouse, Lesmahagow	45	50 —	Walker, John Ewing	Caldercuilt, Maryhill	75	520 —
Tod & Macgregor	Partick, Glasgow	19	5,275 —	Do. do.	Do. (*Minerals*)	—	40 —
Tod, Captain Robert	Burnside, Rutherglen	1	100 —	Walker, Robert, of Lethamhill	Cumbernauld Road, Glasgow	63	230 —
Todd, George	Haghill, Parkhead	11	30 —	Do. do.	Do. (*Minerals*)	—	100 —
Todd, James	Birks, by Shettleston	3	23 —	Walker, Trustees of Robert	Hillhouseridge, Shotts	175	161 —
Todd, John, of Glenduffhill	Woodend House, Cathcart	112	428 12	Do. do.	Do. (*Minerals*)	—	112 —
Do. do.	Do. (*Minerals*)	—	400 —	Walker, Heirs of Thomas	Hawksland, Lesmahagow	9	20 —
Todd, Richard	South Provanmains, Shettleston	60	129 —	Walker, William	99 Sauchiehall Street, Glasgow	20	22 —
Do.	Do. (*Minerals*)	—	100 —	Walker, Trustees of Mrs. Elizabeth	Union Street, Hamilton	1	100 —
Todd, Trustees of Wm.	Birkwood, Lesmahagow	820	437 —	Walker, Mrs. Margaret	North Vennel, Lanark	1	49 —
Tramway and Omnibus Co.	Glasgow	1	125 —	Wallace, James	Rutherglen	6	228 —
Tudhope, Daniel	Netherton, Blackhall	37	68 —	Wallace, James	Kilsyth	72	80 —
Tudhope, George	Abbeygreen, Lesmahagow	80	66 —				

LANARK—continued.

Name of Owner.	Address of Owner.	Estimated Acreage of Property.	Gross Annual Value.	Name of Owner.	Address of Owner.	Estimated Acreage of Property.	Gross Annual Value.
		Acres.	£ s.			Acres.	£ s.
Wallace, Trustees of James C.	Rutherglen	3	62 10	White, John Charles	Auchengeoch, Cadder	3	209 –
Wallace, James F.	Millerston, Glasgow	1	203 6	White, John and James	Rutherglen	36	2,493 –
Walls, William	2 Bellhaven Terrace, Glasgow	2	335 –	White, Trustees of James	Fairfield, Glasgow	28	113 –
Ward, Robert	Baillieston	3	110 –	White, Trs. of Samuel	Lanark	2	37 –
Wardrop, Frederick M., Lieutenant, 3d Dragoon Guards	Norwich	145	230 –	White, Walter	Bankhead, Rutherglen	159	551 –
				White, Walter, and John Hamilton	Bankhead, Rutherglen } Greenbank, Mearns	212	625 –
Wardrop, Trs. of Henry	13 St. James' Terrace, Glasgow	9	35 –	Do. do.	Do. (Minerals)	–	300 –
Wark, Robert, and others	Bargeddie, Old Monkland	95	186 –	White, William	Easter Moffat, Airdrie	13	21 –
Warnock, Andrew	Redmuir, Carmunnock	28	45 –	White, William	Mousebank, Lanark	1,146	595 –
Warnock, David	Rutherglen	3	238 –	White, W. S., of Flowergrove	Flowergrove, Callander	46	60 –
Warnock, Mrs. Jane	Bankhead, Carmunnock	13	44 10	White, Mrs. Jane A.	Cultermains, Biggar	860	1,931 –
Watkins, James Hutton	Blantyre	15	16 –	Whyte, Robert	Carmunnock	5	24 –
Watson, Gavin and Thomas	Wellgate, Larkhall	2	36 –	Wilkie, Major-Gen. John	Knowehead, Uddingston	5	118 –
Watson, James	Lanark	6	85 –	Wilkie, John	24 Blytheswood Square, Glasgow	2	814 –
Do.	Do. (Minerals)	–	16 –	Wilkie, William	Gartferry, Cadder	343	493 10
Watson, James	Larkhall	2	65 –	Williams, John, & Co.	Excelsior Iron Works, Wishaw	12	1,612 –
Watson, James	Roadmeetings, Carluke	3	4 –	Williams, Mrs. Robina	Earnock, Hamilton	620	1,095 –
Watson, James J. D.	46 Miller St., Glasgow	3	22 –	Williamson, George	Wellroad, Moffat	310	125 –
Watson, John	Govan, Glasgow	1	365 –	Williamson, John	Threeneuck, Cambuslang	1	180 –
Watson, John, of Neilsland	123 St. Vincent Street, Glasgow	220	1,129 –	Williamson, Janet and Mary	Bogbead, Tollcross	4	30 –
Watson, Robert	Redsdykepark, Biggar	2	28 –	Wilson, Andrew	Darnhall Mains, Peebles	164	230 –
Watson, Thomas	High Street, Lanark	3	36 –	Wilson, Andrew	Biggar	6	60 –
Watson, Thomas	High Street, Lanark	2	7 –	Wilson, Andrew	Steel's Cross, Lanark	3	8 –
Watson, William	6 St. Colme Street, Edinburgh	8	21 –	Wilson, Andrew	North Provanmains, Shettleston	60	110 –
Watson, William & Janet	Kirkknowe, Wishaw	1	198 –	Do.	Do. (Minerals)	–	120 –
Watson, Mrs. Christina	Woodcliff, Row	8	100 –	Wilson, David	Kilncadzow, Carluke	25	40 –
Watson, Mrs. Agnes	19 Apsley Place, Glasgow	31	186 –	Wilson, Gavin	Westerhouse, Carluke	42	18 –
Watson, Mrs. Elenora	14 Royal Crescent, Glasgow	4	22 –	Wilson, Gavin	Knowetop, Lesmahagow	11	8 –
				Wilson, James	Kirk Street, Strathaven	17	68 –
Watson, Trustees for Mrs. Elenora, and others	Glasgow	189	292 –	Wilson, James	Lowwaters, Hamilton	3	56 –
				Wilson, Heirs of James	Kilncadzow, Carluke	5	20 –
Watt, Alexander	Roughrigg, Shotts	57	28 –	Wilson, James B.	Kilncadzow, Carluke	142	180 –
Watt, Alexander	Stonelaw Tower, Rutherglen	2	70 –	Wilson, James	Fern Cottage, Biggar	1	18 –
				Wilson, James	Riggfoot, East Kilbride	151	130 –
Watt, Alexander	Almadahill, Hamilton	1	65 –	Wilson, James	Coatbridge	2	412 –
Watt, James	Lockhartshields, East Kilbride	76	180 10	Wilson, James	Trinidad Villa, Govan	1	110 –
				Wilson, Rev. John	Crossgates, Bellshill	9	30 –
Watt, James	Rosepark, Bothwell	3	53 –	Wilson, Trustees of John	Dundyvan, Coatbridge	1,123	1,953 –
Watt, Heirs of James	Burnbrae, Wishaw	2	27 –	Do. do.	Do. (Minerals)	–	1,972 –
Watt, John	Drumgray, Airdrie	326	188 10	Wilson, John	Westsidewood, Carnwath	1,810	889 –
Do.	Do. (Minerals)	–	460 –	Do.	Do. (Minerals)	–	22 –
Watt, Robert	Airdrie	2	64 10	Wilson, John	204 Maryhill Road, Glasgow	2	101 –
Watt, Thomas	Milnflat, Carmunnock	25	54 10	Wilson, John, & Company	Troloss, Abington	3,400	600 –
Watt, William	South Flakefield, East Kilbride	82	75 –	Wilson, John Ritchie	Craigend, Airdrie	16	24 –
				Wilson, John	Netherfield, Lesmahagow	54	22 –
Watt, Rev. William M.	Manse, Shotts	50	60 –	Do.	Do. (Minerals)	–	58 –
Do. do.	Do. (Minerals)	–	120 –	Wilson, John and James	69 Great Clyde Street, Glasgow	10	187 –
Waugh, John	St. Johnskirk, Covington, Biggar	474	331 –	Wilson Mortification	Lanark	8	25 –
Waugh, John	Orchardville, Lanark	7	50 –	Wilson, Robert, and others	Braehead, Glassford	50	80 –
Waugh, Stephen	Symington, Biggar	100	80 –	Wilson, Robert	West Merkland, Strathaven	49	75 –
Weddell, John and James	Crofthead, Uddingston	14	189 –				
Weir, James	Shottsburn, Shotts	80	80 –	Wilson, Robert	West Kype, Strathaven	19	20 –
Weir, James	Birkenhead, Lesmahagow	340	245 –	Wilson, Robert	Kirkhill, Cambuslang	4	85 –
Weir, James	Linnville, Lanark	1	5 –	Wilson, Robert	Cross, East Kilbride	107	152 –
Weir, James	Blackburn Mill, Chapelton	11	63 –	Wilson, William	Neukfoot, Strathaven	45	60 –
Weir, John, senior	Leadhills, Abington	1	8 –	Wilson, William	East Merkland, Strathaven	63	86 –
Weir, Walter	Barmulloch, Cadder	1	74 7				
Weir, Mrs. Elizabeth	Braehead, Blantyre	7	45 –	Wilson, William	East Newton, Strathaven	60	110 –
Weir, Agnes and Elizabeth	Braehead, Blantyre	54	50 –	Wilson, Trs. of William	Chapel, Stonehouse	13	34 –
Weir, Ann T.	Blantyre	69	73 –	Wilson, William	Mosshat, Carnwath	8	19 –
Do.	Do. (Minerals)	–	30 –	Wilson, William	Lanark Road, Carluke	3	8 –
Weirholt, Trs. of John B.	Edinburgh	653	230 –	Wilson, William	Forth, Carnwath	1	14 –
Welsh, Archibald	Sandford, Stonehouse	6	10 –	Wilson, William	Old Town, Carnwath	162	137 –
West, Thomas	Larkhall	2	99 –	Wilson, William	Lanark	8	66 –
Wharrie, Rachel	Whitehill, Dalserf	1	20 –	Wilson, William	Thornton, East Kilbride	126	250 –
White, A. C., and Sons	10 Dixon Street, Glasgow	2	196 5	Do.	Do. (Minerals)	–	234 –
White, James	Tweediehall, Strathaven	233	336 –	Wilson, William	Carnwath	150	45 –
White, James L.	11 Seton Terrace, Glasgow	217	246 –	Wilson, Mrs. Ann	North Cairnduff, East Kilbride	55	70 –
White, John	Netherurd House, Noblehouse	10	32 –	Wilson, Mrs. Isabella	Chapel Street, Carluke	28	70 –
				Wilson, Mrs. Marion	108 Gallowgate, Glasgow	13	30 –
White, John	Partick, Glasgow	3	448 10	Wilson, Elizabeth	Bellahouston, Glasgow	1	80 –

LANARK—continued.

Name of Owner.	Address of Owner.	Estimated Acreage of Property.	Gross Annual Value.		Name of Owner.	Address of Owner.	Estimated Acreage of Property.	Gross Annual Value.	
		Acres.	£	s.			Acres.	£	s.
Wilsons & Co.	Summerlee, Coatbridge	125	3,743	–	Young, James	Murrays, Kilmarnock	90	106	–
Do.	Do. (*Minerals*)	–	355	15	Young, John	Easter House, Baillieston	1	191	–
Wingate, Andrew	Oswaldbank, Partick	2	114	–	Do.	Do. (*Minerals*)	–	186	–
Wingate, Trs. of Thomas	Broomhill, Partick	4	180	–	Young, John	Drumgelloch, Airdrie	1	28	10
Wingate, Thomas, & Co.	Whiteinch, Glasgow	11	1,130	–	Young, Robert	58 Kelvingrove Street, Glasgow	25	186	–
Wingate, Margaret, Jemima, and Christina	Burnbank Rd., Hamilton	1	117	–	Young, Trustees of Rev. Robert	Strathaven	18	42	–
Wishaw Flax Company	Wishaw	4	120	–	Young, Stephen	Castleglen, Carmunnock	2	162	–
Woddrop, William Allan, of Garvald	Garvald House, Dolphinton	3,205	3,029	–	Young, William	Holmhead, Strathaven	85	80	–
Wood, James	Lanark	33	52	–	Young, William	32 Wellgate, Lanark	2	7	–
Wood, James	Reddrie, Glasgow	102	242	10	Young, William	23 Elgin Terrace, Partick, Glasgow	2	236	–
Wood, Anne	Lanark	2	7	–	Young, Mrs. Agnes	Claddengreen, East Kilbride	43	60	–
Woodhall Estate Co.	Woodhall, Airdrie	2,398	4,638	–	Young, Mrs. Isabella	Dykehead, Shotts	1	26	–
Do. do.	Do. (*Minerals*)	–	3,996	–	Young, Mrs. George, and another	Springboig, Shettleston (*Minerals*)	–	864	–
Wordie, William	Millersneuck, Cadder	138	200	–	Yuille, Andrew	Hayhill, East Kilbride	62	100	–
Wotherspoon, Matthew, and others	Airdrie	100	182	–	Yuille, Archibald	33 Cathedral Street, Glasgow	190	440	–
Do.	Do. (*Minerals*)	–	130	–	Yuille, John	Newlands, East Kilbride	92	123	10
Wotherspoon, Robert S.	Stonehouse	10	20	–	Yuille, Robert	Newlands, East Kilbride	33	43	–
Wotherspoon, William	302 St. Vincent Street, Glasgow	42	55	–	Yuille, Mrs. Bethia	Eastwoodvale, Thornliebank	1	155	–
Wright, Rev. Stewart	Blantyre	14	47	–	Yuille, Maria P.	Springbank, Lanark	1	8	–
Wyld, Adam	Westraw, Biggar	17	145	–					
Wyld, James	Biggar	28	56	–	Total Owners of Land of one Acre or upwards		1,890	549,232	1284592	18
Wyld, James	Biggar	12	99	–	Total Owners of Lands of less than one Acre in extent		7,227	3,865	451675	9
Wyld, John	3 Sardinia Pl., Glasgow	4	16	–					
Wyllie, Rev. John	Carluke	14	74	–	GRAND TOTAL		9,117	553,097	1736268	7
Wyllie, John	45 Buchanan St., Glasgow	3	800	–					
Young, Alexander	9 M'Auslin St., Glasgow	40	66	–					
Young, George	Millhill, Carmunnock	4	11	10					
Young, James	Bloomshill, Strathaven	87	102	–					
Young, James	East Linnbank, Strathaven	74	120	–					

MUNICIPAL BOROUGH OF GLASGOW.
Population over 20,000.

Name of Owner.	Address of Owner.	Estimated Acreage of Property.	Gross Annual Value.
		Acres	£ s.
Adam, William, & Son	Milnbank, Glasgow	19	667 –
Adams, James, & Co.	7 Scotland Street, Glasgow	3	465 –
Adams, William Y.	Dalmarnock Road, Glasgow	3	296 –
Aitken, James	284 Dalmarnock Road, Glasgow	1	458 –
Alexander, R. F. & J., & Co.	Duke Street, Glasgow	1	1,275 –
Allan, Thomas	Springbank Foundry, Glasgow	9	1,006 –
Alston, Trustees of the late John James	598 Gallowgate Street, Glasgow	2	350 –
Anderson, D. & J.	Walkinshaw Street, Glasgow	3	455 –
Anderston Foundry Co.	Cheapside St., Glasgow	2	1,124 –
Arroll, William	249 Baltic Street, Glasgow	1	140 –
Arthur, James	Queen Street, Glasgow	1	6,923 10
Baillie, Trustees of late Lady Mary	Maryhill	4	10 –
Baird & Brown	Port-Dundas, Glasgow	5	1,945 –
Baird, Robert	2 Clayton Terrace, Glasgow	1	610 –
Bannerman, Walter	Hope Street, Glasgow	2	2,530 –
Barclay, Curle, & Co.	Stobcross, Glasgow	5	4,217 11
Bartholomew, John, & Co.	1 Dundas St., Glasgow	16	3,882 –
Barton, William, & Co.	Scotland St., Glasgow	1	120 –
Beardmore, William & Isaac	Parkhead Forge, Glasgow	28	1,340 –
Belch, John	Pedens Cross, Glasgow	1	2,344 16
Bell, J. & M. P., & Co.	Glasgow Pottery, Stafford Street, Glasgow	5	1,442 10
Bessemer Steel Co. (Limited)	Milton St., Cowcaddens, Glasgow	1	430 –
Black, Robert	Glenarbuck, Bowling	15	6,056 –
Blochairn Iron Company	Blochairn, Glasgow	26	5,048 –
Borron, William Geddes	13 Princes Square, Glasgow	6	409 –
Boyd, Adam	Douglas St., Glasgow	2	3,381 16
Boyd, William, & Co.	North Street, Glasgow	1	675 –
Boyle, Neil	270 London Road, Glasgow	2	1,068 –
Broom & Brownlee	Blochairn, Glasgow	6	240 –
Do.	Do. (*Quarry*)	–	350 –
Brown, Archibald, & Co.	Camlachie, Glasgow	2	465 –
Brown, John	Burnbank, Kilsyth	2	278 –
Brown, Trustees of Moses	87 West Regent Street, Glasgow	31	285 –
Brown, Stewart, & Co.	Springfield Rd., Glasgow	5	889 –
Brownlee James	30 Burnbank Gardens, Glasgow	14	568 –
Bruce, Robert	Woodside Paper Mills, Glasgow	3	365 –
Bryson, William	Crown Street, Glasgow	1	1,652 –
Bulloch, Lade, & Co.	24 Great Eastern Road, Glasgow	3	920 –
Cairns, Moses, & Co.	Rutherglen Rd., Glasgow	1	320 –
Caledonian Railway Co.	302 Buchanan Street, Glasgow	67	6,637 –
Do. do.	(*Railway and Canal*)	202	44391 –
Calton Spinning Company	8 Graham Court, Calton, Glasgow	7	1,586 –
Cameron, James	New Road, Parkhead, Glasgow	3	255 –
Campbell, Sir James, of Stracathro, Kt.	129 Bath Street, Glasgow	3	12912 5
Campbell, John, of Possil	Villa Como, Torquay	11	14 –
Carson, Warren, & Co.	Canal St., Port-Dundas, Glasgow	2	735 –
Cassells, Robert	6 Park Street East, Glasgow	6	270 –
Cattlemarket and Slaughter-House Trust	Glasgow	11	5,073 –
Christie, Thomas Craig, of Bedlay	Bedlay, Moodiesburn	63	133 –
City of Glasgow Union Railway Company	Dunlop Street, Glasgow	42	9,578 –
Do. do.	Do. (*Railway*)	20	16836 –
Clark & Co.	113 South Woodside Road, Glasgow	1	487 10
Clark, George W.	Dumbreck House, Paisley Road, Glasgow	1	1,620 –
Clark, John, junior, & Co.	18/34 George St., Mile-end, Glasgow	3	1,494 –
Clark & Struthers	East Hope St., Glasgow	1	420 –
Clyde Navigation, Trs. of	16 Robertson St., Glasgow (*Harbour*)	33	43349 –
Cochran, Trs. of Robert	Verreville, Anderston, Glasgow	5	1,420 –
Cochrane, J. & R., & Co.	South York St., Glasgow	2	888 –
Commissioners for Repression of Juvenile Delinquency	67 West Regent Street, Glasgow	6	517 –
Connal & Co.	81 St. Vincent Street, Glasgow	3	314 –
Coulson, George F.	80 Canning Street, Glasgow	2	525 –
Couper, James, & Sons	Kyle St., Port-Dundas, Glasgow	2	780 –
Court-House Commissioners	Glasgow	2	2,705 –
Crawfurd, William Stuart Stirling, of Milton	91 Eaton Square, London	16	52 –
Crichton, Mrs. Marion H.	Ardmay House, Arrochar	57	222 –
Crown, The (for Infantry Barracks, Gallowgate; Post Office, Inland Revenue, Custom-House, and Cathedral)	Glasgow	5	3,742 10
Dawson, Adam & John	Linlithgow	1	137 –
Denholm, George, & Co.	Fleming Street, Duke Street, Glasgow	1	102 –
Dennistoun, Alexander, of Golfhill	Golfhill, Glasgow	142	4,537 18
Do. do.	Do. (*Quarry*)	–	800 –
Dixon, Trustees of William	1 Dixon Street, Glasgow	107	5,274 –
Dobbie, Mrs. Alexander	Denny	8	52 –
Downie, Robert	Carntyne, Shettleston, Glasgow	2	100 –
Dunlop & Twaddell	Townmill Road, Glasgow	3	940 –
Dunn, James	43 Burnbank Gardens, Glasgow	4	370 –

LANARK—continued.—(Municipal Borough of GLASGOW.)

Name of Owner.	Address of Owner.	Estimated Acreage of Property.	Gross Annual Value.	Name of Owner.	Address of Owner.	Estimated Acreage of Property.	Gross Annual Value.
		Acres.	£ s.			Acres.	£ s.
Eadie, George & Alexander	Caledonia Road, Glasgow	1	1,314 18	Hannay, Alexander	188 Cowcaddens Street, Glasgow	1	3,705 10
Eastern Necropolis Co.	Glasgow	25	80 –	Harvey, Barnet & John	Port-Dundas, Glasgow	6	718 –
Edinburgh & Leith Roperie Company	Cumbernauld Road, Glasgow	1	250 –	Harvey, Trustees of Robert	100 Acre Hill, Port-Dundas, Glasgow	2	223 –
Edington, Trustees of late A. G.	Garscube Road, Glasgow	3	740 –	Higginbotham, Samuel	M'Neil Street, Glasgow	6	5,862 –
Edington, George B.	Victoria Foundry, Canal Bank, Glasgow	1	120 –	Holms, William, & Brothers	51 Greenhead Street, Glasgow	3	1,132 –
Edington, Thomas, & Sons	Garscube Road, Glasgow	3	785 –	Hoskins, Captain R.	Weston Villa, Abbey Road, London	3	190 –
Elder, John, & Co.	Centre Street, Tradeston, Glasgow	2	1,804 –	Houldsworth, John, & Co.	St. Vincent St., Glasgow	2	748 –
Ewing, James	152 Canning St., Glasgow	1	1,179 –	Houston, John, & Co.	93 Garngad Road, Glasgow	1	250 –
				Howe Machine Company	Avenue Street, Glasgow	2	295 –
				Hozier, James, of Newlands	Mauldslie Castle, Carluke	62	1,514 –
Farie, James, of Farme	Farme, Rutherglen, Glasgow (Minerals)	–	614 14	Hutcheson's Hospital, Trustees of	Glasgow	18	1,080 –
Faulds, Robert	61 Parliamentary Road, Glasgow	3	3,704 –	Hutcheson, Robert	Cowlairs Road, Glasgow	3	82 –
Finlay & Davidson	Victoria Street, Glasgow	1	403 –	Hydepark Foundry Co.	Finnieston St., Glasgow	2	610 –
Fleming, Watson, & Nairn	Govan Street, Glasgow	4	1,496 15	Inglis, A. & J.	Point House, Glasgow	8	3,025 –
Fraser, Duncan	11 Dalmarnock Road	2	2,224 –				
Fraser, John	Govan Street, Glasgow	1	730 –				
Frew, Forrest	354 Main Street, Bridgeton, Glasgow	2	878 –	Jardine, J. & J.	Park Road, Glasgow	2	3,505 –
				Kay, James	82 West Nile St., Glasgow	1	464 –
Galbraith, A. & A.	Oakbank Mills, Glasgow	4	2,393 –	Kelvinhaugh Spinning Co.	Kelvinhaugh, Glasgow	1	1,040 –
Garroway, Robert, James, John, & William	694 Duke Street, Glasgow	7	1,095 –	Kennedy, Hugh	Avenue Street, Glasgow	3	165 –
				Kerr, Thomas Knox	370 Dalmarnock Road, Glasgow	4	889 –
Gilbert, Mrs. Graham, of Yorkhill	Yorkhill, Glasgow	3	265 –	Kyle, James	29 Queen Mary Street, Glasgow	2	884 –
Glasgow Academy Association, Directors of	Elmbank Place, Glasgow	1	625 –	Kyle, William, junior	246 London Road, Glasgow	3	1,750 –
Glasgow, Barrhead, and Kilmarnock Joint Railway Company	Glasgow	20	259 –				
Do. do.	Do. (Railway)	8	1,792 –	Laidlaw, R., & Son	East Milton St., Glasgow	7	2,228 –
Glasgow Bridge Trust	Glasgow	2	11158 –	Laird, George	10 Ann Street, Bridgeton, Glasgow	1	441 –
Glasgow, Corporation of City of	Glasgow	176	6,300 –	Laird & Thomson	14 Broad Street, Mile-End, Glasgow	3	605 –
Glasgow, Gas Commissioners of City of	Glasgow	29	34226 –	Lamb, George & William	St. James' Street, Kingston, Glasgow	1	1,207 –
Glasgow, Improvement Trust of City of	Glasgow	46	46430 –	Lanarkshire (North), Prison Board of	Duke Street, Glasgow	6	1,198 –
Glasgow Iron Company	Garngad Road, Glasgow	10	2,700 11	Lancefield Forge Company	Scotland Street, Glasgow	4	1,120 –
Glasgow Jute Company (Limited)	5 Ingram St., Glasgow	11	5,124 –	Lancefield Spinning Co.	Lancefield St., Glasgow	3	1,880 –
Glasgow, Magistrates of	(For Alexandra Park) Glasgow	69	220 –	Law, David	29 Abercorn Street, Glasgow	1	3,206 –
Glasgow and Paisley Joint Railway Company	16 Bridge St., Glasgow	4	746 –	Law, J. & A.	Pinkston, St. Rollox, Glasgow	2	300 –
Do. do.	Do. (Railway)	16	2,567 11	Law, John, & Co.	Rae Street, Port-Dundas, Glasgow	1	715 –
Glasgow, Parochial Board of City of	Parliamentary Road, Glasgow	10	1,500 –	Lawson, John, Son, & Co.	Mountainblow, Camlachie, Glasgow	3	171 –
Glasgow Police Board	Glasgow	34	2,986 –	Lean, John, & Sons	140 Reid Street, Glasgow	2	608 –
Glasgow and South-Western Railway Company	Bridge Street, Glasgow (Railway & Canal)	13	8,302 –	Leask, James, & Company	Craighall, Possil Road, Glasgow	1	239 –
Glasgow Tramway and Omnibus Company	29 Cambridge St., Glasgow	8	1,631 –	Leck, Henry	33 Renfield St., Glasgow	1	8,355 –
Glasgow, University of	Gilmorehill, Glasgow	18	4,480 –	Little Sisters of the Poor	Garngad Hill, Glasgow	9	304 –
Glasgow, Water Commissioners of City of	Glasgow	10	33612 –	London & Glasgow Engineering Company	Anderston Quay, Glasgow	2	2,030 –
Goold, The Estate of late James—per Robert Gilchrist	116 George Street, Glasgow	1	402 –	Long, John Jex	727 Duke St., Glasgow	3	428 –
Grant, George, & Sons	19 Broad Street, Mile-End, Glasgow	7	2,824 –	Love, Thomas & Moses	London Road, Glasgow	2	360 –
				Lyon, Trs. of late William	Mountainblue, Glasgow	4	330 –
Gray, John, & Co.	Adelphi Terrace, Glasgow	1	835 –	M'Andrew, John	236 Castle St., Glasgow	1	390 –
Gray, Robert, & Co.	Westmuir, Shettleston, Glasgow (Minerals)	–	245 –	M'Aulay, Richard	54 Fisher Street, Glasgow	2	1,152 –
				M'Causland, Capt. Robert	Gartcraig House, Cumbernauld Rd., Glasgow	1	1,230 –
Gray, Trustees of late J. H.	Glasgow	115	227 –	M'Donald, John	Comely Park, Glasgow	2	719 –
Grosvenor, Frederick	Boden Street, Mile-End, Glasgow	1	280 –	M'Dowall, J. S., & Co.	Cumberland St., Glasgow	2	1,541 –
Guild, Heirs of William	Camlachie, Glasgow	10	576 –	M'Dowall, Steven, & Co.	North Woodside Road, Glasgow	8	1,371 5
				M'Farlane, Daniel	Port-Dundas, Glasgow	6	1,200 –

LANARK—continued.—(MUNICIPAL BOROUGH OF GLASGOW.)

Name of Owner.	Address of Owner.	Estimated Acreage of Property.	Gross Annual Value.	Name of Owner.	Address of Owner.	Estimated Acreage of Property.	Gross Annual Value.
		Acres.	£ s.			Acres.	£ s.
M'Farlane, Walter, & Co.	Washington Street, Glasgow	3	1,698 —	Roy, James & George	67 Buchanan St., Glasgow	2	5,057 —
M'Ilquham, Trustees of late Walter	Blochairn, Glasgow	20	291 —	Royal Infirmary	Castle Street, Glasgow	7	100 —
M'Intosh, Trustees of General	114 George Street, Edinburgh	18	1,451 —	Scott, Andrew, & Co.	Main Street, Bridgeton, Glasgow	2	516 —
M'Intyre, John	74 Main Street, Bridgeton, Glasgow	1	1,203 —	Scott, James	Woodside Pl., Glasgow	5	5,782 4
M'Laren, Robert, & Co.	Canal Street, Port-Eglinton, Glasgow	2	640 —	Sighthill Cemetery Co.	Sighthill	44	22 —
M'Lellan, P. & W.	Trongate St., Glasgow	1	494 —	Simpson, Andrew	89 Cubie Street, Glasgow	3	3,973 —
M'Math, J., & Sons	Brookside Factory, Glasgow	2	530 —	Simpsons, Bruce, & Broom	182 Hope St., Glasgow	3	39 —
M'Neil, Alexander	Rosemount, Garngad Hill, Glasgow	4	570 2	Simpson, George	182 Hope St., Glasgow	7	137 —
M'Onie, W. & A.	West Street, Glasgow	2	400 —	Smith, Alexander	Onslow Drive. Glasgow	1	515 —
M'Pherson, Alexander	North Street, Glasgow	1	2,859 —	Smith, A. & W., & Co.	Cook Street, Glasgow	2	840 —
Marshall, Alexander	Havelock Street, Glasgow	4	5,234 5	Smith, George, & Co.	Kennedy St., Glasgow	4	1,838 —
Marshall & Wylie	Swanston St., Glasgow	4	472 —	Smith, Napier	Claverton, Helensburgh, Glasgow	1	246 —
Martin & Miller	847 Duke St., Glasgow	1	297 —	Smith, Reprs. of late Richard	West Street, South Side, Glasgow	1	609 —
Martin, George	142 St. Vincent Street, Glasgow	1	3,928 10	Somerville, John, & Sons	M'Neil Street, Glasgow	2	1,420 —
Mathieson, Donald, & Co.	Govan Street, Glasgow	2	700 —	Somerville & M'Kenzie	81 Cubie St., Glasgow	2	1,339 —
Merchants' House	Glasgow	23	450 —	Sommerville & Co.	99 and 173 Fordueuk Street, Glasgow	1	514 —
Millar, John S.	Eastfield House, Rutherglen, Glasgow	22	3,988 —	Southern Necropolis Co.	South Cumberland Street, Glasgow	20	225 —
Miller, Alexander	Carmyle, Glasgow	1	1,479 —	Steven, A. & P.	Stirling Road, Glasgow	2	820 10
Mirrlees, Tait, & Watson	Scotland Street, Kingston, Glasgow	2	1,280 —	Steven, William	London Road, Glasgow	2	1,585 —
				Stevenson & Co.	Camlachie, Glasgow	2	316 —
Mitchell, James, & Co.	817 Gallowgate Street, Glasgow	2	450 —	Stevenson, Carlile, & Co.	Garngad Hill, Glasgow	11	1,306 10
Mitchell & Whytlaw	Ingram Street, Glasgow	2	775 —	Stewart, Duncan, & Co.	47 Summer Street, Calton, Glasgow	1	360 —
Money, John C.	140 Mains St., Glasgow	1	468 —	Stewart, D. Y., & Co.	Charles Street, St. Rollox, Glasgow	8	830 —
Monteith, Robert, of Carstairs	Carstairs House, Lanark	27	3,727 —	Stewart, Peter	8 York Street, Little Govan, Glasgow	6	89 —
Morrison, James	52 Sauchiehall Street, Glasgow	1	2,549 10	Stewart, Robert	Haghill Distillery, Glasgow	1	22 —
Mucklow, Edward	South York Street, Glasgow	1	320 —	Stewart, Walter	Haghill Distillery, Glasgow	31	124 —
Muir, Brown, & Company	Strathclyde, Dalmarnock, Glasgow	8	1,010 —	Stewart, Mrs. E.	Cumbernauld Road, Glasgow	1	60 —
Murdoch, Alexander	Swanston St., Glasgow	1	162 —	Stobcross Trustees	Minerva Street, Glasgow	10	6,968 10
				Stone Dressing Company	Pollokshaws Road, Glasgow	2	596 —
Napier, J., & Co.	Vinegar Hill, Camlachie, Glasgow	3	462 —				
Napier, Robert, & Sons	Lancefield St., Glasgow	5	2,825 —				
Neilsons & Co.	Hydepark Works, Springburn, Glasgow	8	1,824 —	Taylor, James, & Brothers	Main Street, Anderston, Glasgow	1	1,262 15
Neilson, Walter	172 West George Street, Glasgow	12	90 —	Templeton, J. & J. S.	Crown Point Road	2	950 —
Neilson, Walter M., of Queenshill	Castle-Douglas	19	386 —	Templeton, James & Co.	William Street, Greenhead, Glasgow	1	1,172 —
Nisbet, Thomas	Parkhead, Glasgow	4	291 —	Tennant, Charles, of St. Rollox	Glen, Peeblesshire	116	6,138 —
Normal Seminary of Church of Scotland	New City Road, Glasgow	1	435 —	Tennant, Charles, & Co.	St. Rollox, Glasgow	20	237 —
Norman, John, & Co.	Pulteney Street, Glasgow	1	600 —	Tennent, Trustees of Charles S. P.	Wellpark, Duke Street, Glasgow	11	2,355 —
North British Railway Co.	Edinburgh	4	6,558 —	Tharsis Sulphur and Copper Company (Limited)	136 West George Street, Glasgow	5	1,475 —
Do. do.	Do. (Railway)	169	17987 —	Thomson, Archibald, & Co.	190 Great Eastern Road, Glasgow	2	120 —
Paul, Alexander, & Co.	Fielden Street, Mile-End, Glasgow	3	725 —	Thomson, James and George	Finnieston St., Glasgow	2	1,220 —
Paul, Sanderson, & Paul	Coalhill Street, Camlachie, Glasgow	1	50 —	Thomson, Heirs of late John	Annfield, Duke Street, Glasgow	8	758 —
Peel Street Weaving Co.	1 Peel Street, Glasgow	2	369 —	Thomson, John and James	Finnieston St., Glasgow	1	740 —
Port-Dundas Sugar Refining Co.	Craighall Road	2	1,320 —	Thomson, Robert, & Son	Adelphi Ter., Glasgow	2	1,037 —
Porter, Michael R.	82 Main Street, Bridgeton, Glasgow	4	2,613 —	Todd, George	East Haghill, Glasgow	19	60 —
Preston, James A.	Bernard St., Glasgow	4	239 —	Tramway Cars and Works Company	95 Cumberland Street, Calton	1	160 —
				Tullis, John, & Sons	80 John Street, Bridgeton, Glasgow	1	280 —
Rait & Lindsay	Cranstonhill, Glasgow	1	705 —	Turnbull, John	12 Great Eastern Road, Glasgow	3	166 —
Rankin, William	566 Springburn, Glasgow	1	379 —				
Robertson, John, & Co.	Greenhead St., Glasgow	10	5,297 —				
Robinson, J. & E.	Partick, Glasgow	1	188 —				
Robson, Charles	Lurdenlaw, Kelso	2	373 —	Val de Travers Paving Company (Limited)	88 Hope Street, Glasgow	1	150 —
Rowan, David	Elliott Street, Anderston, Glasgow	1	1,214 —	Waddell, Mrs. Euphemia	3 Annfield Pl., Glasgow	41	247 —

LANARK—continued.—(MUNICIPAL BOROUGH OF GLASGOW.)

Name of Owner.	Address of Owner.	Estimated Acreage of Property.	Gross Annual Value.	Name of Owner.	Address of Owner.	Estimated Acreage of Property.	Gross Annual Value.
		Acres.	£ s.			Acres.	£ s.
Walker, Birrell, & Co.	103 Brook Street, Mile-End, Glasgow	2	800 –	Wordie, Peter	Balgray Cottage, Springburn, Glasgow	2	254 –
Walker, David	103 Sauchiehall Street, Glasgow	3	2,078 –	Wylie & Lochhead	Buchanan St., Glasgow	3	3,310 –
Walker, George L., Trs. of	Victoria Street, Glasgow	1	729 –	Wyper, James W.	Pollokshaws Road, Glasgow	1	357 –
Wallace, James	Burnbank, Cumbernauld Road, Glasgow	15	360 –				
Watson, Gow, & Co.	Lilybank Road, Glasgow	4	1,060 –	York, Trs. of William	156 West George Street, Glasgow	22	185 –
Watt & Wilson	120 Castle St., Glasgow	2	437 –	Young, Strang, & Co.	64 Gordon St., Glasgow	2	1,210 –
White, David	3 Meadowpark Street, Glasgow	2	778 –				
Whitesmith, Isaac	Govan Street, Glasgow	1	223 –				
Williamson, Adam C.	Wellington Pottery, Bellfield, Glasgow	5	212 10	Total Owners of Land of One Acre and upwards 310		3,011	628374 6
Wilson, George, & Co.	Swanston St., Glasgow	2	578 –	Total Owners of Lands of less than One Acre in extent 10,681		1,811	1713789 14
Wilson, Trs. of George	Glasgow	100	258 –				
Wilson, John	Alderwood, Kinnieshead	1	2,136 10				
Wilson, William	Pottery, Campbellfield, Glasgow	2	336 –				
Woddrop, William Allan, of Garvald	Garvald House, Dolphinton	30	84 –	GRAND TOTAL . . . 10,991		4,822	2342164 –

LINLITHGOW.

Population in 1871, - - - - - - **40,695.**
Inhabited Houses, - - - - - - **6,255.**
Number of Parishes, - - - - - **14.**

Name of Owner.	Address of Owner.	Estimated Acreage of Property.	Gross Annual Value.	Name of Owner.	Address of Owner.	Estimated Acreage of Property.	Gross Annual Value.
		Acres.	£ s.			Acres.	£ s.
Aberdour, Lord	Dalmahoy, Edinburgh	91	44 –	Clark, Thomas	Almond Bank, Whitburn	2	79 –
Adie, James Alexander	Rockvale, Linlithgow	17	134 8	Collins, William	Ferry Rd. Head, Yoker	2	36 10
Aitken, Alexander Muirhead	Temple, London	91	205 –	*Coltness Iron Company*	Newmains	10	762 5
				Connell, Mrs. Catherine	Bo'ness	6	31 –
Aitken, John and William Hardie	Falkirk	9	97 15	Corbett, Mrs. Sarah	Orzett, Essex	1	54 –
Aiton, Rev. Thomas	Manse, Livingstone	8	46 5	Cowan, Wm., of Linburn	Linburn House, Mid-Calder	2,231	2,678 –
Allan, James	Bo'ness	1	24 10	Do. do.	Do. (*Minerals*)	–	1,500 –
Anderson, Hugh	364 High St., Linlithgow	5	84 –	Cox, Sir James, Kt.	Kinellan, Edinburgh	65	60 –
Anderson, Trustees of late John	Bo'ness	2	489 4	Crawford, James	Syke, Linlithgow	60	73 10
				Crawford, Thomas	Drumcross Rd., Bathgate	1	84 –
Arthur, John	Otter, Tighnabruaich, Greenock	7	12 –	Crawford, Trs. of Thomas	Bathgate	1	126 –
				Crombie, John	Auchtermuchty	15	90 13
				Crown, The		168	456 10
Baillie, Sir William, of Polkemmet, Bart.	Polkemmet, Bathgate	4,320	2,825 15	Cruickshanks, George	Burnfoot, Bo'ness	1	4 –
Do. do.	Do. (*Minerals*)	–	3,556 –	Dalyell, Sir Robert Alexander Osborne, of Binns, Bart.	Binns House, Linlithgow	820	1,795 15
Baird, Heirs of John	Bo'ness	3	26 –				
Baird, Mrs. Helen	Cross, Linlithgow	2	41 –				
Bartholomew, James	Duntarvie, Winchburgh	8	50 –	Dawson, Adam, of Bonnytoun	Bonnytoun, Linlithgow	409	798 –
Bathgate Academy Trustees	Bathgate	2	64 –				
Bathgate Cemetery Company	Bathgate	2	6 10	Dawson, Adam and John	Linlithgow	10	458 10
Bathgate Foundry Company	Bathgate	3	65 –	Dawson, John	Greenpark, Linlithgow	11	66 15
Benhar Coal Company	Edinburgh	6	240 –	Dawson, John Ramage	Bonsyde, Linlithgow	4	17 –
Bennie, Rev. William	Manse, Bathgate	13	46 10	Denholm, Mrs. Catherine	Bathgate	2	18 –
Blackhall, William	22 Upper Gray Street, Edinburgh	76	115 –	Dixon, William Smith	Glasgow	763	871 15
				Do. do.	Do. (*Minerals*)	–	1,824 –
Blair, William, of Avontoun	Avontoun, Linlithgow	410	830 9	Douglas, James	Leith	1	14 10
				Douglas, William	Coldstream	104	91 5
Boag, John	Dechmont, Uphall	1	12 10	Drysdale, John	Muiravonside, Linlithgow	3	14 –
Boag, John	High Street, Bathgate	2	332 10	Dumbreck, John	Linlithgow	23	79 –
Bo'ness Harbour Trustees	Bo'ness (*Harbour*)	3	340 –	Duncan, Trustees of late Colonel Andrew Henry	Foxhall, Kirkliston	72	257 –
Bo'ness, Kirk-Session of	Bo'ness	6	26 –	Duncan, William	Edinburgh	5	57 –
Bo'ness Representatives	Bo'ness	167	274 –	Dundas, Trustee of George	Linlithgow	2,082	4,723 18
Bo'ness United General Sea Box	Bo'ness	9	336 19	Dundas, James, of Dundas	Dundas Castle, South Queensferry	12	60 10
Braidwood, Mrs. Mary	Chapel Lane, Bathgate	1	110 15				
Bridges, Mrs. Jane Mary	Musselburgh	111	138 –	Dundas, John Francis, and others	Borrowstown, Bo'ness	4	10 –
Branks, Rev. William	Manse, Torphichen	9	49 5				
Brash, James	Hallyards, Kirkliston	121	91 –	Dunlop, Alexander, James, Archibald, and George	Whitburn	5	53 11
Brown, Hamilton	Kilsyth	190	205 5				
Brown, Robert	Lymington, Hants	2	7 10	Durham, Robert Sandilands Weir, of Boghead	Boghead, Bathgate	684	793 2
Brown, Trs. of Thomas	Edinburgh	1	23 –	Do. do.	Do. (*Minerals*)	–	1,859 4
Brownlee, John	Whitburn	11	74 –	Durham, Thomas Maxwell, of Foulshiels	Foulshiels, Whitburn	385	245 15
Brunton, James	Broomlands, Kelso	3	42 –				
Buchanan, David Carrick Robert Carrick, of Drumpellier	Drumpellier, Coatbridge	1,345	706 5	*Dyers, Fraternity of*	Linlithgow	8	16 –
Do. do.	Do. (*Minerals*)	–	1,094 10				
Buncle, John	Springfield, Linlithgow	65	247 10				
				Ferguson, Daniel	Westfield, Torphichen	11	149 –
				Ferguson, Robert	Bathgate	1	80 –
Cadell, Henry, of Grange	Grange, Bo'ness	534	1,973 10	Ferrier, Captain Louis John George, R.E.	Bellsyde, Linlithgow	263	292 –
Do. do.	Do. (*Minerals*)	–	1,747 –	Field, Thomas	Hawkhill, Leith	167	160 –
Caledonian Railway Coy.	Glasgow (*Railway*)	21	4,946 –	Do.	Do. (*Minerals*)	–	30 –
Cardross, Lord	Amondell, Broxburn	2,995	5,693 13	Fleming, James, of Craigs	Craigs, Bathgate	288	200 –
Do. do.	Do. (*Minerals*)	–	2,131 –	Do. do.	Do. (*Minerals*)	–	87 5
Chalmers, Thomas	Longcroft, Linlithgow	88	650 5	Forbes, William Forbes, of Lochcote	Lochcote, Bathgate	1,193	1,204 15
Chapman, James	Ballencrieff Mill, Bathgate	2	117 15				
Chapman, Mungo	Bridgend, Bathgate	3	155 –	Forrest, William, of Netherhillhouse	Easter Ogle, Kirriemuir	146	185 –
Chapman, Thomas	Common Head, Airdrie	111	91 –				
Clark, James, of Wester Inch	Wester Inch, Bathgate	346	230 –	Forrester, John	Hall, Bathgate	1	83 –
				Forsyth, Alexander	Bathgate	8	81 10

LINLITHGOW—continued.

Name of Owner.	Address of Owner.	Estimated Acreage of Property.	Gross Annual Value.	Name of Owner.	Address of Owner.	Estimated Acreage of Property.	Gross Annual Value.
		Acres.	£ s.			Acres.	£ s.
Forsyth, Mrs. Harriet Webster, and others	Redhouse, Bathgate	234	301 10	Jardine, Edward Amory	Newcastle-on-Tyne	1	104 10
Forthbank Foundry Co.	Bo'ness	1	30 —	Johnston, Robert	Dechmont, Uphall	1	8 —
Fraser, Robert	Glasgow	2	75 —	Johnston, Thomas	Glasgow	200	200 —
Fraser, William	Broxburn	3	129 —	Johnston, Thomas	Northbank, Bathgate	2	118 —
Free Church, Deacons' Court of	Linlithgow	4	47 5	Johnston, William	Bathgate	30	270 5
				Johnston, Rev. William	Manse, Uphall	11	55 —
Galloway, Mrs. Elizabeth, wife of John Galloway	Mansgrove, Greenburn	4	20 10	Johnston, Mrs. Margaret	Bathgate	3	45 —
Gardener, David	Middlestrath Mill, Falkirk	1	2 —	Kerr, James	Drumcross, Bathgate	120	120 —
Geddes, Ann	Glasgow	12	39 —	Kidd, Mrs. Mary	Mounthooly, Winchburgh	42	42 —
Gentleman, John	West Craigmaury, Bathgate	50	35 —	King, Mrs. Elizabeth	Bo'ness	5	91 18
Do. do.	Do. (*Minerals*)	—	89 —				
Gentleman, John	Falkirk	44	35 —	Law, Robert	Easter Mains, Broxburn	3	30 —
Do. do.	Do. (*Minerals*)	—	113 5	Lawson, William	Whitburn	63	179 15
Gibson, Mrs. Janet	Cousland, Dalkeith	135	121 10	Learmonth, Representatives of Alexander	Linlithgow	2	7 10
Gilkison, Robert	Glasgow	7	443 —	Learmonth, Mrs. Jane, wife of Wm. Learmonth	Borrowstown, Bo'ness	69	55 —
Gillespie, William Honeyman, of Torbanehill	Torbanehill, Bathgate	709	776 5	Leckie, Mrs. Elizabeth	The Thorns, Uphall	1	30 —
Do. do.	Do. (*Minerals*)	—	13125 5	Liddell, Rev. John Robertson	Manse, Kirkliston	7	73 —
Gillon, Andrew, of Wallhouse	Wallhouse, Torphichen	1,465	1,521 5	*Linlithgow, Guildry Incorporation of*	Linlithgow	11	24 —
Gladdon, Daniel	Sandford Street, Leith	3	10 —	*Linlithgow, Kirk-Session of*	Linlithgow	55	181 8
Glasgow Oil Company	Glasgow	11	484 15	*Linlithgow Union Poorhouse, Managers of*	Linlithgow	6	215 —
Glen, Mrs. Mary Cameron	233 High Street, Linlithgow	4	99 1	Little, Andrew	Whitburn	13	33 —
Gowans, James	31 Castle Ter., Edinburgh	563	327 10	Livingstone, Josiah	7 Roxburgh Place, Edinburgh	1	56 —
Gowans, Walter	Strathmill, Falkirk	43	111 15				
Gray, Patrick	Middlestrath, Falkirk	108	127 —	Livingstone, Thos. Livingstone Fenton, of West Quarter	West Quarter, Polmont	1,500	718 2
Gray, Mrs. Ann	Edinburgh	213	343 —				
Greenshields, John	Bridgeside, Whitburn	5	10 —	Lovel, John	Linlithgow	10	417 15
Grieve, David	Blaeberry Hill, Whitburn	131	178 —				
Grieve, Henry Oliver	Kirkliston	1	67 —				
Hamilton, Trs. of Duke of	Hamilton Palace, Hamilton	3,694	7,445 10	M'Clelland, James and James	140 St. Vincent Street, Glasgow	5	183 16
Do. do.	Do. (*Minerals*)	—	8,076 5	M'Kenzie, Mrs. Agnes Greig	5 North Charlotte Street, Edinburgh	31	45 —
Hamilton, John Wallace Ferrier, of Cathlaw	Cathlaw House, Bathgate	537	833 15	M'Knight, Rev. John	F.C. Manse, Whitburn	8	31 —
Do. do.	Do. (*Minerals*)	—	20 —	M'Lachlan, Rev. James	Torquay	1	74 10
Hare, Stewart Bayley, of Calderhall	Calderhall, Mid-Calder	111	90 —	M'Lagan, Peter, of Pumpherston, M.P.	Pumpherston, Mid-Calder	436	580 15
Heggie, John	Dechmont, Uphall	1	28 8	Do. do.	Do. (*Minerals*)	—	1,200 —
Henderson, John	Linlithgow	2	23 7	M'Nab, John	Glenmavis, Bathgate	1	153 4
Henderson, Thomas, and others	Linlithgow	6	56 —	M'Nair, Robert	Bo'ness	2	168 —
Henderson, William Horn	Linlithgow	4	12 10	Maitland, Sir Alex. Charles Ramsay Gibson, of Cliftonhall, Bart., M.P.	Sauchie House, Stirling	45	104 10
Hog, Thomas Alexander, of Newliston	Newliston, Kirkliston	1,092	2,765 —				
Hope, Honble. Charles	Bridge Castle, Bathgate	197	195 —	Maitland, Rev. James	Kells Manse, New Galloway	207	118 —
Hope, Hugh	London	7	14 10	Marshall, John	Bo'ness	7	392 10
Hope, Admiral Sir James, of Carriden, Kt., G.C.B.	Carriden, Bo'ness	728	1,298 —	Marshall, Marriage Trustees of late Colonel John and late Mrs. Jane	Birkenshaw, Bathgate	140	170 —
Do. do.	Do. (*Minerals*)	—	52 —	Marshall, Thomas	Kelmonhead, Falkirk	80	35 —
Hopetoun, Earl of	Hopetoun House, South Queensferry	11,870	19018 5	Marshall, Thomas	Reeves, Whitburn	39	34 —
Do. do.	Do. (*Minerals*)	—	1,600 5	Martin, James Kennedy, of West Bridgehouse	West Bridgehouse, Bathgate	330	300 —
Hopetoun, Earl of, and others	Hopetoun House, South Queensferry	687	1,029 5	Meikle, Charles William	Crieff	4	11 —
Hopetoun, Earl of and John Smith	Do. do. 20 Charlotte Square, Edinburgh	25	61 11	Meldrum, Edward, of Dechmont	Dechmont, Uphall	1,190	1,859 —
Hopetoun, Earl of and Hugh Bruce	Hopetoun House, South Queensferry Freeland House, Perth	8	40 —	Mickel, Robert	Bellevue Pl., Linlithgow	3	88 1
				Middlemas, John	Dechmont, Uphall	2	7 —
				Millar, Alexander	Low Port, Linlithgow	3	57 10
Hutchison, Trustees of late Thomas	Carlowrie House, Kirkliston	344	1,130 5	Millar, Trs. of late James	Friarsland, Linlithgow	4	25 —
Hutton, Jessie, Catherine, and Christina	South Queensferry	2	50 —	Millar, William	Linlithgow Bridge	8	126 —
				Millar, Elizabeth Jessie, and Ann Isabella	Bo'ness	6	22 —
				Miller, James	Wishaw	3	100 —
				Mills, Peter	Braehead, Bo'ness	1	16 —
Inglis, Charles Halket Craigie, of Cramond	Cramond	226	161 —	Milroy, John	Edinburgh	108	220 15
Inglis, Robert	Linmill, Avonbridge, Falkirk	5	16 —	Mitchell, Agnes and Janet	Standhill, Bathgate	100	85 —
				Do. do.	Do. (*Quarry*)	—	228 —
Innes, George Mitchell, of Bangour	Bangour, Linlithgow	778	1,050 —	Moffat, John, of Barbauchlaw	Ardrossan	943	899 —
				Do.	Do. (*Minerals*)	—	2,017 10

T

LINLITHGOW—continued.

Name of Owner.	Address of Owner.	Estimated Acreage of Property.	Gross Annual Value.	Name of Owner.	Address of Owner.	Estimated Acreage of Property.	Gross Annual Value.
		Acres.	£ s.			Acres.	£ s.
Moir, John M'Arthur, of Hillfoot	Hillfoot, Dollar	3	12 —	Shanks, James	School Park, Whitburn	8	50 5
Morton, Andrew	Bickerton Hall, Greenburn	124	94 —	Shaw, Trustees of William	Trees, Bathgate	50	95 —
Morton, Catherine	Hopetoun St., Bathgate	2	25 10	Do. do. (Minerals)		—	100 —
Muir, Rev. Robert Hugh	Manse, Dalmeny	6	96 —	Shepherd, Rev. Alexander	Manse, Ecclesmachen	9	55 —
				Simpson, Alexander	Royal Bank, Bathgate	3	74 —
				Simpson, Trustees of late Alexander	Gormyre, Torphichen	60	50 —
Napier, Trustees of late George	Kettlestone, Linlithgow	219	210 —	Simpson, David	Royal Bank, Bathgate	17	77 —
Do. do.	Do. (Quarry)	—	14 15	Simpson, Sir Walter Grindlay, of Strathavon, Bart.	2 St. Colme Street, Edinburgh	100	191 5
Newton, Robert Pillans	Polmont Bank, Falkirk	137	170 —	Smith, Rev. Edward	Manse, Carriden, Bo'ness	14	55 —
Nimmo, Alexander	Falkirk	7	85 —	Smith, Thomas	Greenburn	1	47 —
Nimmo, Robert	Compston, Linlithgow	2	36 12	Stables, William Alexander	Cawdor Castle, Nairn	5	110 —
Niven, Rev. Thomas B.	Manse, Linlithgow	6	45 —	Stevens, James	Blackheath, London	3	126 —
North British Railway Co.	Edinburgh (Railway)	368 ⎫	30247 —	Steuart, Captain Robert, of Westwood	Westwood, West Calder	463	593 —
Do. do.	Do. (Canal)	113 ⎭		Do. do. (Minerals)		—	2,937 —
				Stewart's Hospital, Trustees of	Edinburgh	854	1,785 4
Ogilvie, Archibald, of Old Liston	Old Liston, Ratho	9	30 —	Do. do. (Minerals)		—	755 10
				Stewart, John, & Co.	Kirkliston	9	588 —
				Stewart, Robert Houston Johnstone, of Physgill	Champfleurie, Linlithgow	2,036	3,810 1
Pender, John, of Middleton Hall	Middleton Hall, Linlithgow	408	895 18	Do. do. (Quarry)		—	73 10
Do. do.	Do. (Minerals)	—	1,100 —	Stewart, Mrs. Janet Houston D., of Binny	Binny, Linlithgow	372	891 10
Philip, John	Gormyre, Torphichen	6	13 —	Do. do. (Quarry)		—	130 —
Philp, Richard	Linlithgow	2	5 —	Story, John, of Burnhead	Burnhead, Whitburn	786	418 —
Playfair, Rev. David	Manse, Abercorn	9	60 —	Do. do. (Minerals)		—	100 —
Poynter, John Edgar	72 Great Clyde Street, Glasgow	4	139 —	Story, John	Northfield, Greenburn	72	54 —
Primrose, Hon. Bouverie Francis	22 Moray Place, Edinburgh	15	15 —	Strang, George, of Breich	Carleton Place, Glasgow	187	162 —
Pringle, Lieut.-Col. David, of Carriber	Carriber, Bathgate	440	399 15	Taylor, Joseph M'Intyre	Glasgow	104	70 —
Paul, Mrs. Elizabeth	Muirhouse, Bo'ness	3	15 —	Taylor, Heirs of William	Queensferry	1	103 10
				Taylor, Mrs. Marion Brock	Whitburn	1	155 10
				Thomas, Ann M.	7 Viewforth Place, Edinburgh	62	80 —
				Thomson, Alexander	West Croft, Greenburn	5	16 15
				Thomson, Charles Wyville	Bonsyde, Linlithgow	61	125 —
Reid, Trs. of late John	Redmill, Whitburn	43	32 —	Torphichen, Lord	Calder House, Edinburgh	95	60 —
Richard, John Miller	23 Royal Terrace, Edinburgh	107	283 10	Turner, William	Mains, Linlithgow	36	105 —
Robertson, David Soutar	Edinburgh	100	85 —				
Robertson, Rev. Henry M'Intosh	Manse, Bo'ness	13	60 —	*Uphall Mineral Oil Co.*	Uphall	56	2,554 —
Robertson, James	Avonbridge, Falkirk	2	2 15	*Uphall Parochial Board*	Uphall	112	114 10
Robertson, Thomas	Bathgate	1	85 —				
Rollo, Archibald	Sunbury House, Edinburgh	15	12 —	Vallance, John	Edinburgh	1	8 —
Rosebery, Earl of	Dalmeny Park, Edinburgh	5,680	8,902 15	Vannan, John	Bo'ness	1	181 10
Do. do.	Do. (Minerals)	—	2,416 —	Vere, William Edward Hope, of Craigiehall	Craigiehall, Cramond	1,501	3,054 —
Russell, Alexander	Mosside, Bathgate	125	84 5				
Russell, James, & Son	Falkirk	3	441 9				
Russell, Heirs of Thomas	Fauldhouse, Whitburn	505	184 —	Waddell, Heirs of Alexander, of Stoneyburn	Stoneyburn, Whitburn	101	119 —
Do. do.	(Minerals)	—	1,906 15	Do. do. (Minerals)		—	162 —
Russell, Col. Sir William, of Charlton Park, Bart., M.P., C.B.	Charlton Park, Cheltenham	43	85 —	Waddell, John, of Easter Inch	Bathgate	385	591 —
Russell, Mrs. Agnes	Grayshall, Bathgate	3	31 3	Waddell, Mrs. Jane Brown, of Crofthead	Crofthead, Greenburn	670	408 —
				Do. do. (Minerals)		—	86 10
Salmon, Peter	Torbane, Bathgate	4	15 —	Walker, Andrew	Glasgow	174	226 —
Sanders, Robert	Linlithgow	1	5 5	Walker, Henry	Bathgate	2	40 —
Sandilands, Lewis Thomas Nimmo, of Couston	Couston, Bathgate	649	578 10	Wallace, James	Main Street, Bathgate	18	207 10
Do. do.	Do. (Minerals)	—	100 —	Wallace, James	Broxburn	1	155 16
Sawers, Rev. Peter	Craigengall, Bathgate	585	409 5	Wallace, Thomas	Blackburn	1	125 10
Sayer, John	6 Mid Street, Bathgate	19	212 10	Wallace, Trs. of Thomas	Bellamount, Bathgate	230	207 —
Sayers, Curators of Margaret	Bathgate	55	60 —	Wallace, Walker	Bathgate	1	107 15
Scott, Henry	Lochcote, Bathgate	3	12 —	Warden, Colonel Robert, of Binny, C.B.	Binny, Linlithgow	1,279	1,898 15
Selkirk, Earl of	St. Mary's Isle, Kirkcudbright	1,441	1,724 10	Wardrop, William Macfarlane, of Bridgehouse	Bridgehouse, Torphichen	153	257 10
Do.	Do. (Minerals)	—	30 —	Watson, James	Rivals Green, Linlithgow	5	74 —
Seton, Alex., of Preston	Preston, Linlithgow	650	1,230 5	Watson, Thomas, David, and William	Bathville, Bathgate	145	1,141 —
Shairp, Lieut.-Colonel Thomas, of Houston	Houston, Uphall	567	840 —	Do. do. (Minerals)		—	314 10
				Watt, Hugh	9 York Place, Edinburgh	3	20 —

LINLITHGOW—continued.

Name of Owner.	Address of Owner.	Estimated Acreage of Property.	Gross Annual Value.	Name of Owner.	Address of Owner.	Estimated Acreage of Property.	Gross Annual Value.
		Acres.	£ s.			Acres.	£ s.
Watt, Rev. John	Manse, Whitburn	8	33 10	Wood, James	South Queensferry	1	238 15
Waugh, John	Newmill, Avonbridge	38	30 —	Wylie, Executors of Daniel	5 Trinity Crescent, Edinburgh	2	180 —
Weir, James	Bathgate	1	8 —				
White, Thomas	Spring-grove, Bathgate	9	124 5				
White, William	Broxburn	2	35 10				
Whyte, Walter	Bankhead, Rutherglen	313	145 —	Young, James, of Inchcross	Inchcross, Bathgate	383	437 —
Wilkie, Archibald, of Ormiston	Ormiston, Kirknewton, Edinburgh	264	570 —	*Young's Paraffin Oil Co.*	Bathgate	45	2,143 —
Wilkie, David	Larbert	7	46 10	Young, Thomas	Oatridge, Linlithgow	15	35 —
Wilson, Alexander	Dechmont, Uphall	1	8 —				
Wilson, Rev. Alexander M.	F.U. Manse, Bathgate	1	20 —	Total Owners of Land of one Acre and upwards 287		75,286	215,171 15
Wilson, George, & Co.	Kinneil Iron Works, Bo'ness	4	1,598 10	Total Owners of Lands of less than one Acre in extent 1,248		499	33,421 15
Wilson, James	Edinburgh	1	2 —				
Wilson, William Finlay, of Ravestone	11 Florence Place, Glasgow	230	164 —	GRAND TOTAL . . . 1,535		75,785	248,593 10

NAIRN.

Population in 1871,	10,225.
Inhabited Houses,	2,029.
Number of Parishes,	9.

Name of Owner.	Address of Owner.	Estimated Acreage of Property.	Gross Annual Value.
		Acres.	£ s.
Anderson, Robert, of Lochdhu	Lochdhu, Nairn	337	371 3
Auldearn Free Church, Trustees of	Auldearn	1	25 —
Bain, Rev. John, and Thomas Bain	Nairn	3	20 6
Bethune, Mrs. Jane	Nairn	4	91 —
British Linen Company Bank	Edinburgh	1	85 —
Brodie, James Campbell John, of Lethen	Lethen House, Nairn	22,378	4,947 9
Brodie, Hugh F. A., of Brodie	Brodie Castle, Forres	4,407	2,586 —
Bruce, Major Charles Lennox Cumming, of Dunphail	Dunphail House, Forres	740	177 4
Burns, Rev. James	Manse, Nairn	9	63 —
Cameron, Angus	Firhall, Nairn	38	90 —
Cameron, James A.	Nairn	11	23 —
Campbell's School, Trustees of	Achnatone, Ardclach	1	7 —
Cant, Arthur and Matthew	Nairn	6	165 —
Cawdor, Earl of	Cawdor Castle	46,176	7,882 12
Cawdor Parish, Heritors of	Cawdor	2	1 10
Clark, Augustus Terry, of Achareidh	Achareidh, Nairn	233	200 15
Cumming, Sir William Gordon Gordon, of 'Altyre and Gordonstone, Bart.	Altyre House, Forres	2,112	155 15
Davidson, Hugh, of Cantray	Cantray House, Croy, Inverness	6,363	910 10
Drew, Trustees of late William	Nairn	3	37 17
Dunbar, Sir James A., of Boath, Bart.	Boath House, Nairn	1,092	1,012 19
Falconer, Alexander	Nairn	1	91 1
Finlay, Lieut.-Col. Alexander	Ballinder of Nuide, Kingussie	41	262 5
Forbes, Arthur, of Culloden	Culloden House, Inverness	2,011	650 7
Fraser, William, of Newton	Newton, Nairn	100	137 —
Fraser, William	Nairn	1	62 17
Gordon, John, of Kinsteary	Cluny Castle, Aberdeen	3,635	2,536 17
Gordon, Mrs. Mary Ann	Nairn	1	40 —
Grant, Factor loco tutoris of Ian Robert James Murray, of Moy	Glenmoriston, Inverness	10	10 —
Grant, Col. James Augustus, of Househill, C.B.	Nairn	469	555 10
Grant, John, of Broadley	Grantown	152	140 —
Grigor, John	Larkfield, Nairn	16	150 10
Grigor, Heirs of William, of Viewfield and Seabank	Elgin	61	79 3
Highland Railway Company	Inverness	2	47 2
Do. do.	Do. (Railway)	57	3,174 —
Jeans, Alexander	Nairn	1	49 19
Ketchen, Captain James, of Kingillie	India	3	65 —
Leven and Melville, Earl of	Glenferness, Ardclach	7,805	1,317 4
M'Donald, John	Moss Lands, Nairn	4	3 8
M'Gillivray, Alexander	Nairn	1	96 —
M'Gillivray, Neil John, of Dumnaglass	Williamston, Glengarry, Canada	12,600	1,000 —
M'Intosh, Angus	Moss Lands, Nairn	4	3 8
M'Intosh, Heirs of George	Geddes, Nairn	878	982 18
M'Kenzie, Rev. Colin	Manse, Ardclach	10	31 —
M'Kenzie, Donald	Moss Lands, Nairn	4	3 9
M'Kenzie, Kenneth	Moss Lands, Nairn	7	7 5
M'Kissack, Robert, of Ardgye and Roseisle	Ardgye	28	25 —
M'Pherson, John	Moss Lands, Nairn	3	3 6
M'Pherson, Rev. Lewis	Manse, Cawdor	12	37 15
Mann, Alexander	Seabank Cottage, Nairn	2	59 10
Mann, Hugh	Nairn	1	100 —
Moray, Earl of	Darnaway Castle	315	202 18
Murray, Lieut.-Colonel Hugh R.	Lodgehill, Nairn	7	70 —
Nairn, Burgh of	Nairn	315	114 —
Nairn, Trustees of Harbour of	Nairn (Harbour)	9	200 —
Nairn New Cemetery Co.	Nairn	3	9 —
Nairn Seaman's Society	Nairn	2	3 —
Nairn Union Poorhouse Board	Nairn	3	60 —
Nairn, Trustees of U.P. Congregation of	Nairn	2	30 —
Parker, Home S., of Millfield	Kingillie House, Nairn	6	5 15
Reid, Heirs of Rev. James	Manse, Auldearn	7	30 —

NAIRN—continued.

Name of Owner.	Address of Owner.	Estimated Acreage of Property.	Gross Annual Value.	Name of Owner.	Address of Owner.	Estimated Acreage of Property.	Gross Annual Value.
		Acres.	£ s.			Acres.	£ s.
Ritchie, William	Moss Side, Nairn	7	6 –	Turnbull, William	Lodgehill, Nairn	22	129 –
Rose's Academical Institution, Trustees of	Nairn	1	33 –				
Rose, Henry	Rouallan, Nairn	10	70 –	Wilson, Alexander	Rosebank, Nairn	2	80 –
Rose, Rev. Hugh Francis, of Holme	Holme Rose House, Croy, Fort-George	3,672	240 –				
Rose, Major James, of Kilravock	Kilravock, Fort-George	4,395	2,345 5	Total Owners of Land of one Acre and upwards		70,120,636	34,450 7
				Total Owners of Lands of less than one Acre in extent		467 129	7,316 13
Sclanders, William	Forres	1	27 –				
Shireff, Mrs. Elizabeth	Nairn	13	117 –				
Simpson, Robert	Wellington Road, Nairn	1	73 5				
Smith, Trustees of Campbell	Nairn	6	30 10	GRAND TOTAL		537 120,765	41,767 –

ORKNEY.

Population in 1871, 31,274.
Inhabited Houses, 6,288.
Number of Parishes, 18.

Name of Owner.	Address of Owner.	Estimated Acreage of Property.	Gross Annual Value.	Name of Owner.	Address of Owner.	Estimated Acreage of Property.	Gross Annual Value.
		Acres.	£ s.			Acres.	£ s.
Adam, Alexander	Fasque, Fettercairn	30	3 –	Bichan, Robert	Boo-of-Braebister, Deerness	5	8 13
Adamson, William	Lower Palace, Birsay	30	1 10				
Aim, Peter	Hall of Heddle, Firth	24	11 5	Bichan, Robert	Copinshay, Deerness	18	1 10
Aim, Mrs. Robina	Crearhowe, Holm	51	16 10	Birsay, Free Church Congregation of	Birsay	2	14 10
Aitken, John	Wester Sands, Deerness	39	18 10				
Allan, George	Knowe, Stenness	220	63 15	Birsay, Parochial Board of	Birsay	94	2 –
Allan, John	Miffia, Stromness	26	4 –	Black, John	Cairnleith, Ellon, Aberdeen	103	77 –
Allan, Mrs. Janet	Upper Pow, Stromness	6	2 –	Borwick, Charles Flett	Australia	22	10 –
Anderson, James	Appiehouse, Harray	20	18 4	Borwick, John	Quian, Harray	20	9 5
Anderson, John	Brockan, Stromness	19	11 17	Brass, Alexander	Instabellie, Sandwick	8	5 –
Anderson, Rev. John	Ratho, Edinburgh	25	10 –	Brass, David	Moan, Sandwick	90	18 –
Anderson, John	Steadaquoy, Birsay	20	6 5	Brass, John	Newhooveth, Sandwick	8	3 10
Anderson, Thomas	Biggings, Harray	24	9 10	Brass, William	Quoyloo, Sandwick	10	4 12
Anderson, Thomas	Miran, Harray	8	2 18	Brass, Mrs. Elizabeth, and another	Pallast, Sandwick	20	11 5
Anderson, Thomas	Stoneywoo, Harray	19	9 5				
Anderson, William	Lingro, Saint Ola	1	7 –	Breck, Mrs. Margaret	Langskaill, Birsay	7	2 –
Angus, Joseph	Ramsquoy, Stenness	30	11 5	Brock, George	West Greenland, Thurso	90	63 –
				Brotchie, George	Fribo House, Westray	92	86 –
				Brotchie, Robt., of Swannay	5 John's Place, Leith	1,317	343 8
				Brown, George	Hundland, Birsay	220	51 –
Baikie, Andrew	Airsdale, Evie	25	11 5	Brown, Reps. of Hugh	Croval, Sandwick	19	8 16
Baikie, George	Mucklehouse, Walls	2	2 13	Brown, James	Brittabreck, Stromness	25	11 –
Baikie, James, and three others	Nether Linnabreck, Birsay	7	6 –	Brown, James	1 Derby Pl., Glasgow	3	3 –
Baikie, Captain John, R.N.	Kirkwall	108	133 10	Brown, James	Hallbreck, South Ronaldshay	3	7 –
Baikie, Robert, of Tankerness	49 Northumberland Street, Edinburgh	7,846	1,914 13	Brown, John	Hallbreck, South Ronaldshay	5	8 –
Baikie, Thomas	Cloke, Birsay	30	12 –	Brown, William	Hackland, Sandwick	75	28 –
Baikie, William	Mithhouse, Harray	72	9 –	Brown, William	South Heddle, Firth	64	31 3
Baikie, William, and two others	Mithhouse, Harray	34	8 –	Brown, William, junior	Stromness	30	74 –
				Brown, Mrs. Catherine	Stromness	2	7 5
Baikie, Mrs. George	Benlaws, Evie	130	25 10	Brown, Mrs. Cecilia	Stromness	21	28 3
Bain, Alexander	Kirkwall	3	187 15	Brown, Mrs. Margaret	Stromness	40	29 5
Bain, Mrs. Barbara	Mouseland, Westray	14	4 –	Brown, Isabella M.	37 North Bridge, Edinburgh	2	25 –
Bain, Mrs. William Watt	Manse, Lintrathen, Forfar	10	35 –				
Balfour, David, of Balfour and Trenabie	Balfour Castle, Shapinshay	29,054	7,578 1	Bruce, William M'Donald	Birsay	4	2 –
				Buchan, Reps. of Mrs. Ann	Anerly Park, Surrey	76	145 10
Balfour, David, of Balfour and Trenabie, and Captain James William Balfour	Balfour Castle, Shapinshay . Hat House, Wilts	136	30 –	Buchan, Mrs. Mary	Skethquoy, Stenness	4	1 10
				Budge, John	Flaws, South Ronaldshay	5	4 –
				Budge, Representatives of Mrs. Catherine	Flaws, South Ronaldshay	4	7 –
Balfour Hospital, Trs. of	Kirkwall	1	62 12	Burray, United Presbyterian Congregation of	Burray	1	20 –
Balfour, William Sinclair	Berriedale, Westray	240	98 –				
Balfour, Mrs. Jessie	Birstane House, St. Ola	320	187 –	Burroughs, Colonel Fred. Wm. T., of Veira, C.B.	Westness House, Rousay, Kirkwall	6,693	2,116 4
Ballenden, John	Breckan, Evie	14	7 –				
Banks, James	Smiddy Banks, St. Margaret's Hope	152	43 10	Byas, William	Langhouse, Stromness	3	3 10
Banks, William	Angle Cottage, St. Margaret's Hope	158	70 9	Calder, Marcus	Elwickbank, Shapinshay	87	90 –
				Caskey, Rev. Joseph	Manse, Stronsay	53	32 10
Banks, Mrs. Eliza	Smiddybanks, St. Margaret's Hope	4	11 –	Cassie, John	Moa, Rendall	45	16 10
Baptist Congregation	Burray	1	6 –	Christian Knowledge, Society for Propagating	Edinburgh	7	7 –
Baptist Congregation	Westray	2	6 –				
Beatton, John, and another	Rio Grande do sul, Brazil	11	122 8	Church of Scotland, Home Mission Committee of	Edinburgh	5	7 –
Beatton, Peter	Langskaill, Stromness	75	26 10				
Beatton, William	Clovegarth, Stromness	25	9 10	Clark, Mrs. Ann	Bellfield, St. Ola	10	6 10
Beatton, William, and another	Clovegarth, Stromness	60	21 –	Clouston, Rev. Charles	Manse, Sandwick	50	31 10
				Clouston, James	Feolquoy, Harray	14	6 15
Beatton, Mrs. Catherine	Goldigarth, Sandwick	15	9 5	Clouston, James	Navershaw, Stromness	20	8 –
Beatton, Mrs. Euphemia	Newdale, Stromness	3	2 –	Clouston, James	Nisthouse, Harray	19	9 15
Bews, James, senior, and two others	Upper Berryhill, St. Ola	50	5 –	Clouston, James	Wardhill, Stromness	6	1 15
				Clouston, Malcolm	Upper Hammer, Birsay	30	14 –
Bews, John	Hurtisgarth, Sandwick	8	3 –	Clouston, Robert	Balrath, Meath, Ireland	1,336	409 –
Bews, Mrs. Barbara	Kirkwall	2	20 13	Do. do.	Do. (Quarry)	–	3 –
Bichan, George, junior	Oback, Deerness	10	3 –	Clouston, Robert, of Caldale	Plainstones, Stromness	470	135 19

ORKNEY—continued.

Name of Owner.	Address of Owner.	Estimated Acreage of Property.	Gross Annual Value.
		Acres.	£ s.
Clouston, Samuel	Howally, Birsay	60	5 –
Clouston, Thomas, junior	Barnhouse, Stenness	18	8 10
Clouston, Thomas, senior	Nether Bigging, Stenness	30	14 17
Clouston, William	Flaws, Harray	5	2 1
Clouston, William	Garth, Harray	34	12 –
Clouston, William	Nether Bigging, Stenness	18	10 10
Clouston, William, and another	Nether Bigging, Stenness	52	33 –
Clouston, Mrs. Harriet	Nisthouse, Harray	87	33 10
Clouston, Mrs. Marjory	Nearhouse, Harray	12	7 –
Cock, James	Lynn, St. Ola	30	25 –
Commercial Bank of Scotland	Edinburgh	3	70 –
Congregational Church, Trustees of	Harray	2	4 –
Congregational Church, Trustees of	Rendall	1	5 5
Copland, James	Roadside, Holm	2	2 10
Copland, John	Stromness	76	23 12
Copland, Peter	Withaquoy, Holm	40	17 10
Copland, William	Savedale, Sandwick	12	3 –
Cormack, John	Deerness	19	3 –
Cormack, Robert	Newhouse, Deerness	57	28 –
Cormack, William	Skaill, Deerness	20	11 –
Corrigall, Edward Ellicot	Ayre, Walls	522	146 15
Corrigall, Jacob, and another	Upper Bigging, Rendall	24	12 10
Corrigall, James	Appiehouse, Harray	50	9 2
Corrigall, James	Arion, Stromness	330	108 –
Corrigall, James	Australia	45	11 15
Corrigall, James	Georoin, Harray	13	5 5
Corrigall, James	Langalour, Firth	10	3 10
Corrigall, James	Northbigging, Harray	32	12 3
Corrigall, John	Beist, Harray	14	5 10
Corrigall, John	Georoin, Harray	14	5 –
Corrigall, John	North Unigarth, Sandwick	18	11 –
Corrigall, John	Pow, Harray	15	7 8
Corrigall, William	Henchaquoy, Birsay	13	5 –
Corrigall, William	Midhouse, Harray	45	21 –
Corrigall, William	Scuan, Harray	26	9 –
Corrigall, William	Velzian, Harray	16	12 –
Corrigall, Mrs. Jacobina	Mossater, Rendall	58	27 –
Corrigall, Mrs. Margaret	North Bigging, Harray	16	6 14
Corrigall, Ann	Beist, Harray	14	5 –
Corrigall, Jane	Langalour, Firth	8	3 3
Corrigall, Mary	Langalour, Firth	8	3 3
Corsie, John	Wick, Holm Road, St. Ola	1	1 –
Corston, John	Nova Scotia	6	3 15
Craigie, David	Fea, Clouston, Stenness	25	1 15
Craigie, John	Hullion, Rousay	27	18 10
Craigie, John, and another	London, Rousay	5	3 –
Cromarty, James	Bankburn House, South Ronaldshay	91	68 –
Cromarty, James	Gossigair, South Ronaldshay	85	18 –
Cromarty, James	Hestikeldy, Holm	10	7 10
Cromarty, James	Honeysgoe, South Ronaldshay	17	11 10
Cromarty, Mrs. Mary Kennedy	Sandwick, South Ronaldshay	121	67 10
Cross and Burness, Kirk-Session of, as Trustees for 'Fea's Mortification'	Cross and Burness, Sanday	50	14 16
Croy, Peter	Bridge of Waith, Stenness	9	4 10
Cumming, Capt. William	H.M. 48th Regiment	610	85 –
Cursiter, John	Kirkwall	4	61 10
Cursiter, Mrs. Ann	Woo, Rendall	154	17 10
Cursiter, Mrs. Margaret	Stromness	46	14 –
Cusiter, Peter	Quoydandy, St. Ola	50	110 5
Customs, Board of	London	1	17 –
Davidson, Heirs of A.	Stromness	3	5 10
Davidson, Trustees of late William	Aberdeen	1,210	324 –
Davidson, William	Meadowbank, Sandwick	6	1 15
Davie, John	Little House, Firth	29	11 5
Davie, William	Nether Bigging, Firth	7	3 10
Davie, Mrs. Malcolm	Cuppin, Stenness	2	1 15
Deerness, Daniel	Little Halkland, Rendall	10	6 –
Delday, George	Hillhead, Deerness	23	9 –
Delday, John	Gairth, Deerness	4	2 –
Dennison, Jerome	West Brough, Cross, Sanday	60	12 –
Dick, Mrs. Jessie, wife of Rev. James Dick; and another	Ballarat, Australia	204	125 2
Dickson, Andrew	Appiehouse, Stenness	18	12 –
Dickson, Mrs. Elizabeth	Appiehouse, Stenness	18	12 –
Dickson, Mrs. Margaret, wife of Caleb Dickson	Breck, Stenness	8	3 10
Dickson, Mrs. Mary	Feolquoy, Harray	18	5 10
Dinnison, James	Burrowston Hill, St. Ola	35	5 –
Donaldson, William	Bilbster, Wick	79	86 –
Douglas, John	How and Oback, Harray	88	32 5
Drever, James, junior	Askernish House, Lochmaddy	100	23 –
Drever, James, senior	Nestigar, Westray	32	20 –
Drever, Samuel	Quoylet, Westray	4	2 –
Drever, Mrs. Annabella	Kirkwall	34	234 10
Dundas, Hon. John C., of Papdale, M.P.	1 Halkin Street, Belgrave Square, London	274	409 16
Dunnet, George	Windwick, South Ronaldshay	26	13 –
Esson, William S.	Springbank, South Ronaldshay	25	8 –
Eunson, William	Halley, Deerness	35	15 –
Eunson, Mrs. Williamina, wife of Andrew J. Eunson; and two others	Norton, Stenness	274	54 –
Evangelical Union Church Congregation	Shapinshay	14	8 –
Evie, Free Church Congregation of	Evie	1	14 –
Evie and Rendall, Kirk-Session of Parish of	Evie and Rendall	16	6 –
Fea, James	Boloquoy, Cross, Sanday	90	50 –
Fea, William	North Ronaldshay	2	5 –
Fea, Trustees of late Barbara and Helen	Stronsay	459	141 10
Fiddler, William	Innertown, Stromness	3	2 –
Firth, David	Finstown, Firth	2	5 5
Firth, David	Quina, Rendall	395	57 9
Firth, Heirs of David	Finstown, Firth	8	6 5
Firth, James	Boccan, Sandwick	90	11 1
Firth, James	Sunnybank, Stromness	5	13 –
Firth, John	Binnaquoy, Firth	6	3 3
Firth, John	Ness, Harray	23	9 5
Firth, William	Puldrite, Rendall	24	18 –
Firth, Mrs. Elizabeth	Finstown, Firth	30	6 –
Firth, Representatives of Mrs. Margaret	Stromness	1	6 18
Fisher, Rev. Matthew	Manse, Cross, Sanday	42	35 –
Flett, Adam	Handest, Harray	48	13 5
Flett, Adam	Nistaben, Harray	20	10 –
Flett, Adam, and another	Nisthouse, Harray	34	16 –
Flett, Adam, and others	South Wald, Firth	18	8 –
Flett, George	Midhouse, Harray	38	19 10
Flett, James	Australia	8	3 10
Flett, James	Bigging, Harray	55	24 4
Flett, James	Curcabreck, Sandwick	16	11 5
Flett, James	Furso, Harray	30	14 15
Flett, James, and two others	Handest, Harray	15	7 –
Flett, James	Nistaben, Harray	42	13 –
Flett, John	78 Dempsey Street, Stepney, London	200	54 –
Flett, John	Dowiescarth, Stenness	7	3 –
Flett, John	Makerhouse, Birsay	24	8 –
Flett, John	North Bigging, Harray	6	20 4
Flett, John	Windbrake, Flotta	9	8 –
Flett, Magnus	Hallbreck, Sandwick	3	2 5
Flett, Magnus	Nistaben, Harray	35	19 –
Flett, Nicol	Netherhouse, Harray	16	8 –
Flett, Robert	Linneth, Harray	21	6 15

ORKNEY—continued.

Name of Owner.	Address of Owner.	Estimated Acreage of Property.	Gross Annual Value.
		Acres.	£ s.
Flett, William	Easthouse, Sandwick	9	5 10
Flett, William	Græmeston, Harray	8	1 5
Flett, William	Handest, Harray	40	14 15
Flett, William	Horraquoy, Harray	8	3 10
Flett, William	Millygoe, Birsay	20	4 —
Flett, William	Newhouse, Harray	6	3 5
Flett, William	Stonehall, Firth	24	5 —
Flett, William	Stromness	3	13 10
Flett, William	Trettigar, Harray	9	4 —
Flett, Mrs. Graham	Redland, Firth	124	56 15
Flett, Mrs. Jean	Upperhouse, Harray	12	7 —
Flett, Mrs. Mary, wife of James Flett	Yeldavale, Harray	20	11 5
Flett, Elizabeth, and two others	Breckan, Harray	4	2 —
Florence, Peter	Yelda, Stromness	27	4 10
Folsetter, George Taylor	Dale, Evie	158	73 16
Folsetter, James	Howally, Birsay	190	33 14
Fortescue, Archer, of Swanbister	Swanbister House, Orphir	2,620	387 5
Fotheringhame, James	Hescombe, Stronsay	31	18 10
Fotheringhame, Ralph	Lynnfield, St. Ola	15	42 —
Fotheringhame, William	Newbigging, St. Ola	30	19 —
Gardner, Rev. James	Manse, Rousay	40	40 10
Garriock, Gilbert	Sandwick Road, Stromness	18	14 10
Garriock, James Robertson	Stromness	4	33 10
Garriock, John	The Boo, Cairston, Stromness	63	18 —
Garriock, Heirs of Robert	Caviltown, S. Ronaldshay	17	4 —
Garson, George	Newhall, Stromness	50	9 —
Garson, George	Stromness	185	74 15
Garson, James	Gairycot, Sandwick	25	8 10
Garson, Rev. John	F.C. Manse, Birsay	442	150 10
Garson, John	Kirkwall	22	— 5
Garson, Magnus	Millfield, Stromness	8	2 15
Gaudie, Peter	Nether Skaill, Birsay	32	13 12
Geddes, Charles and John	Chesmire, Stenness	80	16 10
Gerrard, John	Trades Park, St. Ola	38	17 —
Gibson, Reps. of Thomas	Malisburgh, Deerness	29	9 10
Gibson, Mrs. Ann	Stromness	10	7 —
Gills, Robert	Stromness	2	27 15
Gilruth, Rev. Patrick Gorthy	Airlie St., Alyth, Perth	65	45 —
Gordon, John	Millhouse, Holm	52	25 17
Gordon, Mrs. Agnes, wife of Adam Gordon	St. Margaret's Hope	25	29 13
Gorie, James	Minehill, Stromness	30	6 —
Gorrie, James	Tullock's Bigging, Stromness	5	3 15
Græme, Alexander Sutherland, of Græmeshall	W. Dome House, Bognor, Sussex	6,444	1,669 14
Gray, Henry	Crooksteths, Orphir	13	5 10
Gray, James	North Halkland, Rendall	26	12 15
Gray, John, of Roeberry	Roeberry House, S. Ronaldshay	425	151 17
Gray, William	Hundatown, Harray	35	16 5
Gray, Representatives of William	Midgarth, Stromness	8	8 —
Gunn, James	Quoyangry, S. Ronaldshay	23	9 10
Gunn, John and Marcus	Buxa, Orphir	134	45 —
Halcro, George	Stromness	94	30 —
Halcro, John	Hogarth, Rendall	36	11 —
Handyside, Maria	Stromness	43	14 —
Handyside, Maria, and two others	Stromness	166	45 10
Harper, James	Neghead, Stenness	4	1 10
Harray and Birsay, Kirk-Session of Parish of	Harray and Birsay	5	3 5
Harray, Thomas	Upper Bigging, Harray	22	10 —
Harvey, George	Chinegar, Orphir	8	6 —
Harvey, George	Vancouver	24	1 13
Harvey, George Philips H.	Banks, Birsay	56	14 2
Harvey, James	Cot, Quoyloo, Sandwick	5	1 —
Harvey, John	Lower Quoys, Sandwick	7	2 —
Harvey, John	Winksetter, Harray	36	22 —
Harvey, Simon	Newhouse, Sandwick	26	12 —
Harvey, William	Lady, Sanday	135	25 —
Harvey, Mrs. Hannah, wife of Magnus Harvey	New Velzian, Birsay	43	6 16
Hay, Charles	Kirbuster, Birsay	20	4 10
Hay, John	Wester Puldrite, Rendall	74	6 —
Hay, Mrs. Margaret	Netherhouse, Sandwick	50	22 —
Hay, Mrs. Margaret, wife of Robert Hay	Myre, Orphir	30	6 5
Hebden, Robert James, of Eday	Sardinia	7,500	1,351 15
Do. do.	Do. (Quarry)	—	40 —
Heddle, James	Horaldshay, Firth	42	21 5
Heddle, John	Horaldshay, Firth	42	21 8
Heddle, John	Rosehill, Stromness	40	8 —
Heddle, John George Moodie, of Melsetter	Melsetter House, Walls	50,410	3,527 6
Heddle, Peter Sinclair	Kirkwall	620	65 —
Heddle, Heirs of William, junior	Stromness	12	19 10
Heddle, Rev. William Sinclair	Kirkwall	2	16 10
Henderson, Forbes	Blinkbonny, St. Ola	229	41 10
Hepburn, David Balfour	Shapinshay	20	3 10
Hercus, William	Bloomfield, St. Ola	30	10 —
Hewison, Mrs. Jane, wife of Murdoch Hewison	Breckowall, Westray	221	80 —
Hiddleston, Rev. Robert	Manse, Orphir	85	32 10
Hiddleston, Mrs. Isabella, wife of Rev. Robert Hiddleston	Manse, Orphir	1,041	274 4
Horrie, John	Park of Heddle, Firth	14	6 10
Horrie, Simon	Upper Lettaly, Firth	19	6 15
Horrie, William	Nether Sands, Deerness	29	10 —
Horwood, Marriage Trustees of Capt. and Mrs. George F. F.	Wargraves, Hurstmonceaux, Sussex	2,650	1,001 8
Hourrie, Mrs. Margaret	Cruan, Firth	2	1 18
Hourston, James	Outbrecks, Stenness	11	6 10
Hourston, John	Eday	56	33 10
Hourston, John	Hallbreck, Sandwick	10	4 17
Hourston, Reps. of John	Stromness	35	8 —
Hourston, Thomas	Quoy of Hozen, Harray	8	2 10
Hourston, William M.	Berlin, Victoria	30	5 —
Hourston, William	Pallast, Stromness	10	5 —
Hourston, William	Stromness	1	10 15
Hourston, Mrs. Margaret, wife of Thomas Hourston	Quoy of Hozen, Harray	11	2 10
Hunter, Alexander	Una, Stromness	25	8 —
Hunter, Jacob	Scorn, Birsay	5	3 —
Hunter, John	Newhouse, Stromness	15	7 10
Hunter, Mrs. Margaret	Howaback, Birsay	3	1 10
Inkster, George	Nistaben, Harray	15	9 5
Inkster, Mrs. Janet	Newhouse, Stromness	2	8 —
Inkster, Margaret	Kirkwall	1	17 —
Ironside, Alexander	East Vetquoy, Sandwick	78	22 10
Irvine, George	Quoyloo, Sandwick	260	71 6
Irvine, James	Stevand, Stromness	19	7 —
Irvine, John	Cumbla, Sandwick	20	6 —
Irvine, John	Tarves, Aberdeen	100	16 10
Irvine, John Wiseman	Upper Garson, Sandwick	90	45 15
Irvine, Peter	Bristol, Sandwick	8	5 5
Irvine, Peter	Brockan, Stromness	10	8 12
Irvine, Peter	Lee, Stromness	53	25 —
Irvine, Robert Graham Watt	Kirkwall	40	12 —
Irvine, Thomas	Sandside, Deerness	14	6 —
Irvine, Representatives of Mrs. Margaret	Hall of Ireland, Stenness	56	33 —
Irvine, Jane, Christina, and Janet	Lower Cottiscarth, Rendall	71	13 12
Isbister, Andrew	Skelday, Birsay	40	14 —
Isbister, David	Upper Onston, Stenness	22	12 10
Isbister, James, and others	Fiold, Firth	6	3 —
Isbister, James	Hybreck, Harray	17	9 —
Isbister, James	Lyde, Firth	3	2 —
Isbister, James Laughton	Upper Scapa, St. Ola	67	53 —

ORKNEY—*continued.*

Name of Owner.	Address of Owner.	Estimated Acreage of Property.	Gross Annual Value.	Name of Owner.	Address of Owner.	Estimated Acreage of Property.	Gross Annual Value.
		Acres.	£ s.			Acres.	£ s.
Isbister, John	Quina, Stenness	12	6 5	Leask, John, and another	Resabreck, Stromness	28	9 10
Isbister, Malcolm	Buckquoy, Harray	28	12 15	Leask, Robert, sen., and Thomas Leask, junior	Agloth, Stenness	37	15 —
Isbister, Thomas	Bluebraes, Firth	13	2 —	Leask, Robert, junior	Coldamo, Stenness	96	32 —
Isbister, Thomas, and others	Garth, Stromness	45	14 —	Leask, William, junior	Agloth, Stenness	29	12 —
Isbister, William	Drydale, Stromness	35	12 —	Leask, Mrs. Barbara	Knockhall, Stromness	49	33 2
Isbister, William	Ingsay, Birsay	256	36 14	Leask, Mrs. Catherine, wife of William Leask	Tormiston, Stenness	32	8 —
Isbister, William	Moan, Harray	15	5 10				
Isbister, William	Nether Lettaly, Firth	2	1 10	Leask, Mrs. Hannah, wife of John Leask	Langalour, Firth	11	4 —
Isbister, William	North House, Harray	15	6 15				
Isbister, William	Upper Bigswell, Stenness	70	36 10	Leith, Benjamin	Burnside, Stromness	8	2 —
Isbister, William	Windywalls, Harray	50	10 10	Leith, Charles	Clouston, Stenness	20	10 —
Isbister, Mrs. Margaret	Nether Geoth, Harray	14	3 15	Leith, Peter	Appiehouse, Stenness	24	12 —
Isbister, Jean, and two others	Queenafineth, Harray	22	9 —	Leith, Thomas	Warthill, Stenness	30	— 10
				Leith, William	Huquoy, Stromness	35	6 —
Iverach, John Guthrie	Kirkwall	121	66 7	Leith, William	Nether Onston, Stenness	35	14 10
Iverach, Mrs. Elizabeth, wife of William Iverach; and Margaret Guthrie	Wideford, St. Ola	579	130 —	Leith, Mrs. Margaret	Stromness	47	12 —
				Leith, Margaret	Grevious, Stenness	12	5 —
				Leonard, John	Housegarth, Sandwick	10	5 15
				Leonard, Mrs. Peter	Comely Bank, Harray	3	4 —
Jack, Rev. David Rait	Manse, Holm	12	22 —	Leslie, Rev. Alexander	Manse, Evie	280	96 17
Johnston, Rev. David	Manse, Harray	216	85 8	Leslie, Robert	Stromness	223	16 10
Johnston, George, and another	Grew, Birsay	36	18 —	Leslie, Thomas	Lesliedale, St. Ola	90	30 —
				Leslie, Thomas	Nearhouse, Lady, Sanday	1	4 5
Johnston, James, of Coubister	Gear House, Orphir	1,280	430 8	Leslie, William	Nearhouse, Lady, Sanday	8	8 8
Johnston, John	Brittavale, Harray	32	12 19	Linklater, Andrew, and another	Quoyscottie, Birsay	15	6 —
Johnston, John	Bannockburn, Stirling	434	86 3	Linklater, David	Aith, Sandwick	34	14 —
Johnston, John G.	Upper Vetquoy, Sandwick	56	25 1	Linklater, George	Flanders, Sandwick	10	2 —
Johnston, John Malcolm	Haugh Head, St. Ola	20	4 4	Linklater, James	Appiehouse, Sandwick	18	7 —
Johnston, Joseph	Nisthouse, Stenness	14	5 15	Linklater, James	Nisthouse, Stenness	34	12 —
Johnston, Magnus	Quoykea, Harray	19	6 10	Linklater, John	Cruan, Firth	30	11 15
Johnston, Peter	Bigging, Birsay	15	7 10	Linklater, John	Housegarth, Sandwick	38	21 10
Johnston, Robert	Congar, Harray	15	4 15	Linklater, John, senior	Nistaben, Stenness	22	11 5
Johnston, Thomas	Overkelday, Harray	15	5 15	Linklater, John	Nisthouse, Stenness	34	12 10
Johnston, William	Haugh Head, St. Ola	20	4 4	Linklater, John	Warth, Sandwick	68	55 —
Johnston, Mrs. Catherine, wife of John Johnston	Houseby, Birsay	35	14 —	Linklater, John	Westhouse, Sandwick	22	10 10
				Linklater, Magnus	Quoy of Hill, Harray	3	2 7
Johnston, Mrs. Janet	Midhouse, Birsay	20	7 10	Linklater, Peter	Flanders, Sandwick	37	2 —
Johnston, Barbara	Bigging, Birsay	3	1 5	Linklater, Thomas	Midbigging, Firth	25	12 5
				Linklater, William	Arion, Stromness	5	2 —
				Linklater, William	Hallbreck, Sandwick	10	4 12
Kay, Rev. Thomas	Manse, North Ronaldshay	5	14 —	Linklater, William	Lyde, Firth	3	2 —
Keillor, Rev. John	Manse, Walls	42	32 10	Linklater, Mrs. Isabella	Hyval, Stenness	8	4 —
Kirkness, Adam	Newhouse, Harray	16	2 10	Linklater, Mrs. Mary, wife of Ebenezer Linklater; and two others	Howaback, Birsay	2	1 10
Kirkness, Adam	Up. Appiehouse, Sandwick	12	5 5				
Kirkness, James	Dillo, Harray	7	2 —				
Kirkness, James	Ezgar, Birsay	15	3 10	Linklater, Andrina, and another	Peace, Sandwick	15	5 5
Kirkness, James	Liverpool	85	45 —				
Kirkness, James	Noltland, Deerness	12	4 4	Linklater, Ann	Quoy of Hill, Harray	22	5 —
Kirkness, Magnus	Cuppin, Harray	3	1 —	Logie, George	Sunnybank, St. Ola	60	30 —
Kirkness, Magnus	Geelong, Australia	18	9 —	Logie, James S. Spence	Kirkwall	4	49 —
Kirkness, Magnus	Moan, Harray	14	5 5	Logie, Trustees of late Rev. William	Kirkwall	840	293 15
Kirkness, Mrs. Ann	Nether Corston, Harray	15	6 5				
Kirkness, Mrs. Margaret	Upper Appietown, Harray	9	4 6	Logie, Helen Elizabeth	Daisy Bank, Kirkwall	4	27 —
Kirkness, Mrs. Thomas	Linklater, Sandwick	11	1 10	Louttit, James	Herston, So. Ronaldshay	4	9 10
Kirkwall Harbour, Trustees of	Kirkwall	3	719 11	Louttit, James	Netherbigging, Rendall	45	11 —
				Louttit, James, senior	Stonepark, South Ronaldshay	9	7 —
Kirkwall, Magistrates and Town Council of	Kirkwall	410	11 5	Louttit, Magnus	Overhouse, Harray	21	7 —
				Louttit, Mrs. Jacobina	Lyron, Rendall	10	3 5
				Lyon, Magnus	Stromness	4	15 10
Lady, Free Church Congregation of	Lady, Sanday	5	15 10				
Laing, Captain Malcolm A.	H.M. 14th Hussars	92	12 —	M'Beath, Andrew	St. Mary's Holm	30	1 10
Laing, Samuel, of Crook, M.P.	1 Eastern Ter., Brighton	944	282 15	M'Beath, Mrs. Isabella	Kirkwall	7	95 16
Laird, Gilbert	St. Margaret's Hope	6	27 —	M'Culloch, Mrs. Elizabeth Ballingall	49 Duke Street, Glasgow	15	10 —
Lamont, Donald	Bendigo, St. Ola	112	25 —	M'Donald, Mrs. Margaret Ann Watt, wife of Donald M'Donald	Appiehouse, Harray	10	1 10
Langskaill, William, jun.	Cuppadee, Sandwick	28	4 —				
Laughton, John	St. Margaret's Hope	81	91 7				
Laughton, John	Valdigar, Holm	134	32 —	M'Kay, William	Nether Ellibister, Rendall	120	25 —
Laughton, William	Grimness, So. Ronaldshay	13	2 10	M'Kay, William	Newhouse, Sandwick	10	2 —
Laughton, Mrs. Jane C.	Fea, Holm	45	13 10	M'Kay, Mrs. Elizabeth	Snucksbrae, Westray	14	4 —
Learmonth, Mrs. Margaret	6 St. Vincent Street, Edinburgh	5	37 7	M'Kenzie, Alexander	Lynnside, St. Ola	19	18 —
Leask, Henry	Boardhouse, Birsay	218	126 —	Malcolmson, Heirs of Margaret	Hilters, Walls	2	1 10
Leask, James, senior	Knockhall, Stenness	12	5 15	Manson, James	Stripol, Harray	5	1 8
Leask, James	Westbank, St. Ola	65	30 —	Manson, John	Appietown, Harray	24	7 10
Leask, John	Niglay, Evie	228	88 5	Manson, Thomas	Australia	4	1 5

U

ORKNEY—continued.

Name of Owner.	Address of Owner.	Estimated Acreage of Property.	Gross Annual Value.
		Acres.	£ s.
Marwick, James	Appiehouse, Sandwick	37	19 16
Marwick, James	Up. Cottiscarth, Rendall	154	21 10
Marwick, Ann	Sandyhall, Rendall	10	2 10
Meil, Thomas	Garson, Sandwick	5	– 10
Merriman, James	Doehouse, Sandwick	9	5 –
Merriman, John	Quarrybank, Stromness	9	5 10
Merriman, John	Rosebank, Birsay	5	– 10
Merriman, Magnus	Somear, Sandwick	15	7 10
Merriman, Thomas	Appiehouse, Harray	9	3 –
Merriman, William	Overhouse, Harray	20	7 10
Merriman, Catherine and Margaret	Planegreen, Sandwick	2	1 6
Miller, James	Refuge, Harray	15	2 4
Miller, John	Nearhouse, Rendall	107	18 –
Miller, William Johnston	Stromness	346	87 –
Miller, Mrs. Ann, wife of James Miller	Aikerness, Evie	3	12 –
Mitchell, Edward	55 S. Clerk St., Edinburgh	110	112 15
Moar, George	Quean, Sandwick	18	7 –
Moar, Hugh	Bought, Rendall	20	5 10
Moar, John	Gyron, Sandwick	13	7 –
Moar, John	Riff, Rendall	25	6 10
Moar, William	Peace, Sandwick	34	14 18
Moar, Mrs. Isabella, wife of John Moar; and another	Holodyke, Harray	9	4 –
Moar, Mrs. Margaret	Horroquoy, Harray	15	10 –
Montgomery, Murdoch	Grimbister, Firth	144	16 10
Morrison, Archibald	Garth, Stromness	13	2 –
Mowat & Hay	Stromness	52	53 –
Mowat, John	South Ronaldshay	72	32 –
Mowat, Representatives of Joseph	Græmsay	3	12 –
Mowat, Nicol	Warth, Birsay	2	1 10
Mowat, Thomas	Langskaill, Birsay	7	4 –
Mowat, Thos. Robertson	58 St. Paul's Rd., Bow Common, London	9	8 –
Mowat, William	Deerness	5	2 10
Mowat, Mrs. Jacobina, wife of John Mowat	Bisgarth, Evie	49	14 –
Muir, Andrew	Craebreck, Holm	61	16 10
Muir, David	Rosebank, St. Ola	17	91 –
Muir, Mary	Innertown, Stromness	1	– 15
Munro, David, and another	Saverock, St. Ola	297	120 –
National Bank of Scotland	Edinburgh	1	71 –
Naughty, George	Summerdale, Stromness	25	2 10
Northern Lighthouses, Commissioners of	Edinburgh	24	156 –
North Ronaldshay, Free Church Congregation of	North Ronaldshay	2	8 10
Oman, Simon	Biggings, Stenness	107	62 10
Omond, James	Savedale, Stenness	32	13 1
Omond, Rev. John Reid	F.C. Manse, Monzie, Perth	150	45 –
Omond, Joseph	Upper Hobbister, Stenness	16	15 10
Omond, Robert	43 Charlotte Sq., Edinburgh	562	230 5
Omond, Mrs. Ann	Kirkwall	66	24 –
Omond, Mary	Cot-on-Hill, Stenness	2	1 10
Orkney, Commissioners of Supply of County of	Kirkwall	1	25 –
Paplay, James	Sandhurst, Stromness	25	4 –
Paplay, John and Allan	Garth, Stromness	45	12 10
Peace, Peter	Castlegreen, St. Ola	16	5 10
Petrie, Alexander	Tradespark, St. Ola	14	6 10
Petrie, David	Stonehall, Deerness	64	21 –
Philip, Thomas	Velzian, Birsay	22	11 4
Pollexfen, James Riddock, of Cairston	6 India St., Edinburgh	1,716	1,215 2
Pottinger, John	Quoylanks, Deerness	51	16 –
Rae, John	2 Addison Gardens, South Kensington, London	155	1 –
Rae, William	Kirkwall	50	13 10
Ranken, Mrs. Janet	Kirkwall	503	154 –
Rannie, Rev. Robert Robertson	Manse, Shapinshay	112	54 12
Reid, Samuel, of Braebister	Papdale House, Kirkwall	837	534 –
Reid, William	Heddle, Firth	45	7 –
Rendall, David	Upper Ellibister, Rendall	45	25 –
Rendall, George	Ness, Rendall	45	12 –
Rendall, William	Gorn, Rendall	20	7 5
Rendall, Mrs. Elizabeth, wife of James Rendall	Arwick, Evie	49	14 –
Rendall, Mrs. Margaret, wife of Adam Rendall	Bisgarth, Evie	49	14 –
Rendall, Mrs. Mary, wife of David Rendall	Midgarth, Rendall	229	54 –
Ridland, Thomas	Conziebreck, Sandwick	5	3 –
Ritch, Andrew	Greenyhall, Deerness	50	6 5
Ritch, Andrew	Upper Linnabreck, Birsay	14	7 –
Ritchie, Alexander	Westshore, Rendall	11	4 –
Ritchie, John	Westshore, Rendall	10	4 –
Robb, James	North America	27	21 –
Robb, Rev. William Donald	F.C. Manse, Deerness	8	10 5
Robertson, Alexander	The Holms, Stromness	65	34 –
Robertson, David	Stromness	24	13 5
Robertson, James and John Robertson	Australia Beaquoy, Harray	90	20 –
Robertson, James	Bigging, Harray	13	5 –
Robertson, James	Lower Lyking, Sandwick	90	49 12
Robertson, James	Quackquoy, Birsay	45	14 –
Robertson, James Spence	Stromness	10	24 –
Robertson, John	Braehead, Stromness	6	5 –
Robertson, John	Fea, Orphir	19	7 10
Robertson, John	Hilltown, Walls	20	2 –
Robertson, John	Tufta, Harray	45	9 3
Robertson, Joseph	Laith, Sandwick	40	21 –
Robertson, Robert	Fea, Orphir	19	7 10
Robertson, Mrs. Ann	Northend, Stromness	19	7 –
Robertson, Mrs. Margaret	Queena, Stenness	61	13 10
Robertson, Jean	Upper Lobady, Birsay	6	2 –
Robson, John	Birsay	6	2 –
Robson, Thomas	Marden, North Shields	12	7 –
Robson, Mrs. Helen, wife of John Robson	Gear, Orphir	9	5 10
Rosey, Alexander	Stromness	2	13 –
Ross, John	St. Margaret's Hope	4	8 5
Ross, William	Stromness	77	66 5
Rousay, United Presbyterian Congregation of	Rousay	1	8 10
Russell, Mrs. Ann, wife of Rev. Thomas Russell	Anerly Grove, Upper Norwood, London	8	20 5
Sabiston, Alexander	Easthouse, Sandwick	26	17 4
Sabiston, Peter	Midhouse, Sandwick	25	16 –
Scarth, James Cathie	Scar House, Sanday	15	18 10
Scarth, Robert, of Binscarth	Binscarth House, Firth	1,807	445 17
Scollay, Mrs. Annabella	Nethertown, Holm	52	42 10
Scott, James	Mithhouse, Harray	23	8 8
Scott, John	East Blett, Eday	8	6 15
Scott, Magnus	Fursebreck, Harray	22	9 –
Scott, Rev. Oliver	Manse, St. Andrews, Kirkwall	69	106 –
Scott, Robert	Wardhill, Stronsay	5	3 –
Scott, Thomas Douglas	Crantit, St. Ola	250	208 –
Scott, Thomas	Sunnybank, Harray	4	1 10
Scott, Mrs. Margaret, wife of Thomas Scott; and another	Fursebreck, Harray	22	6 10
Scott, Mrs. Marjory	Stromness	2	33 –
Seatter, John	Cufter, Evie	44	14 –
Seatter, William	Grittley, Deerness	64	24 –

ORKNEY—continued.

Name of Owner.	Address of Owner.	Estimated Acreage of Property.	Gross Annual Value.
		Acres.	£ s.
Sinclair, David	Stromness	5	62 5
Sinclair, George	Smerquoy, St. Ola	35	5 –
Sinclair, James	Boo of Rapness, Westray	6	1 7
Sinclair, James	Kirkwall	78	179 18
Sinclair, James	Newhouse, Rousay	35	20 –
Sinclair, James	Settiscarth, Firth	55	11 6
Sinclair, James	Upper Bigging, Harray	26	11 7
Sinclair, John	Houton, Orphir	30	5 –
Sinclair, John	Stenness	84	8 10
Sinclair, John	Trattleaquoy, Harray	35	15 10
Sinclair, John	Upper Bigging, Harray	24	10 9
Sinclair, John	Windwick, South Ronaldshay	4	3 –
Sinclair, Robert	Congar, Harray	15	4 10
Sinclair, Thomas	Barm, Firth	8	5 10
Sinclair, Thomas	Beboran, Harray	18	7 –
Sinclair, William	Ness, Sandwick	40	18 10
Sinclair, Mrs. Mary, wife of James Sinclair	Middle Lettaly, Firth	4	1 12
Sinclair, Mrs. Mary	Beboran, Harray	28	15 5
Sinclair, Jessie	Crya, Stromness	13	9 –
Sinclair, Marion	Hooveth, Sandwick	6	3 –
Sinclair, Mary	Burnside, Firth	6	1 5
Skea, Andrew & Robert	Aikerskaill, Deerness	220	140 –
Skea, John	Blubbersdale, Rendall	30	9 –
Skea, William	Daystar, Deerness	7	2 –
Slater, John Miller	Skelbister Cross, Sanday	50	16 –
Slater, Nicol, junior	Kebro, Orphir	24	16 –
Slater, Nicol, senior	Skaill, Orphir	31	32 10
Slater, Thomas	Nearhouse, Orphir	30	13 10
Slater, William	Crya, Orphir	25	12 –
Slater, Mrs. Amelia, wife of Alexander Slater	Liverpool	25	7 –
Smith, David	Quoyloo, Sandwick	10	4 12
Smith, Donald	Craigiefield, St. Ola	50	28 –
Smith, Rev. George	Manse, Westray	80	29 4
Smith, John	Blackbraes, Stenness	15	7 10
Smith, John	Common, Esco, Sandwick	5	1 5
Smith, John	Sandsquoy, St. Andrews, Kirkwall	13	4 10
Smith, John Westgarth, and another	Richmond, Yorkshire	7	21 11
Smith, Magnus	Downby, Sandwick	32	15 5
Smith, Simon, and another	Garth, Harray	19	7 12
Smith, William	Rosemount, Sandwick	3	1 8
Smith, William C.	Westray	2	6 10
Smith, Mrs. Elizabeth	Garth, Harray	36	13 2
Smith, Mrs. Wilhelmina	62 St. Paul's Road, Burdett Road, London	5	6 10
Spark, Rev. William	Springfield, St. Ola	71	98 8
Spence, Andrew	Breckan, Harray	33	12 10
Spence, Andrew	Folsetter, Birsay	40	20 –
Spence, James	Garth, Harray	15	6 –
Spence, Trs. of late James	Kirkwall	329	222 5
Spence, James	Queena, Birsay	10	10 –
Spence, James Bell	Marwick, Birsay	4	1 10
Spence, James	21 Steven Street, Glasgow	3	13 –
Spence, James, of Pow	Stromness	514	282 10
Spence, John	Eastabist, Birsay	35	15 –
Spence, John	Fea, Birsay	47	15 10
Spence, John	Miller House, Sandwick	3	1 5
Spence, John	Redbanks, St. Andrews, Kirkwall	3	16 –
Spence, John	Skethquoy, Sandwick	2	1 10
Spence, Joseph	Millhouse, Sabiston, Birsay	3	10 10
Spence, Magnus	Upper Bigging, Birsay	35	13 –
Spence, Peter	Gorn, Birsay	27	12 10
Spence, Thomas	Curcom, Birsay	30	15 –
Spence, Thomas	Farafield, Birsay	65	18 7
Spence, Thomas	Tufta, Birsay	43	15 –
Spence, William	Bigbreck, Birsay	36	12 –
Spence, William Johnston, and John Fraser	Hall of Rendall	110	94 10
Spence, Mrs. Ann	Cavan, Birsay	24	20 –
Spence, Mrs. Elizabeth, and two others	Stromness	77	15 –
Spence, Mrs. Margaret	Quina, Stenness	13	6 –
Spence, Catherine	Nether Hammer, Birsay	30	14 –
Stanger, James	Ritquoy, Birsay	14	5 5
Stanger, John, of Ness	Stromness	219	155 –
Stenness, Free Church Congregation of	Stenness	3	13 –
Stewart, Trustees of late James, of Brugh	Fribo House, Westray	6,243	1,446 14
Stewart, William	Kirkwall	300	71 –
Stewart, Maria Henrietta	14 Fettes Row, Edinburgh	640	202 –
Still, Charles Stewart, of Burgar	Smoogrow House, Orphir	3,450	856 3
Still, James	Sunnybrae, St. Ola	96	26 –
Stockan, Hugh	Stockan, Sandwick	32	10 –
Stockan, Mrs. Sibella, wife of Samuel Stockan	Scarataing, Sandwick	3	2 –
Stott, Rev. David	Manse, Deerness	4	10 –
Stout, Mrs. Gavin H.	Upperhouse, Feray, Flotta	30	16 –
Stove, Robert	North Windbreck, Deerness	12	5 –
Stromness, Free Church Congregation of	Stromness	2	18 –
Stromness, Magistrates and Town Council of	Stromness	8	7 7
Sutherland, John	Eday	6	4 –
Sutherland, William	Knockhall, South Ronaldshay	9	25 –
Swannay, John	Cot of Rosebank, Sandwick	10	2 10
Swannay, Thomas	Myres Lady, Sanday	4	5 –
Tait, Trustees of late John	Kirkwall	384	293 11
Tait, William	Westbanks, Holm	12	11 17
Taylor, Alexander	Stenisgarth, South Ronaldshay	17	6 –
Taylor, James	Leaquoy, Birsay	40	20 –
Taylor, James	Smoogarth, Firth	12	7 13
Taylor, John	Cumlaquoy, Birsay	11	3 10
Taylor, Peter	Cumlaquoy, Birsay	12	3 10
Taylor, Peter	Geoth, Harray	16	4 5
Taylor, William	New Zealand	59	18 –
Taylor, Mrs. Catherine	Cumlaquoy, Birsay	12	3 10
Taylor, Mrs. Catherine	Mucklewaird, Birsay	25	8 –
Thomson, Rev. David	Manse, Firth	157	84 5
Thomson, Donald	Quoys, So. Ronaldshay	40	14 10
Thomson, James	West Quoys, So. Ronaldshay	12	9 –
Thomson, John	Quindry, So. Ronaldshay	2	1 10
Thomson, Mrs. Elizabeth	Grimness, So. Ronaldshay	14	9 11
Thomson, Mrs. Susanna	Stromness	2	24 –
Thomson, Catherine B.	Banks, Herston, So. Ronaldshay	8	5 –
Tomison's Charity, Trustees for	St. Margaret's Hope	40	22 –
Towers, John	Grind, Voy, Sandwick	33	14 13
Towers, Robert	Warthill, Stromness	7	2 2
Towers, William	Oldhall, Stromness	30	10 –
Trail, Rev. Samuel	University of Aberdeen	500	151 –
Traill, George, younger of Holland	47 Bartholomew Road, Camden Road, London	47	13 5
Traill, Trustees of late George, of Ratter	Thurso	5,031	2,861 12
Traill, Thomas, of Holland	Kirkwall	5,780	1,629
Traill, Thomas, junior	47 Bartholomew Road, Camden Road, London	16	20 –
Traill, William, of Woodwick	St. Andrews, Fifeshire	2,939	917 17
Traill, Mrs. Mary	29 Warriston Crescent, Edinburgh	576	200 –
Tulloch, Andrew	Strathore, Shapinshay	40	10 –
Tulloch, William	Rosevale, Deerness	5	2 10
Twatt's Mortification, Trustees for	Orphir	2	2 –
Twatt, Mrs. Ann	Grind, Sandwick	30	10 10
Twatt, Mrs. Margaret	Appiehouse, Harray	4	1 –
Velzian, John	West Linklater, Sandwick	40	25 –
Velzian, John and Peter	West and Nether Linklater, Sandwick	35	21 5

ORKNEY—continued.

Name of Owner.	Address of Owner.	Estimated Acreage of Property.	Gross Annual Value.	Name of Owner.	Address of Owner.	Estimated Acreage of Property.	Gross Annual Value.
		Acres.	£ s.			Acres.	£ s.
Velzian, Peter	Nether Linklater, Sandwick	30	25 —	Wilson, William	Weardith, Stromness	10	4 5
Velzian, Mrs. Isabella, wife of John M. Velzian	Stromness	29	9 —	Wilson, Mrs. Elizabeth	Upper Fea, Birsay	30	11 —
Velzian, Mrs. Wilhelmina	Upper Lyking, Sandwick	91	47 10	Wingate, Rev. Thomas Daniel	Manse, Stromness	32	20 —
				Wishart, John	Westquoy, Orphir	27	13 10
Walls, John	Easter Greenigoe, Orphir	153	8 —	Wishart, John R.	Stromness	3	6 —
				Wishart, Peter	Howabreck, Sandwick	20	6 5
Walls, Thomas	Skedgabust, Cross, Sanday	6	4 10	Wishart, Robert	Brecks, Orphir	27	13 —
Wards, William	Goodwalter, Rendall	29	6 —	Wishart, William M.	Upperhouse, Sandwick	12	6 —
Wards, William	Hong-Kong, China	105	37 10	Wishart, Mrs. Catherine	Howaback, Sandwick	68	16 —
Wards, William	St. Margaret's Hope	4	12 15	Wood, John	Nether Inkster, Rendall	24	13 —
Wards, Mrs. Jean	Nether Letally, Firth	2	— 15	Wood, John	Park of Lyron, Rendall	30	10 10
Warren, Thomas	Kirkwall	45	63 —	Wood, Mrs. Isabella	Palace Street, Kirkwall	24	10 5
Warren, Mrs. Agnes	Kirkwall	12	119 10	Woods and Forests, Commissioners of H.M.	London	11	28 10
Watson, Rev. Robert	Manse, Hoy	18	20 —	Work, James	Africa	2	6 —
Watt, Heirs of John	Mayfield, Stromness	50	3 —	Work, William	Kirkwall	10	47 —
Watt, William Watt Graham, of Breckness	Kierfiold House, Sandwick	4,946	1,406 15	Wylie, Andrew	Leith	173	55 —
Do. do.	Do. (Quarry)	—	1 10	Wylie, John	Stromness	150	40 —
Watt, Margaret G., and two others	10 Pilrig Street, Edinburgh	270	123 —	Wylie, William	Stromness	1	14 15
Weir, Representatives of Mrs. Julia	Binscarth, Firth	40	14 —	Yorston, John	Orquil, Evie	72	46 12
				Yorston, John	Quoys, Evie	125	38 —
Wheatley, Representatives of Henry	Stromness	19	16 7	Yorston, Mrs. Catherine	Cuppin, Harray	36	20 4
White, Mrs. John	Stromness	1	6 —	Zetland, Earl of	19 Arlington St., London	29,846	5,617 17
White, Margaret and Grace	Ottergill, Stenness	20	8 —	Total Owners of Land of One Acre and upwards		762 220,725	56,728 7
Wick, David	Lydle, Deerness	7	1 10	Total Owners of Lands of less than One Acre in extent		546 148	5,808 6
Wilson, Andrew, and another	Gerwin, Orphir	17	12 —				
Wilson, James	Milldam, Stromness	15	3 15	GRAND TOTAL		1,308 220,873	62,536 13
Wilson, Magnus	Ouraquoy, Firth	22	5 15				

PEEBLES.

Population in 1871, 12,330.
Inhabited Houses, 2,187.
Number of Parishes, 15.

Name of Owner.	Address of Owner.	Estimated Acreage of Property.	Gross Annual Value.	Name of Owner.	Address of Owner.	Estimated Acreage of Property.	Gross Annual Value.
		Acres.	£ s.			Acres.	£ s.
Alexander, Mrs. Archibald	West Linton, Penicuik	1	155 –	Dalkeith, Earl of	Dalkeith Palace	24	46 –
Anderson, Benjamin T. G., of Tushielaw	Cacrabank, Selkirk	2,180	416 10	Dalziel, James	Walkerburn, Innerleithen	6	627 –
				Dick, Rev. John	Tweedsmuir, Biggar	12	44 12
Anderson, William, of Hallyards	Hallyards, Peebles	60	118 –	Dickson, Alexander, of Kilbucho and Hartree	Edinburgh	2,237	2,598 –
Armstrong, Rev. Mathew	Skirling, Biggar	31	76 10	Dickson, Archibald	11 Royal Circus, Edinburgh	15	31 –
				Dickson, James Jobson	20 Young Street, Edinburgh	2	18 –
Ballantyne Brothers	Waverley Mills, Innerleithen	7	519 –	Dobie, Mrs. Agnes	Campend, Dalkeith	215	240 –
				Dobson, J. & A.	Innerleithen	2	231 –
Ballantyne, David	Walkerburn, Innerleithen	2	80 –	Douglas, Alexander Sholto	15 Great King Street, Edinburgh	4	11 –
Ballantyne, David and John	Walkerburn, Innerleithen	8	1,082 –				
Ballantyne, George	The Kirna, Innerleithen	2	55 –	Duncan, William, of Caerlee	1 Heriot Row, Edinburgh	20	125 –
Ballantyne, Trustees of Henry	Walkerburn, Innerleithen	1	43 –	Dundas, Sir David, of Beechwood, Bart.	Beechwood House, Corstorphine	22	10 15
Ballantyne, Capt. James G., of Holylee	Holylee, Innerleithen	2,775	954 –				
Ballantyne, John	Walkerburn, Innerleithen	4	75 –				
Ballantyne, Mrs. Christina	West Linton, Penicuik	4	16 15	Eckford, Janet	Traquair Mill, Innerleithen	1	22 10
Barrett, Rev. Isaac	Skirling, Biggar	1	20 –	Elcho, Lord, M.P.	23 St. James's Place, London	10	17 –
Bell, George Graham, of Crurie	Castleo'er, Langholm	6,600	1,745 –	Elibank, Lord	Darnhall, Eddleston	2,660	2,297 –
Beresford, Mrs. Emily S. M., wife of Very Rev. John M. Massy Beresford	Lisnaskea, Ireland	3,875	2,899 –	Elliot, John Phillips, of Chapelhill	Cambridge House, Leytonstone, Essex	473	327 –
Do. do.	Do. (Mines)	–	180 –	Erskine, Christian, of Venlaw	Portobello	950	669 –
Black, William Connell, of Kailzie	Kailzie, Peebles	1,460	1,441 –				
Blackwood, William	Minden, Peebles	3	64 –				
Booth, Rev. John L.	Stobo	29	76 –	Fergusson, James Ranken, younger of Spittalhaugh	16 George St., Hanover Square, London	10	21 –
Brown, Curators of Horatio R. F., of Newhall	Newhall, Penicuik	1,763	832 10	Fergusson, Sir William, of Spittalhaugh, Bart.	16 George St., Hanover Square, London	1,512	1,784 16
Brown, Heirs of Thomas	Elibank Cottage, Galashiels	1	35 –	Forbes, William, of Medwyn	Medwyn, West Linton, Penicuik	2,600	2,022 –
Buccleuch and Queensberry, Duke of	Dalkeith Palace	248	272 15	Forrester, Rev. Alexander M.	West Linton, Penicuik	5	73 10
Buchan, John	Peebles	8	152 –	Forrester, Rev. Alexander M. and John Forrester	West Linton, Penicuik Edinburgh	237	274 10
Burnett, Arthur	Venlaw Bank, Peebles	9	68 –	Fotheringham, John	Wallacefield House, Biggar	525	141 10
Cairns, John	Winkston, Peebles	1	32 –	Free Church of Scotland, Trustees of	Edinburgh	3	20 10
Caledonian Railway Company	Glasgow (Railway)	132	14516 –				
Campbell, Rev. Colin A.	Lyne, Stobo	21	63 –				
Carmichael, Rev. Sir Wm. H. Gibson, of Durie and Skirling, Bart.	Castle Craig, Dolphinton	8,756	5,795 14	Gibson, James	Springhill, Peebles	3	103 –
Chambers, William, of Glenormiston	Glenormiston, Innerleithen	835	891 –	Gordon, Trustees of Mrs. Catherine	Edinburgh	4,827	2,049 –
Charteris, Lieut. Alfred Walter	23 St. James's Place, London	4	7 –	Graham, William	20 Dean Terrace, Edinburgh	3	40 –
Charteris, Col. The Hon. Richard	16 Grosvenor Square, London	10	17 –	Grieve, William	Branxholm Park, Hawick	22	10 –
Clapperton, Rev. James	Kirklands, Peebles	5	53 10				
Clerk, Sir George Douglas, of Penicuik, Bart.	Penicuik House, Penicuik	500	74 10	Hay, Sir Robert, of Smithfield and Haystoune, Bart.	Kingsmeadow, Peebles	9,155	4,408 13
Cosens, Rev. Alexander T.	Broughton, Biggar	24	70 –				
Covington Kirk-Session	Covington, Biggar	4	6 –	Hay, Sir Robert, of Smithfield and Haystoune, Bart.	Kingsmeadow, Peebles	24	71 –
Cowan, Charles, of Loganhouse	Westerlea, Edinburgh	1,250	294 –	William Ogilvie, of Chesters and William Rutherford	Chesters, Jedburgh Galashiels		
Cunningham, Richard D. B., of Lainshaw and Duchrae	Hensoe, Castle-Douglas	4,195	2,717 –				

PEEBLES—continued.

Name of Owner.	Address of Owner.	Estimated Acreage of Property.	Gross Annual Value.	Name of Owner.	Address of Owner.	Estimated Acreage of Property.	Gross Annual Value.
		Acres.	£ s.			Acres.	£ s.
Henderson, James	Whinnyknowe, Peebles	9	15 –	Newlands Parish, Heritors of	Newlands, Noblehouse	1	8 –
Hicks, Rev. James	West Linton, Penicuik	1	20 –	Nichol, Heirs of Anthony	Marl Hill, Isle of Wight	2,602	486 –
Hope, George, of Bordlands	Bordlands, Noblehouse	2,679	956 10	Noble, Rev. Andrew	Loudoun, Kilmarnock	1	15 –
Hope, Hugh	London	24	11 –	North British Railway Co.	Edinburgh (Railway)	151	10348 –
Hope, James, and James Hope, junior	Kilbucho Old Manse, Biggar } Lamington, Biggar	11	32 –	North Esk Reservoir Co.	Edinburgh	25	250 –
Hope, John	Traquair House, Innerleithen	1	40 –	Peebles, Burgh of	Peebles	22	171 10
Horsburgh, Alexander, of Horsburgh	The Pirn, Innerleithen	4,700	1,857 12	Peebles, Commissioners of Burgh of	Peebles	1	243 –
Horsburgh, Mrs. Helen	The Pirn, Innerleithen	12	84 –	Peeblesshire Poorhouse Commissioners	Peebles	2	40 –
Hunter, Mrs. John	Kingsmuir Cottage, Peebles	1	50 –	Peebles Parish, Heritors of	Peebles	1	10 –
				Plenderleith, Mrs. Isabella	Venlawfoot, Peebles	1	27 –
				Purves, James, and Spouse	Musselburgh	4	39 10
Inch, John	Liberton West Mains, Edinburgh	1,150	414 –	Ramsay, R. B. Wardlaw, of Whitehill	Whitehill, Lasswade	22	10 4
Innerleithen Parish, Heritors of	Innerleithen	1	8 –	Ranken, Thomas	Edinburgh	22	10 11
				Richard, Walter	Kingsmuir, Peebles	3	109 10
Keddie, John	Kingsmuir, Peebles	1	80 10	Roberts, George	Earlston	5	259 –
Kelly, Rev. William	Newlands, Noblehouse	24	52 –	Robertson, Charles	Edinburgh	24	11 5
Kennedy, Major George, of Romanno	Romanno, Noblehouse	595	697 –	Romanes, Robert, of Craigerne	Craigerne, Peebles	27	115 –
Kidd, David, of Woodhouse	Glenternie, Manor, Peebles	782	683 –	Roy, James	Kingsmuir, Peebles	1	40 –
Laidlaw, Thomas	Bonnington Bank, Leith	1	105 –	Scott, Lord Henry John Montagu Douglas, M.P.	Palace House, Beaulieu, Southampton	24	45 –
Leckie, William	11 Carlton Terrace, Edinburgh	6	32 –	Scott, Trustees of Peter	Edinburgh	1,246	1,021 12
Linton Parish, Heritors of	West Linton, Penicuik	1	8 –	Scott, William	Ladhope, Selkirk	1,239	300 –
Lorraine, Rev. John Bell	Peebles	7	67 10	Scott, William	Tweedbank, Melrose	3	201 15
				Smith, David	Edinburgh	22	10 11
				Smythe, William, of Methven	Methven Castle, Perth	24	11 5
Macadam, Stevenson	Portobello	4	50 –	Somerville, Trs. of John; and James Ritchie	Forresthill, Eddleston } Edinburgh	150	90 –
M'Douall, James, of Logan	Logan House, Stranraer	2,900	850 –	Spalding, James	Peebles	8	64 –
M'Gildowny, Romaldo K., of Rozetta	Rozetta, Peebles	70	197 –	Spalding, Trs. of Thomas	Peebles	2	43 –
				Stewart, Duncan F.	Edinburgh	3	73 –
M'Kenzie, Colin James, of Portmore	Portmore, Eddleston	9,403	4,282 –	Stodart, Thomas Tweedie, of Oliver	Oliver, Crook, Biggar	1,144	260 –
M'Kenzie, John Ord, of Dolphinton	Dolphinton House	210	182 –	Stodart, Trs. of Isabella	Peebles	2	16 10
M'Kenzie, Walter H.	Edinburgh	8	6 6	Strain, Right Rev. John	Edinburgh	1	8 –
Mackintosh, James, of La Mancha	La Mancha, Leadburn	953	935 –	Swinton, Mrs. Frances J.	Swinton Bank, Peebles	73	175 –
Macqueen, Arthur James, of Braxfield	Hardington House, Biggar	4,093	2,016 8	Tait, James	Moffat	9	17 –
M'Vicar, Rev. Peter	Manor, Peebles	24	60 –	Tennent, Charles, of The Glen	The Glen, Traquair, Innerleithen	3,500	897 –
Marshall, Archibald	41 Minto Street, Edinburgh	24	164 –	Thorburn, Robert, of Winkston	Viewfield, Lasswade	344	358 –
Meiklem, Rev. Robert	Drumelzier, Biggar	12	37 15	Thorburn, Robert	Peebles	4	76 –
Miller, John, of Leithen, M.P.	2 Melville Crescent, Edinburgh	13,000	2,782 –	Tod, Alexander	St. Mary's Mount, Peebles	5	91 –
Miller, John	West Linton, Penicuik	6	23 –	Traquair, Trs. of Earl of	Edinburgh	10,778	4,846 –
Milne, Rev. John	Kirkurd, Noblehouse	23	50 –	Tweedale, William	Howison Hall, Penicuik	33	69 –
Mitchell, Houston, of Polmood	Bangholm Bower, Trinity Road, Edinburgh	1,609	415 –	Tweedie, James, of Quarter	Rachan House, Biggar	11,151	4,059 5
Mitchell, James	Peebles	1	28 10	Tweedie, Mrs. Benjamina	Merlindale, Biggar	2	40 –
Montgomery, Sir Graham G., of Stanhope, Bart., M.P.	Stobo Castle, Stobo	18,172	6,945 –	Veitch, John	Loanside Lodge, Peebles	18	99 –
Montgomery, John B. H., of Newton	Stobo Castle, Stobo	10	15 –				
Mure, David (Lord Mure)	Edinburgh	25	11 5				
Murray, Rev. Alexander J.	Eddleston	34	75 –	Walker, Gill, & Company	Innerleithen	4	350 13
Murray, James, of Callands	Callands, Noblehouse	389	317 10	Walker, John	Edinburgh	22	10 11
Murray, James, yr. of Callands and John M. Murray	Callands, Noblehouse } London	14	23 –	Walker, William S., of Bowland	Edinburgh	24	11 5
				Wallace, Rev. Jardine	Manse, Traquair, Innerleithen	13	50 –
Murray, James Wolfe, of Cringletie	Cringletie, Eddleston	5,108	2,647 –	Watkins, Lieut. Frederick W., of Medwynhead	Royal Engineers, Gibraltar	1,070	84 –
				Webster, Andrew, of Rutherford Castle	Rutherford Castle, West Linton, Penicuik	492	532 –
Nasmyth, Sir John Murray, of Posso, Bart.	Dalwick House, Stobo	15,485	3,557 8	Weir, Rev. John	Crossford, Lanark	165	228 –

PEEBLES—continued.

Name of Owner.	Address of Owner.	Estimated Acreage of Property.	Gross Annual Value.	Name of Owner.	Address of Owner.	Estimated Acreage of Property.	Gross Annual Value.
		Acres.	£ s.			Acres.	£ s.
Welsh, Thomas, of Earlshaugh	Ericstane, Moffat	2,800	381 10	Woddrop, William Allan, of Garvald	Garvald House, Dolphinton	2,225	760 –
Welsh, Rev. William, of Mossfennan	Mossfennan, Rachan Mill	1,509	634 –	Wyer, Rev. Thomas R.	Summerfield, Peebles	1	45 –
Wemyss and March, Earl of	Gosford House, Longniddry	41,247	14315 16	Total Owners of Land of One Acre and upwards		176	232,302	131,732 15
White, John, of Drumelzier and Netherurd	Netherurd House, Dolphinton	6,366	2,223 9	Total Owners of Lands of less than One Acre in extent		532	108	10,881 5
Wilkie, George	Peebles	1	163 10				
Williamson, Rev. Alexander	Innerleithen	9	57 –				
Williamson, James Montgomery, of Cardrona	Cardrona, Peebles	1,681	1,464 9	GRAND TOTAL		708	232,410	142,614 –
Wilson, Charles	Earlston	2	226 –				

PERTH.

Population in 1871, - - - - - - - 127,768.
Inhabited Houses, - - - - - - 22,134.
Number of Parishes, - - - - - - 78.

Name of Owner.	Address of Owner.	Estimated Acreage of Property.	Gross Annual Value.	Name of Owner.	Address of Owner.	Estimated Acreage of Property.	Gross Annual Value.
		Acres.	£ s.			Acres.	£ s.
Abercromby, Lord	Airthrie Castle, Stirling	10,407	6,007 2	Ballingall, George, of Parkfield	Rewcastle, Jedburgh	230	286 —
Abernethy, Deacons' Court of Free Church of	Abernethy, Newburgh	1	19 5	Ballingall, Mrs. Agnes J., of Altamont	Altamont, Blairgowrie	20	116 —
Abernethy, Kirk-Session of	Abernethy, Newburgh	15	55 5	Balmain, James Forrest, of Ibert of Dalvreck	Manchester	38	95 —
Abernethy, United Presbyterian Congregation of	Abernethy, Newburgh	6	43 —	Balvaird, Trustees of late Col. William, of West Mains of Huntingtower, C.B.	Huntingtower, Perth	52	171 10
Abernyte, Trs. of Free Church Congregation of	Abernyte, Inchture	1	12 —				
Adam, John, of Fala	Larch Grove, Glasgow	58	230 —				
Adams, W. & J.	Callander	4	24 —	Bannerman, Rev. David Douglas, of Abernyte	Dalkeith	250	415 8
Adamson, John	Blairgowrie	1	60 —				
Adie, Rev. Chas. Smith	Tibbermore	12	45 —	Barbour, George F., of Bonskeid	Edinburgh	2,700	1,086 —
Ainslie, Daniel, of The Gart	The Gart, Callander	180	212 —				
Ainslie, John Astley, of Tichardie	Huntington House, Haddington	700	75 —	Barclay, Heirs of Arthur Hay, of Paris	Paris House, Milnathort	1,000	550 —
Airlie, Earl of	Cortachy Castle, Kirriemuir	4,647	6,218 6	Barr, Mrs. Catherine D.	Coupar-Angus	1	12 —
Aitken, John	Methven	3	6 —	Barty, Rev. James S.	Bendochy, Coupar-Angus	7	40 —
Allan, Henry Howard, of Inchmartine	Inchmartine, Inchture	2,855	5,118 10	Barty, James Webster, of Glenacres	Glenacres, Dunblane	4	50 —
Alexander, Trustees of Ebenezer, of Park	Park, Logie, Stirling	21	45 —	Barty, Trustees of Thomas, of Midborland	Midborland, Port of Monteith	86	144 —
Alexander, William, of Longkerse	Longkerse, Logie, Stirling	18	31 10	Baxter, Alexander	Methven	3	15 6
				Baxter, Campbell, of Milton	Ashbank, Blairgowrie	65	150 —
Alyth, Parochial Board of	Alyth	5	75 —	Baxter, James	Little Dunkeld	1	6 —
Anderson, Arthur	Pitlochry	1	40 —	Baxter, John, of Ashgrove	Ashgrove, Blairgowrie	23	288 10
Anderson, David, of St. Fink	Blairgowrie	510	485 —	Baxter, Robert, of Ashbank	America	7	174 —
				Bell, Rev. Herbert	Persie Manse, Blairgowrie	17	28 —
Anderson, David, of Lambhill and Pitfar	Isla Cottage, Coupar-Angus	560	577 10	Bennett, Robert	Blairlogie, Stirling	7	52 19
Do. do.	Do. (Minerals)	—	50 —	Benvie, Rev. Andrew	Scone Manse, Perth	36	70 —
Anderson, Donald	Crieff	1	47 —	Berney, Edmund B., of Carnbostewart	Portobello	315	165 —
Anderson, Rev. James	Manse, Forteviot	7	43 —	Beveridge, Janet, of Easterton	The Elms, Kinross	312	300 —
Anderson, James	St. Fink, Blairgowrie	4	25 —				
Anderson, Trustees of James, of Bleaton	Bleaton, Hallet, Blairgowrie	847	547 10	Bird, John, of Craighead	Craighead, Blair-Drummond, Stirling	147	277 —
Anderson, Rev. John	Manse, Kinnoull	7	65 —	Birrell, Henry, of Rosebank	Gasconhall, Errol	3	24 —
Anderson, Trs. of John	Blairgowrie	3	180 10	Blair, Andrew	Blairgowrie	1	10 —
Anderson, Rev. John A.	F.C. Manse, Doune	2	35 —	Blair, James, of Carsegrange	Carsegrange, Errol	29	120 18
Anderson, Wm., in right of his wife, Maria Eliza Anderson, of Glentarkie	2 Strathearn Road, Edinburgh	517	152 4	Blair, Rev. William	U.P. Manse, Dunblane	1	40 —
				Blair, Christina and Janet	Gartmore, Port of Monteith	3	10 —
Archer, Trs. of Andrew, of Easter Balbrogie	Coupar-Angus	56	110 —	Blairgowrie, Parochial Board of	Blairgowrie	10	5 —
Arnot, James	Abernethy	5	21 19	Bleloch, David	Charlestown, Dunfermline	1	27 —
Arnott, Robert, of Auchengownie	Hatchbank, Kinross	320	140 —				
Armstrong, Mrs. Janet	Arnprior, Kippen	1	3 16	Blyth, John, of Ruthven	Reedieleys, Auchtermuchty	148	320 8
Athole, Duke of	Blair Castle, Blair-Athole	194,640	40758 3	Bogie, George, of Heatherieleys	Gairneybridge, Kinross	303	144 12
Do. (Minerals)	Do.	—	30 —	Bonallo, Rev. David	Manse, Blackford	30	50 —
Athole, Duke of and James Patrick M'Inroy, of Lude	Blair Castle, Blair-Athole Lude House, Blair-Athole	675	100 —	Bontine, Wm. Cunningham Graham, of Gartmore	Gartmore House, Stirling	2,009	1,498 16
				Borrie, David	Rattray, Blairgowrie	2	127 16
Auchterarder, Muir Commissioners of	Auchterarder	233	231 9	Borrie, John	Carnoustie	3	20 —
Auchtergaven, Kirk-Session of	Auchtergaven	21	52 —	Bow, Trustees of Ebenezer, of Wright's Park	Wright's Park, Kippen	229	93 10
Ayton, Ann Rutherford, of Ashintully	Ashintully Castle, Blairgowrie	3,681	1,280 14	Boyd, John	Claremont House, Dunblane	1	40 —
				Boyd, Helen Reid	Allanbank, Dunblane	1	30 5
				Breadalbane, Earl of	Taymouth Castle, Aberfeldy	193,504	28765 13
Baird, Alexander, of Ury	Ury House, Stonehaven	206	378 —				
Balbeggie United Presbyterian Congregation	Balbeggie, Perth	1	16 —	Breadalbane, Trustees of First Marquess of	Taymouth Castle	40,662	7,212 8

PERTH—continued.

Name of Owner.	Address of Owner.	Estimated Acreage of Property.	Gross Annual Value.	Name of Owner.	Address of Owner.	Estimated Acreage of Property.	Gross Annual Value.
		Acres.	£ s.			Acres.	£ s.
Bridge of Earn Free Church, Deacons' Court of	Bridge of Earn	1	32 10	Campbell, John, of Inverardoch	Inverardoch Ho., Doune	518	839 8
Brodie, David	Birnam, Dunkeld	1	60 —	Campbell, John, of Croft of Cultalonie	Croft of Cultalonie, Kirkmichael	84	35 —
Brodie, Trustees of late James, of Polder	Thornhill, Stirling	250	285 —	Campbell, John Livingston, of Achalader	Achalader, Blairgowrie	4,150	2,912 11
Brown, Allan M'Laren, of Marlee	Blairgowrie	952	1,520 4	Campbell, Rev. John R.	Monzievaird, Crieff	12	40 —
Brown David	Cherrybank, Perth	4	32 —	Campbell, Mrs. Bowie S., of Cloichfoldich	Cloichfoldich House, Ballinluig	559	452 4
Brown, Heirs of James, of Croftlands	Croftlands, Abernethy	9	47 —	Campbell, Mrs. Isabella Margaret, and Jane M'Glashan Campbell, of Eastertyre	Eastertyre, Ballinluig	250	134 10
Brown, James	Burgh Acres, Abernethy	20	60 9				
Brown, Trustees of late James, of Lochton	Lochton House, Inchture	1,100	1,122 —				
Brown, Rev. John	Muir of Thorn, Kinclaven	4	15 —	Campbell, Christian, of Eastershian	Eastershian, Amulree	8,598	489 —
Brown, John Harvie, of Shirgarton and Quarter	Dunipace House, Falkirk	190	303 5	Campbell, Janet, and Jane Thomas	Garry, Auchtergaven, Bankfoot	1	6 —
Brown, Peter	Dialfield, Abernethy	2	37 12	Camperdown, Earl of	Gleneagles House, Auchterarder	7,122	3,479 2
Brown, Rev. Thomas	Collace	8	42 15				
Brown, William	Comrie	6	14 12	Carden, Sir John C., of Templemore, Bart.	Torwood, Birnam	16	100 —
Brown, William	Crieff	1	50 —				
Bruce, Andrew	Alyth	1	4 —	Carnegie, Representatives of late John	Manchester	3	5 —
Bruce, David	Bella Vista, Scone	9	89 —	Carmichael, Andrew	Comrie	4	19 15
Bruce, Hugh and George Stirling Home Drummond, of Blair-Drummond	Freeland House, Perth } Blair-Drummond Ho., Stirling	3	25 —	Carmichael, Peter, of Arthurstone	Arthurstone, Coupar-Angus	394	798 8
				Carnegie, David, of Stronvar	Stronvar House, Lochearnhead	22,205	3,558 10
Bruce, Colonel Robert, of Glendeuglie	Glendeuglie, Milnathort	110	197 10	Cathcart, Robert, of Pitcairlie	Pitcairlie, Auchtermuchty	437	354 —
Bruce, William	St. Leonard's Bank, Perth	4	92 —	Caw, James	Milton, Auchterarder	5	45 —
Bruce, William and Andrew, of Flatfield	Flatfield, Errol	69	136 10	Caw, Robert	Methven	2	12 —
				Caw, William	Crieff	12	51 —
Brugh, John Barnet	32 Faulkner Street, Manchester	4	28 15	Chalmers, Trs. of Robert, of Netherton	Blairgowrie	275	214 10
Brugh, Peter	Paisley	2	24 —	Chalmers, Mrs. Jane	Wester Caputh, Dunkeld	20	78 10
Bryce, Robert, of Gallowflat	Saltcoats, Ayrshire	100	218 8	Chapman, John B.	Rattray	3	163 15
Buchan, Trs. of late David	Crieff	1	13 —	Chapman, Robert and John B., of Aitkenhead	Blairgowrie	219	283 14
Buchanan, John	Cauldhame, Kippen	1	1 10				
Buchanan, Mrs. Catherine	Shirgarton, Kippen	1	7 15	Chapman, William, of Lickerstone	Ballomill, Abernethy	2	7 —
Bullions, Robert	Glenfoot, Abernethy	2	10 —				
Burleigh, Lord	Kennet House, Alloa	1,393	766 3	Christie, John, of Cowden	Cowden Castle, Muckhart, Dollar	1,672	1,624 16
Burden, George Spankie Mitchell, of Feddal	Feddal House, Braco	1,835	869 17	Christie, Mrs. Lily	Abbey, Auchterarder	9	64 —
Burt, Arthur, of Deuglie	Deuglie, Milnathort	568	635 13	Clark, Arthur	Blairgowrie	2	40 —
Burt, John	Deuglie Cot., Milnathort	14	20 —	Clark, David	Rattray	5	80 —
Butter, Archibald, of Faskally	Faskally, Pitlochry	17,586	5,670 3	Clark, Robert	Taybank House, Errol	6	70 —
Butter, Trustees of John, of Ardlebank	Blairgowrie	70	148 —	Clark, Captain William, of Princelands	Princelands House, Coupar-Angus	75	287 3
Butter, Robert	Perth	4	15 8	Clark, Rev. William Atkinson, of Bohally	Bohally, Pitlochry	1,800	404 12
Butter, William, of Ballintuim	Ballintuim, Blairgowrie	157	68 —	Clark, William	Rattray	1	26 10
				Clark, Mrs. Susannah, of Heath Park	Heath Park, Blairgowrie	13	70 10
Caird, Edward, of Cromwell Park	Finnart, Garelochhead, Dumbarton	21	380 —	Clinton, Lord	Invermay House, Bridge of Earn	1,198	1,016 6
Cairns, Mrs. Christina, of Lategreen	Bertha Park, Perth	350	75 —	Clunie, James	Abernethy	5	34 5
Caledonian Railway Co.	Glasgow	25	195 5	Clyde, David	Rattray	4	24 10
Do. do.	(Railway)	920	100970 —	Clyde, James	New Rattray	9	17 —
Callander, Free Church Congregation of	Callander	1	50 —	Cochrane, William	Stirling	2	40 —
Callander and Oban Railway Company	Glasgow (Railway)	140	1,579 —	Coffin, Very Rev. Robert A., and others	St. Mary's, Kinnoull, Perth	18	400 —
Cameron, Ewen	Mansfield, Callander	2	140 —	Colquhoun, W. Campbell, of Clathick	Clathick, Monzievaird	1,017	666 —
Campbell, Colin John and Wellesley Campbell, of Conninish	} India	5,000	314 —	Colvill, Thomas, of Barnhill	Downduff, Dunfermline	121	90 —
				Combe, Thomas	Abernethy	1	8 —
Campbell, Rev. David	Fortingall	15	39 —	*Commercial Bank of Scotland*	Edinburgh	3	258 19
Campbell, Rev. Duncan	Moulin, Pitlochry	4	32 —	*Commissioners of Supply for Perthshire*	(Police Stations, &c.)	1	50 —
Campbell, Francis W. Garden, of Troup	Glenlyon House, Aberfeldy	10,516	1,620 14	Comrie, Robert	Cauldhame, Blackford	1	6 —
				Comrie, Mrs. Eliza Sim	Portobello	16	14 —
Campbell, Henry Fletcher, of Boquhan	Boquhan, Kippen	5	97 15	Condie, Trustees of Laura	Perth	450	206 10
Campbell, Major Henry George Lyon, of Wiliamston	H.M. 74th Regiment, Malta	417	835 4	Connal, William, of Solsgirth	81 St. Vincent Street, Glasgow	681	551 5
				Constable, George, of Balmyle	Balmyle, Blairgowrie	1,263	1,211 7
Campbell, Sir James, of Aberuchill and Kilbride, Bart.	Kilbride Castle, Dunblane	5,037	1,949 9	Constable, James Charles, of Cally	Cally House, Blairgowrie	865	770 —

PERTH—continued.

Name of Owner.	Address of Owner.	Estimated Acreage of Property.	Gross Annual Value.	Name of Owner.	Address of Owner.	Estimated Acreage of Property.	Gross Annual Value.
		Acres.	£ s.			Acres.	£ s.
Constable, Trs. of William, of Waterybutts	Waterybutts, Errol	162	502 5	Dougall, Mrs. Mary	Cauldhame, Kippen	5	6 —
Constable, Mrs. Catherine, of Bendochy and Muirhead	Ardgaith, Glencarse	274	630 —	Douglas, Edward O., and wife, of Killichassie	Killichassie, Aberfeldy	7,396	763 19
Constable, Ann	Bertha Cottage, Perth	1	65 —	Dow, John, of Kirktonlees	Manchester	105	182 —
Cook, Rev. John Adam	Bankfoot, Perth	1	49 —	Dow, Trustees of Patrick	Kirkmichael	7	17 —
Cousin, James, of Gowerfield	12 Park Grove Terrace, Glasgow	5	25 —	Dow, Jessie	Newbigging, Methven	4	15 —
Cowpar, Robert S., and Cowpar, John S.	Blairgowrie	4	15 10	Drummond, Hon. Captain Arthur, of Cromlix, R.N.	Cromlix Cottage, Dunblane	7,465	4,240 14
Craigie, Trustees of late Major Robert Collins, of Glendoick	Glendoick House, Errol	1,016	1,798 6	Drummond, Trustee of Hon. Captain Arthur	Edinburgh	218	999 18
Craigie, William Roper	Dull, Aberfeldy	6	30 —	Drummond, George Stirling Home, of Blair-Drummond	Blair-Drummond House, Stirling	13,817	15409 15
Crammond, Heirs of George, of Leitfie	Leitfie, Alyth	128	273 13	Drummond, James	Dalginross, Comrie	22	91 —
Crawford, John	Blairgowrie	6	69 —	Drummond, John, of Blackruthven	Blackruthven, Perth	565	1,114 —
Crawford, Mrs. Janet T., of Mackrieston	Mackrieston, Stirling	10	20 —	Drummond, John, and spouse, of Balquhandy	Balquhandy, Dunning	944	345 10
Crerar, Mrs. Elizabeth	Comrie	2	19 10	Drummond, John Murray, of Megginch	Megginch Castle, Errol	1,000	2,040 18
Crichton, James, of Mains of Rattray	Rattray	197	300 —	Drummond, Peter, of Drumearn	Drumearn, Comrie	104	179 18
Crichton, William, of Viewfield	Viewfield, Perth	4	15 —	Drummond, Mrs. Margaret	Crieff	2	78 —
Crown (Board of Works)	(Dunblane Cathedral, &c.)	1	230 —	Drysdale, James	Bridge of Allan	1	66 —
Cumming, Thomas	Logie, Stirling	1	10 —	Duff, Lachlan	Moulin	1	55 7
Cunningham, Rev. John	Crieff	8	45 —	Dunbar, Rev. Robert Grant	Weem, Aberfeldy	8	34 —
Cunningham, Rev. John	Glendevon Manse, Dollar	12	45 —	Dunblane Building Co. (Limited)	Dunblane	2	83 4
Cunningham, John, of Broadheadfold	Broadheadfold, Dunning	200	108 —	Dunblane Free Church, Deacons' Court of	Dunblane	1	42 10
Cunningham, John, of Balgownie	Balgownie, Culross	40	147 10	Dunblane, Presbytery of	Dunblane	168	163 —
Cunningham, Robert J. B., of Cronan and Balbrogie	6 Walker St., Edinburgh	345	690 —	Duncan, Heirs of Rev. Andrew Bethune	Manse, Culross	8	44 —
Cuthbert, John	Glasgow	3	12 —	Duncan, David	Rattray, Blairgowrie	14	38 —
				Duncan, James	Dunkeld	13	58 12
Dalgety, Mary, Margaret, Hannah, and Helen, of Fernichill and Corb	47 Minto St., Edinburgh	1,050	275 4	Duncan, Heirs of John	Alyth	28	109 3
				Duncan, Patrick Geekie	Kirriemuir	10	21 10
				Duncan, Thomas	Rattray, Blairgowrie	13	25 —
				Duncan, William	Kildare	32	64 —
Dalgleish, John James, of West Grange	Brankston Grange, Culross	2,400	1,483 15	Duncan, Mrs. Elizabeth F. Macduff, of Damside	Damside House, Auchterarder	353	491 —
Davidson, Alexander, of Cauldhame	Cauldhame, Kippen	5	15 —	Duncan, Trs. of Mrs. Elizabeth, of Easter Denhead	Easter Denhead, Coupar-Angus	233	530 —
Davidson, Alexander, of Denbank	Denbank, Abernethy	9	76 2	Dundas, Sir David, of Beechwood and Dunira, Bart.	Dunira, Crieff	5,529	2,725 8
Davidson, Andrew, of Westerdownhill	Balhousie, Perth	1,327	508 11	Dundas, Right Hon. Sir David, of Ochtertyre	Ochtertyre, Stirling	984	1,231 7
Davidson, Rev. George S.	Manse, Kinfauns	6	40 —	Dundas, Edward Thomas, of Manor	Manor, Stirling	198	400 —
Davidson, James Leigh Strahan, of Ardgaith	Dundee	389	957 6	Dundee, Seamen's Fraternity of	Horn, Errol	132	310 —
Davidson, John	Dunning	1	13 15	Dunn, Peter	Kepp House, Kippen	1	3 —
Davidson, Robert H., of The Park	The Park, Culross	35	244 5	Dymock, Mrs. Mary	Gartmore, Stirling	3	12 —
Davie, Alexander	Errol	1	17 10				
Dawson, Archibald	Redgatehill, Kippen	7	9 —	Eadie, Andrew	Blackford	2	8 5
Dawson, John	Blairlogie, Stirling	2	30 —	Eadie, John	Auchterarder	2	63 —
Deans, Helen and Jessie	Alyth	12	55 —	Eadie, Mrs. Elizabeth	Blackbriggs, Muckhart	4	10 10
Dempster, Heirs of James, of Tillyochie	Tillyochie, Kinross	46	42 5	Easson, Alexander, and spouse	Abernethy, Newburgh	2	38 13
Devon Valley Railway Co.	Tillicoultry (*Railway*)	24	457 —	Easton, Heirs of James	Elmswood, Dunblane	2	25 —
Dewar, Trs. of late James	Blairgowrie	5	11 —	Edmondston, Rev. Biot	Manse, Kincardine, Stirling	8	45 —
Dewar, Mrs. Susan, of Overdurdie	Overdurdie, Kilspindie, Errol	637	624 5	Edmonstone, William	Pitversie, Abernethy	3	10 —
Dewhurst, George Charnley, of Aberuchill	Aberuchill Castle, Comrie	3,022	1,242 13	Edward, James, of Balruddery	Balruddery House, Dundee	642	1,223 7
Dick, William, of Tullymet	Tullymet, Logierait	1,000	1,321 18	Elgin and Kincardine, Earl of	Broomhall, Charleston	232	1,870 18
Dick, Mrs. Rachael, of Mountquharrie	Mountquharrie, Abernethy	62	30 —	Elibank, Lord	Darn Hall, Peebles	994	1,871 8
Dickie, John, of Shelterhall	Shelterhall, Dollar	40	37 —	Elphinstone, Lord and Lady Osborne, of Tulliallan	Tulliallan Castle, Kincardine-on-Forth	4,006	5,239 15
Doig, Alexander	Kingower Cottage, Perth	3	8 —	*Errol Chemical Co.*	Inchmichael, Errol	1	35 —
Doig, Paul, of Wester Boquhapple	Wester Boquhapple, Stirling	29	51 —	Erskine, Henry David, of Cardross	Cardross House, Kippen	6,245	4,020 13
Donaldson, George	Balbeggie, Scone	3	14 —	Erskine, Admiral John Elphinstone, M.P.	Lochend, Port of Monteith, Stirling	7	45 —
Donaldson, Robert	Lauglandsteps, Culross	3	7 10				
Donaldson, Margaret, of Cornhill	Cornhill, Perth	43	185 10	Erskine, Trustees of late Mrs. Magdaline Sharpe, of Dunimarle	Dunimarle, Culross	45	178 —
Dougall, Trustees of late John, of Burnhead	Burnhead, Stirling	30	59 15				
Dougall, William	Cauldhame, Kippen	1	6 10	Ewan, John	7 Dalry Park, Edinburgh	2	8 —

PERTH—continued.

Name of Owner.	Address of Owner.	Estimated Acreage of Property.	Gross Annual Value.	Name of Owner.	Address of Owner.	Estimated Acreage of Property.	Gross Annual Value.
		Acres.	£ s.			Acres.	£ s.
Faichney, Peter	South Crofts, Auchterarder	3	13 –	Gerard, Keturah Jane, of Duthieston	Duthieston, Dunblane	3	35 –
Falconer, William	Blairgowrie	4	15 –	Gibson, George, of Kellybank	Kellybank, Dollar	51	105 –
Farney, William M.	Allanbank, Perth	1	40 –	Gibson, Rev. William	Auchterarder	6	45 –
Farquharson, Lieut.-Col. James Ross, of Invercauld	Invercauld, Braemar	20,056	1,508 5	Gibson, William, of Gartwhinzean	Gartwhinzean, Dollar	189	273 12
Fenton, David	Alyth	2	41 5	Gibson, Mrs. Mary C.	Rosebank House, Doune	2	40 –
Fenwick, Robert	Bankfoot, Perth	18	39 16	Gilloch, John	London	1	103 18
Ferguson, Alexander	Blairgowrie	4	12 –	Gilmour, John	Blackford	5	23 5
Ferguson, Alexander	Kincairney, Dunkeld	38	63 –	Glasgow Corporation Water Commissioners	Glasgow	24	6,722 –
Ferguson, Executors of Alexander, of Glenardoch	Glenardoch, Doune	1	156 17	Glen, John, of Easter Pitgobar	Easter Pitgobar, Dollar	72	95 –
Ferguson, Curator of Fergus David, of Linden Park	Linden Park, Auchterarder	6	55 –	Glover Incorporation	Perth	471	1,361 15
Ferguson, James	Woodside, Cargill	6	30 –	Goodall, Rev. Charles	Manse, Dron, Bridge of Earn	5	32 –
Ferguson, John, of Easter Dalnabreck	Australia	477	120 –	Gordon, George, of Donavourd	Donavourd House, Pitlochry	2,760	576 15
Ferguson, John Kinnell	Montrose	1	17 10	Gordon, Rev. William	Manse, Abernethy	6	45 –
Ferguson, Rev. John, and spouse	Coney Park, Bridge of Allan	185	161 –	Græme, Patrick Frederick James, of Inchbrakie	Inchbrakie, Crieff	5,088	3,211 15
Ferguson, Samuel Robert, of Middlehaugh	Pitlochry	140	152 10	Græme, Robert, of Garvock	Garvock, Dunning	644	844 1
				Græme, Mrs. Elizabeth F.	Crieff	1	45 –
				Graham, Alexander	Crieff	1	57 –
Ferguson, Trustees of Thomas, of Balledmund	Balledmund, Pitlochry	1,000	936 11	Graham, Trustees of late David, of Meiklewood	Meiklewood, Stirling	688	1,166 17
Ferguson, William	Rattray, Blairgowrie	3	9 –	Graham, Trustees of Captain Duncan Daniel, of Overglenny	Overglenny, Port of Monteith	300	100 –
Ferguson, Margaret, of Dunfallandy	Dunfallandy, Pitlochry	842	513 –	Graham, James Maxtone, of Cultoquhey and Redgorton	Cultoquhey, Crieff	2,519	3,117 4
Finlay, James, of Deanston, & Co.	Deanston, Stirling	88	1,922 8	Graham, John, of Nether Glenny	Whitecross, Dunblane	479	172 –
Finlayson, Heirs of J. B., of Greenhill	Greenhill, Braco	162	133 –	Graham, John Murray, of Murrayshall	Murrayshall, Perth	1,913	2,678 17
Finlayson, Mrs. Christian, of Greenhill	Greenhill, Braco	10	52 10	Graham, Rev. Robert	Errol	5	38 –
Fleming, Rev. Archibald, of Inchyra	Hamilton House, Perth	341	1,689 10	Graham, Robert, of Coldoch	Coldoch, Blair-Drummond, Stirling	400	696 10
Fogo, Mrs. Janet Laurie, of Row	Row Manse, Helensburgh	450	582 9	Graham, William	Moulin	6	10 –
Ford, John	Comrie Village, Oakley	1	25 –	Graham, William, of Devonshaw	Devonshaw, Dollar	503	490 –
Forfar, Rev. James	Norrieston Manse, Thornhill, Stirling	8	21 –	Grant, Charles T. C., of Kilgraston	Kilgraston House, Bridge of Earn	2,346	3,545 15
Forrester, William, of Arngibbon	Arngibbon, Kippen, Stirling	325	315 –	Grant, James	Blairgowrie	2	16 –
Forth and Clyde Junction Railway	Stirling (Railway)	22	549 –	Grant, Rev. Patrick	Tenandry, Blair-Athole	10	18 –
Fraser, Rev. James	Logierait, Ballinluig	10	34 –	Grant, Peter	Balbeggie, Scone	2	34 –
Fraser, Patrick Allan, of Blackcraig	Blackcraig, Blairgowrie	2,722	1,537 16	Grant, William	Kirriemuir	1	91 1
Fraser, Rev. William	Blairgowrie	15	52 –	Grant, Mrs. Margaret	Australia	6	10 –
Fraser, William, and David Ballingall	Thornhill, Stirling	6	15 –	Gray, George, of Bowerswell	Bowerswell, Perth	2	18 –
				Gray, George, of Bowerswell, and John Conning	Perth	190	40 6
				Gray, Baroness, of Gray and Kinfauns	Kinfauns Castle, Perth	2,631	6,123 9
Gallwey, Mrs. Jane, of Blair	Blair Castle, Culross	526	893 6	*Greenloaning United Presbyterian Church Congregation*	Greenloaning, Braco	2	11 1
Gammel, Major Andrew, of Lethendy	Lethendy, Meikleour	1,262	2,074 17	Greig, Thomas, of Glencarse	Glencarse, Perth	662	1,495 10
Gardiner, John, of Carsegrange	Carsegrange, Errol	90	226 –	Grimmond, Alexander D., of Glenericht	Glenericht, Blairgowrie	1,917	1,148 14
Gardiner, Patrick, of Wester Rottearns	Wester Rottearns, Braco	96	124 9	Grimmond, David, of Oakbank	Oakbank, Blairgowrie	36	323 –
Gardiner, Robert, of Easter Rottearns	Chapelbank, Auchterarder	164	290 –	*Guildry Incorporation*	Perth	663	981 15
Gardiner, Trs. of William	Greenhead, Auchterarder	6	33 10	Guthrie, James	Alyth	5	48 2
Garrick, Reps. of William	Abernethy, Newburgh	1	23 5	Guthrie, James and William	Dunblane	1	134 10
Gartmore Free Church Congregation	Gartmore, Stirling	1	2 –	Guthrie, Joseph	Pitversie, Abernethy	2	20 10
Garvie, William	King's Place, Perth	3	13 –	Guthrie, Christina, Ann, and Isabella	Abernethy	16	81 7
Garvie, Mrs. Elizabeth	276 High Street, Perth	3	13 –				
Geekie, Alexander, of Baldowrie	Baldowrie, Coupar-Angus	891	1,448 6				
Geekie, Alexander, junior	Coupar-Angus	3	29 –	Haig, James Richard, of Blairhill	Blairhill, Dollar	907	1,042 –
Geekie, Trustees of Isabella, of Aberbothrie	West Grange of Aberbothrie, Meigle	130	264 –	Haig, William James, of Dollarfield	Dollarfield, Dollar	1,905	355 –
Geils, John E.	Dunkeld	7	70 –	Haldane, Robert, of Cloanden	Cloanden House, Auchterarder	747	683 –
Gellatly, David	Meigle	2	19 –				
Gentle, Heirs of Robert S., of Parkhead	Perth	276	680 –				

PERTH—continued.

Name of Owner.	Address of Owner.	Estimated Acreage of Property.	Gross Annual Value.	Name of Owner.	Address of Owner.	Estimated Acreage of Property.	Gross Annual Value.
		Acres.	£ s.			Acres.	£ s.
Halkerstone's Trustees	Greenfield Park, Culross	6	25 –	Hosie, Mrs. Emma	Low Valleyfield, Culross	2	40 –
Hally & Son	Crieff	4	125 –	Houston, Heirs of John	Blackford	1	7 –
Hally & Company	Auchterarder	3	98 16	Howard, Trustees of Samuel, of Stanley	Stanley, Perth	131	1,538 6
Hallyburton, Admiral Lord John F. Gordon, K.C.H.	Hallyburton House, Coupar-Angus	361	181 –	Howie, John	Alyth	3	36 15
Hamilton, John Buchanan Bailie, and spouse, of Arnprior and Cambusmore	Cambusmore House, Stirling	12,172	3,207 10	Hunter, Colonel James, of Auchterarder	Auchterarder House	1,500	2,468 11
				Hunter, Mrs. Annie, and Mary Lawson	Auchterarder	13	110 2
Hamilton, Gustavus William Bellew, of Whiteriggs	Carmaerthenshire	380	130 –	Hutchison, Thomas, of Wester Pitgobar	Wester Pitgobar, Dollar	95	260 –
				Hutchison, Trustees of late Thomas	Blairgowrie	127	55 –
Hamilton, John Buchanan, of Leny	Leny House, Callander	3,330	1,334 18	*Hydropathic Company*	Crieff	6	350 –
Hamilton, Joseph Bellew, of Culsknowe	Matlock House, Derby	320	112 –	Inches, Charles, of Hope Park	Rattray, Blairgowrie	14	104 –
Hamilton, Leslie George Baillie	Rycote Knoll, Dunblane	2	45 –	Inches, Heirs of David	Rattray, Blairgowrie	6	25 –
Hamilton, Robert, of Tethyknowe	Tethyknowe, Dollar	90	54 10	Inglis, Major Raymond	Moulin, Pitlochry	2	50 –
Hamilton, Thomas, of Hillside	Threadneedle Street, London	1	60 –	Inglis, Trustees of Thomas H., of Howefaulds	Hutton Park, Largs	111	80 –
Hamilton, Rev. William	St. Martin's Manse, Perth	18	45 –	Irvine, William Stewart	Pitlochry	1	54 –
Hardie, Rev. Thomas	Fowlis-Wester, Crieff	7	45 –				
Harris, David, of Millbank of Aberbothrie	Alyth	120	205 –	Jackson, Mrs. Stewart	St. Johns, Wakefield	125	150 –
Harris, John Archibald	Birnam	1	81 6	Jameson, Melville	Fernhill, Perth	5	95 –
Hart, Rev. Archibald	Bridge of Turret	4	25 –	Jamieson, Michael James, of Arngomery	Arngomery, Kippen	66	162 9
Hay, Edmund Paterson Balfour, of Leys and Mugdrum	Mugdrum House, Newburgh	2,132	5,749 8	Jardine, Andrew, of Lanrick	Lanrick Castle, Stirling	2,821	2,661 –
				Jobson, William	Dundee	3	152 15
Hay, Colonel Henry Murray Drummond, and spouse, of Seggieden	Seggieden House, Perth	800	2,494 13	Johnson, Robert	Sumner Lodge, Dunblane	3	35 –
				Johnston, James	Thornhill, Stirling	6	17 10
				Johnston, Curators of Laurence, of Sands	Sands House, Kincardine-on-Forth	987	1,079 9
Hay, Trustees of John, of Stronphadrick	Letham Grange	7,000	120 –	Johnstone, George, of Monzie	Lathrisk, Fife	3,631	1,409 15
Hay, Rev. Joseph	Lethendy	16	26 15	Johnstone, James, of Kincardine	13 Upper Mount Street, Dublin	1,500	1,272 15
Hay, Trustees of Catherine, of Balendock	Alyth	295	491 17	Johnstone, James, younger of Kincardine	13 Upper Mount Street, Dublin	10	20 –
Hay, Helen Carsewell	Glasgow	37	95 4	Johnstone, James, of Broom	Elmbank Mills, Menstrie	224	120 –
Hay, Jane	Pitlochry	1	40 –				
Hemming, Richard, of Richael and Glaschorie	Worcestershire	10,000	155 –	Johnstone, Rev. John	Manse of Port of Monteith	6	40 –
Henderson, Archibald	Stirling	2	25 –	Johnstone, Mrs. Mary and Margaret Robertson	Perth } Glenfoot, Abernethy	8	12 –
Henderson, Charles James, of Glassingall	Glassingall, Dunblane	650	634 10				
Henderson, Daniel, of Leacocks	Rattray, Blairgowrie	19	20 –				
Henderson, Representatives of David, of Gattaway	Gattaway, Abernethy	350	430 8	Keay, Alexander, of Dalhenzean	Dalhenzean, Kirkmichael	450	90 –
Henderson, George D. C., of Hallyards	Hallyards, Alyth	396	648 16	Keay, Mrs. Elizabeth, of Snaigow	Snaigow, Dunkeld	1,836	1,559 8
Henderson, James	Dundee	6	15 –	Keay, Mrs. Janet	Alyth	16	39 10
Henderson, William, of Blairstruie	Blairstruie, Bridge of Earn	210	215 –	Keillor, Peter	Blairgowrie	5	18 –
Henderson, Mrs. Janet	Balhousie Street, Perth	1	56 18	Keillor, Reps. of Robert	Blairgowrie	1	135 10
Henry, Isaac Anderson, and wife, of Woodend	Woodend, Madderty, Crieff	523	868 –	Keir, Finlay	Duchray, Aberfoyle	2	7 –
Hepburn, Trustees of John Stewart, of Colquhalzie	Colquhalzie, Auchterarder	7,238	2,433 7	Keir, Patrick Small, of Kindrogan	Kindrogan, Pitlochry	10,000	2,445 7
				Keir, William Augustus	Kindrogan, Pitlochry	30	21 10
Herdman, Rev. William	Rattray, Blairgowrie	5	40 –	Kemp, Rev George Wright	Manse of Trinity-Gask, Auchterarder	22	55 –
Herdman, Mrs. Robert	Auchterarder	3	21 10	Kerr, William Wemyss, of East Grange	East Grange, Culross	313	385 11
Heron, Mrs. Isabella	Blairgowrie	3	8 –				
Highland Railway Company	Inverness (Railway)	435	19764 –	*Kettins, Kirk-Session of Parish of*	Kettins	35	95 –
Hill, Trs. of late David	Coupar-Angus	3	98 4	*Kincardine Cemetery*	Tulliallan	2	10 –
Hill, John	Edinburgh	2	37 19	*Kincardine, Heritors of Parish of*	Kincardine, Stirling	1	4 –
Hislop, Mrs. Elizabeth	Auchterarder	8	98 3				
Hogg, Mrs. Eliza	Perth	1	18 10	*Kinglassie, Parochial Board of*	Kinglassie, Fife	120	153 17
Home, George H. M. Binning, of Argaty	Argaty, Doune	2,890	1,460 19	Kinloch, Colonel David J., of Gourdie	Gourdie, Blairgowrie	788	1,269 3
Honey, Rev. John Adamson	Inchture	13	58 –	Kinloch, Sir George, of Kinloch, Bart.	Kinloch House, Meigle	2,854	5,487 –
Honey, Mary and Jane	Methven	2	7 –	Kinloch, George Ritchie	Edinburgh	3	11 13
Hood, Peter	Glenfoot	2	9 –	Kinnaird, Hon. Arthur F., of Kinloch, M.P.	Kinloch Lodge, Dunkeld	4,125	786 10
Horn, James	Blairgowrie	2	7 –				
Horn, Margaret, of Tomanean	Tomanean, Milnathort	134	160 –	*Kinnaird, Kirk-Session of*	Kinnaird, Inchture	4	38 –

PERTH—continued.

Name of Owner.	Address of Owner.	Estimated Acreage of Property.	Gross Annual Value.	Name of Owner.	Address of Owner.	Estimated Acreage of Property.	Gross Annual Value.
		Acres.	£ s.			Acres.	£ s.
Kinnaird, Lord	Rossie Priory, Inchture	7,579	15460 6	M'Callum, Neil	Perth	3	33 10
Kinnoull, Earl of	Dupplin Castle, Perth	12,577	14814 8	M'Cash, James	Burghmuir, Perth	4	7 –
Kippen, James	Blairlogie	4	40 –	M'Cash, John	Burghmuir, Perth	4	12 10
Kirk, John	Bowmore, Islay	4	12 –	M'Culloch, James	Shirgarton, Kippen	1	4 10
Kirkmichael, Heritors of Parish of	Kirkmichael	3	10 –	M'Diarmid, Rev. Hugh	Manse, Callander	11	60 –
Kirkwood, Rev. Thomas D.	Dunbarney Manse, Bridge of Earn	8	48 –	M'Donald, Colonel Alexander M'Ian, of Dun-Alastair	Dover	14,000	2,675 19
Knight, William G., of Jordanstone	Jordanstone House, Alyth	515	603 10	M'Donald, David, of Lassintulloch	Rannoch, Pitlochry	2,561	570 –
				M'Donald, Rev. Duncan	Kirkmichael	8	28 –
				M'Donald, Rev. Hugh	Glenlyon, Aberfeldy	9	10 –
Laing, Rev. Gilbert	Langleybank, Scone	1	20 –	M'Donald, Rev. James	F.C. Manse, Aberuthven	1	24 –
Landale, Robert, of Pitmedden	15 Royal Circus, Edinburgh	258	195 –	M'Donald, James Mitchell	Blairgowrie	2	6 –
				M'Donald, Rev. John	Comrie	16	49 –
Lansdowne, Dowager Marchioness of	Meikleour House, Blairgowrie	9,070	8,025 16	M'Donald, Trustees of John, of Craigruie	Craigruie, Balquhidder	5,525	550 –
Laurence, John	Longshot, Auchterarder	3	19 11	M'Donald, Thomas	Culross	1	36 18
Laurie, David, of Wellfield	Wellfield, Abernethy	25	64 15	M'Donald, William, of Woodlands	Woodlands, Perth	93	213 14
Laurie, Elizabeth, Euphemia, Margaret, and Rev. F. Laurie	Wellfield, Abernethy	6	28 5	M'Donald, William	Low Valleyfield, Culross	1	16 15
				M'Donald, William, of Balnakeilly	Kirkmichael	550	285 11
Lawson, Rev. Alexander, of Cocklaw	Creich Manse, Cupar	84	71 18	Macdonald, William Macdonald, of St. Martins	St. Martin's Abbey, Perth	22,600	9,191 13
Lawson, Charles, of Ballomill	Edinburgh	270	440 –	Macdonald, Margaret Allan and Katherine Ochterlony, of Easter Ballintuim	Arbroath	66	90 –
Lennie, James	Loaningfoot, Kippen	1	6 5				
Leslie, Robert Cargill, of Butterglen	Caputh	25	78 –				
Lethendy Mortification, Trustees of	Scone, Perth	646	1,066 12	M'Dougall, Rev. John, of Orchill	Orchill, Laighdoors, Crieff	966	859 –
Lindsay, Trs. of late John	Almondbank, Perth	16	137 4	M'Dougall, John	Edinburgh	1	7 –
Lindsay, William	Coupsteps, Dollar	6	12 –	M'Dougall, Mrs. Margaret	Blackford	6	231 5
Lochearnhead, Free Church Congregation of	Lochearnhead, Crieff	1	15 –	Macduff, Alexander, of Bonhard	Bonhard, Perth	854	1,187 14
Logan, Rev. Peter	Culross	9	31 10	M'Duff, Donald, of Tomnagrew	Tomnagrew, Dunkeld	584	270 –
Logan, John	Glasgow	1	8 5				
Logie, William	Perth	12	25 –	M'Ewen, Heirs of William	Newton, Perth	6	16 10
Logierait Union Poorhouse, Trustees of	Logierait, Ballinluig	3	150 –	M'Farlane, David and George	Coupar-Angus	2	80 –
Longforgan, Free Church Congregation of	Longforgan	1	30 –	M'Farlane, Walter	Gartmore, Stirling	2	10 –
Low, Alexander, of Butterstone	Caputh, Dunkeld	400	255 5	M'Farlane, Christian, and Mrs. Martha Walker, of Calziemuck	Calziemuck, Ruskie, Stirling	108	158 –
Low, Allan, David, and Edward, of Keithbank	Keithbank, Blairgowrie	12	160 –	M'Farlane, Jane	Woodside, Doune	1	46 10
Low, Isaac, of Welltown	Blairgowrie	63	111 –	Macfee, James	Auchterarder	4	28 9
Low, John	Alyth	46	136 19	Macfee, Mrs. Jane, of Drums	Paisley	1	4 10
Low, Trustees of Thomas, of Mylnefield	Mylnefield, Dundee	566	1,404 13	M'Gavin, David	Dundee	1	56 19
Low, Mrs. Janet, of Borland and Milltown of Glendevon	Borland, Glendevon, Dollar	825	360 –	M'Glashan, Jane, of Eastertyre	Eastertyre, Ballinluig	250	134 10
				M'Gowan, John, of Balrudderie	London	318	297 –
Lowe, Robert, of Fosswellbank	Coupar-Angus	234	182 10	M'Gregor, Rev. Alexander M.	Balquhidder Manse, Crieff	13	30 –
				M'Gregor, Donald	Ballinluig	57	44 11
Lowson, William, of Balthayock	Balthayock House, Perth	1,465	1,306 –	M'Gregor, James, of Fonab	Fonab, Pitlochry	607	371 2
Lyall, Joseph	Blairgowrie	2	13 –	M'Gregor, Trustees of James, of Glengyle	Glengyle House, Callander	2,270	240 –
Lyell, John, of Over Pitcurran	71 Stirling Road, Glasgow	5	58 10	Macgregor, Sir Malcolm Murray, of Edinchip, Bart., Captain R.N.	Edinchip House, Crieff	4,050	1,131 5
Luke, James	Rattray, Blairgowrie	3	35 –	MacGregor, Mrs. Ann	Birnam	1	60 –
Luke & Co.	Blairgowrie	2	332 –	M'Ildowie, Heirs of Peter	Crieff	1	18 –
Lumsden, David, of Fincastle	Pitcairnfield, Perth	561	279 –	M'Innes, Duncan, of Cowden	Cowden, Crieff	102	124 2
Lunacy Board for County of Perth	Perth	60	230 –	M'Inroy, James Patrick, of Lude	Lude, Blair-Athole	15,680	2,460 –
				M'Inroy, William, of Shierglass	The Burn, Brechin	632	290 13
M'Alister, Mrs. Janet	Redgatehill, Kippen	4	8 –				
M'Alpine, William	Gartmore, Stirling	1	14 –	M'Intosh, Trustees of Rev. Alexander	Kirkmichael	50	108 5
M'Alpine, William, of Blacklands	Blacklands, Stirling	5	10 –	M'Intosh, Charles Hill, of Dalmunzie	Torquay	7,000	500 –
M'Ara, Duncan	Rumbling Bridge, Dollar	5	70 –	M'Intosh, George	Newtyle	4	12 –
M'Caill, Donald	Balnald, Monzievaird	110	66 –	M'Intosh, Jane, of Claywhatt	Claywhatt, Blairgowrie	350	228 –
M'Callum, George Kellie, of Braco	Braco Castle, Braco	1,838	1,155 8	M'Intyre, James	Glasgow	3	45 –
M'Callum, James, of Millhills	Millhills, Crieff	34	85 –	M'Intyre, John	Woodvale, Callander	1	121 10
M'Callum, James	Mains of Fullarton, Meigle	1	18 10	M'Intyre & Baxter	Rattray	32	443 –

PERTH—continued.

Name of Owner.	Address of Owner.	Estimated Acreage of Property.	Gross Annual Value.	Name of Owner.	Address of Owner.	Estimated Acreage of Property.	Gross Annual Value.
		Acres.	£ s.			Acres.	£ s.
M'Ivor, John	Greenhead, Muckart, Dollar	5	10 –	M'Whannel, Rev. Alexander	Manse, Blairingone, Dollar	1	12 10
M'Kay, John	Luidburn House, Callander	2	70 –	Mailer, Andrew, of Broadfold	Broadfold, Auchterarder	107	198 10
M'Kechnie, Robert, of Mondowie	Bridge of Allan	500	213 –	Mailer, Andrew	Muirtown, Auchterarder	7	13 10
M'Keith, Donald, of Damside	Sandhurst, Kent	33	47 –	Mailer, Robert	Auchterarder	7	66 2
M'Kenzie, Sir Alexander Muir, of Delvine, Bart.	Delvine House, Dunkeld	4,241	6,419 12	Mailer, Mrs. Jane	Auchterarder	4	18 –
M'Kenzie, Rev. James B.	Kenmore	10	45 –	Mailler, John, of Cornhill	Cornhill, Auchterarder	310	244 10
M'Kenzie, Rev. James S.	Little Dunkeld	14	57 –	Mailler, John, of Eind	Eind, Auchterarder	189	111 –
M'Kenzie, John	Burnside, Mackrieston, Stirling	6	23 –	Main, Mrs. Margaret	Thornyhaw, Culross	3	7 10
M'Kenzie, Georgina Muir	Garry Cottage, Perth	4	85 –	Malahide, Trustee of Lord and Lady Talbot de	Glamis	154	415 –
Mackie, Alexander	Abernethy	2	10 10	Malcolm, William	Edinburgh	4	33 10
Mackinlay, David, of Cordon	Cordon, Abernethy	315	772 16	Malcolm, Margaret and Elizabeth, and Mrs. Butter Malcolm, of Castlemains	Castlemains, Auchterarder	260	572 5
Mackinlay, Trustees of John, of Heathmount	Heathmount, Callander	5	40 –	Manners, Rt. Hon. Lord John, M.P.	Torwood, Birnam	11	130 –
Mackintosh, Alexander, of Collearn	Collearn, Auchterarder	16	160 –	Mansfield, Earl of	Scone Palace, Perth	31,197	23052 6
M'Lagan, Peter	Birnam, Dunkeld	2	60 –	Marshall, Rev. Theodore	Manse, Caputh	16	52 –
M'Laren, Donald	Callander	1	69 19	Marshall, William, of Luncarty	Pooley Park, Manchester	600	1,570 11
M'Laren, Donald	Bogend Orchard, Blairlogie, Stirling	4	20 –	Marshall, William Hunter, of Callander	25 Heriot Row, Edinburgh	393	271 9
M'Laren, Trustees of Donald, of Stank and Kernock	Callander	1,000	165 –	Marshall, Janet Stewart Hall, of Gartchonzie	Roman Camp, Callander	160	130 –
M'Laren, Rev. Duncan	Dunning	1	26 14	Martin, Trustees of George, of Tarhill	Cupar-Fife	220	160 –
M'Laren, Duncan, of Gormack	Blairgowrie	412	336 17	Martin, Rev. James	Manse, Findo-Gask, Auchterarder	27	53 –
M'Laren, John	Blairgowrie	11	88 –	Masson, Rev. Evan M'Kenzie	Dull Manse, Aberfeldy	15	56 –
M'Laren, John, of Middleton and Chapel	Middleton, Stirling	62	110 13	Mathew, Trs. of Robert, of Elmbank	Elmbank, Perth	2	52 14
M'Laren, John, of Beechhill	Coupar-Angus	24	267 4	Mathewson, David, of Nether Balloch	Nether Balloch, Alyth	186	160 –
M'Laren, John Stewart	Auchterarder	2	44 7	Matthew, John Miller, of Glenfarg	Glenfarg, Perth	1,034	1,267 2
M'Laren, Peter	Blairgowrie	7	12 –	Matthew, Patrick, of Gourdiehill	Gourdiehill, Errol	48	200 –
M'Laren, Thomas S., of Dubheads	Edinburgh	79	80 –	Matthew, Patrick Miller, of Newmiln	Newmiln, Perth	434	630 –
M'Laren, Heirs of Catherine	Blairgowrie	4	15 –	Maxton, Mrs. Charlotte, of Easter Kincardine	Crieff	73	145 –
M'Laren, Mary, of Easter Doullater	Callander	500	145 –	Maxtone, Ann, of Ardbinnie	Madderty, Crieff	188	220 –
M'Lay, James	Alloa	1	67 –	Melville, Trustees of late Charles, of Easter Greenside	Easter Greenside, Abernethy	28	40 –
M'Lean, Charles, of Glenearn	Glenearn, Bridge of Earn	640	836 15	Melville, Representatives of James and Representatives of James Hogg	Newmills, Dunfermline Perth	1	3 –
M'Lean, Rev. Malcolm	F.C. Manse, Gartmore, Port of Monteith, Stirling	1	16 –	Menzies, Rev. Allan	Manse, Abernyte, Inchture	13	36 –
M'Leish, Rev. John	Methven	1	20 –	Menzies, James Alexander, of Pitnacree	Pitnacree, Logierait	676	887 9
M'Leish, Euphemia	Coupar-Angus	4	53 3	Menzies, Sir Robert, of that Ilk, Bart.	Castle Menzies	32,784	8,553 15
M'Leod, Rev. Norman	Blair-Athole	110	133 1	Menzies, Trs. of Ranald Stewart, of Culdares	Culdares, Cardney, Dunkeld	33,000	3,824 17
M'Leod, Mrs. Margaret	Blairadam, Kinross	2	6 –	Menzies, William James Breadalbane Stewart, of Chesthill	Chesthill House, Aberfeldy	16,117	2,723 17
M'Minn, Mrs. Elizabeth, and Mrs. Elizabeth Whitson, of Lower Littleton	Edinburgh	37	146 –	Menzies, Hon. Lady	Rannoch Lodge, Rannoch, Pitlochry	35,500	2,914 2
M'Nab, Colin	Upper Canada	1	203 –	Mercer, Graham Reid, of Gorthy	Glentulchan, The Cairnies, Perth	1,753	2,066 17
M'Nab, James	Kirkmichael	4	9 –	Mercer, Trustees of late Major Drummond, of Huntingtower	Huntingtower, Perth	465	1,359 15
M'Nab, John	Blairgowrie	4	15 10	Millar, Andrew	Crieff	2	136 –
M'Nab, Trustees of late Peter	Callander	1	79 –	Millar, James Reid	Broadpot, Culross	1	4 –
MacNaghten, Steuart, of Invertrosachs	Bittern Manor House, Southampton	2,700	310 –	Millar, Thomas, of Balliliesk	Balliliesk House, Dollar	431	367 4
M'Naughton, James	Stewarton, Ayrshire	12	33 –	Miller, David	Auchterarder	2	68 10
M'Naughton, Rev. Neil M.	Kinclaven, Perth	14	30 –	Miller, David, of Nether Kincairney	Hillocks of Clunie	30	71 19
M'Nicoll, Mrs. Barbara	Kinloch, Pitlochry	10	14 –				
M'Onie, Jessie	Gartmore, Stirling	1	5 –				
M'Pherson, Allan, of Blairgowrie	Blairgowrie House	741	1,103 10				
M'Queen, James, of West Kerse of Boquhapple	West Kerse of Boquhapple, Stirling	87	110 –				
M'Ritchie, David	Coupar-Angus	4	16 10				
M'Ritchie, Thomas Elder, of East Logie	Edinburgh	324	360 8				
M'Rosty, James, of Pittacher	Crieff	17	238 –				
M'Vean, Rev. Colin A.	Killin	18	28 –				

PERTH—continued.

Name of Owner.	Address of Owner.	Estimated Acreage of Property.	Gross Annual Value.	Name of Owner.	Address of Owner.	Estimated Acreage of Property	Gross Annual Value.
		Acres.	£ s.			Acres.	£ s.
Miller, Trustees of David, of East Tullyfergus	East Tullyfergus, Alyth	300	232 10	Muckhart United Presbyterian Congregation	Muckhart, Dollar	9	59 15
Miller, George L.	Alnwick	17	14 —	Murdoch, Rev. James M'Gibbon Burn	Inverbraan	13	100 —
Miller, James, of Wester Tullyfergus	Wester Tullyfergus, Alyth	267	181 —	Murdoch, John Burn, of Gartincaber	Gartincaber, Doune	1,496	1,813 11
Miller, Heirs of John	Auchterarder	2	30 —	Muir, Archibald	Leewood Villa, Dunblane	5	50 —
Miller, John	Perth	5	22 11	Murie, James	Burghmuir, Perth	4	7 10
Miller, Robert, of Tweedside	9 Rose Angle, Dundee	20	90 10	Munro, Mrs. Margaret	Blairgowrie	4	37 —
Miller, Elizabeth and Margaret	Methven	1	18 17	Murray, Anthony, of Dollerie	Dollerie, Crieff	1,104	1,768 4
Milne, Robert	Maryland, Abernethy	3	21 —	Murray, Daniel	Gartmore, Stirling	3	15 15
Milroy, Rev. Adam	Moneydie Manse, Perth	14	52 —	Murray, David, of Viewbank	Meigle	132	220 —
Mitchell, Andrew	Balbeggie, Perth	1	9 —				
Mitchell, Ebenezer	Crossmount, Perth	1	16 —	Murray, Captain Jack H., of Croftinloan, R.N.	Croftinloan, Pitlochry	110	225 —
Mitchell, Rev. Gordon	Manse, Kilmadock, Doune	7	61 1	Murray, Mackenzie	Woodside, Cargill	3	40 —
Mitchell, James	Kippen	3	19 —	Murray, Mungo, of Lintrose	Lintrose House, Coupar-Angus	881	1,464 7
Mitchell, James, of Kincairney	Kincairney House, Dunkeld	529	703 15	Murray, Sir Patrick Keith, of Ochtertyre, Bart.	Ochtertyre, Crieff	17,876	11051 9
Mitchell, James	Crieff	4	82 —				
Mitchell, James, and spouse	Exeterbank, Scone	1	30 —	Murray, Trustees of Robert, of Dollarbeg	Dollarbeg, Dollar	6	9 —
Mitchell, John, of Arngask	Dundee	34	82 —	Murray, Thomas G., of Stenton	Edinburgh	185	208 17
Mitchell, Heirs of William, of Crawford Park	Dunblane	1	62 10	Murray, Christian	Morningside, Abernethy	5	52 15
Mitchell, Mrs. Janet E.	Coupar-Angus	28	30 —	Murray's Royal Asylum, Directors of	Perth	50	646 6
Mitchell, Elizabeth	Downhill, Balbeggie	1	11 5	Mustard, John Gardner	London	6	30 —
Moffat, James, of Blairhoyle	Edenhall, Kelso	850	870 15	Mustard, Mrs. Elizabeth	Alyth	8	50 —
Moir, Alexander	North Crofts, Auchterarder	2	26 —				
Moir, A. Erskine Graham, of Leckie	Leckie, Stirling	304	345 —	Nairne, William, of Dunsinaine	Dunsinaine, Perth	3,330	3,529 2
Moir, James	Argaty, Doune	2	34 10	Nairne, William	Stanley	3	9 10
Moir, James M'Arthur, of Lawhill	Hillfoot, Dollar	205	250 5	Neilson, Rev. Alexander	Redgorton	9	56 —
Molison, Francis, of Murie and Errol	Invergowrie House, Dundee	2,135	7,038 18	Nicoll, Rev. John	Meigle	7	46 —
Moncreiffe, Sir Thomas, of Moncreiffe, Bart.	Moncreiffe House, Bridge of Earn	4,673	6,757 19	Nicoll, William	Low Valleyfield	1	23 10
Moncrieff, Major Alexander, of Barnhill	Barnhill, Perth	110	458 5	Niven, James, of Whitehill of Struie	Whitehill of Struie, Bridge of Earn	160	80 —
Moncrieff, Alexander, of Pitcastle	Perth	800	327 —	Niven, Robert, of Craighead of Pitquhanatrie	Craighead of Pitquhanatrie, Bridge of Earn	340	199 —
Moncrieff, D. Scott, of Easter Downhill	Edinburgh	290	140 —	North British Railway Co.	Edinburgh	5	15 —
Moncrieff, Harry	Auchterarder	5	25 —	Do. do.	Do. (Railway)	54	2,960 —
Moncrieff, Rev. W. Scott, of Fossoway	Edinburgh	2,225	1,239 15	Ogilvie, Heirs of Walter	Alyth	10	28 8
Moncur, Heirs of David	Alyth	8	77 17	Oliphant, Captain Laurence James, of Condie	Condie, Bridge of Earn	2,667	2,301 2
Moncur, John Rait	Blairgowrie	20	81 10	Oliphant, Philip Kington Blair, of Ardblair	London	1,318	948 —
Monteath, Alexander, of Duchally and Broich	Broich, Crieff	781	1,243 7	Oliphant, Thomas Truman, of Rossie	Rossie, Bridge of Earn	1,800	1,741 15
Montrose, Duke of	Buchanan House	32,294	5,556 6	Oliphant, Thomas Laurence Kington, of Gask	Gask House, Auchterarder	4,940	4,354 —
Moray, Charles Home Drummond, of Abercairney	Abercairney, Crieff	24,980	14311 9	Omond, John Reid	Monzie F.C. Manse, Crieff	4	35 —
Moray, Earl of	Doune Lodge, Stirling	40,553	10800 —	Orr, James, of Closs	Glasgow	176	201 —
Moray, Captain Henry E. H. D., younger of Abercairney, and William Augustus H. D. Moray	Abercairney, Crieff	3	11 15	Do. do.	Do. (Minerals)	—	150 —
				Orr, Heirs of John	Cauldhame, Kippen	1	5 —
Morgan, George	Monzievaird	2	39 —	Ower, George	Balbeggie, Perth	1	9 10
Morison, James, of Parkhead	Perth	26	86 10	Ower, George, of Graymount	Bendochy, Coupar-Angus	56	150 —
Morison, John Brown Brown, of West Errol	Murie House, Errol	1,918	3,741 7	Panton, John, of Dalnagairn	Blairgowrie	180	200 —
Morison, Robert	Dalreoch, Auchterarder	2	12 11	Partington, William H., and spouse, of Merklands	Ballintuim, Blairgowrie	600	311 —
Morrison, Alexander, of Bellevue	Bellevue, Coupar-Angus	68	185 —	Paterson, David Anderson, of Dalnaglar	Restalrig Park, Leith	630	269 —
Morrison, James Walker, of Bogley	Edinburgh	118	250 —	Paterson, Trs. of George, of Castle Huntly	Castle Huntly, Dundee	2,001	5,320 16
Morrison, Trustees of John	North Crofts, Auchterarder	4	26 9	Paterson, George Frederick, of Castle Huntly	Castle Huntly, Dundee	226	828 4
Morrison, William	Auchterarder	2	19 6	Paterson, George Kinloch Honey	Perth	1	10 10
Morrison's Institution, Trustees of	Crieff	11	120 —	Paterson, Mrs. Margaret	Perth	9	30 —
Moubray, Robert, of Cambus	Cambus, Alloa	300	278 10	Paterson, George, of North Bellfield	Perth	6	18 —
Moulin Episcopal Church, Trustees of	Moulin, Pitlochry	4	60 —				

PERTH—continued.

Name of Owner.	Address of Owner.	Estimated Acreage of Property.	Gross Annual Value.	Name of Owner.	Address of Owner.	Estimated Acreage of Property.	Gross Annual Value.
		Acres.	£ s.			Acres.	£ s.
Patterson, John, of Moss Side of Boquhapple	Moss Side of Boquhapple, Stirling	128	140 –	Ritchie, Trs. of George, of Hill of Ruthven	Hill of Ruthven, Perth	439	920 7
Patterson, Margaret Drummond, of Earn Bank	Earn Bank, Bridge of Earn	8	66 –	Ritchie, Trustees of late James, of Cairey	Cairey, Perth	149	425 10
Patton, Mrs. Margaret Malcolm, of Glenalmond	The Cairnies, Perth	11,079	1,995 15	Ritchie, Rev. William	Longforgan, Dundee	5	45 –
Patton, Margaret Ann, of The Cairnies	Perth	717	651 8	Robb, Mrs. Catherine, of South Kinkell	2 Carlung Place, Edinburgh	29	36 –
Patullo, James, of Persie	Abertay, Broughty Ferry, Dundee	2,214	676 10	Robertson, Alexander, of Blackhill	Blackhill, Dunkeld	95	111 18
Paulin, Rev. George	Manse, Muckhart, Dollar	13	48 –	Robertson, Alexander Gilbert, of Struan	Jamaica	18,000	1,038 18
Pearson, Trustees of Robert	Methven	43	157 15	Robertson, Rev. Alexander Irvine, of Kindrochit	Clunie Manse, Blairgowrie	1,506	382 –
Peebles, David	Rattray	2	8 –	Robertson, Andrew, of Kinburn	Dunning	70	60 –
Penney, Mrs. Christian	Berrydyke, Auchterarder	1	11 10	Robertson, Daniel	Methven	11	22 –
Perth, Community of	(Wellshill Cemetery), Perth	4	48 –	Robertson, Duncan Graham, of East Mains	East Mains, Callander	6	60 –
Perth, Presbytery of, as Trustees for Bellscroft	Dron, Bridge of Earn	9	22 –	Robertson, Edgar William, of Auchleeks	Auchleeks, Blair-Athole	14,732	1,632 17
Petrie, George	Kirkmichael	2	7 –	Robertson, Henry	Findo-Gask, Auchterarder	1	10 –
Philp, William S., of Boghall	Dunfermline	94	148 10	Robertson, Rev. James	Cray, Blairgowrie	1	12 –
Pilkington, Thomas	Crieff	1	17 –	Robertson, James	Bow House, Balbeggie, Perth	1	10 –
Pitcairn or Stoddart, Mrs. Catherine	Kintillo, Bridge of Earn	28	66 –	Robertson, Trustees of James	Corsiehill	3	25 –
Pitroddie United Presbyterian Congregation	Pitroddie, Errol	1	20 –	Robertson, James Stewart, of Edradynate	Edradynate, Ballinluig	1,765	688 8
Place, Edward G., of Lochdochart	Lochdochart, Killin	10,500	1,130 –	Robertson, John	Bendochy	11	12 –
Playfair, Charles, of Islaybank	Islaybank, Bendochy	454	870 –	Robertson, John	Panholes, Blackford	1	6 5
Playfair, Charles George, of Whitehill and Pitkindie	Whitehill, Inchture	1,000	1,020 –	Robertson, Colonel James Peter, of Callander Lodge, C.B.	Callander Lodge, Callander	4	100 –
Playfair, James and David	Auchterhouse, Dundee	3	47 –	Robertson, Peter	Castlebank, Barnhill, Perth	1	28 –
Playfair, Peter, of Couttie	Bendochy, Coupar-Angus	337	787 –	Robertson, Major-General Robert Richardson, of Tulliebelton	Tulliebelton, Bankfoot	4,462	3,719 16
Popham, Admiral B.	Cardean, Meigle	16	32 10	Robertson, Robert	Stanley, Perth	2	30 –
Pople, John Bullen, of New House	New House, Perth	126	334 –	Robertson, William	Blairgowrie	10	60 –
Porteous, Representatives of Alexander	Crieff	3	118 4	Robertson, Mrs. Elizabeth	Kippen, Stirling	5	7 16
Porteous, George Murray	Crieff	2	195 12	Robertson, Mrs. F. C., of Cray	Cray House, Bridge of Cally	437	113 –
Preston, Robert William Pigot Clarke, of Valleyfield	Valleyfield House, Culross	674	883 16	Robertson, Mrs. Mary Stuart, of Struan	Twisaraig, Fortingall	24,000	1,239 –
Do. do.	Do. (*Minerals*)	–	229 –	Robertson, Catherine and Ann	Alyth	4	85 –
Pullar, J. & J.	Ashfield, Dunblane	40	418 –	Robertson, Helen	Comrie	10	75 –
				Robertson, Trustees of Sarah	Brodleton, Stirling	1	18 –
				Rollo, Lord	Duncrub House, Dunning	10,148	8,418 13
Rae, Rev. David Smith	Kinloch	15	58 –	Ross, David	Lilybank, Burghmuir, Perth	3	26 10
Ramsay, Sir James H., of Bamff, Bart.	Bamff House, Alyth	12,845	3,394 1	Ross, Francis Thomas, of Balgerso	Paris	315	594 12
Ramsay, Trustees of late Sir James, of Bamff, Bart.	Bamff House, Alyth	1,865	934 19	Ross, Rev. James	Spittal of Glenshee	1	10 –
Ramsay, Rev. James	Glasgow	5	40 –	Ross, James	Birnam, Dunkeld	1	60 –
Ramsay, Trs. of James, of Viewlands	Viewlands, Perth	3	80 –	Ross, Margaret, of Oakbank	Oakbank House, Perth	69	206 –
Ramsay, Rev. Richard	Manse, Rhynd	7	38 –	Rutherford, Trustees of late Jane, of Glendevon	Glendevon House, Dollar	2,400	872 5
Rankine, Rev. James	Muthill	11	47 –	Ruthven, Lord, of Freeland	Freeland House, Bridge of Earn	2,519	4,083 6
Rattray, Colonel James Clerk, of Craighall	New Rattray, Blairgowrie	3,256	2,927 18				
Rattray, James Clerk, of Coralbank	Coralbank House, Blairgowrie	500	869 3				
Rattray, Robert	Kirkmichael	7	12 –				
Rattray, Thomas	Bendochy	4	10 –	Sandeman, Alexander Boswell, of Huntingtower	Huntingtower, Perth	234	1,277 –
Reid, Alexander G.	Norrieston, Stirling	3	6 –				
Reid, David, of Struie	Struie, Bridge of Earn	168	113 4	Sandeman, Hector, of Tulloch	Tulloch, Perth	168	621 –
Reive, Mrs. Isabella	Newtonshaw, Alloa	1	56 5	Sandeman, Mrs. Margaret Stewart, of Springland	Springland, Perth	4	111 –
Renny, Thomas	Moulin	4	85 –	Saunders, David	Blairgowrie	6	12 –
Richardson, Sir John Stewart, of Pitfour, Bart.	Pitfour Castle, Perth	1,147	4,817 4	Saunders, David H., of Craigmill	Rattray, Blairgowrie	20	379 6
Richmond, George, of Balhaldie	Lawhill, Auchterarder	1,835	1,188 15	Saunders, George, & Son	Rattray, Blairgowrie	4	149 10
Rintoul, Robert	Kincardine-on-Forth	2	65 –				

PERTH—continued.

Name of Owner.	Address of Owner.	Estimated Acreage of Property.	Gross Annual Value.	Name of Owner.	Address of Owner.	Estimated Acreage of Property.	Gross Annual Value.
		Acres.	£ s.			Acres.	£ s.
Saunders, James	London	6	32 2	Sommers, Thomas F., of Little Mill	Rothesay	5	14 –
Saunders, John and David, of Bramblebank	Rattray, Blairgowrie	58	162 –	Soutar, Thomas	Crieff	2	46 –
Scobie, Margaret	Bridgend, Dunblane	3	14 17	Soutar, William Shaw	Blairgowrie	11	46 –
Scone United Presbyterian Congregation	Scone	1	22 10	Soutar, Mrs. Barbara Gray, of Linnbank	Dunfermline	106	147 16
Scott, Heirs of Andrew, of Netherfield of Gattaway	Netherfield of Gattaway, Abernethy	15	47 10	Spalding, Thomas	Woodside, Cargill	3	10 –
				Speedie, Alexander	Perth	4	8 10
Scott, Fredrick Adair, of Fincastle	Fincastle, Pitlochry	4,600	934 –	Speedie, David	Pitversie, Abernethy	2	22 –
				Speid, Mary, and Helen, of Forneth	Forneth House, Blairgowrie	1,929	2,071 3
Scott, James	County Place, Perth	5	15 –	Speirs, Robert Thomas Napier, of Culdees	Culdees Castle, Muthill	1,619	1,971 17
Scott, John, of Lochbank	Bendochy, Coupar-Angus	82	195 –				
Scott, William, of Drums	Drums, Abernethy	4	17 –	Spence, Adam White	Pitlochry	3	45 –
Scott, William, of Burnside	Bendochy, Coupar-Angus	295	350 –	Sprott, Janet, of Mackrieston	Mackrieston, Stirling	25	30 –
Shairp, John C.	St. Andrews	1	30 –				
Sharp, Andrew	Errol	1	56 16	Stalker, David	Galashiels	8	25 –
Sharp, Rev. John	Manse, Aberdalgie	18	62 –	Steedman, Mrs. Elizabeth	Goudiesfold, Abernethy	2	4 –
Sharpe, Trustees of Mrs. Clarissa A. Jelf, of Kincarrathie	Kincarrathie House, Perth	20	180 –	Steel, John, of Blackpark	Fairmount, Perth	347	305 15
Sheddan, Alexander, of Pothill	Pothill, Auchterarder	25	55 13	Steele, Major-Gen. Sir Thos. Montague, of Evelick, K.C.B.	The Royal Barracks, Dublin	2,895	2,911 9
Sheddan, Trustees of John	Auchterarder	3	25 2	Steill, Mrs. Janet	Dundee	10	25 –
Shedden, William, of Lochie	Lochie, Auchterarder	199	206 10	Stephen, Andrew Cree	Kincardine-on-Forth	2	5 –
Shepherd, David	Rattray	1	30 –	Stephen, Rev. William C., of Horsewards	Culross	6	25 10
Sheppard, Rev. Henry A. Graham, of Rednock	Rednock Castle, Stirling	2,775	2,949 10	Stevenson, Rev. Patrick James	Coupar-Angus	2	37 –
Shirrie, Mrs. Elizabeth	Kippen, Stirling	1	6 –				
Sidey, William	Alyth	4	24 17	Stewart, Alexander	Peterhead	3	313 –
Sim, John, of Balnald	Drumcaro, St. Andrews	288	75 –	Stewart, Allan Duncan, of Innerhadden	Innerhadden, Rannoch	4,200	681 6
Sim, Trustees of Robert	Moulin	11	18 –				
Simpson, John	Perth	3	4 –	Stewart, Rev. Archibald F.	Aberfoyle, Stirling	16	43 –
Simpson, John H. Pelly, of Kinmonth	68 Lowndes Square, London	908	1,779 17	Stewart, Sir Archibald D. Drummond, of Grandtully, Bart.	Murthly Castle	33,274	15158 13
Simpson, Mrs. Margaret, of Castlebeg	Threapmuir, Kinross	76	55 –	Stewart, Charles Douglas	Lerwick, Zetland	2	55 –
Sinclair, James	Walnut Grove, Kinfauns, Perth	6	67 2	Stewart, Trustees of late Duncan	Blairgowrie	18	23 –
Sinclair, John	Croftland, Auchterarder	2	35 5	Stewart, Franc Nicholas	Dalpowie, Birnam	30	209 6
Sinclair, Rev. William	Kinnaird Manse, Inchture	8	51 –	Stewart, Francis Archibald	Balmerino, Coupar-Angus	10	13 –
Sinclair, Mrs. Elizabeth	Auchterarder	8	84 2				
Skinner, John, of South Colzie	South Colzie, Abernethy	44	65 –	Stewart, Henry Black, of Balnakeilly	Balnakeilly, Pitlochry	3,535	2,113 –
Skinner, John, of Wester Colzie	Wester Colzie, Abernethy	80	52 –	Stewart, James	Royal Bank, Edinburgh	3	56 –
Sligo, Archibald Vincent Smith, of Comrie	Inzievar, Dunfermline	776	595 –	Stewart, James Arnot, of Struiehill	Struiehill, Bridge of Earn	575	394 10
Do. do.	Do. (*Minerals*)	–	363 10	Stewart, James Horne, of Wester Kinloch	Wester Kinloch, Blairgowrie	82	264 –
Small, James, of Dirnanean	Enochdhu, Pitlochry	9,193	3,043 10	Stewart, John, of Dalguise	Cape of Good Hope	1,750	1,035 13
Smeaton, Rev. John, of Easter Coull, etc.	Tulliallan Manse, Kincardine-on-Forth	474	553 17	Stewart, Malcolm, of Atholebank	Atholebank House, Perth	888	394 –
Smeaton, Patrick Burgh, of Coull	Coull House, Auchterarder	672	885 10	Stewart, Peter	Shirgarton, Kippen	1	5 –
Smeaton, Mrs. Catherine Lawrence, of East Middlethird of Rotearns	Easter Coull, Auchterarder	70	70 –	Stewart, Major Robert, of Ballechin	Ballechin, Ballinluig	10,001	2,654 11
Smith, Andrew	Methven	8	12 –	Stewart, Trs. of Stewart Robertson, of Derchulich	Derchulich, Ballinluig	1,187	717 2
Smith, Andrew	Wallshaugh, Dollar	1	6 10	Stewart, William Arnot, of Wester Clow	Cheltenham	290	250 –
Smith, David	Alyth	2	40 –				
Smith, David	Auchterarder	2	44 –	Stewart, Mrs. Alston, of Urrard	Urrard House, Blair-Athole	5,423	1,205 6
Smith, George Pitcaithly, of Cairnfold	Dollar	60	60 –	Stewart, Mrs. Janetta, of Strathgarry	Strathgarry House, Blair-Athole	237	193 10
Smith, John	Alyth	1	27 –	Stewart, Mrs. Mary	Lorachan House, Callander	1	125 –
Smith, John	Alyth	5	361 10				
Smith, Robert	Edinburgh	2	12 10	Stewart, Charlotte Alston, and Christina Mary A. Stewart, of Killiecrankie	Killiecrankie Cottage, Pitlochry	633	388 5
Smith, Rev. Robert N.	Cargill	4	39 –				
Smith, William, of Finegand	Sheffield	927	100 –	Stewart, Marjory	Ardvorlich Cottage, Lochearnhead	5	35 –
Smith, Mrs. Annie, and Jane Ross	Burghmuir, Perth	3	10 –				
Smithson, Samuel, of Dalnabreck	Lentran House, Inverness	500	200 –	*Stewart's Trade Free School, Trustees of*	Abernethy	27	35 –
Smitton, James	Auchterarder	3	56 –	Stiell, James	Rose Cottage, Scone	1	30 –
Smythe, Trustees of late Robert, of Balharry	Alyth	2,262	5,009 18	Stirling, Alexander	Cultibraggan, Comrie	14	45 8
				Stirling, James, of Garden	Garden House, Stirling	2,620	1,943 10
Smythe, William, of Methven	Methven Castle, Perth	5,128	6,469 11	Stirling, John, of Kippendavie	Kippenross House, Dunblane	6,111	5,586 8
Somervail, William, of Ruthvenbank	Lochgoilhead, Greenock	13	45 –	Stirling, John, of Holmehill	Holmehill House, Dunblane	23	180 12
Somerville, John, of Cairey	Cairey, Abernethy	155	400 –				

Y

PERTH—continued.

Name of Owner.	Address of Owner.	Estimated Acreage of Property.	Gross Annual Value.	Name of Owner.	Address of Owner.	Estimated Acreage of Property.	Gross Annual Value.
		Acres.	£ s.			Acres.	£ s.
Stirling, Robert, of Alexandria	Alexandria, Perth	13	75 —	Turnbull, Archibald, of Bellwood	Bellwood, Perth	60	285 —
Stirling, Thomas James Graham, of Strowan	Strowan, Crieff	3,566	3,385 18	Turner, Angus, of Glentyre and Kippen-Turner	Pitcairns House, Dunning	1,631	684 8
Stirling, Mrs. Christian, of Newtofts of Pitquhanatrie	Borland, Blackford	188	100 —	Union Bank of Scotland	Glasgow	6	95 —
Stirling, Mrs. Isabella, of Garden	Garden, Stirling	1	16 —	Upper Strathearn Combination Poorhouse, Trustees of	Auchterarder	3	100 —
Stirling, Mrs. Morries, of Blackgrange	Blackgrange, Stirling	380	783 14	Urquhart, David, of Mollands	Mollands, Callander	1,858	710 2
Stirling - Maxwell, Sir William, of Pollok and Keir, Bart.	Keir House, Dunblane	8,863	5,731 17				
Stirling and Dunfermline Railway Company	Glasgow (Railway)	39	1,482 —	Vannan, John, of Blalowan	Bo'ness	11	26 10
Stoddart, Rev. William	Madderty Manse, Crieff	10	40 —				
Stoddart, Mrs. Sarah E. Saville, of Ballendrick	Brockhill, Exeter	102	400 10	Walker, Alexander	Findynate, Ballinluig	595	377 5
				Walker, William	Pitversie, Abernethy	3	30 1
Stoddart, Mary B., of Castlelaw	Edinburgh	5	9 —	Walker, Mrs. Helen P.	Manse, Tulliallan	4	22 8
Strathallan, Viscount	Strathallan Castle	7,208	7,611 12	Walker, Mary, of Nether Kincairney	Caputh	18	42 —
Strathmore, Earl of	Glamis Castle	282	362 16	Wallace, James	Blairgowrie	80	73 10
Stuart, Rev. Alexander Moody, and spouse, of Annat	Edinburgh	1,017	1,285 1	Wallace, Heirs of Patrick	Perth	4	70 —
				Wallace, William	Blairgowrie	3	10 —
Syme, Andrew, of Mossside of Boquhapple	Moss-side of Boquhapple, Stirling	150	101 5	Wardlaw, James L., of Easter Fordel	Dunfermline	410	280 —
Syme, James, of Woodend	Auchterarder	161	298 3	Watson, David M., of Bullionfield	Bullionfield, Dundee	4	105 —
Syme, Jessie	Auchterarder	1	6 15	Watson, James, of Inchyra	Grove House, Bowden	136	402 —
				Watson, William	Seaside, Errol	2	51 7
				Welsh, John	Kippen, Stirling	1	7 16
Tait, Rev. Walter	St. Madoes, Glencarse	30	187 10	Wemyss and March, Earl of	Gosford House, Haddington	3,010	7,666 3
Taylor, Alexander	Springbank Cottage, Dunblane	1	23 —	Wentworth, Thomas F. C. Vernon, of Dall and West and East Carie	Wentworth Castle, Yorkshire	3,329	566 10
Taylor, Andrew, of Inveralmond	Cupar-Fife	120	450 9	West, David	Blairgowrie	3	12 —
Taylor, David	Cherrybank, Abernethy	3	11 10	Wharncliffe, Lord	Belmont Castle, Meigle	1,940	4,214 —
Taylor, David	Inglismount, Perth	3	8 —	Whitson, James, of Isla Park	Coupar-Angus	164	456 —
Taylor, Rev. James	Monzie, Crieff	12	47 —				
Taylor, John	Newbigging, Crieff	7	12 —	Whitson, James, of Mudhall	Mudhall, Coupar-Angus	1,040	717 11
Taylor, John Wylde	Highfield, Scone	1	25 —	Whitson, Trustees of late James, of Bardmony	Bardmony, Alyth	196	380 —
Taylor's Institution, Trustees of	Crieff	1	33 —	Whitson, Trs. of late James	Glasgow	271	402 8
Telford, Executors of Rosanna	Boghead, Blairlogie, Stirling	2	20 —	Whitson, Thomas Hunter, of Parkhill	Parkhill House, Blairgowrie	998	1,389 5
Tennent, Trustees of late Hugh, of Dunbarney	Dunbarney House, Bridge of Earn	335	753 8	Whitson, Elizabeth, of Polcalk	Bendochy	92	200 —
Thain, Alexander, of Arthurbank	Coupar-Angus	69	125 10	Whytock & Hardie	Geddochy, Auchterarder	4	10 —
Thom, Andrew, senior, of Kirkton	Rattray	32	96 5	Wighton, John, senior	Balbeggie, Perth	3	10 —
Thom, Robert, of Kirkton	Rattray	18	38 —	Wighton, John, junior	Balbeggie, Perth	1	10 —
Thoms, John	Coupar-Angus	3	78 15	Wighton, William, of Grange of Barry	Grange of Barry, Dundee	60	644 17
Thomson, Andrew	Damhead, Milnathort	2	24 —	Williamson, Trustees of late Andrew	Abernethy, Newburgh	6	30 13
Thomson, John	Wester Moss, Muckhart	19	28 —	Williamson, Rev. David	Manse, Forgandenny, Bridge of Earn	9	42 10
Thomson, Robert	Kippen	1	6 —				
Thomson, William, of Balgowan	Balgowan, Methven	2,953	3,877 17	Williamson, David Robertson, of Lawers	Lawers House, Crieff	29,494	4,543 7
Thomson, William, of Drumquhill	Drumquhill, Dunblane	1	3 10	Williamson, John, of Easter Clunie	Easter Clunie, Newburgh	230	280 —
Thomson, Lilias and Isabella	New Scone	1	8 —	Willison, Trustees of late Rev. John	Croftwillock, Forgandenny	2	9 10
Thriepland, Sir Patrick M., of Fingask, Bart.	Fingask Castle, Errol	2,814	3,019 7	Willoughby de Eresby, Baroness	Drummond Castle, Crieff	76,837	28955 4
Tod, Trustees of late William, of Ayton	Glasgow	350	537 7	Wilson, Alexander	Alford House, Dunblane	4	60 —
Tod, Mrs. Margaret Miller, of Letham	West Brackly, Kinross	85	295 —	Wilson, Rev. John	Manse, Dunning	10	45 —
Torry, Very Rev. Dean	Coupar-Angus	7	50 —	Wilson, Rev. John	Methven Manse, Perth	30	82 12
Tosh, William Henderson	Broughty Ferry	2	59 6	Wilson, John	Bannockburn	5	250 —
Trefusis, Hon. Charles J. R. H. Stuart Forbes, of Balmano and Invermay	Invermay House, Bridge of Earn	3,720	4,396 17	Wilson, John, of Tar of Ruskie	Tar of Ruskie, Stirling	169	190 —
				Wilson, Mrs. Elizabeth	Bannockburn	1	6 10
Trinity College, Trustees of	Glenalmond, Perth	33	240 —	Winter, Rev. David	Bankfoot, Auchtergaven	11	35 —
Trotter, Charles, of Woodhill	Woodhill, Blairgowrie	950	563 7	Wishart, Andrew	Abernethy	5	27 —
				Wishart, David	Muchly, Abernethy	2	18 —
Trotter, Trustees of Col. Robert Knox, of Ballindean	Ballindean House, Inchture	1,175	2,374 12	Wishart, James	Pathhead and Abernethy	2	6 —
				Wood, William Edward C., of Keithick	Coupar-Angus	1,787	2,827 2

PERTH—continued.

Name of Owner.	Address of Owner.	Estimated Acreage of Property.	Gross Annual Value.	Name of Owner.	Address of Owner.	Estimated Acreage of Property.	Gross Annual Value.
		Acres.	£ s.			Acres.	£ s.
Wotherspoon, Rev. Henry William Lang	Kilspindie Manse, Errol	9	64 –	Young, Rev. John	Newburgh	2	12 –
Wright, Colin, of Manor Steps	Manor Steps, Stirling	16	50 –	Young, Rev. Peter William, of Williamfield	Lecropt Manse, Bridge of Allan	134	175 –
Wright, Trs. of Duncan	Kincardine-on-Forth	2	60 15	Young, Peter, & Sons	Milton, Auchterarder	6	46 –
Wright, James A., of Lawton	Lawton House, Coupar-Angus	726	906 1	Young, William	Bankfoot, Auchtergaven	20	40 8
Wylie, George, of Arndean	Arndean, Dollar	595	580 14	Young, William Laurence, of Belvidere	Belvidere, Auchterarder	30	144 12
Wylie, Trustees of Robert	Burghmuir, Perth	6	18 –	Young, Mrs. Fanny, of East Gormack	Blairgowrie	1,342	715 –
Wylie, Thomas, of Airleywight	Bankfoot, Auchtergaven	921	1,159 15	Young, Mrs. Margaret	Caputh	4	20 –
Wylie, Walter	Parkhead, Alloa	1	32 –	Young, Mrs. Thomas, of Newbigging	Methven	35	60 –
Wylie, William, of Culterenny	Bankfoot, Auchtergaven	202	337 17				
Wyllie, John	Methven	3	16 –	Zimmerman, Alexander	Glenfoot, Abernethy	6	23 15
Wyllie, Thomas	Methven	1	20 –				
				Total Owners of Land of one Acre and upwards		1,057	1,610,905 888,722 13
Young, Alexander, of Glenhead Cottage	Keir Mains, Dunblane	6	15 –	Total Owners of Lands of less than one Acre in extent		4,680	1,096 70,642 5
Young, Charles Denoon	St. Leonard's Villa, Callander	1	60 –	GRAND TOTAL		5,737	1,612,001 959,364 18

MUNICIPAL BOROUGH OF PERTH
Population over 20,000.

Name of Owner.	Address of Owner.	Estimated Acreage of Property.	Gross Annual Value.	Name of Owner.	Address of Owner.	Estimated Acreage of Property.	Gross Annual Value.
		Acres.	£ s.			Acres.	£ s.
Bower, John	Montreal Cottage, Perth	1	55 —				
				North British Railway Company	Edinburgh	12	154 15
Caledonian Railway Company	Glasgow	5	506 11	Do. do.	Do. (Railway)	12	1,620 —
Do. do.	Do. (Railway)	39	9,546 —	Paterson, William	Croft House, Perth	2	45 —
Campbell, Peter	Balhousie	1	180 —	Perth, Community of	Perth	206	3,028 —
Commissioners of Supply for Perthshire	(Perth Militia Store-Houses, &c.)	1	300 —	Perth Commissioners of Police	Perth	3	128 —
Crown, The (War Department)	(Perth Barracks, &c.)	8	504 —	Perth Infirmary, Trustees of	Perth	4	220 —
Do. (Board of Works)	(Perth General Prison, &c.)	17	4,141 —	Perth Girls School of Industry, Trustees of	Perth	1	70 —
Dickson, John, of Greenbank	Greenbank, Perth	8	77 —	Pullar, James Frederick	Rosebank, Perth	4	55 —
				Pullar, Laurence, & Co.	Balhousie, Perth	2	230 —
Elibank, Lord	Pitheavlis Castle, Perth	5	70 —	Pullar, John, & Sons	Perth	2	730 —
Faichney Industrial School, Trustees of	Perth	3	77 —	Ramsay, Robert Greig	Rio Villa, Perth	1	60 —
Falshaw, James	Edinburgh	2	224 —	Readdie, John	3 St. Leonard's Bank, Perth	2	330 10
				Ritchie, Trustees of late George, of Hill of Ruthven	Perth	1	221 10
Glovers, Incorporation of Perth	Perth	23	590 6	Rollo, Hon. John	Rodney Lodge, Perth	4	105 —
Gray, George, of Bowerswell	Bowerswell, Perth	4	118 10	Shields, John	Balhousie, Perth	6	400 —
Gray, Baroness of Gray and Kinfauns	Kinfauns Castle, Perth	14	180 —	Skeete, Horace	Bailbroke Lodge, Perth	1	60 —
				Stewart, Mrs.	Taybank, Perth	2	240 —
Hammermen, Incorporation of	Perth	3	359 16	Stewart, Mrs. Johanna	Somerset Villa, Perth	1	70 —
Hay, Robert	Gowanbank	1	50 —	Stuart, Trustees of late Mrs., of Annat	Annat Lodge, Perth	3	74 13
Joint Station Railway Committee	Perth	2	600 —	Todd, Trustees of John	Perth	1	439 15
				Troupe, General George	Pitcullen House	8	100 —
King James VI.'s Hospital, Trustees of	Perth	2	169 4	Wilson, Robert	Durn, Perth	2	60 —
Kinnoull, Earl of	Dupplin Castle	80	599 6				
Malcolm, Robert B.	Perth	2	178 19	Young, Hugh	Low Craigie, Perth	2	145 5
Marshall, Jane, of Rosemount	Rosemount, Perth	6	110 —	Young, C. D., & Co.	Perth	2	200 —
Miller, John Miller	Mayfield, Perth	2	60 —	Total Owners of Land of One Acre and upwards		47	589 28,134 —
Moncreiffe, Sir Thomas, of Moncreiffe, Bart.	Moncreiffe House, Bridge of Earn	70	490 —	Total Owners of Lands of less than one Acre in extent		1,859	250 60,928 1
Moncrieff, Alexander	Tayside, Perth	4	100 —				
M'Leod, Mrs.	Tayhill, Perth	2	60 —	GRAND TOTAL		1,906	839 89,062 1

RENFREW.

Population in 1871, 216,947.
Inhabited Houses, 13,551.
Number of Parishes, 19.

Name of Owner.	Address of Owner.	Estimated Acreage of Property.	Gross Annual Value.	Name of Owner.	Address of Owner.	Estimated Acreage of Property.	Gross Annual Value.
		Acres.	£ s.			Acres.	£ s.
Abercorn, Duke of	Duddingston House, Edinburgh	496	1,680 –	Birkmyre, John	Broadstone, Port-Glasgow	28	130 –
Do. do.	Do. (*Minerals*)	–	2,307 –	Birkmyre, Trs. of William	Port-Glasgow	3	908 –
Adam, George	Greenock (*Timber Pond*)	1	15 –	Do. do.	Do. (*Timber Pond*)	2	75 –
Adam, Mrs. Elizabeth	St. Enoch Sq., Glasgow	2	80 –	Blackwood, Thomas	Woodhall, Port-Glasgow	66	1,520 2
Aitken, James	Woodend, Kilwinning	76	90 –	Do. do.	Do. (*Timber Ponds*)	12	232 5
Aird, Rev. Hugh	Neilston	10	63 –	Blair, James	Wester Kerse, Lochwinnoch	50	80 –
Alexander, John H. I., of Southbar	Southbar, Inchinnan	1,814	2,422 –	Blair, James	Kilmalcolm	15	28 –
Do. do.	Do. (*Minerals*)	–	78 9	Blair, James and David	Lochwinnoch	76	90 –
Alexander, Trustees of Walter	Johnshill, Lochwinnoch	1	14 –	Blair, John	Kilmalcolm	2	32 –
Alexander, Trustees of William	Bridge of Weir	30	108 –	Blair, Mary and Margaret	Lochwinnoch	48	126 10
				Blantyre, Lord	Erskine House, Glasgow	4,449	8,415 17
Algie, David	Old Manse, Inchinnan	5	75 –	Do. do.	Do. (*Quarries*)	–	200 –
Algie, Matthew	Crossmyloof	1	377 15	Do. do.	Do. (*Minerals*)	–	400 –
Allan, Duncan	Rossbank, Port-Glasgow	1	203 –	Bousfield, Charles H.	Johnstone	1	1,076 –
Allan, Trustees of James	Crosshill	3	89 –	Boyd, David	7 Brougham Street, Greenock	1	39 –
Allan, John	Hillhead, Kilbirnie	116	180 –	Boyd, George	Renfrew	12	374 10
Allan, Robert	34 St. James St., Paisley	2	42 –	Boyd, James	Largs	53	56 –
Allison, James	Gatehead, Bishopton	15	22 –	Boyd, James, and another	Lochwinnoch	60	81 –
Allison, Robert	Malletsheugh, Mearns	63	210 –	Boyd, John	149 St. Vincent Street, Glasgow	67	173 12
Alum and Ammonia Co.	Hurlet	2	457 –				
Ancell, John, and others	Cathcart	3	12 10	Boyle, James	150 Main St., Glasgow	1	104 10
Anderson, James, of Highholm	Highholm, Port-Glasgow	360	526 13	*British Linen Co. Bank*	Edinburgh	8	118 –
Anderson, Trustees of James, junior	Port-Glasgow	10	593 3	Brodie, James	Fairhills, Lochwinnoch	42	83 –
Do. do.	Do. (*Timber Ponds*)	2	45 –	Brodie, Trustees of James	109 High Street, Paisley	62	99 –
Anderson, Matthew	Milliken Park	1	65 –	Brodie, John	Kerse, Beith	42	80 –
Anderson, Robert, and another	West Arthurlie, Barrhead	6	594 16	Brodie, Trs. of William	Lochwinnoch	182	196 15
				Brodie, Jane, and others	Nervelstone, Lochwinnoch	50	100 –
Anderson, William	Hurlet	52	238 –	Brodie, Jane, and others	Kilbirnie, Ayrshire	76	60 –
Anderson, Mrs. Jane, and others	Belltrees, Lochwinnoch	73	144 10	Brown, Peter	Rossland, Bishopton	5	62 10
				Brown, William	Water Yetts, Kilmalcolm	255	383 17
				Brown, Mary	Capelrigg, Mearns	299	465 –
				Browns, Malloch, & Co.	Eldersley, Paisley	23	585 9
Anstruther, Heirs of John F.	Bogiewood, Pt.-Glasgow	1	3 16	Brownlie, Archibald	Barrhead	3	96 –
Arbuckle, Matthew	Grey Place, Greenock	1	476 –	Buchanan, D. C. R. C., of Drumpelier	Drumpelier, Coatbridge	2,462	3,112 7
Armour, John	South Hillhead, Mearns	76	120 –	Do. do.	Do. (*Timber Ponds*)	10	294 15
Arrol, James	Rankine St., Johnstone	1	111 –	Bunten, Trustees of James	Braehead, Cathcart	40	372 –
Arthur, James, of Barshaw	Barshaw, Paisley	3	28 –	Bunten, James, and others	Kingston, Greenock	15	533 5
Arthur, Robert	Lochwinnoch	63	158 –	Do. do.	Do. (*Timber Ponds*)	1	15 –
Athya, John	Kirkliuton, Crossmyloof	1	120 –	Burns, George	Wemyss Bay	85	441 –
Aytoun, Mrs. Margaret Ann	33 Upper Brook Street, Park Lane, London	86	170 15	Burns, James	Dodside, Newton-Mearns	1	12 –
				Burns, John	Castle Wemyss, Wemyss Bay	21	183 –
				Burns, Robert	Mid Barnaigh, Lochwinnoch	95	90 –
Bain, Mrs. Janet	Auchneagh, Greenock	2	35 –				
Ballantyne, William	Craigielinn, Paisley	40	85 –	Burns, Mrs. Mary	Sauchiehall St., Glasgow	25	52 10
Barbour, David	Lochwinnoch	6	35 –				
Barbour, John	Lochwinnoch	2	30 10				
Barr, James	Gateside, Greenock	1	50 15	Caird, Trs. of William J.	Port-Glasgow	3	193 19
Barr, Matthew	Houston	2	15 –	Caldwell, Hugh	East Braes, Kilbarchan	47	53 –
Barr, Trustees of Thomas	Lochwinnoch	61	100 –	Caldwell, Hugh	Ward, Lochwinnoch	177	74 10
Barr, Agnes	Carphin, Cupar-Fife	54	60 10	Caldwell, John	37 Milton St., Glasgow	11	48 2
Barrhead Gas Company	Barrhead	1	267 –	Caldwell, John	Earlshill, Lochwinnoch	90	87 –
Bartlemore, James	Lochwinnoch	37	50 –	Caldwell, William	Manchester	75	140 –
Bartlemore, John	Paisley	92	165 –	Caldwell, William	Water Yett, Lochwinnoch	62	70 –
Beckett, James	2 Brougham Terrace, Crosshill	3	565 –	Caldwell, Jane and Jemima	North Muirdykes, Howood	43	60 –
Bell, William J.	Cathcart	1	512 –				
Bennie & Co., George	Kinning Park, Glasgow	1	375 –	*Caledonian Railway Company*	Glasgow	17	45 –
Biggart & Sons, David	High Street, Johnstone	2	207 2	Do. do.	Do. (*Railway*)	172	17777
Birkmyre, Henry	Springbank, Port-Glasgow	2	80 –	Do. do.	Do. (*For Gourock Pier*)	1	187 –

RENFREW—continued.

Name of Owner.	Address of Owner.	Estimated Acreage of Property.	Gross Annual Value.	Name of Owner.	Address of Owner.	Estimated Acreage of Property.	Gross Annual Value.
		Acres.	£ s.			Acres.	£ s.
Cameron, Jane and Helen	Bridge of Weir	1	131 1	Crawford, William	Townhead, Eaglesham	2	28 11
Campbell, Colonel Archibald C., of Blythswood, M.P.	Blythswood, Renfrew	1,826	4,023 16	Crawford, Mrs. Grace, and another	Springside, Howwood	121	145 —
Do. do.	Do. (Minerals)	—	1,906 15	Crawford, Mrs. Mary	Johnshill, Lochwinnoch	15	35 —
Campbell, Capt. Barrington Buckley Douglas	Scots Fusilier Guards, Chelsea	2	9 —	Cross, David	Langbank	128	359 8
Campbell, Rev. George	Pollokshaws	8	65 10	Cross Arthurlie Spinning and Weaving Company	Barrhead	19	889 16
Campbell, Hugh and John	Newmilns, Lochwinnoch	8	31 —	Crum, Alexander and William Graham	Thornliebank	73	4,310 10
Campbell, James	Newhouse, Lochwinnoch	29	36 —	Crum, Alexander	Thornliebank	353	762 —
Campbell, Robert	Burnthills, Lochwinnoch	20	26 —	Crum, Mrs. Agnes	Busby	16	1,189 10
Campbell, William	East Shaw Villa, Shawlands, Pollokshaws	2	195 —	Cuninghame, John C., of Craigends	Craigends, Johnstone	3,136	7,477 7
Campbell, William	Newton Belltrees, Lochwinnoch	2	25 —	Do. do.	Do. (Minerals)	—	2,508 —
Cansh, Thomas	Cathcart	1	100 —	Cunninghame, Allan	Broomstone, Pollokshaws	10	40 —
Carruth, Allan	Cullochant, Kilbarchan	71	130 —	Cunninghame, James, of Tower	Pollokshields	58	110 —
Carslaw, John	Newhouse, Newton-Mearns	45	95 —	Cunninghame, John M.	Stirling	2	300 —
Carswell, Thomas	Neilstonside, Neilston	6	143 6	Cunninghame, Dowager Lady	Maidenhead, Berkshire	265	618 14
Carswell, Rev. William	Eaglesham	123	113 10	Currie & Guthrie	Lynedoch St., Greenock	4	269 10
Cathcart, Earl	Cathcart House, Cathcart	88	567 15	Cuthbertson, John	Cranley Lodge, Helensburgh	137	133 —
Chalmers, Andrew	Waterside, Neilston	6	150 —				
Chalmers, Malcom	Clydeside, Port-Glasgow	2	46 16				
Christie, Robert	Royal Crescent, Crosshill	2	1,649 5	Dalglish, Robert, M.P.	29 St. Vincent Place, Glasgow	63	113 —
City of Glasgow Bank	Glasgow	5	386 11	Darroch, Duncan, of Gourock	Gourock House, Greenock	4,248	4,182 —
Clark, Adam	South Loanhead, Lochwinnoch	30	35 —	Do. do.	Do. (Quarries)	—	205 —
Clark, Andrew	How Barnaigh, Lochwinnoch	29	40 —	Davidson, Mrs. Mary	Ferncliff, Wemyss Bay	2	80 —
Clark, David	Highcraig, Eaglesham	26	70 —	*Deaf and Dumb Institution*	Cathcart	14	250 —
Clark, Samuel	Manswraes, Bridge of Weir	5	47 —	Denholm, Trustees of Mr. and Mrs. John	Mains, Thornliebank	34	80 —
Clark, Mrs. Jean, and another	Auchenhane, Lochwinnoch	55	108 10	Denniston, James W.	Helensburgh	258	217 15
Clark, Mrs. Marion	Tophouse, Howwood	25	25 —	Dick, James	37 Main Street, Pollokshaws	1	102 5
Clark, Elizabeth	20 Hamilton Drive, Glasgow	1	89 —	Dick, Trustees of Quintin	Houston	2	34 —
Clark, Margaret, and others	126 High Street, Renfrew	2	32 —	Dixon, William Smith	1 Dixon Street, Glasgow	160	1,736 10
Clyde Navigation, Trustees of	16 Robertson Street, Glasgow	7	143 5	Do. do.	Do. (Minerals)	—	2,714 —
Coats, J. & P.	Ferguslie	13	330 —	Dobie, James	Glebe Street, Renfrew	1	23 —
Coats, Neilson, & Co.	Thorn	8	911 10	Donald, James and Mrs. Robert	Johnstone	1	120 —
Cochrane, Trustees of Alexander	Kirktonfield, Neilston	24	562 4	Douglas, Trustees of Robert	Elderslie	1	266 1
Cochrane, James, junior	Kirkfield, Bothwell	7	367 6	Douglas, William	Mearnskirk, Newton-Mearns	1	47 —
Cochrane, John	Barrhead	1	153 17	Dove, Mrs. Agnes	7 Newton Terrace, Glasgow	3	295 5
Connell & Co., Charles	Scotstoun, Partick	6	988 15	Drysdale, Thomas C.	Abroad	26	36 —
Connell, William	Lochwinnoch	5	44 —	Duncan, Charles	Woodend, Rothesay	95	130 —
Corbett, Trs. of Thomas	Pollokshaws	2	263 13	Duncan, Robert	Ardenclutha, Port-Glasgow	13	960 —
Couper, James	Holmwood House, Cathcart	3	85 —	Duncan, Robert, and John Laird	Port-Glasgow	3	180 —
Couper, Robert	Sunnyside, Cathcart	2	193 10	Dunlop, James, of Arthurlie	Arthurlie, Barrhead	410	1,210 14
Couper, Agnes, and Mrs. Janet Kennedy	New Cathcart	1	121 17	Dunlop, Robert	7 Richmond Street, Glasgow	1	24 10
Coustonholm Weaving Company	Pollokshaws	2	670 —	Dunlop, Mrs. Margaret	Arthurlie House, Barrhead	205	326 —
Craig, George	Broom, Newton-Mearns	107	290 —				
Craig, John	Westfield, Tarbolton	130	135 —				
Craig, John	Monkland, Kilbarchan	29	63 15				
Craig, William	Whinnerstone, Kilbarchan	45	26 —				
Craig, William	Millthird, Neilston	1	20 —	Eadie, George & Alexander	215 Caledonia Road, Glasgow	3	1,830 —
Craig, William	Cathcart Street, Ayr	1	110 —	*Eaglesham, Feuars of*	Eaglesham	100	18 —
Craig, William B.	Fordbank, Howwood	10	105 —	Edmiston, William T.	128 Crown Street, Glasgow	2	163 —
Crawford, Allan C.	Beith	15	260 17				
Crawford, Andrew	448 Argyle Street, Glasgow	39	222 15	Ellice, Edward, M.P.	28 Grosvenor Square, London	14	50 —
Crawford, Archibald	Kilbarchan	2	199 1	Ewing, James, Trustees of	11 Stirling Street, Glasgow	24	84 18
Crawford, Daniel	St. Albans, Hants	125	168 16	Faulds, Alexander R.	Clark's Land, Stewarton	50	111 10
Crawford, Daniel	Blairside, Kilwinning	110	85 10	Faulds, Andrew	Broadlees, Newton-Mearns	90	140 —
Crawford, George	Banktop, Johnstone	2	218 3	Ferguson, Duncan	Dunterlie, Barrhead	1	203 6
Crawford, Hugh	Burntshields, Kilbarchan	78	140 —	Finlay, James	Langside, Crossmyloof	1	160 —
Crawford, Hugh & James	Beith	12	337 6	Finlay, William	Horswood, Bridge of Weir	48	95 7
Crawford, James	Harplaw, Largs	37	30 —	Finlayson, Bousfield, & Co.	Johnstone	7	302 15
Crawford, John	Sproulston, Howood	143	178 —				
Do.	Do. (Quarry)	—	3 —				
Crawford, Thomas M'K., of Cartsburn	Edinburgh	8	13 —				

RENFREW—continued.

Name of Owner.	Address of Owner.	Estimated Acreage of Property.	Gross Annual Value.	Name of Owner.	Address of Owner.	Estimated Acreage of Property.	Gross Annual Value.
		Acres.	£ s.			Acres.	£ s.
Finlayson, James	Merchiston, Johnstone	14	225 –	Greenock and Wemyss Bay Railway Company	Glasgow (Railway)	76	3,935 –
Fleming, Andrew	Fulwood, Linwood	82	181 5	Greig, Thomas W., of Muirshiel	Muirshiel, Lochwinnoch	3,798	749 –
Fleming, James	Newlandsfield, Pollokshaws	16	765 –	Do. do.	Do. (Minerals)	–	100 –
Forbes, Ninian	Hamilton Street, Govan	1	30 –	Greig, Mrs. Agnes	Edinburgh	260	1,030 13
Fraser, John	Newfield Ho., Johnstone	3	106 15	Grieve, James J., M.P.	Levan, Gourock	4	150 –
Free Church, Deacons' Court of	Barrhead	1	35 –	Guthrie, Robert	12 Kilblain St., Greenock	1	150 3
Freeland & Co., John	Bridge of Weir	7	859 4				
Freeland, Robert, of Gryffe Castle	Gryffe Castle, Bridge of Weir	385	865 7	Hair, Andrew, senior	Glencairn Bank, Port-Glasgow	60	235 –
Fulton, William	Broomknowe, Howwood	40	48 –	Hamilton, George	Blackland Mill, Paisley	15	495 –
Fulton, William	Auchenbathie, Howwood	47	53 –	Hamilton, James	Johnstone	2	221 –
Fulton, William	Glenfield, Paisley	38	697 –	Hamilton, John, of Greenbank	Greenbank, Newton-Mearns	451	955 –
Fyfe, William	Kilbirnie Place, Kilbirnie	37	60 –	Hamilton, James D.	60 George Sq., Glasgow	70	142 18
				Hamilton & Co., William	Bay St., Port-Glasgow	2	340 –
Galloway, William	Fulbar Place, Renfrew	1	32 –	Hardie, Stark, & Co.	Locherbank, Kilbarchan	26	461 –
Gamble, Mrs. Caroline Ann	Ashburn, Gourock	4	220 –	Hardie, William E.	Locherhouse, Johnstone	1	120 –
Gavin & Sons, Ludovic	Eaglesham	12	165 15	Hardie, Marion	West Glenhuntly, Port-Glasgow	9	68 19
Geddes, John	Thornbank, Cathcart	6	55 –	Hart, James	Old Manse, Pollokshaws	2	146 –
Geddes, William	Cathcart	4	417 2	Harvey, Andrew	Nethercairn, Newton-Mearns	156	85 –
Gemmell, John	Overton, Lochwinnoch	73	65 14	Harvey, Charles	Greenlaw, Newton-Mearns	12	63 5
Gibson, Bowman	Snypes, Neilston	41	69 –				
Gilfillan, Rev. Robert	Lochwinnoch	9	45 –	Harvey, Henry Lee, of Castlesemple	Castlesemple, Lochwinnoch	6,500	5,561 15
Gillan, Rev. Robert	Manse, Inchinnan	9	69 –	Harvey, John	Muirend, Lochwinnoch	50	43 –
Gilmour, Allan, of Eaglesham	Eaglesham	16,516	12073 17	Harvey & Co., J. and W.	Yoker, Partick	5	330 –
Do. do.	Do. (Quarry)	–	32 –	Hay, John, and James Campbell	Newton Belltrees, Lochwinnoch	4	14 –
Gilmour, James	Langside, Crossmyloof	1	110 –	Hay, William	Langside, Crossmyloof	2	110 –
Gilmour, Reps. of John, of South Walton	Newton-Mearns	100	295 –	Henderson, Coulborn, & Company	Renfrew	10	1,684 –
Gilroy & Thomas	Crofthead, Neilston	30	668 –	Henderson, James	West Scotland Street, Glasgow	5	4,565 –
Glasgow, Earl of	Hawkhead, Paisley	4,453	6,811 3	Henderson, James M'L.	Renfrew	2	82 –
Do. do.	Do. (Minerals)	–	480 –	Henderson, Robert	7 Mincing Lane, London	464	796 –
Glasgow and Kilmarnock Joint Railway Committee	Glasgow	7	167 10	Do. do.	Do. (Quarry)	–	200 –
Glasgow and Paisley, and Glasgow, Barrhead, and Kilmarnock Joint Railway Companies	Glasgow (Railway)	166	10524 –	Henderson, Mrs. Mary	Park, Inchinnan	13	130 –
Glasgow and South-Western Railway Company	Glasgow	6	351 –	Hendry, John	West Auchengown, Lochwinnoch	25	30 –
Do. do.	Do. (Railway & Canal)	227	29109 –	Herbertson, John	Townhead, Newton-Mearns	247	492 –
Glasgow and Suburban Dwellings Company	Old Cathcart	3	66 10	Heys & Son, Zechariah	Arthurlie, Barrhead	26	1,269 –
Glasgow, Corporation of (for Water Works)	Glasgow	185	9,455 –	Heys, Trs. of Zechariah	Arthurlie, Barrhead	163	379 8
Glasgow, Town Council of	Glasgow	142	400 –	Hill, Rev. Henry D.	Eaglesham	9	55 –
Glen, Thomas	Thornhill, Johnstone	6	110 –	Hill, Mathew	Eldon Street, Greenock	89	34 15
Glen, William	Kaim, Lochwinnoch	72	84 –	Hill, Heirs of Ninian	Levan, Gourock	4	130 –
Glen, Mrs. Margaret	Hillside, Barrhead	8	90 –	Hill, Thomas	Merrylee, Cathcart	43	183 –
Goldie, John	Langside, Crossmyloof	1	120 –	Hodgert, John	Milliken Park, Kilbarchan	2	95 –
Goodwin & Co., James	Russell Street, Johnstone	1	120 –	Holmes, James	Hairlaws, Kilbarchan	25	25 –
Gordon, John, of Aitkenhead	Aitkenhead, Cathcart	333	1,347 4	Holmes, James	Slates, Kilmalcolm	79	117 –
Gormley, William	Newton Ralston, Barrhead	2	37 15	Holmes, John	Girthill, Houston	29	48 –
				Holmes, John	Johnstone	85	183 15
Gourock Ropework Company	Port-Glasgow	18	2,053 –	Holmes, William	Gladstone, Kilbarchan	24	40 –
Gourock, Water Commissioners of (for Water Works)	Gourock	10	150 –	Home, Countess of	The Hirsel, Coldstream	1,325	3,063 13
Govan & Son, William	15 Renfield St., Glasgow	6	676 2	Do. do.	Do. (Minerals)	–	400 –
Graham, Heirs of Alexander, of Fereneze	Fereneze, Barrhead	300	1,050 1	Houston, Campbell and James	Home Cottage, Renfrew	2	231 15
Graham, John G. B., of Fereneze	Fereneze, Barrhead	1,381	726 12	Houston, George Ludovic	Johnstone	1,841	2,800 11
Do. do.	Do. (Quarry)	–	133 –	Do. do.	Do. (Minerals)	–	97 6
Graham, Rev. Robert	Kilbarchan	20	75 –	Howie, John	Hazeldean, Newton-Mearns	165	386 10
Grant, Peter	Johnstone	1	55 –	Howie, Robert	Southfield, Newton-Mearns	80	190 10
Gray, Alexander	14 High St., Johnstone	1	17 10	Howie, Robert	Shanghai	99	120 –
Gray, Dunn, & Company	Stanley Street, Glasgow	2	448 –	Howie, Mrs. Martha	Southfield, Newton-Mearns	1	14 –
Greenock Harbour, Trustees of	Greenock (Timber Ponds)	6	161 17	Huie, James	Crosshill, Cathcart	4	144 –
Greenock, Parochial Board of	Captain Street, Greenock	83	116 10	Hunter, James	Newton-Mearns	1	10 –
Greenock, Water Trustees of (for Water Works)	Greenock	748	9,010 –	Hunter, Thomas O. and Charles P.	24 Forsyth Street, Greenock	2	100 –
				Hurlet and Campsie Alum Company	Hurlet	31	160 –
				Hutcheson, Trs. of David	45 Orchard St., Renfrew	1	45 –
				Hutcheson, James B.	45 Orchard St., Renfrew	1	15 –
				Hutcheson's Hospital Trs.	108 Ingram St., Glasgow	71	350 –

RENFREW—continued.

Name of Owner.	Address of Owner.	Estimated Acreage of Property.	Gross Annual Value.	Name of Owner.	Address of Owner.	Estimated Acreage of Property.	Gross Annual Value.
		Acres.	£ s.			Acres.	£ s.
Jackson, Robert	Huthead, Kilbarchan	38	60 –	M'Connell, Hugh	Nether Kirkton, Neilston	3	461 1
Jackson, Mrs. Janet	Spittal, Cambuslang	72	190 –	M'Cord, Robert	Braehead Villa, Pollokshields	1	90 –
Jamieson, James Fyfe	Rednoch, Stirling	329	345 –	M'Culloch, Trs. of James	Trees, Barrhead	13	146 –
Jamieson, John	Lunderston, Inverkip	5	33 –	MacDowall, Henry, of Garthland	Lochwinnoch	2,825	2,706 15
Jamieson, John	Muirhead, Linwood	7	11 –	MacDowall, Henry, junior	Calderhaugh, Lochwinnoch	2	13 –
Jardine, Walter B.	Mount Florida, Cathcart	1	35 –	M'Dowall, Mrs. Elizabeth	Walkinshaw Street, Johnstone	2	267 –
Jardine, Mrs. Jane	Elderslie	1	120 14	M'Ewan, John	Glenlora, Lochwinnoch	410	457 –
Johnstone, David	Hope Cottage, Shawlands	1	33 –	Macfarlane, Mrs. Catherine	1 Great Western Terrace, Glasgow	4	120 –
Johnstone, David B.	Kaim, Lochwinnoch	169	208 8	Macfarlane, Mary and Christina	Calderhaugh, Lochwinnoch	6	47 10
Johnstone Gas-Light Co.	Johnstone	3	375 –	Macfie, Robert	Airds, Appin, Argyleshire	114	246 11
Johnstone, James	Glenpatrick, Paisley	3	105 –	Do. (*Quarries*)	Do.	–	100 –
Johnstone, Trs. of Robert, of Shieldhill	Glasgow	41	90 –	M'Gaw, Peter	Rosebank, Gourock	1	90 –
Kennedy, Hugh	Partick, Glasgow	40	60 –	M'Ginnes, Daniel	Springfield, Barrhead	3	18 –
Kerr, Mrs. Margaret, and another	Linthills and Newton of Barr	37	40 10	M'Gregor, Patrick Comyn	Lonend, Paisley	140	222 10
King & Co., H. J. H.	St. James St., Glasgow	1	219 –	M'Guffie, Trs. of Thomas	Juniper Bank, Langbank	4	130 –
King, James	Houston	1	24 9	M'Haffie, Reps. of John	Glasgow	197	322 –
King, James K. C.	Millbank, Bishopton	51	103 10	Do. (*Quarries*)	Do.	–	250 –
King, John	South Muirdykes, Lochwinnoch	56	70 –	M'Haffie, Robert	9 Blythswood Square, Glasgow	209	285 –
King, John	Levernholm, Hurlet	8	142 –	Do. (*Quarries*)	Do.	–	904 –
King, John	Houston	3	120 –	M'Hutcheson, James	Renfrew	2	120 –
King, Walter	Houston	2	75 17	M'Ilraith, Rev. John	Erskine, Glasgow	8	55 –
Kippen, Durham	132 St. Vincent Street, Glasgow	15	52 2	M'Ilwraith, James	Kinning Park	1	210 –
Knox, George	Polnoon Lodge, Eaglesham	49	132 –	M'Intyre, Trs. of John	Lorn Terrace, Strathbungo	2	1,090 –
				M'Intyre, John G.	86 High Street, Renfrew	1	51 –
				M'Intyre, Peter, and another	Netherholehouse, Neilston	49	243 16
Laing, Alexander	Comrie, Perthshire	20	18 –	M'Kirdy, A. and J.	Fereneze, Barrhead	2	200 –
Laird, Alexander	Princes Street, Port-Glasgow	3	59 8	M'Lachlan, Neil	Broadley, Neilston	13	40 –
Laird, James	East Knockbartnock, Lochwinnoch	40	75 –	M'Laren, Rev. Alexander	Manse, Houston	10	48 –
Laird, James	Langside, Kilmalcolm	44	70 –	M'Laurin, Peter	Cartside, Johnstone	14	346 8
Laird, John, and others	Port-Glasgow	1	386 12	M'Lean, William	188 West Regent Street, Glasgow	10	475 –
Do. (*Timber Ponds*)	Do.	1	25 –	M'Lean, William	Shields, Renfrew	8	24 –
Lambie, Mrs. Agnes	Paxton Terrace, Crosshill	35	78 –	M'Lellan, Thomas	Barrhead	1	224 –
Lamond, Henry, and John Marshall	64 West Regent Street, Glasgow	13	250 –	M'Lellan, Walter	Clydesdale Iron Works	3	450 –
Lamont, James	Shutterflat, Beith	95	70 –	M'Lellan, Trustees of Mrs. Catherine, and children	Glasgow	1	40 –
Lang, Alexander	Burntshields, Kilbarchan	63	85 –	M'Murtrie, John	Glenclune, Port-Glasgow	2	424 14
Lang, Arthur	West Kilbride, Kilmalcolm	1	6 –	M'Murtrie, Heirs of Mrs. Mary	Glenclune, Port-Glasgow	1	265 16
Lang, Arthur	24 Kinning St., Glasgow	37	50 –	M'Nab & Co., John	Midtonfield, Howood	16	856 6
Lang, George	Cauldside, Kilmalcolm	30	30 –	M'Nair, Trs. of Andrew	Longcroft, Renfrew	2	44 –
Lang, James	East Yonderton, Bridge of Weir	33	115 5	M'Nish, James	50 Castlegate, Nottingham	116	86 –
				M'Onie, Andrew	Bruce Road, Pollokshields	2	130 –
Lang, John	Killochries, Kilmalcolm	64	70 –	M'Phedron, John M'C.	Craigbet, Bridge of Weir	201	403 12
Lang, Mrs. Elizabeth	Burntshields, Kilbarchan	66	87 15	M'Quaker, Robert	Demity Street, Johnstone	1	219 13
Latta, Andrew, and others	Gavilmoss, Lochwinnoch	43	60 –	Macquisten, Rev. Alexander	Manse, Inverkip	10	60 –
Latta, Trs. of William	Boydstone, Lochwinnoch	74	145 –	M'Vicar, Archibald	Shields Cottage, Pollokshields	2	365 10
Leck, Rev. Alexander	Manse, Kilmalcolm	12	30 –	Marr, Richard	Duntocher, East Kilpatrick	3	110 –
Leckie, Robert	Factory St., Pollokshaws	1	330 17	Marshall, John	Westhills, Lochwinnoch	50	90 –
Lindsay, Robert	East Park House, Kilmalcolm	98	127 10	Marshall, William	Ladyburn, Greenock	2	15 –
Lobnitz, Henry C.	Monkdyke, Renfrew	1	15 5	Marshall, Elizabeth, and William Renfrew	Thorn, Johnstone	2	53 9
Lockhart, David	Cogan St., Pollokshaws	1	145 –	Martin, Alexander	Ochil View, Stirling	3	357 –
Logan, William	Little Cloak, Lochwinnoch	28	38 –	Mather, William	Waterfoot, Newton-Mearns	34	122 16
Lounsdale Bleaching Co.	Lounsdale, Paisley	32	506 10	Maxwell, James E. S. S.	Nairn	117	307 3
Love, Alexander and George	Margaret's Mill, Kilmalcolm	18	40 –	Maxwell, Trs. of Sir John, of Pollok, Bart.	Pollokshaws	270	1,233 13
Love, Andrew	Mid Linthills, Lochwinnoch	68	50 –	Maxwell, Trustees of John Hall, of Dargavel	Dargavel	424	526 11
Love, Robert	Braehead, Lochwinnoch	6	89 15	Maxwell, William Hall, of Dargavel	Ryde	803	1,621 –
Love, William	22 Florence Pl., Glasgow	93	143 –	Maxwell, Sir William Stirling, of Pollok and Keir, Bart.	Keir, Dunblane	4,773	13012 –
Lowndes, Robert J.	Crosslees House, Pollokshaws	7	123 15	Do. do.	Do. (*Quarries*)	–	458 15
Lowndes, Symington, & Company	Cogan St., Pollokshaws	3	588 –	Do. do.	Do. (*Minerals*)	–	700 –
Lyle, Alexander	Knightswood, Maryhill	5	9 –	*Mearns, Heritors of*	Newton-Mearns	8	50 –
Lyle, John	Muirshields, Bridge of Weir	2	15 10	Meikle, Robert	Fauldshead, Renfrew	50	140 –
				Meikle, Thomas	Viewfield House, Pollokshields	1	165 –
M'Call, Henry, of Daldowie	Baillieston	791	713 –				

RENFREW—continued.

Name of Owner.	Address of Owner.	Estimated Acreage of Property.	Gross Annual Value.	Name of Owner.	Address of Owner.	Estimated Acreage of Property.	Gross Annual Value.
		Acres.	£ s.			Acres.	£ s.
Meiklejohn, John	Langbank	2	70 –	Paterson, William	129 St. Vincent Street, Glasgow	154	270 –
Merry & Cuninghame (Limited)	St. Vincent St., Glasgow	36	820 18	Paton, William	Clark Street, Johnstone	3	301 5
Middlemas, Mrs. Margaret	Drygate, Kilbarchan	6	15 10	Patrick, John F.	Grangehill, Beith	180	499 18
Millar, Hugh	Newton-Mearns	1	10 10	Patrick, Robert W. C.	Woodside, Beith	295	439 10
Millar, Trustees of John	Picketlaw, Neilston	50	78 7	Pattison, Alexander	Damton, Kilbarchan	88	125 –
Millar, William	Mid Lochead, Lochwinnoch	40	78 –	Paul, William B.	Glen Levan, Gourock	3	70 –
Miller, George	Meikleburntshields, Kilbarchan	92	100 –	Peock, John	Muirdyke, Howwood	19	40 –
				Peock, William	Meiklerigg s, Paisley	10	9 –
Miller, Higginbotham, & Co.	Netherlee, Cathcart	16	653 10	Peock, Jane Eliza	Burnside, Howwood	35	45 –
Miller, William	Eastwoodhill, Thornliebank	5	125 –	Picken, James H.	Titwood, Newton-Mearns	43	55 –
				Pinkerton, John	39 Wellmeadow, Paisley	1	343 1
Milne, Executors of John	Brachead, Paisley	102	145 –	Pinkerton, Representatives of William	Mossend, Lochwinnoch	15	20 –
Mitchell & Locke	West Arthurlie, Barrhead	2	550 –	Pollock, Alexander	Barcraigs, Beith	38	50 –
Mitchell, Mrs. Jean	Blackhouse, by Mearns	139	72 –	Pollock, Alexander	Calderhaugh, Lochwinnoch	176	198 4
Mitchell, Mrs. Margaret	50 South Apsley Place, Glasgow	52	100 –	Pollock, Allan, of Broom	Lismany, Ireland	3,761	4,055 10
Moffat, James	Port-Glasgow	26	548 12	Do. do.	Do. (Quarry)	–	10 –
Do.	Do. (Timber Ponds)	3	110 –	Pollock, James	Blackhouse, Newton-Mearns	129	270 –
Montgomery, James B.	27 North Parade, Penzance	44	80 –				
Montgomery, Mrs. Janet	Sydenham, London	34	120 15	Pollock, James	Titwood, Newton-Mearns	117	234 –
Do. do.	Do. (Timber Ponds)	4	80 –	Pollock, John	Blackhouse, Newton-Mearns	35	88 8
Moody, Robert, and J. H. M'Clure	198 West George Street, Glasgow	1	160 –	Pollock, John	West Walton, by Neilston	51	62 –
				Pollock, John	Springbank, Newton-Mearns	2	73 –
More, James	7 Macdowall Street, Johnstone	1	65 8	Pollock, John	Springside, Howwood	57	52 –
Morrison, John	Newton, Renfrew	2	59 9	Pollock, John	Tophouse, Howwood	51	50 –
Motherwell, Mrs. Mary	Gourock	1	30 15	Pollock, John	Burnthills, Howwood	32	36 –
Muir, Thomas	24 York Terrace, Regent Park, London	103	150 –	Pollock, Robert	North Walton, by Neilston	91	102 –
Muirhead, Andrew	Meiklecloak, Lochwinnoch	90	183 –				
Muirhead, Henry	Bushyhill, Cambuslang	20	19 –	Pollok, Sir Hew C., of Pollok, Bart.	Pollok Castle, Newton-Mearns	2,855	3,339 –
Murdoch, Alexander	Langside	2	120 –				
Murdoch, Trustees of Peter	Todhillbank, Newton-Mearns	32	140 10	Pollok, Lady Crawfurd	48 Melville Street, Edinburgh	290	602 3
Do. do.	Do. (Quarry)	–	20 –	Polson, John	West Mount, Paisley	58	111 –
Murdoch, Peter R.	Todhillbank, Newton-Mearns	5	23 5	Port-Glasgow, Cemetery Board of	Port-Glasgow	6	45 –
Murdoch, Trustees of Mrs.	Todhillbank, Newton-Mearns	90	252 18	Port-Glasgow, Harbour Trustees of	Port-Glasgow	1	100 –
				Do. do.	Do. (Harbour)	3	1,179 –
Mure, Colonel William, of Caldwell	Caldwell, Beith	3,624	4,387 14	Port-Glasgow and Newark Sailcloth Company	Port-Glasgow	1	118 –
Do. do.	Do. (Quarry)	–	52 –	Do. do.	Do. (Timber Pond)	1	15 –
Do. do.	Do. (Minerals)	–	300 –	Port-Glasgow Police Commissioners	Port-Glasgow	3	421 –
Murphy, Henry	Crossmyloof	3	533 –	Do. (for Water Works)	Port-Glasgow	26	300 –
Napier, Sir Robert J. Milliken, of that Ilk, Bt.	Milliken, Kilbarchan	1,280	3,203 4	Queen's Park Bowling Club	Queen's Park, Glasgow	1	20 –
Do. do.	Do. (Minerals)	–	1,183 –				
Neill, Thomas	Hangingshaw, Cathcart	4	62 10				
Neilson, J. and W.	Sussex Street, Glasgow	1	260 –	Ramsay, John	Kilbarchan	3	35 –
Neilson, Macleroy	Wallacebank, Johnstone	2	55 –	Randolph, Charles	The Howff, Pollokshields	2	130 –
Neilson, William	Burnside Cot., Saltcoats	128	135 –	Rankine, James	Dykehead, Stonehouse	4	10 –
Nitshill and Lesmahagow Coal Company	Nitshill	17	356 5	Rankine, William	Thornliebank	4	26 –
				Reddoch, Allan	Laurel Bank, Shawlands	1	85 –
				Reid, James	Johnstone	1	97 15
				Reid, John	Church St., Lochwinnoch	24	107 4
Orr, Robert	Ardencraig, Rothesay	140	238 11	Reid, John	Glenhuntly, Port-Glasgow	20	1,146 –
Orr, Robert	6 Melrose St., Glasgow	38	65 –	Reid, Rev. Mungo	Newton-Mearns	6	53 15
Orr, William	High Linthills, Lochwinnoch	123	66 10	Reid, William	Johnstone	3	19 2
Orr, Tutors of William	Greenbrae, Lochwinnoch	137	230 –	Reid, Mrs. Margaret, and another	Brownhill, etc., by Beith	45	92 6
Do. do.	Do. (Minerals)	–	60 –	Renfrew, Community of	Renfrew	405	1,630 10
Orr, Mrs. Ann	Risk, Lochwinnoch	28	40 –	Renfrew Parish, Heritors of	Renfrew	26	83 –
Orr, Mrs. Jane	Crooks, Lochwinnoch	34	52 –	Rennie, Robert	Moorpark, Renfrew	1	74 –
Oswald, James Gordon	Scotstoun, Renfrew	484	1,527 8	Renton, John	Clynder, Roseneath	6	3,141 10
Do. do.	Do. (Minerals)	–	1,444 –	Richardson, Bruce	53 Virginia St., Glasgow	1	86 –
				Richardson, David	Hartfield, Cove, by Greenock	2,006	1,531 6
Paisley Water Commissioners	Paisley	77	3,624 –	Richardson, Robert Y., of Ralston	Ralston, Paisley	705	2,387 2
Park, William	81 King Street, Tradeston, Glasgow	1	5 –	Do. do.	Do. (Minerals)	–	50 –
Park, Mrs. Ann, and another	Kilmalcolm	2	4 –	Richmond, Mrs. Euphemia	386 Crown St., Glasgow	7	70 –
				Rintoul, David	Canada West	4	30 –
				Rintoul, Robert	8 Crookridge St., Leeds	4	33 –
Parker, Trustees of John	Kilmalcolm	3	181 13	Ritchie, Andrew	Nettlehirst, Beith	56	55 –
Paterson, Thomas Law	Gladstone Pl., Greenock	1	22 –	Ritchie, John	Mansfield, Kilmalcolm	2	115 –

Z

RENFREW—continued.

Name of Owner.	Address of Owner.	Estimated Acreage of Property.	Gross Annual Value.	Name of Owner.	Address of Owner.	Estimated Acreage of Property.	Gross Annual Value.
		Acres.	£ s.			Acres.	£ s.
Robertson, James	Renfrew	4	37 –	Stevenson, William	13 Moray Place, Strathbungo	568	1,259 16
Robertson, Trs. of James	Glasgow	11	170 –	Do.	Do. (Quarry)	–	185 –
Robertson, John M.	Crosshill	2	652 –	Do.	Do. (Minerals)	–	400 –
Robertson, William	Floors, Johnstone	1	100 –	Stewart, Alexander B.	Langside, Crossmyloof	4	180 –
Robin & Houston	Park Street, Paisley Road, Glasgow	1	150 –	Stewart, Andrew	Mosside, Crossmyloof	4	155 10
Robin, Matthew	Croftanreigh Cottage, Renfrew	24	278 10	Stewart, Andrew	Maryfield, Pollokshields	1	105 –
Rodger, Rev. Matthew, and others	St. Andrews	157	741 10	Stewart, James	Williamwood, Cathcart	628	1,094 17
Roman Catholic Association	Johnstone and Bridge of Weir	9	67 –	Do.	Do. (Quarries)	–	394 15
Ronaldson, George	Linwood	8	793 10	Stewart, James, of Garvocks	Southbar, Paisley	2,225	488 13
Ross, James	Titwood, Dunlop	68	50 –	Stewart, Trustees of John	Shawlands, Pollokshaws	14	396 2
Ross, John, junior	West Scotland Street, Glasgow	12	20 –	Stewart, Sir M. R. Shaw, of Greenock and Blackhall, Bart.	Ardgowan, Greenock	24,951	14228 4
Russell, James	Craigton, Mearns	50	84 –	Do. do.	Do. (Quarries)	–	573 –
Russell, James	Newton-Mearns	2	90 15	Stewart, Ninian B.	10 Grosvenor Terrace, Glasgow	4	120 –
Russell, Trs. of William	Barrhead	2	122 10	Stewart, Robert F. S.	Redholm, Wemyss Bay	2	140 –
Rutherford, Mrs. Margaret	Muirhead, by Linwood	6	12 10	Stewart, William	Ocktofad, Port-Charlotte, Islay	178	251 –
				Stewart, William, and another	Factory St., Pollokshaws	1	165 15
Sadler, James S.	Thornliebank	3	65 –	Stirling, James	Glentyan, Kilbarchan	265	786 3
Sawers, Rev. Peter	Gargunnock	66	586 4	Stirling, Robert G.	Woodburn Cottage, Pollokshaws	3	107 –
Scott, Adam	92 Canning Street, Glasgow	1	19 1	Stoddard, A. F.	Broadfield, Port-Glasgow	9	448 –
Scott, William	Mansfield, Kilmalcolm	285	80 –	Struthers, Peter	Sandbank Place, Partick	12	85 –
Scott, Mrs. Margaret	Milliken Park, Kilbarchan	2	60 –	Sutherland, John	Milliken Park, Kilbarchan	1	35 –
Seath, Thomas B.	Sunny Oaks, Langbank	2	230 –	Swan, James	Wattieston, Lochwinnoch	65	104 –
Shanks, Thomas	Johnstone	6	235 –	Swinburne, Capt. Thomas A., R.N.	Eilan Shona, Salen, Fort-William	1	220 –
Shanks, William	Demity Street, Johnstone	2	62 –				
Shanks, William	Bridge of Weir	2	174 –				
Shaw, William	Nithsdale Road, Pollokshields	1	90 –	Tassie, James	Pollokshaws	4	163 12
Simons & Co.	Renfrew	12	1,150 –	Taylor, William	Langbank, Newton-Mearns	13	135 –
Simpson, John & Robert	King Street, Gourock	1	486 10				
Simpson, Robert, junior	Moorpark, Renfrew	4	45 –	Taylor, William	Howwood	3	111 9
Slater, Thomas H.	Oswald Street, Glasgow	1	30 –	Telfer, John	Newark Pl., Port-Glasgow	1	108 7
Smellie, Mrs. Isabella R.	Langside Valley, Crossmyloof	5	51 10	Tennant & Co., Charles	St. Rollox, Glasgow	3	228 10
Smith, Archibald	Lincoln's Inn, London	255	962 11	Thomson, Trs. of Neale	Crossmyloof	113	1,640 12
Do.	Do. (Minerals)	–	2,900 –	Thomson, Nisbet	Johnstone	5	254 16
Smith Brothers & Co.	Park Street, Paisley Road, Glasgow	2	400 –	Tracey, Rev. Bernard	Pollokshaws	1	37 19
Smith, Rev. James	Old Cathcart	6	56 –	Turner, George	Woodlands, Gourock	1	152 –
Smith, James	Ferry Roadhead, Yoker	1	92 10				
Smith, Trustees of John	Ayr	7	150 –	United Presbyterian Church, Managers of	Newton-Mearns	5	22 12
Smith, William	Neilstonside, Neilston	1	17 –				
Smith, Mrs. Marjory	Lochwinnoch	239	441 5				
Sommerville, Robert G.	Jean Street, Port-Glasgow	2	67 –	Waddell, Matthew, and another	Auldmuirfoot, Neilston	2	43 13
Sommerville, William	Langside, Crossmyloof	1	100 –	Wainwright, William J.	Milliken Park, Kilbarchan	1	55 –
Soutar, John	Inverkeithny, Turriff	176	92 –	Wakefield, Joseph C.	Eastwood Park, Thornliebank	63	582 6
Speir, Thomas, of Blackstone	Burnbrae, Johnstone	1,527	3,751 3	Wallace, James	Kilsyth	83	150 –
Do. do.	Do. (Minerals)	–	2,735 15	Wallace, John	Netherplace, Mearns	18	673 –
Speir, William	Hole, Lochwinnoch	40	65 –	Wallace, Agnes	71 High Street, Renfrew	2	39 15
Speirs, A. A., of Elderslie	Elderslie, Renfrew	11,259	14883 8	Watson, Andrew	Bruce Road, Pollokshields	2	120 –
Do. do.	Do. (Quarries)	–	70 7	Watson, Duncan	Pollokshaws	1	336 1
Speirs, Robert T. N.	Culdees Castle, Perthshire	48	157 10	Watson, Duncan, and another	Port-Glasgow	16	380 15
Speirs, William	Barngill, Bridge of Weir	21	63 10	Watson, Henry	Mariaville, Crossmyloof	1	115 –
Speirs, Trs. of Margaret	Shutterflat, Beith	28	55 –	Watson, Robert	Burnstyle, Crossmyloof	7	33 –
Speirs, Margaret & Agnes	Burnbrae, Johnstone	4	100 –	Watson, Robert and William	23 Brown St., Glasgow	2	82 –
Sproull, Robert	Glebe Street, Renfrew	1	15 15				
Steel, John	King Street, Pollokshaws	4	81 5	Watson, William	Overlee, Cathcart	54	100 –
Steel, John	Ardgowan St., Greenock	1	254 –	Watt, Trustees of James, of Ramphorlie	Greenock	470	512 –
Stenhouse, Heirs of Thomas	London	12	158 19				
Steven, James	Glenpark, Port-Glasgow	3	211 –	Weems, John	Walkinshaw St., Johnstone	5	241 2
Steven, Elizabeth & Grace	Polmadie, etc., Govan	93	550 –	Welsh, James	Laigh Cartside, Johnstone	2	30 –
Stevenson, James	Auchenames, Kilbarchan	88	170 –	White, James P.	Kilmun	1	65 –
Stevenson, John	Netherbroadfield, Howwood	148	78 –	White, Matthew	63 Queen St., Renfrew	3	8 –
Stevenson, John	Wardend, Kilbarchan	98	240 –	White, Mrs. Mary	Lonend, Houston	11	42 3
Stevenson, John	Hairlaw, Barrhead	9	25 12	Wilson, Alexander	Overtrees, Lochwinnoch	75	123 –
Stevenson, Robert	Cochranefield, Howwood	12	55 –	Wilson, Daniel	124 Renfield St., Glasgow	1	30 –
Stevenson, Robert	Caulderhaugh, Lochwinnoch	6	76 6	Wilson, John	Kinnieshead, Thornliebank	5	422 –
Stevenson, William	Gateside, Lochwinnoch	4	14 10	Wilson & Sons, John	Nitshill	7	323 13
				Wilson, Matthew	Blackstoun, Paisley	3	45 –

RENFREW—continued.

Name of Owner.	Address of Owner.	Estimated Acreage of Property.	Gross Annual Value.	Name of Owner.	Address of Owner.	Estimated Acreage of Property.	Gross Annual Value.
		Acres.	£ s.			Acres.	£ s.
Wilson, Trs. of Robert	Neilston	4	41 14	Wylie, James	Cragburn, Gourock	2	70 —
Wilson, Trs. of Robert	London	146	203 10	Wyper, John	159 Pollokshaws Road, Glasgow	1	1,235 —
Do. do.	Do. (Quarries)	—	2,931 18				
Wilson, Thomas	Irvine, Ayrshire	5	202 10				
Wilson, William	St. Andrews Road, Pollokshields	1	130 —				
Wilson, William	Lorabar, Lochwinnoch	51	50 —	Young, Alexander	138 Hope Street, Glasgow	150	120 —
Wilson, Trs. of Mrs. Agnes	Johnshill, Lochwinnoch	13	47 17	Young, James	Gallowhill, Paisley	12	36 —
Wilson, Mrs. Janet G. C.	Bandora Hall, Bridge of Allan	250	414 4	Young, James, of Kelly	Kelly, Wemyss Bay	550	856 6
				Young, John	NorthCastlewalls,Howood	76	55 —
Wilson, Mrs. Jean, and others	Easter Auchengown, Lochwinnoch	69	81 —	Young, Trs. of William	Pollokshaws	191	348 4
				Young, Mrs. Jane	11 Victoria Pl., Stirling	12	34 —
Wingate, John	45 West Nile Street, Glasgow	2	55 —	Young, Mrs. Rebecca	Auldhousefield, Pollokshaws	12	1,109 10
Woddrop, William A.	Garvald House, Peeblesshire	250	343 —				
Wood, James	5 Gloucester St., Glasgow	17	30 —				
Wotherspoon & Co., Robert	Great Wellington Street, Glasgow	2	500 —	Total Owners of Land of One Acre and upwards		657	148,679	396,655 16
Wright, Margaret	Calderpark, Lochwinnoch	1	19 —	Total Owners of Lands of less than One Acre in extent		2,558	1,242	165,155 7
Wright's, Duncan, Endowment	Paisley	372	440 —				
Wylie, Hugh	Blackheath Park, London, S.E.	25	22 —	GRAND TOTAL		3,215	149,921	561,811 3

RENFREW—continued.—(MUNICIPAL BOROUGH OF PAISLEY.)

MUNICIPAL BOROUGH OF PAISLEY.
Population over 20,000.

Name of Owner.	Address of Owner.	Estimated Acreage of Property.	Gross Annual Value.
		Acres.	£ s.
Abercorn, Duke of	Duddingston House, Edinburgh	166	733 —
Abbey Parochial Board	Craw Road, Paisley	32	551 —
Aikman, James	Camphill, Paisley	3	222 —
Allison, William	Love Street, Paisley	2	135 —
Armour, Robert, and others	Paisley	3	636 15
Arthur, James	Barshaw, Paisley	52	451 —
Barclay, James	Canal Bank, Paisley	4	109 15
Barr & Reid	Shambles Road, Paisley	2	130 —
Bell, Archibald	48–50 Causeyside, Paisley	1	390 —
Bowie, John	31 Glen Street, Paisley	2	239 10
Brough, Peter	Oakshawhead, Paisley	2	70 —
Brown, Andrew	George Place, Paisley	2	436 5
Brown, Hugh	Egypt Park, Paisley	3	143 5
Brown, John, and others	Collinslie, Paisley	47	1,604 5
Brown, Robert	Underwood, Paisley	34	1,264 15
Buchanan, Henry	25 Well Street, Paisley	2	253 —
Caldwell, James	Craigielea Place, Paisley	3	155 15
Caldwell, Rev. Robert R.	Bishopton	1	92 5
Caledonian Railway Co.	Glasgow (Railway)	15	1,436 —
Campbell, Colonel Archibald C., M.P.	Blythswood, Renfrew	28	71 10
Campbell, William	Camphill, Paisley	1	155 —
Campbell, Mrs. Margaret	Tarbert, Lochfine	14	64 10
Cattanach, Alexander	Auchentorlie, Paisley	17	169 —
Cattanach, Alexander, and another	King St., Sacell, Paisley	4	1,445 —
Carlile, Sons, & Co., James	New Sneddon, Paisley	2	611 10
Cemetery Company	Paisley	22	69 —
Clapperton & Co., William	New Sneddon, Paisley	1	268 —
Clark, James	Camphill, Paisley	1	456 —
Clark, James	Chapel House, Paisley	3	551 10
Clark & Co., J.	Gordon's Lane, Paisley	4	617 10
Clark & Co., J. & J.	Seedhills, Paisley	9	3,532 —
Clark, Stewart	Kilnside, Paisley	7	127 10
Coats, J. & P.	Ferguslie, Paisley	3	2,907 15
Coats, Sir Peter, Kt.	Woodside, Paisley	12	448 —
Coats, Thomas	Ferguslie, Paisley	326	1,080 —
Cochrane, Mrs. Agnes	6 Hamilton Crescent, Partick	18	93 —
Craig, Archibald	5 Gateside, Paisley	9	503 15
Craig, Agnes	Saltcoats	4	32 —
Craw, William	Caledonia Street, Paisley	3	205 —
Crown, The	(For Greenlaw and West Lane, Paisley)	15	220 —
Dalglish, Robert, M.P.	29 St. Vincent Place, Glasgow	13	37 —
Donald, James	Riccartsbar, Paisley	6	75 —
Dunn, Heirs of William, senior	Barterholm, Paisley	14	151 5
Edmiston, William	34 Canal Street, Paisley	1	122 15
Educational Association	Paisley	1	56 —
Fisher, John	4 Causeyside, Paisley	2	152 5
Forbes, James—per William Forbes, factor *loco tutoris*	Paisley	5	529 15
Forbes, Mrs. William	1 Underwood Lane, Paisley	3	510 15
Fraser & Co., Alexander	Blackhall Printworks, Paisley	1	38 —
Fullarton, Alexander	Crossflat, Paisley	19	196 15
Fullarton, Hodgert, & Barclay	Renfrew Street, Paisley	2	372 —
Fullarton, John	Merksworth, Paisley	4	89 10
Gardner, Archibald	Nethercommon, Paisley	7	510 —
Gardner, Mrs. Margaret	West Greenhill, Paisley	4	15 10
Gibson Brothers & Co.	47 Queen St., Glasgow	4	790 —
Glasgow, Earl of	Hawkhead, Paisley	126	630 10
Glasgow and Paisley Joint Railway Co.	Glasgow (Railway)	33	3,834 —
Glasgow and South-Western Railway Co.	Glasgow (Railway & Canal)	38	6,268 —
Greenlees, Trustees of Mrs. Elizabeth	Paisley	2	7 —
Hamilton, Hugh	4 Bank Street, Paisley	1	253 10
Hanna, Donald, & Wilson	Smithhills, Paisley	3	612 —
Holmes, Archibald C.	Sandyford, Paisley	6	118 10
Holmes, William	Brabloch, Paisley	12	134 10
Hutchison, Archibald	Fairhill, Paisley	2	211 15
Infirmary, Directors of	11 Bridge Street, Paisley	1	210 —
Jack, Peter, junior, & Co.	Nethercommon, Paisley	1	230 —
Johnstone, William	Beauchamp, Paisley	3	94 10
Kerr, Robert	4 Elmbank Crescent, Glasgow	2	889 —
Kerr, R. & J. P.	Underwood, Paisley	6	1,396 5
Kerr, Curators of Eliza Ann—per Stewart Clark	Gallowhill, Paisley	63	368 5
Kibble, Trs. of Elizabeth	Greenock Road, Paisley	3	89 10
Langs & Semple	Seedhills, Paisley	1	200 —
Lees, Rev. James C.	Garthland Street, Paisley	6	103 10
Leishman, Mrs., and another	Gockston, Paisley	4	13 —
Logan, Crawford B.	Liverpool	35	167 5
M'Allister, Robert D.	Blackland Place, Paisley	2	93 5
M'Alpine, Thomas W.	Castlehead, Paisley	2	201 —
M'Farlane, Janet, Elizabeth, Helen, and Agnes	Canal Bank, Paisley	2	293 15
M'Gregor, Patrick Comyn	Lonend, Paisley	74	527 10
M'Innes, John, and others	Paisley	2	6 —
M'Intyre, William, junior	Castlehead, Paisley	3	302 15
M'Kean, William	5 Garthland Pl., Paisley	2	425 —
M'Kenzie, Archibald	North Greenhill, Paisley	5	149 —

RENFREW—continued.—(MUNICIPAL BOROUGH OF PAISLEY.)

Name of Owner.	Address of Owner.	Estimated Acreage of Property.	Gross Annual Value.	Name of Owner.	Address of Owner.	Estimated Acreage of Property.	Gross Annual Value.
		Acres.	£ s.			Acres.	£ s.
M'Kenzie Brothers	Gateflat, Paisley	4	296 —	*Saucel Brewery Company*	Saucel, Paisley	3	553 5
M'Walter, Robert	45 Causeyside, Paisley	2	777 5	Slater, Mrs. Jane	150 Holland St., Glasgow	4	108 5
Maxwell, James E. S. S.	Acre Street, Nairn	25	122 10	Smith, John T.	Wester Carriagehill, Paisley	4	450 5
Millar, James	41 New Sneddon, Paisley	2	274 15				
Morgan, John	Greenlaw, Paisley	54	515 5	Smith, Mrs. Mary	1 Minto St., Edinburgh	3	10 —
Morrison, Mrs. Mary	Chain Road, Paisley	2	257 —	Snodgrass, John	21 Gauze Street, Paisley	1	264 —
Muir, John	Moss Street, Paisley	2	401 5	Speirs, A. A.	Elderslie	28	41 —
Muir, Mathew	Greenhill, Paisley	4	55 —	Speirs & Co., David	167 George St., Paisley	4	453 10
Muir, Hugh B.	London	3	118 —	Speirs, Gibb, & Young	Greenlone, Paisley	12	204 —
				Spence, John	62 Storie Street, Paisley	1	76 —
				Stewart, John M.	Greenhill, Paisley	7	108 10
Neilson, Trustees of John	Oakshawhead, Paisley	4	165 —	Stewart, Sir Michael R. Shaw, Bart.	Ardgowan, Greenock	295	572 —
Orr, Robert	Rothesay	56	134 10	Symington, John M.	44 Oakshaw St., Paisley	3	130 —
				Thomson, Rev. John	Blackhall Terrace, Paisley	1	55 —
Paisley Burgh, Community of	Paisley	126	980 15				
Paisley Burgh, Parochial Board of	New Sneddon, Paisley	7	416 —	Watson, James	118 Union St., Glasgow	20	74 —
Paisley, Corporation of	Paisley	2	148 10	Weir, Andrew	Williamsburgh, Paisley	2	285 10
Paisley Gas Light Commissioners	Gas Work Road, Paisley	4	2,910 —	Whitehead, Representatives of the late Joseph	Paisley	21	82 12
Pattison, Trs. of Robert	Paisley	19	480 15	Wotherspoon, William	Maxwellton, Paisley	17	731 —
Peock, William	Meiklerigs, Paisley	54	234 10	Wright, Trustees of Daniel	Paisley	1	343 —
Pinkerton, John	53 High Street, Paisley	2	385 —				
Pollock, Alexander R., and another	Paisley	26	112 —				
Pollock, Marriage Trustees of Alexander R.	Underwood, Paisley	3	74 —	Young, James	Gallowhill, Paisley	89	361 —
Pollock, William	25 Moss Street, Paisley	3	73 —	Young, John	Fulwood, Houston	35	132 —
Polson, John	West Mount, Paisley	19	125 —	Young, John	Castlehead, Paisley	2	150 —
Polson, William	5 Gauze Street, Paisley	2	373 —	Young, Mrs. Mary	39 Canal St., Paisley	4	56 15
Porteous, Dundas S.	50 High Street, Paisley	2	175 5				
Priorscroft Bowling Club Trustees	Storie Street, Paisley	1	28 —				
Procurators, Faculty of	Paisley	3	74 5	Total Owners of Land of One Acre and upwards		137 2,675	61,202 17
Ragged School, Directors of	Albion Street, Paisley	3	150 —	Total Owners of Lands of less than One Acre in extent		1,258 669	79,481 15
Renfrewshire Prison Board	County Buildings, Paisley	1	465 —				
Richardson, Robert Y.	Ralston, Paisley	273	971 —				
Robin & Houston	New Sneddon, Paisley	3	432 —	GRAND TOTAL		1,395 3,344	140,684 12
Rowat, Robert	Prospecthill, Paisley	2	80 —				

MUNICIPAL BOROUGH OF GREENOCK.
Population over 20,000.

Name of Owner.	Address of Owner.	Estimated Acreage of Property.	Gross Annual Value.	Name of Owner.	Address of Owner.	Estimated Acreage of Property.	Gross Annual Value.
		Acres.	£ s.			Acres.	£ s.
Adam, George	43 Eldon St., Greenock	1	212 —	Glasgow and South-Western Railway Company	Glasgow	7	1,091 10
Agnew, Alexander	8 Margaret Street, Greenock	1	656 3	Do. do.	Do. (Railway, Stations, Depots, etc.)	37	6,269 —
Aitken, James	78 Eldon St., Greenock	8	1,427 6	Glebe Sugar Refining Co.	West Blackhall Street, Greenock	2	2,318 —
Allan, Heirs of George	27 Union St., Greenock	2	181 4	Greenock Academy, Directors of	Greenock	3	160 —
Allan, George, & Sons	East Hamilton Street, Greenock	1	263 10	Greenock Corporation	Greenock—		
Allison, Mrs. Mary	East Blackhall Street, Greenock	1	767 8	Town Proper		4	3,660 16
Anderson, Alexander	7 George Sq., Greenock	4	550 —	Do. for Cemetery and Burying Grounds		44	400 —
Arbuckle, George	65 Eldon St., Greenock	2	1,340 —	Do. for Public Parks		20	100 —
				Harbour Trust		33	2,909 15
Ballantine & Rowan	Dellingburn St., Greenock	2	580 —	Do. (Quays, Sheds, and Graving Docks)		27	31662 —
Barnard, James	9 George Sq., Greenock	3	903 15	Do. for Timber Ponds		26	863 —
Birkmyre, William and Adam	Lynedoch St., Greenock	2	630 —	Police Board		3	606 2
Black, James	11 Kelly St., Greenock	1	664 14	Do. for Gas Works		7	6,125 —
Blair, Reid & Steele	Ingleston St., Greenock	2	1,345 —	Water Trust		1	121 —
Blake, Barclay & Co.	Macdougall St., Greenock	1	115 5	Do. for Waterworks		17	4,448 —
Brown, Matthew	10 Ardgowan Square, Greenock	1	156 —	Greenock Cotton Spinning Company	Greenock	1	333 8
Brown, Stewart, & Co.	Overton, Greenock	3	416 4	Greenock Foundry Co.	Greenock	5	1,170 15
Buchanan, Trs. of Walter Washington	Eldon Street, Greenock	3	160 —	Greenock Infirmary, Trs. of	Greenock	1	400 —
				Greenock, Parochial Board of	Greenock	2	300 —
				Greenock Provident Investment Company	Cathcart St., Greenock	3	1,119 6
Caird & Co.	Arthur Street, Greenock	16	4,348 4	Greenock & Wemyss Bay Railway Company	Glasgow	1	37 10
Caird, Colin S.	Newark Street, Greenock	2	165 —	Do. do.	Do. (Railway, Stations, Depots, etc.)	38	1,350 —
Caird, James T.	Arthur Street, Greenock	5	402 —	Grieve, Walter	60 Union St., Greenock	2	500 —
Caledonian Railway Co.	Glasgow	5	1,063 16				
Do. do.	Do. (Railway, Stations, Depots, etc.)	45	4,911 —				
Cameron, Allan	Macdougall St., Greenock	1	124 —				
Carbery, Charles	21 Eldon St., Greenock	1	888 13				
Carmichael, Andrew	Finnart Street, Greenock	1	130 —	Haddow, Trustees of Andrew Carmichael	Ardgowan St., Greenock	2	1,096 11
Cartsburn Sugar Refining Company	Crescent St., Greenock	1	514 —	Hill, Trustees of Mr. and Mrs. Lawrence	Port-Glasgow Road, Greenock	2	80 —
Clyde Sugar Refining Co.	Drumfrochar Road, Greenock	2	55 —	Houston, Robert	Esplanade, Greenock	3	360 19
Cooper, Alexander	Rothesay, Bute	1	547 17	Hunter, John C.	Forsyth Street, Greenock	2	373 5
Cram, Peter	13 Mount Pleasant St., Greenock	1	1,155 19	Hutcheson, George	St. Lawrence Street, Greenock	2	1,123 6
Crawford, Alexander	Finnart Street, Greenock	1	617 9				
Crawford & Fulton	Terrace Road, Greenock	1	533 19				
Crawford, Thomas M'Knight	Murrieston House, Mid-Calder	53	233 8	Jamieson, Robert W.	1 Brisbane St., Greenock	2	1,136 7
Crawhall, Allison, & Co.	Rue End St., Greenock	1	843 —				
Crown, The	(Government Property)	4	1,009 10				
Cunliffe & Dunlop	Inchworks, Greenock	8	605 —	Kerr, Heirs of John	Eldon Street, Greenock	1	370 —
Currie & Guthrie	Lynedoch St., Greenock	3	550 17	Kerr, Mrs. Margaret	Eldon Street, Greenock	2	125 —
Cuthbert, Robert	Newark St., Greenock	2	160 —	Kincaid, Donald & Co.	East Hamilton Street, Greenock	3	303 7
Ewing, Alexander	56 Hope Street, Glasgow	1	1,100 —	Lang, James	27 Regent St., Greenock	2	907 4
				Latham, Mrs. Elizabeth Isabella	1 Margaret St., Greenock	1	157 —
Findlay, James	Newark Street, Greenock	2	140 —	Leitch, Mrs. Mary O.	Newark Street, Greenock	1	80 —
Fleming, Reid, & Co.	Drumfrochar Road, Greenock	8	560 —	Leitch, Quintin, & Co.	Whinhill Ropewalk, Greenock	3	160 —
Forrest, Heirs of William	Greenock	2	1,327 19	Lennox, John	Bogston, Greenock	2	120 —
				Lyle, Abram	Eldon Street, Greenock	3	1,035 —

RENFREW—continued.—(Municipal Borough of GREENOCK.)

Name of Owner.	Address of Owner.	Estimated Acreage of Property.	Gross Annual Value.		Name of Owner.	Address of Owner.	Estimated Acreage of Property.	Gross Annual Value.	
		Acres.	£	s.			Acres.	£	s.
M'Clure, William	56 Union St., Greenock	1	481	9	Scott, Alexander, & Sons	20 Baker St., Greenock	3	1,676	—
M'Intyre, Thomas	2 Wilson St., Greenock	1	1,177	19	Scott, Captain Edward	27 Esplanade, Greenock	1	459	—
M'Kay, Peter	98 Eldon St., Greenock	2	549	9	Scott & Co.	Main Street, Greenock	5	800	—
M'Kenzie & Walker	Dellingburn Square, Greenock	2	300	—	Shaw, Henry	Millport, Bute	1	30	—
					Steele, Robert, & Co.	4 Rue End St., Greenock	12	2,574	15
M'Millan, James	20 Margaret Street, Greenock	3	648	—	Stewart, Sir M.R.S., Bart.	Ardgowan, Inverkip	1,130	2,378	—
					Do. do.	Do. (Timber Ponds)	4	60	—
M'Whirter, Robert	5 Caddlehill Terrace, Greenock	2	482	—	Sword, Trs. of Archibald	36 Eldon St., Greenock	1	529	12
Marine Investment Company	Gracechurch St., London	20	483	7					
Do. do.	Do. (Timber Ponds)	7	104	—					
Marshall, William	Ladyburn, Greenock	5	474	12	Thomson, John	Caddlehill, Greenock	4	112	—
Morton, James	Newark Street, Greenock	4	190	—	Tough, Alexander, & Son	Clyde Ropework, Greenock	2	160	—
Muir, Heirs of Andrew	London	2	290	—					
Neill, Dempster & Neill	Drumfrochar Road, Greenock	4	1,283	3	Walker, Hugh	2 Newark St., Greenock	3	110	—
					Walker, John, & Co.	Nicholson St., Greenock	5	2,384	—
Neill, Mrs. Marion	Octavia Terrace, Greenock	2	137	10	Walker, Robert S.	66 Eldon St., Greenock	1	297	10
					Watt, Margaret and Agnes	Ardgowan St., Greenock	2	130	—
Orr, Hunter & Co.	43 Wellington Street, Greenock	1	210	—	Wood, Trustees of Sir Gabriel	Mariners' Asylum, Greenock	8	898	13
Patten, Archibald, & Co.	35 Baker St., Greenock	3	1,120	—					
Paul, Sword & Co.	Ingleston St., Greenock	2	855	—	York, James	5 Campbell St., Greenock	1	826	3
Poynter, John E.	Clydeneuk, Uddingston	2	400	—					
Rankin & Blackmore	Baker Street, Greenock	2	570	—	Total Owners of Land of One Acre and upwards		102	1,788 130366	7
Richardson, James, & Co.	Roxburgh St., Greenock	1	176	5	Total Owners of Lands of less than One Acre in extent		1,026	268 158036	6
Richmond, Archibald F.	Patrick Street, Greenock	1	701	4					
Robb & Fullarton	Bogston, Greenock	1½							
Do. do.	Do. (Timber Ponds)	2½	220	—					
Robb, John, & Co.	Greenock	8½							
Do. do.	Do. (Timber Ponds)	7½	358	10	Grand Total		1,128	2,056 288402	13

ROSS.

Population in 1871,	77,593.
Inhabited Houses,	15,028.
Number of Parishes,	32.

Name of Owner.	Address of Owner.	Estimated Acreage of Property.	Gross Annual Value.	Name of Owner.	Address of Owner.	Estimated Acreage of Property.	Gross Annual Value.
		Acres.	£ s.			Acres.	£ s.
Ainslie, Robert, of Muirton	Elvingstone, Gladsmuir	4,500	663 10	Dingwall, Parish School Board of	Dingwall	2	25 —
Ankerville, Heirs of Lord	Tain	2	5 —	Dingwall & Skye Railway Company	Inverness (Railway)	383	2,274 —
Ashburton, Dowager Lady, of Kinlochluichart	Loch Luichart Lodge, Dingwall	28,556	1,885 —	Dunlop, George	Roxburgh St., Greenock	179	18 1
Avoch Free Church, Trustees of	Avoch	10	30 —				
Avoch and Rosemarkie, Ministers of	Avoch and Rosemarkie	12	31 11	Easter Ross, Poorhouse Combination of	Tain	5	100 —
				Edwards, William	Craigton, Inverness	11	25 —
Baillie, Evan, of Dochfour	Dochfour Ho., Inverness	24,500	1,650 —	Edwards, Mrs. Helen	Strathpeffer	1	45 —
Baillie, Right Hon. Henry James, of Redcastle	Redcastle, Inverness	6,512	6,276 6				
Bain, Murdoch	Hillockhead, Fortrose	1	11 10	Ferguson, Trustees of late Colonel Robert Munro, of Novar	Raith, Kirkcaldy	440	302 16
Balfour, Arthur James, of Whittinghame	Whittinghame House, Prestonkirk	71,778	3,032 15				
Bankes, Meyrick, of Letterewe	Letterewe, Dingwall	69,800	2,463 2	Ferguson, Tutors of Ronald C., of Novar	Raith, Kirkcaldy	14,582	3,602 18
Barnet, Rev. James	Manse, Croich, Ardgay	7	10 —	Ferguson, John	Conon, Dingwall	1	7 —
Black Isle, Poorhouse Combination of	Ness of Fortrose, Fortrose	3	100 —	Fingal Mason Lodge	Dingwall	1	68 10
Blyth, Peter	Culrain, Ardgay	590	59 —	Fletcher, James, of Rosehaugh	Rosehaugh, Inverness	11,095	8,545 —
Bremner, Alexander	Hill of Fortrose, Fortrose	3	14 —	Fodderty, Heritors of Parish of	Fodderty, Dingwall	3	5 —
Bruce, William	Dingwall	3	70 —				
				Forbes, Arthur, of Culloden	Culloden House, Inverness	6,393	3,814 17
Caledonian Banking Co.	Inverness	1	140 —	Forbes, Rev. Daniel	F.C. Manse, Edderton, Tain	1	22 5
Cameron, Alexander	Leanaig, Dingwall	90	25 —				
Cameron, Duncan	Beauly	2	40 —	Forbes, Rev. Donald	F.C. Manse, Lochcarron	1	14 —
Cameron, John	Muckernish, Munlochy	13	3 —	Forbes, William	Allangrange Moor, Munlochy	23	9 —
Cameron, Rev. William	Manse, Lochbroom, Dingwall	2,000	170 5	Forsyth, John	Ness, Fortrose	5	8 —
Campbell, Rev. Duncan	F.C. Manse, Evanton	1	15 —	Forsyth, John	Dingwall	1	221 7
Campbell, Rev. Ewen	Manse, Keose, Stornoway	531	45 —	Forsyth, William	Allangrange Moor, Munlochy	17	3 —
Campbell, Rev. George	Manse, Tarbat, Tain	12	30 —				
Campbell, Rev. George L.	F.C. Manse, Crossbost, Stornoway	5	21 —	Fortrose, Magistrates of	Fortrose	29	88 15
Campbell, Rev. John	F.C. Manse, Uig, Stornoway	5	24 5	Fowler, Henry Mackenzie, of Raddery	Raddery, Fortrose	950	1,024 8
Campbell, Mrs. Barbara	Dingwall	2	95 15	Fowler, John, of Braemore	Braemore, Lochbroom, Dingwall	39,530	2,995 —
Carloway Free Church, Trustees of	Carloway, Stornoway	5	27 —	Fraser, Andrew, of Glastullich	Glastullich, Tain	660	611 8
Cattley, William E., of Edderton	Ospisdale House, Dornoch	1,300	353 —	Fraser, Arthur, of Arabella	3 Inverness Terrace, Bayswater, London	625	995 10
Catton, Trs. of Alfred Robert and Mrs., of Strathnashallag	43 Castle St., Edinburgh	12,000	600 —	Fraser, Donald	Tain	39	157 —
Chapelhill, Kirk-Session of	Nigg, Parkhill	4	6 —	Fraser, Tutors of Hugh Kenneth, of Braelangwell	Cromarty	580	50 —
Chisholm, James Sutherland, of Chisholm (The Chisholm)	March Hall, Edinburgh	18,927	2,034 6	Fraser, Rev. Hugh	Manse, Fearn	8	30 —
				Fraser, John	Ness, Fortrose	9	24 —
Chisholm, James Taylor	New York	5	70 —	Fraser, Rev. John	Manse, Nigg, Parkhill	7	30 —
Christie, Trustee for Mrs. Ann	Wester Teaninich, Alness	1	15 —	Fraser, Rev. John W.	F.C. Manse, Rosskeen, Invergordon	2	16 —
Clarke, Alexander	Eriboll, Tongue	228	125 —	Fraser, Roderick	Bogton, Forres	8	18 18
Craig, Hugh	84 Richard St., Glasgow	16	8 —	Fraser, Rev. Roderick	Manse, Uig, Stornoway	33	46 —
Crown, The		2	363 —	Fraser, Rev. Simon	F.C. Manse, Fortrose	1	32 —
Darroch, Duncan, of Torridon	Torridon, Dingwall	32,000	1,062 —	Gair, George	Conon, Dingwall	1	13 —
Davidson, Duncan, of Tulloch	Tulloch Castle, Dingwall	36,130	6,093 15	Gairloch, Heritors of Parish of	Gairloch, Dingwall	4	6 —
				Gardener, John	Conon, Dingwall	1	27 —
Davidson, Heirs of William	Tain	684	292 —	Gibson, Rev. John	Manse, Avoch	5	30 5
Dingwall, Burgh of	Dingwall	15	48 5	Gillanders, George	Rosemarkie	2	23 10

ROSS—continued.

Name of Owner.	Address of Owner.	Estimated Acreage of Property.	Gross Annual Value.	Name of Owner.	Address of Owner.	Estimated Acreage of Property.	Gross Annual Value.
		Acres.	£ s.			Acres.	£ s.
Gillanders, James Falconer, of Highfield	Highfield House, Tarradale	10,000	2,255 6	Macdougall, Alexander William	Battlefields, Bath	400	30 —
Graham, Paul, of Drynie	Drynie House, Inverness	1,806	1,402 7	Macdougall, Alexander	Hill, Fortrose	8	8 —
Graham, William	Tullich, Parkhill	8	22 10	Macdougall, Rev. John	Manse, Carnoch, Beauly	4	13 —
Grainger, John	Aberdeen	1	35 —	Macewen, Rev. Ewen	Manse, Edderton, Tain	40	49 —
Grant, John	Glenaldie, Tain	25	20 —	Macfarlane, Rev. John A.	Manse, Urray, Beauly	20	38 —
Grant, Rev. Thomas	F.C. Manse, Tain	5	25 —	Macgregor, Rev. John	Manse, Knockbain, Inverness	52	77 —
Guest, Sir Ivor Bertie, of Canford Manor, Bart.	Canford Manor, Wimborne	33,971	1,180 18	Macgregor, Rev. Malcolm	F.C. Manse, Ferrintosh, Dingwall	8	26 —
Hadwin, Sidney, of Balblair	Kildonan Lodge, Golspie	2,517	59 —	Machardy, Rev. James	Manse, Alness	6	30 —
Haggart, Rev. John	Manse, Lochcarron	250	64 —	Macintyre, Rev. Alexander	Manse, Shieldaig, Dingwall	2	10 —
Hall, Andrew, of Calrossie	Blaireich, Golspie	2,059	1,835 8	Macintyre, Donald	Mains of Avoch, Avoch	6	15 14
Hall, George Ross	Belleport, Invergordon	1	32 10	Macintyre, Hugh, of Coulpleasant	Coulpleasant, Tain	200	60 —
Hanbury, Charles Addington, of Garve	Garve Lodge, Dingwall	3,200	823 7	Macintyre, Lieut.-Col. John	Fortrose	2	35 —
Hay, Roderick	Invergordon	2	72 —	Macintyre, Rev. Neil	Manse, Lochalsh	222	80 —
Heron, Peter	Lamington, Tain	206	28 5	Maciver, Alexander	Courthill, Fortrose	6	22 —
Highland Railway Company	Inverness (Railway)	311	16605 10	Mackay, Alexander	Arcan, Urray, Beauly	1	54 —
Hogarth, Alexander Pirie	Aberdeen	55	40 —	Mackay, Alexander	Hilton, Tain	175	15 —
Holehouse, John, of Mount Pleasant	Mount Pleasant, Fortrose	96	75 —	Mackay, Donald, of St. Vincent	Tain	455	110 —
				Mackay, Rev. Donald	Manse, Cross, Stornoway	6	21 —
Holmes, William James Owen, of Monar	Monar, Struy, Beauly	12,950	402 —	Mackay, George G., of Raasay	Raasay, Portree	3,962	630 10
Home, John	Rosemarkie	5	15 10	Mackay, George	Culrain, Ardgay	8	5 —
Hood, Alexander	Fortrose	3	29 —	Mackay, John	Munlochy	12	3 —
Hossack, Alexander	Fortrose	1	46 5	Mackay, Rev. John S.	Manse, Poolewe	5	18 —
Humphrey, John, of Bayfield	Bayfield, Tain	662	632 5	Mackay, Kenneth	Portnalick, Ardgay	22	18 —
				Mackay, Rev. William	Manse, Killearnan, Inverness	9	40 —
Inglis, George, of Newmore	Inverness	2,918	1,777 14	Mackenzie, Alexander, of Scatwell	Scatwell, Beauly	10,052	899 5
Jamestown Free Church, Trustees of	Jamestown, Strathpeffer	6	3 —	Mackenzie, Alexander	Dingwall	1	92 15
				Mackenzie, Alexander	Muckernish, Munlochy	10	5 12
Johnstone, Henry A. Munro Butler, of Novar, M.P.	8 Seymour Place, London, W.	24,350	3,294 8	Mackenzie, Rev. Alexander	Manse, Logie, Parkhill	28	45 —
Junor, Donald, senior	Fortrose	6	27 7	Mackenzie, Alexander Robertson	Fortrose	3	29 10
Junor, Donald, junior	Fortrose	5	21 —	Mackenzie, Captain Alexander W.	Forest Hill, Beauly	14	64 10
Junor, Duncan	Hill of Fortrose, Fortrose	4	6 —	Mackenzie, Curators of Charles, of Kilcoy	21 St. Andrew Square, Edinburgh	24,658	7,257 15
Junor, James	Hill of Fortrose, Fortrose	4	4 —	Mackenzie, Colin	28 Castle Street, Edinburgh	11	37 10
Junor, John	Ness of Fortrose, Fortrose	2	2 10	Mackenzie, Colin	Allangrange Moor, Munlochy	12	4 10
Junor, Heirs of Robert	Rosemarkie	1	8 12	Mackenzie, Heirs of Colin	Conon, Dingwall	1	14 —
Kilmuir-Easter, Heritors of Parish of	Kilmuir-Easter, Invergordon	1	2 10	Mackenzie, Colin Lyon, of St. Martin's	Inverness	341	356 —
				Mackenzie, Donald	Culrain Hill, Ardgay	30	2 —
Knockbain, Heritors of Parish of	Knockbain, Inverness	2	4 —	Mackenzie, Dowager Lady	Kinellan Lodge, Dingwall	4	45 —
				Mackenzie, Rev. Duncan S.	Manse, Gairloch, Dingwall	150	60 —
Lochbroom, Heritors of Parish of	Lochbroom, Dingwall	1	2 —	Mackenzie, Captain James Dixon, of Findon	Mountgerald House, Dingwall	5,804	4,022 5
				Mackenzie, James	Poolewe	2	20 —
Macainsh, Peter	Woodburn, Crieff	370	100 —	Mackenzie, James Fowler, of Allangrange	Allangrange, Munlochy	2,742	1,692 18
Macallister, Rev. Ronald	Manse, Dingwall	14	78 —	Mackenzie, James Thompson, of Kintail	Glenmuick, Aberdeen	25,500	1,982 16
Macandrew, John	13 Hill St., Edinburgh	8	15 15	Mackenzie, Heirs of John	Poolewe	2	17 —
Macarthur, Rev. Allan	F.C. Manse, Barvas, Stornoway	5	21 —	Mackenzie, John A. Shaw, of Newhall	Newhall, Invergordon	573	436 —
Macdonald, Alexander, of Trinity	124 Skidmore Street, Bancroft Place, Stepney, London	12	88 —	Mackenzie, James A. F. H. Stewart, of Seaforth	Brahan Castle, Dingwall	8,051	7,905 7
Macdonald, Rev. Colin	Manse, Knock, Stornoway	6	21 —	Mackenzie, Kenneth, of Dundonell	Dundonell House, Ullapool	64,335	3,671 15
Macdonald, Duncan	Dingwall	11	14 —	Mackenzie, Kenneth	Courthill, Fortrose	5	44 10
Macdonald, Rev. George	Manse, Rosskeen, Invergordon	7	48 —	Mackenzie, Sir Kenneth S., of Gairloch, Bart.	Conan House, Dingwall	164,680	7,842 15
Macdonald, George	Allangrange Moor, Munlochy	13	6 —	Mackenzie, Osgood H., of Inverewe	Inverewe House, Poolewe	10,000	510 —
Macdonald, James and John	Viewfield, Ardgay	120	20 —	Mackenzie, Rev. Peter	Manse, Urquhart, Dingwall	40	60 —
Macdonald, Rev. Kenneth	F.C. Manse, Applecross	1	12 —	Mackenzie, Col. Roderick	Dingwall	2	5 —
Macdonald, Margaret	Dingwall	1	219 10	Mackenzie, Trustees and Curators of Sir Arthur, of Coul, Bart.	Coul House, Dingwall	43,189	5,214 17
Macdonald, Rev. Murdoch	F.C. Manse, Logie, Parkhill	1	15 —				
Macdonald, Robert	Warranaburn, Ardgay	34	7 —	Mackenzie, Captain Roderick, of Kincraig	Kincraig, Invergordon	1,086	1,215 16
Macdonald, William	Allangrange Moor, Munlochy	11	4 —				

ROSS—continued.

Name of Owner.	Address of Owner.	Estimated Acreage of Property.	Gross Annual Value.	Name of Owner.	Address of Owner.	Estimated Acreage of Property.	Gross Annual Value.
		Acres.	£ s.			Acres.	£ s.
Mackenzie, Roderick	Hilton, Culrain, Ardgay	142	21 —	Murray, Colonel John, of Polmaise	Polmaise, Stirling	1,080	75 —
Mackenzie, Roderick Grogan, of Flowerburn	Flowerburn, Fortrose	1,931	1,817 17	Murray, Rev. Donald	F.C. Manse, Portmahomack	8	15 —
Mackenzie, Thomas	Shandwick, Tain	2	9 —	Murray, Fitzgerald L. Ross, of Pitcalzean	Reform Club, Pall Mall, London	1,296	1,201 16
Mackenzie, Thomas, of Ord	Ord House, Beauly	21,229	2,460 4	Murray, Joseph	Fortrose	1	8 —
Mackenzie, William	Culrain Hill, Ardgay	62	5 —	Murray, Kenneth, of Geanies	Geanies, Tain	5,303	4,400 18
Mackenzie, William	Allanfearn, Inverness	1	189 19	Murray, Mrs. Maryann	Tain	169	54 —
Mackenzie, William	Achendunie, Alness	1	3 —				
Mackenzie, Lady	Belmaduthy, Munlochy	18	50 —	Nicolson, Major Charles Arthur, of Hawkhill	Hawkhill, Fortrose	63	117 —
Mackenzie, Rose C.	Poolewe	2	13 —	Nicolson Institute, Trustees of	Stornoway	1	30 —
Mackichan, Rev. Alexander John	Manse, Kinlochluichart, Dingwall	9	14 —	Nicolson, Rev. Roderick	Manse, Applecross	42	71 —
Maclean, Rev. Alexander	Manse, Kiltearn, Dingwall	12	36 —	Northern Lighthouses, Commissioners of	Edinburgh	53	245 —
Maclean, James and Barbara	St. Martin's, Invergordon	24	73 —				
Maclennan, Roderick	Muckernish, Munlochy	10	3 —	Otty, William	Conon, Dingwall	1	10 —
Maclennan, Mrs. Jane	Fairburn, Beauly	1	4 —				
Macleod, Rev. Alexander	Manse, Kincardine, Ardgay	10	30 —	Paterson, John	Allangrange Moor, Munlochy	10	3 10
Macleod, Robert Bruce Æneas, of Cadboll	Invergordon Castle, Invergordon	11,827	10761 —				
Do. do.	Do. (Harbours)	3	260 —	Reid, Robert Montgomery	Culrain, Ardgay	74	50 —
Macleod, Thomas	Conon, Dingwall	1	17 10	Reid, Bernard	Ness, Fortrose	5	11 —
Macleod, Mrs. Isabella	Culross	2	14 10	Reid, Trustees of Elizabeth	Dingwall	2	60 —
Macmaster, Rev. Donald	Manse, Back, Stornoway	5	20 5	Robertson, Charles, of Kindeace	Kindeace, Invergordon	16,800	2,056 4
Macniel, Daniel	Kirriemuir, Forfar	389	45 —	Robertson, James	Hill of Fortrose	6	21 10
Macpherson, John, of Heathmount	Heathmount, Tain	335	51 10	Robertson, John, of Rhynie	Rhynie, Fearn	528	1,098 —
Macpherson, Rev. John	Ardelve, Lochalsh	1	15 —	Robertson, John Gordon	Dingwall	3	130 —
Macpherson, Mrs. Janet	Strath, Gairloch, Dingwall	5	20 —	Romanes, Mrs. Isabella, of Dunscaith	Dunscaith, Parkhill	8	30 —
Macrae, Donald, of Kirksheaf	Kirksheaf, Tain	321	230 —	Rose, Hugh Law, of Tarlogie	Tarlogie House, Tain	3,039	2,029 4
Macrae, Rev. Donald	Dell, Barvas, Stornoway	5	21 —	Rose, Rev. Lewis	Manse, Tain	13	46 —
Macrae, Duncan	Munlochy	17	4 —	Ross, Alexander	Highmills, Tain	6	37 15
Macrae, Rev. John	Manse, Stornoway	10	48 —	Ross, Colin George, of Weavis	Brooke Lodge, Cheadle, Cheshire	15,850	950 —
Macritchie, Rev. Malcolm	Knock, Stornoway	5	16 17	Ross, Commissioners of Supply of County of	Dingwall	1	420 —
Mather, Robert	Druid Temple, Inverness	2	40 —	Ross, Donald, of Moorfarm	Castlecraig, Parkhill	450	169 14
Matheson, Alexander, of Ardross, M.P.	Ardross Castle, Alness; and 38 South Street, Grosvenor Sq., London	220,433	20245 12	Ross, Donald	Chanonry Point, Fortrose	5	10 —
Matheson, Rev. Alexander	Manse, Glenshiel, Lochalsh	60	40 —	Ross, Donald	Hill of Fortrose, Fortrose	22	46 2
Matheson, John	Munlochy	28	5 —	Ross, Donald	Munlochy	10	4 —
Matheson, Sir James, of the Lews and Achany, Bart.	Lews Castle, Stornoway	406,070	17676 7	Ross, Donald Gordon	Dingwall	2	121 —
Matheson, William James, of Milton	23 Abercromby Place, Edinburgh	500	272 6	Ross, George, of Pitcalnie	Rhives, Parkhill	10,618	1,269 10
Menzies, Rev. John	Manse, Fodderty, Dingwall	15	45 —	Ross, George Balfour M'Kenzie, of Aldie	Abercorn Gardens, Edinburgh	1,086	500 —
Methuen, Heirs of James	Leith	1	17 10	Ross, Col. George William Holmes, of Cromarty	Cromarty House, Cromarty	1,646	1,340 —
Middleton, Lord	Applecross House, Dingwall	63,000	1,919 18	Ross, Hector	Midoxgate, Fearn	50	45 —
Miller, Colin Milne, of Kincurdy	Kincurdy, Fortrose	400	359 10	Ross, James	Ardival, Tain	70	5 —
Miller, Heirs of John	Rosemarkie	1	13 —	Ross, Heirs of John	Tain	1	41 18
Morison, Alexander	Bayhead, Stornoway	1	20 —	Ross, John	Janefield, Fortrose	3	10 —
Morison, Rev. James	Manse, Kintail, Lochalsh	200	40 —	Ross Memorial Hospital, Trustees of	Dingwall	1	20 —
Morrison, James	Allangrange Moor, Munlochy	12	4 10	Ross, Sir Charles William Augustus, of Balnagown, Bart.	Balnagown Castle, Parkhill	110,445	12652 16
Morrison, John	Munlochy	12	4 10	Ross, Robert Ferguson, of Invercharron	Invercharron, Ardgay	1,420	484 6
Munro, Alexander	Ochto, Ardgay	60	15 —	Ross, Heirs of William, of Shandwick	Golspie	2,869	2,721 8
Munro, Andrew, and William Ross	Invergordon	1	150 —	Ross, Mrs. Daniel, of Hartfield	Castlebrae, Tain	152	256 9
Munro, Alexander P. C., of Rockfield	Rockfield, Tain	382	502 5	Ross, Helen	Cromarty Ferry, Parkhill	1	8 —
Munro, Rev. Alexander Rose	F.C. Manse, Alness	2	20 —	Ross, Williamina E. F.	Brighton	6	14 —
Munro, Charles, of Foulis	Foulis Castle, Dingwall	4,458	3,780 11				
Munro, David, of Allan	Allan, Fearn	965	1,680 —	Sellar, Robert, of Aldie	Huntly	272	452 —
Munro, George	Munlochy	5	12 —	Shaw, John R., of Glencarron	Glencarron, Dingwall	8,300	645 —
Munro, James	Alness	2	10 —	Sim, Peter	Inverhouse, Ardgay	40	35 —
Munro, James, of Highfield	Highfield, Tain	160	50 —				
Munro, Heirs of Lieut. John	Tain	2	16 —				
Munro, Stewart C., of Teaninich	21 Hill Street, Edinburgh	2,729	1,460 16				
Munro, William, of Swordale	Swordale, Dingwall	3,930	1,236 12				
Munro, Catharine, of Balcony	Balcony, Dingwall	280	390 —				

ROSS—continued.

Name of Owner.	Address of Owner.	Estimated Acreage of Property.	Gross Annual Value.	Name of Owner.	Address of Owner.	Estimated Acreage of Property.	Gross Annual Value.
		Acres.	£ s.			Acres.	£ s.
Simpson, James, of Culrain	Fort-William	523	310 10	Urquhart, Lewis Carmichael, of Knockbreck	West Villa, Elgin	100	222 13
Simpson, John	Muckernish, Munlochy	14	6 –	*Urquhart, Ministers and Kirk-Session of*	Urquhart, Dingwall	3	16 5
Smith, Rev. Farquhar	Arpafeelie, Inverness	1	14 –	Urquhart, Thomas, of Kinbeachie	Cujiwa, Belvoir, Australia	400	344 5
Smith, John, senior	Ness of Fortrose, Fortrose	18	40 –				
Smith, John	Inverallan, Grantown	300	29 4				
Smith, Peter	Culrain, Ardgay	150	8 –				
Steel, James	Wishaw	48	4 –				
Stewart, Colin	Kempfield, Dingwall	7	13 10	Vass, David R.	Ayr	67	84 10
Stewart, Donald	Dingwall	3	132 4				
Stewart, Rev. Donald	Kilmuir-Easter, Invergordon	16	39 15	Watson, James	Fortrose	2	26 11
Stewart, William	Conon, Dingwall	1	17 –	Watson, Mrs. Eliza; and Eliza Watson	Tain	16	50 10
Storie, Sophia R.	Porchester, Hants	15	49 –	Watters, John	Culrain, Ardgay	82	5 –
Strachan, Rev. James	Manse, Barvas, Stornoway	640	88 –	White, Henry W., of Monar	Carlton Club, Pall Mall, London	6,800	345 –
Stuart, Right Hon. Sir John, of Lochcarron, Kt.	Courthill, Lochcarron	32,450	2,661 4	Wilson, John	Rosemarkie, Fortrose	1	10 –
Sutherland, George	Culrain, Ardgay	30	2 10	Wood, Rev. Alexander	Manse, Rosemarkie, Fortrose	10	60 –
Sutherland, George	Rosemarkie	2	63 –				
Sutherland, Duke of	Dunrobin Castle, Golspie	120	210 –	Wood, George, of Inveroykel	Inveroykel, Ardgay	4,800	150 –
Sutherland, Duchess of	Dunrobin Castle, Golspie	149,879	11792 16	Woodhouse, Samuel	Norly Hall, Cheshire	7	7 10
Sutherland Railway Company	Inverness (*Railway*)	27	74 –	*Works, Her Majesty's Board of*	London (*Fishings*)	–	5 –
Tain Academy, Trustees of	Tain	2	30 –	Young, Donald	Ness, Fortrose	10	49 16
Tain, Burgh of	Tain	1,834	431 15	Young, Simon	Cloy, Fortrose	11	40 –
Tain, Burgh of, and other Claimants of Morrich Mor Commonty	Tain	2,010	50 –				
Tain, Parochial Board of	Tain	5	8 –				
Thomson, John	Inverness	45	13 –	Total Owners of Land of One Acre and upwards		324 1,971,309	247,833 17
Tolmie, Rev. John W.	Manse, Contin, Dingwall	34	50 –	Total Owners of Lands of less than One Acre in extent		1,719 373	21,508 3
Turnbull & Co.	Avoch	1	150 –				
Urquhart, Heritors of Parish of	Urquhart, Dingwall	4	4 –	GRAND TOTAL		2,043 1,971,682	269,342 –

ROXBURGH.

Population in 1871,		53,974.
Inhabited Houses,		7,829.
Number of Parishes,		35.

Name of Owner	Address of Owner.	Estimated Acreage of Property.	Gross Annual Value.	Name of Owner.	Address of Owner.	Estimated Acreage of Property.	Gross Annual Value.
		Acres.	£ s.			Acres.	£ s.
Aitchison, William, of Glenkerry	Brieryhill, Hawick	81	151 10	Brunton, Trustees of William, of Ladhope	Ladhope, Galashiels	303	555 —
Aitken, George	Morebattle	1	16 —	Buccleuch and Queensberry, Duke of	Dalkeith Palace, Dalkeith	104,461	39457 18
Aitken, Rev. William F.	Midlem, Selkirk	1	11 —				
Allan, Francis	Hawick	3	9 17	Buccleuch and Queensberry, Duke of	Dalkeith Palace, Dalkeith		
Allan, Richard	Howden, Jedburgh	1	162 10	and Alexander Curle	Melrose	26	39 17
Allan, Richard	Bowmont Street, Kelso	3	184 5				
Allardyce, Rev. James M.	Manse, Bowden	15	52 8	Bunyie, Mary	Newstead, Melrose	8	36 10
Ancrum, Heritors of	Ancrum	2	2 —	Burn, Isabella Jeffrey	Highcross, Melrose	1	60 —
Anderson, Benjamin Thos. G., of Tushielaw	Cacrabank, Selkirk	3,183	763 8	Burnie, Rev. William	Manse, Oxnam, Jedburgh	13	48 10
Anderson, Mrs. Margaret	Midlem, Selkirk	6	16 —	Calvert, Thomas	Morebattle	1	4 17
Antrobus, Sir Edmund, of Antrobus and Rutherford, Bart., M.P.	37 Eaton Square, London	1,796	2,499 —	Cameron, Mrs. Elizabeth Louisa, wife of Alexander Cameron of Mainhouse	Elgin	400	700 —
Armstrong, Colonel Adam	St. Petersburgh	3	76 9	Campbell, Lord	Hartrigge, Jedburgh	1,600	2,277 9
Baird, Trustees of late George, of Stitchell	Stitchell House, Kelso	4,339	8,374 17	Carre, Walter Riddell, of Cavers Carre	Cavers Carre, Selkirk	174	291 5
Balfour, Heirs of Charles, of Newton Don	Newton Don, Kelso	318	780 —	*Castleton, Heritors of*	Castleton, Hawick	1	1 —
				Chalmers, Rev. John	Manse, Ashkirk, Hawick	15	55 —
Ballantyne, Heirs of John	Laret, St. Boswells	13	34 —	Charters, George	Kalemouth, Kelso	2	67 10
Bell, Alexander	Linton, Kelso	22	73 5	Chisholm, Mrs. Jessie	Lilliesleaf	8	33 —
Bell, Gideon W., of The Woll	The Woll, Hawick	762	505 10	Chisholme, Lieut. John J. S., of Stirches	H.M. 9th Lancers	1,155	1,397 10
Bell, William	Cortleferry, Stow	1	23 —	Church of Scotland	Roxburghshire	9	10 —
Berwickshire Railway Co.	Edinburgh (*Railway*)	10	464 —	Clapperton, Robert	Gattonside, Melrose	3	25 —
Betts, Mrs. Mary Ann W.	London	24	35 —	Clark, Capt. James A., of Langhaugh	York	60	221 —
Black, Adam, and Mrs. Isabella Black, his spouse	Priorbank, Melrose	36	208 —	Clark, James	Lauder	3	11 —
				Cleghorn, George, of Weens	Weens House, Jedburgh	531	825 10
Black, Rev. John	U.P. Manse, Newcastleton	1	17 —	Cochrane, Alexander, of Ashkirk	Gort House, Surrey	1,500	1,199 12
Black, William, of Nether Wells	2 Osborne Place, Manchester	255	390 —	Cochrane, Trustees of late Mark	St. Boswells	3	26 10
Blaikie, Trs. of late Robert	St. Helen's, Melrose	26	154 —	Cochrane, Thomas	Ancrum	1	9 10
Blair, James	Edinburgh	6	15 —	Cochrane, William	Greenbank, Galashiels	21	27 —
Blythe, James	Drygrange Mains, Melrose	17	64 15	Cockburn, Trustees of late Thomas, of Menslaws	Menslaws, Jedburgh	150	330 —
Bogue, Thomas	Berwick	4	329 —	Cotesworth, Robert	Cowdenknowes, Earlston	6	10 10
Bonnington, Robert	Bowden	1	12 12	Cotesworth, Trustees of late Robert, of Cowdenknowes	Cowdenknowes, Earlston	1,420	1,404 —
Boston, James	Easter Deloraine, Selkirk	1	24 —				
Boston, Mrs. Euphemia	Gattonside, Melrose	93	117 5				
Bowden, Feuars of	Bowden	23	9 19	Cowan, James	Edinburgh	26	33 10
Bowden, Heritors of	Bowden	1	1 —	Cowan, John	Edinburgh	2	12 —
Boyd, John, of Maxpoffle	Maxpoffle, St. Boswells	248	664 19	Cowan, Samuel Hunter, and Heirs of Margaret Campbell	Bengal Staff Corps Kirkcudbright	24	60 —
Boyd, John Brack, of Cherrytrees	Cherrytrees, Kelso	670	850 —				
Boyd, Trs. of late Charles W.	Kelso	15	77 —	Craig, Rev. Archibald	Manse, Bedrule, Jedburgh	15	52 —
Brewster, Dame Jane Kirke Purnell	Allerly, Melrose	8	65 —	*Crailing, Heritors of*	Crailing	1	1 —
				Craw, John	Jedburgh	58	319 14
Broad, John	Ashby, Melrose	1	55 —	Crawford, Thomas	Middle Blainslie, Lauder	77	90 —
Brodie, Walter	Wyndhead, Lauder	1	12 —	Crozier, Mrs. Margaret	Newcastleton	1	18 3
Bromfield, Rev. Robert	Manse, Sprouston, Kelso	9	50 —	Cunningham, Rev. Adam	Manse, Crailing, Jedburgh	11	65 —
Brown Brothers	Galashiels	4	851 —	Cunningham, Henry	Edinburgh	7	40 12
Brown, John J. E.	Rosebank, Kelso	15	147 5	Curle, Alexander, of Morriston	Abbey Park, Melrose	140	494 6
Brown, William Nimmo	St. John's, Melrose	1	50 —				
Brown, Rev. William	Craigiebank, Perth	2	94 15	Curle, James, of Evelaw	Harleyburn, Melrose	46	234 14
Brown, William	Jedburgh	11	91 10	Curle, Mrs. Isabella	St. Cuthbert's, Melrose	2	80 —
Brunton Bequest Trustees	Harcarsetree, Bowden	12	18 —	Currie, William, of Linthill	Linthill, St. Boswells	1,020	1,389 —
Brunton, John Stenhouse, of Hiltonshill	Ladhope, Galashiels	130	147 —	Dalrymple, Hon. George Grey, of Elliston	Elliston, St. Boswells	158	379 —
Brunton, Thomas Lauder, of Arthurshiels	23 Davies Street, Berkeley Square, London	174	170 7	Dalrymple, James, of Langlee	Langlee, Galashiels	719	1,172 10
Brunton, Trs. of late James	Bowden	22	75 —				

ROXBURGH—continued.

Name of Owner.	Address of Owner.	Estimated Acreage of Property.	Gross Annual Value.	Name of Owner.	Address of Owner.	Estimated Acreage of Property.	Gross Annual Value.
		Acres.	£ s.			Acres.	£ s.
Darling, Margaretta Elizabeth and Jane	Edinburgh	1	60 —	Erskine, George O. H. E. Biber, of Dryburgh	Dryburgh, St. Boswells	139	472 10
Davidson, Rev. Adam	Manse, Yetholm	20	59 —	Erskine, James, of Shielfield	The Priory, Melrose	3	60 10
Davidson, Rev. Alexander	Manse, Cavers	11	39 —	Erskine James, and Alexander Curle	Melrose	210	215 10
Davidson, Gilbert	Hawick	17	91 3	Ewen, Rev. John	Manse, Hobkirk	41	67 —
Davidson, Gilbert	Hawick	3	6 —				
Davidson, John	Lanton, Jedburgh	9	27 7				
Davidson, Trustees of late John S.	Alnbank, Ancrum	4	49 —	Fair, James S. E.	Overwells, Jedburgh	29	120 —
Davidson, William Scott	Ancrum	7	55 12	Fairbairn, John, of Fens	Grizzlefield, Earlston	280	607 10
Dawson, Rev. John	Manse, Makerstoun, Kelso	23	63 —	Fairbairn, John James	Grizzlefield, Earlston	1	3 5
Deans, William	Jedburgh	6	54 12	Fairholme, George Knight Erskine, of Old Melrose	Bregenz, Austria	1,300	1,700 8
Denholm, Feuars of	Denholm	5	16 19				
Dickinson, John	Bemersyde Cottage, St. Boswells	9	28 —	Fairholme, Trustees of Caroline Elizabeth, of Chapel	Chapel, Lauder	419	721 3
Dickinson, Robert	Longcroft, Lauder	5	45 —	Ferguson, Rev. John	Manse, Edgerston, Jedburgh	2	20 —
Dickinson, Trustees of Thomas	Eildon, Melrose	18	45 —	Fiddes, John and James	Chesterhall, Ancrum	15	40 —
Dickson, Captain Sir Alexander Collingwood T., of Hardingham, Bart.	Sydenham, Kelso	234	754 —	Finlay, Mrs. Mary Ann, of Coldhouse	37 South Clerk Street, Edinburgh	194	194 5
Dickson, James, of Chatto	Bughtrig, Coldstream	4,139	3,531 8	Fraser, Robert	Philadelphia	2	8 —
Dickson, William	Hawick	5	102 —	Frater, Trs. of late John	Westfields, Kelso	40	115 —
Dickson, Wm. Richardson, of Chisholme	Chisholme, Hawick	3,551	2,164 16	Free Church of Scotland	Roxburghshire	8	109 10
Dicksons and Laings	Hawick	5	772 —	Freer, Allan	Melrose	16	207 —
Dobie, Alexander, of Raperlaw	Eskbank, Dalkeith	333	272 6	Gibb, George G. S.	Boon, Lauder	3	20 —
Dodd, William	Newcastleton	1	10 10	Gibson, Mrs. Margaret	Dingleton, Melrose	4	14 10
Dodds, Rev. Andrew	Avonbridge, Falkirk	42	70 —	Gladstone, Heirs of Andrew	Bloomfield, Ancrum	5	10 —
Dodds, John	Bowden	5	21 —	Gourlay, Rev. Adam	Manse, Lilliesleaf	11	48 —
Douglas, Christopher, of Chesterhouse	Edinburgh	1,356	1,771 16	Govenlock, Peter	Yetholm, Kelso	3	218 —
Douglas, Sir George H. S., of Springwood Park, Bart.	Springwood Park, Kelso	5,568	6,730 5	Govenlock, Trustees for Mrs. Jessie	Lilliesleaf	12	36 —
				Graham, John	Newmills, Lauder	3	26 5
Douglas, James, of Cavers	Cavers House, Hawick	9,840	7,937 6	Graham, Rev. M. H.	Manse, Maxton, St. Boswells	10	55 —
Douglas, Mrs. Margaret	Ulston, Jedburgh	1	26 —	Graham, Mrs. Elizabeth	Berwick	6	81 14
Dove, Helen	Midlem, Selkirk	6	10 10	Gray, Andrew	Lilliesleaf	4	13 —
Dryden, Robert	Midlemburn, Selkirk	78	75 —	Gray, Isabella and Agnes, and Mrs. Jessie Hogg	Ancrum	9	22 10
Dudley, Earl of	Witley Court, Stourport	1,086	2,825 3	Gray, Peter	Midlem, Selkirk	6	18 5
Dunlop, Charles Walter, of Whitmuirhall	Whitmuirhall, Selkirk	469	434 —	Gray, William	Sharplaw, Hownam, Kelso	5	105 10
Dunlop, James	Rachelfield, Smailholm, Kelso	5	64 10	Greenhill, Rev. Charles K.	Manse, Roberton, Hawick	13	18 —
Dunglas, Lord and Hon. James A. D. Home	Newton Don, Kelso } The Hirsel, Coldstream }	5	11 —	Gregory, Mrs. Mary Somerville	Greycrook, St. Boswells	5	60 —
				Grieve, James	North Sinton, Hawick	40	70 —
				Grieve, Robert, senior	Bowden	5	38 —
Dunn, Andrew	Kelso	2	165 —	Griffith, George Waldie	Hendersyde Park, Kelso	9	120 —
Dunn, Thomas	Kelso	1	55 —	Guthrie, Trustees of late John	Jedburgh	3	44 5
Dunn, Thomas John	Melrose	2	55 —				
				Haddington, Earl of	Mellerstain, Kelso	4,708	5,079 4
Easton, Trs. of late George	Melrose	3	22 10	Haddon, Andrew	Honeyburn, Hawick	6	45 —
Easton, Robert	Melrose	2	131 5	Haldane, William	Galashiels	3	114 10
Easton, William	Jedburgh	4	112 —	Hall, David	Hawick	1	28 —
Eliott, Sir William F. Augustus, of Stobs, Bart.	Stobs Castle, Hawick	16,475	8,934 2	Hamilton, John R.	Minto, Hawick	2	10 10
				Handyside, Robert	Morebattle	9	19 —
				Hardie, James	Edinburgh	26	60 —
Eliott, Trustees of late Sir William F., of Stobs and Wells	Hawick	2,870	2,575 6	Hardie, Isabella	Newtown, St. Boswells	4	20 10
				Harkness, John	Castlehill, Jedburgh	5	24 4
Elliot, Adam	Newcastleton	1	14 3	Hart, George	Newstead, Melrose	1	12 15
Elliot, Hon. Arthur R. D.	London	3	10 15	Hart, James	Lockiesedge, Hawick	1,172	969 9
Elliot, Hon. George F. S.	London	4	5 4	*Hawick, Burgh of*	Hawick		
Elliot, James	Galalaw, Kelso	3	53 —	Hawick Combination Poorhouse, Managers of	Hawick	1	100 —
Elliot, John, of Binks	Burnmouth, Hawick	550	275 —	*Hawick, Heritors of*	Hawick	1	4 2
Elliot, Robert, of Redheugh	24 Abbey Street, Carlisle	271	185 —	*Hawick, Parochial Board of*	Hawick	5	57 17
				Hawick Working Men's Building and Investment Society	Hawick	2	29 10
Elliot, Robert Henry, of Clifton	Clifton Park, Kelso	5,258	5,178 5	Heiton, Andrew	Perth	9	118 10
Elliot, Sir Walter, of Wolfelee, K.C.S.I.	Wolfelee, Hawick	3,030	2,284 5	Henderson, David, of Abbotrule	Abbotrule, Hawick	2,340	2,503 13
Elliot, Trustees of late William	Knowes, Kelso	5	91 —	Henderson, John	Kelso	1	187 15
Elliot, William	Jedburgh	3	80 —	Henderson, Mrs. Margaret	Lanton, Jedburgh	16	20 —
Elliot, William B., of Benrig	Benrig, St. Boswells	38	163 —	Henry, Hon. Mrs. Louisa, of The Pavilion, wife of Col. Charles S. Henry	Winchfield, Hants	690	1,275 2
Elliot, William Claude, of Harwood	Pall Mall Club, London	4,900	2,379 15	Herdman, Rev. James C.	St. Mary's, Melrose	10	111 10

ROXBURGH—continued.

Name of Owner.	Address of Owner.	Estimated Acreage of Property.	Gross Annual Value.	Name of Owner.	Address of Owner.	Estimated Acreage of Property.	Gross Annual Value.
		Acres.	£ s.			Acres.	£ s.
Hilson, George, senior	Jedburgh	3	262 –	Lees, George, & Company	Galashiels	2	138 10
Hilson, George, junior	Jedburgh	63	191 9	Leishman, Rev. Thomas	Manse, Linton, Kelso	10	62 –
Hilson, John and William	Jedburgh	1	292 12	Leith, Lady Eliza Caroline, of Drygrange, wife of Sir George Hector Leith, of Burgh St. Peter's, Bart.	Drygrange, Melrose	1,315	1,724 4
Home, George H. M. B., of Softlaw	Argaty, Stirling	605	1,059 6				
Home, Hon. Cospatrick Douglas, Lieut. Rifle Brigade	The Hirsel, Coldstream	7	5 5	Little, James	Newcastleton	1	31 7
				Little, Matthew	Oxnam, Jedburgh	1	8 –
Home, Hon. Wm. Sholto Douglas, Lieut.-Colonel Grenadier Guards	The Hirsel, Coldstream	6	5 5	Lockhart, Allan Eliott, of Borthwickbrae	Borthwickbrae, Hawick	1,884	1,036 15
Home, Hon. G. Douglas	The Hirsel, Coldstream	8	5 5	Lockie, George	Newtown, St. Boswells	1	105 10
Home, Countess of	The Hirsel, Coldstream	25,380	7,995 –	Lothian, Marquess of	Monteviot, Jedburgh	19,740	23684 5
Humble, George, of Old Graden	Old Graden, Kelso	304	355 17	Lunacy Board of Roxburgh, Berwick, and Selkirk	Melrose	28	475 –
Humble, George and John	Kelso	7	31 2				
Humble, John	Waverley Lodge, Kelso	3	149 19				
Hume, George	St. Boswells	2	36 15				
Hume, John	Gledsnest, Hawick	1	10 10	Macallister, Rev. Dugald	Manse, Stitchell, Kelso	8	50 –
Hunter, Rev. George	Manse, Kirkton, Hawick	7	30 –	Macgregor, Robert	Dingleton, Melrose	1	5 10
Hunter, James	Kelso	1	65 –	Macmorland, Rev. John P.	Manse, Minto, Hawick	36	100 –
				Maconochie, John Allan	Gattonside Ho., Melrose	5	16 10
Jackson, Trustees of late John	Friarsmount, Jedburgh	14	118 10	Maconochie, Robert Blair, of Gattonside House	Gattonside House, Melrose	298	485 5
James, James, of Samieston	Les Vauxbelets, Guernsey	805	917 –	Macpherson, Lieut.-Col. David E., of Belleville	Belleville House, Kingussie	145	152 5
Jamieson, John	Bowden	2	9 15				
Jamieson, Mrs. Margaret	Bowden	2	18 –	Macrae, Rev. John	Manse, Hawick	16	131 12
Jardine, James, of Larriston	Dryfeholm, Lockerbie	4,293	1,372 10	Makdougall, Maria Scott, of Makerstoun	Makerstoun House, Kelso	2,513	4,763 17
Jardine, John, of Thorlieshope	Arkleton, Ewes, Langholm	2,000	844 9	Mair, Rev. John	Manse, Southdean, Hawick	41	85 10
Jardine, Robert, of Lawstone and Langraw, M.P.	Castlemilk, Lockerbie	1,198	989 10	Mallandain, Mrs. Elizabeth, and Mrs. Jessie Mitchell	Manchester	11	33 –
Jedburgh, Heritors of	Jedburgh	1	2 –	Mann, George & Charles	Darnick Vale, Melrose	4	31 6
Jedburgh, Union Board of	Jedburgh	2	71 –	Manuel, William	Darnick, Melrose	1	37 –
Jerdan, Rev. Charles S.	Loanhead, Denny	6	29 10	Marr, Robert	Gattonside, Melrose	3	31 10
Jerdan, David	Dalkeith	10	30 –	Marshall, Christian	Newcastle-on-Tyne	3	16 10
Jerdon, Archibald	Allerton, Jedburgh	2	58 –	Martin, John, of Firth	Headington Lodge, Oxford	450	440 –
Johnson, Edward	Tweedbank, Kelso	4	75 –				
Johnstone, John	Gattonside, Melrose	3	11 10	Martinson, John N.	St. Boswells	1	19 –
Johnstone, Rev. Thomas F.	Manse, St. Boswells	8	49 –	Mather, Catherine Isabella	St. John's, Melrose	42	156 1
				Matthewson, John	Ashkirk, Hawick	52	74 –
Karr, Rev. John Seton, of Kippilaw	Strachur Park, Greenock	920	924 16	Maxwell, Edward Heron, of Teviotbank	Teviotbank, Hawick	295	500 –
Kelso, Heritors of	Kelso	4	10 –	Mein, Alexander	Jedburgh	8	27 –
Kelso, Parochial Board of	Kelso	4	70 –	Mein, Andrew W., and John E. Mein of Hunthill	Hunthill, Jedburgh	1,097	1,502 2
Kennedy, Thomas	Kelso	19	58 –				
Kerr, Andrew	Newtown, St. Boswells	2	78 10				
Kerr, Lord Charles Lennox	Perth	8	18 –	Mein, Surgeon Thomas, R.N.	St. Boswells	13	73 17
Kerr, Captain Lord Ralph Drury	H.M. 10th Hussars	4	10 –	Melrose Parochial Board	Melrose	2	15 –
				Mercer, George	Cotgreen, Melrose	36	106 –
Kerr, William Scott, of Sunlaws	Sunlaws, Kelso	2,662	3,154 5	Mercer, James	Galashiels	1	71 10
Kerr, Mrs. Helen	Newcastleton	1	8 13	Merchant Maiden Hospital	Edinburgh	874	1,475 12
Kerr, Mrs. Margaret, wife of Thomas Kerr, of Craighouse	Craighouse, Earlston	148	140 –	Michie, John	Kelso	1	82 12
				Millar, Robert	Lochgilphead	2	41 –
Keir, William, of Whithaugh	Whithaugh, Newcastleton	768	329 2	Millar, William	Jedburgh	26	293 9
				Miller, Hew	Ochtertyre, Crieff	24	37 –
Kidd, Charles George, of Lowood	Lowood, Melrose	98	264 10	Miller, William	Dovecote, Hawick	1	10 10
				Milligan, Robert	Hawick	2	90 16
Knox, David	Martinshouse, Hawick	2	43 15	Mills, Thomas	Morebattle, Kelso	1	10 10
Knox, John	Melrose	4	32 –	Milne, Nicol, of Faldonside	Faldonside, Galashiels	1,100	1,499 5
				Milne, Nicol, of Whitehill	Dryhope, Selkirk	192	228 15
Laidlaw, Peter	Jedburgh	8	416 5	Minto, Andrew	Lilliesleaf	2	32 –
Laidlaw, Thomas	Hawick	51	1,914 4	Minto, Earl of	Minto House, Hawick	8,633	6,888 4
Laidlaw & Fairgrieve	Galashiels	1	770 5	Mitchell, Heirs of Alexander, of Stow	Carolside, Earlston	2,000	1,303 10
Laing, Alexander	Hawick	4	76 –				
Lamb, Rev. William	Manse, Ednam, Kelso	5	50 –	Mitchell, James	Oakendean, Melrose	10	65 –
Lauder, Alexander	Midlem, Selkirk	3	9 –	Mitchell, Thomas	Melrose	3	31 5
Lauderdale, Earl of	Thirlestane Castle, Lauder	756	740 10	Moffat, Douglas, of Harpertown	New University Club, St. James', London	998	2,168 18
Laurie, James	Jedburgh	8	27 –				
Laurie, Walter	Jedburgh	23	69 10	Morton, Robert	London	4	13 –
Law, Archibald	Selkirk	3	23 10	Moscrip, Richard	Morebattle	3	15 –
Law, Heirs of Robert	Lilliesleaf	4	13 15	Muir, James Lauder	Melrose	20	39 –
Lawrie, James Hill	St. Boswells	6	28 10	Muir, Mrs. Margaret Flora, of Ormiston, wife of Rev. R. H. Muir	Manse, Dalmeny	688	731 10
Lawrie, John	Dingleton, Melrose	1	10 –				
Lawrie, Robert	St. Boswells	1	21 10	Munro, Rev. William	Hawick	3	132 2
Lee, Rev. William	Manse, Roxburgh	10	50 5	Murdie, Henry	Lanton Mains, Jedburgh	1	4 10

ROXBURGH—continued.

Name of Owner.	Address of Owner.	Estimated Acreage of Property.	Gross Annual Value.	Name of Owner.	Address of Owner.	Estimated Acreage of Property.	Gross Annual Value.
		Acres.	£ s.			Acres.	£ s.
Murray, James	Newcastleton	1	14 10	Pott, Robert	Newcastleton	1	11 —
Murray, John, of Wooplaw	Wooplaw, Melrose	611	540 —	Pott, Captain William	H.M. 27th Regiment	9	14 —
Murray, John	Glenmayne, Galashiels	6	151 —	Potts, William	Edinburgh	3	21 10
Murray, Sir John, of Philiphaugh and Melgund, Bart.	Philiphaugh, Selkirk	942	981 —	Pringle, James Thomas, of Torwoodlee	Torwoodlee, Galashiels	2,500	1,357 —
				Pringle, Thomas	Newstead, Melrose	6	24 —
Murray, Richard	Newcastleton	1	19 —	Pringle, Mrs. Mary, of Wilton Lodge	Wilton Lodge, Hawick	150	206 2
Murray, Mrs. Janet	Bridgend, Melrose	11	45 10	Prison Board of Roxburghshire	Jedburgh	2	110 —
Nichol, James	Newcastleton	1	3 10	Purdom, Thomas	Hawick	3	50 10
Nichol, John	Newcastleton	1	17 3	Purves, Trustees of late John	Whitehouse, Ancrum	72	135 —
Nichol, Thomas	Broomilees, Melrose	2	54 —				
Nimmo, James	Ashton, Gourock	2	114 —	Purves, Eleanor R., Christian W., and Eliza J.	Pointfield, Kelso	1	50 —
Noble, Rev. James	Manse, Castleton, Hawick	30	45 —				
North British Railway Company	Edinburgh (Railway)	780	31204 8				
North-Eastern Railway Company	York (Railway)	34	1,543 8	Rae, Robert	Temple, St. Boswells	40	90 —
				Ramsay, Elizabeth Williamson, of Maxton, and Sir William G. H. T. Fairfax, of Holmes, Bart.	Maxton 16 Queen's Gate, Hyde Park, London	664	1,222 —
Ogilvie, Alexander	Chesters, Jedburgh	26	6 7				
Ogilvie, Thomas Elliot	Chesters, Jedburgh	40	27 15	Rea, Charles, of Halterburnhead	Doddington, Wooler	730	425 —
Ogilvie, Lieut. W. F.	Chesters, Jedburgh	26	6 7				
Ogilvie, William, of Chesters	Chesters, Jedburgh	1,721	2,171 15	Redford, James	Lilliesleaf	23	43 —
Oliver, Andrew	Jedburgh	1	52 15	Redford, William	Selkirk	1	23 —
Oliver, James	Thornwood, Hawick	71	340 —	Redpath, James, and Mrs. Logan	Goshenbank, Kelso	2	220 —
Oliver, James	Hawick	8	137 5	Renton, Rev. Henry	U.P. Manse, Kelso	1	42 —
Oliver, John	Borthaugh, Hawick	27	145 10	Renwick, Francis	Morebattle	1	15 —
Oliver, John, of Overton Bush	Kelso	460	278 —	Renwick, Robert, of Halkburn	Halkburn, Melrose	886	670 —
Oliver, Robert, of Blakelaw	Lochside, Kelso	1,999	2,355 —	Richardson, Trustees of late John, of Kirklands	Kirklands, Ancrum	70	188 —
Oliver, Mary	Edinburgh	3	14 —	Riddell, Captain George W. H., of Muselee	Muselee, Hawick	1,933	1,553 12
Ord, John, of Muirhouselaw	Nisbet, Kelso	1,112	1,404 —				
Ormiston, Andrew	Gattonside, Melrose	7	24 —	Riddell, Major-General William, of Camieston, C.B.	The Anchorage, Melrose	297	441 —
Ormiston, William Thos., of Glenburnhall	Glenburnhall, Jedburgh	381	1,054 —				
Ormiston, Trustees of late Mrs. Jane	Melrose	2	122 —	Riddell, Major-Gen. William, of Camieston, C.B., and Mrs. Margaret Riddell	The Anchorage, Melrose	3	75 —
Ormiston, Mrs. Janet	Langland's Bank, Hawick	8	17 —				
Ormiston, Isabella	Edinburgh	11	26 —	Riddell, William	Hundalee, Jedburgh	28	45 —
Ovens, Trs. of late Thomas	Galashiels	1	132 —	Riddell, William	Lilliesleaf	4	23 —
Oxnam, Heritors of	Oxnam, Jedburgh	1	1 —	Ritchie, Rev. George	Manse, Jedburgh	5	61 —
				Roberts, William, & Co.	Galashiels	1	433 —
Panton, Patrick	Edenbank, Kelso	80	289 6	Robertson, John	Nether Blainslie, Lauder	19	28 10
Parnell, Richard	Gattonside Villa, Melrose	41	154 —	Robertson, Richard	Blainslie, Lauder	18	43 —
Paterson, Adam, of Whitelee	Edinburgh	335	572 19	Robertson, Richard	Glasgow	7	13 —
				Robertson, Heirs of Mrs.	Ednam House, Kelso	4	358 10
Paterson, Trustees of late Adam	Galashiels	1	235 —	Robertson, Thomas	Blainslie, Lauder	5	24 5
Paterson, Heirs of James	Bowden	1	15 —	Robson, Charles	Kelso	5	139 —
Paterson, Robert	Edinburgh	2	19 15	Robson, Rev. George	U.P. Manse, Lauder	43	80 —
Paterson, William, of Ettrickhall	Ettrickhall, Galashiels	630	1,149 19	Robson, John	Linhope, Teviothead	2	7 19
				Robson, Thomas	Jedburgh	10	37 —
Paton, Andrew	St. Boswells	1	45 —	Roman Catholic Church	Roxburghshire	2	78 10
Paton, John	St. Boswells	18	90 10	Romanes, Robert	Lauder	7	25 15
Paton, John, of Crailing	Crailing House, Jedburgh	1,493	2,322 14	Roxburghe, Duke of	Floors Castle, Kelso	50,459	43820 8
Paton, Walter	Hawick	1	31 —	Roy, Frederick Lewis, of Nenthorn	Nenthorn House, Kelso	48	80 —
Patterson, Rev. James	Manse, Ancrum	14	71 8				
Pattison, Mrs. Ann Elizabeth Pringle, of The Haining, wife of J. Pringle Pattison	Melrose	2,527	1,410 —	Royds, Arthur	St. David's, Newtown, Montgomeryshire	5	116 —
				Russell, Francis	Jedbank, Jedburgh	2	60 —
Paul, Rev. David	Manse, Morebattle	13	60 —	Rutherford, Andrew	Kittyfield, Melrose	10	11 —
Pearce, Robert Finlay	London	3	43 —	Rutherford, George, of Sunnyside	Sunnyside, Melrose	258	408 5
Pennycook, Peter, of Newhall	Peebles	384	724 10	Rutherford, George	The Scaurs, Jedburgh	13	86 15
Philips, Harriet Elizabeth	Oakendean Cot., Melrose	18	69 —	Rutherford, Robert	Corsock, Dalbeattie	14	52 —
Pirie, Rev. James	F.C. Manse, Bowden	1	22 5	Rutherford, Robert	Paradise, Kelso	4	64 —
				Rutherford, Thomas	Hayclose, Penrith	1	10 —
Plummer, Charles Scott, of Sunderland Hall	Sunderland Hall, Selkirk	1,748	1,913 —	Rutherford, Trustees of Thomas S.	Jedburgh	84	144 —
Polwarth, Lord	Mertoun House, St. Boswells	4,102	5,280 2	Rutherford, Walter	Crailing Tofts, Jedburgh	67	137 8
				Rutherford, Isabella	Lanton, Jedburgh	2	11 5
Pott, Colonel George, of Todrig	Borthwickshiels, Hawick	782	457 —	Rutherfurd, Henry, of Fairnington	Fairnington, Kelso	1,784	2,012 10
Pott, Gideon, of Knowesouth	Knowesouth, Jedburgh	1,832	1,158 —	Rutherfurd, William O., of Edgerston	Edgerston, Jedburgh	7,703	3,463 —

ROXBURGH—continued.

Name of Owner.	Address of Owner.	Estimated Acreage of Property.	Gross Annual Value.	Name of Owner.	Address of Owner.	Estimated Acreage of Property.	Gross Annual Value.
		Acres.	£ s.			Acres.	£ s.
Rutherfurd, W. O., of Edgerston, and W. A. O. Rutherfurd, yr. of Edgerston	Edgerston, Jedburgh	20	40 –	Sprot, Lieut.-Col. John and Edward W. Sprot	H.M. 91st Highlanders, Edinburgh Castle Riddell, Selkirk	14	16 –
				Sprot, Mark, of Riddell	Riddell, Selkirk	3,278	3,426 19
				Stavert, Archibald, of Hoscote	Edinburgh	1,938	1,065 –
Sanderson, Thomas	Melrose	1	20 –	Stedman, Mrs. Sophia	Edinburgh	84	405 7
Sanderson & Murray	Galashiels	1	509 –	Stenhouse, Andrew	America	1	2 –
Sanderson, William	Galashiels	9	162 19	Stenhouse, John	Midlem, Selkirk	7	12 –
Scott, Adam	Lanton, Jedburgh	10	14 –	Stevenson, Henry	Hunthill, Jedburgh	3	14 –
Scott, Alexander, and Elizabeth Scott, of Falla	Hopetoun House, South Queensferry Ormiston, Tranent	669	300 –	Stevenson, Thomas	Lanton, Jedburgh	4	7 –
				Stevenson, Thomas	Bleachfield, Melrose	6	69 –
				Stevenson, William	Lanton, Jedburgh	4	8 5
Scott, Archibald, of Howcleuch	Hawick	350	233 10	Stewart, Andrew, of Cotfield	Cotfield, Lilliesleaf	583	495 –
				Stewart, George	Gattonside	46	48 –
Scott, Colonel Arthur	H.M. 5th Fusiliers	2	34 –	Stewart, Rev. James	Manse, Wilton, Hawick	75	265 5
Scott, Charles, of Langlee	Langlee, Jedburgh	485	488 1	Stewart, John	Galashiels	1	6 –
Scott, Francis	Newcastleton	1	19 15	Stewart & Mein	Kelso	5	180 10
Scott, George	Gattonside, Melrose	2	42 –	Stirling, Adam	Galashiels	1	53 15
Scott, George, of Overwells	Mosstower, Kelso	377	550 2	Storie, Thomas and William	Lanton, Jedburgh	6	18 10
Scott, Henry	Newton, Hawick	5	12 10	Storie, William	Lanton, Jedburgh	2	19 10
Scott, James	Lanton Park, Jedburgh	46	70 –	St. Boswells, Proprietors of Undivided Green of	St. Boswells	3	4 16
Scott, Heirs of James R. Hope	Abbotsford, Melrose	25	60 –	Suddens, Mrs. Margaret	Bowden	4	15 –
Scott, Heirs of J. R. Hope; and Mary Monica Hope Scott, of Abbotsford	Abbotsford, Melrose	1,237	1,585 6	Swan, Rev. David	Manse, Smailholm	12	50 –
				Swan, Robert	Kelso	37	109 –
				Sword, George	Midlem, Selkirk	48	55 –
Scott, James Robson, of Ashtrees	Belford, Kelso	272	253 2	Tait, James	Kelso	9	105 –
Scott, John, of Samieston	Dolphinston, Jedburgh	500	510 17	Talbot, Hon. Gilbert C.	London	10	23 12
Scott, Curators of John Corse, of Sinton	Sinton, Hawick	401	232 10	Telfer, John	Langleyburn, Newcastleton	1	19 15
Scott, John Scott Elliot, of Riccalton	Buckholm, Galashiels	3,242	979 14	Telfer, William, junior	Newcastleton	1	6 10
Scott, Trs. of late William, of Raeburn	Lessuden Place, St. Boswells	121	433 10	Thomas, James, of Pinnacle	Forthar, Fife	655	612 3
Scott, Thomas	Kersknowe, Selkirk	9	10 –	Thomson, Andrew, and Mrs. Wilhelmina Thomson, of Mainhill	Mainhill, St. Boswells	146	270 –
Scott, Trs. of late Thomas Macmillan, of Wauchope	Hawick	55	177 10	Thomson, James, of Merwick	Merwick, St. Boswells	65	165 –
Scott, Thomas Robson, of Newton	Newton, Jedburgh	938	1,113 –	Thomson, James	Croupyett, Ancrum	4	18 10
Scott, Lieut. Walter Macmillan, of Wauchope	H.M. 6th Dragoon Grds.	3,488	2,352 5	Thomson, John	Jedburgh	1	187 17
				Thomson, Rev. John	Rosalee, Hawick	12	135 –
Scott, Sir William, of Ancrum, Bart.	Ancrum House, Jedburgh	2,131	3,201 17	Thomson, Heirs of Robert G., of Templehall	Jedburgh	192	372 –
Scott, William	Lanton, Jedburgh	6	6 –	Thomson, Mrs. Martha	Jedburgh	19	129 –
Scott, Rev. William	Laurelbank, Partick	20	130 –	Thomson, Mrs. Mary Ann, of Allanshaws, wife of Rev. John Thomson	Rosalee, Hawick	1,077	650 –
Scott, Mrs. Helen	Newton, Hawick	383	590 –				
Scott, Jessie, of Wooden	Wooden House, Kelso	260	785 –				
Scott, Hon. Katherine	Mertoun Ho., St. Boswells	29	209 –	Thomson, Jessie	9 Kew Terrace, Glasgow	132	169 6
Scott, Violet	Melrose	1	50 –	Thomson, Violet	Morebattle	1	10 –
Scottish Episcopal Church	Roxburghshire	2	24 –	Trotter, Trustees of late Alicia Alison	Easter Housebyres, Melrose	600	387 2
Shedden Park Trustees	Kelso	8	77 –				
Shiel, Andrew	Hassendean, Hawick	3	43 8	Tudhope, James	Deptford	3	12 5
Sibbald, Heirs of Alex.	Gattonside, Melrose	2	6 –	Tully, James	Bowanhill, Hawick	22	34 –
Simson, Charles S. Rankine, of Threepwood	Threepwood, Melrose	1,000	521 –	Turnbull, Heirs of George	Brae, Jedburgh	9	127 8
				Turnbull, James	Ancrum	8	31 10
Simson, James	Melrose	5	167 10	Turnbull, John	Hendersyde, Kelso	1	17 –
Simson, Thomas, and Executors of Rev. Charles Simson	Middle Blainslie, Lauder	770	605 –	Turnbull, Michael	Sunlaws Mill, Kelso	3	26 5
				Turnbull, Robert, of Galalaw	Galalaw, Hawick	158	135 10
Sinclair, Lord	Stonedge, Hawick	2,251	1,242 16	Turnbull, Robert Laidlaw, of Merrylaw	Falnash, Hawick	930	152 6
Smail, William Archibald	Overmains, Coldstream	8	28 15				
Smail, Walter	New Zealand	3	21 15	Turnbull, Heirs of Walter	Ancrum	6	29 –
Smith, Adam	Australia	4	25 10	Turnbull, Trustees of William, of Fenwick	Hawick	2,482	2,262 11
Smith, John Alex., M.D.	Edinburgh	71	357 15				
Smith, Alexander	Appletreehall, Hawick	1	28 –	Tweeddale, Marquess of	Yester House, Haddington	4,425	4,774 19
Smith, James	Australia	4	12 15				
Smith, Rev. James	Manse, Kelso	7	96 –	Union Poorhouse Trustees	Kelso	5	111 5
Smith, John	Leaderfoot, Melrose	9	45 10	United Presbyterian Church	Roxburghshire	3	15 16
Smith, Trs. of late John	Darnick, Melrose	7	53 4	Usher, Thomas	Hawthornside, Hawick	17	50 –
Smith, Peter and George	Smailholm, Kelso	20	40 –				
Smith, Stephen	Stockbridge, Hants	5	33 –	Vair, Thomas	Stafford	5	31 12
Smith, William	Australia	18	41 10	Veitch, Rev. William	Edinburgh	8	29 –
Society for Propagating Christian Knowledge	Edinburgh	1,650	767 17	Veitch, William	Inchbonny, Jedburgh	21	109 17
Somervaille, Robert, of Charlesfield	Charlesfield, St. Boswells	168	270 –	Walden, Viscount	Chislehurst, Kent	80	200 –
Spottiswoode, Joseph	Gattonside, Melrose	6	18 –	Waldie, Trustees of late John, of Hendersyde	Kelso	1,661	3,592 15

ROXBURGH—continued.

Name of Owner.	Address of Owner.	Estimated Acreage of Property.	Gross Annual Value.	Name of Owner.	Address of Owner.	Estimated Acreage of Property.	Gross Annual Value.
		Acres.	£ s.			Acres.	£ s.
Walker, William Stewart, of Bowland	Bowland, Stow	3	2 10	Williamson, Thomas	London	3	4 –
Warrender, Sir George, of Lochend, Bart.	Bruntsfield House, Edinburgh	2,260	1,665 –	Williamson, Elizabeth	Newstead, Melrose	10	37 –
				Wilson, George	Newcastleton	1	11 2
Waters, Robert Rankine	Edinburgh	1	101 19	Wilson, George, of Heronhill	Heronhill, Hawick	105	1,186 –
Watson, Rev. George	Manse, Hownam, Kelso	11	31 –	Wilson, James	Earlston	1	3 10
Watson, Thomas Lindsay	Hawick	10	35 –	Wilson, John	Hawick	8	1,063 5
Watson, William, & Sons	Hawick	15	531 10	Wilson, Trustees of late John, of Otterburn	Otterburn, Kelso	2,590	1,464 16
Watson, William Scott, of Burnhead	Bucklands, Hawick	1,219	1,522 12	Wilson, Richard Jackson Walker, of Graden	London	700	1,234 3
Watson, Mrs. Janet	Wiltonbank, Hawick	12	40 –				
Watson's Hospital	Edinburgh	690	1,394 16	Wilson, Robert	Edenside, Kelso	2	6 15
Wauchope, Andrew, of Niddry	Niddry House, Edinburgh	3,335	4,478 11	Wilson, Walter	Hawick	8	909 12
				Wilton, Heritors of	Wilton, Hawick	4	10 –
Waugh, Richard	Melrose	1	87 –	*Wilton, Parochial Board of*	Wilton, Hawick	3	20 15
Waverley Hydropathic Co.	Skirmish Hill, Melrose	23	365 –	Wintrup, James	Ashyburn, Ancrum	15	30 –
West Croft Trustees for Poor of St. Boswells	St. Boswells	4	9 –	Witherspoon, William	Stouslea, Hawick	1	6 10
				Wood, George	Earlston	5	12 –
White, Michael	Hawick	4	157 4				
White, Rev. W. S.	Potter Hanworth Rectory, Lincoln	3	73 –	Yair, Rev. Joseph	Manse, Eckford, Kelso	8	32 5
				Young, Andrew	Morebattle	1	9 5
White, William	Morebattle	1	10 –	Young, Rev. Robert	Manse, Teviothead, Hawick	11	25 –
Whillans, Aaron	Smailholm, Kelso	1	23 10	Young, William	Galashiels	1	23 15
Wight, Rev. George and John R. Wight	Manse, Wamphray, Dumfries / Edinburgh	24	34 15	Total Owners of Land of One Acre and upwards 575		422,780	392,005 14
Williamson, James, of Laretburn	Laretburn, St. Boswells	101	249 –	Total Owners of Lands of less than One Acre in extent 1,880		683	64,877 13
Williamson, Trustees of late Robert	Kerfield, Kelso	25	139 10	GRAND TOTAL . . . 2,455		423,463	456,883 7

2 B

SELKIRK.

Population in 1871, - - - - - - - 14,005.
Inhabited Houses, - - - - - - - 1,741.
Number of Parishes, - - - - - - 10.

Name of Owner.	Address of Owner.	Estimated Acreage of Property.	Gross Annual Value.	Name of Owner.	Address of Owner.	Estimated Acreage of Property.	Gross Annual Value.
		Acres.	£ s.			Acres.	£ s.
Aimers, Thomas	Galashiels	7	182 15	Edmond, Robert	Galashiels	2	30 17
Aitchison, William, of Glenkerry	Brieryhill, Hawick	1,345	400 —	Elibank, Lord	Elibank, Selkirk	1,168	360 11
Alexander, David Carnegie	The Firs, Selkirk	4	52 —				
Anderson, Benjamin T. G., of Tushielaw	Cacrabank, Selkirk	2,300	725 —	Falconer, Rev. John	Manse, Ettrick, Selkirk	22	30 —
				Farquharson, Rev. James	Selkirk	6	62 —
Anderson, George, of Broomhill	Broomhill, Selkirk	177	379 1	Fisher, Robert F.	Galashiels	1	40 —
Anderson, Henry Scott	Selkirk	10	87 15	Forbes, William, of Callendar and Patrick B. Smollett	Callendar House, Falkirk Cameron House, Alexandria	8	10 1
Anderson & Scott	Selkirk	2	50 —				
Ballantyne, Capt. James George, of Holylee	Holylee, Innerleithen	2,885	852 10	Forsyth, Agnes	Selkirk	2	16 15
Bathgate, Trs. of Simeon	Selkirk	1	98 —	*Galashiels Gas Light Company*	Galashiels	10	265 —
Blackstock, Rev. Robert	Galashiels	1	35 —				
Borthwick, John, of Crookston	Crookston House, Stow	8	10 10	Gibson, Rev. John Sharpe	Manse, Kirkhope, Selkirk	5	27 8
				Gloag, Rev. Paton J.	Manse, Galashiels	6	28 15
Brown, Adam	Galashiels	5	80 —	Greenhill, Rev. Charles K.	Manse, Roberton, Hawick	2	22 —
Brown Brothers	Galashiels	9	327 2				
Brown, James	Galashiels	2	92 —				
Brown, James	Kirkwynd, Selkirk	4	39 —	Haldane, William, Richd., and Robert	Galashiels	38	449 3
Brown, James	Thornfield, Selkirk	7	80 —				
Brown, J. H., & Co.	Selkirk	9	1,526 10	Haldane, William	Galashiels	4	59 —
Brown, Trustees of James	Helmburn, Selkirk	296	185 —	Hall, John	Galashiels	1	209 5
Brown, Thomas	Selkirk	1	30 —	Hall, Thomas	Selkirk	2	97 9
Brown, William	Galashiels	7	111 10	Hay, Sir Robert, of Smithfield and Haystoune, Bart.	Kingsmeadow, Peebles	600	106 15
Brown, William	Galashiels	3	367 —				
Brown, William	Selkirk	4	97 7				
Brownlee, James	Galashiels	12	78 —	Heatlie, Andrew	Selkirk	4	74 —
Brydon & Brown	Selkirk	4	347 —	Herbertson, Andrew, & Sons	Galashiels	7	230 1
Buccleuch and Queensberry, Duke of	Bowhill, Selkirk	60,428	19828 3	Herbertson, Andrew	Galashiels	2	294 4
Burns, John	Selkirk	1	21 —				
Carmichael, Heirs of James	Hawick	13	25 —	Jardine, John, of Thorlieshope, and Thomas L. Jackson	Arkleton Ewes, Langholm	10	22 —
Carnegie, David, of Stronvar, and James Carnegie, yr. of Stronvar	Stronvar House, Lochearnhead	9	10 3				
				Jenkins, Rev. Alfred	Galashiels	1	48 —
Chisholm, Margaret	Selkirk	1	2 —	Johnstone, Daniel and Archibald	Philiphaugh, Selkirk	1	53 16
Chisholme, John	Selkirk	3	6 7				
Church of Scotland	Selkirkshire	2	4 —	Johnstone, James, of Alva	Alva House, Alva	8,614	2,505 4
Cochrane, Adam Lees, and Archd. Cochrane	Galashiels	60	972 —				
Cochrane, Adam Lees	Galashiels	12	103 —	Laidlaw, William	Galashiels	4	72 —
Cochrane, Adam, jun., and Kenneth Cochrane	Galashiels	4	853 14	Lamb, George	Selkirk	2	77 5
				Lambert, James	Springbank, Selkirk	7	38 10
Cochrane, Adam	Galashiels	2	76 —	Lang, Hugh M., of Broadmeadows	Broadmeadows, Selkirk	785	824 14
Cochrane, Smith, & Bathgate	Selkirk	1	94 —	Lang, Trs. of late John	Selkirk	2	6 10
Craik, James, and James A. Jamieson	Edinburgh	6	10 3	Lang, Patrick Sellar	Selkirk	6	80 —
				Lee, Alexander H., and Robert Cowan	Edinburgh	6	10 3
Cumming, Thomas	Selkirk	7	99 10	Lees, George	Galashiels	5	366 —
Dalgleish, Adam	Ladylands, Selkirk	4	44 10	Lees, Robert	Galashiels	2	60 —
Dalgleish, James Russell	Selkirk	1	220 —	Leitch, Richard	Selkirk	1	62 10
Dalgleish, Walter	Galashiels	2	25 10	Leny, William Macalpine, of Dalswinton and Frederick Pitman	Dalswinton, Dumfries Edinburgh	14	58 10
Deans, William	Selkirk	4	45 —				
Dickson, Arthur	Galashiels	7	352 13				
Dickson, William Richardson, of Alton	Chisholme, Hawick	1,105	450 —	Lockhart, Allan Eliott, of Borthwickbrae	Borthwickbrae, Hawick	2,028	757 12
Dobie & Locke	Selkirk	3	477 —	Lockhart, Sir Simon Macdonald, of Lee and Carnwath, Bart.	Lee Castle, Lanark	8	10 1
Dun, Trustees of Major-General John, of Shawpark	Shawpark, Selkirk	167	320 6				
Dunn, Trustees of James	Ladylands, Selkirk	3	24 5	Lockhart, William Eliott, yr. of Borthwickbrae	Borthwickbrae, Hawick	950	258 —

SELKIRK—continued.

Name of Owner.	Address of Owner.	Estimated Acreage of Property.	Gross Annual Value.
		Acres.	£ s.
M'Currick, David	Byethorn, Selkirk	3	46 –
M'Dougall, Trs. of Mrs. Christina	Galashiels	2	270 5
Mark, William	Selkirk	2	82 –
Mercer, Robert, of Scotsbank	Ramsay Lodge, Portobello	2,000	842 5
Minto, Earl of	Minto House, Hawick	1,032	264 5
Mitchell, Heirs of Alexander, of Stow	Carolside, Earlston	3,124	1,663 10
Mitchell, James	Galashiels	2	252 –
Morrison, John	Galashiels	3	58 –
Muir, William	Selkirk	4	33 13
Murray, David, and Archibald Stavert	Edinburgh	4	14 8
Murray, John	Glenmayne, Galashiels	38	165 10
Murray, Sir John, of Philiphaugh and Melgund, Bart.	Philiphaugh, Selkirk	1,857	2,054 2
Napier and Ettrick, Lord	Thirlestane Castle, Selkirk	6,988	2,066 17
North British Railway Co.	Edinburgh (Railway)	60	4,951 –
Ogilvie, George	Holefield, Kelso	12	37 –
Ogilvie, Robert G., of Hartwoodmyres	Edinburgh	886	361 10
Oliver, Trs. of James D.	Selkirk	2	5 –
Paterson, Adam	Galashiels	2	166 6
Paterson, Mrs. Adam	Galashiels	1	58 –
Paterson, John	Galashiels	2	124 –
Paterson, William, of Ettrickhall	Ettrickhall, Galashiels	950	934 12
Pattison, Mrs. Ann E. Pringle, of The Haining, wife of J. Pringle Pattison	Melrose	4,800	3,307 13
Plummer, Charles Scott, of Sunderland Hall	Sunderland Hall, Selkirk	1,735	1,495 4
Polwarth, Lord	Mertoun House, St. Boswells	3,595	1,760 –
Pott, Colonel George, of Todrig	Borthwickshiels, Hawick	3,090	1,061 10
Pott, George, of Potburn	Linthaughlee, Jedburgh	5,660	1,240 –
Pringle, Alexander, of Whytbank	Yair House, Selkirk	3,397	1,791 12
Pringle, James Thomas, of Torwoodlee	Torwoodlee, Galashiels	5,401	2,723 6
Pringle, Sir Norman William Drummond, of Stitchill, Bart.	Newhall, Selkirk	419	278 –
Rae, Agnes	Selkirk	2	27 –
Roberts, Alexander F.	Manorhill, Selkirk	3	43 –
Roberts, George	Selkirk	7	68 –
Roberts, George and Jas.	Selkirk	10	908 –
Roberts, James	Bannerfield, Selkirk	3	57 –
Roberts, William	Galashiels	6	75 –
Roberts, William, & Co.	Galashiels	1	315 2
Robertson, Jane, Helen, and Elizabeth	Bridge Park, Selkirk	4	124 3
Rodger, George, of Bridgelands	Bridgelands, Selkirk	135	402 –
Rodger, George	Selkirk	5	12 –
Rodger, Peter	Selkirk	2	58 15
Russell, Helen Jane Montstuart, of Ashiesteel	Ashiesteel, Galashiels	889	545 –
Russell, James	Ladylands, Selkirk	1	3 –
Russell, Rev. James	Manse, Yarrow, Selkirk	14	31 10
Sanderson, Peter	Galashiels	5	75 –
Sanderson, Peter & Robert	Galashiels	6	637 –
Sanderson, Robert	Galashiels	2	97 –
Sanderson, William A., Robert, and James	Galashiels	5	706 –
Scott, Archibald, of Howcleuch	Hawick	289	225 –
Scott, Henry, of Overkirkhope	Crosslee, Selkirk	1,900	613 –
Scott, Hugh, of Gala	Gala House, Galashiels	3,600	3,396 7
Scott, John Corse, of Sinton	Sinton House, Hawick	2,130	2,069 17
Scott, Robert	Kingcroft, Selkirk	9	31 10
Scott, Lieutenant Walter M'Millan, of Wauchope	H.M. 6th Dragoon Guards	1,450	335 –
Scottish Episcopal Church	Selkirkshire	5	7 10
Selkirk, Burgh of	Selkirk	1,800	1,059 12
Selkirk Gas Light Company	Selkirk	2	247 –
Selkirk, Heritors of	Selkirk	1	13 –
Selkirk, Parochial Board of	Selkirk	5	19 –
Shaw, James	Galashiels	2	404 17
Sibbald, John	Galashiels	4	415 –
Sime, James	Galashiels	1	440 6
Simson, Trs. of late James	Selkirk	11	73 8
Somerville, Robert	Galashiels	1	64 –
Sprot, Mark, of Riddell	Riddell, Selkirk	1	3 –
Stavert, Archibald, of Hoscote	Edinburgh	201	335 –
Steedman, John	Ravensheugh, Selkirk	5	40 –
Stirling, Adam	Galashiels	5	299 –
Stirling, Robert	Galashiels	1	246 16
Swinton, Archibald Campbell, of Kimmerghame, and John W. Todd	Kimmerghame, Dunse; Edinburgh	6	10 5
Tait, Peter Guthrie	Edinburgh	3	7 –
Tait, William	Selkirk	1	2 10
Tawse, John	Edinburgh	7	10 3
Thomson, William	Clovenfords, Galashiels	3	210 –
Traquair, Trustees of late Earl of	Traquair House, Innerleithen	9,765	1,757 –
Turnbull, John	Selkirk	1	30 –
Turnbull, Trustees of William, of Fenwick	Rodono, Selkirk	6,440	1,980 –
Union Poorhouse, Managers of	Galashiels	2	100 –
Waddell & Turnbull	Selkirk	5	1,000 –
Waddell, Thomas	Selkirk	3	48 –
Walker, James Scott	London	15	23 1
Walker, William Stuart, of Bowland	Bowland, Stow	1,531	745 6
Walker, William C., yr., of Bowland	Bowland, Stow	15	23 1
Williamson, James M., of Cardrona	Cardrona House, Peebles	3,015	894 7
Wilson, Thomas	Roberton, Hawick	1	10 –
Total Owners of Land of One Acre and upwards . . . 168		161,691	87,501 17
Total Owners of Lands of less than One Acre in extent 538		124	15,527 16
GRAND TOTAL . . . 706		161,815	103,029 13

STIRLING.

Population in 1871,	98,218.
Inhabited Houses,	13,275.
Number of Parishes,	26.

Name of Owner.	Address of Owner.	Estimated Acreage of Property.	Gross Annual Value.	Name of Owner.	Address of Owner.	Estimated Acreage of Property.	Gross Annual Value.
		Acres.	£ s.			Acres.	£ s.
Abercromby, Lord	Airthrey Castle, Stirling	1,150	1,753 17	Bell, Mrs. Fanny	Portobello	6	20 –
Adam, James	Nicolswalls, Denny	92	70 –	Benn, Mrs. Helen, wife of Col. Anthony Benn; and Mary Moseley Munro	Stirling	52	120 –
Adam, John	Buckieburn, Denny	213	110 –				
Adam, Trustees of John	Denny	67	63 5				
Adam, Trustees of Robert	Falkirk	5	257 –				
Adam, Mrs. Jane Brown	Glasgow	6	17 –	Bennet, Adam	Causewayhead, Stirling	27	80 –
Aitken, Trustees of Henry	Falkirk	50	176 5	Bennie, William	Kirk o' Muir, Denny	20	22 –
Aitken, James	Auchengillon, Strathblane	133	100 –	Benny, Robert	Underwood, Denny	48	184 10
				Berry, Rev. James	U.P. Manse, Buchlyvie	1	20 –
Aitken, James, of Darroch	Falkirk	85	295 10	Beveridge, Mrs. Jemima	Culross	22	68 15
Aitken, James, and others	Falkirk	290	528 5	Bilsland, Archibald	Gartness, Killearn	6	30 –
Do. do.	Do. (Minerals)	–	920 –	Binnie, John	Avonbridge, Falkirk	10	40 –
Aitken, James, & Co.	Falkirk	2	194 10	Black, Trustees of late James	Sydenham House, Bridge of Allan	1	91 –
Aitken, John Gillespie	Snowdon Place, Stirling	2	276 10				
Aitken, John	Gartcows, Falkirk	61	242 15	Black, Ann	Hillend, Avonbridge	130	140 –
Alexander, Charles Jamieson	Jawcraig, Falkirk	8	142 15	Blackburn, James	Temple, London	4	10 5
Alexander, Rev. George	Manse, Stirling	7	92 –	Blackburn, Trustees of late Peter, of Killearn	Killearn	2,739	2,220 12
Alexander, Sir James Edward, of Westerton, Kt.	Westerton House, Bridge of Allan	181	1,045 10	Blair, Duncan William	Edinburgh	53	60 15
				Blair, Mrs. Agnes	Balfron	4	6 –
				Bolton, John Cheeny, of Carbrook	Carbrook, East Plean	129	263 18
Alexander, William	Longkerse, Blairlogie	8	12 –				
Allan's Hospital	Stirling	171	853 5	Bontine, William Cunningham Graham, of Gartmore	Gartmore	6,931	4,118 15
Allan, James	Cauldhame, Falkirk	1	56 10				
Alva Gas Company	Alva	1	189 –	Do. do.	Do. (Quarry)	–	15 –
Anderson, Finlay	Inchyra Grange, Polmont	95	307 –	Borthwick, Francis Laura	Westfield, Falkirk	29	65 15
Anderson, James	Kirkcaldy	23	67 10	Bow, Trustees of late Ebenezer	Stirling	860	403 –
Andrew, George Robertson	Falkirk	3	33 –				
Angus, James	Kilsyth	4	24 –	Bow, James	27 Castle Street, Glasgow	66	67 15
Arnot, David	Falkirk	3	109 16	Bow, Robert	Bogside, Kilsyth	23	55 10
Arthur, John	Balcastle, Slamannan	73	65 –	Bow, William	Halls of Airth, Falkirk	13	35 –
Arthur, Mrs. Marion Muirhead	Stirling	65	150 –	Bowie, James	Torrance of Campsie	50	91 15
				Bowie, John	Crosslands, Campsie	2	18 15
				Bowie, Robert	Pleasance, Falkirk	1	84 10
				Boyd, Trs. of late Alexander	Falkirk	3	54 4
Bain, Edwin Sandys, of Livilands	Livilands, Stirling	349	788 –	Boyd, Trs. of late David	Milton of Campsie	3	130 16
				Boyd, John	Crosshill, Slamannan	3	21 –
Baird, James	Denny	4	10 –	Boyd, John	Whitepiece, Slamannan	167	139 10
Baird, James	Sunnyside, Falkirk	7	23 –	Boyd, William	Moss Castle, Slamannan	10	30 –
Baird, Trustees of late Robert	Airdrie	408	174 –	Boyd, William	South Greens, Airth	5	15 –
Do. do.	Do. (Minerals)	–	2,072 10	Boyd, Trustees of Mrs. Jean	Kirkintilloch	1	19 15
Baird, William, & Co.	Gartsherrie, Coatbridge	119	476 –	Braidwood, Thomas	Carmichael, Lanark	1	150 –
Baird, William, & Co.	Gartsherrie (Private Railway)	4	120 –	Brechin, Archibald	Mealybrae, Torrance of Campsie	23	30 –
Baird, Mrs. Helen	Dennyloanhead, Denny	4	40 –	*Bridge of Allan Hydropathic Company*	Bridge of Allan	4	310 –
Baird, Mrs. Janet	Craigford, Bannockburn	5	36 10				
Baird, Mary	Edinburgh	60	264 10	*Bridge of Allan Water Company*	Bridge of Allan	4	245 10
Baldie, Robert	Bridge of Allan	1	75 –				
Balderston, Robert Glass	Bishopbriggs	40	45 –	Brisbane, John	Miln Park, Bannockburn	6	28 –
Ballingal, Rev. James	Manse, Balfron	18	60 –	Brodie, Trustees of late James	Fintry	509	212 10
Barr, John	Ardrossan	402	530 –				
Do.	Do. (Coal)	–	212 –	Broom, Wm., and others	182 Hope St., Glasgow	126	123 –
Barr, Mary	Chapelton, Milngavie	30	72 –	Brown, Andrew, of Flatt	Flatt, East Kilbride	125	212 –
Barrie, John	Blacklock, Slamannan	36	21 5	Brown, George	South Broomage, Larbert	2	5 –
Bartholomew, Hugh	Glenorchard, Torrance of Campsie	270	628 –				
				Brown, George	Kerse Lane, Falkirk	3	161 15
Bayley, Heirs of Isaac, of Manuel	Manuel, Linlithgow	338	467 10	Brown, Hamilton	Kilsyth	7	205 10
				Do.	Do. (Private Railway)	3	90 –
Bayne, John	Bridge of Allan	6	722 –	Brown, John Harvie, of Quarter	Dunipace House, Falkirk	1,436	1,411 –
Begg, Rev. William	Manse, Falkirk	6	47 10				
Belfrage, Mrs. Margaret	Rosepark, Falkirk	3	47 15	Do. do.	Do. (Minerals)	–	403 15
Bell, Trustees of late Alexander	Falkirk	83	455 5	Brown, John	Bennetston, Falkirk	2	18 10
				Brown, Rev. Robert Hope	Manse, Kilsyth	15	61 –
Do. do.	Do. (Minerals)	–	180 5	Brown, Mrs. Elizabeth	Maydub, Denny	2	6 –

STIRLING—continued.

Name of Owner.	Address of Owner.	Estimated Acreage of Property.	Gross Annual Value.	Name of Owner.	Address of Owner.	Estimated Acreage of Property.	Gross Annual Value.
		Acres.	£ s.			Acres.	£ s.
Brown, Mrs. Helen	East Plean, Stirling	2	8 —	Campbell, Trustees of late Marion	Falkirk	162	115 —
Brownlee, James	Meikle Finnery, Alexandria	4	24 —	*Campsie, Heritors of*	Campsie	2	6 —
Bruce, Sir William Cuningham, of Stenhouse, Bart.	Stenhouse, Falkirk	780	1,531 5	Canning, Rev. Alexander Colquhoun	Antrim, Ireland	90	71 10
Do. do.	Do. (*Minerals*)	—	518 10	Carr, Thomas	Whitegate, Kilsyth	2	12 —
Bruce, Lady Elma Thurlow, of Kinnaird, wife of the Hon. Thomas John Hovell Thurlow Bruce	Kinnaird House, Larbert	1,107	1,590 4	*Carron Company*	Carron, Falkirk	3,143	7,142 8
				Do. (*Minerals*)		—	112 10
				Carss, Robert Meiklem	2 Bridge Street, Maryhill	9	63 —
Do. do.	Do. (*Minerals*)	—	258 15	Chalmers, Trustees of late James	Overblelloch, Stanley	22	35 —
Bruce, Mrs. Isabella	Whins of Milton, Stirling	1	13 10	Chalmers, William	Old Town, Kilsyth	1	35 10
Bryce, Andrew	Blackstone, Avonbridge	138	117 5	Chapman, Lawrence	Blairgowrie	213	203 10
Bryce & M'Laren	Dualt, Killearn	5	10 —	Christie, George	Stirling	3	172 —
Bryce, Margaret, Agnes, and Mrs. Eliza Meikle	Bridge of Allan	1	35 —	Christie, John	Forthbank, Stirling	117	488 —
				Christie, John	Park Terrace, Stirling	2	995 10
Bryson, Mrs. Margaret	Graham's Road, Falkirk	1	28 —	Chrystal, Executors of Mrs. Christina	Gargunnock	2	90 —
Buchanan, Alexander	Gartaharn, Drymen	151	202 —	Clark, Alexander	Meadowbank, Torrance of Campsie	58	176 10
Buchanan, Alexander	Whitehouse, Stirling	36	107 10	Cochrane, Thomas	Falkirk	3	34 —
Buchanan, Rt. Hon. Sir Andrew, of Craigend, Kt., G.C.B.	British Embassy, Vienna	883	948 —	Colquhoun, John	Corkerhill, Pollokshaws, Glasgow	23	50 —
Buchanan, Andrew	Cowiebank, Stirling	4	17 —	Colquhoun, Rev. John Erskine Campbell, of Killermont	Killermont, Maryhill	193	403 10
Buchanan, Colonel David Carrick Robert Carrick, of Drumpellier	Drumpellier, Coatbridge	868	350 —	Connal, Michael	Glasgow	184	223 10
Do. do.	Do. (*Minerals*)	—	150 —	Connell, George	Skipperton, Denny	62	76 —
Buchanan, David M'Laren	Boquhan, Killearn	721	500 5	Cooper, Henry Ritchie, of Ballindalloch	Ballindalloch, Balfron	627	753 10
Buchanan, Duncan	Bogend, Bannockburn	5	50 —	Copland, Thomas	Herbertshire St., Denny	1	18 15
Buchanan, Major Herbert, of Arden	Arden, Callander	830	1,644 13	Cousin, William	Bridge of Allan	2	78 —
Buchanan, John	Coldroch, Drymen	3	39 —	Cousland, James	Denny	3	107 5
Buchanan, John	113 Virginia Place, Glasgow	90	189 15	Cousland, Trustees of late William	Denny	4	92 —
Buchanan, John	108 Hutchison Street, Glasgow	24	49 10	Cowan, Alexander	Glasgow	5	30 —
				Cowan, Peter	Bannockburn	1	27 —
Buchanan, Robert	St. Thomas's Well, Stirling	226	204 5	*Cowane's Hospital*	Stirling	439	1,891 3
				Cowie, James	Falkirk	1	99 —
Buchanan, Robert	Park House, Killearn	4	20 —	Cox, James	Dublin	10	36 —
Buchanan, William	Burnside, Kippen	1	14 10	Cox, Josiah	Falkirk	11	66 10
Buchanan, William	Crosshouse, Campsie	81	115 —	Craig, Walter, junior	Colbeg, Torrance of Campsie	39	68 —
Buckie, John	East Balgrochan, Torrance of Campsie	50	98 10	Crombie, James	Standrig, Avonbridge, Falkirk	40	30 —
Bulloch, James	Canglour, Stirling	50	40 —	Crombie, Mrs. Margaret	Avonbridge, Falkirk	1	6 10
Bulloch, John	Boards, Denny	112	75 —	*Crown, The*		359	1,238 8
Bulloch, Robert	76 Wilson St., Glasgow	66	236 10	Cruickshanks, Ferguson, & Co.	Denny	2	30 —
Bulloch, Thomas	Boards, Denny	25	24 —	*Culcreuch Spinning Co.*	Fintry	17	376 15
Burleigh, Lord	Kennet House, Clackmannan	379	595 —	Cumming, Wright	Stirling	2	120 10
Burns, Robert	East Plean, Stirling	1	10 10	Currie, John	North Third, St. Ninians	120	100 —
Burns, William Hamilton	Falkirk	2	202 16	Cuthil, John	Banknock, Denny	58	70 5
Burns, Trustees of late Mrs. Margaret	Denny	100	169 15				
				Dallas, Mrs. Amelia Kidston	Bowtrees, Airth	109	200 —
Cadell, Henry, of Grange	Grange, Bo'ness	1,129	1,193 5	Dalrymple, David	Haughhead of Campsie	2	53 10
Do. do.	Do. (*Minerals*)	—	180 —	Davidson, James	Buchlyvie	3	6 10
Calder, Alexander	Hillhouse, Linlithgow	30	23 —	Davie, James	Muirhead, Larbert	3	32 —
Calder, John	Hill, Linlithgow	75	117 —	Davie, John	Newlandshill House, Dunfermline	6	40 10
Caldwell, William	Denny	5	151 10				
Caledonian Railway Co.	Glasgow (*Canal*)	58	} 52025 15	Davie, Heirs of John	Denny	3	14 —
Do. do.	Do. (*Harbour & Docks*)	15		Davie & Sons	Stirling	1	151 10
Do. do.	Do. (*Railway, &c.*)	258		Dawson, William, of Powfoulis	Carron, Falkirk	1,241	3,808 18
Callander, George Frederick William	Ardkinglas, Cairndow	601	1,885 15	Do. do.	Do. (*Minerals*)	—	685 10
Callander, Henry, of Preston Hall	Preston Hall, Ford, Dalkeith	95	313 —	Dick, John, of Craigengelt	Stirling	1,140	547 —
Do. do.	Do. (*Minerals*)	—	282 —	Dobbie, Trustees of Janet	Airdrie	11	22 10
Callander, Thomas	Linkfield, Airth	1	57 —	Dobie, Mrs. Elizabeth	East Craigannet, Denny	192	105 —
Cameron, Heirs of John	Whitehill, Denny	3	1 10	Donald, George	West Blairskaith, Campsie	123	182 —
Campbell, Sir George, of Succoth, Bart.	Garscube House, Glasgow	926	1,567 5	Donald, Trustees of late Robert	Greenock	90	180 —
Campbell, Henry Fletcher, of Boquhan	Boquhan, Stirling	5,679	3,185 5	Donald, Robert	Low Blochearn, Milngavie	116	124 —
Campbell, Sir James, of Stracathro, Kt.	Stracathro House, Brechin	24	25 —	Donaldson, George	South Alloa	4	160 —
Campbell, Thomas Hinton	Millfield, Falkirk	135	494 5	Donaldson, William	North Street, Bo'ness	1	24 —
Campbell, Mrs. Catherine	Kippen	1	9 14	Dougal, Robert	Kippen	4	21 11

STIRLING—continued.

Name of Owner.	Address of Owner.	Estimated Acreage of Property.	Gross Annual Value.	Name of Owner.	Address of Owner.	Estimated Acreage of Property.	Gross Annual Value.
		Acres.	£ s.			Acres.	£ s.
Douglas, Archibald Campbell, of Mains	Mains House, Milngavie	297	533 8	Finlay, Heirs of William	Blackhill, Denny	25	17 —
Douglas, Edmund Ralston	15 Howard Place, Edinburgh			Fisher, Daniel	26 Bothwell St., Glasgow	40	84 —
Do. (Minerals)		—	7 10	Fleming, Hon. Cornwallis, of Cumbernauld & Biggar	Cumbernauld House, Glasgow	2	8 —
Douglas, James Crawford	15 Howard Place, Edinburgh	100	80 —	Do. do.	Do. (Minerals)	—	782 —
Dow, Mary	Glasgow	19	40 —	Fleming, James Simpson, of Balquharrage	16 Grosvenor Terrace, Edinburgh	181	494 3
Drummond, George Stirling Home, of Blair-Drummond	Blair-Drummond, Stirling	372	700 —	Fleming, John, senior	Clayfaulds, Denny	19	80 —
Drummond, John	Spittal, Buchlyvie	35	83 —	Fleming, John, junior, and James	Clayfaulds, Denny	20	18 —
Drummond, Heirs of John	Gateside, Milton	13	25 —	Fleming, Robert	High Street, Falkirk	3	34 10
Drummond, Mrs. Mary	83 Green Street, Calton, Glasgow	2	15 10	Flynn, Trustees of Wilhelmina Jane	Cornton, Stirling	81	180 —
Dun, Andrew	West Third of Kepdowrie, Buchlyvie	75	65 —	Foord, Mrs. Jean	Brackinlees, Airth	34	81 —
Duncan, Alexander	Herbertshire, Denny	65	142 —	Forbes, William, of Callendar	Callendar House, Falkirk	13,041	12795 16
Duncan, Alexander	Shieldhill, Falkirk	23	35 —	Do. do.	Do. (Minerals)	—	3,419 10
Duncan, Heirs of Andrew	Herbertshire, Denny	20	450 —	Forbes, William Forbes, of Lochcote	Lochcote House, Bathgate	14	33 15
Duncan, Henry	23 Castle Street, Dundee	63	90 —	Forgie, John	Falkirk	1	49 5
Duncan, John	Broomridge, Denny	19	40 10	Forrest, John Clark	Hamilton	120	66 —
Duncan, Walter	Gateside, Banton, Denny	100	121 —	Forrester, Gabriel Napier, of Craigannet	Southfield, Stirling	516	300 —
Duncan, Mrs. Marion	Camelon, Falkirk	1	31 5	Forrester, Peter	Drumquharn, Killearn	139	80 —
Dundas, Heirs of Colonel Joseph	Carronhall, Falkirk	1,989	2,704 —	Forrester, William	170 Renfield St., Glasgow	4	38 —
Do. do.	Do. (Minerals)	—	500 —	Forsyth, Charles	Gargunnock	6	35 15
Dunlop, Alexander, of Clober	Clober, Milngavie	60	511 —	Forsyth, Heirs of James	Campsie	5	28 10
Dunlop, Robert	87 West Regent Street, Glasgow	87	180 —	Fraser, Robert Hugh	Carbeth Guthrie, Strathblane	286	269 10
Dunmore, Earl of	Dunmore Park, Stirling	4,620	8,072 10	Fraser, William	Bridge of Allan	2	40 —
Do.	Do. (Minerals)	—	850 —	Free Church, Trustees of	Bridge of Allan	2	76 —
Dunn, Alexander	Kilsyth	3	45 10	Frew, David	Kingston, Kilsyth	1	8 10
Dunn, Mary, and William Wilkie	128 Ingram Street, Glasgow	115	122 5	Fulton, Heirs of William	Falkirk	3	144 —
Duthie, Alexander, of Ruthriestone	Edinburgh	500	488 5	Gaff, Thomas	Falkirk	12	77 —
Duthie, Mrs. Mary	Melville Terrace, Stirling	1	133 10	Gair, John	Falkirk	8	102 —
				Galbraith, James, of Balgair	Loughrea, Ireland	1,427	570 —
Edmond, David	Ballochruin, Balfron	190	135 —	Galbraith, Thomas Littlejohn, of Blackhouse	Stirling	302	428 5
Edmond, Heirs of James	Muirhead, Denny	4	10 —	Galbraith, Jane G. and Anna B.	Stirling	1	26 10
Edmond, Representatives of Thomas	Balfron	1	56 —	Galloway, James	Clayslaps, Stirling	28	71 —
				Gardner, William	Bathgate	70	71 —
				Garrow, John	Kelt, Denny	30	37 —
Edmonstone, Rear-Admiral Sir William, of Duntreath, Bart.	Colzium, Kilsyth	9,778	7,677 18	Gibb, James	Edinburgh	3	30 —
Do. do.	Do. (Minerals)	—	8,451 —	Gilchrist, William	East Borland, Denny	9	20 —
Elphinstone, Lady Georgina A. H., wife of Lord William G. O. Elphinstone	Tullyallan Castle, Kincardine-on-Forth	42	100 —	Gillespie, David	Causewayhead, Stirling	2	119 —
				Gillespie, James	Cowan Street, Stirling	4	257 5
				Gillespie, William Honeyman, of Torbanehill	46 Melville Street, Edinburgh	3	160 —
Erskine, Alexander	Crosshill, Falkirk	15	26 10	Gillespie, Mrs. Jean	East Seamores, Denny	35	143 10
Erskine, Henry David, of Cardross	Cardross, Port of Monteith	40	60 —	Gillies, David	Bonnybridge, Denny	2	30 5
Espie, James	Kerse Lane, Falkirk	8	114 10	Glasgow Corporation Water Commissioners	Glasgow (Reservoir)	61	16126 —
Ewing, Archibald Orr, of Ballikinrain, M.P.	Ballikinrain, Killearn	4,520	3,065 15	Glen, Robert	Cross, Kilsyth	5	68 10
Do. do.	Do. (Quarries)	—	20 —	Glen, Catherine	Kilsyth	5	28 5
				Gordon, Edward Strathearn, of Auchenreoch, M.P.	Edinburgh	875	1,009 —
Fairlie, Walter	Spittal, Balfron	21	30 —	Gordon, William Eagleson	Homehill, Bridge of Allan	2	100 —
Falconer, Rev. Alexander	Manse, Denny	5	36 —	Govane, Agnes, of Park	Drymen	563	672 —
Falkirk, Commissioners of Police	Falkirk	1	38 10	Gow, James	Drumbeg, Drymen	106	172 4
Falkirk, Feuars of	Falkirk	33	64 5	Gow, Robert	Bonhill, Dumbarton	100	115 —
Falkirk Iron Company	Falkirk	19	982 14	Gow, Mrs. Catherine	Rothesay	4	10 —
Falkirk, Parochial Board of	Falkirk	12	52 10	Gowans, James	Edinburgh	265	130 —
				Gowans, Trustees of John	Stirling	114	238 —
Fenton, Mrs. Mary, and Mrs. Catharine Rennie	Australia / Glasgow	4	13 —	Graham, Alexander	The Brooklet, Birkenhead	19	128 13
				Graham, Trs. of David	Meiklewood, Gargunnock	288	514 —
Ferguson, Alexander	Parkside, Bannockburn	8	10 10	Graham, James	Auchencloch, Denny	38	78 —
Ferguson, David	Croftside Muir, Bannockburn	15	20 10	Graham, John Cameron	Ballewan, Strathblane	1,205	423 —
Ferguson, Janet and Marion	Falkirk	51	140 —	Graham, John Graham Barns, of Craigallion	Fereneze, Barrhead	637	557 —
				Graham, Captain Thomas	Dalquharn, Renton	547	558 —
Ferrie, James	Balgrochan, Torrance of Campsie	59	218 5	Graham, William	Middlekerse, Kippen	160	212 18
				Graham, William, of Airth	Airth Castle, Falkirk	1,145	3,141 15
				Do. do.	Do. (Minerals)	—	100 —
Ferrier, Mrs. Eliza, wife of Rev. John Ferrier	Tain	10	52 10	Graham, Janet Gloriana, of Ballagan	Ballagan, Strathblane	914	612 15
Finlay, John	Seamores, Denny	5	11 —	Gray, Trs. of late Charles	Denny	29	42 —

STIRLING—continued.

Name of Owner.	Address of Owner.	Estimated Acreage of Property.	Gross Annual Value.	Name of Owner.	Address of Owner.	Estimated Acreage of Property.	Gross Annual Value.
		Acres.	£ s.			Acres.	£ s.
Gray, George	Windyyett, Falkirk	248	150 –	Jamieson, Graham	Gartness, Killearn	30	56 –
Gray, James, and others	58 Rose Street, Glasgow	1	6 5	Jamieson, Michael James, of Arngomery	Arngomery, Kippen	475	891 12
Gray, John	The Hall, Denny	78	188 –	Jamieson, William	Gargunnock	1	8 10
Gray, Thomas	Stoneywood, Denny	9	146 –	Jamieson, Mrs. Catherine	Glasgow	60	60 –
Gray, Mrs. Mary	7 Young Place, Helensburgh	33	28 15	Jenkins, George	Whins of Milton, Stirling	1	8 10
Grangemouth Coal Company	Grangemouth	13	395 8	Johnston, Archibald	Falkirk	2	184 5
Grieve, James	St. Ninians, Stirling	2	90 8	Johnston, Charles C.	Stirling	6	85 –
Grindlay, Trustees of late Charles	Stirling	16	121 15	Johnston, Trustees of William	Barraston, Torrance of Campsie	107	172 –
Grindlay, John	Bonnyside, Denny	3	12 10	Johnston, Mrs. Margaret	Bathgate	14	42 –
Grindlay, Heirs of William	Kilsyth	3	19 –	Johnstone, Trustees of late Alexander	Stirling	20	70 10
Grossart, James	Falkirk	8	82 7	Johnstone, James, of Alva	Alva House, Alva	5,340	4,004 10
Guild, Janet, and Mrs. Beatrice Lyons	Broomhill, Denny	50	116 10	Do. (*Minerals*)	Do.	–	500 –
				Johnstone, John	Muirhouses, Falkirk	1	13 –
				Johnstone, Robert	Windyrigg, Falkirk	14	10 10
Hagart, Colonel Charles	Craigend, Stirling	40	169 10	Johnstone, Thomas	Hallhouse, Denny	13	34 –
Hagart, Major-General Charles, C.B.	Tockington, Bristol	99	266 –	Johnstone, Thomas	Redding, Falkirk	37	80 –
Haldane, William	Bridge of Allan	1	165 –	Johnstone, Thomas	Lodge, Slamannan	30	16 –
Hamilton, Duke of	Hamilton Palace, Hamilton	810	911 –	Johnstone, William	Whitehill, Denny	41	36 10
Do. do.	Do. (*Minerals*)	–	2,011 –	Johnstone, Mrs. Jane	Dykehead, Slamannan	36	15 –
Hamilton, John Buchanan, of Leny	Leny, Callander	582	925 17	Johnstone, Grace and Mary	Bridge of Allan	2	54 –
Do. do.	Do. (*Quarry*)	–	11 10	Jones, Heirs of Thomas	Compthall, Falkirk	4	25 –
Hamilton, John	16 Finlay St., Glasgow	35	36 –	Kay, John	Gateside, Stirling	29	30 –
Hamilton, John	Kingston, Kilsyth	3	28 15	Kay, Janet	Music Hall, Kippen	2	6 –
Hamilton, Robert	Kilsyth	3	49 10	Keir, Duncan	Buchlyvie	6	27 –
Hamilton, William	Greenhill, Denny	33	40 –	Keir, Thomas	Falkirk	180	115 –
Hardie, Alexander	Avonbridge, Falkirk	3	13 –	Keir, Mrs. Margaret	Torwood, Falkirk	1	9 10
Hardie, Graham	Burnbrae, Falkirk	3	35 –	Keith, Rev. George	Manse, Muiravonside	5	35 –
Hardie, Robert	Glenrath, Manor, Peebles	3	20 –	Kelly, Rev. Andrew	Manse, Alva	13	58 –
Hardie, Mrs. Mary	Grahamston, Falkirk	1	20 –	Kennedy, William	The Allen, Buchlyvie	20	20 –
Hart, Alexander	6 Gauze Street, Paisley	7	25 –	Kerr, John	Bankhall, Bannockburn	7	10 –
Hastie, John	Pirney Lodge, Slamannan	103	50 –	Kerr, Robert, of Dougalston	Dougalston, Milngavie	1,790	3,574 16
Hay, James	Hayfield, Denny	30	45 –	Kerr, Thomas	East Lochdrum, Denny	72	30 –
Hay, James, and others	Manse, Lochgoilhead	18	25 –	Do. (*Quarry*)	Do.	–	20 –
Hay, John	Glenbo, Denny	12	55 15	Kidd, James	Hookney, Denny	28	19 –
Hay, William	Glenhead, Denny	69	80 –	Kincaid, Heirs of John Buchanan	Carbeth, Killearn	780	645 –
Hattersley, Thomas	Lennoxtown	1	116 10	Kincaid, Jane Clark and Margaret	Orchard Hall, Falkirk	26	90 15
Henderson, James Alex.	Falkirk	1	45 –	King, John, of Campsie	Glasgow	680	857 6
Henderson, Thomas	Springfield, Falkirk	25	147 15	Do. do.	Do. (*Minerals*)	–	610 –
Henderson, William	8 Brunton Place, Edinburgh	390	354 –	King, Heirs of Mrs. Margaret	Milngavie	3	50 –
Do. do.	Do. (*Minerals*)	–	50 –	Kinross, William	Stirling	1	165 –
Henry, Robert	Falkirk	1	34 15	Kirkwood, Mrs. Mary	Westgarth, Denny	18	32 –
Hill, Alexander	Stirling	10	150 5				
Hill, William	Bannockburn	30	52 10	Laing, Alexander	Kernock, Carronbridge	157	76 –
Hodge, James	Chartershall Mains, Stirling	19	36 15	Laing, James	Birdstonebank, Kirkintilloch	122	293 –
Hodge, William	Awells, Falkirk	84	408 10	Laing, John	Langhill, Denny	234	154 –
Home, George H. M. Binning, of Argaty	Argaty, Doune	17	40 –	Laing, John	Leys, Denny	7	15 –
Honeyman, Mrs. Christina	Broomage Loan, Larbert	2	9 10	Laing, John	Tops, Denny	22	18 –
Hood, John	Cathcart Road, Glasgow	35	52 10	Laing, William	Loanhead, Denny	45	52 10
Horne, Rev. Robert S.	Manse, Slamannan	22	36 –	Lamont, James, of Knockdhu	Gartmore House, Gartmore	403	562 –
Howie, John	Glasgow	8	21 10	Lang, Alexander	Kilsyth	1	35 14
Hunter, Rev. William	Baldernock	10	35 15	Lang, Mrs. Janet S.	Torrance of Campsie	7	97 15
Hurlet and Campsie Alum Company	Campsie	39	1,117 5	*Larbert Institution for Educating Imbecile Children*	Larbert	9	140 –
Imrie, Rev. David Neil	Logie, Bridge of Allan	8	70 –	Lawrie, Alexander Campbell, and Tredway Clark Dickson	9 Nelson Place, Edinburgh Warwick, Carlisle	650	457 10
Inglis, John Russell	Linmill, Falkirk	88	148 –	Do. do. (*Quarry*)		–	10 –
Inglis, Robert	Linmill, Falkirk	281	66 –	Lawrie, James	Parkhead, Polmont	4	17 10
Inglis, Jane Donald	190 St. George's Road, Glasgow	5	45 13	Lawrie, Mrs. Lillias	Brightons, Polmont	8	34 15
				Do. do. (*Quarry*)		–	70 –
Jaffray, William, and others	Campvale, Pollokshaws, Glasgow	9	41 10	Learmonth, Richard	Little Kerse, Falkirk	3	31 10
Jaffray, William, and others	Hong-Kong	5	16 10	Learmonth, Thomas Livingstone, of Parkhall	Parkhall, Linlithgow	896	925 18
Jeffray, James	8 Elmbank Crescent, Glasgow	3	72 10	Do. do. (*Minerals*)		–	70 –
Jeffrey, Robert, & Son	Ballindalloch, Balfron	76	391 10	Leckie, Andrew	Partick, Glasgow	1	10 –
Jamieson, Alexander	Midquarter, Stirling	34	30 –	Leckie, Mrs. Janet	Glentirran Muir, Kippen	2	9 10
Jamieson, George Auldjo	Edinburgh	149	162 –				

STIRLING—continued.

Name of Owner.	Address of Owner.	Estimated Acreage of Property.	Gross Annual Value.	Name of Owner.	Address of Owner.	Estimated Acreage of Property.	Gross Annual Value.
		Acres.	£ s.			Acres.	£ s.
Leishman, Mary	Camelon, Falkirk	1	51 10	M'Lachlan, William Alexander, of Auchintroig	Auchintroig, Balfron	1,200	478 —
Leith, Sir George Hector, of Burgh St. Peter's, Bart.	Ross Priory, Alexandria	1,314	422 10	M'Laren, David	Bridge of Allan	4	648 —
Lennie, Trustees of late Moses	Woodlee, Denny	18	20 10	M'Laren, George Adinston	Thornhill, Falkirk	86	175 —
Lennox, Peter	Oakfield, Helensburgh	397	410 —	M'Laren, James	Torwood, Falkirk	8	25 —
Lennox, Hon. Mrs. Margaret C.B.H.K., wife of Hon. Charles Spencer Bateman Hanbury Kincaid Lennox	Lennox Castle, Lennoxtown	7,606	8,313 10	M'Laren, Rev. John	Manse, Larbert	9	57 —
				M'Lay, Robert	Garden, Buchlyvie	3	6 —
				M'Lay, William	Laurieston, Falkirk	3	6 —
				M'Lean, James Grant	Bridge of Allan	1	60 —
				M'Lean, John	Grahamston, Falkirk	1	64 5
				M'Leish, John Meiklam	Glasgow	400	361 —
Do. do.	Do. (Minerals)	—	610 —	M'Math, Mrs Mary	Larbert	13	30 —
Leny, James Cunningham, of Bent	Gartocharn, Kilmaronock	130	120 —	M'Millan, Trs. of Duncan	45 Dunlop St., Glasgow	150	304 —
Liddell, Janet	Wardhead, Denny	21	59 5	M'Nab, Alexander	Lillyburn, Milton of Campsie	38	507 —
Lilburn, Heirs of John	Loch, Airth, Falkirk	24	70 —	Macnaughton, Rev. Colin	Manse, Killearn	8	32 —
Linlithgow Foundry Co.	Linlithgow	1	40 —	M'Naughton, Mrs Janet	Heatherbank, Milngavie	2	35 —
Lithgow, William	Torrance of Campsie	4	79 15	M'Nee, John	Kirkintilloch	1	16 —
Livingstone, John	Beanscroft, Torrance of Campsie	6	12 —	M'Nicol, Mrs Mary	W. Balgrochan, Torrance of Campsie	4	7 5
Livingstone, Trustees of Thomas Fenton, of Westquarter	Westquarter, Falkirk	440	800 5	M'Owan, James	Rashiehill, Denny	96	65 —
				M'Phedran, Duncan	Bridgehill, Falkirk	25	40 —
Lochore, Rev. Alexander	Manse, Drymen	8	45 —	M'Pherson, Hugh	Townfoot, Denny	902	341 —
Logan, Alex. Christopher	Edinburgh	113	360 —	M'Pherson, James	Milton of Campsie	3	140 10
Lowis, John Mangles, of Plean	Plean, Stirling	1,300	1,327 —	M'Pherson & M'Laren	Grangemouth	1	87 —
Do. do.	Do. (Minerals)	—	300 —	M'Symon, John	Arbuthnot, Falkirk	6	46 —
Lucas, Trustees of Robert	Bridge of Allan	1	127 15	Main, Alexander	Glasgow	73	24 —
Lyle, James	Glasgow	5	12 —	Maitland, Sir Alexander Charles Ramsay Gibson, of Cliftonhall, Bart., M.P.	Sauchie House, Stirling	6,023	5,479 5
				Do. do.	Do. (Minerals)	—	329 10
				Maitland, James	West Balgrochan, Torrance of Campsie	194	285 —
M'Adam, John	Blairoer, Drymen	113	111 10	Maitland, James, and others	Do. (Minerals)	—	350 —
M'Adam, Mrs. Margaret	Mains, Kilmaronock	900	258 —				
M'Alley, James	Newmarket, Bannockburn	5	51 15	Malcolm, Heirs of Archibald	Dunmore, Stirling	6	26 —
M'Allister, Alexander	58 Rose Street, Garnethill, Glasgow	141	160 —	Mar, Earl of	Hilston Park, Monmouthshire	4	18 —
M'Allister, Robert	Easter Glinns, Kippen	2	8 —	Marshall, James	Mineral Cottage, Coatbridge	2	94 —
M'Alpine, James	Garrauld, Balfron	140	48 —				
M'Alpine, James	Craigs, Stirling	2	126 10	Marshall, John	Edinburgh	2	6 —
M'Arthur, Alexander, and others	6 Chatham Place, Glasgow	25	117 15	Marshall, John	Stonehouse, Falkirk	50	55 —
Maccall, Thomas Smith	Haypark, Polmont	49	167 —	Marshall, John	Laverockhill, Torrance of Campsie	173	250 —
M'Callum, George Kellie, of Braco	Braco Castle, Braco	100	295 5	Marshall, William	Newhouse, Falkirk	79	188 —
M'Callum, John George	Duchlage, Drymen	141	127 —	Marshall, William	17 Monteith Row, Glasgow	150	80 —
M'Callum, John	Lochard, Aberfoyle	2	12 —	Do.	Do. (Minerals)	—	250 —
M'Cash, Mrs. Janet	Hillhead, Glasgow	2	90 —	Marshall, William	East Acredyke, Torrance of Campsie	10	15 —
M'Culloch, Trs. of John	88 Great Clyde Street, Glasgow	194	220 —				
M'Donald, Mrs. Helen	Bannockburn	2	15 5	Marshall, Mrs Marion	Avonbridge, Falkirk	20	49 10
M'Dougall, Mrs Isabella	Bridge of Allan	1	127 —	Marshall, Jane and Margaret	Townhead, Kilsyth	122	154 —
M'Ewen, Heirs of James	Stirling	4	105 —				
M'Farlane, Duncan	Glentirran Muir, Kippen	2	1 10	Martin, Robert	Easter Jaw, Slamannan	9	17 15
M'Farlane, James	North Shields, Denny	95	70 —	Maxwell, Sir William Stirling, of Pollok and Keir, Bart.	Keir House, Dunblane	1,487	2,370 —
M'Farlane, Captain John Warden, of Ballancleroch	Ballancleroch, Haughhead, Campsie	2,844	971 —				
M'Farlane, Trustees of late John	Bridge of Allan	2	280 —	May, George	Earlsburn, Denny	306	165 —
M'Farlane, Malcolm	Townhead, Balfron	19	26 —	Meek, Heirs of George	Falkirk	58	228 —
M'Farlane, Robert	Oxhill, Kippen	31	66 10	Meikle, Rev. Matthew	Manse, Fintry	11	38 —
M'Farlane, Mrs. Agnes	Braes, Denny	234	255 —	Melville, Mrs. Christian	Kersehill, Falkirk	9	203 7
M'Gregor, Alexander Bennet, of Cairnock	Glasgow	2,003	575 —	Menzies, Alexander Henry Murray, of Coxpow	Largs	150	350 —
M'Indoe, Mrs. Isabella	W. Carbeth, Strathblane	44	57 —	Menzies, Gilbert Innes Murray, of Avondale	Largs	238	539 15
M'Intosh, Rev. William	Manse, Buchanan, Drymen	43	62 —	Millar, James	Stirling	1	413 10
M'Intosh, Mrs. Grace	Glasgow	150	363 4	Miller, George	Glasgow	10	24 —
MacKay, James	Temple of Ballat, Balfron	113	90 —	Miller, James, and others	Compston, Linlithgow	45	80 15
MacKay, John Selby, and George	Grangemouth	46	157 —	Miller, John	Bridge of Allan	7	20 —
Do. do.	Do. (Coal)	—	580 15	Miller, John	Carrongrove, Denny	43	725 10
M'Kenzie, Colin	28 Castle St., Edinburgh	189	97 15	Miller, John	Orchard, Denny	54	86 —
M'Kie, William	East Kirkton, Auchterarder	11	35 10	Miller, Robert	Westerbankhead, Denny	65	120 —
				Miller, Thomas	Myers, St. Ninians	64	45 —
M'Kinlay, Alexander	Musselburgh	23	65 —	Miller, Mrs. Janet	Butterflats, Stirling	3	32 —
M'Kinlay, Alexander	Oldtown, Kilsyth	1	51 14	Milroy, Rev. Andrew Wallace	Forthside, Stirling	11	180 10
M'Kinlay, Trs. of James	1 Princes Street, Glasgow	4	210 —	Mitchell, Andrew	Whins o Milton	3	31 10
M'Lachlan, Archibald	Whins of Milton, Stirling	3	45 —	Mitchell, Duncan	Glasgow	460	90 10

STIRLING—continued.

Name of Owner.	Address of Owner.	Estimated Acreage of Property.	Gross Annual Value.	Name of Owner.	Address of Owner.	Estimated Acreage of Property.	Gross Annual Value.
		Acres.	£ s.			Acres.	£ s.
Mitchell, Duncan William	Stronechriggan, Fort-William	350	80 –	Neilson, James	Rosehall, Falkirk	3	63 10
Mitchell, William	Livilands, Stirling	5	128 –	Neilson, Trustees of James	Rosehall, Falkirk	2	10 –
Mitchell, William Thomson	Grahamston, Falkirk	6	124 6	Neilson, William	Glasgow	75	114 –
Moffat, Rev. William, and William Nicol	Cairnie, Huntly } Denny	21	55 15	Neilson, William	43 Renfield St., Glasgow	15	15 –
Moffat, William	Cross, Kilsyth	2	28 –	Newton, Robert Pillans	Polmont Bank, Falkirk	14	110 –
Moir, Trustees of Allister Erskine Graham, of Leckie	Leckie House, Stirling	3,450	3,471 5	Nicol, Andrew	Beancross, Falkirk	28	70 –
				Nicol, Trs. of late John	Glasgow	130	100 10
				Nicolson, Michael Hugh Stewart, of Carnock	Ardgowan, Greenock	1,421	1,862 15
Monro, Alex. Binning, of Auchenbowie	Auchenbowie, Stirling	438	588 –	Nimmo, Alexander	West Bridge St., Falkirk	79	371 10
Do. do.	Do. (Minerals)	–	50 –	Do. do.	Do. (Minerals)	–	253 5
Monro, Rev. Thomas	Manse, Campsie	8	45 –	North British Railway Co.	Edinburgh (Canal)	67 }	26699 11
Monteath, Alexander	Broich, Crieff	119	120 –	Do. do.	Do. (Railway, &c.)	580 }	
Monteath, Mrs. Ann, and Bethia K. and Mary Bow	Wrights Park, Kippen	272	204 10	Norval, John	Braehead, Strathblane	5	14 –
Montrose, Duke of	Buchanan House, Drymen	68,878	15706 1	Ogilvie, Charles E. Walker	Peterborough	186	687 10
				Do. do.	Do. (Minerals)	–	200 –
Moray, Charles Home Drummond, of Abercairney	Abercairney, Crieff	5	8 5	Oliphant, James	Broad Street, Denny	2	106 –
				Oliver, Richard	Camoquhil, Balfron	2	4 –
Morehead, Trustees of late Robert	Dunipace, Denny (Minerals)	–	1,815 10	Oliver, Janet	North Broomage, Larbert	1	9 10
				Orr, William	Boxton, Falkirk	100	88 –
Morrison & Cunningham	Stirling	1	105 –	Oswald, James	Milton, Stirling	45	54 –
Morrison, James	Bridgend, Falkirk	33	40 –	Oswald, Mrs. Andreas	North Broomage, Larbert	3	12 5
Morrison, Heirs of James, of Livilands	Livilands, Stirling	85	527 15	Paisley, Rev. Robert	St. Ninians, Stirling	10	63 –
Morrison, John	Nelson Place, Stirling	2	394 –	Park, Rev. William	Manse, Airth	10	63 5
Morrison, Joseph	11 Monteith Row, Glasgow	6	23 5	Paterson, Alexander	Bridge of Allan	1	135 –
				Paterson, Andrew	Williamfield, Stirling	7	55 10
Morrison, William, and James Inglis	Torrance of Campsie	6	14 –	Paterson, James	Glasgow	99	58 10
				Paterson, William	Barnego, Dunipace, Denny	96	110 –
Morrison, Heirs of Mrs. Margaret	Campsie	1	13 –	Paton, George	Bottom, Falkirk	16	67 2
				Paton, James	Viewforth, Stirling	7	150 –
Morrison, Mrs. Margaret, and Helen Bayne Morrison	Chartershall, Stirling	3	13 10	Paton, James	Edinburgh	192	173 –
				Patterson, Robert	73 Lucas St., London, E.	3	8 –
Morrison, Trustees of Janet	Glasgow	1	4 10	Pearson, Rev. James	Manse, Strathblane	10	44 –
Morton, Isabella and Catherine	Ferniebank, Bridge of Allan	1	110 –	Philips, Andrew	Milngavie	3	60 –
				Philp, Robert	Bridge of Allan	1	383 –
Motherwell, William	Airdrie	190	46 –	Pollock, John, of Auchineden	Auchineden, Killearn	2,641	847 –
Muir, Rev. Pearson M'Adam	Manse, Polmont	5	35 –	Pollock, Walter Whyte	Glasgow	103	85 –
				Potter, James	Glenfuir, Falkirk	20	102 –
Muir, William Hamilton	Edinburgh	40	100 –	Pringle, Lieut.-Col. David	Carriber, Bathgate	21	12 12
Muir, Mrs. Mary	Wellbank House, Campsie	50	65 –	Do. do.	Do. (Minerals)	–	10 –
Muiravonside, Parochial Board of	Muiravonside, Linlithgow	40	28 –	Provan, James	Glasgow	4	32 15
				Provan, James	Prospect Bank, Dunoon	180	160 –
Muirhead, Trustees of late George	Denny	2	25 –	Provan, Trs. of Moses	17 Gordon St., Glasgow	100	95 –
Muirhead, John	Burnhouse, Denny	214	186 –	Provan, Trustees of Moses, and Peter M'Intosh	Glasgow	45	35 –
Muirhead, Heirs of John	Borland, Denny	4	10 –	Provan, Margaret Stevenson	Glasgow	2	11 –
Muirhead, Mrs. Elizabeth	Graham's Road, Falkirk	1	19 –				
Muller, Charles William Maxwell	Glenyards, Denny	68	113 2				
Mungall, John	Leith	1	30 –	Rae, Michael	Stenhousemuir, Falkirk	1	14 15
Mungall, Robert	Bulliondale, Falkirk	130	120 –	Rae, Peter	Forge Row, Carron	2	22 –
Mungall, William	Newlees, Falkirk	4	17 –	Ralston, William	Little Barnego, Denny	58	60 –
Munnoch, Alexander	South Lodge, Stirling	841	124 –	Ralston, Mrs. Eliza G. Waddell	Balquhatstone, Slamannan	797	551 10
Murdoch, Rev. Alexander Higgin Burn, of Neuck	Nice	180	521 5	Ramsay, Mrs. Christian, wife of John Ramsay	Linlithgow	81	34 –
Murdoch, David	Falkirk	2	45 –	Rankine, Patrick	Moffathills, Airdrie	75	40 –
Murdoch, Rev. James Burn, of Greenyards	Seven Oaks, Kent	552	1,052 5	Rankine, Patrick, yr. of Otter	Kilfinan, Kyles of Bute	956	719 –
Murdoch, Rev. John, and others	Kirkpatrick-Fleming	35	91 –	Do. do.	Do. (Coal)	–	893 –
				Rankine, Peter	Glasgow	1	24 15
Murdoch, Trustees of late Thomas	Springkerse, Stirling	62	230 10	Rankine, Robert William	Rosebank, Falkirk	2	226 10
Murdoch, William	Fleuchams, Gargunnock	3	15 10	Reid, Hugh	Shieldhill, Falkirk	74	45 –
Murdoch, William	Milton of Campsie	3	27 10	Reid, James	Woodville, Stirling	4	449 –
Murdoch, Mrs. Mary	West Gateside, Drymen	10	25 –	Reid, James	Strathblane	9	60 –
Murray, Heirs of James	Whins of Milton	1	25 –	Reid, John, of Hayston	Kirkintilloch	270	660 –
Murray, Lieut.-Col. John, of Polmaise	Polmaise, Stirling	6,813	9,047 10	Reid, John Robert	Prospecthill, Falkirk	96	109 5
Do. do.	Do. (Coal)	–	846 10	Do. do.	Do. (Coal)	–	44 15
Muschet, John Saunders	Birkhill, Stirling	54	267 4	Reid, Robert	Bridge of Allan	2	50 –
				Reid, Thomas, of Carlston	Carlston, Torrance of Campsie	250	361 –
				Reid, William	Sappieside, Stirling	4	21 18
Neil, William	West Mailings, Denny	30	40 –	Reid, Mrs. Janet	Smallburn, Polmont	7	54 15
Neilson, James	Runnions, Balfron	93	86 –	Reid, Mrs. Margaret	Barnsdale House, Stirling	3	26 15

STIRLING—continued.

Name of Owner.	Address of Owner.	Estimated Acreage of Property.	Gross Annual Value.
		Acres.	£ s.
Rennie, Alexander	Bankhead, Denny	42	113 5
Reoch, Andrew	Oakwood House, Buchlyvie	30	68 —
Reoch, James Miller	2 Irvine Place, Stirling	113	73 —
Risk, James	Bankier, Denny	24	315 —
Ritchie, James	Craigmore, Strathblane	23	50 —
Ritchie, William	Milton of Campsie	139	319 —
Ritchie, Mrs. Jane	Falkirk	40	71 10
Robb, Alexander	Stokie Muir, Strathblane	6	7 10
Robertson, Alexander	Liverpool	52	142 —
Robertson Brothers	Forthvale Mills, Stirling	4	300 —
Robertson, David Soutar, of Lawhead	Edinburgh	200	510 —
Robertson, James	Maddistonbrae, Linlithgow	4	7 4
Robertson, Heirs of James	Cornton, Stirling	79	306 10
Robertson, Michael	Balfron	12	185 —
Robertson, Trustee of Mrs. Jean	Mileburn, Gourock	38	25 —
Robertson, Catherine Georgina	Beechwood, Stirling	15	115 —
Robison, James	Ayr	297	379 14
Ronald, Michael	Hill of Kinnaird, Falkirk	15	64 15
Ross, Alexander, of Balwill	Ballochneck, Buchlyvie	678	839 —
Ross, William	Toll Road, Alva	3	449 10
Russell, Alexander Turnbull	30 Hope St., Glasgow	175	254 —
Russell, James	Broadyett, Denny	31	50 —
Russell, James	Longcroft, Denny	110	146 10
Russell, Trustees of James	Falkirk	677	1,583 10
Do. do.	Do. (Coal)	—	300 —
Russell, John	Drum, Denny	46	39 10
Russell, John	Mayfield, Falkirk	7	71 —
Russell, John	Broompark, Denny	88	51 —
Russell, John	Seamores, Denny	57	56 10
Russell & Aitken	Falkirk	76	85 10
Russell, Mrs. Amelia	Kerse Lane, Falkirk	1	17 14
Russell, Janet	Broompark, Denny	2	25 —
Rutherford, Rev. Alexander Cumming	11 Mount Pleasant, Portobello	165	207 —
Scott, Andrew	Woodend, Denny	32	54 15
Scott, James Stenhouse	Blairlodge, Polmont	27	130 —
Scott, John	Milngavie	3	211 8
Scott, William	South Woodend, Denny	68	45 —
Scott, William	Stirling	150	145 —
Scottish Spelter Company	Greenhill, Denny	2	60 —
Sewell, Robert	Balfron	1	12 10
Shand, George	Denny	4	42 —
Shanks, David	High Street, Denny	4	32 —
Shanks, James	Cuthelton, Denny	3	7 15
Shanks, John	Wester Jaw, Falkirk	113	90 —
Shanks, Thomas	Headswood, Denny	62	129 15
Shaw, Trustees of late William	Bathgate	31	60 15
Shearer, John	Thrushville, Stirling	2	442 —
Shedden, John	Doups, Denny	185	87 10
Sheppard, Rev. Henry Alex. Grahame, of Rednock	The Holmwood, Surrey	4,082	560 —
Sheriff, John Bell	Carronvale, Falkirk	164	363 —
Sheriff, Thomas	Abbotshaugh, Falkirk	3	40 —
Simpson, Robert	Halls of Airth, Falkirk	12	41 10
Simpson, William	Carlston, Torrance of Campsie	75	76 5
Simpson, Trs. of William	79 George St., Edinburgh	1,033	1,274 5
Do. do.	Do. (Coal)	—	439 —
Simpson, Mrs. Agnes	West Mains, Falkirk	8	32 —
Sloss, Isabella and Mrs. Mary Campbell	Lennoxtown	1	136 5
Smart, William	Charlotte St., Glasgow	3	26 10
Smith, Adam	Falkirk	342	468 9
Smith, Alexander	Falkirk	2	124 —
Smith, Andrew	Willowbrae, Edinburgh	89	232 10
Smith, David Ross	Calfmuir, Kirkintilloch	3	4 10
Smith, Fullarton, & Co.	Lock 16, Falkirk	3	22 —
Smith, John	Falkirk	6	244 —
Smith, Captain John Kincaid	Polmont House, Polmont	281	819 18
Smith, Robert	Stirling	18	877 —
Smith, Heirs of Mrs. Mary	Stirling	4	62 —
Snell, James Anderson	Redding House, Falkirk	12	118 15
Society for Propagating Christian Knowledge	23 York Pl., Edinburgh	116	253 —
Somerville, William	St. Ninians, Stirling	1	113 —
Speirs, Alexander	Kilsyth	5	80 —
Speirs, Alexander Graham, of Culcreuch	Culcreuch, Fintry	7,172	2,397 14
Speirs, Mrs. Elizabeth, wife of John Speirs	Burnhouse, Denny	30	35 —
Speirs, Mrs. Mary	Fintry	91	239 15
Speirs, Elizabeth	Laurelhill, Stirling	14	118 —
Spens, Mrs. Henrietta O'Valiant	Lathallan, by Falkirk	284	419 15
Spiers, Trustees of late Andrew	Lochgreen, Denny	600	298 —
Spittal's Hospital	Stirling	19	378 11
Spreull, Andrew	North Blochearn, Milngavie	250	62 —
Stainton, Josephine, of Biggarshiells	Lutterworth, Leicestershire	389	1,232 11
Stalker, Robert	Stirling	1	86 —
Stark, John	Woodburn, Falkirk	38	25 —
Stark, Rev. John	Manse, Gargunnock	9	35 15
Stark, Ralph	Camelon, Falkirk	25	263 10
Steuart, Sir Henry James Seton, of Touch and Allanton, Bart.	Touch House, Stirling	4,801	2,676 —
Stevenson, James	Mount William, Gourock	10	23 —
Stevenson, James	Rowantreehills, Slamannan	27	42 —
Stevenson, Robert	Beechmount, Kirkintilloch	2	79 —
Stevenson, William	The Lea, Bridge of Allan	2	85 —
Stevenson, Rev. William	Manse, Bothkennar, Falkirk	5	38 —
Stevenson, Mrs. Mary	Jawhills, Slamannan	100	22 10
Stewart, Captain David, of Stewarthall	Stewarthall, Stirling	276	726 5
Stewart, Duncan	Drymen	3	40 —
Stewart, John	Milton of Buchanan, Drymen	4	11 10
Stewart, Robert	London	450	310 —
Stewart, William	Donaldson's Hospital, Edinburgh	3	14 10
Stewart, Mrs. Isabella	Castlehill, Stirling	1	8 —
Stewart, Mrs. Janet	Parkfoot, Falkirk	1	12 —
Stirling, Andrew	Haggs, Denny	344	646 —
Stirling, Captain Andrew, of Muiravonside	Muiravonside, Linlithgow	688	638 —
Stirling, Major Charles Campbell Graham, of Craigbarnet	Craigbarnet, Lennoxtown	3,343	1,691 —
Do. do.	Do. (Quarry)	—	25 —
Stirling, Sir Charles Elphinstone Fleming, of Glorat, Bart.	Glorat House, Lennoxtown	2,700	1,793 12
Do. do.	Do. (Coal)	—	246 15
Stirling, David	Garngrew, Denny	35	71 10
Stirling, Trs. of Gilbert	Larbert House, Falkirk	899	1,610 15
Stirling, James	Haggs, Denny	1	19 —
Stirling, James, of Garden	Garden, Buchlyvie	618	808 17
Stirling, James	Kippen	3	16 6
Stirling, James	Gargunnock	3	11 10
Stirling, Major John Stirling, of Gargunnock	Gargunnock House, Stirling	1,881	1,488 10
Stirling, William, of Tarduf	Tarduf, Linlithgow	260	295 —
Stirling, Mrs. Ann Craigie, of Glenbervie	Glenbervie, Falkirk	778	1,367 5
Stirling, Burgh of	Stirling	5	739 2
Stirling, Commissioners of Supply of	Stirling	1	236 6
Stirling Gas Company	Stirling	2	653 17
Stirling, Lunacy Board of	Stirling	74	680 —
Stirling, Managers of Combination Poorhouse of	Stirling	2	200 —
Stobie, Trustees of late Thomas, of Ballochneck	Kinross	720	600 —

STIRLING—continued.

Name of Owner.	Address of Owner.	Estimated Acreage of Property.	Gross Annual Value.	Name of Owner.	Address of Owner.	Estimated Acreage of Property.	Gross Annual Value.
		Acres.	£ s.			Acres.	£ s.
Storie, William	Falkirk	285	228 15	Watters, Alexander Wm. Dunn	Craigton, Fintry	721	383 10
Stott, John	Whins of Milton, Stirling	2	20 -	Watters, Andrew	Glenample, Lochearnhead	105	212 -
Strachan, Mrs. Eliza Jane, of Thornton	Thornton, Falkirk	212	401 4	Waugh, Heirs of George	Loanrig, Slamannan	46	36 -
Strode, Nathaniel William John	Albany, Piccadilly, London	223	168 10	Waugh, James	South Arnloss, Slamannan	150	55 -
				Do.	Do. (Coal)	-	160 -
				Waugh, James	North Arnloss, Slamannan	185	84 -
				Do.	Do. (Coal)	-	50 -
Taylor, James	Sunnyside, Falkirk	9	45 -	Waugh, James and John	South Arnloss, Slamannan	94	60 -
Taylor, James	Holehouse, Falkirk	53	31 10	Waugh, John	Newmill, Avonbridge, Falkirk	128	124 -
Taylor, Rev. James Wm.	Criech, Cupar-Fife	10	21 -				
Taylor, John	Redding, Falkirk	4	4 -	Waugh, John	Hillhead, Slamannan	66	45 -
Taylor, William Forrester	Carronbridge, Denny	2	16 -	Waugh, John and George	North Arnloss, Slamannan	150	54 -
Taylor & Company	Abbey Road, Stirling	6	163 -	Waugh, Thomas	Holehouse, Slamannan	98	80 -
Taylor, Catherine and Agnes	Bonnybridge, Denny	3	12 -	Webster, John	Herdshill, Falkirk	1	30 -
				Weir, Robert	Waterslap, Falkirk	1	10 -
Taylor Institution	Crieff	36	123 10	Weir, Mrs. Jane	Barrachan, Milngavie	119	120 -
Tennant, Colonel Hamilton Tovey	Annfield, Stirling	10	110 -	Do.	Do. (Quarry)	-	10 -
Thomson, Alexander	Backdales, Denny	181	84 -	*Westquarter Chemical Co.*	Westquarter, Falkirk	2	30 -
Thomson, Alexander	Johnstone	82	40 -	White, Trustees of late Alexander	114 George Street, Edinburgh	353	353 -
Thomson, Trustees of late George	Park Terrace, Stirling	2	250 -	Whitehead, William	Bradford	1	76 -
Thomson, James David	Grangemouth	1	3 15	Whyte, William	Allander Mills, Milngavie	19	233 -
Thomson, John	Cornton Vale, Bridge of Allan	30	100 10	Wilson, Charles Henry Haldane, of Endrickbank	Endrickbank, Drymen	251	411 10
Thomson, John	Shielwalls, Denny	88	40 -	Wilson, James	East Shieldhill, Falkirk	8	12 10
Thomson, Mrs. Christina	173 George St., Glasgow	134	94 -	Wilson, Trs. of James	Bannockburn	3	395 15
Todd, John	Melville Terrace, Stirling	4	91 10	Wilson, John, of Hillpark	Hillpark, Bannockburn	459	857 -
Todd, John, of Finnick	Finnick, Drymen	526	419 10	Do. do.	Do. (Coal)	-	50 -
Towers, James	Grahamston, Falkirk	2	96 5	Wilson, John, of South Bantaskine	South Bantaskine, Falkirk	271	615 5
Towers, Robert and James Towers Clark	Glasgow Wester Moffat, Airdrie	80	81 10	Do. do.	Do. (Coal)	-	300 -
				Wilson, John	Grahamston, Falkirk	1	12 -
Towers, Mrs. Agnes	Grahamston, Falkirk	3	45 2	Wilson, John, of Auchineck	Auchineck, Drymen	2,510	609 -
Towers, Trustees of late Helen	Glasgow	22	22 -	Wilson, John, and Benjamin Cox	Falkirk	2	3 -
Turnbull, James	Hallquarter, Canglour, Stirling	119	118 -	Wilson, William, and others	Broomfield, Davidson's Mains, Edinburgh	165	85 -
Turner, Robert	Burntisland	10	22 -	Wilson, Trustees of late William and John	Bannockburn	23	139 15
				Wilson, Trustees of late William	Bannockburn	123	766 15
Ure, George	Bonnybridge, Denny	23	137 -	Wilson, William, of Banknock	Banknock, Denny	370	1,037 -
Ure, William	Grayswalls, Denny	30	25 -				
*Ure & Co.	Bonnybridge, Denny	9	476 -	Wilson, William	East Drumclair, Falkirk	70	55 -
Urquhart, John Grubb	Vellore Castle, Linlithgow	78	135 -	Wilson, Rev. William	Manse, Kippen	5	34 10
				Wingate, Charles	Stirling	12	64 10
				Winning, Andrew	Balmore, Torrance of Campsie	47	72 -
Waddell, Alexander Peddie, of Balquhatston	Edinburgh	945	638 15	Wood, Trs. of late Ellis	Blanefield, Strathblane	19	753 6
Do. do.	Do. (Coal)	-	1,580 -	Wordie, William	Stirling	2	471 10
Waddell, Matthew	Meadowbank, Polmont	124	310 -	Wright, James	Herbertshire St., Denny	5	24 -
Waddell, Gaston Margaret Ann	Balquhatston, Slamannan	32	33 5	Wright, Heirs of John	Killearn	4	10 12
Walker, James	Candyhead, Linlithgow	19	19 -	Wright, William, of Broom	Stirling	117	311 -
Walker, Trs. of late James	5 Hart Street, Edinburgh	113	359 15	Wright, Mrs. Elizabeth	Stirling	30	57 -
Walker, John	Lennoxtown	4	24 15	Wright, Margaret and Agnes	Clifford Park, Stirling	10	116 -
Walker, Robert	Balmore, Torrance of Campsie	11	31 -				
Walker, William	Whins of Milton, Stirling	1	28 -	Yellowlees, David	Stirling	1	62 -
Walker, Heirs of Wm.	Wholeflatts, Falkirk	10	63 4	Young, John	Overton, Denny	40	65 -
Walker, Heirs of Mrs. Jean	Falkirk	3	50 -	Young, Peter	3 Irvine Place, Stirling	88	210 -
Wallace, James	Kingston, Kilsyth	4	220 -	Yuill, Walter	Little Camoquhill, Balfron	30	35 -
Wallace, William and James	Canglour, Stirling	21	18 -				
Wardrop, John	Camelon, Falkirk	1	28 10	Zetland, Earl of	Kerse House, Falkirk	4,656	9,552 -
Watson, David, of Bardowie	Bardowie, Milngavie	175	148 4	Do. do.	Do. (Coal)	-	4,256 -
Watson, George	Blackbraes, Falkirk	3	16 -				
Watson, John	123 St. Vincent Street, Glasgow	5	503 10				
Watson, Trs. of late John	Wester Barnego, Denny	110	80 -	Total Owners of Land of One Acre and upwards 848		283,468	413,190 2
Watt, Heirs of James B.	9 York Place, Edinburgh	6	13 10				
Watt, Rev. John	Candy, Ceylon	22	67 5	Total Owners of Lands of less than One Acre in extent 3,409		1,283	108,216 9
Watt, Thomas	Roughrig, New Monkland, Airdrie	60	35 -				
Watt, Margaret Rennie	Renfrew Street, Glasgow	12	56 10	GRAND TOTAL . . . 4,257		284,751	521,406 11

SUTHERLAND.

Population in 1871, - - - - - - - **24,317.**
Inhabited Houses, - - - - - - - **4,914.**
Number of Parishes, - - - - - - - **14.**

Name of Owner.	Address of Owner.	Estimated Acreage of Property.	Gross Annual Value.	Name of Owner.	Address of Owner.	Estimated Acreage of Property.	Gross Annual Value.
		Acres.	£ s.			Acres.	£ s.
Aird, Rev. Gustavus	F.C. Manse, Migdale, Ardgay	15	17 10	M'Kenzie, Rev. Kenneth	Manse of Kinlochbervie, Lairg	3	10 —
Anderson, Andrew	Altas, Rosehall, Ardgay	50	6 —	M'Kenzie, Rev. Kenneth	Manse of Strathy, Thurso	10	10 —
				M'Kinnon, Rev. Neil	Manse of Creich, Ardgay	7	26 —
				M'Lean, Hugh	Badfluich, Rosehall, Ardgay	29	5 —
Birnie, Charles	Altas, Rosehall, Ardgay	50	7 —				
Brooks, John	Altas, Rosehall, Ardgay	52	6 —	M'Leod, Executors of Gordon, of Glencassley	Glencassley, Rosehall, Ardgay	11,000	412 —
Brooks, Theophilus	Altas, Rosehall, Ardgay	28	4 —	M'Leod, John and David	Altas, Rosehall, Ardgay	32	10 —
Brown, James	Rosehall, Ardgay	100	13 —	M'Millan, Rev. Gilbert	Manse of Loth, Helmsdale	15	33 —
				M'Pherson, Rev. John	F.C. Manse, Lairg	4	12 —
Cadger, George	Rosehall, Ardgay	74	9 —	Matheson, Rev. Farquhar	Manse, Lairg	27	33 —
Cameron, Ewan	Altas, Rosehall, Ardgay	20	8 —	Matheson, Sir James, of The Lews and Achany, Bart.	Achany, Lairg	18,490	1,812 10
Clarke, Rev. Patrick F.	Manse of Kildonan, Helmsdale	26	48 —				
Clarke, Robert	Dornoch	2	15 —	Meldrum, Rev. Andrew	Manse of Clyne, Golspie	13	32 —
Cooper, George Murray	Altas, Rosehall, Ardgay	70	12 —	Morrison, Alexander	Rosehall, Ardgay	30	4 —
				Munro, John	Altas, Rosehall, Ardgay	30	7 —
				Munro, Nathaniel	Meikle Altas, Rosehall, Ardgay	27	8 —
Falconer, Rev. John	F.C. Manse, Rosehall, Ardgay	11	20 —	Murray, Donald	Meikle Altas, Rosehall, Ardgay	17	5 —
Findlay, William	Dykehead, Huntly	118	14 —				
Fraser, Donald	Helmsdale	1	97 —	Murray, James	Altas, Rosehall, Ardgay	40	10 —
Free Church, Trustees of	Edinburgh	1	2 10	Murray, Peter and Alexander	Rosehall, Ardgay	100	13 —
Gilchrist, Dugald, of Ospisdale	Ospisdale House, Dornoch	3,600	800 —	Northern Lighthouses, Commissioners of	George Street, Edinburgh	77	70 —
Gow, William	Pulteneytown, Wick	2	66 —				
Grant, Rev. William C.M.	Manse of Durness, Lairg	50	50 —				
				Pirie, Alexander	Altas, Rosehall, Ardgay	40	5 —
Hadwen, Sidney, of Balblair	West Garty, Helmsdale	2,991	394 10	Pope, Eliza	Navidale, Helmsdale	4	25 —
Horn, George and Alexander	Rosehall, Ardgay	30	4 —				
Horn, Joseph	Little Altas, Rosehall, Ardgay	40	13 —	Readman, Robert	32 Lynedoch Street, Glasgow	174	40 —
				Ross, Alexander	Altas, Rosehall, Ardgay	22	9 —
Joass, Rev. James M.	Manse, Golspie	11	35 —	Ross, Sir Charles William Augustus, of Balnagown, Bart.	Balnagown Castle, Parkhill	55,000	970 —
				Ross, Charles	Altas, Rosehall, Ardgay	12	2 —
Loban, Charles	Altas, Rosehall, Ardgay	40	5 —	Ross, Donald	Meikle Altas, Rosehall, Ardgay	20	7 —
Loch, George, of Embo	Uppat, Golspie	320	300 —				
Logan, Rev. Angus	Manse of Tongue, Lairg	260	55 —	Ross, Donald (Bain)	Meikle Altas, Rosehall, Ardgay	28	9 —
				Ross, John	Meikle Altas, Rosehall, Ardgay	8	3 —
M'Ainsh, Peter	Woodburn, Crieff	370	125 —	Ross, Joseph	Meikle Altas, Rosehall, Ardgay	60	12 —
Macaulay, Rev. Donald	Manse of Eddrachillis, Lairg	315	35 —	Ross, Robert	Meikle Altas, Rosehall, Ardgay	13	6 —
Macdonald, Rev. Colin	Manse of Rogart, Golspie	20	30 —	Ross, William	Meikle Altas, Rosehall, Ardgay	13	3 —
M'Donald, Donald	Meikle Altas, Rosehall, Ardgay	16	7 —				
M'Donald, John	Meikle Altas, Rosehall, Ardgay	19	8 —				
M'Donald, William	Rogart, Golspie	1	10 —	Sim, John	Rosehall, Ardgay	120	12 —
M'Intosh, John	Altas, Rosehall, Ardgay	24	10 —	Stevenson, William, of Invernauld	The Lea, Bridge of Allan	1,125	180 —
Mackay, Rev. Donald	Manse of Stoer, Lairg	12	13 —				
M'Kay, John	Rosehall, Ardgay	170	15 —	Stewart, Charles, of Dalcrombie	Inverness	2,000	300 —
M'Kay, William	Meikle Altas, Rosehall, Ardgay	20	7 —	Stewart, Rev. Duncan	Manse, Dornoch	9	35 —
M'Kay, William	Dornoch	4	15 —	Strachan, Joseph	Altas, Rosehall, Ardgay	50	6 —

SUTHERLAND—continued.

Name of Owner.	Address of Owner.	Estimated Acreage of Property.	Gross Annual Value.	Name of Owner.	Address of Owner.	Estimated Acreage of Property.	Gross Annual Value.
		Acres.	£ s.			Acres.	£ s.
Sutherland, Duke of	Dunrobin Castle, Golspie	1176343	56395 13	Tennant, Robert, of Rosehall	Scarcroft Lodge, Leeds	2,080	651 —
Do. do.	Inverness (*Railway*)	111	542 —	Thompson, John	Clayhills, Aberdeen	500	90 —
Sutherland Combination Poorhouse Committee	Bonar Bridge, Ardgay	4	60 —	Wallace, James	Rosehall, Ardgay	50	6 —
Sutherland Railway Company	Inverness (*Railway*)	184	1,113 —	Williamson, Rev. David	Manse of Assynt, Lairg	1,800	50 —
Sutherland and Caithness Railway Company	Inverness (*Railway*)	195	(Under construction.)	Total Owners of Land of One Acre and upwards		85	1,299,194 68,602 7
Sutherland, Rev. David	Manse of Farr, Thurso	325	40 —	Total Owners of Lands of less than One Acre in extent		348	59 2,892 —
Sutherland, John	Darcha, Rosehall, Ardgay	20	10 —	GRAND TOTAL		433	1,299,253 71,494 7
Sutherland-Walker, Evan Charles, of Skibo	Skibo Castle, Dornoch	20,000	3,231 14				

WIGTOWN.

Population in 1871, - - - - - - - **38,830.**
Inhabited Houses, - - - - - - **6,739**
Number of Parishes, - - - - - - **17.**

Name of Owner.	Address of Owner.	Estimated Acreage of Property.	Gross Annual Value.	Name of Owner.	Address of Owner.	Estimated Acreage of Property.	Gross Annual Value.
		Acres.	£ s.			Acres.	£ s.
Adair, Heirs of John	Stranraer	1	57 15	Dunbar, Sir William, of Mochrum, Bart.	Merton Hall, Newton-Stewart	3,674	2,612 4
Adamson, John	Agnew Crescent, Wigtown	5	208 14	Dunn, Trs. of late Henry	Wigtown	7	52 10
Agnew, Sir Andrew, of Lochnaw, Bart.	Lochnaw Castle, Stranraer	12,962	9,229 4				
Agnew, Robert Vans, of Sheuchan and Barnbarroch, M.P.	Barnbarroch, Kirkinner, Wigtown	6,777	6,996 14	Ewart, Trs. of late James	Newton-Stewart	1	95 —
Agnew, Mrs. Catharine Vans	Corsbie, Newton-Stewart	5	62 12	Faed, James, of Craigenveoch	14 Comely Bank, Edinburgh	905	248 4
Allan, Rev. William	Manse of Mochrum, Port-William	15	55 —	Ferguson Bequest Fund, Trustees of	66 George Sq., Glasgow	1,274	1,028 14
Anderson, Charles	Barsalloch, Port-William	3	42 —	Fergusson, Mary M.	Sheuchan St., Stranraer	8	155 —
				Forsyth, Alexander, of Valleyfield	Valleyfield, Kirkcolm, Stranraer	80	80 —
Balmer, Rev. Stephen	Manse of Portpatrick	13	30 —	Forsyth, Rev. William	Manse of New Luce, Glenluce	20	88 —
Barty, Rev. Thomas	Manse of Kirkcolm, Stranraer	13	45 —	Frederick, David, of Gass	Drumbreddan, Stoneykirk	1,000	150 —
Beddie, John and David	Kirkchrist, Newton-Stewart	5	27 10	Frood, Rev. Bryce	Manse of Old Luce, Glenluce	15	50 —
Bennett, Rev. David	Sheuchan Cottage, Stranraer	25	20 —	Galloway, Earl of	Galloway House, Garlieston	23,203	24864 6
Black, Ebenezer Stott	Wigtown	6	29 10				
Blair, David Hunter, of Dunskey	Dunskey, Portpatrick	8,255	4,948 16	Garlieston Harbour Trs.	Garlieston (Harbour)	1	228 10
Blair, Edward Jas. Stopford, of Penninghame	Penninghame House, Newton-Stewart	37,268	9,035 16	Gibb, John, senior	Hanover St., Stranraer	1	158 9
Boyd, Mark Sprott, of Merton Hall	Walton-on-Thames	1,524	814 —	Gordon, John	George Street, Stranraer	1	169 10
British Linen Co. Bank	Edinburgh	1	165 —	Graham, John	71 West Nile St., Glasgow	8	55 —
Broadfoot, James	Westmains, Kirkinner	5	32 15	Grahame, Barron, of Morphie	Bowbutts House, Kinghorn	1,524	300 —
Broadfoot, Peter, of Wards	Wards, Whithorn	40	126 —	Gulline, Mrs. Jessie	Dewsbury	1	46 6
Broadfoot, Robert	Whithorn	20	52 —	Hamilton, William Charles Stewart, of Craighlaw	Craighlaw, Kirkcowan	6,300	2,576 11
Bute, Marquess of	Mount Stuart, Rothesay	20,157	2,936 12	Hannah, Heirs of Mrs. Grace	Wigtown	6	49 17
Caird, James, of Cassencary	Cassencary, Creetown	4	100 1	Harriott, George Robert, of Killiemore	Killiemore Lodge, Kirkcowan	481	316 19
Campbell, Patrick	Belmont, Stranraer	5	55 —	Hathorn, Lieut.-Col. John Fletcher, of Castlewigg	Castlewigg, Whithorn	3,582	5,169 —
Charles, Rev. James	Manse, Kirkcowan	19	45 —	Hay, James Francis Dalrymple, younger of Dunragit	108 St. George's Square, London	906	70 —
Craig, Margaret, and Heirs of William Craig	Queen's Terrace, Ayr	211	187 6				
Crown, The	(Government Property)	59	696 —				
Cullen, Rev. James	Manse of Wigtown	10	72 —	Hay, Rear-Admiral Sir John Charles Dalrymple, of Park Place, Bart., M.P.	Dunragit House, Glenluce; and 108 St. George's Square, London	7,400	6,601 2
Cumming, Trs. of late James	Douriebank, Port-William	2	212 4				
Cumming, Mrs. Mary Honeyman	84 Great King Street, Edinburgh	4	37 10	Hay, William Archibald Dalrymple and James Stewart	108 St. George's Square, Edinburgh	3	42 —
Cunningham, Rev. Robert	Cairnryan Rd., Stranraer	1	60 —				
Dalrymple, Heirs of Thomas	Stranraer	2	118 —	Heron, James	Ardwell Inn, Stoneykirk	7	24 —
Davidson, John	Lochans, Stranraer	1	13 —	Hill, Francis Chorley, of Changue	Changue, Port-William	444	400 15
Dean, William, of Polbae	Polbae, Kirkcowan	1,905	200 —				
Dougal, Rev. James	Manse of Stoneykirk	8	43 —				
Douglas Academy, Trs. of	Newton-Stewart	3	35 —	Ingram, Alexander	Stranraer	1	177 —
Douglas, Trustees of late George Agnew	33 Heriot Row, Edinburgh	14	95 17				
Douglas, Mrs. Jeanie	Grosvenor Road, Claughton, Birkenhead	4	105 —	Jardine, Rev. Matthew	Manse of Whithorn	10	53 —
Drew, James, of Craigencallie	Doonhill, Newton-Stewart	5	107 10	Johnstone, Mrs. Lillias Miller	Minnigaff Manse, Newton-Stewart	1	45 —
Dunbar, Robert Lennox, of Machermore	5 Brompton Sq., London	15	20 —	Jones, James	Burgess Croft, Stranraer	4	11 —
Dunbar, Uthred James Hay, and William Cospatrick Dunbar	7 Princes Terrace, Princes Gate, London	6	14 —	Kennedy, John	Woodside, Newton-Stewart	2	278 —

WIGTOWN—continued.

Name of Owner.	Address of Owner.	Estimated Acreage of Property.	Gross Annual Value.	Name of Owner.	Address of Owner.	Estimated Acreage of Property.	Gross Annual Value.
		Acres.	£ s.			Acres.	£ s.
Kirkcolm, Free Church Congregation of.	Kirkcolm	1	29 –	Service, Rev. John	Manse, Soulseat, Stranraer	31	63 –
King, James Bowie	Ayr	8	81 –	Simson, John, and Mrs. Christian D. S., of Barrachan	Wigtown	720	622 16
M'Connell, John and Charles Magee Routledge	Rock Cottage, Whithorn } Port-William }	2	10 –	Stair, Earl of	Lochinch Castle, Stranraer	79,174	40425 7
M'Cormick, Alexander	Lochenkit, Corsock, Dalbeattie	4	17 –	Stair, Trustees of late Earl of	Lochinch Castle, Stranraer	3,492	3,084 17
M'Culloch, Heirs of David, of Little Torhouse	Little Torhouse, Wigtown	833	767 11	Steel, John	Schoolhouse, Glasserton, Whithorn	3	10 –
M'Douall, James, of Logan	Logan, Stranraer	16,290	11785 12	Stewart, Rev. Archibald	Manse of Glasserton, Whithorn	18	46 –
M'Dowall, Alexander H.	Church Street, Stranraer	1	64 10	Stewart, Horatio Granville Murray, of Broughton	Cally, Gatehouse	1,584	1,707 –
M'Dowall, Thomas	Woodside, Wigtown	11	45 –	Stewart, Hugh, of Tonderghie	Tonderghie, Whithorn	662	948 –
M'Geoch, John	Duncan Villa, Wigtown	4	72 –	Stewart, Mark John, of Blairderry	Ardwell, Stranraer	1,578	306 7
M'Haffie, George William Gordon, of Corsmalzie	Corsmalzie, Bladnoch, Wigtown	3,420	990 18	Stewart, Robert Hathorn Johnston, of Physgill	Glasserton, Whithorn	5,552	7,619 5
M'Haffie, William James, of Torhousemuir	Torhousemuir, Wigtown	761	531 10	Stewart, Heirs of Robert, of Omoa	Omoa, Glasgow	8	10 10
M'Keand, Andrew, of Airlies	Airlies, Kirkinner	775	542 2	*Stoneykirk, Heritors of Parish of*	Stoneykirk	2	56 –
M'Kenna, Alexander, of Clantibuies	Low Malzie, Kirkinner	153	102 10	*Stranraer, Commissioners of Police of*	Stranraer	1	60 –
M'Kenna, Fergus	Newton-Stewart	1	23 –	*Stranraer, Harbour Trustees of*	Stranraer (Harbour)	4	600 –
M'Kie, John	Kilquhirn Cottage, Wigtown	2	28 10	*Stranraer, Magistrates and Town Council of*	Stranraer	1	159 –
Maclaurin, Dugald	8 Great George Street, Westminster, London	1	8 6	*Stranraer Poorhouse, Directors of*	Stranraer	2	150 –
MacLean, Peter, of Duchra	Bellevilla, Stranraer	320	296 –	Stroyan, David, of Culvennan	Newton-Stewart	709	286 2
M'Lean, Rev. William	Manse of Penninghame, Newton-Stewart	11	81 –	Stroyan, John, of Kirkchrist	Boreland, Kirkcowan	302	260 –
M'Meikan, William	Low Salchrie, Stranraer	6	15 –	Taylor, Samuel, senior	London Road, Stranraer	2	179 –
M'Micking, Thomas, of Miltonise	Burnbrae, Helensburgh	2,477	195 10	Wallace, Charles, of Dally	Dally, Kirkcolm, Stranraer	119	116 17
M'Millan, William	Newton-Stewart	1	139 19	Wallace, Lieut.-Col. Sir William T. F. Agnew, of Craigie and Lochryan, Bart.	Lochryan House, Cairnryan, Stranraer	5,785	1,373 5
M'Queen, Alexander and George, of Chippermore	Chippermore, Port-William	483	270 –	Wallace, Mrs. Margaret	Wigtown	6	43 –
M'Taggart, John M'Taggart Ellis, of Grennan	Grennan, Glenluce	1,614	499 12	Warrack, Rev. Alexander	F.C. Manse, Leswalt, Stranraer	3	28 –
M'Taggart, Mrs. Susannah Ommanney, of Ardwell	Ardwell, Stranraer	5,998	6,616 10	Warren, Rev. Robert Sharp	Stranraer	46	143 –
M'William, Alexander	Barvernochan, Kirkinner	2	11 –	White, Major-General H. Dalrymple, of High Mark	32 Lowndes Square, London	827	65 10
M'William, James, of Garrochar	Bank Street, Wigtown	11	61 –	*Whithorn, Magistrates and Town Council of*	Whithorn	2	183 16
Maitland, William, of Freugh	Balgreggan, Stranraer	7,848	5,881 11	*Wigtown, Magistrates and Town Council of*	Wigtown	114	393 17
Maxwell, Sir William, of Monreith, Bart.	Monreith, Port-William	16,877	15289 10	*Wigtown, Trustees of United Presbyterian Church of*	Wigtown		53 5
Milligan, James, of Tannielaggie	5 Royal Terrace, Edinburgh	1,600	225 –	Williamson, Rev. William	Manse of Kirkmaiden, Stranraer	6	40 –
Milroy, Thomas	Tarff Mill, Kirkcowan	2	13 –	Wright, Trustees of late Bryce	Stranraer	2	101 –
Milroy, Thomas, William, and John	Tarff Mill, Kirkcowan	4	65 –	Wright, Hugh, of Alticry	Alticry, Port-William	461	368 10
Milroy, William	Waulk Mill, Kirkcowan	6	65 –				
Minot, Jane Susan	Braefield, Portpatrick	1	40 –				
Mitchell, John	Princes Street, Newton-Stewart	3	84 19				
Monteith, Mrs. Frances	Duncree, Newton-Stewart	1	50 –				
Moore, John Carrick, of Corsewall	Corsewall, Stranraer	3,362	2,920 5				
Murdoch, Rev. Alexander	Manse of Sorbie	13	47 –				
Murdoch, Rev. Alexander and George Agnew Main	Manse of Sorbie } Whithorn }	2	31 7				
Parlane, James, of Craigdhu, Craiglemine, and Appleby	Park Crescent, Victoria Park, Manchester	1,410	1,739 12	Young, Captain William, of Gillespie	Craig Lodge, Glenluce	1,997	852 15
Portpatrick Railway Co.	Stranraer (Railway)	343	6,839 –				
Pringle, James Hall, of Dirrie	Cleithaugh, Jedburgh	618	432 8	Total Owners of Land of One Acre and upwards 146		308,800	200,836 1
Reid, Rev. James	Manse of Kirkinner	12	57 –	Total Owners of Lands of less than one Acre in extent 1,674		287	29,753 3
Ross, Rev. Andrew, of Knocknassie	Knocknassie, Kirkcolm, Stranraer	38	25 15				
Routledge, John	Mill of Mochrum, Port-William	7	62 12	GRAND TOTAL . . . 1,820		309,087	230,589 4

ZETLAND.

Population in 1871,	31,608.
Inhabited Houses,	5,667.
Number of Parishes,	12.

Name of Owner.	Address of Owner.	Estimated Acreage of Property.	Gross Annual Value.
		Acres.	£ s.
Anderson, Trustees of late Arthur	London	2	75 —
Anderson, Daniel	Killister, North Yell	70	5 —
Anderson, Gideon	Ollaberry, Northmavine	4,256	323 —
Anderson, John, and another	Moorfield, Delting	12	10 10
Anderson, Thomas	Clothen, Yell	3	1 10
Anderson, Mrs. Ursula	Midby, Yell	105	3 —
Bain, Rev. James	F.C. Manse, Delting	1	15 5
Bain, Nichol	Aithsetter, Cunningsburgh	36	4 5
Bain, Mrs. Phillias	Gord, Cunningsburgh	34	3 2
Barclay, Rev. James	Manse, Sussater, Yell	700	82 1
Barron, Laurence	Hammer, Delting	5	10 —
Bayne, Rev. Alexander	Manse, Tingwall	50	44 —
Beatton, Charles Clouston	Schoolhouse, Tingwall	3	10 —
Black, David Dakers, of Kergord	Brechin, Forfarshire	4,600	402 14
Boag, Rev. William Goldie	Manse, Voxter, Delting	47	25 —
Brand, Rev. William	Manse, Dunrossness	56	32 —
Bressay, Kirk-Session of Parish of	Bressay	318	12 4
Brown, James	Cunningster, North Yell	145	4 10
Bruce, James	Schoolhouse, Urafirth, Northmavine	10	6 —
Bruce, John, of Sumburgh	Sand Lodge, Sandwick	12,338	1,791 12
Do. do.	Do. (Quarry)	—	4 —
Bruce, John, yr. of Sumburgh	Sumburgh, Dunrossness	240	71 —
Bruce, Tutors and Curators of William Arthur, of Symbister	Lerwick	25,180	2,354 8
Bruce, Elizabeth	Sand Lodge, Sandwick	8	33 —
Budge, Mrs. Sinclair	Seafield, Yell	1,700	154 11
Busta Estate, Trustees on the	Busta House, Delting	29,820	2,707 10
Calder, Laurence	Hillister, Whiteness	33	12 15
Cameron, Major Thomas Mouat, of Garth	Annsbrae, Lerwick	24,363	2,035 6
Campbell, Trustees of late John Deans	Kilmarnock	2	139 —
Cheyne, Harry	56 Frederick Street, Edinburgh	2,000	81 2
Do.	Do. (Quarry)	—	14 —
Cheyne, John	Dundee	220	18 2
Cheyne, William Watson	Edinburgh	168	8 —
Cheyne, Mrs. Barbara	10 Rutland Square, Edinburgh	1,900	130 1
Christian Knowledge, Society for Propagating	Edinburgh	41	34 10
Chromate of Iron Quarries, Proprietors of	Unst (Quarries)	—	1,000 —
Church of Scotland, Home Mission Committee of	Edinburgh	15	36 —
Clark, Oliver, Andrew, and James	Burragarth, Unst	90	12 —
Clarke, Magnus	Holygarth, Yell	120	8 —
Cogle, Mrs. Margaret, wife of Robert Cogle	Gord, Cunningsburgh	14	1 5
Congregational Church, Trustees for	Greenvale, Sandsting	17	9 —
Cormack, Mrs. Jane, wife of John Cormack	South Hall, Yell	76	17 15
Crabb, Rev. James	Manse, North Yell	6	10 —
Craig, Rev. John	Manse, Sandwick	2	10 —
Craigie, Mrs. Margaret	Milby Cot., North Yell	20	8 6
Cunningsburgh, Free Church Congregation of	Cunningsburgh	2	13 15
Davidson, George	Scalloway, Tingwall	1	4 —
Davidson, Thomas	Culbinsgarth, Cunningsburgh	85	10 —
Dickson, Adam	Vementry, Aithsting	1,033	59 10
Duncan, Charles Gilbert	Lerwick	12	20 —
Duncan, Mrs. Helen	Lerwick	50	21 —
Edmondston, Laurence	Hallygarth, Unst	19	19 —
Edmondston, Mrs. Ursula, wife of Thomas Edmondston, of Buness	Buness House, Unst	5,000	758 —
Fea, Representatives of Magnus Sinclair	Baltasound, Unst	51	20 —
Fetlar and North Yell, Free Church Congregation of	Fetlar and North Yell	3	8 —
Fraser, Mrs. Joan	Murraster, Sandsting	197	5 —
Galloway, James Kirkland	Lerwick	100	7 12
Garriock, George	Hillister, Whiteness	21	5 —
Garriock, James	Hillister, Whiteness	3	3 10
Garriock, Lewis Francis Umphray, of Berry	Gibbleston Lodge, Scalloway, Tingwall	756	125 2
Garriock, Peter	Lerwick	100	103 12
Garriock, Thomas	Wadbister, Whiteness	7	4 —
Georgeson, George	Kinkwall, Walls	68	5 —
Gifford, Thomas	Busta House, Delting	340	29 4
Gifford, Mrs. Elizabeth, wife of Thomas Gifford; and another	Busta House, Delting	800	139 9
Gilbertson, John	Maill, Dunrossness	190	12 12
Goodlad, James	Swinister, Tingwall	106	24 10
Goudie, James	Levenwick, Sandwick	27	2 16
Goudie, Mrs. Jessie	Mountfield Villa, Lerwick	216	128 8
Goudie, Mrs. Ursula	Linds, Sandwick	9	4 —
Gray, Representatives of John	Valant, Unst	64	4 —
Greig, Archibald Forbes, of Sandsound	Reawick, Sandsting	2,201	302 5
Greig, Louisa and Emma	Lerwick	730	116 6
Grierson, Andrew John, of Quendale	Quendale House, Lerwick	22,006	1,131 10
Halcrow, Edward	Ockraquoy, Cunningsburgh	6	1 17
Halcrow, Henry	Ealdigarth, Cunningsburgh	12	2 10
Halcrow, John	Tow, Tingwall	60	10 —
Halcrow, Laurence	Fladabister, Cunningsburgh	15	3 15
Do.	Do. (Quarry)	—	1 10
Halcrow, Laurence	Hoswick, Sandwick	126	18 2

ZETLAND—continued.

Name of Owner.	Address of Owner.	Estimated Acreage of Property.	Gross Annual Value.	Name of Owner.	Address of Owner.	Estimated Acreage of Property.	Gross Annual Value.
		Acres.	£ s.			Acres.	£ s.
Halcrow, Laurence	Scarpigarth, Cunningsburgh	10	1 16	Jamieson, Charles Dunbar, and another	Lerwick	6	41 —
Halcrow, Malcolm	Fladabister, Cunningsburgh	66	3 15	Jamieson, James	Still, Unst	150	5 —
Do.	Do. (Quarry)	—	1 10	Jamieson, James	Swinister, Sandwick	17	2 —
Halcrow, Malcolm	Hoswick, Sandwick	58	5 8	Jamieson, John A., and Mrs. Jane Jamieson	Housegarth, Uyasound, Unst	30	2 10
Halcrow, Nicol John	Stove, Sandwick	130	20 10	Jamieson, Magnus	Brough, Delting	60	3 10
Halcrow, Peter	Aithsetter, Cunningsburgh	6	— 18	Jamieson, Peter	Gerragarth, Unst	48	2 —
Halcrow, Thomas	138 Duke Street, Leith	25	7 —	Jamieson, Thomas	Swinister, Sandwick	18	2 —
Halcrow, Walter	Uradale, Tingwall	90	15 5	Jamieson, William	Hoswick, Sandwick	20	2 —
Halcrow, William	Fladabister, Cunningsburgh	66	5 5	Jamieson, Mrs. Ann	Ollaberry, Northmavine	21	2 10
Halcrow, Ursula	Keotha, Cunningsburgh	10	— 12	Jamieson, Mrs. Thomas	La' Hammer, Unst	19	12 15
Hamilton, Rev. Zachary Macaulay	Manse, Bressay	540	37 —	Jamieson, Ann Person	Ockraquoy, Cunningsburgh	4	1 10
Harrison, Gilbert	Lerwick	256	170 10	Jeromson, Thomas	Naverhouse, Fetlar	50	2 10
Harrison, William Baillie M'Kenzie	Lerwick	1	51 5	Johnson, Adam	Quarff	14	1 8
Hawick, John	Crooksetter, Northmavine	50	8 —	Johnson, Basil	Freedom House, Yell	2	— 5
Hay, Charles	Dollar, Clackmannanshire	300	54 12	Johnson, James	Hestinsetter, Sandsting	500	26 17
Hay, George Husband Baird, of Hayfield	Hayfield House, Lerwick	11,105	1,759 15	Johnson, James	Upper Sound, Yell	90	14 —
Hay, Hay	Scatsta, Delting	63	2 13	Johnson, John	Clothen, Yell	14	4 —
Hay, John Ogilvy, of Quarff	Rangoon, India	800	80 14	Johnson, John	Lindburn, Yell	4	6 5
Heddell, Andrew Gordon	Victoria, Australia	5	41 10	Johnson, John Gilbert	Raga, Yell	94	5 —
Heddell, Charles Hope	Gord, Cunningsburgh	160	17 3	Johnson, John Ingram	Bighton, Unst	77	5 —
Heddell, Francis, of Uresland	Helleness, Cunningsburgh	258	137 9	Johnson, Magnus	Bremer, Cunningsburgh	20	2 1
Heddell, Peter	New Zealand	22	36 1	Johnson, Theodore	Clothen, Yell	14	4 15
Henderson, Bruce	Arrisdale, Yell	84	5 —	Johnson, Mrs. Hannah	Clothen, Yell	3	1 —
Henderson, Gavin	Scousburgh, Dunrossness	5	14 10	Johnston, George	Tresta, Aithsting	5,000	241 4
Henderson, George, of Pettister	Burravoe, Yell	666	121 18	Johnston, James	Bixter, Aithsting	599	62 —
Henderson, James Cheyne	Bardister, Northmavine	160	34 —	Johnston, James	Cuppaster, Yell	24	4 —
Henderson, John	Roe, Delting	33	2 —	Johnston, John	North Huxter, Weisdale	60	5 —
Henderson, Magnus	Bothen, Haroldswick, Unst	76	9 10	Johnston, John	Stennesstwatt, Walls	88	6 14
Henderson, Captain William John, of Gloup	Yell	1,250	75 16	Johnston, John Alexander	Bridge of Walls	30	18 10
Henry, Archibald Scott	Bayhall, Walls	65	13 11	Jolly, Rev. Archibald	F.C. Manse, Greenland, Walls	8	14 —
Henry, John Thomas	Burrastown, Walls	893	61 11	Laurence, Mrs. Jessie, wife of William Laurence	Vatchly, Dunrossness	397	21 7
Henry, Mrs. Lillias, wife of John Thomas Henry; and another	Burrastown, Walls	2,204	113 6	Laurenson, Arthur	Lerwick	1	87 9
Hoseason, Arthur C., and five others	Australia	108	3 10	Laurenson, Charles	Gord, Cunningsburgh	17	1 17
Hoseason, David Arthur	Bayanne, North Yell	190	13 15	Laurenson, Gifford	Westerhoull, Scalloway, Tingwall	2	4 —
Hoseason, Captain George	Australia	600	33 8	Laurenson, Laurence	Kirkhouse, Whiteness	14	5 5
Hoseason, Trustees of late James, of Aywick	Leith	480	90 15	Leask, Joseph, of Sand	Sound, Lerwick	11,847	1,099 15
Hoseason, John	Gutcher, North Yell	230	29 11	Leisk, George Thomas	Uya, Unst	787	126 10
Hoseason, Robert	New Zealand	300	64 7	Lerwick, Commissioners of Police of	Lerwick	1	8 4
Hoseason, Trustees for Thomas White	Leith	310	13 15	Lerwick, Trustees for Feuars and Heritors of	Lerwick	60	143 4
Houston, John S.	Schoolhouse, Braeside, North Yell	3	5 —	Do. do.	Do. (Quarry)	—	18 —
Hughson, Hugh	Beddins, Walls	100	7 —	Levie, Rev. William	Manse, Neep, Nesting	103	25 16
Hughson, Thomas	Sandside, Delting	180	15 10	Linklater, Trustees of late Andrew	Linkster, Tingwall	30	14 —
Hunter, Peter	Kirkhouse, Whiteness	84	2 4	Lunna Estate, Trustees on the	Sand Lodge, Sandwick	13,330	1,052 4
				M'Kenzie, Hector	Schoolhouse, Greenland, Walls	3	3 —
Inglis, David	Flemington, Weisdale	300	17 15	M'Queen, John Rainier	Brookhouse, Chailly, Sussex	4,000	286 7
Ingram, Rev. James	Hillside, Unst	190	13 —	Malcolmson, Mrs. Agnes	America	30	2 —
Ingram, Rev. John	Hillside, Unst	190	13 —	Manson, James	Gord, Cunningsburgh	22	1 16
Inkster, James	Westerhoull, Scalloway, Tingwall	1	2 17	Manson, John	Pickgarth, Sandwick	36	4 5
Irvine, Charles	Houlland, Tingwall	60	6 —	Matthewson, Andrew Dishington	Schoolhouse, Aywick, Yell	180	11 19
Irvine, Gilbert	Grutness, Dunrossness	27	9 —	Miller, Rev. Duncan	U.P. Manse, Tuftan, Delting	5	13 —
Irvine, John	Scalloway, Tingwall	53	4 10	Mitchell, James	Sandsting	160	18 —
Irvine, John William	Grutness, Dunrossness	10	— 12	Moar, Daniel	Cunnister, North Yell	10	3 10
Irvine, Robert	Lochside, Lerwick	438	108 18	Moar, John David	Moarfield, North Yell	71	10 10
Irvine, Thomas	Midbrake, North Yell	1,074	68 12	Moar, William	New Zealand	60	4 6
Irvine, William	Lerwick	2	59 —	Moodie, Andrew	South Moustoft, Weisdale	41	5 16
Irvine, Mary Elizabeth	Bellevue, Lerwick	1,731	172 7	Moodie, Peter	South Moustoft, Weisdale	42	4 4
				Mouat, Andrew Malcolm	Nether Levenwick, Sandwick	67	15 —
Jacobson, James	Setter, Delting	200	13 15	Mouat, Andrew Walter	America	45	9 10
Jamieson, Charles Dunbar	Lerwick	190	18 15	Mouat, Henry	Girlsta Mill, Tingwall	48	3 —
				Mouat, James	Canada West, North America	150	37 6

2 D

ZETLAND—continued.

Name of Owner.	Address of Owner.	Estimated Acreage of Property.	Gross Annual Value.	Name of Owner.	Address of Owner.	Estimated Acreage of Property.	Gross Annual Value.
		Acres.	£ s.			Acres.	£ s.
Mouat, James	North Hammersland, Tingwall	48	3 —	Sievwright, William	The Mount, Lerwick	2	63 —
Mouat, John	Laurence, New Zealand	280	40 —	Sinclair, Alexander	Petries Pund, Dunrossness	18	3 —
Mouat, John and William G.	Springfield, Baltasound, Unst	154	20 10	Sinclair, Charles	Gravin, Delting	4	5 —
Mouat, Thomas	Cullister, Sandwick	36	5 17	Sinclair, Hercules	Cova, Whiteness	35	15 10
Mouat, William	Lerwick	220	101 10	Sinclair, Magnus	Snarraness, Sandness, Walls	252	12 18
Mouat, William	Levenwick, Sandwick	27	2 16	Sinclair, Mrs. Catherine	Braeside, Unst	4	7 —
Mouat, Anne Cameron, of Bressay	Gardie House, Bressay	4,400	696 3	Smith, Arthur	Islesburgh, Northmavine	35	3 —
Do. do.	Do. (*Quarries*)	—	4 2	Smith, James	Clivocast, Unst	365	43 5
Mullay, Robert	Lerwick	2	24 10	Smith, James	Hill Cottage, Sandwick	5	3 —
				Smith, James	Nether Levenwick, Sandwick	30	3 —
Nichol, Rev. Archibald	Manse, Walls	13	27 5	Smith, John	Aithsetter, Cunningsburgh	36	4 5
Nicolson, Charles	Scalloway, Tingwall	6	82 7	Smith, John	Greenland, Walls	8	5 —
Nicolson, Gideon Scott	Hill of Houll, Scalloway, Tingwall	16	3 —	Smith, Laurence	Beolka, Cunningsburgh	20	2 2
Nicolson, Robert	Springfield, Walls	2	28 —	Smith, Peter Leslie	North Ness, Lerwick	2	63 12
Nicolson, Mrs. Agnes, wife of Henry Nicolson	Wick, Lerwick	73	11 18	Smith, Thomas	Brindister, Lerwick	93	7 10
Nicolson, Lady, of Nicolson	Shelburne House, Landsdowne Road, Cheltenham	24,785	1,314 7	Smith, Thomas	Greenland, Walls	7	5 —
				Smith, Rev. William	Manse, Unst	115	31 —
Nisbet, Mrs. Christian	Cunnister, North Yell	50	5 10	Spence, Gilbert William	Glendye, Banchory	190	35 5
Northern Lighthouses, Commissioners of	84 George Street, Edinburgh	51	186 —	Spence, James	Houston, Unst	60	8 10
				Spence, John	Haroldswick, Unst	25	37 —
				Spence, Trustees of late Robert Niven, of Windhouse	Lerwick	3,005	204 17
Ollason, William	Bardister, Walls	215	18 —	Spence, William	Haroldswick, Unst	8	15 10
Omand, Mrs. Catherine	Springfield, Yell	80	4 5	Spence, Mrs. Jane Fea	Hammer, Unst	895	101 4
				Spence, Mrs. Jane	Lerwick	300	29 10
Peterson, Reps. of Arthur	Collafirth, Delting	11	10 —	Spence, Mrs. Clementina Scott, and Grace Eliza Scott, of Scalloway	Musselburgh, Edinburgh	4,378	332 —
Peterson, Helen	Greenwall, Tingwall	24	5 —	Steuart, Grace M. T.	Lerwick	30	38 5
Pole, Basil	Gardie, Yell	72	9 —	Stout, Thomas	Lerwick	28	36 14
Pole, William	Greenbank, North Yell	800	61 5	Stove, Magnus Laurence	Killister, Burravoe, Yell	12	2 15
Pole, William, jun.	Mossbank, Delting	30	23 12	Strong, Robert	Hoswick, Sandwick	29	5 7
Pryde, Robert	Stapness, Walls	320	27 —	Sutherland, Donald	Cuppaster, Yell	19	3 —
				Sutherland, Rev. James R.	Manse, Northmavine	19	20 —
Ridland, Reps. of Andrew	Scarvister, Sandsting	35	5 —	Tait, George Reid	Helendale, Lerwick	19	179 —
Ridland, James	Westerskeld, Sandsting	44	3 —	Tait, Sir Peter, Kt.	Tingwall House, Clapham Park, London	1,287	134 —
Ridland, Jerome	Westerskeld, Sandsting	44	3 —	Taylor, James	Bellister, Tingwall	164	15 10
Ridland, Laurence, jun.	Scarvister, Sandsting	35	5 —	Taylor, Thomas	Wormadale, Whiteness	19	16 —
Robertson, Duncan Irvine	Schoolhouse, Papa-Stour	5	5 —	Taylor, Walter	Catwells, Tingwall	50	3 —
Robertson, Gilbert	Brough, Delting	30	2 15	Thirde, Rev. James Young	U.P. Manse, Ollaberry, Northmavine	1	12 —
Robertson, John Finlayson	Viewfield, Ye	90	5 10	Thomason, Representatives of Robert Magnus	Swarrister, Yell	85	6 5
Robertson, Robert	Setter, Weisdale	48	8 —	Thomson, John	Houll, Walls	17	11 10
Robertson, Scott	Grutquoy, Walls	100	10 —	Thomson, John	Squarefield, Unst	16	10 15
Robertson, Thomas	Lahore, India	90	9 10	Thomson, William	Skurran, Weisdale	20	8 —
Robertson, Thomas	Nether Houll, Yell	4	2 12	Thomson, Margaret	Balliasta, Unst	81	7 12
Robertson, William	Lerwick	152	48 5	Tulloch, Gilbert	Scalloway, Tingwall	12	16 —
Robertson, Mrs. Barbara Grace Henderson	Lerwick	13,700	384 —	Twatt, John	Voe, Walls	243	20 —
Robertson, Mrs. Jean, wife of Robt. Robertson	Setter, Weisdale	245	30 —	Twatt, Mrs. Jane A.	Voe, Walls	134	27 —
Robertson, Mrs. Sarah	Cuppaster, Yell	1	1 —				
Rose, Rev. William	Manse, Sandsting	767	32 10	Umphray, Andrew, of Reawick	Reawick, Sandsting	3,896	333 11
Ross, John	Schoolhouse, Bressay	4	10 —	Umphray, Andrew, of Reawick; and Lewis Francis Umphray Garrioch, of Berry	Reawick, Sandsting	100	26 15
Royal Bounty, Committee for	Edinburgh	6	6 —	*Unst, Free Church Congregation of*	Unst	4	13 10
Russell, Rev. James	Schoolhouse, Happyhansel, Walls	46	8 —				
Russell, Rev. John	Manse, Whalsay	2	12 —				
Sandison, Henry	Gardens, Delting	5	3 —				
Saunders, Rev. Alexander Reid	Manse, Lerwick	6	35 —				
Scalloway Estate, Trustees on the	Scalloway, Tingwall	600	27 7	Walker, John	Marine Terrace, Aberdeen	50	73 —
Scollay, Judicial Factor on estate of Robert	23 Gordon Street, Leith	109	3 —	Walker, Miles	Swinkle House, Longleddell, Kendal	3,370	122 3
Scott, Robert Thomas C., of Melby	Melby House, Walls	13,020	1,205 17	*War Department*	London	3	75 —
Scott, Thomas	Scottfield, Scalloway, Tingwall	2	9 12	Watson, Representatives of Rev. William	Fetlar	520	22 15
Scott, Walter	North Park, Scalloway, Tingwall	2	2 5	Webster, Rev. David	Manse, Fetlar	300	29 —
Shewan, Laurence	Goat, Dunrossness	10	6 —	*Wesleyan Conference*	England	2	16 10
				Williamson, David, and another	Navy Lane, Lerwick	500	10 1

ZETLAND—continued.

Name of Owner.	Address of Owner.	Estimated Acreage of Property.	Gross Annual Value.	Name of Owner.	Address of Owner.	Estimated Acreage of Property.	Gross Annual Value.
		Acres.	£ s.			Acres.	£ s.
Williamson, Gilbert	Schoolhouse, Twatt, Aithsting	600	38 15	Zetland, Earl of	19 Arlington St., London	13,600	858 11
Williamson, Representatives of James	Upper Gardie, Yell	6	7 —	Total Owners of Land of one Acre and upwards		309 305,303	30,030 9
Williamson, Laurence	Mid Yell	200	14 10	Total Owners of Lands of less than one Acre in extent		240 80	3,528 10
Williamson, Robert	Everland, Fetlar	300	15 3				
Williamson, Robert	Gord, Cunningsburgh	20	2 10				
Williamson, Thomas	Haggersta, Whiteness	13	2 —				
Williamson, Thomas	Millbrae, Unst	131	11 —				
Williamson, William	Fogrigarth, Aithsting	200	12 10	GRAND TOTAL		549 305,383	33,558 19
Williamson, William J.	Burravoe, South Yell	1	— 7				

ABSTRACT.

	COUNTY.	Number of Owners.	Estimated Acreage of Property.	Gross Annual Value.
			Acres.	£ s.
1.	Aberdeen	4,489	1,253,358	851,516 3
	Do. Borough of Aberdeen	2,983	1,780	267,333 —
2.	Argyll	2,864	2,030,948	430,151 10
3.	Ayr	8,370	720,910	1,061,903 15
	Do. Borough of Kilmarnock	1,006	1,037	59,348 5
4.	Banff	4,025	407,501	227,025 —
5.	Berwick	1,743	292,139	377,211 3
6.	Bute	737	138,972	86,178 6
7.	Caithness	1,030	471,763	136,885 13
8.	Clackmannan	1,227	30,189	97,482 6
9.	Cromarty	231	18,206	11,964 8
10.	Dumbarton	2,346	153,736	325,407 —
11.	Dumfries	4,177	676,971	595,511 17
12.	Edinburgh	3,237	226,778	581,603 6
	Do. Borough of Edinburgh	11,546	3,738	1,294,331 —
	Do. Do. Leith	2,189	1,226	253,104 —
13.	Elgin	2,564	303,168	203,705 —
14.	Fife	10,410	304,363	905,577 7
15.	Forfar	4,898	553,852	795,581 7
	Do. Borough of Dundee	4,445	2,142	447,528 1
16.	Haddington	1,511	171,739	349,209 17
17.	Inverness	1,867	2,589,408	361,848 5
18.	Kincardine	1,384	244,585	253,392 12
19.	Kinross	725	44,888	64,471 14
20.	Kirkcudbright	2,386	571,950	360,960 7
21.	Lanark	9,117	553,097	1,736,268 7
	Do. Borough of Glasgow	10,991	4,822	2,342,164 —
22.	Linlithgow	1,535	75,785	248,593 10
23.	Nairn	537	120,765	41,767 —
24.	Orkney	1,308	220,873	62,536 13
25.	Peebles	708	232,410	142,614 —
26.	Perth	5,737	1,612,001	959,364 18
	Do. Borough of Perth	1,906	839	89,062 1
27.	Renfrew	3,215	149,921	561,811 3
	Do. Borough of Paisley	1,395	3,344	140,684 12
	Do. Do. Greenock	1,128	2,056	288,402 13
28.	Ross	2,043	1,971,682	269,342 —
29.	Roxburgh	2,455	423,463	456,883 7
30.	Selkirk	706	161,815	103,029 13
31.	Stirling	4,257	284,751	521,406 11
32.	Sutherland	433	1,299,253	71,494 7
33.	Wigtown	1,820	309,087	230,589 4
34.	Zetland	549	305,383	33,558 19
	Total	132,230	18,946,694	18,698,804 —